TROUT

PHOTOGRAPHS OF FLY-TYING BY

CHARLES S. KRUG

ALSO MANY DIAGRAMS IN LINE BY

IVIN SICKLES

&

G. DON RAY

TROUT

By RAY BERGMAN

Fly plates in full color painted by
DR. EDGAR BURKE

THIRD EDITION, ENLARGED
with new material
by Edward C. Janes

ALFRED A. KNOPF: NEW YORK

1976

PUBLISHED, NOVEMBER 1938
REPRINTED THIRTEEN TIMES
SECOND EDITION, REVISED AND ENLARGED,
RESET AND PRINTED FROM NEW PLATES,
NOVEMBER 1952
REPRINTED ELEVEN TIMES
THIRD EDITION, ENLARGED APRIL 1976

LIBRARY OF CONGRESS CARD NUMBER: 75-10592
ISBN: 0-394-49957-3
ISBN: 0-394-73144-1 (paperback)

MANUFACTURED IN THE UNITED STATES OF AMERICA

To you all

*The many good fellows I know and
have fished with,
and those whose paths may never cross mine except
through the medium of these pages.
This is my visit with you,
our fishing adventure together.
I trust it will be
enjoyable, instructive, and memorable.
When I am gone, when all who now read these pages
have passed beyond,
I hope that* TROUT *will continue to live,
perhaps to instill in future generations
a love and understanding
of angling*

Introductory Note to the Third Edition

Fundamentally, angling has not changed since the beginning when man first impaled a bait upon a bone hook and lowered it into the water on the end of a plant or animal fiber line. Only the materials and the techniques have changed.

Limber saplings cut beside the water have given way to processed rods made from hickory, lancewood, greenheart, bamboo, metal, and fiberglass. Bone hooks have been replaced by hooks of steel. Animal and green plant fibers have been superseded by other fibers —among them hemp, linen, silk, and nylon—which are wound upon reels and which provide greater control in playing a hooked fish. Natural baits have been supplemented by artificial flies, plugs, and metal spoons and spinners. But the basic objective remains: to attract fish, hook them, and eventually bring them into possession.

At first, this pursuit was carried on for the serious purpose of obtaining food, but even the early prehistoric fishermen must have thrilled with pleasure and pride when they landed the occasional lunker fish. Through the ages, as wider food sources became available, angling gradually metamorphosed into a sport rather than a strictly utilitarian endeavor.

Every era has produced gifted individuals who through interest, opportunity, study, and native skill have stood out as anglers. Some troubled to write on the subject and left their mark upon the sport. Dame Juliana Berners and her *Treatyse on Fysshynge with an Angle*, Izaak Walton and *The Compleat Angler*, Alfred Ronalds with *The Fly-Fisher's Entomology*, and W. C. Prime, who wrote *I Go a-Fishing*, are names that come to mind.

In our day such a man was Ray Bergman, who was born in Nyack, New York in 1891 and died there in 1967. His book, *Trout*, became a classic in his lifetime. First published in 1938, it was reprinted thirteen times before a second edition appeared in 1952.

The second edition has been reprinted eleven times and the book remains today a textbook and bible for trout fishermen everywhere. The book still has a freshness and timeliness which is remarkable. The tenets laid down by Ray Bergman and the theories he set forth are as valid today as they were in 1938.

On nymph fishing: "You should always approach still clear waters with great care. If they are a bit shallow you should keep very low, on your knees if necessary, and make your first cast from some distance below, letting the nymph alight on the water of the tail of the pool. If the water below the pool is too fast to make such a cast feasible, then work up to the pool with as little disturbance as you can and wait there five or ten minutes before you make your first cast."

On dry-fly fishing: "Here is an important thing to learn when fishing any shallow water. Often trout will travel some distance in order to take the fly. When they do, you can see the wake they make as they come after the fly. This is exciting, so that your reactions may cause you to strike too quickly and hard. Whereupon you either take the fly away from the fish or break the leader, leaving the fly in its mouth. Until you can control this violent reaction you will never become consistently successful at fishing for large trout in shallow water. From my experience I find that it usually pays to wait until a fly disappears from the surface before you strike; or more efficiently, just manage to bring the line taut, something that hooks the fish but doesn't break the leader."

And again, on the effects of sunshine and shadows: "Remember that on gray days there is no area where the fly is indistinct, and that this applies to any day when the sun does not cast a clearly defined shadow. On bright days, even under the shadow of the trees, the water may catch the reflection from a rock or cliff or the leaves of trees on which the sun is shining brightly, and so obscure the vision of the fish when a fly floats by in that area affected by the reflection.

"All these things must be taken into consideration when choosing the most advantageous position to fish from, and the combinations you run into are many and complicated. . . . I will say this, if you can ascertain the exact location of a large trout, the depth of water he lies in, and then figure out the angles of sunlight so that you can place your fly in that area of sufficient but sometimes indistinct vision, you stand a good chance of taking him, perhaps not the first time you try, but eventually, if you keep at it and make sure you have the thing figured out correctly."

These observations are still true today and will be equally sound a hundred years from now and, indeed, as long as there are trout to be sought after and anglers to seek them.

However, despite the timelessness or timeliness of Ray Bergman's instructions, new developments in tackle and, as a result, new techniques have come about since the last revision of *Trout* in 1952, developments the publisher feels should be incorporated in the book to bring it up to date. Hence this latest revision.

The publisher has remade nearly all of the sixteen color plates using the originals of Dr. Edgar Burke's magnificent paintings and wishes to thank Mrs. Norma Christian, Mr. James Sterns, Dr. George Looser, and Mr. Joseph Weise, who are fortunate enough to own these paintings and kind enough to make them available for new plates for this book.

It is too bad that Ray could not do the revising himself, giving us at first hand the results of his tests of new equipment and his experimentation with new angling methods. Since this is impossible, it has been decided by the publisher and myself that, instead of interpolating notes into each chapter, it would be preferable to include the new material in an appendix consisting of two parts—one describing new developments in tackle which have appeared since the last edition was published, and the second discussing angling methods which the appearance of this new tackle has brought about.

We hope this appendix will inform the reader of recent developments in tackle and will provide suggestions concerning new techniques. For the benefit of beginning fishermen I have explained some fundamentals of fishing tackle and its use.

No attempt has been made to update the book so far as changes in the waters Ray wrote about are concerned. Ray fished in a day before developers, highway builders, dams, and suburban sprawl had ruined much of the countryside and when many streams still flowed clear and unpolluted.

Let them remain so in his book, a nostalgic memory of what this country once was like, a rebuke to what it has become, and a challenging goal for the future. In *Trout*, waters will forever run pure and sparkling and fish will rise in clear, untrammeled streams.

Edward C. Janes
Westfield, Mass. 1975

A NOTE ABOUT

The Second Edition of TROUT

Since *Trout* was originally published in 1938 I have been steadily gathering new material about trout and have covered more than one hundred thousand additional miles in the United States and Canada in quest of interesting fishing to write about. In this completely revised edition I have brought things up to date.

The original text has been checked, corrected, and sections not strictly important have been deleted. Much new material has been added. This covers angling experiences, methods of fishing, flies, lures, lines, leaders and other things. When *Trout* was first published spinning had not been introduced in the United States. Since that time it has become very popular and I took up the method at once. There are two lengthy and complete chapters on this method of fishing. They cover tackle, methods, and experiences.

All of the original color plates of flies have been retained and four new plates have been added, two of flies and two of spinning lures. These were painted by Dr. Edgar Burke who did the rest of the plates but who will do no more because he died not long after completing these last four. Countless anglers will mourn the passing of this grand friend and surgeon who made his paintings so alive and compelling. Where needed, new diagrams have been added and old ones redrawn.

Altogether this new edition of *Trout* is twenty-five per cent longer than the original and I have kept in mind that you want sound, unbiased ideas about tackle as well as entertaining reading. I hope it will please all my old friends who have been so kind and loyal and gain many new ones.

RAY BERGMAN

Introduction

Perhaps an introduction to a book such as this should be written by someone else, especially someone prominent in the field of fresh-water fishing. But because I have always fought my own battles through the business of life, I felt that *Trout* also should go out into the world without any outside help from a name that might increase its sale. I felt that it should stand on its own merits, on the strength of its character, on my own efforts in my chosen field of endeavor. Therefore I did not ask anyone to write an introduction.

But it seems that this type of book must have one. It is customary and expected. So I had to do it myself.

Many hours of hard work, sacrifice, and self-denial went into these pages. What has been written is frank and accurate according to my personal experiences. There has been an earnest desire to segregate important facts and to present them graphically. When a problem has been encountered it has been met and overcome, even though in some cases it took hours to write a single page. I have relaxed and written from the heart as well as the brain of experiences since 1904 gained in waters from coast to coast. I have written it as if it were addressed directly to a dear friend who had stopped in to see me and to ask for information. As the pages were written I relived the experiences described—became transported to the localities where they occurred even though actually they were written at home.

To pick out a title for this volume was a difficult job—or at least I made it so. For days I struggled with ideas. Then one evening Herbert S. Pettit, friend and neighbor, dropped in to see how I was progressing with the manuscript, and I told him what a time I was having with this simple problem. Why not call it "Trout," he suggested. Why not indeed? As always, simplicity proved to be the need, and so Pettit's suggestion was used.

Because *Trout* is sincere in purpose and thought, I know it is genuine and think you will like it. I hope we will become friends because of it.

RAY BERGMAN

Contents

CONTENTS

Plates

[all color plates will be found following page 260]

TROUT

CHAPTER I

Early Experiences

As FAR back as I can remember I have been passionately fond of the outdoors. Memories of childhood are mostly vague and dreamlike, but I have some recollections of these early days which have survived the years. Oddly enough, they are of rainstorms, and in them I am either fishing with a hand line from a long stone dock jutting out into the Hudson River or else I am wandering along the rocky shores of the river in the vicinity of Hook Mountain, that isolated northern rampart of the Palisades.

With startling reality I can still feel the sting of rain on my face, blown against it by the eastern gale. Vividly I can see the angry waters of the river buffeting the dock and the shore, the border of light gray along the eastern horizon, and the restless black clouds that seemed to form directly on that border of light and then rush madly across the sky, finally to bank in huge masses against the western horizon.

The catching of fish seems insignificant in these memories of the play of the elements. I don't remember much about it, but as I see it now, I believe that the fishing was simply an excuse to get out in the open, to breathe air that came to me directly over open spaces, to face nature when she bared her soul. I remember plainly that my favorite wind was a howling northeaster, the sort of wind that usually brought a three-day storm. During such periods even the village streets were deserted and quiet. To me this condition was ideal and I could not be kept indoors. Wild storms appealed to me, transported me back through the ages to primitive days, brought me thrills that made my body quiver with sheer physical delight. I would rather face the storms at the river's edge or on a mountain top than have many dollars' worth of fireworks on the Fourth of July, and in the eyes of youth during that period this was a mighty comparison indeed.

[3]

Somehow I feel that the elements and all life are directly related, so much so that anyone who is sincerely enraptured by nature stands very close to the great beyond. To such souls, fishing is an outlet to the feelings, a surcease from life's trials. Being closely attuned to nature's whims I drifted naturally into out-of-door pursuits, and fishing seemed to be the one sport that best gratified my innate craving for an intimacy with those forces of which I knew so little.

When I was a boy, conditions were quite different from what they are today. I am old enough to have experienced the old-fashioned ways of the latter part of the nineteenth century and the rapid-fire progress of the twentieth. I saw the horse and carriage give way to the automobile, the dusty roads change rapidly from macadam to Tarvia and then to concrete. Each advance of progress had its effect on the fishing. I started writing about angling when the outdoor magazines paid little or nothing for stories, when their files were filled with material submitted without any thought of recompense, submitted simply because the contributors wanted to see their names in print. I saw these conditions gradually change as more people became interested in fishing and demanded first-class articles in the magazines they read. The leading magazines grew in size, and their contents in quality, which was as it should be. I received only thirty-five dollars for my first story, and it ran through two issues of the magazine in which it was published. This periodical was later absorbed by another and has since lost its identity.

Naturally my early fishing was confined to bait, which was good because it taught me where the trout were located. As a matter of fact no one in our territory ever used flies, nor did they know anything about fly fishing. Even as recently as 1920 I doubt if there were more than six fly fishermen in our community. I had a fairly accurate check-up on this because at the time I happened to own a sporting-goods store. I tried my best to get others interested in fly fishing but it was slow work, and when I sold out, most of the fly stock was left on the shelves. There were fifty buyers of bait hooks to one customer for flies. It is different today. There are now enough fly fishermen to make flies and fly-tying materials a principal stock in trade of many tackle dealers.

Considering these things it is somewhat remarkable that I started fly fishing so early in life. However this was due mostly to chance, although my keen desire to find out the hidden secrets of fishing had something to do with it. You see, even after everyone else had quit for the season I kept on trying. I felt sure there was a way to catch trout at that time of the year and kept experimenting to find out how to do it. So one day I happened to be at the right place at the right time and met a man who was able to show me that trout could be taken late in the season.

I shall never forget that day. It was early July and I was eating lunch on the bank of a meadow stretch of my favorite stream. I had fished down some two miles and had caught only two six-inch trout. When this angler came along he stopped for a chat and showed me his catch, eight beautiful brookies, none under ten inches and several better than twelve inches.

Here was a chance to find just what I wanted to know, so I started asking questions. I told him of the poor luck I had experienced since the middle of June, and how the other fellows in town said all the fish were caught out during April and May and made fun of me because I felt differently about it. "I just couldn't believe that," I said, "because if it were true we wouldn't get any fish the next spring and we always do. Now you have proved that I was right and they were wrong." [1]

The man smiled. "All the trout are never caught out. Sometimes they get very scarce, and the fewer there are the wiser they seem to get. Some become too smart to be taken even by the most expert, and these fish constitute the seed that keeps the streams stocked. But around here there are always plenty of trout left after the bait fishermen get through. You see, hardly anyone ever fishes these streams with a fly, and that is about the only way to take them during the latter part of the season—except after a heavy rain, when worms are best. That is why you hear that cry of 'fished out' so often. Now just watch. See that clump of alders?"

---

[1] At this time restocking streams was very uncertain and legal-sized fish were not used for the purpose. The stream in question had not been stocked for several years.

TROUT

He pointed to a group of bushes at a bend some forty feet downstream. "It is quite deep there," he explained, "and the trout stay
well under the brush at this time of day, but I think I can stir up
some action."

He made a cast of some forty-five feet, dropping the flies lightly
at the very bend of the stream and so close to the alders that they
almost snagged. He let them sink for a few moments and then with
a slight twitch of the rod started them jerking through the water.
On the third jerk I saw a flash of pink and the water boiled. His
first cast had brought results. He landed the fish and killed it by
tapping it on the head with his knife. He then placed it on some
green moss near by and we looked at it exultingly. The man dis-
mounted his rod and made preparations to leave. "Well, good-by,"
he said. "Take that fish home and show it to the boys who make
fun of you."

Such generosity overwhelmed me! I stammered my thanks in-
coherently. After he was gone I was sorry that I had not asked his
name and address or perhaps I might have made arrangements to
meet him on the stream again. There were so many questions I
would have liked to ask him. It seemed to be so hard to find out
anything about fly fishing in those days. Nevertheless, the incident
had been very enlightening and the knowledge gained was absorbed completely, so that the effects were lasting. The man probably forgot the incident within a few days, but I never did and I
often wonder what he would think if he knew the thought his
passing interest had provoked.

I did not have any fly outfit or enough money to buy one immediately, so I spent the next few weeks observing the stream instead of fishing. In the meantime I saved every cent of my allowance and what I made on my paper route against the purchase of
an outfit, which I hoped I could get before the close of the season.
Incidentally, I found the occupation of watching the stream so
fascinating that temporarily I forgot the fishing. This was the best
thing that could have happened, and I learned more during this
time than I had in all my previous fishing experience. I spent tedious hours crouched in the alders that sheltered deep holes, and
from these vantage points I could see how the trout acted. I did
not realize that I was building up my fund of fishing lore that
would be invaluable to me in the years to come. I did it simply

because I was intensely interested and wished to find out how and where the trout did their feeding in the late season. Here are some of the important things I discovered that later improved my game.

First, that most of the trout, when not feeding, stayed close to the bank in the deepest parts of the deepest holes near their feeding grounds.

Second, that nearly all of the trout in the brook preferred shade and thick cover when not actually engaged in feeding, also that they had certain hours when they fed most. These were in the late afternoon as soon as the direct rays of the sun left the water and in the early morning, immediately after daybreak, up until the time that the full force of the sun made its presence felt on the water. During these periods they left the deep holes and took strategic locations along the shallow stretches that connected the various holes.

Third, that these particular trout preferred to feed under water rather than on the surface. I couldn't tell what they were taking because whatever it was could not be seen, but when I cleaned a trout I caught just before the end of the season, I found it was filled with a solid black mass that looked like scum but that I diagnosed as very small underwater insects. Occasionally when some large, juicy-looking flies floated down on the surface they would take them, but by far most of the action took place under water.

Fourth, that the effects of vibration were very disturbing. The surrounding ground, being very boggy, trembled on the slightest provocation and sent the warning vibrations down to the bed of the stream. The instant the trout felt these vibrations they immediately scurried for cover, where they stayed for considerable time before venturing forth again. This time varied greatly. Sometimes they would stay under cover for only a half hour. At other times they would not come out again until the next feeding period. It showed clearly how one could easily spoil his chances of taking fish by making a careless approach. Six times while I was watching, a cow caused the vibrations and in each case the trout went for cover. If the cow stayed on the bank for a half hour or longer, the trout came out again and did not seem to mind the presence of the animal. They seemed to know that the cow was harmless, and associated with the animal the vibrations that frightened them.

I managed to get a nondescript fly outfit together before the end of the season and started fishing again. The results were far from satisfying. I ruined my chances on every stretch at the very first cast. Because I did not know any better I thought my outfit quite swell, but in reality the rod was heavy, cumbersome, and dead, and the line did not fit it. Besides, the guides were spaced so far apart that the line kept wrapping around the bamboo between them. Of course it was a cheap outfit, so one could not expect much, but it was certainly discouraging to learn to cast with it. This first experience with fly casting was a veritable nightmare. All I had to guide me was that memory of one cast I had seen made by an accomplished fisherman. Half the time the line was tangled around my body, and countless times I had to cut the fly away from my clothes or my person. I always frightened the trout at the first cast and then struggled with the outfit for an hour after, fishing water from which the fish had disappeared. On the last day of the season I caught one trout by accident, and this saved me from utter rout. With this fish to cheer me I faced the closed season with a peaceful mind filled with dreams of the season to come. For I had caught a trout on a fly, and had done it at a time when the other fellows said it couldn't be done. That was glory enough for an unsophisticated fisherman.

It took time and many a headache to correct the faults of my outfit and my casting. More than a year had passed before I knew that the line I had was entirely too light for the rod and that the guides had to be spaced much closer than they were on my rod to give best results. I have no vivid memories of this period, so can't tell much about it, but I must have succeeded in getting things ironed out very well, judging by the following notes made several years later, in 1914 or thereabouts.

I find that these trout of the Crumb Creek meadow stretch cannot be taken during July and August unless I use extreme care, not only in the approach, but in the cast and the selection of flies. The flies must be of subdued coloration, they must alight on the water softly and sink immediately, and the retrieve must be made slowly and with deliberation. It takes from fifteen to twenty-five minutes to work to a suitable casting location, and the slightest misstep on the way is fatal to my chances.

When I started fishing this water the trout weren't so particular. As long as the fly alighted softly and you did not frighten the trout by your approach, they would rise no matter how you handled the retrieve. This last season it has been different, and for some time I haven't been taking any fish. I felt sure that the way I handled the flies was the cause of the trouble, and as I had been retrieving them rapidly close to the surface, I changed today and fished them slow and deep. It seemed to be the solution, because I took a good trout from each stretch. Would probably have taken more but they ran so large that I had to go to the water's edge to land them and so spoiled my chances of taking any more from those particular locations.

My notes for the next six years are of scattered experiences and rather incomplete, but through them I find a continual striving to perfect my fly fishing. Some of the experiences are worth recounting, especially the early trips to the Catskills. Such trips were real events in those days. They took a lot of time and were quite expensive. We did not have cars to carry our duffel. It had to be carried by hand, and our means of transportation were the railroads and the old horse and wagon at the end of our journey. There was something sweetly pleasant about those days which seems to have vanished with the coming of the automobile. Our simple pleasures were most enjoyable, and the air did not carry the taint of gasoline or the atmosphere of irreverence that seems to be generated by the numbers of people who now frequent the mountains and who are not in accord with the true spirit of nature. All lovers of the out-of-doors can sense this disturbing influence, although they probably do not give much thought to the real cause of the feeling. The streams alone offer relief that is complete. When one feels the rush of cold water against his waders, and pits his skill against the natural instincts and wariness of the trout, everything else is lost in the sheer joy of the moment.

It must be admitted that our early fishing in the Catskills was crude. There were plenty of fish and no competition to speak of, so we did not have to be very skillful to be successful. The notes I made in those days do not offer much in the way of angling knowledge. They are simply accounts of the fish caught. We fished with worms more than we did with flies, and when we used flies it was with a hit-or-miss carelessness that did not tend to develop one's fishing technique. I believe that during this period I really went backward rather than forward. It shows how one's progress may be retarded by fishing places where the trout are easy to catch.

But as time went on and automobiles became more plentiful, there began to be a vast difference in these conditions. Here and there we came across skillful anglers who took trout when the rest of us could not do a thing. A few such experiences started me thinking, and from then on, my notes began to show the influence of constructive thought, thus becoming of some value. Consider the following quotation, which was taken from the first notes worth mentioning since the experiences on Crumb Creek three years before.

It is becoming increasingly difficult to catch trout. Our last three trips to Sundown have been very poor. Lots of fishermen, and no one caught anything except one fly fisherman I met who was far above the average. He did not seem to have the least trouble catching them and thought the fishing exceptionally good. Clearly something is wrong with our methods and our tackle. I didn't want to bother the man, but I did find out that he used nine-foot leaders about half as thick as our three- and six-foot ones. I also noticed that he did not give the flies any motion, just let them float as they would with the current. It has started me thinking, and my thoughts are not very complimentary to us.

After seeing this man I found a pond, formed by a small spring brook, which is filled with trout, a few as large as fifteen inches, as far as I could judge from seeing them under the water. Tried my best to get one, but my coarse tackle scared them. I finally put on a worm, cast it out, and waited. After two hours I got a bite and took a ten-incher. Don't feel a bit satisfied with myself. It all shows that I've been standing still for several years—worse than that, I've been sliding backward. Next week I'm coming back with suitable tackle and really try to do some fishing.

That I meant what I wrote is proved by the notes made the following week.

It was dumb of me to forget my experiences on Crumb Creek. It was all due to the easy fishing we've been having in the Catskills. Here I have been fishing like a novice when I have had experiences that should have taught me better. It all came back today as I stood on the banks of the spring pond. Here were trout in absolutely still water that was clear as crystal. You could not get near the bank by walking in an upright position without causing a lot of excitement among the trout living in it. I found that out as I approached the first time. I sat down and stayed perfectly still for an hour before attempting to fish. Made a bungle with my first cast and scared the fish again. This necessitated another wait, and I made it more than an hour to be sure that the trout had forgotten about it. Remembering Crumb Creek I wet my flies and leader thoroughly before making the cast. Still influenced by old memories I let the flies sink before starting the retrieve and placed the cast so that they went to one side of the school instead of directly over them. As the retrieve progressed I saw some shadowy forms start after the flies, and then the reflections on the surface hid them from my sight. The next instant I felt a tug and connected with a really good fish—about 1½ pounds. Of course I was elated and proud, in fact I was so excited that I quit fishing and rushed back to camp to show my fish.

Subsequently my experiences at this pond taught me many useful facts. It was there that I discovered you could approach trout with less chance of disturbing them if you did so with the sun at your back. At the time I did not know why this was so, but later on I realized it was because the sunlight blinded them and so they did not see you silhouetted against the sky. There are many interesting angles to this, which I shall take up exhaustively in another chapter. I think that the most important thing that the spring pond taught me was the necessity for perfect casts, with fine long leaders and proper manipulation. After I learned how to take trout from this place consistently, my results in the main stream immediately showed improvement. I was able to get fish from the most difficult still waters, places we had formerly passed by unless the stream was discolored, when we fished them with bait. Of course I was not a master at the game. Usually I was satisfied with one or two fish from each still water. But it was a step in the right direction, and as long as I kept thinking constructively, I was bound to improve as the years went by.

The medium-fast smooth-topped glides bothered me for a long time. Occasionally the fast, skittering method worked but it was very uncertain. When I fished from the side I was invariably too late on the strike, especially when I let the flies float down on a slack line, which seemed to be by far the most effective way of fishing them. Finally I overcame the trouble by a very simple thing. Far up on the leader, near the line, I tied on a Coachman or a White Miller so that I could follow the progress of the flies as they floated downstream. On my first attempt with this cast I noted that the light-colored indicator fly made several peculiar motions during the course of its float, but because I didn't know any better, I thought they were caused by the water currents. Once, however, I felt a slight tug at the moment the motion occurred, and then I realized that it was caused by a trout taking one of the lower flies. From then on I struck no matter how slight the motion of the indicator fly was, and at once began to catch trout. I advanced rapidly. It seemed to be the one thing needed to spur me on to greater efforts. I learned to keep my nerves at hair-trigger tension so that I reacted instantaneously to anything that was the least bit suggestive of a contrary action on the part of fly, line, and leader. Every shadow or flash of light was treated as a striking fish. After a time I found that I could sense things my eyes did not see, but I must admit that sometimes my nerves played me false and I found myself striking to the shadow of a bird flying overhead or to the flash of a leaf or twig twisting and turning in the current. But this all went with the game, and more often than not these never-failing reactions produced a fish when the strike was made. Usually I was more surprised than the trout every time this happened, even after the method became an old story as far as I was concerned.

It was subtle fishing and developed intuitive reactions to a remarkable extent. Before long I was doing it all unconsciously and was seeing things that happened under water. That is one of the important educational angles of wet-fly fishing. It trains the eye to recognize significant trifles and to pick out both fish and pocket holes from the confusion of rapidly moving water.

At the same time I found that I had to be in the proper mood to have success when fishing a wet fly. If I wasn't, I usually failed miserably. It was this fact that started me fishing with a dry fly. I found that I could handle the floating fly easier than wet flies, and it did not make so much difference if I felt a bit out of sorts. This is readily understandable. The dry fly is always in plain sight. I could tell just what was going on, so it was much easier to do what I wanted to do. Then too, it did not require such nerve tension. However, I must warn all beginners that the dry-fly game is an insidious one. It creeps upon you unawares, and unless you fight the tendency you will eventually fish in no other way. And to keep in the pink of wet-fly perfection you must practice this form of fishing consistently. It takes only a few weeks to lose that fine sense of perception which is needed to do it properly, but it often takes much longer than that to regain it once you get out of practice.

Sometimes I wonder if it isn't best to have plenty of hard knocks when learning how to fish. There isn't any doubt that the things we learn from our own observations and mistakes stay by us, while the things we learn from reading and study are easily forgotten. I know that I never gained any substance from what I read until after I had started to think things out for myself. After that the experiences of others were real, and I learned a great deal from them because I could put myself in the place of the writers. Always keep in mind that the way to get the most out of reading and study is to supplement it with actual practice.

Many years have passed since my first experiences at fishing, but the memories of them remain to keep me company during many a thoughtful hour. If you would like to preserve your memories, keep a diary of your experiences. In later years it will serve to bring back to you many of the days you would like to live over again. No fish will ever give you the same thrill as your first good trout. One of the penalties of becoming experienced is the fact that you become somewhat blasé and lose some of the acute sensations that attend first experiences. Not that you like fishing less. Far from it. You find that your love for the sport grows with the years. But you will no longer tremble and throb as you put your net under a large old trout. It will be just another fish. I know I wish I could once again experience the thrill that came with the catching of my first big fish. There was something about it that cannot be compared with any other sensation. But on the other hand, there are other interests to absorb the old-timer, the greatest of which is to get the best of some knotty angling problem. If this book serves to stimulate your own powers of observation and common sense, then I shall feel that it has served its purpose.

❧ CHAPTER II ❧

Wet-Fly Methods

IN DISCUSSING the methods and uses of wet flies it is necessary to reduce all explanations to the simplest form so that beginners at wet-fly fishing will derive some benefit from them. I trust that the experienced angler will forgive me when I appear too obvious, and will realize that it is only by so doing that I can hope to be of some help to those who have not had previous training in the art. It is a common fault for experts at any game to overlook many things that have an acute bearing on it simply because they are so well versed that they cannot conceive of anyone else's not knowing the fundamentals.

As a matter of fact, apparently it is the insignificant things that really mark the dividing line between success and failure. That you cast so well that others compliment you for your skill is not so important, but that you handle the flies in some particular and almost indescribable way may be very important indeed. You may gather from this that I am not particularly interested in perfect-form casting, and that is very true. The main thing is to have the flies alight correctly on the place where they are most likely to produce results. After that they should be handled in the most efficacious way for the time, location, and type of water. If you become a perfect-form caster while achieving the necessary results, so much the better; but it is best to concentrate on the other points rather than on form, and the casting will usually take care of itself. In this connection let me say that some of the best fishermen I know could not be called "pretty" casters, but they do cast their flies so that they act the way they should and catch the fish.

One of the most important methods of fishing the wet fly is the "natural drift." There are several ways to accomplish this, the most generally useful being the up-and-across-stream cast. You take your position directly opposite the water you wish to fish, and

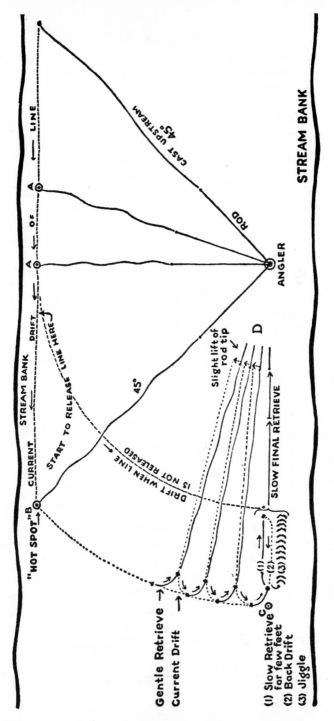

WET-FLY "NATURAL DRIFT"

make a cast at about a forty-five-degree angle upstream to the opposite side (*see sketch*). As soon as the cast is completed, the tip of the
rod is lowered a trifle and then kept pointed directly at the flies, as
they sink in the water and the current carries them downstream.
The line should be slack and yet just on the verge of being taut.
This allows the flies to be affected naturally by the current and yet
leaves you in perfect command if you get a strike.

If you desire a longer drift than that obtained by the original
cast, you may get this by "mending." To accomplish this, bring
the rod slowly to a position slightly back of vertical and then make
a sort of push forward, using enough force to cause the fly to
swish back and then forward to arrive in a different position. This
also provides extra slack, and you gain some additional natural
drift.

If the water below you is not likely to be occupied by fish, then
the float of the flies may be terminated at an angle of about forty-
five degrees below you (B) or just when they have started to drag
across the stream. Watch and be prepared for a rise at this particular position, as it often occurs at this point. However, if the water
directly below you is likely to hold some trout, then let the flies
drag all the way across the stream until they come to a stationary
position below you. Let them play in this water a moment or two,
and then if a strike is not forthcoming, retrieve them for a few feet
and immediately let the current pull them back to their original
position. Vary this procedure by a slight lift and drop of the rod
instead of the longer retrieve, even jiggle them a bit several times.
If this does not bring a strike, then start retrieving the flies very
slowly until only ten or fifteen feet of line and leader remain below the end of the rod. At this point lift the flies preparatory to
another cast. Sometimes you will get a rise at the very moment you
start to make the lift, so be prepared for it.

As a rule, if you have placed your flies in the right place to
start with, most rises will occur at the following locations: from
A to A; at B just at the moment the flies begin to drag; at C when
you are working the flies in the small area below you as described;
or between C and D when you are retrieving (*see sketch*). Inasmuch
as the positions from A to A are the most likely places for the trout
to be, provided you have started your flies at the most effective
point, most of the rises will occur in this locality or at B, which is

well known to wet-fly anglers as a "hot spot." I have often watched a trout look over the flies between A and A, but refuse them for some reason, only to follow and rise viciously just where the flies started to drag. I have also noticed that many anglers miss this chance to take a trout by lifting their flies too quickly. Many fishermen seem to think that it is absolutely necessary to get in as many casts per hour as possible, that the number of casts made will determine the size of the catch. This does not work out in practice, because a desire to make casts rapidly tends to make the angler slight the actual fishing of the flies, which, after all, is the thing that catches the trout. Fish out each cast completely. Flies will not catch fish while they are in the air.

As a general rule it is best to have the sun at your back when fishing with this method—first, because it allows you to see the flies clearly; and, second, because it decreases the chances that the fish will see you. Even if the hole under the bank or brush is in deep shade, it is to your advantage to have the sun at your back, because the glare on the water between you and the fish acts as a cover to your operations. Of course under some conditions rocky cliffs or bright-colored light reflecting vegetation will create counter rays of light, which changes this condition to a certain extent; also when the sun is near the horizon your shadow may have some effect on the fish, but on the whole you cannot go far wrong by following this hint. Just remember that fish are blinded by direct bright light the same as we are, and choose your fishing locations accordingly. The accompanying diagram will serve to illustrate this graphically. Naturally a reversal of this condition would mean that your eyes are disturbed by the sun and that the trout can readily see you unless you are far enough away so that his line of sight does not carry to you.

Every rocky stream contains many pocket holes that are a bit difficult to locate. Unless you fish very carefully you are bound to skip many of these pockets. If they are shallow you can see the trout rush away from them as you get close. For this reason, unless you know the water thoroughly, it is best to fish all broken water in a very painstaking manner, being sure not to miss any part of it. Often you will go through most of a pocket stretch without getting a rise, so that you get discouraged and start skipping places here and there. As a rule this means that you are passing up opportunities to take fish—the very best chances of all, according to my personal experiences. It was only after I made it a point to fish these places ordinarily neglected that I began to show a decided improvement in my average catch. Of course when you have been over a section of pocket water a great many times you get to know it so well that you do not miss these spots, but even here you must

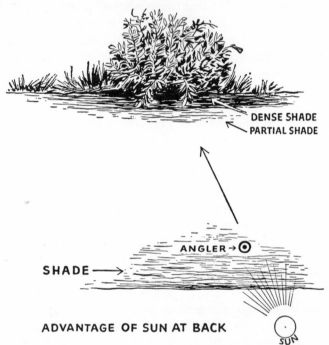

DENSE SHADE
PARTIAL SHADE

ANGLER →

SHADE ——→

ADVANTAGE OF SUN AT BACK

SUN

not be guided too much by past experiences. Every once in a while I find that pockets which have been unproductive for a long while will suddenly start to be very productive. For this reason I do not hesitate to advise a minute covering of all pocket stretches regardless of what your personal opinion of them may be. Only by doing this can you be sure that you have taken advantage of all opportunities.

This type of water requires different technique than fishing bank pockets that have no badly broken water between them and the angler. It is quite imperative to use a short line, not more than twenty feet at the most, and in many cases even less than that. Fortunately this is possible in water of this character as long as you proceed cautiously and do not cause too much disturbance with your feet when wading. You really do nothing more than flick the flies to each spot, but you do it systematically so that you do not skip any hidden pockets. You should pay especial attention to the sides, back, and front of all sizable rocks, both sunken and those which show above the surface. Let the flies float around the rocks with the rod handled so that they do it quite naturally even though the line is kept taut. Following the course of the flies with the tip of the rod makes it possible to do this. Let the flies rest in the pocket behind the rocks and occasionally manipulate the cast so that the dropper fly dances on the water above the most likely locations. Probably the best way to fish this type of water is downstream, but do not confine your casts to sections below you. Also cover the stream on both sides of you.

On some occasions and in some streams a variation of this method is to be recommended. Fish the water thoroughly as described but use a cast of three large flies, about 6's, and work them over the pockets with fast jerks. Do not use any slack line in doing this, in fact do not use your retrieving hand at all. Everything is accomplished with the rod and a short line, which is kept taut against the reel. The very instant all the flies touch the water on the forward cast, you start them moving, bringing the rod back and upward with a speedy, jerky movement. The instant the tail fly reaches the surface of the water on the retrieve, the rod should be in a position to make a quick lift and a new cast. Avoid fishing the flies after the rod reaches a vertical position, because in that case a striking fish may break the tip. I have had many occasions to bless this method of fishing, although I must admit that I had neglected it for many years until it was again brought to my attention in the following manner.

We were on the lower stretches of the Neversink River, in New York State, where the fish run large and are exceedingly temperamental. Three of us had been fishing for more than five hours without seeing a trout. We had fished upstream with a dry fly and had worked back with a wet fly, fishing it in the regulation ways. On the way back we caught up with another fellow, who was also fishing with wet flies. But instead of using only one small fly, his cast was made up of three large flies dangling on a heavy leader. His casts were short and quick. Within one minute he made twelve.

He paid particular attention to all the rocks and could certainly make those flies flutter across the little pockets in a teasing manner. Even as we watched he took two brown trout that were better than fourteen inches in length.

It brought back memories of the old days when I had used this method for brook trout. Because I had become interested in more advanced ways I had forgotten this old one, or to be really candid, I had come to consider its use out of the question when it came to brown trout. But when I saw how it produced for this angler on the Neversink when our fancy methods had failed, my feelings in the matter experienced a sudden reversal.

We could not take advantage of the idea at this time. All our wet flies were small and delicate, and our leaders too fine. I did try it a while with large dry flies, but somehow they would not work. I have since found that the best combination is a three-loop heavy trout leader six to nine feet in length and three bushy wet flies, size 6, of various colors. (See Chapter III for specifications and other wet-fly tackle information.) With this combination it is possible to get the right effect, and the heavy leader enables you to hook a large fish, on the jump as it were, without breaking the gut. Incidentally, the heavy leader is not detrimental in this case because it is above the water practically all the time. In some cases a six-foot leader is better than a longer one.

But do not get the idea that this method is infallible. As a matter of fact it is worth while only in streams of very fast flow. But for fishing pocket water in rapids and also for fishing the speedy parts of riffles, it is invaluable.

Here is another way useful for almost any type of water ranging from fast to medium slow and particularly for steelhead. The cast is made quartering downstream. At the completion of the cast the rod is immediately manipulated with a rhythmic up-and-down motion, the movement being very slight and slow. To be specific the wrist should not move more than seven inches, and there should be about twenty-eight upward movements to the minute. As the fly proceeds downstream you retrieve line slightly, about a total of six inches for the entire float, that is until the fly comes into position directly below you. When this point is reached, several different ways of finishing the cast may be used. One is to keep the fly working slowly upstream, using the "hand twist" retrieve.

Another is to release the small quantity of line that was gathered in, and when the line comes taut, work the fly up and down in an area of from six inches to one foot. If no strike is forthcoming within a couple of minutes, it should then be retrieved. Last, you may strip off six to eight feet of line when the fly comes taut, and then release this footage of line all at once so that the fly will sink and at the same time go a bit further downstream. When it comes taut again, you may either retrieve it by the "hand twist" method or else reel it in slowly. Incidentally, this reeling-in process is often deadly, so much so that I rarely fail to give it a try when fishing wet.

Sometimes it is advantageous to strip off six or seven feet of line at the moment the cast has been completed—before the fly has floated downstream. This gives the fly a greater depth and, if the fish are "using" on bottom, results in better catches. In all these methods it is imperative to have the fly sink as soon as it touches the water. All that is needed to accomplish this is to soak the fly thoroughly before making the cast.

In addition to these various methods of fishing the wet fly, there are some others that, while not so well known, are equally important. For instance, there is the count system for still waters, which I believe Clyde Post and I originated at Brandy Brook in the Adirondacks. We stumbled on this method by chance. We had been fishing in the late afternoon without success when Clyde suddenly became tired and let his fly sink at the completion of his cast. He came to life just in time to keep it from getting caught in the snags, and as he brought the line taut he felt a tug. Of course we both started letting our flies sink after this, and several times we felt fish as well as snags but did not connect with any trout. Because we noted that all the hits came just at the moment we were likely to get snagged, we decided to see just how long it took for the fly to reach bottom. To ascertain this we counted. Before long we knew exactly how much to count for the fly to reach a point just above the snags, and when we got that we started striking at the very moment the total count was reached. About every fifth cast our blind strike was rewarded with a trout. This simple idea is most useful under many conditions, and by adopting it you can often successfully fish tough spots that otherwise would be exasperating rather than productive.

In all still-water fishing it is usually best to let the flies sink before starting the retrieve. The depth to let them sink depends on the circumstances, and it pays to try all depths until the best one is reached. As a rule the "hand twist" retrieve is best for waters of this type. The name of this retrieve is my own, and right here I shall describe it. It is really the most important in wet-fly fishing, and yet I've never seen it described so that anyone not knowing it could tell what it was. At the start of the retrieve take the line between your thumb and forefinger. With them pull the line in as far as your fingers will normally move. Then immediately reach up with the other three fingers and pull the line with them as far as they will move normally. This brings your thumb and forefinger into position again, and you simply keep repeating this performance, building up an orderly roll of line in the palm of your hand. This, you'll find, will pay off easily and evenly, without snarling on the next cast. In making this retrieve, maintain a steady and even rhythm until it is completed. This may be regulated as to speed, and this regulation is often necessary.

This is an antique method of retrieving, but it has never lost its effectiveness, as those who use it will readily testify. I shall no doubt mention this retrieve by name from time to time in subsequent chapters, so to those who are not conversant with it I would recommend that you string up a rod at this time so that the principle of it will be impressed on your mind. If you can visualize these things as you read of incidents where the methods are used, what you read will have much more interest and value.

Another method is one that came from watching an angler fish from a high point on the bank, from where I could see the flies and the creek bed while he could not. At this time the trout were apparently off feed, and I had quit fishing, preferring to wait until they started to rise. I watched this fellow carefully. I felt sure that he wouldn't get any fish, but if he did I wanted to see how he did it. Then I saw something that made me sit up and take notice. The fisherman had stopped his retrieve shortly after starting it to turn around to speak to his guide. It was only a slight pause, and then he started moving the flies again. A second later he again paused as he spoke to the guide a second time. As the fly started sinking on the slack line I saw the flash of a trout as it took the fly and then immediately spit it out. A fraction of a second later the angler resumed the retrieve, but by this time the fish was gone. Of course he knew nothing about it. A little while later I tried the stunt a bit further downstream, and it produced a limit catch even though others on the stream failed to take a fish. Following is the method which is very useful in spring holes or in the still waters of any stream.

At the completion of the cast, start the flies moving rapidly with an upward movement of the rod. Make about three fast jerks, and then lower the rod tip and allow the flies to sink for a count of fifteen or longer if the water is more than five feet deep. Then make three more jerks and follow it again by the pause and lowering of the rod tip. Continue this procedure until the retrieve is completed. Whenever the fly is sinking, watch it carefully. If you see a flash or see the line twitch, strike hard and quickly. If you are too slow or don't strike hard enough to offset the disadvantage of the slack line, the fish will spit out the fly before you can set the hook.

When a similar but faster action than can be maintained by the "hand twist" retrieve is needed, you may use what I call the "line retrieve." In making this you hold the line with the thumb and forefinger of the rod hand. Then with the other hand you strip in the line with jerks. These may be short and deliberate or fast and erratic, in fact you should mix up the speed and the length of the jerks to suit the conditions.

A variation of this retrieve is made by using both the rod and the line at the same time. In this case the rod supplies most of the action during the start of the retrieve, while the hand finishes it when the rod has reached a point slightly under vertical. This method is used when you wish the flies to come along rapidly near the surface of the water and is very effective with a bucktail, as I discovered while fishing Encampment Creek in Wyoming. A nine- or nine-and-a-half-foot rod is needed to do it effectively, and it is rather exhausting because you must not let the flies rest on the water a second after the cast is completed, and the faster you get the next cast back, if you miss a fish on the first retrieve, the better chance you have of taking him.

Occasionally I use a style of wet-fly fishing that I call the "continuous roll." It is really nothing more than one switch or roll cast after another. You start with a regular cast across and downstream.

When the fly comes taut below you, the rod is lifted slowly to the perpendicular and then given a quick downward movement, which is completed with the rod pointing toward a spot several feet further upstream. If this is done correctly, the fly will alight some five or six feet nearer shore and a bit further upstream than it was at the end of the drift. Since no back cast is needed in making this cast, it proves very useful in fishing narrow and brush-lined streams, or when you are fishing one side of the stream and your comrade the other and you have the side where you cannot make a regular cast without getting hung up. It is also very useful on a flooded stream when the trout are in the backwaters and eddies under low-hanging trees and brush or under the banks. The fly stays low and so can be put under obstructions, and in addition it stays so water-logged that it sinks deeper than it would when making an ordinary cast. No motion is given the fly when fishing in this manner. It is allowed to float as it will, and the line must be watched carefully for any indications of a strike that is not felt.

When fishing very deep water it may be necessary to use a split shot, but avoid this unless it is an absolute necessity. After the fly reaches bottom, bring it in slowly, using the "hand twist" retrieve. As a rule it is best to fish upstream. However, if there are many irregular boulders in the water, a weighted fly fished upstream may prove very troublesome because it frequently snags. In this case you might make out better, particularly when fishing fast water, by using more weight and fishing downstream. Fly fishing with a sinker is similar to bait fishing except that it is more difficult; but if flies will not produce without lead, and you want to use them, then there's nothing else to do.

Remember that wet flies may represent many different things, so that various methods are needed to make them consistently effective. The trout may take them for nymphs, drowned surface flies, minnows, or small crustaceans. In subsequent chapters I shall illustrate by actual experiences how these different styles of wet-fly fishing brought results, and also explain some variations of the different methods needed under certain conditions.

Avoid being a slave to one style. It may be all right for the particular stream you fish most and know intimately, but it may not be a bit satisfactory for other streams you may fish. The man who is well informed on different methods and has had practice in using them has a decided advantage over one who fishes the same way no matter what the conditions. I know it is easier to follow along the lines of least resistance and keep fishing one way because it does not require any mental effort. You can do the same thing in the business of life, but it doesn't get you anywhere. It will pay you to get out of the rut and try different things, to experiment a bit. Only by doing this can you expect to overcome a few of the obstacles that prevent you from being successful. No one can possibly hope to overcome them all.

A Discussion of Wet-Fly Tackle

FLIES

THIS subject of fly patterns is a complicated and absorbing one. There is hardly an angler who hasn't some pet fly that he considers better than any other. Often it is a well-known standard pattern, but sometimes it is a fly that is known very little or that perhaps he may have designed himself. It would be an endless task to try out all these patterns so that one could talk about them intelligently. For this reason I shall take up only those flies which have served me through the years and which I know make a well-balanced assortment. However, in addition I have assembled a large number of patterns that have been successful all over North America, and from them Dr. Edgar Burke has made accurate color plates. This is probably the largest collection of flies to be reproduced in color in any one book. With these color plates, and descriptions of the flies, you can either reproduce any of the patterns yourself or have someone make them for you.

Obviously no one could possibly carry and use all the flies shown in this book. Nor are they needed. But the average angler likes to experiment, and any fly pattern, new or old, is of great interest, whether or not it is extensively used for fishing. The recommended patterns I shall discuss never lose their usefulness. New flies are born at a rapid rate these days, but this basic assortment is as sound today as it was when I first started to fish in 1900. I have, however, expanded the list somewhat to make it wider in scope, but not too unwieldy. Note then when 2XL follows a hook size, it means that the shank is two sizes longer than a standard hook of that number. All the other hooks are regular 2X Stout hooks in standard length, or standard wet-fly hooks.

BLACK ANT. Sizes 8, 10, 12, 14.

While the fly pattern called Black Ant is very old, this particular design is far more lifelike in appearance than the usual ties, and is quite new. It was specifically developed for brown trout in the streams of Pennsylvania. However I have found it excellent in many other waters in the East, the Rockies, and the Far West.

The pattern shown on the plate was sent me by Charlie Wetzel, of Newark, Delaware, author of *Practical Fly Fishing*, who mentioned it as one of his favorites. He did not say who originated it and I'm not positive just where the development began, but the first sample of this particular type that I obtained and used came from Bob McCafferty, of Pennsylvania. All the fellows in Central Pennsylvania I've talked or corresponded with consider this fly one of their musts. Because it proved quite generally useful, I decided it deserved a spot in my basic list.

On the whole sizes 8 and 10 are most popular, but in some Western waters I've had better results with sizes 12 and 14. One of the advantages of this fly is the ease with which it sinks. It is made by building up winding silk, to shape, in several stages; each stage is varnished and given time to harden before the next one is wound on. Thus the fly sinks quickly and is of particular value for use in fast channels, swirling eddies, and similar situations when the trout won't rise and the water is deep.

BLACK GNAT. Plate 1. Sizes 8, 10, 12, 14.

Especially effective in the Northern brook trout country where the black flies make life miserable in the early season, this old-timer will always come in handy at some time or other if you will give it a chance.

On the whole sizes 10 and 12 are most useful, but often in spring-hole fishing in the North sizes 6 and 8 will interest the best fish. Sometimes, too, I find that this pattern makes a splendid nymph. For this purpose simply cut the wings off close to the head, leaving just enough stub to give the effect of shoulders.

BLACK QUILL. Plate 1. Sizes 12, 14, 16, 18, 20.

Under many conditions a quill-bodied fly does better execution than the heavy-bodied Black Gnat, particularly in the small sizes. Sometimes, when a midge hatch is in progress, a wet Black Quill in size 18 or 20—the smallest you can get is best—will bring results when fished on the surface with a long leader, not less than nine feet, tapered to 4X or 5X. At times I've used even finer, and got more rises but also more breakages on the strike. Silk-worm gut is best in these fine calibrations provided it is top grade. But fine leaders can't take a sudden jerk no matter what they are made of, and you must remember this when using them.

However, the use of very fine leaders is necessary if you expect to get rises; and for some reason floating and dragging wet flies will sometimes get results when the same patterns in a dry-fly tie, doing the same thing on the water, fail to interest a single fish.

One thing is sure. A combination of tiny midge wets, and I mean tiny in tie as well as in hook size, in combination with a fine and long tapered leader, will often induce trout to take when every other allurement fails. The system may prove costly in lost flies because you are working on the border line of impracticability, but it will also provide you with thrills that you'd otherwise miss.

It may be difficult to purchase tiny flies. Not many tiers like to make them, some simply can't make them properly. They may be expensive, and they should be; it takes more time to tie such tiny flies, and it is hard to find hackles narrow enough. But if they are made right the cost is well worth while.

BLACK WOOLEY WORM. Sizes 6, 8, 10, 2X Long.

This creation caused me some thought in making a classification. It isn't a true wet fly, a nymph, or a dry fly. It is what I would term a caterpillar, made so that it may be fished wet without too much effort. Caterpillars in natural state float very well. It isn't entirely black, only the body being that, and the grizzly hackles (barred or Plymouth Rock) are soft and sparsely tied. It has proved to be a great fish-catcher. I felt that it should be included in this basic assortment.

The fly in the plate was furnished by Don Martinez, of California. He explains: "This is probably the most popular number that was ever commercialized. They were not original with me (they are made in several color combinations) but were derived from a very old Missouri bass fly of somewhat similar design. I was merely the first to make them commercially as a trout fly, or to be more accurate, trout lure. Black is perhaps the best number."

BLUE DUN and BLUE QUILL. Plate 1. Sizes 10, 12, 14, 16, 18, 20.
The prevalence of natural flies running to gray makes a fly of this color essential. I have never been able to decide if both the Dun and the Quill are necessary, although I find that I favor the Dun. There is something about the blue-gray fur body that makes a juicy-looking fly when wet. But others feel that the quill body more nearly imitates nature, and will use nothing else. You take your choice or try both.

Some of the lighter shades in gray also serve well as imitations of the olives. In selecting the pattern, hold the feathers so that the light shines through them instead of on them. You will notice that although two flies may look the same when examined *under* the light, they may look entirely different when seen *against* the light. In some the fibres take on an olive hue, others show a pale lavender tint, while some look decidedly bluish. I've found need for all of these tints, and would suggest that you try to get all three for your assortment. In my opinion this difference in shadings answers that often-repeated question why one fly of a given pattern takes fish, while another fly looking apparently the same, and fished over the same spot, doesn't work.

Often in the past, on losing a fly that had been taking fish, I tied on an apparent duplicate and failed to get a touch. It wasn't until I discovered this subtle difference in the hackles that I started to remedy the trouble. On the whole I find the lavender and the olive tints most useful, but there are times when blue is needed. This particular color difference is more important when fishing dry than when fishing wet, but it also makes a difference in wet-fly fishing when the fish see the fly against the light instead of the bottom or the banks, something that often happens.

Some anglers prefer the Quill Gordon or Dark Hendrickson patterns. These both have speckled Mandarin duck or wood duck wings, which have a brownish cast. They are usually tied dry, and may be seen in color on Plates 14 and 15 respectively. To make wet, simply use soft hackles and slant them back, and tie the wings along the top of the body instead of vertically.

I must admit that I too like these flies and often use them in preference to either the Blue Quill or Blue Dun. But here again we get into differences in the tints as seen against the light, and usually they are made with the Blue Quill shades of gray rather than the sooty-smoky gray the Hendrickson should have.

Blue Quills and Duns are variations of the English Blue Upright, and the variations in color appear in both the American-made flies and those of foreign manufacture. As advised, it makes sense to have several variations in your box. No one tie is tops everywhere or always. And the variation preferred by one person or fish may not be endured by another.

Ordinarily, either pattern is an early-season fly, and I've yet to find a section of the country where they will not produce at one time or another. They have proved most effective for me in the Eastern states of New York, New Jersey, Pennsylvania, Vermont, New Hampshire, and Connecticut; the Western states of Colorado, Idaho, Montana, and Wyoming. This does not mean that they may not be just as effective in other states and parts of Canada.

CAHILL, Regular or Dark. Plate 2. Sizes 8, 10, 12, 14.

This rather dull-looking brown fly with its blue-gray body is a standard pattern that you can rely on whenever a brownish dull fly is needed. I have successfully used it from coast to coast on brown trout, and have sometimes found it most killing for brook trout in the North in the larger sizes—say 6 and 8.

On the whole it is a brown-trout pattern, and the sizes most generally useful are 10 and 12, but 14 is often needed on low and clear water.

CAHILL, Light. Plate 14. Plate shows dry fly. Slant hackles and wings backward to make wet variety. Sizes 8, 10, 12, 14, 16.

I could easily wax poetic and become boresomely enthusiastic about this fly. If it was necessary to confine my assortment of flies to only two or three, this would be one of them. Basically it is an Eastern pattern, particularly effective in the Catskill waters and similar Eastern mountain streams. However it has served me well in many other states, including Michigan in the Middle West, Wyoming and California in the Far West.

The Light Cahill Quill is a splendid variation of this pattern—see Plate 14 dry for color. While ordinarily the fox-fur body of the regular pattern is all that one needs, there are times when the quill body does better on selective rises.

In purchasing flies of this pattern you will find great variation in the shades of ginger; in fact often the color isn't ginger at all, but a light brown. Personally I like them in two shades, one a definite ginger (almost brown) and the other a very light ginger, almost wheat-straw color. I like the fur body on each to run close to white—it might be better to say pale cream. This shade can be found in the belly fur of the red fox and in the fitch or European polecat. And one of my neighbors has a Persian cat with just the right color under-fur. I often gather it from the floor and make flies with it. Any well-defined quill is all right for the quill pattern.

COACHMAN. Plate 2.	
COACHMAN, Leadwing. Plate 2.	Sizes 6, 8, 10, 12, 14, 18.
RIO GRANDE KING. Plate 7.	Steelhead sizes 4, 6.
ROYAL COACHMAN. Plate 8.	

I have listed these four patterns together because I'm not too sure that you need more than one of them. They are all excellent, the Leadwing being of particular value in Eastern waters, the Rio Grande King in Western waters. All stem from the original Coachman. Personally I'll use any one of them indiscriminately, and I'd feel lost without one or another in my box. Certainly one of them would be my choice if I were confined to the use of only a few patterns; but which one to choose would indeed be a problem.

On the whole I'd recommend the large sizes for lake and pond fishing, for heavy fast water, or water that is discolored. I'd consider sizes 10, 12, and 14 most generally useful for ordinary stream fishing, with 18 excellent for some clear water and wary trout conditions, particularly in the late season. But always carry one or more, because they will most assuredly take trout under many and sundry circumstances.

GINGER QUILL. Plate 14. Plate shows dry fly. Slant hackles and wings backward to make wet variety. Sizes 8, 10, 12, 14, 16, 18, 20.

The dry Ginger Quill shown on Plate 14 is tied with Mandarin or wood duck wings. I've also tied it with teal or mallard feathers

TROUT

dyed bluish gray or slate. The true Ginger Quill is made with slate or bluish-gray wings cut from flight feathers of a duck, the same as shown on the wet Blue Quill on Plate 1. As a matter of fact if you simply substitute ginger hackle and tail in the Blue Quill, then you have the Ginger Quill.

If you use the Light Cahill Quill in two shades of ginger hackle —that is, both dark and light—then you may not need this pattern. However, there are times when the slate wing may be needed to get best results. So here is a suggestion. Most Ginger Quills with the slate wing are tied with a dark ginger hackle—as on the dry Ginger Quill (Plate 14). So make this one of your ginger patterns. The other could be the Light Cahill Quill as shown on Plate 14, but tied wet, that is with hackle and wings slanting back. This will give you a good contrast in ginger-colored quill patterns, and both will produce well if given a chance.

In the small sizes—16, 18, and 20—I would definitely suggest the slate-colored cut duck wings. But I admit this is prejudice on my part, because such flies have produced best for me. The contrary is true in sizes 14 and larger. Then I prefer the Cahill type wings.

GOLD RIBBED HARE'S EAR. Plate 3. Sizes 8, 10, 12, 14.

This fly will also take fish almost anywhere, at one time or another. I have very successfully used it as a nymph by cutting off the wings close to the head, scores of times; and when tied without wings and tail it serves nicely as a fresh-water shrimp. In the latter case, however, the hare's-ear fur should be on the light side to bring best results. The color does vary, and in my opinion it is good to have tints ranging from brownish-gray to a definite gray. As a basic pattern it holds a high position. Other patterns can easily stem from it.

GRAY HACKLE, YELLOW and GRAY HACKLE, PEACOCK. Any size according to needs.

Although this fly is very old, it is a good basic design with either peacock herl, yellow floss silk, or fluorescent body. This last, a recently developed material, is brighter than silk. The tie is simple. It consists of only the body and the hackle, which is grizzle or grizzly, also called barred and Plymouth Rock.

Flies such as Silver Ghost, Spencer (a gray palmer with green

[32]

under-body and yellow tag as a tail), and Teal, a splendid pattern, will all serve in place of the Gray Hackles; in fact they are frequently far more effective. See Plate 8. Also you might use Witch Silver (Plate 9) which is simply a variation of the Gray Hackle. This is illustrative of the way in which you can use the fly plates in *Trout* to your benefit. When you feel the need of a certain general coloration such as gray, and have none that is suitable, go through the plates carefully, study them, and look for variations on the basic colors.

GRIZZLY KING. Plate 4. Sizes 4, 6, 8 for Northern brook trout. Sizes 8, 10, 12 for rainbow trout. Sizes 10, 12, 14 for grayling.

Even this fly is a variation of the Gray Hackle. Its general tone is gray. But the teal or mallard wing adds something and there are plenty of times when its green body and dash of scarlet or crimson will make the trout take when another gray fly fails to attract.

This is another very old pattern which I neglected for many years, because there were so many claims made for other and newer patterns. It was originally made to seduce brook trout, but I've found it just as good for other trout, provided it isn't used when they refuse everything else. You will note that I particularly specify the sizes and uses for this fly. This selection is based entirely on my personal experiences. I've never used the pattern for browns enough to know whether or not it really is outstanding for them. But it might be, especially for freshly stocked browns, as the following story seems to indicate.

As I was writing about the Grizzly King, a friend dropped in for a visit. I didn't mention this fly, or even say I was working on the book, but just before he left he took extra time to tell me of this experience.

He had received an invitation to fish a private stretch of stream, so he went early in the morning and fished hard all day. After working like sin until about 5 P.M. he finally got his limit. But his friend, the club member who had invited him, worked just as hard and never caught a fish.

As they sat on the bank talking over the day, an elderly man started fishing the pool directly in front of them. He caught a nice trout on the first cast, and then proceeded to take his limit in rapid-fire order. Of course this made my friend and his companion sit up and take notice.

The trio met when the patriarch came ashore. My friend, being much impressed, said: "That was the best bit of fishing I've ever seen. Would you mind telling me what fly you used?"

Without hesitation the old man took hold of the fly still tied to his leader and handed it to my friend. "Just a fly the boys tied on for me when I started out," he answered.

It was a Grizzly King. My friend's unsuccessful companion tied on one of this pattern and went down to fish the pool. Just as quickly, he also took his limit.

"I've never seen such fishing!" exclaimed my friend. "It amazes me. Do you have this sort of fishing regularly?"

"No," answered the old gentleman. "The boys knew I'd be here this afternoon, so they stocked the pool for me."

Of course it might be that the trout just got the urge at that particular time—or it might have been a major solunar period. Maybe they'd have taken anything just then. I don't know for sure, because I wasn't there, and the dates and time periods were not available.

But sometimes freshly stocked trout are difficult to catch, even with bait, let alone with a fly. Keeping this in mind, we might give the old-time Grizzly King a pat on the back as a good fly. It was proved to be that in my experience within the limitations stated.

IRRESISTIBLE (WARF VARIANT). Plate 16. Sizes 8–2XL, 10–2XL, sometimes 6–2XL.

This name is not, properly speaking, the name for this pattern, which may be tied wet or dry. It is merely a descriptive tag, indicating a variation of the original Irresistible, a dry fly designed by Joseph Messinger and shown on Plate 16. This wet fly was first tied by a Missouri fisherman having the name of "Ozark" Warf. It resembles the Irresistible only in the body, which is the same except that Ozark makes it quite fat. It is too new to be included in the color plates, but if you look at the body of the dry Irresistible and make the changes indicated you should be able to picture it without too much trouble. Here is the description:

Body—Clipped deer hair, tied fat, although tight and smoothly clipped like the dry pattern.

Wing—Black hair; bear or similar, tied slanting back and just a bit shorter than the body.

Tail—Fox-squirrel tail hair, quite bushy, not quite as long as the body.

Hackle—Ordinary dark ginger or regular red brown, tied in slanting backward to the hook barb and "bearded," that is, not wound on in the usual way but fastened in as a bunch on the underside of the hook at the head end. In other words it is tied on the same as the hair wing, except that it is underneath instead of on top.

Ozark sent me a few of these flies in the summer of 1948. Since then I've used them enough to know they have something that clicks. During 1949 they produced for me many times when some of my old favorites failed entirely or did very poorly. But my experience with the fly has been confined to its use as a dropper on a wet-fly cast for brookies. However, I have used the same body on dry flies with great success since about 1940.

Because this fly is a newcomer, and my experience with it is so limited, I hesitate to call it basic. But I do believe that it fills a definite need and deserves your consideration. I feel quite sure that it will live up to my expectations, at least when used as a dropper.

McGinty. Plate 6. Sizes 4, 6, 8, 10. See also Bee, Plate 1.

While this isn't a generally popular fly it will often produce nicely in the summer months. I find only occasional need for it when fishing for browns, lots of use for it fishing for Northern brookies during warm weather. It is a good Canadian and Maine pattern, with specially tied variations good for steelhead.

March Brown, American; March Brown, English—Male and Female. Plate 5. Sizes 10, 12, 14, sometimes 8.

These flies don't get enough attention from the average angler. The American March Brown is a decidedly brownish fly that has proved very effective in many Eastern waters. It is well known, and you shouldn't have any trouble either purchasing or making it. It has usually worked best for me early in the season—say from opening day to June 15—with variations, of course, according to the season.

[35]

The English March Browns are extremely buggy, the female lighter in color than the male. Both are most effective, and have served me well in both the East and West. Grayling seem particularly fond of either.

When the wings of these flies are cut off stubby, they make excellent nymphs. I find, however, that it is difficult to purchase these patterns from American makers, probably because of the popularity of the American design.

You will note that the steelhead version is a fancily dressed English pattern.

MONTREAL. Plate 6. Sizes 2, 4, 6, 8, 10.

While I've occasionally taken trout other than brooks with this pattern, I'd definitely call it an essential for Northern brook trout and usually unnecessary for other species. The plate shows the original tie, and two variations. All three are good, and in recent years I find that I lean to a pattern with a white-tipped wing, but otherwise the same as the regular. Sometimes, too, the fly works better if you get it with a fuzzy, instead of a smooth, body.

OLIVE DUN and OLIVE QUILL. Plate 6. Sizes 10, 12, 14.

As a rule I do not find much need for these two patterns, but when I do, I need them very badly indeed. I'm sure that I do not always use them when I should, simply because the color has never appealed to me. But there are sometimes worms and flies of pale-green coloration in our lakes and streams, and we are often missing a bet by neglecting these two flies.

ORANGE FISH HAWK. Plate 14. Plate shows dry fly. Slant hackles back for wet fly. Sizes 10, 12, 14.

I prefer this pattern to the Gray Hackle Yellow. It is a most effective wet fly for all species of trout. It has often produced for me when getting fish was tough. It is also just as good as the Gray Hackle Peacock, the one tied with a peacock herl instead of orange floss silk. The difficulty these days is getting badger hackles with good black centers and light outsides. As a matter of fact they are hard to get even in the more honey-colored shades. Fancy birds that produce this sort of hackle are becoming more and more difficult to obtain, and I doubt if the situation will get better. It is more likely to get worse, because the present trend in fowl is toward fast breeders, growers, and layers, rather than toward beautifully feathered birds. If there is any improvement, it will stem from someone who starts raising cocks for fly tiers. Of course hackles from such a source would need to be expensive, but critical anglers who want the best wouldn't find that objectionable, provided the price is within reason.

If you can purchase or make Orange Fish Hawks, I'd say to do it. The pattern does catch trout.

PALE SULPHUR. Plate 6. Sizes 12, 14, 16. See also Mealy Moth and Pale Watery Quill.

You need some flies that range from a pale sulphur to cream, particularly in the middle of the season. This suggests a range of colors rather than a specific pattern. As a matter of fact just one shade will not be enough to take care of selective hatches. A paper-match-stick yellow is good for one design, and for another a deep cream or light honey. Then if you can get a White Miller that is off color —faintly creamy and without any tinsel on the body—it will be found most useful in filling out a rounded assortment of flies in these shades.

PARMACHENE BELLE. Plate 7.

This fancy pattern is primarily best for brook trout in Northern waters, and for sea-run steelhead on the West Coast. In my opinion it is the popular fly substituting for the colorful paired fins of the brook trout, which have always been a killing bit of bait. Other imitations of this natural lure are Fontinalis Fin and Bergman Fontinalis. See Plate 10. (I didn't name the last one. It was named for me by the friend who designed it, Phil Armstrong, of Michigan and Pennsylvania.) Of course natural fins vary in color, so that any fly made along these lines should be satisfactory as a basic.

But while I have specified this pattern for certain fish, you may find it useful for browns and other species. Often I have used it with good effect when the water has been high and slightly discolored.

PROFESSOR. Plate 7. Sizes 4, 6, 8, 10, 12.

This English pattern seems to have become more renowned in America than it is in the land of its origin. In the large sizes, 4, 6, and 8, it is excellent for Northern brooks. I find it also very good for the other species when used in sizes 8 through 12. It is particularly effective when there are plenty of yellowish grasshoppers in the meadows.

QUEEN OF THE WATERS. Plate 7. Sizes 10, 12, 14.
While I hesitated to call this a basic pattern, I decided it was worth a place in your box if you fish Eastern waters. It has proved particularly good for me in some New Jersey and New York streams of the Delaware watershed.

QUILL GORDON. Plate 14. Plate shows dry fly. Wings and hackle should be slanted back for wet fly.
See remarks relative to Blue Dun and Blue Quill.
Unless this fly is tied with a different color hackle than the blues, I do not see its imperative need. However, if you can't get different shades of hackle, I would suggest that, because of the Quill Gordon's speckled brown wood duck wing, it would be well to have the Blue Dun and the Quill Gordon rather than both the blues. But if this fly is tied with really smoky-bronze hackle, it serves a need distinct and separate from that of either the Blue Dun or the Blue Quill.
While I wouldn't consider this a Northern brook-trout pattern, I have found that in a special tie it is often a winner with these fish. For this purpose I use a size 10 or 12 hook, 2X long. The wing, a single one, is tied upright and not divided. The hackle and tail are very sparse, the body quill well defined. Give this a try some time. It is particularly effective at dusk and through the night. Of course be sure that night fishing is allowable.

SILVER DOCTOR. Plate 8. Sizes 4, 6, 8, 10.
If you can get this pattern tied at least somewhere near the correct dressing, it is excellent for certain conditions. Although primarily a Northern pattern it has proved useful on brown trout streams in the thickly settled regions, and for steelhead waters in the West.
On the brown-trout streams it is particularly good for night fishing, or for high discolored-water conditions. Sometimes it gets good results when live minnows are making the best catches. It is

a handy fly to have available. You may go a long time without using it, but it will serve a need some day, provided you think of it at the right time.

In recent years the Silver Doctor has lost much of its prestige to the many excellent and fancy streamer and bucktail flies used for similar purposes.

WICKHAM'S FANCY. Plate 9. Sizes 6, 8, 10, 12, 14, 16, 18.

CAMPBELL'S FANCY. Plate 14. Plate shows dry fly. Slant wings and hackles backward to make wet variety.

I have listed these two flies together because they are of the same type, and where one is good the other usually is also. Personally I prefer the Campbell's Fancy, but as the Wickham's is better known and easier to obtain from the average tackle shop, I've given it top billing. Cahill Gold Body, Plate 14 (dry fly), is another pattern in this group.

In my opinion, the yellow tail and the black-and-white teal wings of the Campbell's make it more generally attractive and useful coast to coast. This seems particularly true in the larger sizes, all patterns running very uniform in performance in sizes 10 through 18.

THIS concludes my list of essential wet flies. I do not dispute that many others are good, and no doubt needed for special conditions. But the purpose of these recommendations is to simplify your assortment and not to make it more complicated. You can, you know, get so much varied information that you become quite confused, and unable to make a wise selection. I'm also listing some flies from the various plates which you may study and consider as additions to your assortment, or even as replacements for some of these that I have personally found adequate in fishing from coast to coast.

As a rule sparsely tied flies are better for hard-fished waters, and heavily dressed flies are best for the wilderness. However, the reverse is sometimes true, so that it always pays to have some of each style.

The following are some other flies shown in the plates that I have used to advantage. There are many others that I know will fill a definite need at some time or another. I have not listed the patterns already mentioned and discussed in the text. The remarks indicate my personal experience with the patterns.

Plate 1. ALDER. Good for all trout and in many places.
ALEXANDRA. A fancy pattern that often proves surprisingly effective.
BLACK JUNE. An all-around pattern.

Plate 2. BRUNTON'S FANCY. A variation of a Gray Palmer.
CARDINAL. For Northern brook trout.

Plate 3. GORDON. Almost a basic fly for the author's money.
GOLD MONKEY. A good all-around fly.
GOOD EVENING. For both browns and brooks in the East.
GRANNOM. For brown trout in the East.

Plate 4. GRAVEL BED. For browns, rainbows, and graylings, both East and West.
GREEN COACHMAN. For browns in the East, occasionally useful in the Yellowstone country.
GREENWELL'S GLORY. Considered practically a basic by the writer. Has been effective all over the country.
IRON BLUE QUILL. A generally useful fly.
JOCK SCOTT. For Northern brook trout, Western steelhead, and Atlantic salmon.

Plate 5. KINGDON. One of the rather numerous brownish flies which make good variations of the March Brown.
LADY MILLS. A fine buggy pattern for general use.

Plate 6. MOTH BROWN. An excellent night pattern.

Plate 7. RED TAG. A great brook-trout pattern. Also excellent for browns, especially without the bright red tag.

Plate 8. SASSY CAT. For Northern brook trout.
SHEENAN. A splendid all-around orange-bodied pattern.
ST. PATRICK. An excellent minnow-type pattern for browns, rainbows, and brooks.

Plate 9. WARWICK. An outstanding all-around fancy fly.
YELLOW DRAKE. Useful when yellow is needed.

Below are listed all of the wet flies not already discussed in the preceding text:

BLACK BUG. This design, by Ray Allinger, of California, was supplied to me by Harry Huffman, of the same state. It is really nothing more than a development of the Black Hackle. However, the body design makes it entirely different, both in looks and in usage.

BROWN HELGRAMMITE NYMPH. This one, also by Mr. Allinger, is a variation of the Brown Hackle but with the body differing as in the Black Bug. While called a nymph, it really should not be so classified.

[Note that both of these flies have a thorax, or at least the body extends on both sides of the hackle. This idea is used in the construction of dry flies by Vincent C. Marinaro, of Pennsylvania. He is not acquainted with Mr. Allinger, yet by an interesting coincidence they both had the same basic thought, one for a wet fly, the other for a dry fly. Of course the Allinger patterns could also be made as dry flies.]

FISH FLY. This pattern by Charlie Wetzel is one of his own design. He recommends it in sizes 6 and 8, medium long or 2X long hooks. To quote Mr. Wetzel: "This fly loves the bright sunshine and if the weather is propitious it may be noticed in good numbers, flying sluggishly here and there among the willows bordering the stream. During the latter part of May and early in June (Eastern waters) it appears over the water and its imitation is rated as a killing fly on large brown trout. When I originally constructed this pattern it was tied dry but in more recent years I have changed it over to a wet fly, in which state (no doubt due to its large size) it has proven far more successful."

GREIG QUILL. A good design.

JOCK SCOTT (SHERBROOKE). Percy F. Buckland, of Sherbrooke, Quebec, Canada tells me that this version of the Jock Scott is demanded by many anglers in some sections of the province. They do not want the standard.

LORENZO. By Mr. Buckland. A Northern brook-trout pattern. Size 6 has been very successful for large fish.

RED QUILL SPINNER. Another by Charlie Wetzel. Recommended in size 12. To quote from his book, *Practical Fly Fishing:* "This is one of the earliest May flies and it usually arrives when the snow water is running off. It is typically a cold water fly and is usually seen in the bright sunshine, rising and falling over the water. Hatches at this time of the year usually occur in the heat of mid-day and as a rule very few trout are interested in the dry fly. For that reason its imitation is most successful when tied and fished wet."

STONE FLY. Also by Charlie Wetzel. Hook size 10 medium or 2X long. He says: "It favors those stretches where water flows swiftly over a rocky bottom. Its imitation will be found most successful in such riffles."

WHITE CADDIS. Still another from Charlie Wetzel. He writes: "Without doubt this insect is the prototype of that old favorite erroneously named the Deer Fly. It is commonly found from Canada to Florida and is over the water from twilight until early morning. Its imitation, wrongly named the Deer Fly, has stood the test of time."

NOTE. Plate 2 shows an old Deer Fly tie. This isn't anything like the Deer Fly that Mr. Wetzel refers to. His reference is probaby to the pattern shown in color in the famous old book *Favorite Flies* by Mary Orvis Marbury. The comments on the fly in this book say in part: "It is probable that calling the fly pictured in the plate the Deer Fly began with a mistake by someone." This ties up with Mr. Wetzel's statement.

Wet-Fly Leaders

Probably the most generally used length of leader for wet-fly fishing is six feet. However, I believe that seven and a half feet is better, and that nine feet is best when the water is very clear and quiet, and the trout wary.

Despite the fact that nearly all angling writers recommend eyed hooks, there are still many snelled flies in use, so that the old regulation wet-fly leader is still needed. These looped leaders should be purchased in a calibration to fit the snelled flies you buy; otherwise the results will be unsatisfactory.

For instance, if the fly snells calibrate .014 inch, the leader should measure at least that much or a trifle more. Leaders of this weight are generally used only in Northern brook-trout waters or where there are large fish like the steelhead of the coastal streams, or the rainbows of Michigan's Soo rapids and the Finger Lakes streams of New York State. Such leaders need not be tapered, but if they are it is wise to start the butt length with material calibrating .019 or thereabouts.

Personally I do not see the need for such heavy leaders for average Northern brook-trout fishing, where fish up to two pounds are tops. But where fish range from two pounds up to five, there might be good reason for them, particularly if the waters were snaggy and strong-arm tactics were needed to keep the fish from getting into the hazards.

While eyed flies have some advantages over the snelled variety, one being the ease with which a large number may be carried, the snelled flies are a great aid to any one with poor eyesight. But I would suggest that the person needing or preferring snelled flies buy only those snelled to eyed hooks, and that he insist on getting leaders to match the flies he buys.

If you can get snelled flies made with fine gut, then of course you may and should use fine leaders. But if you can't locate such snells, and you wish to fish fine, it will be necessary to use eyed flies. To use an ordinary looped leader for this, simply add a dropper snell to the loop and cut off the end fly loop. When choosing or making a fine leader you might use the following procedure.

I would designate leader material calibrating .008 inch as fine for wet-fly fishing. This would be 3X nylon or 2X silk-worm gut. Now you *can* use a level leader of this weight, but believe me, a level leader of seven and a half feet in this size is difficult to cast. Therefore it will be to your advantage to use a tapered leader. Following are some tapers that work nicely in a seven-and-a-half-foot leader, allowing plenty of waste for knots and loops:

	Using 16-inch strands	Using 20-inch strands
For .008 leader	.015; .014; .012; .010; .009; .008.	.015; .013; .011; .009; .008.
For size heavier (.009) leader	.016; .014; .012; .011; .010; .009.	.016; .014; .012; .010; .009.

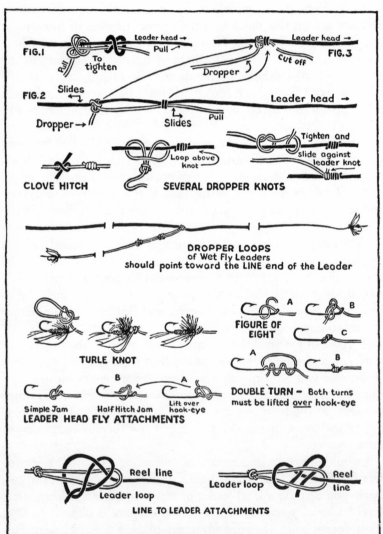

The dropper loop would be best for average purposes if tied near the upper end of the second strand from the fly end of the five-strand leader, or in the third strange of the six-strand leader. Occasionally, though, it may be of advantage to have the dropper loop midway up the leader. You may use a snell or tippet two sizes smaller than the loop calibration, but it is usually best to keep the

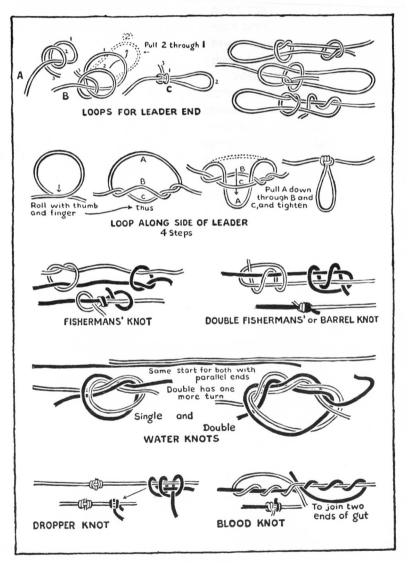

LOOPS FOR LEADER END

Roll with thumb and finger → thus

Pull A down through B and C, and tighten

LOOP ALONG SIDE OF LEADER
4 Steps

FISHERMANS' KNOT

DOUBLE FISHERMANS' or BARREL KNOT

Same start for both with parallel ends
Double has one more turn
Single and Double
WATER KNOTS

DROPPER KNOT

BLOOD KNOT

To join two ends of gut

difference to .001 inch or to have no difference at all. But never have a tippet of greater diameter than the leader because this will make for poor results; the leader and the flies will tangle quite easily.

Nylon comes in twenty-inch and twenty-two-inch lengths, as well as longer ones. Some may object to cutting the lengths of nylon to the above specifications because of the waste. But to get proper tapering you must do this, or else have a longer leader than you want. In fact, a clever tier won't need strands as long as I have specified. But the cost of nylon strands is so small that the waste is hardly an item to consider.

Even silk-worm gut is well down in cost. With this material you may need to change the formula somewhat. Perhaps you won't be able to get all sixteen-inch strands. I know that you won't get all twenty-inch strands. So you must arrange the set-up accordingly, for instance something like the following, assuming you could get only those lengths:

14 inch	*14 inch*	*16 inch*	*16 inch*	*18 inch*	*18 inch*
.015	.014	.012	.010	.009	.008

Or if the strands are all short, you may add an extra strand in one of the missing sizes such as .013 or .011. With this basic information you should be able to figure out your own tapers without any difficulty. Of course always carry proper tippets for replacements. The list on page 47 will give you manufacturers' numbers for various calibrations. These actual measurements are the most sound and sure way of giving the correct information.

Wet-Fly Rods

In the last century, when the fly rod as we know it was relatively new and flies were almost always fished wet, all fly rods were very limber. But when the dry fly came into use it demanded a change in fly-rod action. It was found that the false casting necessary to keep the fly dry, as well as the power needed to propel the fluffy, air-resisting fly against the slightest wind, called for a rod with considerably more backbone and stiffness than those which had been made up to that time.

This chart has been prepared for the convenience of those who buy nylon and gut when marked without calibrations by the manufacturers. The pound test is not given because it varies in different brands. To make proper leaders the calibrations must be followed.

Calibration	Nylon numbers and sizes in thousandths of inch	NAT. A.A. & C. CLUB list for S. W. Gut
.023	0/5	—
.021–.020	1/5	1/5
.019	2/5	2/5
.018	3/5	3/5
.017	4/5	4/5
.016	5/5	5/5
.015	6/5	6/5
.014	7/5	7/5
.013	8/5	8/5
.012	9/5	9/5
.011	0X	10/5
.010	1X	0X
.009	2X	1X
.008	3X	2X
.0075		3X
.007	4X	3X
.0065		4X
.006	5X	4X
.0055		5X
.005	6X	6X

Today nearly everyone wants a stiff rod. They even go too far and get rods that are too stiff to be pleasant for fishing, rods requiring such heavy lines to bring out their action that it actually cuts down one's score when fishing clear, shallow and quiet water, and perhaps other types of water as well under certain conditions. Personally I find a rod of medium stiffness ideal for use with either wet or dry fly. An eight-foot split bamboo rod, of the best grade, weighing three and five-eighths to four ounces, is a good choice. If more power is needed, as on large streams or on windy lakes and ponds, then it will be best to have an eight-and-a-half- or nine-foot rod, ranging in weight from four and five-eighths to five and one-quarter ounces. It is impossible to give exact weights because of variations in the bamboo, also in accessories. For instance I have one eight-footer weighing three and one-half ounces that has the same power and action of another weighing four ounces. The four-ounce job has a locking reel seat that makes part of the difference; the difference in the bamboos must make the rest.

One should not overlook steel rods. These have been improved in action to such an extent that the good ones perform very well indeed. And they keep nearly all their action in use, while the best of split bamboo rods lose ginger in time. I don't like the feel of steel rods, but I must admit that when I get the right line on one and

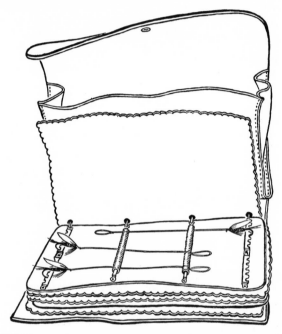

FOLDING LEATHER WET-FLY BOOK FOR SNELLED FLIES

fish it long enough to become used to its action, it will do just as good work as my pet split bamboo.

In recent years glass fibre rods have come into the picture. Some fellows like them very much, others do not. However, they are being steadily improved, and as the prices have also come down to a reasonable figure, they are now giving steel and bamboo some stiff competition.

But because stiff rods are not needed for most wet-fly fishing one may use very light rods and thus get the maximum of sport in playing a fish. I find that an eight-foot rod weighing three and one-quarter ounces and a nine-foot rod weighing four and one-quarter ounces are great tools for Northern brook-trout fishing from boat or canoe. But they are not necessary, so I would not recommend them except as extras to your regular equipment.

All these remarks about rods refer to the better grades. It would be difficult to give such information about low-priced rods because there are so many of them. At the same time let me point out that you may often pick up a gem when purchasing a cheap rod. If it does have good action it may pay to change the ferrules, add extra guides if needed, and give it a good finish. Considerable cost is added or saved by items like these.

Fly Books and Boxes

The carrier for your wet flies depends on their type and size. If you insist on snelled wet flies, then the fly book is the only satis-

ALUMINUM CLIP BOX FOR EYED WET FLIES

factory container. The type with springs to hold the gut straight and a clip to hold the hook of the fly are satisfactory.

For eyed wet flies the clip-style boxes are excellent. See illustration on page 49 for one type. I like these boxes rather small, approximately four and three-quarters by three and one-half inches and not too deep. The depth of the box shown is nine-sixteenths of an inch, and it suits me fine. I have many others, but one of these dimensions seems to be the one I most often choose to take with me.

Magnetic boxes are liked by many. These boxes are equipped with magnets that hold the flies secure. You may prefer them to the clip or other types, so give them a look-over before making up your mind. As personal tastes vary, neither of these types may please you, so take time out for some shopping. It's lots of fun, even if you don't buy.

Fly and Leader Sink

Often it is advantageous to have both the leader and the fly sink quickly. You may get this result by using mud and water, but to hurry things along, you may use one of the excellent wetting agents now on the market, and obtainable at completely stocked tackle stores. If you can't locate any, you will find aerosol fairly good. It is used as a wetting agent in photography and you may purchase it from a photographer. But don't expect too much of this stuff. You must apply it frequently unless you keep your flies in the water continuously all day. If the leader and fly dry out between fishing periods, then apply some more before starting to fish again.

Nymphs and
Methods of Fishing Them

NYMPH fishing is simply a method of wet-fly fishing with artificials that are supposed to imitate underwater creepers.

While you can successfully fish wet flies in the nymph manner,
often some of the wet-fly methods fail to work with close imitations of natural nymphs. For instance, wet flies will frequently
produce best results when they are moved rapidly. In my experience nymphs are rarely effective when used in this manner. The
inference is clear. The natural creepers do not move with pronounced darts and jerks when they are adrift from their home
rocks and logs. They are primarily crawlers rather than swimmers,
although there are a few forms that can move rapidly through the
water. When the artificial looks much like a natural that doesn't
move like a minnow or bug, then the trout are suspicious of it
when it acts unnaturally.

This brings up the question of what the trout think fast-moving
wet flies are. Personally I believe they are taken for small minnows,
or shrimp, or some other form of underwater life that might move
about speedily when feeding or frightened. Certainly a drowned
fly does not move except as carried along by the current. It is even
likely that fish do not take our wet flies for any specific insect at
all, but because they look like something to eat and act as if they
were trying to escape, the fish strike them out of curiosity. Of
course this does not explain why they might prefer certain patterns
on some days and not on others. Often the most killing fly is one
that to our knowledge does not imitate anything in nature. But
then we do not know just how our imitation looks to the fish or
how the different degrees of light affect its appearance.

The first nymphs I ever used were made in England. They were
nothing more than bodies of flies made a bit thick near the head,

with a few turns of hackle constituting the feelers. I never did any better with them than I did with a wet fly with the wings cut off, so I finally discontinued using them. Then Louis Rhead brought out his series, which were supposed to be close imitations of the nymphs found in American streams. As even fair copies of the natural, they were failures. It would have taken a vivid imagination to see the resemblance, but some of them, especially the pink pattern, were very effective in certain waters.

An outstanding contribution in the way of nymph imitations was Hewitt's Hard Body Nymph. It has a flattened body and is quite realistic, although the opaque body does not imitate the translucent body of the natural. My first attempt at a nymph design resulted in a lure that, while not actually imitating the natural, did bring good results in many waters, especially on the Beaverkill, in New York, for which it was originally tied. It was impressionistic rather than imitative, and the guinea-fowl feelers gave it movement and life that others lacked. Then Herbert Howard and I, in working out a formula for translucent bodies, discovered a combination of materials that made it possible to make a flat body imitation that was also semi-transparent. Also it could be shaped so that it looked like a natural and could be colored in any shade. I made some up in amber, brown olive, dark green, and dark orange red and they proved quite successful under certain conditions. However, they require a lot of time to make, and unless a way is found to overcome this, I doubt if they will ever become widely known. Paul Young, as his contribution, brought out the Strawman Nymph. Although this looks nothing like a nymph, it is one of the most effective lures of this type. It may be that the rough construction closely imitates a cased caddis. Oscar Weber's contribution was an assortment of nymphs in various stages of development. While I haven't had much experience with these nymphs, having had only one—the Phurea—my success with this pattern was sufficient to have me mention the entire assortment. Another good nymph is the "Dickie," especially useful on the Beaverkill and other Catskill streams.

I have used many other excellent designs with success and there are probably many more patterns just as good that have escaped my attention. While I endeavor to keep up with the new items, it is impossible to keep track of, and try out, the many new nymphs that are continually making their appearance. Nor do I think it necessary in order to catch fish. However, all new fly patterns are of great interest and I regret my inability to give each one a fair trial. Without a doubt I would find many of surpassing merit if I could. Needless to say, all the types I have mentioned have won their spurs. Sometimes when one won't produce, one of the others will. Sometimes none are worth a damn. Much fishing lore is based on personal experience in special locations so that it is impossible to make hard-and-fast rules about it. One man may make a killing with X nymph pattern while another can't catch a fish with it. This happens with well-known flies more than it does with nymphs, probably because they are used more. The more you learn about fishing, the more experience you get in widely separated sections, the more you will realize the truth and humility in this assertion.

There are a number of methods with which nymphs may be successfully fished. As with wet-fly fishing, these are hard to describe because so much depends on one's ability to feel and sense both the progress of the lure and the strike of the fish.

I don't pretend to be a good nymph fisherman—in fact I often feel a bit uncertain when using them. However, they have served me well and I always use them in apparently hopeless cases when dry and wet flies have failed to produce. Many times the habit of giving them this last chance has resulted in my getting the finest fish of the day, which is a real recommendation when you consider that the other flies get all the best opportunities to prove their worth. Because of these occasional successes under adverse conditions, I feel that my descriptions of the methods used will be of some value to the reader.

If I seem to use excessive detail in describing these methods, I hope the experienced nymph fisherman will overlook it and realize that many beginners at the game will read these pages. Even at that, I fear the descriptions may be inadequate. Besides, the intuitive reactions of the angler mean more than the application of advised mechanical operations. Such things cannot be expressed by words. They are too elemental and elusive.

The first method to learn is what I call the "downstream drift." Let us take up each move separately. First, if the nymph is one of the type that requires wetting before it sinks, be sure it is well soaked so that it goes down readily. Then make a cast either across stream or slightly down and across stream. As the current carries the lure along, follow its progress with the tip of the rod. This allows it to float naturally without drag and is practically the same system with which you would fish a worm. In this method of fishing you really need not see a rise to your nymph. If you do the job correctly you will feel a tug, and the tautness of the line will set the hook. If the trout is small, then a slight lift of the rod is necessary to set the hook, but inasmuch as the natural reaction when feeling a strike is to do this, it will probably be done without the angler being conscious of it. Of course there will be many misses, but usually they will be small fish even though you might think differently. I have had large trout take a nymph so hard when fished in this way that the sudden pull made the click of the reel sing, and that is music every angler likes.

Another method, which I use more frequently than any other, is the "upstream drift." It is accomplished by casting the nymph either directly upstream or quartering up and across stream. It is practically the same as dry-fly fishing except that the lure is under water instead of on the surface. In my estimation this is the most effective way to use nymphs, but unfortunately it is also the most difficult method to learn. In the beginning it may be advisable to use a dry fly on the leader as an indicator. In attaching this dobber or float, tie it on as short a tippet as you can manage and attach it to the leader from four to six feet above the nymph. A fly with good floating qualities is necessary, say a heavily tied palmer hackle of a color most visible to you.

The purpose of this dry fly is to give you something to watch for indications of a strike. Sometimes it will disappear quickly, at other times it will simply stop floating with the current, and often it will simply twitch slightly without going under the surface. All these signs signify a strike, and you must react quickly by striking back or you will miss the fish. As an example, suppose the fly is floating along with the current and suddenly stops or goes a bit slower than the current. At the very instant this happens you should set the hook; otherwise it will be too late. Of course it may be that the nymph touched a rock and caused the dry fly to act peculiarly, but this is a chance you must take. As a matter of fact, if the dry fly acts in the slightest degree unnaturally in relation to the flow of the water, it usually means that a trout has taken the nymph. Sometimes these indications are so slight that it takes a very observant eye to see them. The more you can develop this keenness of observation the better wet-fly and nymph fisherman you will become.

Incidentally, this sort of fishing demands a thorough knowledge of water currents as well as a keen judgment that tells you when the fly is drifting as it should. To develop these talents will give you some invaluable practice in the science of reading a stream. After a time you will be able to discard the dry-fly indicator and fish the nymph without its aid. However, I have found that it helps considerably in getting one acquainted with nymph-fishing technique and is likely to make it possible for those who have never been able to do anything with these lures really to accomplish something with them.

The "upstream drift" method is extremely useful for fishing under banks, log jams, or anything else that might afford a hiding place for trout and that may be reached in this manner. To fish such a location successfully it may be wise first to float a dry fly to it in order to ascertain just how long it will take your nymph to reach the spot, of course allowing a bit for extra time so that the sunken lure will get down into the hole.

After you have figured this out by watching the performance of your dry fly, then you may fish your nymph in the same way, being sure that it sinks. When the estimated time has elapsed, pull the line taut and be ready to strike. You are very likely to lose nymphs fishing this way and will also miss many strikes, but every once in a while you will take a good trout that otherwise never would have found its way into your creel.

Although I have taken a good many fish with this method of nymph fishing, I rarely use it except after I have had a rise and missed it near one of these natural haunts of trout. Invariably a nymph drifted down to such fish will bring a ready response, and if I am clever or lucky enough, I connect; otherwise all I get is the thrill of the second chance. However, I realize that I miss many an opportunity to take fish because I do not fish every one of them with a nymph—rise or no rise on the dry fly.

Fish that are "tailing" in the shallow water fall readily for a nymph fished with the "upstream method." Don't overlook the fact that trout busy at this game of dislodging nymphs from the rocks are quite likely to be "cruisers." That is, they sometimes dislodge nymphs from the bottom and then chase after them. I've often had trout follow my artificial from six to eight feet before taking it; so do not be in too much of a hurry to lift the nymph from the water to make another cast. If you fish each cast out to the limit, it is my humble opinion that you will take more fish than you will if you let it float only a few feet and then lift it. The place for your lure is in the water and not in the air, and yet I see many anglers expending more energy in casting than they ever do in actually fishing their fly. I'm inclined to be that way myself and often find it very necessary to curb the impulse.

As an illustration, let me tell you of an experience that shows how stupid we may be at times. It happened on a stream in northern New York. I had fished a mile of excellent water and hadn't taken a fish although I had frightened many of them as I waded along. The longer I fished the more discouraged I became and the more I flicked my fly here and there instead of fishing it in the water. It got so that the fly barely had time to float a foot before it was lifted and cast to another spot. Finally I caught up with another angler and, rather than break in ahead of him, I stopped to watch. Within five minutes he had taken two fair fish and I had discovered the reason for my failure. Both the trout he took had struck after his fly had floated at least fifteen feet; in fact they hit so close to him that he was just about ready to lift for another cast when it happened. Incidentally, this fellow was just two trout short of his limit, and seventy per cent had struck after the fly had made a long float. I turned around, went back to where I had first started, and fished the same water again. However, I didn't get very far this time. I kept the fly in the water and was kept busy with rising fish. Practically every one I hooked followed the fly for quite a distance before taking it. A premature lift had been the only cause of my previous failure. While this case is a bit extreme, it is applicable to some extent at all times. You never lose anything by keeping the fly in or on the water, and you may gain much.

I have a mania for fishing still waters with a nymph. No other fly is better adapted for the work. They sink readily—or should—and are realistic enough to be attractive to the fish. The method of fishing is simple and yet subtle. Of course a long cast is necessary because the trout are able to see you for some distance or otherwise notice disturbing influences that come too close. You should always approach still clear waters with great care. If they are a bit shallow you should keep very low, on your knees if necessary, and make your first cast from some distance below, letting the nymph alight on the water of the tail of the pool. If the water below the pool is too fast to make such a cast feasible, then work up to the pool with as little disturbance as you can and wait there for five or ten minutes before you make your first cast.

If you know where the fish usually congregate in any particular still water, then make your first cast directly to this spot. Otherwise start with a short cast until you have covered the entire piece of water or find the fish.

On completion of the cast, the nymph should immediately sink, and it is allowed to descend until it reaches bottom if it does so without being taken. During this period the line should be watched for any movement not in keeping with the normal process of the sinking of the nymph and leader. The line should be dressed so that it floats. Should it jerk slightly or suddenly straighten out after it has started to curve, you should be prepared to strike without the slightest delay. If nothing occurs, or if it does and you miss the fish, start retrieving very slowly with the "hand twist" retrieve, about sixteen thumb-and-forefinger movements to the minute being a good speed. Sometimes it is best to let the nymph rest on bottom for several moments before starting the retrieve. When this is done, the first movement is a cautious raising of the rod to start the nymph moving, after which the retrieve is made as described. This can be done best on a sandy or gravelly bottom. When there are boulders or weeds you sometimes get into difficulties, though not completely if you come clear when the lift from bottom is made.

Once you locate a spot where you get strikes, fish it carefully. Retrieve the lure until you can lift it from the water without making a disturbance. A sloppy lift will often spoil your chances of taking any more trout. Always take a few minutes between casts and make each one perfect. If it should land in the wrong spot, do not pick it up and make another one. Fish it out just as if it went to the very place you intended it to go. Haste in this sort of fishing is very disastrous. If you are deliberate and careful, you may nurse a still water for considerable time and take far more fish than you could by racing along the stream trying to fish in as many spots as possible.

Still another method of fishing the nymph is one I call "dabbling" for want of a better name. Only a very short line is used, in fact often just the leader comes into play. It is not applicable to all conditions, but where it can be used, it frequently brings good results when other methods fail.

It works best in a small, deep pool where it is possible to get directly over the deepest part without showing yourself to the fish that may be in it. If the bank is covered with thick vegetation, it helps because the trees, bushes, or high grass will neutralize your figure and there will be no silhouette. The approach must be exceedingly cautious, and under some conditions it is best to keep low down.

By careful maneuvering, you may get into a position where you can see the bottom of the hole without alarming the trout, and then you are in a good position to fish by "dabbling." With a roll cast, propel the nymph to the head of the pool where the current is sufficient to carry it back into the deepest water. With a bit of practice you will be able to keep the line taut while doing this. The nymph will probably touch bottom before covering the entire pool, in which case a slight lift of the rod tip will start it on its way again. During most of this time the progress of the lure is guided by the rod, and care must be taken not to give it any violent action. All that is necessary is an occasional short lift, made deliberately and smoothly, and then a drop of the rod tip to allow the nymph to sink to bottom again and thus come taut against the rod.

Personally I do not care to fish with a nymph steadily because it is tedious and tiring. Instead, I use it as an extra ace for the purpose of getting another chance at a good fish that has missed my dry fly. At least thirty per cent of the time I have taken such fish by doing this, and on the whole, some sixty per cent rise to it. To me this constitutes the principal charm of nymph fishing. It so often gives you that additional opportunity to take a good fish.

Tackle for Nymph Fishing

Rods—The same recommendations as for wet flies.
Leaders—12-foot tapered .017 to 3X or 4X (.007 to .0065) for

ordinary conditions, although 9-foot will usually turn the trick. The only reason for a long leader in fast or medium-fast water is the fact that the longer the leader the more detached the nymph appears and thus the more natural. However, when fishing still waters, a leader of fifteen to eighteen feet tapering from .018 to 3X, 4X, or 5X may be found a distinct advantage.

Nymphs—All the nymphs shown in Plate 10 are good. The following, though, are my personal favorites.

#1 R.B. Plate 10. Sizes 10, 12, 2X or medium long shank. An all-around job.

#2 R.B. Plate 10. Sizes 10, 12, 2X long shank. Mostly useful for brook trout.

#1 HEWITT. Plate 10. Sizes 8, 10, 12, regular shank.

#2 HEWITT. Plate 10. Sizes 8, 10, 12, regular shank.

ED BURKE. Plate 10. Sizes 10, 12, 14, regular shank.

AMBER TRANSLUCENT. Plate 10. Sizes 10, 12, regular shank.

GREEN TRANSLUCENT. Plate 10. Sizes 10, 12, regular shank.

HENDRICKSON. Size 10, regular shank. This was designed by Art Flick in imitation of one of the nymphs found in Schoharie Creek, in the Catskills.

TELLICO. Sizes 10, 12, regular shank.

This pattern, designed particularly for use in the Smoky Mountains of Tennessee, is a newcomer to me. Rev. Edwin T. Dalstrom, of Tennessee, sent me the first one I ever saw, and recommended it as the one best wet fly for the region. Since then I've had such success with it in other waters, both East and West, that I've added it to my personal list.

Incidentally the Fuzzy Bear Brown and Yellow patterns, as developed by Dan Bailey, of Montana, deserve your consideration. They are made with rubber and hair, and Dan says that many say they're worm fishing when they use them.

Don't buy very many nymphs to start. A dull-colored one will serve for the experimental stage. You may not like the game at all, so it is foolish to get too many patterns in the beginning. If you like it, then go the limit and it will pay you good dividends—at least according to my experiences.

≈§ CHAPTER V §≈

Experiences with
Wet Fly and Nymph

IN THIS chapter of anecdotes pertaining to sunken-fly fishing
I have drawn from some outstanding experiences in different locations. I have refrained from taking any lone exceptions as examples,
because while interesting, they would not prove of any particular
benefit. The incidents I have chosen have been duplicated in some
degree many times, and so may be considered at least logical answers to the problems they solved. If at times my conclusions seem
a bit weak or theoretical, it is because they are candid and because
the actual results left me groping. After all, nearly every angling
experience is subject to qualification. No matter how conclusive
anything seems, it is always assailable, in fact in many cases it may
be torn apart and completely discredited. It is this very angle to
fishing that makes it the fascinating study it is. We cannot look
upon it as an exact science, because the same applications will not
invariably produce the identical results. For instance, perhaps we
discover some method of fishing a certain stream that proves very
successful. For some time we get consistent results with the method
and think we have solved the problem. Perhaps we even get a bit
puffed up over it and do some bragging. Then something happens.
We don't get the results we did. Perhaps the fishing gets so poor
that we say the stream is fished out, and believe it. Just about this
time someone else comes along using a different method and fly.
He makes a series of good catches, and so disproves all our conclusions. The following account of some experiences on Beaver
Brook, New York, illustrate how easily this may happen.

For two years I had fished with a wet fly on this stream using
the across-and-downstream "drift" method. It was consistently
effective and produced good catches. When it didn't work I used

a dry fly with fair success. But as time went on, the catches be-came smaller and finally petered out altogether. Because one never saw many trout rise on this stream and the water was of a color that hindered one from seeing the bottom, it was hard to tell whether the trouble was caused by the lack of fish or not; but be-cause I had previously taken trout and couldn't do it now, I sur-mised that this was the trouble.

I had about decided to give up fishing the brook for good when something happened to change my mind. One day on the way down the brook after a blank morning I spied a man fishing one of my favorite pools. I had fished it that very day without rising a fish. As I watched this man through the rhododendron that bor-dered the creek I saw him take three good trout. He was fishing with bait, and I noted that he cast the worm directly upstream and stripped in line fast enough to keep the line taut. Each fish he caught seemed to take the bait at his very feet.

His success gave birth to an idea. I quietly withdrew from my vantage point and went downstream to another pool that had for-merly been productive. Instead of fishing it in the old way I now fished it from the lower end, sending the fly to the head of the pool and then letting it drift with the current. The movement of the water wasn't strong enough to carry the fly more than halfway through the pool, so when it reached the slow eddy in the center it wabbled uncertainly and gradually settled to bottom. During this time I did not see any flash or movement that could be inter-preted as the action of an interested fish. It seemed that the idea was doomed to failure, but something caused me to fish out the cast completely instead of impatiently lifting the fly from the water. After it had reached bottom I left it there a moment or two and then lifted the rod tip slightly in order to dislodge it. Then I started pulling it in with the "hand twist" retrieve, doing it very slowly. When it had reached a point some fifteen feet above me, I saw a shadow behind it, a shape in the water that hadn't been there before and that moved at the same speed as the fly. Although it was difficult I controlled my feelings and kept the retrieve steady. Just when a few more twists of the wrist would have taken the fly from the surface, the trout took it and hooked himself.

I took two more fish from that pool in the same manner and, before leaving the stream that day, took seven more—all good fish.

It was the solution to my problem and proved that the brook was still well populated with trout, even though the "downstream-drift method" had failed to take them.

Why the trout in this brook suddenly ceased taking a wet fly when fished in a manner that had formerly proved most effective has always puzzled me. The only solution I can offer is that the larvæ which might have been their favorite food had disappeared, and so the old method failed to simulate the action of the larvæ they had been forced to take as a substitute. At any rate the new method proved most effective, not only in this stream, but in many others from coast to coast.

However, in order to get any results from this sort of fishing you must have patience and be very deliberate in anything you do. Haste, unnecessary movements, in fact any movement that is likely to transmit light reflections on the water, may easily ruin any chance of success you might possibly have. It is not easy to keep making perfect casts and to let your fly drift to your feet time after time when you don't get results immediately. You are likely to feel that it isn't any use, and so hurry the drift and pick the fly from the water in such a way that it informs every fish in the pool that there is something wrong. Right here we have one of the most common reasons for angling failures—intolerance for things we can't control. Impatience makes us do things carelessly and heedlessly, and by so doing we only aggravate the condition that caused our irritation in the first place. No one ever accomplished much by letting impatience upset his judgment. When there are factors present that are likely to make you lose patience, it is just the time when you must exercise rigid self-control so that you do nothing that may impair your chances of success.

Often fish will rise cautiously to the fly when it starts drifting at the head of the pool. They will follow it until it sinks to bottom, when they retire from the vicinity, but not so far that they cannot keep watching this thing which acts and looks a bit strange. When it starts moving again and begins drifting with the slight action given by the "hand twist" retrieve, they become interested once more, and usually desire and curiosity finally get the best of their judgment and they take the fly. I have seen this happen in clear water, but always any degree of haste, undue motion, or a change in the speed of the retrieve would make the fish leave the scene.

Even when the trout seem to be hitting your fly at the head of a riffle or pool, it usually pays to take the time necessary for it to sink and get into an eddy or back current from which it is necessary to retrieve it. The "hand twist" method is ideal for this purpose. Some of the best trout I have ever taken have come from the backwashes or holes that are caused by the current action of fast water. Consider the following experience, which is one of many. I happened to be fishing a long riffle that led into a shallow pool. The fish had been rising steadily in the fast water, and I had taken eight nine- to ten-inchers on a six-foot maximum drift of the fly. Of course this did not keep up, and when the action got slow on one occasion, as I lighted a cigarette I let the fly drift past the regular productive section on a slack line. When I tried to lift it from the water, I found that it had caught on the bottom. A partial roll cast released it, and more from habit than anything else, I started to bring it in with the "hand twist" retrieve. I had made about five completed motions with my hand when I got a strike so hard that the reel sang a merry tune as the fish rushed upstream. This trout weighed 3¼ pounds, and the incident happened on one of the famous Catskill streams.

Of course locations of this kind are likely to be inconstant—that is, they vary from time to time. Naturally the most logical positions for large fish to choose are those into which the most amount of food drifts because of water action. Large trout prefer to get food that is obtainable with the least effort. But the same force that pulls the food into such places also brings in all the other loose matter stirred up by freshets, and so the very spot that might be most productive is also subject to the hazard of being spoiled by the very action that makes it a preferred location for large fish. Often many of the changes in these locations are very slight. A hole may fill up in one place, and another may be formed a few feet in some other direction from the original spot. For this reason you should study the stream bottom after each heavy rain or after you have failed to fish some favorite riffle for a long time. Never let your judgment be swayed by past experiences. This is another common failing of fishermen, myself included. Just because one method, fly, or location has proved productive in the past does not mean that it will always remain so. Never feel that a pool, riffle, or any stretch of water you are familiar with is no longer any good because it fails to produce when fished in the way you have been accustomed. Try other places in the stretch besides the spots where you have formerly taken fish; fish it from new angles. You may get surprising results.

As an illustration showing further uses of the "hand twist" retrieve, let me give you an account of a rather unusual experience on a small pond near Lowville, New York. It was a somewhat weedy bit of water, and because there were no boats, we had to fish from shore. When we got there in the early afternoon no fish were rising within casting distance, and although we tried as far out as we could cast, not one rise resulted from the efforts of our party.

I soon tired of casting over apparently fishless water, so I wandered along the shore looking for favorable cover that trout might like. Coming to a log at the water's edge, I sat on it to rest. The water at this point was about knee deep at the shore line, so I felt sure the trout would come in there if any place. Besides, about a dozen good fish were rising some two hundred feet out, and I thought that they might move in at any time.

About twenty minutes later I spied a succession of rises that were progressing toward shore. They seemed to be made by one fish that had started "cruising." Thinking that this trout might come in close enough to be fished for, I changed to a dry fly and waited. The rises continued until they reached a distance of about a hundred feet from shore and then stopped. It seemed as if my chance was gone. Then I saw the rises start again within three feet of shore and some forty feet to the left. Each rise was closer to me, so I figured out the speed of the trout's approach and cast the fly so that it alighted in front of his line of movement. Nothing happened. Then I saw the fish advancing slowly. He suddenly rose to the surface and took something I could not see. I quickly cast the size 18 Blue Dun I happened to be using. He started toward the fly when it alighted about three feet in front of him, but soon changed his mind and went on his way. Directly in front of me he rose again. Although this happened within six feet, I could not see what he took, if anything. Then I made a rapid change from dry fly to nymph, and although the fish was now out of my sight, I had seen him rise several times and had a good idea where he was. I cast the nymph so that it curved slightly over his line of march, and started bringing it back with the "hand twist" retrieve. About six feet of line had been brought in when the fish took the lure. The barb took hold, and a few minutes later the fish was in my creel.

The incident gave me a new burst of energy. I first worked the shore line carefully and then combed the rest of the water as far as I could reach. Not a single rise was forthcoming. Again I became discouraged and sat down on the log. As it was a cloudy day, twilight came early and persisted for an amazingly long time. During this period I noticed a difference in the action of the fish. The rises became more frequent, more splashy, and were definitely moving shoreward.

Soon several trout were within reach. Twenty minutes later at least fifty were within casting range. Because the fish seemed to be feeding on the surface, I had taken off the nymph and had returned to a dry fly. I lost count of the number of dry flies I tried, but I know I tried everything from tiny dark patterns to large gaudy ones without getting a single indication. By the time I got through experimenting, it was getting so dark that I could barely see the fly, but even at that I took six good fish with a nymph and the "hand twist" retrieve before it got completely dark.

As I landed my last fish, the clouds broke on the western horizon and let through a narrow streak of light that colored the water with the orange and gold of sunset. Then came a sight I had never seen before and never expect to see again. The rises came so close together that the pond took on the appearance of being pelted by large hailstones. In addition, an intense nervousness seemed to have affected all the fish. When I made a cast, it seemed as if all the fish within a radius of three hundred feet instantly splashed the surface, and when they did this it carried through to the fish beyond them and so progressed across the entire lake. It was mysterious, incomprehensible, and after it happened the first time, I never got another rise.

Then I felt something tugging at the rawhide laces of my shoes. I brought out the flashlight and looked down into the water. Two trout and a score of very small bullheads evidently thought my laces were worms and were trying to make way with them. I have since wondered whether many of the rises that evening hadn't been bullheads. I'm sure they couldn't have been all trout—there weren't that many in the lake. As I think back I remember a great many peculiar little tugs at my nymph which felt like tiny fish, and there were very few trout in the pond under eight inches. I imagine it was the bullheads tugging at the fly.

Here is another incident that shows the value of nymphs and the "hand twist" retrieve. It took place in September in New Brunswick, Canada. I had become a bit tired of catching grilse and salmon, and thought I'd like to try some trout fishing. Our guides, Boyd Hovey and Claremont Moon, did not think much of the idea—first, because they would rather have us fish for salmon, and second, because they didn't think there was much chance of taking any trout at that time with conditions the way they were.

This only intensified my desire to catch trout. If they were hard to get, then it gave us something to strive for. So we went up what they called a "bogan." It was what we call a "flow" in the Adirondacks—that is, the lower stretches of a small stream into which the waters of a big stream backed. In the South they often call the same type of water a "slough." Personally I think "backwater" a good universal name for it. However, in this particular case the water of the Miramichi River was so low that it no longer backed up into the lower stretches of the brook. Instead, the overflow from the small stream ran into the river, and we had quite a job getting across the shallows with our canoes.

The water in the bogan was as clear as crystal. The bottom was a delight to the lover of trout. It was grassy, mossy, and covered with gravel where the vegetation did not grow. We advanced carefully until we reached a place where Boyd claimed we'd get trout if anywhere. I started fishing with my regular salmon leader and a size 6 Parmachene Belle, the approved sort of fly for the region. Nothing happened. I changed patterns and sizes several times, and finally put on a regular medium-weight, six-foot, wet-fly trout leader. Still no results. I fished always with the approved Northern method, bringing the flies rather swiftly through the water with the rod retrieve. After this I tried the "hand twist" retrieve, using the same flies and medium-weight leader. Still no response.

The guides did not say anything, but in their eyes I saw an "I told you so" look. This put me on my mettle. I must do something to show them that trout could be taken from that bogan. It was noon. The sun was bright, and the bottom of the stream showed up clearly without a trout in sight. It looked hopeless and my heart sank. "Perhaps," I thought, "there isn't a trout here anyway."

Then I got an idea. Why not use the methods we did under similar conditions when fishing the hard-fished streams near New York City? I started searching through my equipment. I found a few nymphs, two of a salmon-red color and one with a gold-ribbed gray body and brown back. A little more search uncovered a number of gut strands of various sizes. After a little work I transformed a nine-foot light salmon leader into an eighteen-foot nymph leader tapering to 4X. Then I looked the situation over while I soaked one of the salmon-meat-colored nymphs (R.B. No. 2, Plate 10), so that it would sink readily on touching the water. Over on the far side of the still water a large bush shadowed what appeared to be a hole deeper than the rest of the bogan. It looked like a logical place to concentrate on. All this took time, and when I took a side glance at the guides, I could see they were getting more impatient every moment. They wanted to get back to the salmon and couldn't see any sense in my killing time fussing with tackle.

But at last everything was ready, so I made a cast that dropped the nymph close to the bank under the attractive-looking bush. I sat motionless while the lure sank to bottom. Guide Hovey looked at me questioningly, in fact a bit disparagingly. For the moment I know my standing with him dropped considerably. I didn't blame him, but I had hopes that my experiment would work. The motion of the line stopped, so I knew my nymph had reached bottom. I started retrieving slowly with the "hand twist" system. I had hardly started this when I got a vicious strike and connected with a pound-and-a-half brook trout. The bored looks on the faces of the guides disappeared and were replaced by expressions of keen interest.

Outwardly nonchalant, but inwardly seething with pride and gratification, I proceeded to fish that bogan as if it were the simplest thing in the world. Twice I hooked fish as the lure sank. I saw the line twitch slightly and struck. I took the rest of the fish when the nymph was being retrieved. Boyd tried it for a while, and so did my wife. But they both retrieved the fly too fast. My retrieve was about eighteen movements to the minute or about nine complete wrist motions. They made about three jerks to my one. Believe me, getting the right speed and timing to this retrieve is very important, and it varies with conditions.

During our stay at Jack Russell's camp my wife and I spent many pleasant hours fishing for brook trout in this bogan. The best lures were the R.B. Nymphs, numbers 1, 2, and 5 as shown on color plate No. 10. The best wet flies were Gold Ribbed Hare's Ear and Greenwell's Glory. Not once did the Northern patterns produce, such as Parmachene Belle, Montreal, Professor, and others that are normally good in this territory.

Just the simple process of letting a fly sink to bottom on a slack line sometimes leads to worth-while results. In this connection consider the following incident. Quite a number of years ago, in fact before I knew anything about nymph fishing, I spent considerable time on the western slope of the Adirondacks. Because we occasionally enjoyed a mess of small brook trout, I sometimes quit fishing for sport and spent a few hours fishing for eight- to nine-inch fontinalis.

One of the best places for these small trout was the Peavine Creek, which emptied into the Oswegatchie River about a mile below the dam of Cranberry Lake. It required a little effort to reach this spot. After reaching the location on the river opposite the entrance to the Peavine, one had to pole a raft across the river and then up the creek until the first beaver dam was reached. Here the raft was anchored so that it was possible to stand on it and fish into the pool above the dam.

The surroundings were wild and impressive. Directly bordering the brook were the usual alders. Beyond that on either side, and seen through the openings in the brush, a swamp meadow spread out with all its isolated grandeur and mysteriousness. Beyond the meadow was a rise of land, which was densely covered by spruce and other evergreens, lending its touch of the unfathomable to the general outlook. I never went up this meadow stretch of the Peavine without trembling with excitement. It was primeval, elemental. I expected to see bears, deer, almost any wild creature at any moment.

Above the dam the heights of land on either side closed in on the meadow. Here the forest crowded the brook, and the alders limited one's vision to their sky lines.

On this particular morning, dawn was just breaking as I poled the raft across the Oswegatchie. As I moved slowly along, the scarlet and maroon of the eastern horizon gradually spread out until it covered a third of the firmament. It transformed the misty gray atmosphere into a riot of color. The scene changed with every moment, and when I reached the beaver dam I stopped a while to enjoy it. The sun suddenly poked over the eastern horizon, and the witchery of the scene departed. Its bold rays quickly dispelled the mist, and the scene became comparatively commonplace.

Because I had business to attend to, I quickly set up my rod and got ready for fishing. In a half hour I expected to have enough trout for our breakfast and dinner.

But something was wrong. The usually agreeable pool was extremely disagreeable. For one hour I worked carefully and hard, changed flies many times, but never got one sign of encouragement. At last I came to the last pattern in my box, a No. 14 Iron Blue Dun. I cast it out and retrieved it several times without results.

It was very discouraging. I began to lose interest and thought more about breakfast. A careless cast to the left side of the pool, and close to a thick clump of alders, brought a sickly little rise. I was sure that it was a redfin minnow, so didn't even bother to strike. Feeling that it was useless, I let the fly sink to bottom as I placed the rod partly on the raft and partly on the dam while I smoked a cigarette.

About five minutes passed. The cigarette was finished, and I knew it was time to leave for camp, because breakfast would be ready by the time I got there.

When I took up the rod I received a shock. Instead of the line pointing upstream and to the left, it now pointed toward the right. A subtle warning flashed through my brain. It made me cautious. I retrieved the slack line gingerly, and as I brought it taut against the rod tip, I felt a throbbing. It was the signal to strike, and I did. The resulting commotion turned the quiet pool into a cauldron of boiling water. I knew I had something large, but didn't know what.

Some ten minutes later I saw the fish clearly for the first time. It almost caused disaster. For the moment I got a bad case of buck fever and froze solidly to the reel. Only the fact that I had a very light rod, which absorbed the strain, saved me from losing the fish. Before the rod broke I awoke to the precariousness of the situation and released the line, which the fish took upstream at record speed.

But he was a fool trout like so many of the big ones we land under bad conditions. Without any effort he could have dashed into the alders, where my light tackle would have broken. Instead, he simply raced up and down stream and acted like a senseless maniac. Finally he became tired and flopped helplessly on his side. I slipped my long-handled net under him and, although the frame almost collapsed under the strain, succeeded in getting the fish to the raft, where I dropped on my hands and knees to keep him from flopping overboard. When weighed on the scales of the general store, he proved to weigh 6 pounds 9 ounces, as pretty a specimen of brown trout (*Salmo fario*) as anyone would want to see.

Needless to say, I felt quite elated over my success. When I heard the complimentary remarks of those who saw the fish and later experienced the exhilaration that accompanies such local renown, I became quite haughty. Fortunately this feeling did not last long. I soon realized that it is on such lucky instances that many reputations are made, and that the person reaping the glory from such happenings really does not deserve it as a result of his skill and knowledge of fishing. I knew that I did not deserve any credit for my part in this affair. Luck alone had been responsible. The lure had been neglected, and the fish already had it in his mouth when I started to bring the fly in. The fish itself did not have brains enough to get away. Of course I used good judgment when I felt the first pull of the fish, but if any credit is due anything except luck, it should go to the little Iron Blue Dun, which was left to shift for itself while I smoked a cigarette.

Everywhere we go we shall find the sunken fly and some form of the "hand twist" retrieve useful. Let me take you now to Pennsylvania, to the upper reaches of the Brodhead's Creek. The time of the year was early May, the weather clear—frosty at night and pleasantly warm during the day, although when the sun went under a cloud, the moderate northwest wind made us wish that it would keep shining.

My companion and I started fishing at the small pond located just a short distance above the lake near Sky-Top Lodge. Because a few fish were rising we first used dry flies, but after a half hour without results we changed to wets. I don't know how many times Fred changed his flies, but I know that I tried a dozen patterns before I got a rise—to a size 14 Orange Fish Hawk that was being manipulated close to the surface by the "hand twist" retrieve. Because occasionally the trout were breaking on the surface, we kept fishing our flies near the top, but after an hour of hard work we still had only one fish, which had taken the Orange Fish Hawk the first time it was used.

As this fly had given me the only action so far, I decided to keep it on but also felt that I should try sinking it deep before giving it up as a hopeless undertaking. This I did, and when some ten completed movements of the "hand twist" retrieve had been made, I saw the line twitch and immediately hooked a trout. This combination of depth and retrieve proved to be what was needed, and we both took quite a number of fish before tiring of the location.

Of course we thought that we had solved the secret of catching fish for the day, so we went confidently to the first pool above the dam. But here we struck a snag. The trout would not respond to the Orange Fish Hawk and the "hand twist" retrieve. We fished several more good-looking pools in the same manner and with the same fly, and still failure dogged our footsteps. Because we had taken fish in the pond with this combination, we thought it should work everywhere else, and so we decided that there were not many fish above the pond. We came to this decision while we were fruitlessly fishing one of the most enticing pools of the entire stream. But at this very moment the light changed so that it disclosed the bottom to our eyes. What we saw made us gasp. About twenty feet above us the gravel was covered with so many trout that they made a black spot of several square yards on an otherwise light-reflecting bottom. Of course we started fishing for them, at first without any idea of what we were doing. But as I let the fly sink to bottom and then retrieved it with the "hand twist" retrieve, the following facts forced themselves into my unwilling brain. First, that the fish appeared slightly interested, but not enough to strike, and second, that the instant the retrieve was started, they immediately lost all interest.

It suggested two things: that the fly wasn't just right, and that the manipulation was all wrong. Working on this, I tied on the R.B. No. 2 salmon-colored nymph. Because the trout seemed to become interested only when the fly I had been using had reached a point a foot or so above them, I let this nymph sink before attempting a retrieve. It never reached bottom. Several fish rushed for it before it had sunk three feet, and one of them got it. Once again this happened, and then the trout refused to bother with the lure when it was sinking. I let it sink until it rested on the gravel, let it stay there perhaps half a minute, and then started it moving at the very least speed possible. I had hardly started when I got a solid hit and connected.

There was no doubt about the effectiveness of this salmon-colored nymph, but we soon found out that we had to fish it just so or else there wasn't any response. The retrieve was effective only when the movements were made so slowly that no jerks were in evidence—about six completed hand movements of the "hand twist" retrieve to the minute being just right, provided they were made with slow deliberation. In addition, the retrieve wasn't the least bit effective unless the nymph was allowed to reach bottom before the movement was started.

It may seem odd to some of you that such slight differences in manipulation as changing the speed of retrieve three or four movements a minute, or regulating the depth of the sinking fly a foot or so, would make the difference between success and failure, but it is often on such trifles that our success depends.

On this very day we had experienced two entirely different conditions that required special methods of attack in order to take fish. Still another was in store for us. In the afternoon we fished the lake above the falls. It was really nothing more than a widening of the stream caused by a dam. Here our nymphs and "hand twist" retrieve were worthless. By mere chance I put on a No. 6 Black Gnat, a regular Northern pattern, and began playing with it, jerking it speedily through the water with the regular rod retrieve. A missed rise showed us the possibilities of the combination, so we started using it seriously. It resulted in the best fish of the trip besides several others that we lost. But even at that the method was not effective unless the fly sank considerably before the retrieve was started.

The combination of sunken fly and slow retrieve is particularly useful when the streams are so low and clear that it seems useless to fish and when the general consensus of opinion is that small dry flies are the only thing that will possibly produce. As a matter of fact the sunken fly is by far the best bet. When a dry fly alights on water that is clear and still and on which the sun is shining, it causes a shadow quite unlike that of a natural insect. You see, the artificial is opaque while the natural is semi-transparent; thus the shadows made by them are quite different. Then too, the leader, when used with a dry fly, is quite likely to float instead of sink. We know that it is best for it to sink, but more often than not it floats despite our efforts to make it do otherwise. This makes shadows that are very disturbing to the fish and does far more harm than most of us realize.

On the other hand, a wet fly or nymph, thoroughly soaked before using, will sink the instant it touches the water, and it takes a well-soaked leader down with it. The instant the fly and leader go below the surface, the telltale shadows almost disappear. All that results is a shadow so slight that its effects are negligible. Also, the instant the fly or lure starts sinking, it becomes an object of interest rather than alarm, thus increasing our chances of success.

The first time I became fully aware of these phenomena I happened to be fishing one of the crystal-clear streams of the Catskills. We were using dry flies, but although trout were rising we could not take a fish; in fact every time we made a cast, no matter how delicate and perfect, the fish immediately stopped rising and stayed down from periods ranging from forty-five minutes to an hour and a half. If we waited until the fish began rising again, it did not do any good because the very first cast put them down once more, and this second time they frequently stayed down for good.

It was very discouraging, and I would have quit except for a circumstance that led to some enlightening observations. Coming to a long and rather shallow pool, I approached as carefully as I could and, on reaching an advantageous position, made ready to fish it. It was then I noticed that the light was just right for revealing the bottom to my searching gaze. In the deepest part were some thirty fish, most of them apparently inactive on the bottom. A half dozen were working near the surface and rising occasionally when some fly that appealed floated over them. This hole was located in the center of the stream. Some fifteen feet to the right and close to shore was another hole. The bottom here was not distinctly visible, although I could see that there were trout in it even though none were rising.

Although I was using an eighteen-foot leader and directed the cast so that the fly dropped on the water below the fish instead of over them, the very first false cast caused them to scatter like leaves in a wind. By the time the fly touched the water the entire school was darting and milling around as if greatly agitated. I let the fly lie there for about ten minutes. There was an almost imperceptible eddy current at the location, which made the fly circle slightly. During this time the trout settled back to the bottom of the hole. Not one fish had shown the slightest bit of interest in the fly floating above them. I began moving the fly slightly. This caused very evident nervousness on the part of the school. Several moments later the line began to belly and sink badly, so that it was necessary to retrieve the fly. This action caused the trout to scatter wildly again.

The situation fascinated me. I decided to wait until the fish had recovered from their fright, until some of them started rising again. An hour later a few fish started taking flies from the surface and the rest seemed perfectly at ease, so I made another try. This time, however, I used a No. 14 eyed wet Gold Ribbed Hare's Ear. When I made the cast, the fish scattered as before, but because no false casts were made previous to the drop of the fly, it did not cause as much excitement as my first effort with the dry fly. As I let the Hare's Ear sink I noted one great difference in its effect and that of the dry fly on the trout. The dry fly, when motionless on the surface, did not seem to frighten them; but neither did it attract attention, or perhaps I should say interest, as it is quite certain that the fish saw it. Not one fish made the slightest move toward it in the spirit of investigation. On the other hand, the sinking of the wet fly created quite a bit of interest. Even though the trout had scattered at the cast, at least a half dozen came toward the fly before it had reached a depth of three feet.

When it reached bottom I knew that these fish were near the place. I let it lie there several moments and then lifted the rod tip enough to start the fly from the bottom. I did not see any fish take it, but I suddenly felt a tug and reacted quickly enough to set the hook in a fairly decent fish.

Subsequent experiments on this day and many other days and in different localities proved conclusively that trout, after being frightened, resumed feeding on bottom or in midwater before they did on the surface. They also proved that if the leader readily sank, a dry fly did not cause as much disturbance as it did when the leader floated, and that a sparsely tied translucent-body fly caused less suspicion than a heavy-tied fly with a dense body.

The experiments also disclosed the fact that while the trout, after being scared, were soon susceptible to a sinking fly, they were rarely interested in a floating one. There is a reasonable answer to this. Trout feel safe in deep water. Water is their element, just as air is ours, and they know that the deeper they get, the safer they are from dangers that threaten from outside their world. If you doubt this statement, just try the following experiment. First locate some trout in shallow water. Then frighten them. What happens? They immediately go for deep water, if it is available, or hide under anything that will provide shelter. After this, go to a pool of deep water where you can see the fish. Frighten them. They will not leave this hole. If it is filled with rocks that provide shelter, they will hide under them; but if not, they will simply rush frantically around, never leaving the pool unless you get in it and actually force them out. If the bottom is soft or has any muddy portions, the trout will hide in such places, burying themselves in the soft substance.

Speaking of mud brings to mind a small stream in the extreme northern section of New York State. The upper reaches wander through a meadow, and here the water ranges from a few inches to a couple of feet in depth. The bottom is soft sand, mud, and weeds. Throughout the entire stretch, trout are scattered everywhere. Many bends, where the water deepens slightly, contain as many as thirty fish ranging from four to fifteen inches. If you should walk along the banks of this brook, every trout will have disappeared by the time you turn around to retrace your steps. However, if you look closely you will see an occasional tail showing itself in the silt of the bottom. These fish bury themselves in this soft substance and stay there until the threatening danger has passed. Incidentally, this is one of the most fascinating streams I've ever fished. I call it "Spring Brook," and the stream into which it runs "River X." Needless to say, these are not the real names. I withhold them for obvious reasons—one, that I do not want them publicized for personal reasons; and the other, that a friend who loves the place first brought me there, and I could not betray his confidence. You'll read more about both of them in this chapter and in subsequent ones.

Here is an incident that illustrates the usefulness of "dabbling" a nymph as described in Chapter IV. The location was the north branch of Callicoon Creek. The fishing was very poor. In the morning we fooled around with nymphs, wet flies, and dry flies but didn't get very far. Of course we fished in the orthodox manner and, for the time being, felt that we were doing the best we could and that the fish were simply off feed. Fortunately for us I finally got tired of casting and started to think. Years ago I did not have any trouble taking fish under these conditions. I simply went to work gathering live nymphs from the rocks in the stream and then fished them from suitable spots in deep holes. Such methods always brought results. Why wouldn't they do the same now if I tried them?

When this thought first occurred to me, we were in a shallow stretch. For some distance beyond this spot the stream was unsuitable for the idea I had in mind. The water was too fast and there were no deep holes. We fished it without results in various ways and with many different flies. Then we came to a pool that looked just right for the experiment.

On one side it was bounded by a flat and open gravel bar. On the other side the bank was high and well undermined. It was also well covered with brush and trees. The hole itself was normal—fairly shallow at the head, where the current ran with fair speed, deep and quiet in the center, and shallow, although smooth and quite fast, at the tail.

It was one of those spots which anyone who has ever had anything to do with fishing would enthuse over. By this time I had become quite subdued by failure and did not rush headlong into the project in mind. Instead I looked the situation over carefully and then made a wide circuit of the hole so that I could approach it from the wooded side. When I got within fifteen feet of the pool,

I dropped to my hands and knees and crawled the balance of the way, stopping some six feet from the edge of the bank to string up my rod and get it ready for the job at hand.

Before starting on the expedition I had tied a nymph to a nine-foot 3X leader (.007) and had placed them in a well-soaked leader box. Now I looked at them and, because they were not wet enough, waited about fifteen minutes more until I knew they would handle properly. I couldn't bring myself to use a live nymph until every other possible experiment with artificials had been tried. The nine-foot leader proved too long. It would not straighten out. You see, it was simply a proposition of flipping a few feet of line with just the leader dropping on the water. This entailed another wait until a seven-and-a-half-foot leader tapering from .017 to .007 was soaked and so made ready for use.

I must admit that I was impatient and very nervous by the time this second leader was ready. I wasn't even sure that it would be satisfactory, and it took all my will power to resist fishing anyway, even though the tackle wasn't just right.

At last the cast seemed pliable enough to work with. Restraining my impatience a bit more, I looked the pool over carefully. Just below me was the deepest part. It was so deep that even though the water was extremely clear I could not see the bottom plainly. However, I could dimly see a score of trout, who seemed to be moving slightly here and there in the eddy of the pool, so I knew I had something to fish for.

With a flip of the rod I sent the nymph to the lower part of the current leading into the pool. It sank at once and drifted down into the deep water. Here a slight eddy caught it and kept it whirling around some three feet below the surface for a few moments. Then it started to descend rapidly. Soon the slack in the leader was all gone, so I lowered the rod tip in order to let it go as deep as possible. Just as the line touched the water I saw a flash deep down and felt a tug. I was a bit slow and missed the hit. A few seconds later I saw another flash, and this time I struck instinctively and connected with a twelve-inch trout. The disturbance caused by landing this fish scared the rest of the trout in the pool, so I left it and went searching for another.

The balance of that day was spent in fishing suitable locations in this manner. The net result was seven fish, running from ten inches to fourteen inches. Each time a fish was taken, it spoiled the pool for further fishing.

Since that time I have frequently used this method when conditions were so contrary that fish could not be taken by ordinary methods. Just to show you how useful it is, let me tell you of an experience that took place on May 20, 1933, on the same stream.

Although it was still early in the season the water was clear and low. In addition there were not many flies hatching, and rising trout were few and far between. My companion was a well-known member of the Anglers Club of New York, A. W. Miller—known as Sparse Grey Hackle—a good fisherman and student of fishing. However, at the time he didn't think much of nymphs, and while he was too much the gentleman to say anything derogatory about them, I could see skepticism in his eye every time I mentioned their importance.

When we first started fishing, a trout was rising under the bridge that covered the first hole we selected for our starting-point. Although Sparse was quite insistent that I fish the water first, I refused to do so, because I can never bring myself to fish a good piece of water before my guest has his try at it, and because I knew the water, realized the conditions from previous experiences, and was pretty sure that a nymph would be better than a dry fly.

At this time Sparse was a dry-fly purist. Unless he could get them by this method he preferred to do without any fish. He placed as pretty a fly as anyone could wish to see in just the right position under the bridge. He did it, not only once, but a score of times. Once he got a half-hearted splash, but from where I stood I could see that it wasn't a "business rise," so that he could not be blamed for missing it. As a matter of fact the trout never touched the fly. Some fifteen minutes later he conceded defeat and told me to try my luck.

During this interlude I had not been wasting my time. I had looked over the situation carefully and had decided that I could move thirty feet closer to the fish than Sparse. Because I did not know this particular bit of water perfectly, I used a dry-fly dropper on the leader above the nymph. This was to help me in floating the nymph perfectly, and at the same time it enabled me to see any action that might occur from the performance of the dry fly.

I selected a position about twenty feet from the fish, at the left side of the stream. When ready to cast I was almost opposite the trout, but because of the broken water where the fish was located I felt sure that he did not see me. Nevertheless I waited until he rose again before I cast. The moment he did, I cast the lure about four feet above him and in the correct position so that the current would carry it within his vision. This was easy because the cast was short and yet brought into play the required quantity of line to make it accurate. I watched the dry fly closely. For several feet it floated the same speed as the current, and then it hesitated—stopped. Immediately I struck and hooked a ten-inch brown.

But this incident did not help us much. As we went upstream we were discouraged by the absence of rising fish. Coming to an ideal pool for the purpose, I decided to do some "dabbling." The background was so perfectly wooded that it completely concealed my person. Also the bank was high and the pool small, so I knew I could see everything that happened as well as handle the nymph correctly.

Although I knew just what I was doing, I made a mess of the fishing in this pool. Somehow I could not connect with the fish that hit my lure, even though I saw them take it. I know I had ten good hits from fish ranging from ten to fifteen inches, and I missed every one, even though I felt a decided tug each time one struck.

At the next suitable hole I thought I would try some natural nymphs, so I upturned a number of rocks to get several large enough to use. The net results were two more fairly decent trout. This restored my confidence, so I discontinued using naturals and returned to artificials. The brief interlude of using naturals had affected the desired result. Now I hooked at least fifty per cent of the fish that took the artificial. Sparse was becoming more interested in nymph fishing every time I got a strike.

By the time evening came I had a nice creel of fish, but nothing better than twelve inches and only one of that size. The balance of the day has nothing to do with nymph fishing except to show that when conditions are not right for them they are worthless, just as dry flies are when conditions are not right for them. It is a matter of record that as the sun approached the western horizon the nymph became less effective, and finally absolutely useless as the sun disappeared behind the hills.

At this time Sparse and I separated. There were several hundred yards of good fishing water ahead of us, and we could both fish good water without disturbing the other. Because the trout no longer took the nymph, I changed to a dry fly—a Fan Wing Royal. Instead of fishing all the water I had allotted to myself, I decided to head straight for a long pool that I knew contained several good fish. When I got there I saw several trout rising in the fast water at the head. This was good. In water of this sort it does no harm to hook a fish. The other fish would not become suspicious unless the hooked one fought directly where hooked—something that was hardly likely to happen, because a hooked fish usually immediately leaves the spot where something he thought good to eat turns out to be a stinging, resisting bit that continually forces him to use all his strength to oppose it. (NOTE. In quiet water a struggling fish might make all the other fish within sight of the disturbance suspicious. However, this is not always true, because often the rest of the fish in the immediate location will follow the hooked fish—no doubt thinking that it has captured something good to eat that they should have a share of.)

It was one of the times in my life when I did not get excited. I sat down on the shale rock at the edge of the pool and considered the situation carefully before making the first cast. The flies on the stream were quite large—about No. 10's—and of a light-ginger color. Certainly my Royal Coachman did not imitate them in the slightest. By a lucky chance I happened to have a Fan Wing Light Cahill in my fly box—a delicate mixture of light-ginger hackle and ginger-dyed mallard wings. As far as I could see, this imitated the natural better than anything else I had. Whether it really did remains a debatable question. It is true that the first cast with this dry fly took a twelve-inch trout and the second cast a fifteen-incher, but inasmuch as the Royal Coachman was not used and did not have a chance to prove itself, I cannot say that the Light Cahill was necessary. There is a good chance that the fish would have taken any fly that was cast over them in the right way.

As I landed the last fish, Sparse appeared on the scene. He was very enthusiastic over my good fortune but a bit disgusted with himself. "I muffed my chances," he said. "Had several good rises, but the trout are still in the stream." He knew why he had failed to put one of these fish in his creel. He had spent the entire day fishing with a dry fly when the fish refused to take anything on the surface. Being a sportsman of the highest type, he repressed his feeling of discouragement and disappointment, and so his nerves were on edge by the time his chance came. Because of this he "blew up" when he saw success in his grasp, and struck too hard and fast. Need I say more? I've done the same thing many times and shall probably do it many times in the future. On this particular evening I was in good condition for taking advantage of any opportunity that presented itself. I had a fair catch of fish, and there had been so many strikes I had missed that I had used up all my excess nervous energy, that tension which so often causes faulty striking. When the rise to the surface came, I was as cool as a cucumber. Therefore I calculated my chances carefully and fished with deliberation and steady nerves. That was why I had good luck.

The experience was of real benefit to Sparse. Although he kidded me about the nymph fishing, he was genuinely interested in the game and was soon experimenting with it. Before long he began to get results and so made a step forward in his progress as an all-around angler. Besides having a higher percentage of good fishing days when the trout refused to take a surface fly, he also became a more efficient dry-fly fisherman because the use of the nymph taught him some things that the dry fly could not.

Often good fish will feed in locations that the angler can reach only by a downstream or an across-and-downstream cast. A nymph is sometimes the best answer to this problem, as illustrated by the following incident that occurred on a Wyoming stream.

Picture this scene. There is a deep hole on the side of the river opposite you, barricaded both upstream and downstream by dense log and debris jams. Also, that side of the river is heavily forested, so much so that you couldn't possibly reach the hole from there. The main current, quite swift, flows between this pool and the near shore, brushing the bank from which you must fish for its entire length. So you cannot fish the hole or the fast water from pool side, nor is it possible to get into the stream and fish it from a wading position on the near side.

So you are forced to fish from the right bank looking downstream. This is about three feet high and covered with tall grass, except for the lower end which is barren. At this lower end, or foot of the entire hole, a three-pound brown made a practice of feeding day after day, no matter what time I happened to get there.

I tried for that fish with a dry fly a dozen different days. I fished from all possible positions and picked up a number of inconsequential fish up to a pound and a half. But I always succeeded in putting the big one down, usually by trying to get in good dry-fly casting position below him or by the drag of the fly when I attempted to fish from above.

I finally decided to try a nymph. It was one picked from my box at random, straw-colored and black-ribbed. I carefully planned a cast that would drift the fly downstream directly in front of the fish. I had done this several times with the dry fly, so knew it wasn't difficult. I had learned just how far to cast across the current into the pool in order to let the current do the rest.

The light was good, so that I could follow the course of the line from my casting position until the fly got within a few feet of the trout; then I lost sight of it. But I could still see the line where it left the rod tip, and I watched it intently. This suddenly twitched. I struck and was fast.

He was a young fish in excellent condition, so that I had plenty of trouble on my hands for a few minutes. Several times I feared for the 3X (.007) gut leader I was using as I applied extreme pressure to keep him away from the snags. The third time seemed to break his spirit and he came in without too much further fuss.

It gave me great satisfaction when I lay on my stomach to reach down so that I could land this trout with my hand. It gave me greater satisfaction a few minutes later to place him gently back into the stream, after weighing him in a wet cloth. For a few minutes he rested there, dazed. Finally I gave him a slight touch with a stick, and he sped away toward the snag-bordered pool.

Sometimes ponds are tough problems, so tough in fact that often we must resort to worms or methods other than fly fishing in order to be successful.

The first lake I ever fished, aside from those which were merely widened spaces of streams, was Cranberry Lake in the Adirondacks. At the time this was really wild country. The only road that connected the place with the outside country was a miserable affair and tough going for the few automobiles then in use. I know that we found it much more satisfactory to take the railroad, inasmuch as the state roads were still in their infancy and the cars themselves were very different from the smoothly riding auto of today. Even as close to New York City as Nyack and Suffern the main roads were bumpy, full of curves, and exceedingly dusty.

Our first camp on Cranberry was at the mouth of Brandy Brook Flow, and it got a full sweep of wind from the south and west. The first afternoon we reached there the water was like glass. I hurriedly rigged up a rod, put on a worm (it was early spring and the water was deep), and dropped it over the end of the dock. It never stopped sinking until I checked the reel, because a fish had taken it at once and kept running with it—a three-pound brook trout.

It seemed like heaven. I had found the place to get them. But it didn't work out that way. It was almost two weeks later before I took the next trout from this spot, and then I took two on minnows. Casting a fly was a heartbreaking job. I spent three solid days fishing the shores of the neighborhood and took one nine-incher. This was before I knew anything about the lake. If fishing it now I'd stick to the rock shoals and troll with a spinner.

After a week of rather slow fishing someone told us about Dog Pond. It was quite a trip getting there, and on the way we met a party coming out who said they couldn't find it. It was rather late in the afternoon when this happened, and it put a damper on our enthusiasm. Nevertheless we kept on. The last identification spot was a deserted lumber camp that was supposed to be close to the pond. The party we had met had reached this. Knowledge of the woods solved the difficulty for us. In searching for the pond I came to a small brook, the waters of which were too warm to be spring-fed. I followed it and almost immediately came to the pond.

We had no tent, but on the pond was a cabin in the last stages of disintegration. About the only place that was usable was the porch, so we gathered a bunch of spruce boughs and large ferns and made our beds there. It was dark before we finished this job and the cooking of our evening meal. I gathered a goodly supply of wood, built up the fire so it would burn for some time, and then we all crawled under the blankets.

Then I fell asleep—for how long I do not know. I was awakened suddenly—startled, just a wee bit terrified. Something was scuffling out there in the black. I grabbed the flashlight and threw its rays out on the clearing. The white light caressed a furry foot, a big furry foot. That was all I saw. The foot disappeared and I heard the sound of quick-moving, heavy steps. Had I seen a bear? Perhaps, and again perhaps not. It might have been a raccoon. But I wanted to believe it a bear, and really it might have been one, so I leaned over to the others and whispered hoarsely: "Did you hear that?" "Yes," came the quavering answer. "What was it?" And what a thrill I got when I answered dramatically: "A bear!—A big bear!" Bear or not, I wish I could again experience the thrill of that night. To me that is the only penalty of growing old—the inability to get thrills from little things that experience finally teaches you are nothing at all. I am still imaginative, but now the imagination merely takes me on momentary journeys into the realms of fairyland. In those days I really lived what I now imagine. I even wonder now if there was any reality then.

I fell asleep again. Some time later I heard my wife shriek.

"What's the matter?" I asked with my heart in my throat.

"Something is moving around at my feet," she replied.

Again the flashlight came into use, and this time revealed a porcupine who turned when the light shone in his eyes and made for the doorway of the cabin, which he entered. This time it wasn't any imagination or guesswork—it was the real thing, but only a porky.

And so the night passed. Exhaustion finally overcame excited nerves and we all fell into a sound sleep. We awoke to a cheerful, sparkling world. Close by, the waters of Dog Pond danced in the sunlight and invited us to fish. But I was the only one who responded. The others were more concerned in making up lost sleep.

On this first attempt flies would not work. I wasted a good hour trying them—in fact I had fished over at least a hundred rises without getting one sign of encouragement. Fortunately I had brought along a can of worms—I did that in those days—but because I had always fished ponds with a dobber when using bait, I did so now and used my bait-casting rod for the job, because I didn't want to strain my precious fly rod.

The raft was drifting quietly and slowly, so I made a cast off the side and released slack line. The dobber caught the rays of the rising sun and bounced brightly over the tiny waves. Suddenly it started making quick darts, upending once in a while but not going under the surface. I thought: "It must be a tiny fish. He can't even pull that small dobber under." Then I struck and got a surprise. Instead of a small fish I had one that fought against the bait-casting rod harder than any largemouth bass I had ever caught. If you've never taken a trout on a bait-casting rod, try it sometime. If he's any size, he'll make you step—far more than he ever would on a fly rod, which does most of your fighting for you. It took fast work with the reel and careful release of the line on the vicious tugs to bring the trout to the raft, and then I lost him. I had left the net on shore and made a sorry attempt at landing the fish without it. I won't mention what I thought of his size. I'd probably exaggerate if I did.

At any rate I had a swell morning's sport before breakfast, and then as the weather looked threatening, and we had supplies for only one meal, we went out.

I fished this pond many times after this and got to know it like a favorite poem. The only consistently successful way to fish it was with worms, and the best way to do that was to drag the worm behind the drifting raft. As long as you adjusted your line so that the worm touched bottom occasionally, you got trout; and as the bottom was singularly free from snags and sharp rocks, you rarely had any trouble. But as the years passed by, the fishing became different. The drag method became less successful, and we had to try different ways. It was during this period I had the best results with bucktails and spinners, casting them to shore close to overhanging or fallen trees or among the boulders that skirted the shore in many places. When you found one trout you always found a half dozen or more, and it was a common sight to see three or more fish following the trout you were playing. This was before spinning tackle invaded the United States. See Chapters IX and X.

There was one spot that was great fishing when the trout came to it. It was a shallow bay into which ran a tiny spring brook where some of the trout spawned. The bottom of this bay was thick with weeds, which came to within a foot of the surface. Crawfish by the thousands lived in these weeds, and at night the trout would often go in to feed on them. We never had any luck getting fish at night, but occasionally they would come in early in the evening or stay after daylight in the morning; in that case we could sometimes take them readily, occasionally with flies, but always with worms. When fishing this water with worms a tiny dobber was needed to keep the line from tangling in the weeds.

I would not call this pond good for fly fishing. Bait or spinners of some sort would always produce but flies were a very uncertain proposition, as far as it concerned the larger fish. My biggest from the pond went two and three-quarter pounds, but we caught quite a number that went better than a pound. One thing that might be of interest and value to the reader is the fact that the raft itself had plenty to do with the success or failure of the worm-dragging system. If the raft was too buoyant and drifted too fast, it reduced our catches. If it was low-floating and water-logged and drifted slowly, our catches increased. We had several opportunities to test this, and it was proved beyond a shadow of a doubt. The reason is simple. A bait dragging too fast made the fish suspicious, but a bait barely moving over the bottom looked all right.

Whenever I've had the opportunity to check a raft against a boat since those days, the raft has always proved the least frightening to fish. Drifting with a boat over shallow waters was a sure-fire alarm, while drifting over the same water with a raft large enough to hide you from the fish below never caused any disturbance. In fact the trout were likely to congregate under it even while it was drifting, and they generally used it as cover if it drifted against shore in the right sort of spot.

We once had a narrow escape on a raft. It happened this way. On getting to the pond we couldn't find the old raft in the accustomed place. We started searching for it, and while we didn't find it we did find two extremely large logs held together with three cross logs and a few boards. It didn't look any too safe, but night was close and we wanted to get our duffel across, so we took a chance. We got across safely and made camp and then went down on the raft to wash. My comrades, Clyde Post and Fred Geist, went first while I stopped to finish some little job.

Finishing the work and feeling rather exuberant, I ran down to the raft and ran out on the board with a hop, skip, and a jump. It was too much for it. It parted in the middle and deposited us in the water. Clyde was straddling a log when it happened and came bouncing along it for all the world like a big frog. Fred went in completely and waded to shore like a drowned rat. I had felt the logs go and turned quickly to run back in. I did famously for a few feet, then the log turned and in I went. Drenched and shivering, we got to the fire and stripped.

It was lucky this accident happened when it did. We fixed the raft after that. It might have happened when all our duffel was on it or while we had been fishing in the middle of the pond. And Fred was the only one who could swim. Incidentally, we packed two good paddles to the pond and left them under the tar-paper roof of the old boathouse. We haven't been back for years now, and I have often wondered who eventually got them and what they thought about it.

In this same country was a series of ponds that provided good fly fishing. The one I fished most was Cat Mountain Pond. This pond was thick with fish, but they ran small—on the average about six to the pound—although once in a while a half-pounder would show up.

These trout would take almost anything you fished with. While experimenting I tried as many as five flies on a leader, and with this string took from three to four fish on a cast. Doubles were a common thing even when using only two flies. I even caught them on a bare hook that was fairly new and shiny. I always broke the hook barb off when fishing the pond.

Most of the time we took these trout from the weed beds in comparatively shallow water. Once in a while, however, they couldn't be found in the shallows, in fact I didn't think we could find them anywhere until I happened to sink a worm down in the deepest part of the pond and got an immediate response. It wasn't much sport, but a few trout were needed for food, so I decided to take enough for that and quit.

It was here that an amusing incident happened. Although from experience I knew the trout in this pond ran small I had a net with me.

Well, the fish were biting fast, and I was kept busy carefully releasing the small ones and keeping the best ones when I got a peculiar strike. The fish took, I struck, and then came a dead weight with a peculiar little wiggle. I happened to be using an eight-foot, two-and-a-half-ounce rod, and it could not lift that fish. When after some three or four minutes I did not get anywhere, I put the rod down and started pulling the line in hand over hand. The wiggle persisted all the way up, and you may imagine my astonishment when I saw a net appear in which was a nine-inch trout. The net looked familiar, so I turned around to look at mine—and it was gone. In some way I had knocked it off the raft without noticing it, and a trout had taken my worm and then entered the net. When I brought the net aboard, the fish was thoroughly enmeshed—so much so that it took a good ten minutes to unravel the snarl.

While I did not fish Cowhorn or Basshout ponds to the extent that I did Cat, I did fish them enough to find that the catches in Cowhorn might be anything from a six-incher to a two-pounder by actual experience, and up to a five-pounder according to old-timers; while the Basshout fish ran three to the pound as a general average. Cowhorn was inclined to be very spotty. Sometimes it would produce fish anyone would be proud to catch, and at other times the best one could do would be to take six- to eight-inchers.

Beaver and their dams, in my estimation, are detrimental to trout in most instances. They flood areas, which turns the water sour after a time when the rotting wood gets in its work. To start with, the beaver dams seem beneficial. In them one gets some grand fishing, and the trout run of good size. But this condition does not last. Gradually the fishing becomes poorer, and finally all one gets is a race of stunted trout. They also ruin many spawning beds, flooding the natural sand and gravel shallows and covering them with a muddy, sour silt. The following quotation from the New York State College of Forestry Bulletin is interesting. (Syracuse University: Vol. II, No. 1A, February 1929, p. 241. Subject: Clear Pond, Adirondacks.)

There were four beaver dams not far apart, counting the one at the foot of the pond, which was the largest and which had flooded a considerable area and killed much small spruce, etc. It had raised the pond about 5 feet above the former level and obliterated the only suitable spawning beds for trout in the pond.

In most cases the beaver's damming streams or small ponds has resulted in just this destruction of trout life. Even if the flooded area does not stop reproduction, it eventually creates an inferior race of trout—black and poorly conditioned. There may be conditions under which beaver dams would be permanently beneficial, but if so I've never come in contact with them. It may be that in the high altitudes where the water remains excessively cold and where the vegetation is not so thick they may be beneficial in raising the water temperature enough to further the growth of some species. It is also possible that the type of soil and vegetation flooded would make a difference in one way or another. In excessively sandy soil, for instance, the creation of a dam might create new spawning beds in place of the old. Study, much time and research, as well as careful observation are required to learn the good or evil effects of the places I have seen. I am sure that beaver often endanger trout existence. They make mud puddles out of pretty little natural ponds and in heavily wooded spring brooks. As far as the angler is concerned, the temporary benefits of their work are usually followed by serious consequences.

There is one thing of which I am convinced. If a pond or lake is suited for the well-being of trout, they will cruise all over it in search of food. If only parts of the pond or lake are suitable, the fish will settle in such places. Of course concentrations of food will cause concentrations of fish even in those ponds that are completely suitable for trout. These locations sometimes change, as illustrated by the following notes on a wet-fly experience while pond fishing in Maine in 1949.

The location was Penobscot Lake, still reasonably isolated considering present-day conditions in the East.

Before we got there Mrs. Woodward, the owner, and Bert Quimby, the manager of the camp, had made it a point to locate all the "hot spots" so that we could get the most from our stay. But a few days before we arrived all these places save one went bad.

There were other guests and they were fishing the remaining active location, so we spent some time on the ponds near by, as well as scouting around and trying here and there in hopes of finding where the fish had gone.

In the course of these trips it was interesting to note that each one of the small and detached ponds had a particular location where you could catch fish. For instance, there was the Dingley chain of three ponds, called First, Second and Third Dingley respectively.

In First Dingley there was only one small pool. This produced only once in a while. I tried it each time when going through, and also tried casts while we went across the lake to the portage to Second Dingley, but never did get a rise. Neither did any one else during our stay.

In Second Dingley the range of the trout occupied perhaps a quarter of an acre all told. Perhaps I'm generous in making this estimate, which is based entirely on fishing it three times and on what I saw in the way of rising fish within and out of our range. Our guide explained that where we fished were the best places in the ponds and that these locations held up throughout the fishing season; that you could not take fish anywhere outside of these territories. I neither saw nor heard anything that contradicted this statement although I am well aware that there may be some other spot in each, not yet discovered, where one could get action.

The Third Dingley fishing spot was smaller than that of Second Dingley, but this pond had the reputation of providing either a good catch of large fish or nothing at all. I'll tell you about my experience there when you read the chapters on spinning.

We had one good wet-fly afternoon at Second Dingley. The winning combination was a cast consisting of a straw-colored nymph as tail fly, and a dropper that I called the Irresistible (Warf Variant), described in Chapter III. This put dry fly and spinner to shame.

On the other hand a pond called North Bay—really a part of Penobscot Lake, to which it is connected by a rather narrow channel called the Thorofare—was entirely different. In this water the trout might be anywhere, and on different days we picked them up at different places.

Then one day we had a chance at the one known hot spot. This was located in the Thorofare. We'd been told that the best spot in the pool was close to a floating log which projected from a bog.

I was using the nymph and fly combination successfully used on Second Dingley. It was calm at the time, and the nymph just brushed the near edge of the log and disappeared under the surface. I was watching closely and imagined I saw the line twitch ever so slightly, so I struck to find I'd hooked a very nice fish on the nymph. In two successive casts two more good fish responded in the same manner. These were all fish better than average. After that they ran to average size.

I can't say definitely that I actually saw the line twitch, and yet

I felt that I did, and each time the result was a hooked fish. I knew that a fish had my fly, even though I couldn't swear that I'd seen anything to apprize me of the fact. It was the intuitive fisherman's response, something I had more strongly when I was young than I have now.

It is a question whether I would have been as successful if the water had been rough at this spot. It is quite likely that, if the cast had dropped and sunk in the same place, the fish would have taken it, but in this case I wonder if I would have known that a trout had taken the fly? Perhaps I wouldn't have known, which would prove either that I did see the take in the smooth water, or else that the fish didn't strike at all in rough water. I bring this up to show that one can't be positive in matters concerning fishing, that in case of doubt there are other sides to the question.

We kept trying here and there on Penobscot and the ponds, but didn't get any other action except some spotty responses to dry flies and spinners. These incidents will be discussed in the proper chapters.

But on the day before our last at Penobscot Lake, Mrs. Woodward and I went out with determination in our hearts. At the first place, a new location to me, we got some nice trout, but not on flies. It took a spinning outfit to turn the trick. As we were really looking for fly fishing we kept cruising. Not far from the dam we finally spotted some rises in a shallow bay. The wind, which had been blowing quite hard, suddenly died out completely, so that any action could be seen for long distances.

When we got within casting distance of the rises the action was immediate and continuous. I used the combination of the Irresistible (Warf Variant) and the straw-colored nymph. Doubles were common, and there would have been trebles and more had I been using more than two flies. However the Warf did the greatest execution.

Up to this time Mrs. Woodward hadn't fished. She wanted to watch me, and was very pleased that she had found an active location for me. But now, at my persuasion, she also joined the game. Then we discovered that the trout were somewhat selective. They didn't fall for her original cast of flies, so we went through our respective boxes and dug out a couple of flies that somewhat resembled the patterns of my two. Her best fly turned out to be a small brown-and-gray bucktail, its general colorations and material similar to the Warf except that it didn't have the deer-hair body.

Before the trout quit the frantic rise, which probably started about 2:45 and ended at 4:30 P.M. on September 30, 1949,[1] I released with my own hands twenty-five good-sized fish. There were many more that were lost in the fight. When trout are coming as fast as this, one doesn't play them carefully. From the strike on, the fight is forced to make them jump and splash and fight back. Thus many of them get off, particularly when there are doubles— something for which you are thankful because it saves you the task of unhooking, with the outside chance of fatally injuring some of the trout.

These, combined with the fish I'd taken on spinning tackle, made my total put-back score thirty trout, some of them mighty fine specimens of *Salvelinus fontinalis*. It was one of those days that are sometimes experienced by the brook-trout fisherman. I usually get one such chance on every trip of at least one week. It is always an exciting occasion.

The number of trout in a lake or pond depends upon the food supply and natural spawning conditions. Given plenty of food, sufficient area, and suitable spawning grounds they will prosper and grow to a fair if not large size. If these things are limited the trout will be limited also, sometimes to a large number of small and poorly conditioned fish and at other times ending up in mostly large fish but very few of them. The restocking of any water is not satisfactory unless these things are taken into consideration and often it would be of greater benefit to feed the present population rather than to increase it.

Brown trout in particular seem to be more inclined toward cannibalistic tendencies under these conditions. In many cases brook trout seem to degenerate into an inferior race, small and poor. Browns are more inclined to keep eating each other until the few overcome the balance. Glasby Pond in the Adirondacks illustrated this. It was originally stocked with browns. Fishing was good for a time, with the trout getting larger but more scarce each year. The last record made of any fish being caught in the pond was in 1917

---

[1] The date is given here for the benefit of those who may wish to check it against one of those tables giving specific times when fish are most likely to strike. R.B.

when Richard Jessup caught two which weighed respectively three pounds fourteen ounces and four pounds four ounces. From what can be ascertained these were the last two fish left of the original stocking. The pond, incidentally, didn't have any trout in it to begin with.

The same thing also happens with brook trout at times. The late Chan Wescott, of Cranberry Lake, told me about Curtis Pond. He said that once there was very good fishing there, that the trout grew to large size, and that each year they got larger and were scarcer. No small trout seemed to come along as they do in the usual course of events. Finally there came a year when only three very large fish were caught and from that time on no one ever took another one from that stocking.

One thing seems to be sure. These complete disappearances of trout from ponds seem to be confined mostly to those ponds which were not natural trout waters. Again let me quote from a bulletin published by Syracuse University: "Hedgehog (Clear Pond on the U. S. Geological Survey Topographic Map) and Glasby ponds were also visited. The steep, absolutely dry bed of the outlet of Hedgehog was followed to the pond. It is said not to have been a natural trout water, but it has been stocked and trout of large size have been caught there. As usual in such instances where suitable spawning beds are lacking, as they appear to be in this pond, the fish taken are or were only grown-up individuals of the original fish planted."

Once you find the key to any pond it simplifies the problem. You keep following the same formula, and it usually works. The trouble is that ponds and lakes vary and you have little help from the appearance of the surface, something that aids so much in the reading of streams. So unless you take the trouble to sound and drag an unknown water you are at a loss to know just what to do until you see fish making a disturbance. Weed-beds and rock shoals are the two best bets to look for, and in the late summer a knowledge of the coldest spots is absolutely essential.

Out at Spring Creek, which was Ollie Deibler's pet project when he was Fish Commissioner of Pennsylvania, I had some interesting experiences with wet flies. For instance, one morning a lightly cast fly was absolutely ineffective. The results were so poor that I finally became careless and slapped the fly on the water so hard that it made a splash. It brought a rise from a good fish, which I hooked and landed. I recognized this as a hint and took advantage of it, slapping the fly on the water as hard as I could. For two hours I had some rare sport and took a lot of fish, all of which were returned to the water after being carefully unhooked.

After lunch this method failed to produce. I fooled around with one thing or another for some time and finally started fishing upstream with a heavy fly that sank deeply. I let it sink as it would and simply kept the line from coming taut against the fly. The first time I did this the fly drifted some fifteen feet and was quite deep when I saw the line twitch slightly. I struck and connected with a nice brook trout. Fishing from the same spot and making the same drift each time, I took six more good fish on six casts.

Then this method failed. Trying all sorts of things, I finally put on a split shot and sunk the fly to the bottom before moving it. Then I worked it very slowly with the "hand twist" retrieve. The results were quite pleasing—three fish larger than any I had caught previously. But toward evening the fish started rising and would not take wet flies or nymphs regardless of how they were fished.

Just consider this one day on a stream that probably has more fish to the square yard than any other stream in the country except perhaps those in some private preserves—four changes in method needed in one day. Do you wonder that I stress the importance of knowing many methods of using flies and lures? One must do so in order to get even fair results, especially in these days of concentrated fishing when the fish are becoming wiser every season.

An interesting angle to the fishing at Spring Creek was provided by the fact that the fish were fed regularly with a reddish conglomeration of ground lights and salt-water fish, a combination that, they told me at the hatchery, had been found very satisfactory. This feeding of the fish in the stream was absolutely necessary because there were far more trout in the water than it could sustain naturally.

The food was thrown on the water with dippers, and, being rather soggy in texture, it kept together well enough to fall on the stream in rather large chunks, thus causing an audible "smack" and some surface disturbance. Because of this I realized that when I cast a large fly so that it slapped the water, it was imitating, to some extent, the food the fish had become accustomed to, thus accounting for my success when fishing a fly in this manner.

But this conclusion did not explain why the fish suddenly refused a fly slapped on the water and preferred one that drifted naturally. Neither did it explain why the fish suddenly refused all artificials except dry flies AND YET TOOK GROUND-UP FOOD AT ANY TIME, EITHER ON OR BELOW THE SURFACE. My first reaction to this thought was to tie a fly of the same color as the food being fed the trout. "They will do the work," I thought as I looked at my creations, which resembled the ground-up lights.

But while the idea was sound enough, it did not work. The fish took the fly that looked like meat, but not any better than they did any other artificial. When my "meat" fly worked, so did any other fly. Here another fact showed up. You could fish a stretch of water without a single rise to your credit and then, when food was thrown in, take fish after fish on the same fly that had been refused a moment before. When the food was thrown on the water, the fish seemed to lose all caution and took anything that floated along with it. Why? Was it because the appearance of the food they were accustomed to getting made them feel safe in taking anything that looked edible? Or did the appearance of the food make them excited and "piggish," so that they dashed at anything that drifted along with the current? Perhaps in such cases each fish tried to get at the food first and selfishly attempted to get more than the rest. According to my personal observations I'd say that the latter reaction was the true one. I feel sure that large quantities of food excite the cupidity of fish. Certainly anyone who has observed at all must know that no individual fish ever gives any other fish any part of what he gets himself. "To the victor belong the spoils" is a law of nature that cannot be disputed. When one fish gets something, he keeps it unless some other fish takes it away from him by force or superior agility. Any fish that has more than he can swallow immediately is followed and harassed by many others and often loses part of what he has secured. No one can possibly deny this.

Of course the fish in Spring Creek were not usually fed when anglers were on the stream. But for experimental purposes we did have some food thrown out while the section was open to fishing. The results were interesting and thought-provoking. At the time we selected, the fishing was at a low ebb. Not one of the fishermen within our immediate vicinity had had a rise for several hours. It seemed as if there weren't any trout in the water. All true anglers will recognize this feeling. Of course we always know better, but we do have our doubts at times.

But the first dipper of prepared food brought at least thirty trout to the surface, and several anglers who happened to have flies on or in the water at the time took trout. The next few dippers caused the water to boil, and at least seven fishermen connected with good fish. Inasmuch as the flies being used ranged from delicate dry flies to coarse streamers, it clearly showed that what they were using had nothing to do with their success. The reason they caught fish was the appearance of food the trout were looking for. They expected it and waited until it appeared, unless a particularly appetizing and abundant hatch of natural insects appeared, in which case they started feeding on them and were susceptible to any artificial that imitated them.

To my mind this suggests possibilities for the angler's campaign. I wonder how a concentrated effort on the part of many fishermen would react on trout? Suppose a group got together and all fished the same water with large flies? Would the fish think that the artificials were real and start feeding? I am not in the least sure they would, but there is an idea here that might result in something worth while. After all, heavily stocked waters in which the fish are fed regularly require special thought, and as such streams are becoming more necessary with each advancing season, they deserve some consideration.

It is quite likely that the fish would not be fooled by the concentrated attack at all. It is almost certain that the reason they hit the artificials floating down in company with the prepared food was because they knew that in order to get their share of "easy pickings" they had to grab anything they saw quickly and did not wait to investigate its quality or genuineness. It may be that the odor and the flavor of the raw meat spread rapidly through the water and made them ravenous, as no offerings of odorless and tasteless artificials could do. One thing is sure: fish definitely know the difference between the real thing and an imitation. Sometimes they are momentarily fooled by the artificials, but it doesn't take them long to get wise. I'm puzzled and uncertain about it all as it pertains to fishing, but I feel that my idea might find root in the mind of some other angler who will delve deeper into the subject.

Writing about this brings back some old memories. Years ago I found out that the sudden appearance of muddy water often started the trout feeding and invariably made them less suspicious. To take advantage of this fact after the streams had become low and clear, I used to pick out a suitable stretch, go above it, and cause a good supply of dirt to muddy the water. Then I would go below and fish the water with a wet fly. Time after time it resulted in good fishing when it was absolutely impossible to get trout by ordinary means. Of course the stream cleared quickly from the results of my work so that the activity was short-lived, but it did serve to pep up the blank days of July and August.

Some fifteen to twenty miles from New York City, in the state of New Jersey, the Hackensack River glides smoothly through meadow and swampy forest land. It doesn't look like a trout stream, nor was it one when I was a young man. As far upstream as the Congers–New City Road in New York State this river was populated by pickerel. From this point on, one began to take an occasional trout, and the brook above the junction at Verdin Brook was one of the best brook-trout streams one would ever hope to find. But the lower stretches were pickerel water pure and simple, and although once in a great while someone would pick up a large trout, we all knew that it was because the fish was large enough to be immune from the attacks of the pickerel and that no small trout could survive in the water.

When the New Jersey authorities became conservation-minded and began their program of restocking, they decided that the Hackensack River near the New Jersey–New York line deserved some attention. Their efforts in its behalf were well worth while. The trout put in here seemed to do very well. Many of them moved upstream and provided trout fishing in the New York part of the stream, but many of them stayed in the vicinity of the "Old Tappan" stretch.

However, the type of water at this point does not lend itself to easy fishing, and while at first fishermen made wonderful catches without much effort, after a time the fish seemed to get wise and only accomplished anglers could get worth-while results.

While I never happened to fish this particular stretch of the river, I have two friends who did. They are Al Argenti and Tony Savoca of Northvale, New Jersey. Al is a "natural" who instinctively short-cuts through any problem. He seems to know just what to do without fussing or fuming. He does not analyze the problem, but he unerringly puts his finger on the things that solve it. Tony, while not possessing Al's intuition, has the analytical sort of brain that searches for and isolates the reasons for Al's success. Between the two they made a great pair and certainly went places when it came to taking fish under adverse conditions.

As I worked on this chapter of *Trout* these boys came in to see me. Because I believed that their views on wet-fly fishing would be worth while passing on to others, I turned the conversation into these channels and we checked up with their experiences on the Hackensack and compared them with mine on waters of similar type.

"The flies must be fished slow," asserted Tony.

"With this retrieve?" I questioned, getting a rod and demonstrating the "hand twist."

"Yes," was the reply. "But sometimes it's best to let them float without any motion except that supplied by the current."

Before we got through we found that the following methods, both of which have been described in previous pages, were the reasons for their success:

Hand-twist retrieve—SLOW.

Natural drift—both upstream and down- and across-stream methods.

"Most fellows fish their flies too fast," they insisted. They also stressed the importance of using the pattern and size of fly for the prevailing conditions. This confirmation of my own ideas, coming from two fellows who have shown time and again that they know their fishing, is very gratifying. Only thoughtful, constructive articles and books are capable of gaining and holding their interest.

Several years ago these two men accompanied me to a pet stream of mine in northern New York. We were out primarily for dry-fly fishing and didn't spend any time trying other methods. But one afternoon, while we were walking downstream to place ourselves in scattered positions along a favorite stretch, we passed a pool in which we saw the splash of a large fish.

Of course we stopped to look and presently saw another wrinkle on the water that looked like a rise. We decided to investigate.

The boys refused to fish—said it was up to me. Before starting I looked the situation over carefully. At the head the riffle hugged the far shore and was quite narrow. About ten feet lower down, the riffle changed into a smooth glide with fair speed. This glide also hugged the far shore, and the water looked about twice as deep as the riffle. Below the glide the stream spread out into a fairly deep and very quiet stretch some thirty feet wide and seventy feet long.

The first rise had been seen about halfway down the glide. The second rise had occurred at the foot of the riffle. Now as I got ready I saw a rise at the tail of the glide. At first I thought that there were several fish feeding, but closer observation disclosed that they were all caused by one fish that seemed to be cruising up and down the stretch. I saw the trout working up through the glide, and saw him take several insects that seemed to be drifting down at various depths. He then proceeded almost to the top of the riffle, where he started "tailing." After several moments of this he came swiftly back to the tail of the glide and started upstream again.

It didn't take long to see just what he was about. He was dislodging nymphs from the bottom in the riffle and then working the water below to feed on what he had uprooted. At this time the boys were frankly skeptical about nymph fishing. They had tried it without success. I believed it to be a good opportunity to present an object lesson on the value of nymph fishing, so I proceeded to make what I hoped would be a spectacular demonstration. First I fished with a dry fly. I wanted to show the boys that this fish would not take the floating fly. I felt reasonably sure that the dry fly would be ignored, because there were quite a number of duns on the stream and this fish had not taken one while I watched. I gave the dry fly plenty of chance and changed patterns several times, but the trout did not take the slightest notice of them. Then I went a bit further and tried the ordinary variety of wet flies. These also were ignored. "So far, so good," I exulted inwardly. "If he'd taken any of these flies it would have spoiled everything."

Now came the ticklish part of my demonstration. I knew that any error would be fatal so deliberately prepared to make the try a good one. Tying on a No. 1 R.B.—size 12LS nymph, I waited until the fish had finished his grubbing job in the riffle and was on his way downstream. As he turned to work back upstream my nymph dropped in the riffle and started drifting downstream. It required all my attention to keep the lure located and the slack line at proper length, so that I could not see where the fish was, but as my fly reached the center of the glide I saw a swirl by it, lifted the rod to take up the slack, and felt that electric thrill caused by the hooking of a good fish.

You should have heard Tony and Al yell. You never saw two more enthusiastic anglers. They were all for nymph fishing now. But strangely enough, on this day that one trout was the only one that seemed to be interested in nymphs. The rest all preferred a light-ginger fly floating on the surface. Of course I had been lucky in making my demonstration. Everything had worked according to Hoyle, and that is quite extraordinary, as everyone knows who has tried to illustrate some particular point about fishing to someone he is trying to impress. But the boys stoutly claim that luck had nothing to do with it. I'm glad they feel that way about it, because it certainly gives you a moral lift to know that someone thinks you are a pretty good fisherman.

And here is another incident illustrating the value of nymphs. This took place some two thousand miles away from New York on a Wyoming stream. Although at this particular time dry flies produced very well, certain sections that contained large fish were so situated that dry flies did not interest the trout living in them. You see, there were rather deep holes located under banks and undermined tree roots against which the current ran rather swiftly and then turned at an abrupt obtuse angle. Such holes rarely extended more than eight or ten feet below the point where the current gouged out the bank, and while the lower portions always yielded some medium-sized fish, I felt certain that the undercover portions contained larger ones. So I determined to experiment a bit.

Picking out one particularly attractive-looking spot, I first fished it with a dry fly, making the cast from the tail and placing the fly well up in the riffle. I did this several times until I had impressed on my mind the time required for this fly to float down the riffle and to the alder-covered bank. Once I got this point well established, I changed to a nymph that I soaked well and then cast it to the same spot. When I figured that it had reached the bank, I allowed some thirty seconds additional time to let it get under the cover and then raised the rod cautiously. I felt a slight pull and instinctively reacted with a strike. Instantly I was playing a fish that felt heavier than any I had previously taken, and subsequently landed a three-pound brown trout, dark and brilliantly colored.

I soon found out that I had been lucky in hooking this fish. Later experiences brought many misses, and I could not seem to get the technique of striking down well enough to get a better average than twenty-five per cent. However, strikes I did get, and many of them; so I considered the experiment of exceeding value.

Incidentally, this method is very useful when you get a rise to a dry fly that you miss, especially when it occurs a few feet above locations like the one just mentioned. Such rising fish rarely return for another dry fly, but will usually take a nymph fished so that it drifts under the bank. From observation I find that when a trout rises to a surface fly and misses, he usually returns to his normal home and is a bit startled over the occurrence, besides being suspicious of surface food. However, his appetite has not been appeased; so when an attractive-looking morsel appears down in his hole, he is quite likely to take it. Experiences proving this have happened to me so often that I feel my observations about them are sound and worth while. But you must calculate the drift of the nymph to perfection; otherwise you will become discouraged and think it all a lot of worthless talk. The average nymph fishing does not lend itself to careless work or superficial study. You must know what you are doing and do it well; otherwise the results will not encourage you to further trial.

One can never tell just what to do or be sure that because one method works between certain hours, it will continue to do so for the balance of the day. Here is an incident pertinent to this situation. The location was northern New Jersey. I had never fished the stream, and two friends who considered it ideal took me there to show me what a real stream was like.

Of course it was the same old story. "It was never this way before," and "Something is wrong today," were remarks I heard frequently. At noon not one of us had taken a fish—in fact we hadn't had even a rise.

After lunch, things weren't any better. "Let's sit by the stream and watch," I suggested. "Certainly there isn't any use in pounding water the way we've been doing. Either the fish aren't taking at all or else we're using the wrong methods."

The boys were willing; so we sat. I happened to take a position directly at the edge of the stream alongside a rather sizable riffle that contained some good-looking pockets. More to pass the time than anything else, I rigged up a cast of three wet flies and, when it was finished, started whipping it carelessly over the riffle. I got tired of this, so I let the current take the flies downstream and then amused myself by dancing the two droppers over the water, as the tail fly held the leader reasonably taut against the current. It was interesting to see flies skip on the waves of the riffle, and I had become quite absorbed in seeing how well I could do the job when a trout rose swiftly to the hand fly, which was touching the water only once in a while. He hooked himself securely, and I had the pleasure of landing an eleven-inch brook trout.

Without moving from my comfortable seat, I tried the stunt again. This time I skipped the center fly over the water, the hand fly being a foot or two in the air. A trout grabbed the skipping fly and pulled it under the surface. This brought the hand fly to the top of the water, and instantly a fish hit it so hard that he broke the fly from the tippet. However, the other fish was still on and soon was in the creel.

Of course this incident woke us up and we went at the fishing with great enthusiasm, using the method I had stumbled upon while idling. As a matter of fact I had often used it in the past but had somehow forgotten it until I started playing with the flies. Even then I did not expect it to produce, but it did and for three hours we had some good sport.

Then came a change. Suddenly the trout would not take our dancing flies. For an hour I worked diligently without getting a rise. As is usually the case under such circumstances, I felt sure that the fish had stopped feeding. But on coming to a long glide, I saw a good-sized trout breaking at the lower end, and I knew that the trouble was with my method and not the fish. I first tried the dancing flies over this fish, but he ignored them. Then I tried all the other methods of wet-fly fishing, but it did no good. Although I'm not fond of spinner fishing, I decided to try one at this time just to see if the trout would take it. Instead of rigging up a special leader, I took off the tail fly and tied the spinner in its place.

The ruse taught me something. The trout did not hit the spinner, but he did take the center fly. At first I thought it an accident, but when I took another fish on the next cast, also on the first dropper, and then caught a half dozen more in other pools, some on the center fly and some on the hand fly, I began to realize that in some way the spinner on the end of the leader had something to do with my success. Not wanting any more fish anyway, I did a little experimenting. The cast of flies alone, no matter how fished, would not produce, but the moment a spinner was placed at the end of the leader, action began. Observation showed that the spinner imparted a peculiar action to the flies that seemed to be what the fish desired—*at this particular time*. Not one of the fish hit the spinner, and I found that when the hooks were taken from it the results were even more satisfying. Incidentally, on subsequent experiments I discovered that sometimes the method worked and at other times it did not. Often the trout would hit nothing but the spinner, and sometimes they would hit neither fly nor spinner but would take flies manipulated in some other way. The experiences clearly showed the necessity of variation in one's fishing.

Whatever you do, don't overlook the possibilities of very small nymphs and wet flies, that is 14's and 16's and even smaller if obtainable. There is a preponderance of tiny larvæ and flies on most of our streams, and while we can't hope to ever imitate the smallest ones, we can get some artificials tied as small as possible and so be in a position to take advantage of many rises and feeding periods when the trout refuse our larger flies. Several years ago I tied up two dozen No. 18 translucent nymphs. It took me two days to do it, but I've never regretted having spent the time. In ponds and streams from New York to Wyoming they have sometimes turned a day of failure to one of success. To carry these midge wet flies and nymphs in your kit is to be prepared for emergencies. Just remember that one of the toughest times to take trout is when they are feeding on very small insects or larvæ. Although the smallest artificials possible will not take care of all such hatches, they will produce results often enough to make having them worth while.

As an illustration let me tell you of an experience that took place late one afternoon in the High Sierras of California. During the last hour before sunset the fish had responded well to a dry fly, but after the sun disappeared behind the peaks the trout suddenly refused the floating fly, even though they continued to break the surface of the water.

After several changes in sizes and types of dry flies that failed to interest the fish, I started experimenting with nymphs. Nothing happened until I tied on one of the tiny 18's. By this time it was getting too dark to fish a nymph well, but at that, during the brief period between then and total blackness, I rose twelve fish and hooked two. What might have happened if I had used this midge nymph sooner is a question. Perhaps the fish would have taken it eagerly; perhaps they wouldn't have taken it at all until that last moment when I started using it—perhaps the moment they began to refuse the dry flies was the time they changed their selection of diet. We have no way of absolutely proving things that happen this way, since we have no check against them. Nevertheless the small nymphs did the work and took the two best trout of the evening. I missed the others because I could not see what I was doing, and I had to strike blindly at swirls that caught the fast fading light in their waves or at slight tugs that carried through to the tip of the rod.

While the above experience deals with nymphs, the same thing holds true with tiny wet flies. As a general rule 14's are the smallest you will need, but once in a while a much smaller fly will bring better results. In my experience with these midges I've never found a large variety of patterns necessary. In fact almost any pattern seems to be O. K. as long as it is small enough. It is also best when tied very sparse with a small body and just a few wisps of hackle. Strangely enough I've found these tiny flies just as effective in fast water as I have in still water. It hasn't been necessary to use them often—the notes of the last twelve years reveal only some eight times when it was essential to use them to catch fish.

Some of the most fascinating wet-fly fishing may be found in Quebec, Maine, and other parts of northern North America. Some of my most recent experiences in this section were enjoyed in the Laurentides Park of Quebec. Since about 1938 I've spent quite some time in this inspiring country, which was introduced to me by Gustave Bedard, then Superintendent of the park, and further shown to me by the Assistant Superintendent Laurent Talbot, while Gus was overseas in the war.

Between the two of them I became completely sold on what they had to offer. Of course the only selling really necessary was to get me there. The forests with their deep moss floors, the lakes with their entrancing shore lines, the streams with their ever-changing beauty, and, above all, the beautiful brook trout, *Salvelinus fontinalis*, in such pleasing numbers and size, did the rest. And if I needed additional prompting, it was there in the occasional glimpses of wild life that came now and then, like the sparkle of sunshine breaking through the clouds on a gloomy day. We've had otters, in military array, inspect us as we passed by in our canoes, so close that we could see their whiskers bristle. We've had Roger Durocher, one of our guides, call a bull moose so close that even he got frightened at the beast's anger when it found out that we weren't a girl friend. We've heard the wolf packs howling close by while we cast our feathery offerings, perhaps over the rise of a coveted fish, perhaps simply over a place where trout were supposed to lie. And in the fall, when the northern lights send a mystical glow over the heavens and the waters, one who loves the wilderness finds there a fulfillment of desires that date back to ages long past, when man's only pleasures came from what nature had to offer in the raw.

I've written about most of our fishing experiences in the park, and you may read about them in another work of mine as well as in the chapters on spinning in this book. As a matter of fact outstanding happenings do not come along like leaves from a tree disrobing for winter, and as this book describes only actual fishing experiences I can't supply much more about the Laurentides. But I can tell you about the places we have fished, and about our last experiences there with a wet fly.

First of all let me explain, for the benefit of those who do not know, that the Laurentides Park is brook-trout country. While the old "cast and fast retrieve" method is used more than any other by the guests, it isn't always the best method by any means, particularly after the first marvellous fishing of springtime has passed by. The hand-twist retrieve, described in Chapter Two, is of course always in order, but so also are some of the more difficult methods of wet-fly fishing.

For instance, take the fishing the last week of the 1948 season,

September 23 through 30, from the base camp on Lake aux Ecorces. One of the good spots reached from here is the narrow stretch of water between the lake proper and the dam.

Ordinarily there is always current in this reach, but this time when we fished it the water was faster than we'd ever seen it, due to some heavy rains that had fallen just before our arrival.

The trout were definitely selective. You could make hundreds of casts without getting a fish, but when you dropped the right fly or lure in the right place, at the right time, with the proper technique, then you got a strike.

Usually Laurentides trout respond best to large, fancy flies, sizes 2 and 4 being quite suitable. But these fish would not have anything to do with such truck. They wanted something more natural looking. My wife took her best fish, a three-pounder, on a March Brown, size 8. It was a sparsely tied job, made particularly for brown-trout fishing in Catskill Mountain and similar streams. The fish took it for a nymph. I took my best fish, also a three-pounder, on a silvery gray streamer pattern, size 6, made by a New Zealand angler who had sent it to me for trial in this hemisphere. To the trout's eye, it probably resembled a small fish.

The best results were obtained by casting slightly up and across stream, then letting the fly drift on a slack line while watching closely for the tell-tale twitch that denoted a strike. See the NAT-URAL DRIFT METHOD description in Chapter II, Page 14. When the fly started to drag it was retrieved, by the hand-twist method if it was a regular fly or nymph pattern or a jerky and twitchy action if it was a minnow imitation.

We fished this water only the first two days after arrival, and while we managed to take a fair number of fish, our score was very poor compared to the fishing others got there on the days we were angling somewhere else. It seemed that, as the water-flow decreased, the fishing got better, at least for large fish.

There are some places in this country where you can always catch trout—for instance, the river that connects Big Lake Metascouac with Lake Hirondelle. This is a stream of short length, and in the fall there are only three holes or pools where the trout may be found in quantity. Whenever you fish these pools you are amazed at the response you get.

On this 1948 trip four of us fished two of the holes in this river. We all caught trout without any effort, frequently two at a cast, with quite a number of quarter-pound to three-quarter-pound fish among them.

This sort of fishing becomes boring after an hour. It is too easy. When we quit, the trout were taking just as readily and as fast as when we started. This may seem incredible, but do not overlook the fact that this fishing is not abused. Most of the anglers fishing it are satisfied with one visit and they rarely keep any fish except the injured ones. As only guests of the Park get to fish the waters (anyone is eligible who makes a reservation in time) and as they are always with guides, there isn't much chance of dangerous sabotage.

While most of the trout in these pools run small, occasionally one catches a large one. My best so far has been a two-and-three-quarter pounder that I caught in Gracie's Pool, so named for my wife because she loves it.

One of the famous pools of this territory is named Roseberry. This name was not derived from a berry but from the name of a guide who, not knowing the rest of the country well and getting good results for his "sports" there, fished it to the exclusion of any other place.

When you strike this pool right (it is like a small pond), you may get plenty of large fish. One year my wife and I had great fishing there; in another year Laurent Talbot tried it early, before any guests had arrived, to find plenty of really large fish present and willing, including some that he couldn't handle with the tackle he had.

But even if the large fish aren't there, you can always pick up a fair number ranging from a quarter to three-quarters of a pound, provided you fish it right. The fish may not be where you expect them, but in a place where you might easily scare them. During the 1948 trip this pool provided very poor fishing. But my guide, Roger Durocher, was a young man with vision, and we started cruising cautiously, with my flies searching out all likely looking spots. Finally, in shallow water that was heavily weeded, I connected with a nice little trout of twelve inches. It happened that we had found a large school of them, the sizes ranging from ten inches to fourteen inches. They were all concentrated in a spot not more than twenty-five square feet in area.

After catching a dozen or so I called the other canoes. But although we carefully explained how to reach these fish my wife's guide, who was inclined to be stubborn and who didn't seem to know too much about fly fishing, paddled right over the hot spot and ruined it for further action.

But when one fishes the Ecorces-Metascouac region it is definitely for the purpose of taking some large trout. Now, in my estimation, a large brook trout is one of two pounds and over. While I've taken quite a number of two- to three-pounders, I've connected with and landed only two four-pounders in a matter of four trips. But each time we return, my hopes are for a five-pounder or better. This hope is one of the most compelling influences in keeping fishing interest at fever heat.

Another section I like very well is the Metabetchouan. This is reached from Kiskisink, an Indian settlement on the Canadian National Railway. To reach it you take the night train to the village where a truck picks you up and carries you some thirteen miles to the river. From there you go by canoe and portage, usually stopping at the Lake St. Henri camp for a while before proceeding to Camp Metabetchouan.

There is sometimes excellent fishing in the rapids below the falls close to the St. Henri camp, and also at Brule Lake where there is also a camp, one that is on the rough side but nevertheless very comfortable. There are some large fish in this territory, and the fishing locations are easily reached.

Camp Metabetchouan is located at the upper end of small Lake Metascouac, or rather where the upper Metabetchouan River joins the lake. There are some great fishing holes up the river. On one trip three of us each took a trout of four pounds or better, besides several others of three and a half pounds. Streamers and bucktails often produce in this water, but I took my best fish with a size 4 tandem Parmachene, that is, two flies of this pattern and size connected by a short piece of gut. As a matter of record both of my best Laurentides trout fell for this pattern and size, although the other one took a single and not a tandem.

There are also some good holes in small Lake Metascouac as well as in Lakes La Place, Page, Loiselle, and St. Patrick.

Incidentally the water feeding the Upper Metabetchouan comes mostly from Lakes Hirondelle and Big Metascouac. One can come in to Ecorces from the east, and then by canoe and portage work down to the Kiskisink landing on the lower Metabetchouan, fishing all the waters in between if you allow enough time and if the interchanging of party dates at each camp can be synchronized. Gustave Bedard and I had this trip all planned one year, but fate took a hand and stopped it. We both got extremely bad colds before we even reached the jumping-off place. But I'm still hoping we can make it one of these days. It should be a wonderful trip, providing plenty of thrills and good fishing. Oh, to be young again!

On the whole this wilderness brook-trout fishing is mostly a wet-fly proposition. However, there are times and places where the dry fly does good work. I've written about a few such experiences in the chapters on dry-fly fishing.

Always keep in mind that wet-fly fishing is a game in which intuitive reactions are most important. The most infinitesimal happening should be remembered and analyzed if possible so that it may be used on future fishing trips. It is the accumulation of such incidents and the absorbing of them, so they become an unconscious part of your angling technique, that make for perfection.

CHAPTER VI

Bucktails and Streamers

IN FLIES of this type we have a welcome and needed aid for the angler who does not care to use bait under any circumstances and who might otherwise quit without a fish. These flies are excellent for use under conditions when dry flies and ordinary wet flies are ineffective and are also generally useful throughout the season.

I am somewhat surprised to note how many anglers have the idea that flies of this type are adaptable only in the case of high and discolored water or in the early season before good fly fishing starts. As a matter of fact, frequently they produce during low and clear water conditions, and there is hardly a day's fishing that can't be made a bit better because of the wise use of such flies in some particularly baffling situation.

By this I do not mean to imply that they are adaptable on all occasions—that you could use them to the exclusion of everything else and benefit thereby. Rather do they serve as an additional artifice with which you may succeed in deceiving some wary specimens or perhaps overcoming the difficulties of certain stream conditions not controllable by other methods and flies. At the same time they are quite sporty to use, in many cases the rises to them being as perfectly visible as those made to a floating fly.

In my opinion a large assortment of patterns is not necessary, but the assortment should be varied, both in colors and sizes. One type, originally conceived by a Mr. Hobbs in Connecticut and since continued by a reputable New England firm, has always been most satisfactory. It is really nothing more than a regular bucktail fly but has the addition of an enamel head, on which an eye is painted. Whether this eye means anything is subject to debate. Some experiences I have had seem to prove that the eye did make a difference. In searching around for a reason for this I noted that some small minnows and other tiny specimens of different species had conspicuous eyes, and that these eyes were visible in the water even when you could not distinguish the rest of the fish. It is possible that an eye painted on the head of an artificial may produce an effect particularly acceptable to some trout under certain conditions. At any rate, while these flies are not infallible, any more than many other varieties of artificials, I do think the idea has enough merit to be worth considering.

This original Optic (trademarked) bucktail set others working on eyes for flies, with the result that you may now purchase both glass and plastic eyes to be tied in at the head of a lure. I like the plastic better than the glass because they are lighter in weight, easier to tie on, and much more difficult to break. However, the glass eyes do have a transparency not present in any others, so that for some purposes or conditions it is quite likely that they would be best.

My favorite colors for a straight bucktail fly are brown and white, black and white, yellow and orange, and red and white. As a rule, when fishing for ordinary stream trout, sizes ranging from 6 through 10 on 2X or 3X long hooks, and sizes 8 through 12 on 6X long hooks, will cover most needs. On the whole I've found the medium to small sizes most useful although for heavy and deep waters I prefer sizes 6 and 8, 6X long.

The streamer fly, tied with a combination of feathers and hair or with feathers alone, can be made into most minnow-like combinations with the right materials. While these are not as durable as the straight bucktails because of the comparative frailty of streamer feathers, they do have additional life and action in the water, and sometimes excite or fool the trout into striking when regular bucktails fail. In fashioning these flies the maker has the choice of a great variety of feathers which tend to make the minnow effect. In hackles there are various shades of badger, from white with black center to deep honey with dark center. Then there are the furnace and cochybondhu colors, in tones from light ginger to dark red or almost entirely black. Dyes may be employed to produce a greenish or bluish color, both effective for some conditions, as for instance when you wish to imitate the smelt runs. Mixing these feathers with deer hair, polar bear hair, squirrel hair, and what not provides a vast combination of designs for the imaginative fly maker.

Nearly every angler has some ideas along these lines, which is a good thing. It continually creates new interest and provides new topics for discussion. Every once in a while some fellow has an unusually clever idea and produces a fly that is outstanding in performance no matter where used, while patterns for specific localities are continually making their appearance. These patterns for specific places are sometimes necessary, but usually some standard pattern will do the same work. This is not intended as a criticism of patterns that have no national standing. It is intended only to show prospective anglers that they need not worry if they don't have every known pattern. No one could possibly expect to carry all the different flies and be able to find just what he should have at some particular place at the very time he needed it. There is a decided need for simplification, and whether you use Tom's, Dick's, or Harry's particular killer, it does not matter as long as you have some fly that will work at the required time. Remember that no one yet has ever devised a fly that always catches fish. It isn't likely that anyone ever will. If someone claims this distinction for a certain pattern, just make a bet with him. Then fish side by side with him day after day and see what happens. I know some fellows who carry so many different flies that they spend valuable time trying out their stock when they could get better results if they used only one fly and concentrated on fishing in places where there might be a willing fish. From my observations I think most of us spend too much time worrying about our tackle and too little time learning the intimate characteristics of the fish in the streams we fish most. Don't forget that a person who has exceptional knowledge of trout, even though his equipment may be nothing more than a cane pole and a crudely fashioned fly, can take some trout under conditions that might well tax the ingenuity of the most elaborately equipped angler whose knowledge of fish is somewhat above the ordinary. This does not mean that the fellow with nondescript tackle would do poorly with a good outfit. On the contrary, he would do much better than with his crude outfit, once he learned how to handle it. But it does mean that no matter how good your outfit, it won't be worth anything to you unless you first assimilate enough fishing sense to make it possible for your outfit to do its part. After all, tackle is not alive. It cannot think. It cannot perform by itself. It needs your controlling influence, and if that is misdirected, the best tackle in the world can't do anything for you.

It is a good rule always to blame yourself if you have poor luck. Be unmerciful in your judgment of *you*—in the way you fish, in the places you fish, in every motion you make. Only in this way can you expect to progress. Each time you discipline yourself, you recognize faults that should be corrected. This means advance, for once you admit a fault, you instinctively try to correct it.

Sometimes extra large and outlandish-looking flies are extremely effective, even on small streams. Two such patterns are the Marabou and the Black Ghost. As landlocked salmon and bass patterns these look swell—but for trout? Well, I know I was laughed at several times when I first brought them out in front of conservative anglers, but they didn't laugh after they saw the effect they had on trout. The original pattern of the Marabou was described in my book *Just Fishing*. It was white, and the photographed pattern was tied by A. M. Ballou, of North Dighton, Massachusetts. The colored engraving of the one in this book is approximately the same, but was tied by myself. Since the advent of this fly other patterns have appeared. One in particular, the Yellow Breeches, a combination originating in the brains of Charlie Fox and Bob McCafferty of Pennsylvania, has proved itself an excellent addition to a family which most likely will grow. In the color plates this is designated by the name "Yellow Marabou," simply to avoid confusing the reader and to keep the type classification apart from the regular flies. But "Yellow Breeches" is the real name, and while my pattern, as shown on the plate, is tied a bit differently from Charlie's and Bob's, the general effect is the same. I have tried out Blue Gray, Scarlet, and Green Marabou, but the results I obtained with them were not sufficiently outstanding to deserve more than a passing mention. However Bob McCafferty tells me that black is good. It should be. He gave me one. I'm sold on it. I only wonder how I overlooked it in the first place.

One of the logical developments of the Marabou fly was the final appearance of very small ones, even down to 10's and 12's, on 2X long shank hooks, and sometimes smaller. In making these miniatures be sure that enough of the fluffy feathers are used to make a fairly thick mass when wet. There are times when these tiny Marabou streamers prove very effective, so I feel they are worth calling to your attention.

It is unnecessary to elaborate extensively on streamers and bucktails, although I shall discuss some additional patterns at the end of this chapter. Almost any combination of colors and materials will prove effective at one time or another. The patterns shown in Plates 10 and 12 have all proved to be excellent. There are two types to keep in mind. They are the fancy, or any bizarre combination of colors and materials you might fashion; and the imitative, or flies made with a specific natural fish food in mind. But be sure that you have a diversified assortment and a comprehensive range of sizes.

While one may fish streamers and bucktails with short and coarse leaders, care in the selection of terminal tackle is just as important for consistent success with them as it is with any other fly.

For the smaller sizes, say from 10 through 14, 2X by 3X long, leaders of six feet, seven and one half feet and nine feet, tapered to .007 or .008 work best. For longer shanks and heavier wire in sizes 8 and 10, I would suggest the same lengths but a size or two heavier on the fly end, say .009 or .010. For flies larger than this it may be best, for the purpose of casting, to use leaders tapering to .010 or .012.

Keep in mind that the leader is used mostly for concealment, to fool the fish into thinking that the fly is free and unattached to anything. Thus the more wary the fish, the finer the leader one might need. But if the fly is heavy and the leader very fine, you may find that you make a mess of the cast, and so hurt your chances rather than help them. In this case it would be greatly to your advantage if you used a heavier and perhaps shorter leader in combination with a perfect fly delivery. It is definitely a matter of balance, and this is one of the things that helps make fly fishing complicated. For instance, suppose you were using a nine-foot 3X leader (.007 silk work gut, .008 nylon) and it worked perfectly with a size 10 2X long streamer. If you changed to a size 6 6X long streamer using the same leader, you would find that something was drastically wrong, that you couldn't make the perfect casts you had been making with the other fly. This sort of thing happens constantly when it comes to casting, either with fly, lure, or natural bait. You should always keep this in mind and work out the answers by experimentation.

Deciding the length of the leader is another problem. A good general length is seven and one half feet. This length handles well and serves to cover all ordinarily wary trout, even under clear water conditions. Sometimes a six-foot leader is plenty long enough, for instance where the water is even slightly clouded or extremely rough and white.

Under any conditions where extreme caution is required to keep trout from becoming suspicious, twelve- to fifteen-foot leaders will be found more effective than those ranging from seven and a half to nine feet. I want to call your attention to a special reason for this. When a fly splashes on the water, something that is likely to happen with bucktails and streamers, it either frightens or attracts. Observation has shown me that in low, clear water when the trout are wary and skittish they will often be frightened by a splash of a fly tied on a seven-and-a-half-foot leader but will be attracted to the same fly making the same sort of a splash when tied on a fourteen-foot leader. Of course it does not always work out this way. Sometimes it does not make the slightest difference, but it does make a difference often enough to be worth trying.

As an illustration of the value of both bucktails and long leaders when fishing low, clear water, here is an experience that took place on Encampment Creek in Wyoming. While ordinarily we considered this an ideal dry-fly stream, on this occasion our drys did not produce during the first three days of our stay. For instance, there is one bit of water at the upper end of the canyon stretch that is literally alive with fish. Three days we went there, and each day the trout appeared to be rising enthusiastically, but unfortunately they were taking minute flies impossible to imitate successfully. For at least three hours of this third day Fred Gerken and I worked over these fish with dry flies. We bent pattern after pattern on the leader, tried each one from five to ten minutes, and then discarded it. The smallest sizes we had with us were 16's, and these looked like giants compared to the microscopic specimens the trout seemed to be taking. However, the 16's did do a bit better than the larger flies, getting a few splash rises and accounting for two hooked fish, but the results weren't anything to get excited about.

After a time I began to lose interest. I sat down on a rock in midstream and started flipping the fly haphazardly in an absent sort of manner. As I did this I started speculating and suddenly got an idea. We hadn't tried bucktails or streamers, and we were using nine-foot leaders. Perhaps our leaders were too short for the conditions, and perhaps a bucktail of some kind would excite the trout into taking what we had to offer. We already knew that our dry flies were too large.

There wasn't anything to lose by trying, so I took a fourteen-foot leader tapered from .018 to .008 (2X) from my chamois dry-leader case and put it in the soak box. I believe I dozed while it softened. At any rate there was a blank period between. Suddenly I was wide awake. I could see Fred a quarter of a mile downstream, and ten feet from the rock on which I sprawled three or four good trout were disporting themselves on the surface of the water. No one ever moved more cautiously than I did in getting the leader and bucktail attached to my line. It was done without disturbing these fish. It was a bit difficult to cast that short distance with such a long leader, but somehow it was accomplished and the fly alighted with an audible smack, although only a small portion of the leader touched the water. I started it back to me immediately, but it didn't move three inches before I was fast to a fourteen-inch brown and the other fish were trying to take the fly away from him. Landing this fish frightened the others, but not badly. They went out to the quiet water some thirty feet away and started feeding.

But getting these fish to take the fly required a change in tactics. They boiled to it when I fished it slowly, but they wouldn't take. This happened so many times that I finally got a bit peeved and slapped the fly over them, bringing it back so fast that it skipped over the water. There were several frantic jumps and then I was fast, this time to a fifteen-incher. This seemed to be the answer to the problem—*bucktail fly thrown carelessly, in fact a bit sloppily, and then skittered speedily through or over the top of the water.* From every part of the eddy section this brought rises and hooked fish. Then I worked the shore on the opposite side of the stream, casting the fly to the very edge of the bank and starting it back almost before it landed. Several very large trout were thus enticed into striking, but I hooked only one and this was lost during the resultant fight. From here I worked upstream into the faster water that led into the eddy. Trout appeared from behind every rock, and sometimes there were half a dozen trying to get the fly at the same time. Finally I became tired of catching them, so started experimenting simply to see what would happen. It was soon apparent that any bucktail fly in size 8 or 10 produced when fished fast, but that large bucktails, streamers, marabous, and others of this type were not so good. Regular wet flies proved absolutely useless, and what dry flies I tried still failed to bring anything more than a few half-hearted rises.

I then changed back to a nine-foot leader. While using this, even the favored flies of the moment failed to produce very much response. I realized that this might be because of the many trout that had been hooked or nicked in the comparatively limited area, so I changed back to the fourteen-footer to check up on this point. The results were somewhat amazing and considerably out of the ordinary. In fifteen casts I got fifteen rises and hooked eight fish.

One thing besides the leader was very important. It was the action given the fly. It had to be just right to produce satisfactorily. It was obtained by a combination rod-and-hand synchronization— the rod being raised by short jerks to the vertical at the same time the hand applied additional speed and erratic jerks by manipulating the line.

Because of the outstanding results of this entire combination, you might get the idea that it is an infallible method and that the fly which produced was better than the ones that failed to make a good showing. Please don't be so misled. There is no one best method or fly. What may be excellent on one occasion may be useless on another. The lesson this teaches is to try various methods and flies until you get results. Sometimes, no matter what you do, you won't get anywhere, but keep trying anyway. The leader dope is sound. No one ever harmed his chances by using the lightest and longest he can handle, but many fishing trips have been failures because the leader was too short or too stout. But you must be able to handle the leader or else it won't work.

Encampment Creek proved to be a grand experimental stream. For this reason I picked it to illustrate things that have happened in many other small streams. There were plenty of trout, it was quite small, and the water was as clear as crystal. Conditions changed from day to day, and what worked well in one stretch didn't always work so well in another.

An experience with the Marabou streamer used over a large gathering of rainbow trout is worth telling. The pool that was the locale of this incident didn't seem to have any particular advantages—in fact, except for the reason that I saw trout rising there and that my comrade Glenn Jones, from Colorado Springs, said he had made several large catches in it, I wouldn't have given it a tumble. On both sides the bottom was mud and silt, and the channel ran over a bottom of rather small gravel. The deepest part barely reached the tops of my waders, and the only good hiding spot was several rocks at the head, where the current from the rocky riffle above broke and skirted both sides. Around this rock and along the entire main stem of the channel we saw a continuous rise of fish, and most of them were good ones. We each took a side and fished with dry flies. After a full hour of this we still had to catch our first trout.

I had changed patterns so many times that I grew a bit tired. Besides, I had gradually increased the length of the leader until it was now about eighteen feet, and it hadn't helped a bit. It seemed useless. Retiring to the bank, I watched Glenn. He finally succeeded in hooking a ten- or eleven-incher, but after that he just cast, as we had been doing ever since arriving there.

A sudden impulse swept over me, a desire to investigate those rising trout, to get as near them as I possibly could. I wanted to see what they were doing. The canyon wall behind me was high and rugged and acted as a perfect neutralizing background for my person—I got within twenty feet of the fish without disturbing them. Feeling that I would ruin any chances of seeing anything if I got any closer, I let well enough alone and watched closely. I soon saw that they were not rising directly to the surface, but instead were taking something just under it—so close in fact that, when taking, first their noses, then their dorsal fins, and finally their tails broke through the water in rapid succession. Nearly every time a fish rose, it was like three quick rises in a row, making it appear that more fish were rising than was actually the case.

This fired my ambition again. A nymph would surely work! But it didn't—neither the first one I tried nor any other of the dozen or so I tried after. Remembering past experiences when some crazy pattern of fly had produced under trying circumstances, I tied on a large white Marabou and cast it so that it raked directly through the thickest of the rise when I retrieved. As it darted through the ranks, the water boiled. I felt several hard tugs and hooked a ten-incher. It looked as if the entire school followed this fish as it was being landed. Then they saw me and disappeared. Once again this happened, but this time not so many fish followed. When they scurried for middle of the stream, the rise stopped abruptly and did not resume, even though we waited an hour. In the meantime we both kept fishing. But not another fish followed my Marabou, while Glenn got only one rise from the far side of the pool on the very edge of the current stem.

In further experiments both the Marabou and the Black Ghost brought strange reactions. They would usually account for two or three good rises in each choice location of every riffle or pool, but they also seemed to kill those places for further effort unless you waited for considerable time after disturbing them. These flies were great for the purpose of locating good fish. Many a speculative cast in places where we never got a rise to a dry fly brought a big fellow out of hiding. Occasionally we'd hook one, but in the majority of cases it would be either a follow-up or a half-hearted hit we missed. On the other hand, they frequently brought to the net good fish that dry flies did not seem to attract; so they were well worth using.

We finally devised a method that seemed to be ideal. First one would fish the water with a dry fly, and then the other would follow through either with a bucktail, a Marabou, or a Black Ghost. Working it the opposite way was not satisfactory. Dry-flying a stretch did not seem to hurt it for the other type of fishing, but reversing the procedure seemed to spoil it for the dry fly. From this it seems that using these excitement-makers is not so good for those who may be following close behind you. At any rate that is the conclusion reached from careful observations and many notes made subsequently.

Since a most effective way of fishing the flies is either slightly up and across, directly across, or slightly down and across stream, it is possible to work either up or down stream when fishing with them. The main requisite, to prevent spoiling water, is to keep away from the edge of the stream except when you want to fish a particular place, and then advance with extreme caution. In the case of slightly sloping shores that blend in with the water, it may be best to remain far back and when casting to the fish let the near portion of the line drop to the ground. When you make the retrieve, let it drag earth if necessary. This same idea is useful when fishing across weed beds, flat rocks, or high grass. Often it provides just the right concealment and gives the right action to the fly.

It didn't take long to find out that the Black Ghost seemed to have a peculiar fascination for big trout. Besides quite a number of really splendid specimens it produced for me, it almost got me a record-breaker. That it did not was my fault and not the fault of the fly. It happened this way.

Below the road bridge that crosses the river near Wilcox Ranch an island divides the stream. Both sides being good fishing, one may spend a full half day there without any trouble. On this afternoon I had fished both sides with a dry fly and was working back on the right-hand side, picking out hidden holes where I had received good rises that had been missed. On reaching the last pool of the stretch I saw a peculiar-looking wrinkle in the water near the far bank. It was a long distance to make with a delicate delivery, and as the water was almost still at this point, I felt that the slightest sloppiness in a cast would ruin my chances. So I walked past the scattered bushes until I came to the main riffle leading from it. Although the amount of water coming over this lip was not great—in fact it was quite thin—there was a decided drop, so much so that when I knelt I felt sure I would be hidden from the fish in the pool.

I was soon convinced that this was a large fish. Occasionally his movements sent out waves a small fish could not have made. I expected that he wouldn't be interested in the dry fly, and this proved to be the case. Two dozen perfect floats over him failed to bring the slightest response. Besides, many juicy naturals floated over him and were neglected just as much as my artificial. So I changed to a Bucktail. He made a couple of swirls but did not take it. Then I tried the Marabou. This brought one splash, and then he ignored it. I had only one Black Ghost left. It was a large one—about three inches long, hook size 4, 6X long shank. The first time this fly darted past him he struck and missed but kept following. He came to the very lip of the break from which I was fishing. I could see him plainly, in fact his back was out of water. As I lifted the fly he made a grab at it and then went out a few feet to reach water that covered him, and he lay there looking like a miniature submarine. If an inch long, he was three feet in length. It was a ticklish situation. The movement of the rod in making the cast might make him suspicious—wise to what was going on. With a supreme effort I controlled my impulse to cast. I waited patiently. Finally he seemed to decide he had lost his opportunity to get the morsel that had disappeared in the air, and it wasn't coming back to give him a second chance. At any rate he turned and started slowly out to deep water.

This was my opportunity. With as little effort and movement of the rod as possible, I sent the Black Ghost out on its mission—directing it so that it would fall within his line of vision but not in front of him, where he might possibly see the leader. Of course it was luck—I know that, even though I like to imagine it was skill. That fly alighted just in back of his eyes. He turned like a flash, and before I knew it he had the fly and was making for midstream with great speed.

Right there I made my mistake or perhaps used faulty judgment. It's not easy to analyze reactions at such an exciting moment. I knew I was using a 3X leader. I knew the slightest untoward strain would break it. Even as he went rushing to deep water I regretted not having changed to a heavier one. Anyway, because of this, I did not strike, and when he got to midstream he came to the surface, gave a sudden flip, and my line went slack. The barb of the hook had never penetrated into the hard mouth of this old-timer.

There is something to be learned from this experience—always take time to change to suitable tackle when you know the quarry is larger than ordinary and is likely to have a mouth that will require a decided strike to set the hook. In the case of a large fly, a really fine leader is not so necessary, especially if you cast so that the leader will not be over the fish. A 1X leader would have turned the trick in this instance of course if I had used the pressure it could stand. I feel sure that the 3X leader caused my failure. It had instilled in my unconscious reasoning the necessity to be careful in the event of the rise of a large fish. This feeling was so strong that I neglected to strike at all. In this connection, remember that the larger and heavier the hook, the more pressure you need to send the barb home. 4X gut may set a size 16 short barbed and light wire hook in the mouth of a fish like this, but you can't expect it to do so with a size 4 heavy wire hook. It is such things that make it so difficult to prescribe generally when advising what weight leaders to buy. It all depends, and there are many ifs. That is why almost any statement regarding fishing and tackle must be qualified. Conditions, size of fish and flies, type of water, and other things all have a bearing on what is best to use.

Even the angler's state of mind enters into the problem. Nervous reaction, excitement, overanxiousness, uncertainty, optimism, and despondency all have an effect on our fishing, and the right tackle combination for the mood helps in making a successful day. When we are in good spirits, sure of ourselves and confident that we can succeed, we can use lighter tackle than when we are out of sorts, nervous, and anxious. Far more necessary than perfect casting is the control of emotion and the ability to see and do the right thing at the right time.

In Michigan, bucktails and streamers are of the utmost value. One of their most important uses is for night fishing. The late Tom Harris, a well-known angler who fished considerably on the Au-Sable near Roscommon, would never have taken the number of large fish that he did except for this type of fly. His favorite, as I recall it, was made with badger streamer feathers. I fished with Tom the last time, in a pool a short distance below Charlie Merrill's camp.

Charlie and I were old friends, and we both preferred dry-fly fishing to anything else, so that Tom's insistence and coaxing that we do some night fishing with large streamers never had an effect when we were together. But Charlie became seriously ill. We had planned to be with him at his camp, but instead my wife and I visited him at the Ford Hospital in Detroit.

This visit took away all our desire to fish in Michigan that year. As cheerful as Charlie was, in our hearts we knew that probably we would never see him again. We didn't. But he was so insistent that we go to his camp, made it so apparent that he would be keenly disappointed if we did not, that we could not deny him.

Tom Harris was holding the fort. He was to be our host in place of Charlie. The sight of the cabin made us more gloomy than ever. Charlie's cabin was Charlie—it breathed his personality. Everything we looked at brought back visions of him showing it to us. Somber Tom fitted in this background. He had always been with us when we fished with Charlie, but now his concern for his friend had put an unaccustomed look on his face—a look that had erased the witty twinkle in his eye and lowered the cheerful wrinkles at the side of his mouth so that they expressed worry and sorrow.

Of course we avoided the topic as much as possible and talked of fishing. Tom took us to the icebox, where he displayed several splendid specimens of *Salmo fario*. "Night fishing," he explained. "You've got to go out with me once, anyway." I wasn't particularly thrilled but acquiesced. "Perhaps," I thought, "it might make me feel better."

About an hour before dark we arrived at the place Tom had selected for the night's operations. It was beautiful water, and under different circumstances I would have been thrilled with the prospects. With his innate courtesy Tom let me fish all the choice locations on our way down to the "night pool." He followed behind and fished water I had spoiled. As I remember, I rose three fair fish, which I missed, and took one small rainbow. Tom thought this was a good sign that the fish would surely take after dark.

Once at the pool, before we cast a fly we waited until the shore line had come indistinct and the sky above formed a luminous milky way between picturesque borders of the tops of evergreens. In the meantime Tom had explained the method of fishing so that I would know how to handle my fly. While it was still light enough to see what we were doing, we got into position about a fair cast apart.

It was slow that night. I have no idea how many casts I made, but I know I was weary and ready to quit when I got my first hit. It was a vigorous one and caught me so much off guard that the line slipped from my fingers. Of course the point of the hook didn't penetrate, and I lost my only chance. But the incident gave me added enthusiasm, which kept me fishing.

Tom was below me. By this time it was so black that I seemed to be enclosed in a vault. But the quiet, which could be felt, intensified individual sounds, so that the swish of Tom's rod and line in casting gave rhythm to my thoughts and told me he was still there.

Suddenly the dreamy harmony of the night was shattered by a human shout and a tremendous splash in the water. Tom had hooked a fish and was exultant. Of course I quit casting and listened. Somehow it was too quiet—it didn't seem right. Then I heard again the music of Tom's casting. "What happened?" I called. "Don't know," was the reply. "The hook pulled out. Guess he struck a bit short and was hooked lightly." And that was our net catch for the evening.

We left camp the next afternoon. As we said good-by, the old twinkle came into Tom's eyes. "I'll get some fish tonight," he said. "It always happens this way when I want to show someone how good night fishing is." And he did—took too grand specimens. This is not a "fish story." Tom could always prove his catches, and I never knew him to say he took a fish if he didn't.

No matter where I've fished, bucktails and streamers have been effective at some time or another. Often it is necessary to change the pattern and style, but their value to the fly assortment cannot be questioned. For instance, take the Madison River in Yellowstone Park. The first time we fished this water it was not very productive to dry flies, but wets and streamers were excellent. The fish didn't give a darn for any of the patterns in my box, but were particularly attracted to a Royal Coachman streamer of fairly large size—about a No. 4, 2X long. Don Martinez tied the ones I used. He didn't think much of them as fish-getters himself, but finally he had to admit that they did take fish, especially when other fishermen consistently proved they did, even when other patterns failed.

But they had to be fished a certain way; otherwise they wouldn't produce. The method used was similar to bait fishing—that is, to let the fly drift on a slack line and take in that slack when a fish struck. Sometimes you saw the flash of a fish as it took, sometimes you saw the line twitch, and at other times you couldn't see a thing but merely felt a heavy pull as the fish came taut against the rod. In either case you had to strike hard and quick; otherwise you lost out.

This made it necessary to use a rather heavy leader, one that calibrated at least .011 at the fly end. You see, you had to take up all the slack that might be bellied against a strong current—otherwise the hook would not go home—and this calls for real "muscle striking." When using a light leader, one will occasionally strike too hard for the depth of the fly and the amount of slack, and when this happens, any leader that cannot stand the strain of that strike will break.

Scotty Chapman, a local resident of the section, was an artist at this sort of fishing. He knew the currents of the Madison in this section so well that he had no difficulty in gauging the strike when it came. Personally I didn't make out very well. I got strikes from quite a number of fish but failed to set the hook, so they got off almost as soon as I felt them. Besides, I wanted to watch what those who knew the stream did when they were really after fish, so I spent more time watching than I did fishing. There's no doubt that practice and experience plus a thorough knowledge of the stream are very essential for success in fishing of this sort. However, Scotty said that this type of fishing was of limited duration on the Madison, that not long before I arrived, normal conditions existed, and that as soon as the first snow came, which was expected within a day or so, it would become normal again. This meant that regulation methods of fishing a wet fly or bucktail would once more prevail. Incidentally, we got the snow, but I had become fed up on much bucktail and wet-fly fishing before arriving at West Yellowstone and after this experience I had found a stream in the park that provided dry-fly fishing of excellence. So I did not get back to the Madison that year to check on the boys. But I have fished this stream many times since then and have found it to be the same as any other. At times the regulation wet-fly methods worked O. K., but at other times you had to try all the tricks in your bag, and even then you might not have the right one.

On the whole I have found the natural drift followed by the hand-twist retrieve most productive. (See Chapter II.) Often the fish struck when the natural drift was in operation, particularly when the fly had been cast all the way across stream and was drifting along an overhanging bank. However, many strikes came at the end of the drift, or during the swing of the fly across stream after drag had set in, and sometimes when the retrieve was in progress.

There is a decided similarity between this fishing and angling for the rainbows of Sault Sainte Marie rapids. I first fished these rapids in the fall of 1948, when conditions were decidedly unfavorable.

Here are first impressions of these Soo rapids. In case you do not know exactly what they are, let me explain that they are formed by the waters of Lake Superior plunging down a series of drops to form Saint Mary's River.

Of course this isn't a natural flowage. It is controlled by a great many dam gates, and few of those who inspect the locks and watch the lake boats pass through are aware that beyond these locks rush the white and green waters of the rapids.

When we arrived at the Soo all the gates except one were closed, and this one was only partially open. And it had been that way for considerable time, which is likely to stop fish from running. So the water was low and very few fish were moving up or down.

Let me describe my first morning on the rapids. My host and guide, Earl Leitz, had said the night before: "Be ready at five." At this time of the morning in early October it was pitch black. But by the time we had coffee and toast and reached the parking space near the locks, it was nearly dawn. I had no idea where the rapids were, and when Earl had parked the car and started walking across the locks I began to wonder what was going on.

Earl said: "There are some boats going through. Guess we'll have to go around."

At the moment this meant nothing, but I soon found out that it meant a very long walk. When you walk in tune with Earl Leitz you move fast, a bit too fast for a man of sixty. I kept up fairly well, and didn't puff too much, but I did wish that he would go a little slower.

After going to the foot of the locks and all the way across them, we had to turn and go nearly to the head. Finally we came to a large building, a power house. Earl tried the door, but it didn't open. Then we noticed a sign. It mentioned a new regulation; the door would be opened to anglers if they would ring the bell.

We were admitted, and with Earl throwing out a few words to the men in the power house as we passed, we rushed to the opposite end of the building. There Earl grabbed a couple of long, sturdy poles and indicated that I open the back door. I did and now Earl's pace increased, like a hunting dog getting hot on a trail. We rushed across a narrow walk with a thin railing. Suddenly Earl ducked under the handrail and started down a steep earth embankment. I slid after him and found that we were in the no-man's-land of an excavating job. We rushed toward another high and rugged embankment. By this time I thought we must be almost to Canada. It was getting light. When we reached the pile, Earl stopped to say: "Let's go up on top so that you can see where we are going to fish."

Then I saw the rapids quite a drop below us. Foaming white areas were margined by greenish, clear water. It looked wild and fascinating, and my blood tingled while my casting arm started to itch. Earl took a moment to point out the several drops we would fish, and then we went off—this time almost at a dog trot. Believe me, I became in just as much of a hurry as my comrade.

We clambered over some jagged rocks and then scrambled down to the river edge, at a small bay protected from the rushing waters by a sharp point of land and rock at the upper end. On this placid surface floated the largest canoe I'd ever laid eyes on.

"It's a freighter," explained Earl. "Bought it from Scotty." Scotty Stevenson, by the way, is one of the old-timers. He has been fishing the rapids for many years—did it long before they had cut it down, for the sake of commerce, to the size it is now.

It takes both skill and strength to pole a canoe in this surging, treacherous water. On the way to our first fishing stop I alternately gazed down into the greenish depths and across the tumbling expanse to the Canadian shore. It was like four large rivers made into one. It both thrilled me and caused, momentarily, a slight chill of fear.

Finally, by extreme effort Earl managed to get the canoe alongside a boiling drop and indicated that I cast the fly directly into it.

We were both soon working our fly rods. Earl's rod was a brute of a tool that needed a B level line to bring out the action. The leader he used was at least a ten-pound test. Before leaving I found out that this heavy stuff is needed, especially the line and leader. However, a rod like Earl's is too much for me to handle without fatigue, so I chose to use my nine-and-a-half footer of five and three-quarter ounces. This wouldn't put out as much line as Earl's, so some spots couldn't be reached. I did not consider this much of a handicap, because it was only an occasional place that couldn't be covered, and all the fish that Earl took hit within the limits of my rod's best distance.

Earl used a Bali Duck fly in a large size—perhaps No. 2—while I decided to try a fly sent me, with a message of good luck, by the late Ken Cooper, of Michigan.

The first three holes did not produce for either of us, but at the fourth Earl took two medium-sized fish almost at once. Twenty minutes later I thought that luck had deserted me, especially as Earl picked up another in the middle class. But then, just as my fly had started to swing after a rather long natural drift, I felt a welcome tug and my reel sang a merry tune as the fish made its initial run. It was disappointingly small, perhaps a trifle over two pounds. At the start of the fight and until it jumped, I thought it was much larger, so hard do these Soo rapids fish fight.

That ended the first morning's fishing. Earl had to get back to work and besides, so they said at the time, there were only two times of the day to bother with fishing. These were early in the morning and late in the afternoon.

The other few mornings that I fished were almost like this one except that I did better, once taking three fish. But never did I hook into a trout of more than three and a half pounds. However, one morning Earl took me down to the lower rapids. We first tried it from shore. Before I had my rod ready he had hooked a fish on his first cast, a comparatively short one. It weighed a full five and a half pounds. But not another strike came from that particular hole, something that illustrates the value of getting the first fly to a location.

As far as catching fish went, my afternoon attempts were failures. Neither the fellows who generously guided me nor I took any fish, but I did the most casting. To at least one of these friends I was something of a hoodoo. This was Dr. Marks. When Earl and I were fishing the first morning, the Doctor fished below us at the highest point in the rapids that could be reached with a motor. He took one fish of six pounds. Of course we took four during the same period, but they were fish ranging from two to three and a half pounds. The afternoon I fished with the Doctor we didn't get a single touch, even though we both fished like Trojans. But on the afternoon I went out with Scotty Stevenson in the upper stretches, Marks fished the lower water and took a most beautiful rainbow weighing six and three quarter pounds, while I did not get a strike, even though Scotty placed me in the same spots that had been productive when I'd fished them in the morning.

But to show how luck sometimes enters into the game, let me give you Dr. Marks's explanation of his good fortune. He said that he'd become tired of automatically casting and not getting any strikes, so started aiming at some mergansers, which were fishing in the rapids. He was making long casts at these birds, in a vain hope of snagging one. After each cast he fished the fly out to the limits of the downstream drift, and on one of them the fish took.

Contrary to the usual reaction this fish ran upstream with a rush, moving so fast that before the Doctor knew it the line had fouled on the anchor rope at the bow of the boat. Rod pressure proved futile, so Marks laid the rod down and started pulling the line with his hand. After some steady but cautious pressure, the line suddenly pulled free with the trout still fast. The fish started downstream, the Doctor picked up his rod, and the rest of the fight followed a normal pattern.

The Doctor was helped a lot by the stout line and leader that he uses, like the rest of the regular and successful Soo rapids fishermen. He explained that in landing a large trout in these waters it is best to drop the rod when the fish is played out, and finish the job by hand. This saves the rod from excessive strain and often prevents the loss of a fish because of the excessive time needed when landing one on the bend of a rod against the heavy rushing water. The hand pull brings the fish in quicker and much more efficiently, provided the line and leader are strong enough to take the strain.

You might ask, why not take the extra time and forget about the strain on the rod? This is all right, if you don't care about the punishment to your rod, or if you are using one made of a material that can take it—except for one thing, a most important consideration. The hook may pull out. The fly may have caught in a soft part of the mouth, where it may hold for five or ten minutes. But after fifteen minutes the flesh may tear, and if this happens the fish is lost, no matter how skillful your handling. The tackle should fit the conditions.

This doesn't mean that you must kill every fish you catch. The quicker you land one, if you want to release it, the less chance there is of it dying. Playing a fish to exhaustion on excessively light tackle

TROUT

can do just as much harm as anything else. If you wish to kill the
fish you hook, then why not use suitable tackle? I have always con-
tended that the tackle should fit the condition, and after some
forty-eight years of angling I am more convinced than ever that
this is a sound and logical viewpoint.

Before experiencing this Soo fishing I would have been shocked
at landing fish in the manner of Marks, and would have scorned
such heavy tackle. While I'd fished considerably for heavy and
hard-fighting game fish in fast water, I'd previously always done
so where it had been possible to follow a bad actor and eventually
get it in a place where it could be landed without using excessive
force. But when this cannot be done, then heavy tackle and rough-
landing tactics must be considered best and most sensible.

During a good part of our stay at the Soo the barometer was
unsteady. Then it dropped very low, and we had four days of
extremely strong wind and heavy rain. It was after the wind had
subsided that Dr. Marks got his best fish, while I didn't get a rise.
That was the last chance I had that year, as we left the following
day. But while I was working on this chapter a letter from Earl
Leitz reported that the fishing never did get any better that autumn;
so it would appear that the poor fishing of the fall of 1948 was
definitely the result of the small amount of water coming through
the one gate.

In the year following this visit to the Soo rapids I returned for a
second try. I fished twice in the canoe, once for about an hour and
again for two hours. Not a fish was caught, by either me or the
others. There were a few fish taken during our stay of some ten
days but with the exception of one, taken on a fly by Dr. Marks,
they were caught with natural bait, and all in one hole that could
be fished from the bank. This time the trouble was too much
water, too many gates open. You couldn't get to the fish, or fish
properly when you did. One friend there said: "I love these rapids,
but I've never had any luck fishing them." But don't think we
wasted time. There's some great smallmouth bass fishing on the
lower stretch of Saint Mary's River. We had a taste of it and it was
good. And one of these days I may get to the rapids when they are
hot.

The fellows with whom I fished on the Soo were all good fishermen who knew the waters well. Each one has caught his share of its battling rainbows, but there is a slight variation in the way they fish their flies. In watching Earl Leitz I noted that he was continually making the lure work by giving the line a spirited up-and-down action. I could always see it twitching from the corner of my eye, and hear the swish of his line, as I fished out my own casts. Garl Chambers and Doctor Marks both favored the natural drift and slow retrieve. Scotty Stevenson, the real old-timer, didn't fish enough for me to get the lowdown on his style. He wanted me to have all the chances. However, I would say, from the few casts he made and from his conversation, that he favored the natural drift and slow retrieve. All of them used the drift to the extent of getting the lure deep and down into the flow of the current. It was on the retrieve that the variation occurred. They all fed out a lot of line after making the cast. This is an easy matter in this strong water, but you need heavily-hooked flies to get sufficient depth.

As to these flies, the main requirements seem to be heavy hooks, to insure proper sinking and strength for holding the heavier fish; a wide gape for easy hooking; and plenty of color or sparkle, or both, to attract attention. Just to give you an idea of the types used, here are three of them:

Soo. This is a bit difficult to describe because about two thirds of the way from the bend of the hook some claret bucktail is tied on streamer fashion with black silk. Then the body continues as usual, and the balance of the fly is finished in the regular manner.

Tail—two hackle tips of Barred Rock cock dyed a deep Montreal claret.

Tag—Yellow chenille.

Body—Embossed silver tinsel ribbed with broad, flat, silver tinsel, separated by the binding-in of the lower bucktail wing. The bucktail is the deep, rich, claret red, and the winding is black silk finished off with shiny lacquer or enamel.

Wings—Tied above the claret wings is a rather wide band of yellow bucktail, and a topping that is a sparse batch of brownish-black bucktail.

Head—A plain head may be used. My sample has a red head with painted eyes—black pupil with white iris.

BALI DUCK. This fly may be tied in many variations, as indeed you may do with these colorful patterns. I give you the most simple, which is definitely an effective one.

Tail—Golden pheasant tippet.

Hackle—Brown, soft.

Wings—Two Bali duck (Yanosh) streamer feathers—tied streamer fashion, that is, horizontally along the shank of the hook.

Head—Black.

Except for the tail and the Jungle Cock eye, this fly is similar to the Jess Wood streamer, as shown in Plate 10 in color with Tandem hook. An original dressing, one given me by Jess Wood, appears in a black-and-white plate in *Just Fishing* (page 356). The original hackle is either cochybondhu or furnace, instead of straight brown or red.

SCOTTY.

Tag—Gold tinsel with black chenille egg sack.

Tail—Barred wood duck.

Body—Seal fur dyed garnet red.

Hackle—Dyed garnet red.

Wings—Six matched furnace.

Can be darker but illustration is a good color. If you can't get furnace, use red-brown, but in large feathers it isn't too difficult to get the black centers in the red necks.

Head—Black.

For Eastern fishing I prefer the smaller bucktails not too heavily tied, and the combination feather-and-hair type, also tied as sparsely as possible. My notebooks are filled with experiences with such flies on Eastern streams, but for our purpose here I shall select only those incidents which are particularly outstanding.

First, let us go to a stream in northern New York, a stream I shall call River X because it is small, not well known, and is incapable of withstanding the onslaughts of such concentrated fishing as we have today. At the time of these experiments, the flow of this stream was controlled by human agencies—a saw mill and a cheese factory. If you wished to fish dry fly when these places were in operation, which was almost every weekday, you had to watch your chances and do it when the stream was normal.

When first I fished this water I stopped every time the stream became high or discolored. Often, just when fishing was at its best, the flood from above would come along and the rise would instantly stop. On some trips I was lucky to get in three hours of fishing a day, especially when I got up late.

On one occasion I was up for a scant two days. Evidently the factories were busy at this time because the first day I barely started out when the water became milky and until late in the afternoon it was unsuitable for a dry fly. As a matter of fact it wasn't normal until 6 P.M. It was an hour later before the trout started rising and this left very little time for fishing, although it must be admitted that at the last half hour before dark the fish rose well.

The following morning I got up quite early and started up what we called the "high banks" stretch—a section bordered by high cliffs, and heavily wooded. For the first half mile it was ideal. The trout were willing, and each pool provided plenty of action when the dry fly floated over them. But just as I got to one of my favorite spots, a place I knew contained quite a number of large fish, the water started to rise and got very muddy. For the moment I became angry and my language was not all that might be desired. I had to leave that afternoon at four, and this meant my fishing was over, unless—the thought came to me suddenly—I fished with a method that suited the conditions.

There were only two alternatives—bait and sunken flies. I had no bait and I did not care about fishing with it—but in my fly box were several bucktails I had put there for emergencies. This was an emergency if there ever was one, so I took one out and tied it on my dry-fly leader. By this time the water had come up considerably and looked like weak coffee colored by skim milk—the condition caused by the sawmill. The pool I stood by did not yield anything. The one below was a considerable distance away, and the rise was just beginning as I got there. I carelessly dropped the bucktail in the fast water leading into it and woke up with a start when I immediately felt a heavy surging tug and saw the rod bend almost double. The result? A fifteen-inch brown, fat and yellow. Two more fish hit here, and then the sport stopped. The next pool was close by. It did not produce a strike. The following one was a five-minute walk away, and here again I caught up with the advancing rise. As in the second pool the first cast resulted in a good fish besides two other good hits with which I failed to connect. The net results of this trip proved that if one fished likely water with a bucktail at the start of the discoloration, the results were sure and satisfactory; but if one waited until the rise of water had been on for fifteen minutes or more, it was almost impossible to take fish no matter what fly was used. Later on, careful observations and experiments along these lines confirmed these first findings. As a matter of record I have notes concerning two consecutive days' fishing which are quite illuminating. First day: Followed the rise in water and fished each hole during the first fifteen minutes of discoloration. Results: fourteen holes fished, twelve trout caught, twenty strikes received, three holes unproductive. Second day: Waited until the rise had been on twenty minutes before starting. Results: fourteen holes fished, five fish caught, seven strikes received, ten holes unproductive. *The identical section of stream was fished in both instances.* Each day the reaction of the trout to dry flies before and after the water rise was the same.

Just a note on more recent developments in this connection. During World War II both the mill and the factory ceased operations. Only once during this period was I able to fish this water due to travel restrictions. There seemed to be fewer trout in the stream and they weren't quite as fat, probably because of the absence of the whey from the cheese factory. But the fishing followed a more normal pattern. Formerly a hatch of flies that occurred during the factory and mill discharges failed to interest the fish, so that once these water disturbances started, the dry-fly fishing stopped even though the fly hatch was most substantial. But during the war-time visit the hatches definitely brought good rises during those times of the day when the factory discharges formerly had stopped them.

Up to this writing the cheese factory has not resumed operations; and neither has the upper stretch of the stream produced the numbers and sizes of fish that it did when the whey was mixed daily with the water, and the sawmill operations raised and discolored the stream periodically.

The lessons learned in this stream about the artificial rise and fall of streams have helped me elsewhere where conditions followed such a pattern. It takes time to learn just what effect these man-made changes have on the reactions of fish, but it is well worth any angler's time to study them. When you learn the answers you may bring many more fish to net.

Incidentally, a small spring brook, not subject to these unnatural conditions, that flowed into this stream never reacted favorably to bucktails or to any of the streamer types, even though many of the trout of the main stream made a practice of running up this brook for a considerable distance. Here the dry fly was best most of the time, although occasionally, especially during a rise caused by rain, artificial caddis and small wet flies were most effective.[1]

Coming down to southern New York, to a stream approximately fifty miles from New York City and directly at the Jersey line, some experiences with the combination of bucktail and feather streamers proved quite interesting.

On the whole this was usually a disappointing dry-fly stream even though most of the water looked ideal for the method. Once in a blue moon we'd have a good day with the floaters, but mostly our attempts were a joke. On the other hand, regular wet flies and methods were excellent if one knew the stream well enough as to the lay of the trout and the special tricks necessary to get them to take. This was proved by Ferrier Martin, whose uncle owned a farm bordering it. His favorite flies were the Whirling Dun and the Coachman, and he seldom failed making a fair catch no matter how poor conditions were.

However, the rest of us—and we were many—did not have such consistent results. We really didn't do so badly, but Ferrier did so much better that it piqued us. Then one day Bill Randebrock brought with him some flies that he called Kienbush Streamers. They were those combination flies made with both bucktail and streamer feathers. On the very first pool he rose a half dozen good trout and hooked two. This excited us, and we went at the game in earnest, with the result that we had a wonderful day. Not only that, but these flies served to bring us results at any time when we couldn't do anything with dry flies. The best method of fishing these flies here seemed to be mostly down and slightly across

[1] All observations on both these streams were made between July 1 and August 31.

stream. When the fly pulled taut in the current below you, it was jiggled a bit and finally retrieved jerkily until it was close enough to lift for the next cast. Of course the stream was quite overgrown, so that in most places it was necessary to fish the flies in this way or not at all. So perhaps that had something to do with it. However, in the few locations where a cross-stream retrieve could be managed, it did not seem to work as well as the other method unless you forgot the retrieve and simply let the fly drift with the current, giving it a slight twitch now and then.

A few miles south of this stream there was another one, a meadow creek called Black Brook. This was in New Jersey. It was sluggish and the banks were muddy and swampy, so that it wasn't particularly attractive. However, in those days it contained quite a number of fairly large brook trout, so we overlooked the other disadvantages. Most of the trout lay close to or under the banks, which made fly fishing rather difficult, especially since these fish didn't care much for a dry fly that could be dapped [2] in the best places after you had crawled to the necessary position to turn the trick—a logical way to fish under such circumstances. Of course a worm worked when fished this way. It was also possible to fish a worm downstream along the bank after you were in a good location, and this always produced. But flies were different—the very casting of them seemed to spoil your chances. Several times I gave up in despair and used bait, but each time I came back I had a new idea and started fly fishing with great hopes. Finally I found the partial solution—that is it was partial because it worked only under certain stream formations. This was where the stream made a bend at right angles. If the bends were as in Figure 1, you could approach carefully and, by keeping low, fish successfully the entire stretch from where you were to location B. Usually the right bank in this instance was most productive, and before casting to the bend at A, I always fished first with a short line to both banks, alternating at each increased length until reaching C on the right bank and A on the left bank. On reaching A, the fly was allowed to drift as it would with the current, which usually brought it to B. Then it was retrieved slowly and carefully so that it would not catch the grass

[2] Dapping. A fishing term meaning to let the fly touch the water as the leader hangs straight down from the rod tip. The fly is repeatedly allowed to touch, then lifted off the surface and dropped back, to make it appear like a real insect doing this sort of caper.

drooping over the bank between B and C. From C it was brought back slowly and with slight jerks.

When fishing the banks from where I sat to A and C, the fly was manipulated on a partially slack line. That is, it was first thrown into the current close to the bank on a slack line. When the line came taut, the fly was given a slight jerk. Then the rod tip was

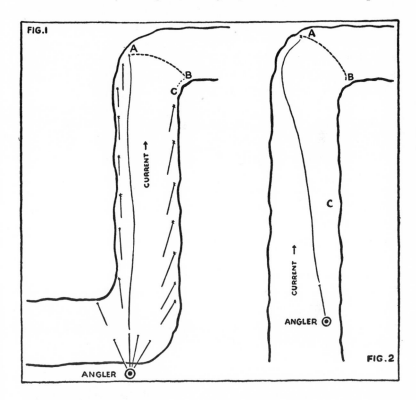

lowered and more line released, if possible, giving more slack. When this straightened out, the fly was given another twitch. Usually two of these twitches were all that one could manipulate on a cast. After that the cast was lengthened and the same procedure followed. In this way with successive casts the water was covered thoroughly and in what seemed the most attractive way as far as the trout were concerned. In most cases the right bank between the angler and C would produce from one to four rises. The left bank rarely produced more than one, and often not that.

The drift between A and B produced some of the best fish—on one occasion a three-pounder.

When a bend came at the end of a long, straight stretch as in Fig. 2, it complicated matters somewhat. To fish it from either the left or the right bank was awkward, and besides it was almost impossible to fish close to the banks of the run leading into the "bend pool." After considerable experimentation I found that by easing myself over the bank into the water, making each movement slowly and with utmost caution, I could get into casting position without spoiling more than ten feet of water below me. However, I did find that to do this it was best to wait from fifteen to twenty minutes after getting in the water before casting the fly. From then on, the procedure was the same as when fishing the double bends, except that you had to keep your back cast higher than ordinarily because of the high banks.

Sometimes when letting the fly drift from A to B it would snag on the right-hand bank. While this was troublesome, it was also very effective if you could manage to get it loose by a delicate switch cast and then let it settle a bit before starting the retrieve. More than one fish was taken because of this, even though these same fish had refused the identical fly a number of times when the drift was made without getting the fly snagged.

This releasing a snagged fly by a switch cast is often productive. In one bend hole there was a sunken log located just where the fly was quite likely to catch when making the drift. I lost at least a dozen flies on this log without getting a fish, but finally I learned how to handle one so that it didn't get snagged too badly. A switch cast, followed by a quick retrieve, both released the fly and brought it away from the danger point. The first time I succeeded in doing this I took a good trout, and after that, fifty per cent of similar manipulations in this particular hole brought results. If I had become discouraged before learning how to do this with a minimum of disastrous snaggings, it would have meant one less productive place to fish. Since you are always running up against propositions of this kind, or some others equally exasperating, you can readily see how giving up too easily may reduce your chances of success. Sticking to individual problems until you master them will ultimately increase your catch. As in any other line of endeavor, each tough problem you solve makes it easier to solve the next one.

Of course this sort of thing is often quite expensive. It frequently means lost or broken leaders as well as flies. But inasmuch as the returns on an angler's investment are computed by the number of fish hooked, I believe that it pays to take the chances that might mean a loss of tackle. Even a successful bait fisherman loses plenty of hooks. He knows that many of the fish lie in places where he must take chances with tackle if he expects to get them.

It is always worth the time and effort that you spend in learning how to fish difficult spots without getting hung up. What if you do spoil your chances a dozen or even two dozen times and lose tackle while doing it? Trout like such places; the average individual gets hung up while fishing it, or else he is too cautious and casts his fly so that it isn't in any danger of getting snagged and so is useless in attracting the fish in that particular spot. Usually after one snagging he quits and doesn't fish the place again. Once you learn how to be fairly consistent in getting the fly in such places without getting snagged you have overcome one of the greatest obstacles to really successful fishing. This advice is well worth storing in the back of your mind for future use.

For your convenience, I am listing here the various methods of bucktail fishing that I personally have found successful. No doubt there are others I do not know, but these are all proved by long and varied experience and so should be of instrinsic value to the reader.

ROD-JERK METHOD: This is accomplished entirely by the rod and the casting arm. No line is held in the retrieving hand. Only enough line should be cast to allow you to handle the fly satisfactorily without the aid of the retrieving hand. This, of course, varies with the length of the rod—the longer it is, the further you may cast your fly and yet manipulate it as it should be. To ascertain the limit of the possible satisfactory cast, experiment with different distances until you find the farthest distance at which you can work the fly in a satisfactory manner. The cast should never be made beyond that point where the fly cannot be under instant control at the moment you start the retrieve. In other words, you should be able to give the fly instant action the moment it touches the water. This does not mean that you should always start it moving just as it strikes the surface. Sometimes it is best that the retrieving action start *before the fly touches the surface,* and at other times it may be best to let it sink slightly before starting the retrieve. Different methods are needed for certain days and conditions, and you should ascertain first which method is best for the particular time. But you must always be in command of your line and fly so that without effort you can make it do what you want without excessive slack line. In manipulating the retrieve after the fly is started, bring the rod upward in short jerks, using the wrist and forearm. When the rod reaches a point just below vertical, lift the fly and make a new cast. While this method is particularly effective when used across stream, it is also useful and productive when used in any other way. The speed of the retrieve should be varied according to conditions.

SUNKEN COMBINATION HAND-AND-ROD RETRIEVE: In this method it is not necessary to limit your cast for best results. After making the cast, let the fly sink. Sometimes only a few inches is necessary; at others it is advantageous to let it sink to bottom. When the depth desired is reached, start retrieving by jerking in the fly with your hand, for a few feet or until the rod is in full control of the fly. Then finish out with the rod lift-and-jerk method.

HAND-TWIST RETRIEVE: This is exactly as described in the chapter on wet-fly fishing and is used under identical conditions, being particularly effective in deep, still waters and ponds.

NATURAL DRIFT: This also is described in the chapter on wet-fly fishing and is effective when the trout want something large and yet do not wish to rush after it or anything that is moving against the current. Personally, I believe this method is best for bucktail fishing when the fish are feeding on bottom—on large larvae that are drifting deep. As a rule the across-and-downstream cast is best for this method, but it is also good when used on upstream casts— in which case it is necessary to retrieve slack at the same rate of speed as the current without pulling against it. If you allow the line to get too slack, you won't feel the strike if a fish hits. Besides, the line is quite likely to become entangled with some rocks and cause you real trouble.

Another method used considerably in Maine is a very fast and energetic arm retrieve. The fly is cast and allowed to sink. Then, with the line held loosely under the hand holding the rod handle, the other hand takes hold of the line below the handle and starts retrieving with fast forearm jerks which are continued until the fly is ready to be picked from the water. These jerks are long and vigorous, starting just below the handle and ending at the side with the arm held straight down. You must stand up to do it right. To me the method is tiring and uninteresting, but it does produce and is particularly effective for lakes and big waters.

Variations of these methods may be used to advantage, and frequently you will find a combination of two or more worth trying. These attempts at describing the basic methods of manipulation are in the hope that they will enable the reader not versed in bucktail fishing to get started along the right track. If in some cases I repeat, it is because of the importance of these things. Incidentally, all the methods in the wet-fly fishing chapter may be used for bucktail fishing.

Always keep in mind that for this type of fishing, a long rod may be used to advantage. It is always good policy to carry along both an eight-foot rod, for dry fly, and a nine-foot rod, which will also handle a dry fly and yet be better for bucktails than the smaller tool. If you start off dry-fly fishing with your seven-and-a-half- or eight-foot rod and find that the trout won't rise to them but will take a bucktail, it will really pay you to go back to the car or the camp for your longer rod. No one ever lost anything by spending the time necessary to be properly prepared. In this particular case there is nothing truer than the fact that struggling along all day with your short rod is a loss in efficiency. Of course I expect I shall be challenged about this contention, but all I can say is let those who dispute it compare both the long and short rods honestly and with unbiased judgment when fishing with bucktails. If the long rod doesn't do a better job, then I'm having a brain storm and I apologize. And this comes from one who prefers a seven-and-a-half-foot rod for dry-fly fishing.

Notes about the streamer and bucktail flies in the color plates.

Plate 10:

GRIFFEN	
GRAY SQUIRREL SILVER (R.B.)	Sizes 12, 6X long;
RED SQUIRREL GOLD (R.B.)	8, 10, and 12, 2X long.
BELL SPECIAL	

These four flies are all excellent stream patterns. There is an-other in the R.B. series that I use also. It has white badger streamer feathers, white bucktail or impali under feathers, a silver tinsel body and a red hackle under the head. The Bell Special is a fascinating job tied with ostrich feathers. These are soft and fluffy and when wet they mat together in such a way that the effect is very min-now-like, at least to anglers.

The Jess Wood, already mentioned in connection with the Sault Sainte Marie fishing, is primarily a Northeastern pattern, made for the lakes of Maine and Quebec. However, it makes a most minnow-like fly and is useful anywhere that a large fly is indicated. The tandem hook shown in the illustration is effective, but the fly is just as good when tied on a single 6X long or longer hook. The tandem hook is best when you run into short strikers, and also takes those fish that strike at the head. To make the hooking even more sure one could, if desired, make a three-hook tandem job, the extra hook being centered between the other two, probably facing up in-stead of down like the others.

One thing is sure, there isn't any cut and dried way in which a trout strikes a streamer fly, nor can one predict the manner in which they will. Personally I'll keep to the single hook with the barb set about two thirds of the way toward the end of the streamer feather. However, I must admit that many fish are missed when us-ing a large single hook fly, fish that would have been hooked had there been a tandem or similar arrangement.

BROWN AND WHITE BUCKTAIL. This is a simple, original tie made for the Esopus River in New York State. It is a sound design, and useful in all sizes on all waters. An excellent variation is one made with black top hair instead of the brown hair shown.

EDSON TIGER DARK and EDSON TIGER LIGHT. Sizes 4, 6, 8, 10, 6X long. These two patterns, which made their debut on New England waters, became very well known and popular. While I've taken lots of fish on them, it has been mostly in Maine, Quebec, and Vermont lakes. However, this is because I've used them more in such places, having other patterns I like better for other waters.

Here are some other streamer patterns that have been found outstanding for one reason or another.

ADELE. By Joe Fandel, of Massachusetts. Sizes 2, 4, 6X long or longer. This a typical Maine pattern for landlocked salmon. Mr. Fandel uses it successfully in Sebago, Belgrade, and Pierce Pond, Maine. It has also produced well for Atlantic salmon on the Miramichi, near Doaktown, New Brunswick, Canada, in early spring.

BROWN MALLARD. Sizes 8, 10, 12, 2X long. I've been using this successfully for many years but unfortunately I do not know who originated it. As I find it effective from coast to coast, used as both a streamer and a nymph, I think it a worthy addition to any angler's fly assortment.

DOUBLE-TROUBLE, BADGER STREAMER. Sizes 4, 6, 8, 10, 12, 6X long. Nymph sizes, 6, 8, 2X long. This is one of my own patterns that was inspired by some flies sent me by a New Zealand correspondent. It is a sort of double streamer, the tail serving as the second. Strangely enough this fly, besides being a good streamer pattern, works very well as a nymph.

DOUBLE-TROUBLE, BLENDED (Grizzly and Blue). This is simply a variety of the foregoing design. You may make a large number of combinations. Incidentally the placing of bright streamer feathers between two dull colors makes a fine effect. For instance, tie on two bright-yellow feathers. Then on each side of these feathers tie a blue-gray feather of the same size. This will give you the general idea.

MICKEY FINN. This pattern was made popular by John Alden Knight. Originally it was simply called Red and Yellow Bucktail. I used the pattern tied on the old-style snelled hooks as far back as 1926 or thereabouts. It is a very effective pattern and well deserved the boost given it by Jack in his writings.

O'DONALD (JOE). Tied by Harry Huffman. Designed by Butch Wilson. Sizes according to needs.

O'DONALD (JIM). Tied and designed by Harry Huffman. While both of these flies were originally made for bass fishing in the

Far West, they proved so good for me when used for Northern brook trout and large rainbows in the Mountain States that I thought them worth showing. They should also be excellent for landlocked salmon and so forth.

PROVO STREAMER. Sizes 6, 8, 10, 12, 6X long. This pattern by Clarence M. Wanke, of Utah, has proved very effective for me. When he first sent me the description he wrote: "It is a composite of Alaskan Mary Ann and the Erskine Streamer." Both of these are good patterns. My personal experience with it has been in stream fishing for brown trout, where it has done very well.

ROOST DACE. This is an Eastern stream pattern designed by Jimmie Deren, of New York.

RED TROUT MINNOW. Tied and designed by Joe Fandel. This is another of the imitation-minnow types, tied small and delicate for fishing over educated and wary trout in areas where fishermen crowd the streams. Joe Fandel fishes it in such waters as the Charles River near South Natick, Mass. I find that it works well wherever a small minnow fly is needed.

CHAPTER VII

Dry-Fly Fundamentals and Tackle

THERE are two very essential requirements that the angler must master for consistently successful dry-fly fishing. These are: delicacy in presenting the fly, and the ability to float that fly in a natural manner, the same as a natural fly would float if carried along by the current. Sounds simple, doesn't it? It is, providing you overcome the difficulties that might prevent their fulfillment.

Delicacy is attained through an ability to cast properly, together with a rod, line, and leader that work in perfect harmony with the caster. So much has been written about rods, balance, lines, leaders, and how to cast that I doubt if I shall be able to add anything to the sum total of knowledge. But it is necessary to say something about these things in order to make this work complete, and I offer the following suggestions.

First, for delicacy in casting it is best not to have a rod that is too heavy or stiff. Usually better-grade rods ranging from seven-and-a-half to nine feet in length and from three and three-quarter to five-and-a-half ounces in weight will fill the bill. However, in the matter of weight it is a good idea not to be too particular as some rods of identical length and weight may have actions as different as night and day. For instance I have one seven-and-a-half-foot rod of three-and-three-quarter ounces that is like a poker and, as far as I am concerned, fit only for spinner or bait fishing. At the same time I have several others of the same length and weight that are stiff and powerful without being pokers. Also I have a couple of four to four-and-a-half ounce (glass) rods of the same length that are just right. It's all in the feel, with power and stiffness being combined with resiliency and suppleness. Some rods have this; others do not. Now this "right" feel is an elusive thing. It is indescribable—that is, to the extent that you can't possibly pick out a rod from the description. The nearest I can come to giving you an impression of it is that you feel a rigid resistance but at the same time feel the rod live and breathe right down to the grip. The action is distributed with a decreasing, even power from the hand grasp to the tip.

Very few anglers are able to recognize this quality when they have a new rod in their hands. Only much experience in handling rods can develop one's senses to the point where it is possible to recognize this quality. For this reason it is best to buy your rods from reliable dealers or makers, from those who have had plenty of experience either in making or handling rods, from those who know what a good dry-fly rod should possess, or from someone who has had contact with so many good fishermen that he has absorbed those niceties of judgment which are necessary in order to accurately judge action in a rod.

This is possible, you know. One salesman I knew well who rarely fished for trout instinctively knew a good dry-fly rod the instant he felt one and it was seldom that his judgment was at fault. This skill had come from many years of experience in catering to customers who knew rods and who knew what they wanted.

On the other hand, when you find a salesman who has had the angling as well as the merchandising experience, you will find a certain sympathy and understanding that is hard to beat, as well as someone who really knows what it is all about.

Remember this. The fellow who really knows things will not try to impress you with his knowledge. Only those who have a limited experience are likely to do that. *The experience of years and the knowledge gained from it are ingrained in the personality of the possessor.* You don't need to be told if a fellow really knows anything about fishing. You sense it after talking to him only a few moments. We who have fished for a good many years can tell the moment he takes a rod in his hand if a man is a fly fisherman. The way he handles it immediately tells the story far better than any words.

Many years ago I bought a seven-and-a-half-footer that proved perfect as far as I was concerned. In the hands of the average caster it would cast forty to fifty feet without undue strain and yet was ideal for close work. It was accurate and delicate—good for either a large or small stream. Since then I have purchased three more—had them made to imitate the action of this original. One was the unsuitable stiff rod previously mentioned, but the others were positive

duplicates. Every angler I have ever let try one has become enthusiastic over their feel and performance, even though not one of
these anglers believed in a rod as short as seven and a half feet. By
actual test I have found that they will do everything that is possible
with an eight-foot rod and at the same time give you that additional
advantage of less length when on a brushy stream.

I have several objections to short rods for dry-fly fishing. They
are not satisfactory when it is necessary to wade deep—that is in
any water that reaches six inches or more above the knees. Most
of us when fishing are inclined to drop our backcast, and the deeper
the water the more this tendency causes trouble. A long rod aids

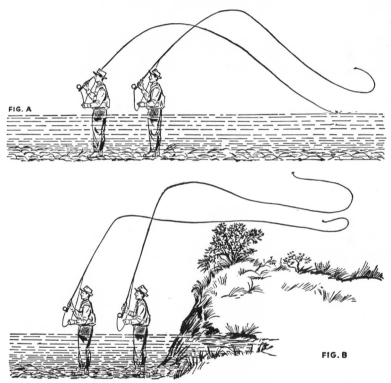

SHOWING A SHORT AND LONG ROD IN ACTION *under identical con-*
ditions and in hands of fair caster. With the short rod the fly
will catch on bush. With the long rod it will probably miss it.
Of course if you learn to keep your back-cast high, which is
most important anyway, you can get by with the shorter rod.

in overcoming this fault, which, even though it is correctable by casting, won't be corrected by the average individual except by mechanical means. (See Fig. A.) Naturally, the longer the cast attempted, the greater the possibility of the line's dropping because of the extra line weight in the air on the back cast. In addition, when

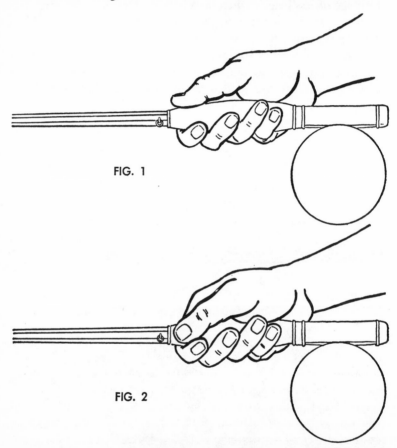

FIG. 1

FIG. 2

the angler has a high background (Fig. B) the longer rod helps in lifting the line high enough to avoid snagging. But even more important than these two things is the advantage you get from using a long rod when standing in deep water when it comes to lifting the fly from the water at any considerable distance for the next cast.

Regarding the tendency of the average fly fisherman to bring his rod too far back on the cast, here is a simple yet extremely helpful hint to cure the fault. It actually works. First, grasp the rod as usual, with the guides underneath and the thumb lined up on the grasp directly above them. (Fig. 1.) Then simply shift the thumb to the side of the grasp, keeping the rest of the hand in the same position. (Fig. 2.) (Drawings made of the right hand.) You will find that this simple procedure automatically aids in preventing you from bringing the rod too far back. It is also the easiest and most natural hold for the average human hand.

Even so, the longer rod will prove advantageous when you are standing in deep water, if only for the reason that it allows better handling of the fly when it is floating on the water (you are able to fish the fly with less line touching the surface), aids in the hooking of the fish because of this, and makes the pickup for the following cast easier. Besides it makes it possible to drop the fly more gently, because of better control of the line *when making a long cast*—something that may be frequently necessary when fishing large, turbulent, or deep streams. Then, too, it is sometimes necessary to reach across a fast rapids to fish a feeding groove of water on the other side. To do this successfully you must avoid drag, and you can best do so if neither line nor leader touches the fast current between. Naturally, the longer the rod the greater the distance you can span, which is definitely an advantage.

On the other hand, it should be kept in mind that the longer and heavier the rod, the more tiring it will be for the user. One simply can't have everything in one length and weight. If you can have only one rod it might be wise to compromise. I would call an eight-and-a-half-footer a good middle-of-the-road job. One of four-and-a-half to five ounces, with what is often referred to as dry-fly action, should be about right. In the average run of rods you are more likely to find the right action in a five-ounce weight than you are in anything lighter. A nine-foot rod of five-and-a-half to six-and-a-quarter ounces is enough rod for any trout fishing, while a seven-and-a-half- or eight-footer ranging from three and three-quarter to four ounces will be found more generally satisfactory and pleasant to use for average stream fishing.

If you are considering glass or steel rods, you will find something around seven and a half feet the most satisfactory, at least at the present time (1952). There is one great advantage that rods made of these materials have over split bamboo. They do not lose much of their original action in use. On this point, let me quote from a letter from my good friend Arthur E. Low, of California, who probably knows more about trout tackle than any other individual in this country. I had written him for his opinion on steel rods, the modern ones. He wrote in part: "Some time ago the factory made up about ten different weights and actions of steel rods for me to experiment with. The best one, as far as you and I are concerned, was a three-piece four-ounce rod with a soft action. I mean soft for steel, and about like a fairly good dry-fly action in bamboo.

"Such rods in bamboo definitely will not last over three hundred hours of casting without losing at least thirty per cent of their original action. I have one of these tubular steel rods above mentioned that has been used, and by hundreds of different people—something that would immediately ruin a bamboo—about six thousand hours, and it is within one and a half per cent of its original tip-action, etc."

Glass fibre is the strongest of all rod materials, but the fibre strands must be held together by a laminating agent. It is this bonding material that gives way in use, and thus the glass fibre rods are only as strong as the plastic used in holding them together. At the time of this writing there is a new agent being used by one manufacturer that is supposed to match the characteristics of the glass fibres, and because of this, and the manner in which the fibres are tapered, they claim to have a practically unbreakable rod. So far the company has not made any trout rods. I suppose that in the future they or someone else will. A number of anglers resent the creation of anything unbreakable for fishing, on the grounds that it doesn't give the fish a fair chance. But of course one could easily handle that situation by never using a leader so strong that the fish can't break it.

In the short time that glass rods have been in existence they have been steadily gaining in favor. Also, as the manufacturers keep experimenting, the glass rods are getting better in every way. In action particularly this has changed my first opinion of them. Candidly, the first fly rods I tried I thought abominable. But this last year I obtained two new jobs that I'm getting to like very well. One in particular feels very much like a pet bamboo of mine. I must say, however, that it weighs nearly an ounce more than the bamboo of the same length and while the action seems very similar it has considerably more power than the bamboo and will handle a size larger line.

One important point to be considered in casting is the necessity of getting the proper weight line for the rod. Often this is troublesome, and if one doesn't get properly fitted at the beginning it can become quite expensive.

There are two general types of tapered lines; the double-taper, and the three-diameter, torpedo-head, or otherwise specially constructed taper having only one casting end.

A double-taper line is one made with a taper at each end. Each taper starts as a fine level which gradually increases until it arrives at the desired body size, or center of the line. This remains level for most of the line's length, until it starts tapering down to the opposite end. The sizes of level fly lines are designated by letters, I being the smallest. From there on up, to a maximum weight usually not heavier than B, the line gets one size heavier as you back down the alphabet. Thus C line would be heavier than D. A tapered line is marked with both the size of the fly end and the body. Hence a line marked HCH means that both ends of the line are tapered to size H and the body of the line is level C. Size HCF means that the leader end of the line is size H, then it tapers up to C (of which there may be from fifteen to twenty-five feet) and then it gradually tapers to a level F which remains constant for the balance of the line. A four-diameter line of HDBG would consist of four sizes between the tapers from one size to the other.

There isn't any question that the special tapers cast best for distance, and they are often to be recommended for bucktails and streamers of the larger sizes. But the heavy front end bothers me in dry-fly fishing, and for this work I use a double-taper. I would suggest a double-taper for casts up to fifty feet; special tapers for casts longer than that.

Another point to remember is that three-diameter lines have only one casting end. When this gets shortened with use, it progressively loses its value; and when the small end is all gone, your line is useless as a taper unless you splice on some more small-diameter line at the cut-down end. But in a double-taper you really have two lines in one, provided you make use of them. This is done easily enough by simply turning the line end to end rather frequently, so that the end near the bottom of the reel spool doesn't become so badly kinked that it presents a tough problem. And if you want two separate lines from your double-taper, you can make them by simply cutting it in half and then splicing level G or F to the heavy body ends. Of course the splicing must be smoothly and securely done, which does mean work—unless you do it as a hobby, when of course it becomes play.

Regarding the respective qualities of nylon and silk fly lines I can report only on developments up to the date of this writing. Inasmuch as manufacturers and scientific researchers are continually striving for better finishes at lower costs, some new process may come up at any time to change the picture.

Silk lines can be finished to a greater degree of perfection, even now, than can nylon, but they are subject to a chemical change while aging that causes some of them to get sticky. Now this doesn't always happen, in fact often it does not. The trouble is that there isn't any way of telling if one will or will not get that way after you purchase it—or when, as a matter of fact. Also, while the best finish for silk fly lines is called vacuum, there are a lot of lines made that have a nice looking and feeling surface, but are not impregnated and finished properly because of the excessive labor costs involved in such a process. If the line does not get sticky, then the vacuum finish will outlast the other finishes by many years. Here is another warning about silk. After years of use the line may still seem in wonderful condition, and yet not have much strength left due to a slow rotting process. However, ordinarily this does not apply to lines less than seven to twelve years old.

Nylon is not subject to this deterioration, and I've had only one line get sticky. On the other hand the material will not take a finish that will stand up. I know that I can never get more than sixty full days of fishing from a double-taper nylon line, using both tapered ends. It is claimed by at least one manufacturer that the material will not permit the use of enough heat for a better finish. However, there is a new process that is supposed to reduce this fault. I'll say more about that later. Also they are working on a new process that might make possible a longer lasting finish for nylon lines simply because the excessive stretch of the material is greatly reduced. It is, of course, mainly the stretch that causes the finish to go bad, and the last lines I've used are far better in this respect than the first ones I tried.

Nylon lines float much better than the average silk, hence they make excellent dry-fly lines. In this connection I must mention the hollow fly lines. I used these when they originally came out, and at that time they weren't very good because, when the finish cracked, water got into the hollow core, and the line became a dud. But now, because of the use of a special coating on the braided silk before the finishes are applied, this fault has been eliminated. This together with the superb finish makes them beautiful lines; their greatest drawback is the price, which is quite steep.

Because I wanted the unbiased opinion of someone else on this subject, I asked Arthur Emery Low for his opinion on nylon versus silk, and on double-tapers versus three-diameters. Here are some pertinent excerpts from his reply.

Up to this time [1949] I have been against this material [nylon] for fly lines except where a man could really afford two lines, one of silk and one of nylon, and of course use the nylon only for dry-fly fishing. Nylon lines have never lasted me, one tapered end alone, more than 200 hours of use without "breaking down" because the too much stretch of the material "pulled off" the finish. Each season I have always used and spoiled at least two double-taper nylon lines, using both ends, and one three-diameter.

As far as silk is concerned we have all been able to float such lines in almost any water, when we had to, for dry-fly fishing. Sometimes, it is true, we had to redress them at lunch time on an all-day fishing trip, but that wasn't too bad except for the fellows who wanted to fish an eight-hour day without getting out of the stream. And of course the line was heavy enough to sink for wet-fly fishing. And the finish would last several years if properly taken care of. I have seen some good quality lines that seemed perfect after ten years of fishing.

I would say that until the new nylon process is perfected [this refers to taking out the stretch and so forth], silk lines are tops for the average man.

Now about three-diameter, torpedo, bug or call them what you will lines. These came out for only one purpose and it may be that I had a lot to do with pushing the idea. After publicity about the success of the distance tournament casters using such lines took hold on the public, many anglers shifted to them. In the case of tyros this was generally to their sorrow.

There are several things involved when comparing the use of these two lines, but in all but one instance they favor the double-taper. First, it has a double life, since you have two ends to wear out. Second, it casts much more evenly and you get a straighter line in casting when casts are of permissible length, that is as far as the rod action and the skill of the angler can throw it without the belly of the line sagging. It is at this point that double-taper fails and three-diameter has value. You can definitely get longer casts with a minimum of belly sagging with the three-diameter or torpedo-head lines. However, after the belly of the three-diameter gets about ten feet beyond the tip, then it is extremely hard to properly lay a fly *on top of the water*. One great trouble with these tapers is that the bellies are too short. Generally, to be most effective, they should be from twenty to twenty-five feet long.

Another trouble with these special tapers is that the stream current drags them down much faster than other lines. This is because the heavier belly gives more water tension and forces a kink, or doubling of line, at the rear taper where the light, level part begins.

These remarks by Mr. Low concerning double-taper and torpedo-head lines should be taken very seriously by both consumer and manufacturer. Not only do they give the reasons for a double-taper and a torpedo-head, but they also point out a fault in the latter, which if corrected might well make the lines far more popular than they are.

Just a short bit of general advice on the care of fly lines. Keep them clean and never put them away wet, whether they are silk or nylon. To clean, wipe them with mild soap and water, then with a clean, wet rag, and finally allow them to dry thoroughly. In the case of a dry-fly line you may add a thorough rub-down with a good line dressing, but never put the dressing on to excess or fail to rub it in well. I would not dress a wet-fly line. You don't want that to float unless the conditions call for fishing just under the surface, in which case you should use your dry-fly line and grease the leader to the point needed to keep the fly from sinking deeper than desired.

Be careful with nylon fly lines. Do not stretch them to clean and dress, unless you are sure that you have a non-stretchable nylon line. You might hurt the finish if you do.

For the out-of-season period it will aid in keeping the lines in good condition if they are coiled, to about the size of the original factory coil or larger, and placed where the temperature is neither excessively hot nor cold. Line-carriers are all right, but I've never used one that didn't have some faults. Fly lines should always be kept away from excessive heat.

I mentioned that I'd have more to say about the new finish for nylon lines. Following are a few quotations from the correspondence of the inventor of the process, not a line maker, when he sent me two lines to experiment with, one for a bass rod and the other for a trout rod. I shall, of course, be giving them the works. Because the lines look and feel good to me, I'm very anxious for a chance to use them.

The HCH taper is one of the first made on production equipment, and while we have to have better controls, to get the maximum toughness, we are sending you one of the first, knowing that if this one passes the test, all of them will.

Frankly, to the best of our knowledge, you are the only fishing editor, or writer, who has had the courage to tell the world that a nylon line is not worth a damn.

We feel that here is a nylon line that will match a silk line on any point, weight, durability, pliability and far better for water absorbent resistance, shooting, and above all has a balance or feel that you will sense on the first cast. It would be only cricket to inform you of this development in view of your stand on the nylon of today [1950] and let you judge if this line could well be the fly line of the future.

Our objective is to keep the diameter one or two thousandths under silk lines, but have the same weight. You might think this is carrying the decimal point a little too far, but try our HCH line on your heavy rod that handles well an HCH silk but not the HCH nylon you now have.

Well, I did just that, trying the two lines out on the snow, and the new finish worked just as well as the silk line I used for this rod and better than the GBG nylon I had found necessary to use with it. The GBG was too heavy and the HCH old nylon was too light for this particular rod, a rather limber nine-and-a-half-foot, five-and-three-quarter-ounce rod that I like very well. The new HCH nylon was perfect. Whether or not the finish will stand up as well as the best silk finish is something for the future to decide, and with me that means at least a year or two of extensive use. Otherwise the finish is the best I've ever seen on a nylon line. It is quite likely that most manufacturers will be wanting to use it in time.

Since first procuring this line I have now given it two full years of use. It is still in first-class condition.

To get the right size line for any rod is not simple, and to be absolutely sure one should really try it before buying, something that is usually impossible. However, the following table will be found reasonably accurate for dry fly rods unless the nylon line being chosen is one of the type that weighs as heavy as the silk in the same calibration. In that case use the silk line recommendation.

ROD	NYLON	SILK
8 ft.−4 oz.	HDH *or* HEH	HEH
8½ ft.−4½ oz.	HDH	HEH
8½ ft.−5 oz.	HCH	HDH
9 ft.−5–5½ oz.	HCH	HDH
9 ft.−6 oz.	GBG	HCH

If you try on your rod the line selected according to this table, and find that it doesn't cast well, it may be that cutting off some of the end will make it work all right. In illustration of this let me tell you of a recent experience. I had a new rod to try out, an eight-foot two-piece five-strip bamboo, weighing four ounces. I had picked an HDH nylon for it, but when I started fishing it simply would not throw the fly well enough to make a decent cast, no matter what the distance. I started cutting off the H part of the line, a few inches at a time. It wasn't until I'd cut off four and a half feet of the six feet of level H line that it would perform properly. By the time I got it fitted I was beginning to think I'd made an error in judgment and that the rod really required an HCH. Nearly all lines need some adjustment in this manner when fitting to the rod. In some cases it is very slight, so try just a few inches at a time. In others the slicing off must be considerable, as in the case just cited.

The list of line sizes on page 157 is that recommended by the National Association of Angling and Casting Clubs. I have included them to give you an idea what the diameter of fly lines should be.

The leader, or cast, is a most important item for consideration on the part of a fly fisherman. While silkworm gut held the star position and the spotlight as a supreme leader material for many years, it now has at least one serious rival among the synthetic products. That is nylon.

There are a number of synthetics on the market and doubtless there will be many more. A product that is tops today may take second place tomorrow. The best of these recent synthetics do not need soaking to be used, but in my experience I have found that

NAACC OFFICIAL STANDARD TABLE OF
FLY LINE CALIBRATIONS WITH LETTER DESIGNATIONS,
MAXIMUM PERMISSIBLE TOLERANCES,
AND MAXIMUM PERMISSIBLE AVERAGE DEVIATIONS

Letter Size		Nominal Diameters in 100ths of inch
I	....	.022
H	....	.025
G	....	.030
F	....	.035
E	....	.040
D	....	.045
C	....	.050
B	....	.055
A	....	.060

1 The maximum permissible tolerance, plus or minus, shall be one-half of the difference between the nominal diameter and the nominal diameters of the adjacent sizes or 2½ thousandths on all letter sizes, except I and I to H which are 1½ thousandths.

2 The maximum permissible average deviation throughout the length of the line shall not exceed one thousandth of one inch, plus and/or minus.

they *do* work best when they have absorbed all the water they can. So I soak them along with the silkworm gut I still prefer for certain purposes.

Personally I see the need for both synthetics and the animal product. I choose silkworm gut for heavy calibrations because it gets pliable when wet, while the heavy non-soaking synthetics stay very stiff and have a tendency to coil. Of course this coil may be stretched out but often it occurs at most inopportune times. I also choose the natural gut, of the best grade of course, in the small calibrations because it is slightly stiffer, even when saturated, than are the water-resisting types of synthetics. Roughly I'd place the heavy limit at .016 and the light limit at .009. However, this applies only to dry-fly fishing for which I prefer silkworm gut. For other work, where the flies are heavy, and even fairly small ones gain weight readily when fished wet, this fault of nylon is not noticeable. Also, nylon is being constantly improved. Some makes are now very soft.

Many of you may disagree with these conclusions. That is your right and your privilege. My calculations are based on personal fishing and on the things I've seen happen to others while they were fishing.

Keep in mind that a synthetic such as nylon is extremely slippery, its knots have a tendency to slip if poorly tied, and you will get in trouble if you are the least bit careless. The trouble may not occur at once, but it is quite likely to happen at the worst of times *unless the knot has been perfectly made*. It is surprising how the stuff will slip. You can't be too careful in making the knots very tight. This slipping does not happen with natural gut or a synthetic that swells when it gets wet. The very swelling process acts as a preventive.

A dry-fly leader should be selected according to the needs of the moment. A good basic one for the average dry-fly rod and conditions is seven and a half feet long, tapering from .015 to .008. By "average rod" I mean one that uses a line no heavier than HDH and no lighter than HEH, and by "average conditions" I mean air that ranges from zero movement to a fair breeze, or even wind that is causing you trouble in making a good cast, but with water broken enough to conceal the line and perhaps the leader. Most pocket water is of this type, and so are riffles and the rapids leading into pools.

But suppose the wind is strong, and from such a direction in relation to where you want to fish that you must cast with it. Then this seven-and-a-half-foot 2X silkworm gut or 3X nylon leader may prove unsatisfactory. You may find it difficult to drop the fly without slapping the water. Here a longer and finer leader will perform far better. In many cases a nine-foot leader tapering from .015 or .014 to .007 or .0065 will be sufficient. The taper should jump fast down to .009, and then be finished off with a long tip taper running from .008 to .007 or smaller. If these end strands are 17 or 18 inches long or longer, two will suffice if the fly is size 14 or larger; but if size 16 or smaller flies are being used, then you need an extra strand; in other words the end should run .008, .007, .0065 or .006. In this connection it may be advantageous to use even finer material than .006—if you can obtain it and if you can hook a fish with it without getting a break.

The reversing condition, that is, casting into a strong wind, requires a heavy leader. If the water is rough enough to make excessive caution unimportant, and the fly being used is large, say anything from size 6 through 12 inclusive and heavily dressed, then a seven-and-a-half-foot leader tapered from .017 to .009 (1X gut or 2X nylon) will handle far more easily than the same length tapered from .015 to .008. As a matter of fact I often use a leader of this length and butt calibration tapered to .010 (0X gut or 1X nylon) finding it sometimes better because it is stronger.

There is another seven-and-a-half-foot leader needed if you expect to use flies smaller than size 14. If you haven't yet used flies in sizes 16, 18, and 20, then you should consider doing so because there are times when only little ones will interest the trout. A good taper for small flies is .015 or .014 to .007 (3X gut or 4X nylon)—this for flies not smaller than size 18 on stout wire, or for fast water.

But for 2X fine wire flies, or for quiet water conditions, you may need a taper down to .006, especially when using flies as small as sizes 18 and 20. This leader will also fill the need when fishing for wary trout, under conditions where only the leader should touch the water. If a long cast is needed, where the water is exceptionally clear and quiet and the trout wary, then you will need a longer leader.

For ordinary clear slow-moving water, or water very clear but having a slightly roughened surface, a nine-foot leader tapering from .016 to .008 will serve nicely. But if the trout are extremely cautious it may pay to use a taper of .015 to .007, or if very small flies are needed to .0065 (4X gut) or .006 (5X gut or nylon).

For very clear water with a glassy surface, the longer and finer the leader the better. But of course the limit here is governed by your skill in handling the outfit. Some say they can handle fifteen to twenty feet of leader with ease. Personally I can not, nor can the great majority of fishermen. My limit is a twelve-footer, and I can't satisfactorily use a large and fluffy fly with this length unless a light to moderate wind is with me. Without the wind, or with too much of it, I get into trouble. But I can handle such a leader with regular winged flies, not too heavily tied, in sizes 14 through 20; and with hackle or divided-wing flies up to size 12, or even size 10 under the right conditions. But if I have a wind blowing into my face I have difficulties. The smaller the fly the better in such a case, but often I must reduce the leader length to get good results.

Of course if the wind roughens the water you may not need so long a leader. During a single day's fishing you may find it advantageous to change leaders several times, the better to cover the water and meet the conditions encountered.

My choice of length and taper for the twelve-foot leader is one strand of each of the following calibrations, beginning at the line end: .017; .016; .014; .012; .011; .010; .009; .008; .007; .006.

The number of strands used is based on an average of sixteen inches to a strand with allowance for tying, this last without too much waste. It might be easier to allow more for waste and add an extra strand, say size .013. I've used the sixteen-inch basis because, in silkworm gut, it is difficult to get longer strands than this, and in the larger calibrations you can't be sure of getting even that length except once in a while. In such a case you make up the difference by using seventeen-inch, eighteen-inch, or longer strands in the calibrations available. Actually an average length for the ten strands of seventeen inches, or one hundred and seventy inches over all, would make for easy and quick tying. Nylon you may cut to exactly the length desired. If you find that your skill prevents much waste and thus you get a leader longer than desired from the lengths you are using, then cut the average strand length accordingly. The cost of nylon is so low that cutting inches from a twenty- or twenty-two-inch strand doesn't mean much; and the cost of drawn silkworm gut is now low enough to make it attractive to the fishermen that prefer it. Undrawn silkworm gut in the heavier calibrations is still excessively high in price, especially when you consider the loss incurred from culling out the unusable strands. However, in tying seven-and-a-half- and nine-foot nylon leaders with twenty-inch strands, you can use five strands for the shorter leader and six strands for the longer one, against possibly one extra strand for each leader made from available silkworm gut.

The following are the tapers of the leaders that I have discussed in the foregoing. I've given alternatives to take care of both gut and nylon leaders, basing the tapers on silkworm gut strands averaging seventeen inches in length, and on nylon in either twenty- or twenty-two-inch lengths. Often twenty-two-inch nylon is available rather than twenty-inch, and at the same price. Of course you may use the gut tapers when using nylon, or the nylon tapers when using gut, if you have this material in sufficient average lengths to do so. Avoid joining strands more than two sizes apart. To tie .006 to .009 is to invite disaster, because the difference in the sizes usually makes a poor and weak knot. Probably the best knot for joining two strands of leader material is the "blood" or "chator" knot; the best one for making the line loop is called the "perfection loop" knot. (See diagrams of knots on pages 44–5; the "perfection loop" is at top, left, on 45.)

Length	Taper	Silkworm gut	Nylon

This is a splendid all-around leader.

7½ feet	.015–.008	.015; .014; .013 or .012; .011; .009; .008.	.015; .013; 012 or .011; .010 or .009; .008.

For casting into the wind when a fine leader is unnecessary.

7½ feet	.017–.010 or .009	.017; .016 or .015; .014; .013; .012 or .011; .010 or .009.	.017; .015; .013; .011; .010 or .009.

For any condition where a small calibration at fly end is needed, but a long leader is not important.

7½ feet	.015–.007 or .0065	.015 or .014; .013 or .012; .011 or .010; .009 or .008; .007; .007 or .0065.	.014; .012; .010; .008; .007; .006.

NOTE: Joining .008 to .006 is difficult; so is joining .009 to .007. This illustrates the disadvantage of using five twenty-inch strands to make a seven-and-a-half-foot leader in a low calibration, yet with a butt heavy enough to be satisfactory. You would do better to cut the strands shorter and use extra strands of intermediate calibration.

The basic nine-footer, as the .008 is the basic seven-and-a-half-footer. If you wish to cut your outfit to the simplest possible, then these two basic leaders—seven and a half feet to .008 and nine feet to .007—would be splendid choice.

9 feet	.016–.007	.016 or .015; .014; .013; .011; .009; .008; .007.	.015; .013; .011; .009; .008; .007.

Length	Taper	Silkworm gut	Nylon

For all-around work, where slower and clearer water may require more leader length than seven and a half feet between fly and line. Like the basic seven-and-a-half- and nine-footers, this is a splendid cast to have in your leader assortment.

Length	Taper	Silkworm gut	Nylon
9 feet	.017 or .016–.008	.017 or .016; .015 or .014; .013 or .012; .011; .010; .009; .008.	.016; .014; .012; .010; .009; .008.

For fishing with the wind when a longer leader is unnecessary.

Length	Taper	Silkworm gut	Nylon
9 feet	.015 or .014–.007, .0065, or lighter	.015; .013; .011; .009; .008; .007; .0065 or .006.	.014; .012; .010; .009; .008; .007; .007 or .006.
12 feet	.017–.0065 or .006.	.017; .016; .014; .012; .011; .010; .009; .008; .007; .0065 or .006.	.017; .015; .013; .011; .009; .008; .007; .0065 or .006.

As to the jumps of two sizes between strands, let me advise that cutting the strands shorter, and inserting the missing sizes between, makes a more gradual taper that sometimes casts better than the faster taper. But let me warn you on this: a slow-tapered leader starting with a small calibration at the butt is a sorry affair and makes for very tough casting. The lower priced leaders are of this type. The tapers I have given have butts heavy enough to be satisfactory and work in very well with average material lengths. If you wish your leaders tapered with only one step between each strand you must be prepared to pay more for them, if you do not tie them yourself. Each extra knot means that much more time in the making.

As I see it, the leader is used for three reasons; to promote invisibility, to make the fly appear detached from the angler, and to drop the line down to cobweb thinness to conform with the delicate feathered creations we fondly hope imitate the natural insects on which trout feed. Either natural or synthetic gut seems to be in keeping with the water, and it is true that trout are less suspicious of it, most of the time, than they are of a line.

Keep in mind that you can't very well use a leader tapering to .009 or .010 with a size 18 fly, and it is correspondingly poor practice to try using an .006 leader on a size 8 fan-wing fly. In the first case the leader would dominate the fly; and in the second case you'd have the very dickens of a time to straighten out a cast, if indeed you ever could except by holding it in a strong wind and letting this do the work for you.

When conditions are such that a combination of large flies and fine gut is needed to produce results, then use the finest gut you can and yet make an excellent delivery. You might better make perfect deliveries with gut somewhat heavier than you think will work than make sloppy casts with gut finer than you actually need. Incidentally, length of leader helps out here. The trout seem more fearful of line than leader, and you may find it to your advantage to use a twelve-foot leader tapering to 1X or 2X rather than a seven-and-a-half-footer tapering to .006 or .0065.

But this small calibration (5X) is sometimes the only answer to success, in fact sometimes you may find it advantageous to go finer —say down to .005 or .0055 calibration. But watch out with this fine stuff. It hasn't much strength, and you must be most skillful to hook and land a good fish with it. Besides that, you must have luck with you as well. You can hold a fish only to the strength of the leader. If you go beyond that or the strength of a small and very fine wire dry-fly hook, in order to keep a fish from getting into a snag, then something has to give. But always keep in mind that you do not need fine leaders or delicate flies in heavy water, so it is foolish to use them there. You often do need such stuff in still water that is very clear and in which the fish are very wary. When you have bad hazards in such places, your chances of successfully landing a large fish on light terminal tackle are very slight. But in such cases watch for favorable times to fish, when you can use stronger tackle —such as when the water is slightly discolored or after dark.

Recently some anglers have been trying out double-tapered nylon leaders. In this leader the material is smaller at the line than it is further on. To let you visualize this I give below a couple of working examples.

#1 — GENERAL PURPOSE	#2 — TO CAST INTO HIGH WIND
.015 — 13 inches	.016 — 13 inches
.016 — 8 inches	.018 — 13 inches
.017 — 8 inches	.020 — 13 inches
.018 — 14 inches	.018 — 13 inches

#1 — GENERAL PURPOSE	#2 — TO CAST INTO HIGH WIND
.017 — 10 inches	.016 — 12 inches
.015 — 10 inches	.014 — 12 inches
.013 — 10 inches	.012 — 10 inches
.011 — 12 inches	.011 — 10 inches
.009 — 14 inches	.010 — 17 inches
.008 — 14 inches,	or longer
or longer	

From this you may experiment to suit yourself and perhaps you will find the exact tapers that best suit your tackle and yourself.

There are also knotless tapered nylon leaders now available. Some anglers claim that they are ideal. I haven't tested them long enough nor comparatively enough with knotted leaders to pass along any opinion as to their relative value. Of course it won't take much time, if changing flies frequently, to need at least one knot at the fly end.

Fortunately for the angler it is quite normal for small flies to work best when fine gut is needed, so the problem of large flies and fine gut is not a common occurrence; but if you do run across conditions when it is necessary, you will find that if you use a leader consistent with the size of your fly, it will work out better than if you try doing otherwise. But always keep in mind that long leaders will consistently bring more uniform success than short ones, and that the finer the gut you use, *consistent with the conditions and the size of fly used*, the better chance you have of outwitting wary trout.

Proper care of silkworm gut and leaders is important. The method I've found satisfactory is to keep the excess stock in a chamois pocket leader case, or some other good container, and wherever possible away from heat. The leaders in current use I keep wet in a soak-box from the day I start using them for the season until it is over. If there is extra stock at the end of the season it is stored in a drawer away from direct furnace heat.

For any trip of short duration it is wise to carry two each of the various weights and lengths of leader previously specified—that is, of course, if you take your dry-fly fishing seriously. You may make out very well with one length and calibration. For longer trips, and in any case for emergency, it is always a good idea to have extras of leaders and points on hand.

As for nylon leaders and strands, you need not carry them in the soak-box. However it does not harm them to do so, in fact I think it makes them a bit more pliable and satisfactory to use at the start. Neither do these leaders and points need the special care necessary for silkworm gut, but I would suggest that you test them when they get a few years old. There have been cases when the material has become very weak with age.

A leader soak of glycerine and water (one ounce of glycerine to four ounces of distilled water plus a pinch of baking soda) seems to preserve silkworm gut, but personally I do not care to use it. The mixture fails for me in that it does not make the gut pliable enough for immediate satisfactory performance. I have recommended this soak and still do if the main purpose is to preserve gut. But in my experience the leader has never acted properly when so treated until the glycerin was off the gut and the water had time to put it in perfect condition for fishing. Of course the use of such a preservative for nylon and other synthetics is unnecessary.

I'm suspicious of metal soak-boxes that are not enameled or painted on the inside. I may be all wrong about this, but I do know that I've had far better wear from silkworm gut leaders when using a celluloid soak-box and distilled or rain water than I have when using anything else.

When in use, the leader should be examined frequently. Often, when casting, a wind knot is a danger spot. It makes a weak place in an otherwise good leader and will break easier than the material at that point. If the knot occurs in the fine points, you are quite likely to have the leader break when a fish strikes. Sometimes if caught in time these knots may be picked out with a pin or stiletto. If pulled too tight so that you injure the gut in attempting to pick them out, it is best to cut the strand and tie it together again with a blood knot. (See page 45.) Remember that these knots tied in the leader from casting may well cause you the loss of the prize fish you are always striving for.

Of course it takes time to do these things. Of course it is troublesome. But if you wish to make the best of your fishing, then you must take care of these details or else suffer the consequences with a smile when things go wrong. It is my frank opinion that more fish are lost by carelessness than by any other reason, except perhaps excitability. I'll venture to say that every person who reads this will recall some incident where he would have taken some especially good fish if he'd only taken the time to be careful.

Often we know well enough that our leader is becoming frayed and weak in spots. We know that it has acquired some knots it shouldn't have. But because we don't want to miss any possible chance, because we keep seeing water ahead we want to get to quickly, because we see some rises ahead that we feel sure mean fish in the creel for us, we keep rushing along instead of taking the moment or two it would need to either repair our injured leader or replace it with a new one. The one we are using seems to be holding out all right; we catch several nine- or ten-inchers with it, and nothing goes wrong. Or perhaps fishing is so slow that we feel it isn't worth while to make a change. Probably we won't rise a fish anyway.

And then it happens—the rise of a good fish. Just before it happened we might have been snapping at the rises of small fish; we might have gone partially asleep on our feet because of inaction, casting mechanically and without thought of what we were doing. We may even be in a state of "blue funk" because of our failure to rise some fish that were working but that we put down instead. At any rate we're in a bad state of mind, in no condition to take care of the rise of a really good fish.

Our reaction to the event is violent—all out of reason. Our strike is mighty, almost hard enough to break the tip of our rod if something else doesn't give way. The leader parts company with the fly. We have what remains of the leader, the trout has our fly, and we have lost the one big chance of the day—perhaps of the season.

Of course this fiasco can't be completely blamed on a frayed and weakened leader. As a matter of fact, under such conditions any leader tapering smaller than 2X is sure to break, and even this size may not stand the strain. It depends greatly on which way the fish happened to be moving at the time of the strike. If the fish was moving toward you, or if your strike was made before the trout had completed his taking of the fly, the strain would be lessened to such an extent that the leader might hold. But if the fish took the fly going away from you, or had completed the take and was on the way to bottom with it, even a 2X point would be likely to break.

On the other hand, perhaps you don't strike too hard. Perhaps you gauge the rise accurately and set the hook perfectly, and the fish dashes away on its first vigorous run. It is then that you may have occasion to worry about your frayed leader, and if the fish is a real fighter you are almost sure to come to grief and lose him before the fight is over. The slightest rub of a frayed spot against a sharp rock is quite likely to finish the job. When this happens, do you blame yourself for having been careless? Or do you blame your tackle and everything else except yourself? Of course you may not have been at fault in any way. If not, then you have good reason to feel "sore" about that something which caused your loss. But before blaming that something else, first consider your own part in the affair. If you find that you have been negligent, make up your mind to avoid a recurrence of the fault. By so doing you build up a resistance against failure. Remember that when your good chances do come, being prepared in every way will be a long step forward to being successful.

There isn't any doubt that trying too hard, letting trifles upset your temper, and attending to mechanical details rather than to natural problems militates against successful fishing. Unconscious rhythm, careful observation of natural stream phenomena, and a relaxed state of mind are synonymous with really good fishing. Observation relaxes, relaxation brings rhythm to your movements and so aids your manipulation of the fly. Study the currents, the bottom, the insects on the rocks and in the air. If you concentrate on these you will find the mechanical problems taking care of themselves as long as you possess the rudimentary training and know what should be done.

Anglers have long been confused about the calibrations of silkworm gut. One manufacturer calls a size one name, another calls it something different. Or they name it by numerical characters such as 4/5, 2X, to mention only two calibrations out of many, and these naturally differ according to the maker. The manufacturers of nylon have also used the numerical characters but in most instances the distributors and wholesalers of this material also give the calibration measurement as well—the only sensible thing to do.

I believe that as long ago as 1930 a movement was started to make a standard list of gut sizes, so that all manufacturers would use the same terms for the different sizes. As far as I know, this never materialized. I have long believed that all natural and synthetic gut should be marked in thousandths of an inch. It is the only method that makes sense. Suppose inches were named by some terms such as 1X, 2X, and so forth, but when you bought a foot of material made by one manufacturer it measured more or less than an actual foot? Since 1930 I've been advocating actual measurements in place of the other system, and while the old way is still in use many firms now include the actual calibrations as well.

A tolerance must be allowed in calibrations for both materials, as the synthetics do not run any truer in calibration than does best grade drawn silkworm gut. This should not exceed more than .000½ (one half of one one thousandth of an inch) either plus or minus. Thus in the smallest sizes you may find 4X and 5X, or 5X and 6X running to the exactly same calibration.

There are at least five different grades of silkworm gut, and a number of basic manufacturers. Undrawn gut is the strongest but it is difficult to get long strands of even calibration. "Selecta" is the best grade, and much more expensive than the others. Drawn gut is natural gut that has been pulled through a perfectly round hole in a diamond. Its sizes range from .016 through .005, and of course the strands are round and uniform in calibration, thus making the manufacture of leaders with it comparatively simple. In sizes smaller than .009 or perhaps .008 it is rare to find perfect undrawn strands, and as a rule the drawn sizes .009 through .005 are used for leader making even though the balance of the leader is of undrawn strands.

Silkworm gut, incidentally, is not the intestine of the worm; it is the viscous material from which the creature spins its silk, taken from the silk gland just before the worm is ready to spin. Drawn out, while still soft, to the desired thinness, it hardens soon after exposure to the air and takes on the familiar form in which it is used for making leaders.

A good floating preparation for your fly is quite important. Something that cleans as well as waterproofs is an advantage. As far as I am concerned, two ounces of paraffin dissolved in one pint of non-leaded gasoline makes a good concoction for the purpose.[1] It not only waterproofs the fly by depositing a film of wax on it, but also acts as an efficient cleanser. This last property is especially acceptable after a trout has taken a fly deep and when you take it

[1] Ethyl gas is no good for this. It must be non-treated gasoline.

out of the mouth it is bloody and matted. Simply dropping the fly in the bottle and giving it a few shakes with your thumb over the top will make it sprightly and fresh. Of course the fly is left on the leader. This is the best way to use this dope. To put it on with a brush is not so good—you might just as well use any other mixture. For this reason a large-necked bottle is necessary. These are easily obtained from any druggist. After the fly has been dipped, it should then be whipped in the air a few times. This gets rid of the excess gasoline and starts evaporation of the balance. Then you should dap it on the water of the stream. This congeals the diluted wax film. By the time you make the cast, the liquid oil has disappeared and you have a treated fly that does not leave a film on the water. Carbon tetrachloride, ether, or benzine may be used in place of gasoline.

There are two objections to using this preparation. One is serious. In dipping the fly the oil gets on the leader and sometimes makes it brittle. However, I have never had much trouble in this respect myself, although some others have. The other is that when the temperature gets below 60° the wax congeals. To prevent this I carry it in such a way that the bottle may be slipped under the jacket at times when it is necessary. The warmth from the body then keeps it in good condition.

To make this preparation, shave the wax and put it in the bottle with the gasoline. If you feel like fussing, keep shaking the bottle to dissolve the wax; otherwise place it in the sun and let the heat do it. Don't put it on a stove.

There are, of course, many excellent fly-floating preparations on the market, and if you do not feel like making your own, you may find one that suits your particular needs among them. However, I would advise against too oily mixtures and ones that do not evaporate or harden readily. This type is not particularly satisfactory and of course does not clean your fly. Some anglers prefer using a paste grease, rubbing it on with the fingers. This is excellent on a new fly, if done carefully so that the hackles are not matted. However, when using it on a fly that has caught a fish, it is first necessary to wash and dry the fly. This not being necessary with the gas-wax combination, you can readily see where the latter can save you much time when experiencing a short but spirited rise of trout. Under such circumstances the time spent in drying out a fly may well reduce your chances from fifty to a hundred per cent or even more. By actual tests we have shown that under such circumstances an angler using the gas-wax preparation has been able to make as many as five perfect floats of the fly to one made by the fellow using paste grease. When the fish are taking fast, anything that will enable you to get your fly in floating condition most quickly is the best preparation to use. When fish are coming slowly, then it doesn't matter much if you must dress a fly occasionally to make it float; in fact doing so gives you something to occupy your time.

Since World War II the silicone floating preparations have come into rather wide favor, and they are fine except that they are also expensive. One of the newest I've tried comes nearest to being like the compound for which I have given the formula in that it dries off a bit faster than the others. One objection I have to the silicones is that it takes longer to prepare a fly with them, for they should be allowed to dry as much as an hour to be effective; and while they are supposed to last the life of the fly, you won't find this of much aid when the fish are taking fast. Unless you clean and dry the fly thoroughly, which takes time, it will not float. On the other hand, as stated, the old gasoline-and-wax formula which I started publicizing about 1929 is excellent when you want a fly cleaned, dried, and redressed in a matter of moments. Good rises are often of short duration, and to change a fly or wait too long between fish before the next cast can prove most aggravating and distressing. Ether works best in this case because it evaporates very fast. You may need a doctor's prescription to get it, but keep in mind that the most volatile liquid that will dissolve paraffin wax will definitely do the best work. A New England firm, Decto Products, had a fly dressing that met these qualifications but they have discontinued the making of sporting products as of 1951, and perhaps forever. I am mentioning it here in the hope that they will bring it back on the market some day, because it was good stuff and not costly. (This firm never advertised or produced a fancy package, which is probably the reason why their products in the fishing line had to be discontinued. And yet of all the fly-floaters and line-dressings I've ever used, theirs were tops, and discriminating anglers who used them from coast to coast so considered them.)

On the other hand some conditions call for a wait between casts. For instance, if you rise some good fish and miss them you may ruin your chances if you cast back to them too quickly. In such a case, the longer it takes to get a drowned fly back into good floating condition the better.

The dry-fly box has long been a problem. The aluminum individual spring-cover types have never been entirely satisfactory. The average compartment is too small for many flies, the metal dents quite easily, and the springs that work the covers get out of order easily. The less mechanism on articles of this type, the better I like them.

In comparatively recent years, plastic boxes have made their appearance in ever-increasing styles, shapes, and qualities. The small ones, of one compartment only, are often quite useful. If you use

TYPICAL COMPARTMENT DRY-FLY BOX

only a few patterns or sizes, you may work out a quite satisfactory method of finding the fly you want when you want it, with six or seven of these scattered in various pockets. This applies to either round or oblong boxes. Representative sizes would be three inches by two inches by three-quarter inch deep; or two and three-quarter inches in diameter by three-quarter inch deep. You may like others of slightly different specifications. Some are made in transparent green and red. These different colors may be utilized to hold flies of different sizes.

Round boxes made of celluoid, without hinged covers, and of the size given, were the first to make their appearance; and they were launched by Gene Connett, a name I'm sure is well known to the readers of *Trout*. These were naturally followed by compartment boxes made of improved materials. They are very sturdy, and yet very light in weight.

Some fishermen object to boxes with a one-piece cover, claiming that the flies blow out in a heavy wind. I've never had this trouble even when fishing in Wyoming, Idaho, Montana, or parts of the High Sierras of California, where day after day the wind blew a gale such as is seldom experienced in the East. If you do not like this type of box, there are now available magnetic fly-boxes of various sizes and construction. These run higher in price than the plain boxes and the weight is considerably greater because of the magnets. However, they do have their points, and some folks like them very much. Another type in some favor here and there is the box that hangs over the neck and on the chest. It folds back when not in use, and opens in front of you when in use. Ken Reid, at one time an angling editor and later tops in the Izaak Walton League, originated the idea many years ago.

But fly boxes are very personal. What you like, another may not like at all. Do not rush when making the original purchase. Look over different items, ask questions about them, and make your own final decision.

A line-carrier of some sort is always in order. It comes in handy for carrying extra lines and also to change your line from end to end so as to get the full use from it.

The use of two reels is also to be recommended for getting the full value from your double-tapered line. Transferring the line frequently from one reel to the other keeps both ends in use and so in good shape. Like rubber tires, fly lines deteriorate quicker without use than when being used.

The creel situation has never troubled me much since I passed the days when I wanted to bring home fish to show admiring friends. Today I keep very few fish except on occasions when someone who really enjoys eating them puts in a request for a few. For this reason I have abandoned the regulation creel, and when I carry anything at all it is the grass market-bag type—a flat grass bag that lies against the body and weighs practically nothing.

There is one objection to these carriers—they do not wear well. About the best wear you can get out of one is a single season of use. If you keep lots of fish, you won't get even that. In addition they are not readily obtainable. Some have been, and perhaps now are, made in the United States, but the original supply came from England. Just before World War II, I purchased a dozen, and now have two left, one unused, the other still capable of handling some more special fish I want to keep. I hope that I may be able to purchase a few more when I need them. If not, I'll revert to the cloth-wrapped fish or fishes in the jacket pocket. Or if I really want a mess for some appreciative people I'll use the standard creel, which is a splendid article except for its bulkiness.

FLAT GRASS CREEL

The canvas creel has its advantages. If kept wet the evaporation keeps the contents cool, and this helps to save the fish carried in it, particularly on hot days when meat spoils quickly. Under cool and dry air conditions one can get by, even if neglectful, for a considerable time. However, unless you thoroughly scour and wash such creels after each use they soon smell so badly that even an insensitive person will object, while a sensitive nose will make its owner ill. And not even a wet canvas creel will preserve fish indefinitely. For that you need ice, either natural or dry.

A number of persons I know use neither a creel nor a grass bag. They simply wrap a desirable specimen in moist cheesecloth or some other suitable material, and place it in the large pocket of their fishing jacket. When the jacket pocket is unprotected cloth, the same as the rest of the article, this has the disadvantages of the canvas creel, without the advantage of evaporation; because you surely would not wet your jacket in the stream from time to time as you would a creel, even if you knew that doing so would help keep your fish in edible condition. All in all, except for the bulk and weight, it is hard to beat the willow creel, either whole or split, if you want to keep all the fish you catch up to your limit each day. If you do use a creel, I would suggest a long, narrow, and low one, so that it will take a really nice fish without doubling it up and ruining its looks before you get it home or anywhere that you might like to display it.

The choice of a wading jacket is very personal. I'll just point out some things that make such an article of clothing an item of pleasure rather than an aggravation. There are limits to the number of pockets that you can use to advantage. I have some with so many pockets that if I put something in each one the thing bulges out like a balloon. The jacket should have enough pockets for your needs, and they should be of a size that will properly carry those items you most like to have with you; plus an extra pocket or two to take care of things you didn't think of to begin with. Before you buy such an item, make a list of the things you just know you could not be without. Then assemble them and see if you can find a jacket that will carry them all.

You really need two jackets, or perhaps I should say one jacket and a vest, because one of the two should have sleeves and the other should be sleeveless. The one with sleeves should also be shower-proof. The vest is best for clear and hot weather. If neither of these suits you, then you may get a neck-strap tackle container that is similar to the dry-fly box already mentioned.

The fishing hat is an important item. It should have a brim all around that is wide enough to shield the eyes from the sun and to protect you from the rain. I note that some advocate the use of long peaked caps. These are fine provided it doesn't rain; but nature has a great trick of pelting us with raindrops when we least expect it. These caps offer no protection against rain except to the face. On the sides and at the back, the rain simply drains freely down the neck, so that even if you are wearing a raincoat you get soaking wet, literally from the neck down. Incidentally there are water-proofing materials that will make a regular felt hat quite rainproof, and there are other hats, already waterproofed and rather snappy looking, that you may buy for a few dollars. These are more widely distributed in the South and West than they are in the North and East, at least at this writing (1952).

The raincoat should be of light weight so that it may be rolled into a small package. The place for this item is on your person. If it is in camp, at home, or in the car it won't do you any good in a sudden shower; and it may take you away from some good fishing if you are some distance from your raincoat and find that you really need it to keep on fishing. If you wear waders, a short-length raincoat will be just right. If you wear boots, it will be best to have a long coat. If you don't use either, or simply wear rubber-bottom hunting shoes, you may find that the rain-suits of nylon are very nice. These are extremely light in weight, and come as a pair of pants and a short-length coat.

Now for waders, probably the item that hurts the pocketbook as much as any equipment the angler buys. For average streams, use the type that come above the waistline. Besides these it pays one to have either a pair of hip-length wading-stockings or a pair of hip-length rubber boots soled with either felt or leather and hobnails. For extra-deep streams, such as the steelhead rivers of the west coast, it is wise to get waders that fit well up under the arms. There are some excellent waders of this type manufactured in California.

In this matter of waders I don't believe that it is any longer necessary to buy a foreign make. American manufacturers are continually improving their product, and today I would just as soon have them as any of the best made in other countries.

There are always many discussions on the relative merits of felts and hobnail shoes. Of course there is need for both. On well-scoured, hard-rock bottoms the felts are usually the best. On mud, slippery moss, and slimy rocks I believe that hobnails will give one the best service. However, most hobnails loosen in the soles as soon as the shoes have been wet and dried a few times. I've had this happen with the highest-priced shoes. The hobs should really be riveted on the soles. When having a resole job done, see that the repairman does this. But be sure that the rivets do not come in contact with the wader-foot. The best way is to have the hobs riveted on the sole before it is sewn to the welt. If the hobs are simply tacked on, replacing them is a continual and annoying performance. Screw calks are not bad for emergency work, but those I have used seem to be excessively hard and so do not hold on the rocks as well as the soft hobs.

Felts are quite satisfactory for comfort, but the felt wears down quickly, especially if you do much walking out of the stream.

One of the objections to some felt-soled shoes is the high price. During 1949 an enterprising and sympathetic Connecticut business man produced a "felt sole kit." These kits, consisting of two felt soles, sufficient cement, and instructions are definitely a boon to the wader. You may cement these soles to your slippery-bottomed boots and save yourself many a bad, and perhaps a dangerous, fall. If you have high-priced and high-quality shoes with welts and uppers in good condition but with the soles worn out, you may with this outfit make them as serviceable as they were when new. Of course care and time are needed to do a good job as the instructions advise. A kit like this has been long needed. I remember paying much more for a piece of piano felt, and then having a shoemaker cut soles from the material and sew them to the tops at a rather stiff price. Now the replacement is much simpler, and you can do it yourself if you take the time. It should also be easier for the repairman if you would prefer to have him do it.

From a fishing standpoint, I think felts are the best. One can wade softly and quietly no matter how rocky the bottom. Hobs grit against the rocks and send out vibrations that may frighten the fish or at least make them suspicious. This doesn't mean anything in fast water, but it does in other circumstances. So each style has both good points and bad. Really, one should have several pairs if his angling adventures take him to places where the streams vary considerably. If the streams you fish most are all of the same type, then get the shoe most adaptable to those conditions. The same thing applies to the types of boots.

Here is a general rule to follow. For clear, smooth, hard-rocked, plant free, or sandy streams, a soft shoe is very satisfactory. If it is a small or shallow stream where all holes can be reached without wading deep, the hip waders or hip-length rubber boot will be the best bet. If the stream is very rough, with rocks of all sizes cluttering the bottom, with crevices between them for the foot to get jammed in, with water of a dark color that dyes the rocks and hides the bottom from your view, then you need foot protection in the way of a hard reinforcement in the toe of the shoe, stiff leather all around the lower part, and reinforcement at the heel. Then just remember that mud, slime, or anything that must be penetrated in order to get a footing on the solid beneath, demands hobs for complete satisfaction, and that for any other condition, felt will no doubt give you the most comfort.

The average angler has a few streams to which he is partial and he fishes them more than any other. It is for these streams he should buy his equipment, and not for some stream that a salesman might be thinking of. I find that sometimes the salesman in the average store recommends what he or some good customer uses, rather than considering the customer's personal needs. If you happen to be fishing under the same conditions as this, everything is swell; but if, as often is the case, you fish under different conditions, what you buy may not be suitable at all. For this reason be wary of a salesman who knows just what you need without first asking you pertinent questions.

One must not overlook the service given by the outdoor magazines. They give free advice by letter whenever it is asked for. However, when writing them do not ask for too much information at one time. Having been an angling editor for some magazines since 1927 (*Outdoor Life 1934*), I have had plenty of experience in this respect. While it always gives me great pleasure to answer all the questions I am able to, I must admit that to answer some letters as they should be answered would require an exhaustive article, which of course is impossible. It would help a lot if folks would study what they read, and when asking questions confine themselves to one or two specific ones.

A fishing knife is a great comfort. I have one I wouldn't be without. It is quite small, light in weight, and yet contains a serviceable blade, a pair of scissors, a stiletto, a file, a disgorger, and a screw driver. In addition the handle is a three-inch rule and all steel parts are magnetized, a handy thing when handling small hooks. If you don't care for a knife of this type, or if you don't care about paying the price for it, you may carry a knife separately and get one of the clips, which sell for seventy-five cents. They contain a disgorger, clipper, and stiletto and are very satisfactory. As a matter of fact, tying one of them on each fishing jacket, shirt, and trousers is a very good idea. Then you will always have at least one when you need it.

A few safety pins, attached here and there on to your clothes, come in handy for many things, from picking out knots and the eyes of flies to providing a temporary line guide on a rod. They are cheap insurance against some exasperating trifles.

I almost forgot the net, and this is natural because I rarely use one. The trouble with them is that you don't need one for the average fish, and if you carry one large enough for the fish you do need it for, it is rather inconvenient, at least for me. Probably as satisfactory a net as any is the solid-wood-frame type equipped with a snap catch on the handle. This snaps on the sling ring, or you can have a ring sewed on your wading-jacket wherever it is most convenient to you. Some like a ring sewed on a loose bit of tough tape attached to the shoulder. With this arrangement you may carry the net over your back, well out of the way, and at the same time reach it easily by taking hold of the tape and pulling it to the front.

There are all sorts of nets to be had. There is one of the telescope variety, which some prefer. The handle telescopes and the net ring folds when not in use. When needed, a flip of the arm opens and snaps the net securely in place, and the telescope handle lengthens without much effort. This net is also made with the non-telescope handle.

Some persons like the elastic shoulder net. I detest it because when going through the brush it can catch hold of a bush and suddenly let go, thus socking you on the back with plenty of force.

A net is of advantage when fish are taking fast. They may be landed faster without taking extra chances on breaking fine gut. For the sake of small fish the mesh should be small. If it is too large the gills of small fish get caught in the cord and this means an injured and almost always a dead fish, even though it is put back.

Before delving into the natural float, the second requisite of successful dry-fly fishing, I wish to call your attention to the artificial fly itself. I purposely left this out of essentials because I'm not so sure that it is necessary that the fly be perfection. In other words, the crudest, most poorly tied fly in the world may take trout if it is cast and floated properly. At the same time a fly that is nicely balanced and tied with proper dry-fly hackles helps the angler because it fishes better. It alights nicely and rides upright and stays on the surface, thus imitating a live natural and not one that is drowned or spent.

Let us discuss the artificial fly, looking at the thing sensibly. To begin with, I doubt that exact imitations of naturals are essential to success. As a matter of fact I believe that it is impossible to create an artificial *duplicate* of a natural insect. No matter how cleverly we tie our flies we can never attain that ethereal lightness, delicacy, and lusciousness which is so apparent in the real thing. If we do create an exact copy, the few hackles (legs) will not float the product, especially when tied on a hook, and the hook is the one thing we must have if we expect to feel the fish for a time in addition to rising them. The hook certainly isn't an imitation of anything in nature, although it does vaguely resemble the extended body of a dragon fly or related insect when curved downward. But we don't tie most of our trout flies in imitation of dragon flies. So how can you explain away that unnatural appendage when you call your copy of a fly a close imitation?

However, we must admit that either we do fool the trout to some extent, or they look on our offerings as something different to be sampled. In this connection keep in mind that fish will pick up pieces of wood, leaves, and other items that drift down with the current, and, pertinently enough, where anglers are not allowed to fish for them they will take anything thrown on the water, including popcorn and other things you wouldn't consider being trout food. This isn't theory, it is fact.

Nevertheless there are some qualities that tend to make our manufactured flies more lifelike and consequently more productive. One is the lightness of wire of which a hook is made. There isn't any doubt that a fly tied on a light-wire hook is more advantageous to the angler than one tied on a heavy-wire hook. For one thing, the light-wire hook enables the fly-tier to use less hackle and yet have a fly that will float. Besides, if on a lightweight hook you used the amount of hackle needed to properly float a heavy hook, you would have a fly that would probably keep the hook from going under the surface of the water at all. In that case it would seem that you more nearly imitate a natural live fly than you do with a sparse tie that allows the barb and point of the hook to go under the water, where it must be seen more clearly than the feathers and body ma-

[179]

terials comprising the pattern, which are above the surface. Now just let me point out that this is theory, as the need for exact imitation is theory. Both the sparse ties and the high floaters do good execution. But I believe that you should be realistic in your thinking. Simply because you have a fly tied very sparse you should not consider it a better imitation than a fly so tied that the hook doesn't penetrate the surface. From a practical standpoint I find that sometimes a sparse tie, with the hook point and barb getting below the surface, is best. At other times I find that fairly heavy hackles and a heavy tail work far better than the lightly tied job. Finally we have the bivisible and spider types. The latter in particular is a high floater when tied on a small hook, and it will often get rises when all the other varieties fail. Note that I'm not claiming that they catch more fish. This is a distinction that you must keep in mind in regard to the different ties. But if we admit that the hook does not imitate any appendage that may be present on a natural insect, then we must also give credence to the theory that the more the hook is concealed, the more lifelike the artificial will appear.

Comparing the appearance of a light-wire-hook fly to a heavy-wire-hook fly on the water shows the following. The first alights softly in ratio to the thickness of the hackle and the tail, because the hackles offset the weight of the hook sufficiently to prevent a fast and unnatural drop. Also, when it reaches the water it floats well, with the hackle and tail both doing their job as intended. On the other hand, a heavy-wire fly, unless it is considerably overhackled, will drop like a piece of lead, hitting the water so forcefully that often the tail submerges. This brings the hook under the surface and puts the entire fly out of balance as far as it was originally supposed to float. This does not mean that a fly floating this way will not catch some fish, because it will, but certainly it does not imitate a natural as well as the light-wire-hook fly. From my personal experience I find that when it comes to catching fish under difficult conditions, the way a fly floats does make a difference and under such circumstances the light-wire hook is far superior to the heavy-wire hook. This might also account for the success of the spider and variant type flies. When tied properly they float high and lightly. However, there are two disturbing contradictions to this reasoning. They are the spider fly tied without a tail and the parachute or Gyro construction that can't float any other way except with the hook under water. Both of these flies are very effective at times. However, I find flies on which the hook is somewhat concealed when floating more consistently effective, covering all conditions. Pertinent to this hook concealment I must here mention a different idea in fly construction, a fly that up to now has not been made commercially. Marvin K. Hedge and Phil Gootenburg were jointly responsible. Having the same idea as I about the hook being the most disturbing factor of the artificial fly, they were clever enough to think of a solution. It was simple. They merely tied it in reverse—put the wings on upside down. In order to make it act right they tied on the hackle crossways and in bunches instead of winding them on in the regulation way. They named it the Visa Phledge Fly. It has possibilities. Of course it is not infallible any more than any other fly, and it also presents some complications in making, but as another aid to bring success to the long-suffering angler it should not be overlooked.

To illustrate these various remarks about flies, I had the artist make some sketches. Without explaining the reasons behind my request, I asked him to make drawings of the different flies as they actually appeared under two conditions—first, on a table as you see them when buying; second, as they appeared when looking at them floating on water with the eyes held at water level. These sketches are self-explanatory provided you study them carefully. After that use your imagination and visualize a natural fly under the same conditions, remembering that the natural fly has no hook in its body and that it rests on the water with its feet, that are only six in number. Then compare your mental pictures with these sketches. This may help you to arrive at sensible conclusions. In this connection I must call your attention to the spent flies, which are naturals that are not sitting delicately and upright on the water's surface. They are flies that for one reason or another have come under control of the water, in other words they are either drowned or are drowning, their wings are spread out flat, and they look wet and bedraggled. But even here the hook is an unnatural appendage, in fact even the finest of wires weighs far more than the fly it is supposed to imitate.

And do not overlook the fact that the fine-wire hooks needed for well-floating, sparsely-tied flies will not take too much punishment. There are limits in this respect. If very fine wire is tempered hard enough so that it won't bend under the pull of a good fish, then it is likely to break under the same pressure. If it is too soft it may straighten out on a good fish, but if it is too hard it may break on a rock. Tempers vary in hooks of the same make, but if the wire is on the heavy side it doesn't make too much difference as long as they are not too brittle. Often one one-thousandth of an inch (.001) will make a difference in the floating qualities of a fly, but will also give the angler a break as far as strength is concerned if the small fraction of an inch is on the heavier side. For dry flies, 2X fine, 1X

NAACC OFFICIAL STANDARD TABLE OF
REGULAR FLY HOOK MEASUREMENTS
WITH SIZE DESIGNATIONS, DEVIATIONS
AND PERMISSIBLE TOLERANCES

NOTE

1. The length is the over-all measurement of the shank, excluding eye. (See Diagram)

2. Sizes No. 22 to 13 increase in size by 1/32 inch for each number.

Sizes No. 12 to 3 increase in size by 1/16 inch for each number.

Size No. 2 to 5/0 increase in size by 1/8 inch for each number.

The maximum permissible tolerances, plus or minus, shall be one-half of the difference between sizes.

3. Odd number sizes, in all respects, measure midway between the even number sizes.

4. Deviations from regular sizes are indicated by X's, either long, short, stout or fine. Each X denotes a single number size either above or below the standard. Size 12–2X fine is size number 12 on a number 14 wire. Size 10–4X long is size number 10 with a length of size number 6.

FLIES ON HARD SURFACE

FLIES ON WATER

LIGHT WIRE HOOK

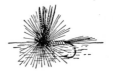

MEDIUM WIRE HOOK

VISA PHLEDGE FLY

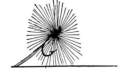

SPIDER FLY

SPIDER FLY WITHOUT TAIL

SPARSE TAIL FLY

GYRO FLY

fine, and regular or standard fine are good hooks. If the fish run large it may be best to use the standard, otherwise the 1X and 2X fine will take care of the situation.

Fly patterns probably are more discussed than any other item of tackle. The number of patterns reaches a tremendous total, and they will all catch fish at some time or other. The number of patterns we actually need remains a moot question and provides many spirited hours of debate. No matter what any individual decides is the correct assortment, there will be many others who disagree with him. This is good medicine. It keeps the subject eternally alive. Candidly I don't believe anyone can be positive about this thing. Even after individuals arrive at definite conclusions they are likely to change their opinions after further experiences bring new flies to their attention, especially when they find that someone else has made a catch at a time when their flies didn't produce. Often new patterns appear, shine like a shooting star for a short time, and then are forgotten except by a few to whom the fly has a sentimental interest. Other flies have become bywords among anglers and persist throughout the years no matter how much competition they have. No matter what other flies you may be partial to, no matter what anyone says, put plenty of faith in these non-dying patterns. Remember that they keep living and stay at the top of the heap because they fill a decided need. Just to see how these preferences to patterns work out, let us take a candid look at my own experiences and reactions along these lines.

In the beginning I used the old-type double-winged style of dry fly. My pet patterns were the Royal Coachman and the Whirling Dun. These two flies gave good results, so I clung to them through good fishing and bad. But there came a time when new flies appeared on the horizon and piqued my interest. Besides, others were catching fish with them when I couldn't take fish with my old favorites. The first different fly I tried was a Brown Bivisible. It didn't look like much, being simply a Brown Palmer tied with a white face. But the results were gratifying that first day I used it. In fact the trout liked it so well that they wore it out before I had caught all I wanted, and after that they wouldn't take anything else. At the time this sold me on the Bivisible. It certainly was a marvelous fly. Today, being somewhat skeptical from the hard knocks of experience, I wonder if the trout didn't simply stop rising about the time that particular Bivisible wore out. In the light of subsequent experiences I'm inclined to think that they did, but since at the time I had no Bivisible to continue with and the other flies did not work, the honors must go to the Bivisible. At the time I was extremely enthusiastic. I gave Bivisible flies complete and indisputable credit. I believe that I even intimated that they were the last word—the ultimate in dry flies.

True, they didn't take trout every time I went fishing. In fact they were refused time after time by rising trout. But I didn't blame this on the flies or myself. Of course not. The trout were simply selective, that was all. They were taking a fly we could not imitate, so nothing would work. I was so sold on the Bivisibles for one complete season that if the trout wouldn't take one, I figured they wouldn't take anything, and I was perfectly satisfied with this decision.

Then one day I watched a man fish a pool I had just left. As a matter of fact it was the fourth pool I had left that day without rising a fish with my Bivisibles. This fellow promptly proceeded to take a half dozen splendid specimens on a Royal Coachman Fan Wing, a fly I had previously scorned. Not only that, but he quit after this because he had his limit and was going home. And I didn't have a single fish.

Of course the Fan Wing Royal was added to my collection, and following this came the Light and Dark Cahill, the Quill Gordon, Pale Evening Dun, and many others that gradually blossomed out with fan wings instead of the ones they were originally born with. They were all swell, with the Royal being tops. I really became quite rabid on the subject of fan wings. I even fished them exclusively for two years. "Here is one fly," I stated more than once, "that is infallible. If a fan-wing fly won't take trout, then nothing else will."

I had the same sort of crush on the Spider flies. They, also, were the last word for a few months or so. But these infatuations did not last. In rapid succession I fell in love with Quill Gordon, Light Cahill, and a score of others. Once I took them on I kept them, but I also kept continually adding to my harem. At last it got so extensive that it was a burden to carry them. Every pocket was filled with boxes, and every box was jammed to the cover. When I wanted to use any particular fly I was lucky if I found it after fifteen minutes of careful searching. Obviously something had to be done about it. Many of the patterns were rarely or never used and took up room that could be used to better advantage. Most of them were unnecessary.

This led to an extremist move in the other direction. I felt that I could get along well with not more than seven patterns and that for most patterns a size 12 hook was the best size. This first list I give here.

> Blue Bivisible—12
> Badger Bivisible—12
> Brown Bivisible—12
> Royal Coachman—10 and 12
> Black Gnat—12
> Brown Spider—14 and 16

The Royal 10 was for evening fishing, and of course the Spiders were made with the small hooks and wide spread of hackle to give the buoyancy that was the charm of this type.

This assortment seemed just right when I compiled it and until I had given it a thorough workout. Then I discovered that smaller flies were a positive necessity at times and that the color range of the assortment was far from complete. The list started to grow again until it reached the proportions of that shown in my book *Just Fishing.* I used this list for some five years without change, but since then experiences steadily changed that list to another one. I'm giving you both the *Just Fishing* list and the new list side by side so that you may compare them.

While these lists show some differences, most are unimportant, being merely slight changes in the patterns and names. For instance, the Bataviakill was originally made for an Olive. In subsequent experiments we found that an Olive Brown was better than any other shade, so the Brown Olive took the place of the Bataviakill. The Bridgeville Olive is the original from which I designed the Green May as shown on the color plates. There are slight differences in the body, length of hook, and the hackle, and the name May Fly is more appropriate than Bridgeville Olive, inasmuch as either pattern is supposed to represent the *Natural Green May.*

In place of the Brown Spider I prefer the Ginger Furnace, the main difference being the black center, which seems to give an added effectiveness to the pattern. This has become a scarce item,

1932 *Just Fishing* LIST OF DRY FLIES

Fly	Size of Hooks
Badger Bivisible	8–10–12–14–16
Basherkill	10–12–14
Bataviakill	10–12–14
Black Bivisible	12– 16
Blue Cahill Spider	14
Bridgeville Olive	10–12
Brown Bivisible	8–10–12–14–16
Brown Spider	14–16
Cahill	10–12–14–16
Cahill Light	10–12–14–16
Campbell's Fancy	12–14
Hendrickson	10–12–14–16
Hendrickson Light	10–12–14–16
Hendrickson Egg Sac	12–14
Owre	12–14
Paulinskill	10–12–14
Quill Gordon	10–12–14
Queen of the Waters	12–14
Royal Coachman Fan Wing	8–10–12–14

Also an additional supplementary list without sizes.

Black Gnat Silk Body
Coachman
Gold Ribbed Hare's Ear
Grannom
Iron Blue Dun
Little Marrayatt
March Brown
Orange Fish Hawk
Pink Lady
Royal Coachman
Wickham's Fancy

1938 *Trout* LIST OF DRY FLIES

Fly	Size of Hooks
Adams	10–12–14–16–18
Badger Bivisible	12–14
Badger Furnace Spider	14–16
Black Angel	12–14–16
Blue Dun or Coty Light	16–18
Blue Fox (R.B.)	10–12–14
Blue Spider	14–16
Brown Olive	12–14
Cahill Gold Body	12–14
Cahill Light	10–12–14–16
Coty Light	12–14
Flight's Fancy	16–18
Fox (R.B.)	10–12–14
Ginger Furnace Spider	14–16
Gray Wulff	8–10
Green May Fly	8–10–12 LS.
Hendrickson Dark	12–14
Henderson Light	12–14
Honey Dun	
Multi-Color Variant	12–14
Quill Gordon	10–12–14–16
Royal Coachman Fan Wing	8–10–12–14
Royal Coachman	16–18
White Wulff	8–10
Yellow May Fly	8–10–12 LS.

so use plain brown if nothing else is available. The Blue Cahill Spider has been replaced by the Blue Spider, which has a gold tinsel instead of a gray fur body. This is merely my preference. Others prefer the fur body. The Gold Body Cahill is practically the same as the Campbell's Fancy; in the dry, the Gold Body Cahill. The Cahill—now usually referred to as the Dark Cahill—I do not consider sufficiently necessary to be included in a specific list, although it would be necessary in a general list.

The Paulinskill also changed a trifle, and because the name meant nothing in particular I changed it to Honey Dun to designate a color between ginger and cream. Whether you buy a fly tied after the original Paulinskill pattern—and called that—or buy the new pattern called Honey Dun, you will get the color intended, provided they are tied according to specifications. The name change was made merely to have it conform somewhat with the color of the fly.

The Coty flies are really offsprings of the Blue Dun and the Iron Blue Dun. Quite a number of years ago Victor Coty, who makes a specialty of taking outdoor movies, was confronted with the problem of finding a fly that would work on the still waters of the Ausable. His first idea was that something in a light blue-gray would be the ticket. At the time I happened to be a salesman in a New York City tackle shop, and we had just brought out a light Blue-Gray Bivisible. Victor tried these, but while they produced better than other flies he tried, they still lacked something. Art Defaa and Victor, both staying at Byron Blanchard's at the time, then got together and produced a light Blue-Gray Bivisible with hackles much shorter than those used in tying a regulation fly. This increased the effectiveness of the pattern, but Coty still wasn't satisfied. He felt that the bivisible idea didn't quite fit in with the picture.

After that Victor and I experimented with different shades of blue-gray, both in bodies and in hackles. The final result is shown in this book, and accurate descriptions of the materials used as well as the color plates will enable any fly-tier, professional or otherwise, to duplicate it. It is a good fly in both patterns. The only objection I have to it is the difficulty of seeing it on the water, in which respect it is as bad as the Quill Gordon. There are two shades, light and dark.

While I list the Hendricksons as well as the Cotys, I'm not so positive that you need both. The colors are different, it is true, but the general effect is similar so that if you wish to cut down on the number of patterns for your specific list, choose the one you like best and discard the other. However, I must say that I have had plenty of experiences when the Coty worked and the Hendrickson didn't, and vice versa. The Quill Gordon also comes under this general color range. One might well get along with the Blue Dun or Light Coty and the Quill Gordon, provided the quill fly is tied dark. Otherwise, either the Dark Hendrickson or the Dark Coty would become absolute necessities. I mention this because the shades of these flies vary considerably, not only when made by different makers but when bought at different times from the same makers. This is the reason I had a color photograph taken of the various hackles. They will give you a guide in selecting flies, regardless of name, so that you get an assortment of necessary color variations to meet the majority of conditions you come in contact with. Simply buy your patterns according to the shade of the hackles, and you can't go far wrong in getting a balanced assortment in the more neutral shades. In decided colors, such as scarlet and yellow, it really doesn't make much difference. The trout that will take them are susceptible to gaudy colors, and if your patterns are somewhat near the shade desired they will be all right.

The Wulff flies were designed by Lee Wulff and fill a decided need in large sizes. As the wings and tails are made of bucktail, the flies are very durable and in many cases take the place of fan-wings. I consider them necessary to the well-balanced fly box. New Wulff patterns, Black Wulff and Grizzly Wulff, have been added to my color plates because they are considered very important by fishermen in the Rockies as well as in other sections. They were designed by Dan Bailey, of Montana, and are really good medicine.

The Multi-color Variant such as I have listed was born from necessity. A. C. Barrell wrote an article about a Multi-color Variant made from a single hackle which was varicolored. His story caused such a demand for the fly that a shortage of these hackles resulted. I didn't get any of the originals, and the subject intrigued me, so I made up some Multi-colors by combining black, ginger, and white hackles. To this I added a black badger tail hackle and a pair of spent grizzly wings. It was a tremendous success—so much so that now I'd feel lost without it.

You will note a few other comparatively recent flies in the list. The Adams, Blue Fox, and Fox are all designs wherein two different colors of hackles are intermingled. This mixing of hackles is very effective. It promotes life in the fly, and light shining through the combinations gives an iridescent effect that trout seem to like. I've used all three in many states between the Atlantic and Pacific seaboards, and they've all proved consistent producers. They also serve to complete a balanced assortment, combining as they do colors that give you a pattern between blue dun and grizzly (Blue Fox), red and grizzly (Adams), and between ginger and honey (Fox). The Yellow May has been included but is not a necessity. It comes in mighty handy once in a while and gives you a fly with a yellow cast when needed, but you may get along without it.

You will note the addition of some size 18's in the new list. There isn't any doubt about the necessity of having these small sizes, only be sure that they are really the size stated and not simply the size hook requested, with hackles large enough for size 14. Not that the 16's and 18's with 14 hackles won't take fish, because they will; but in that case they aren't really a standard tie, becoming more of the variant type.

The real need for the small flies is when midges are on the water, and the smaller your 16's and 18's are tied, the more chance there is that they will be effective. These tiny flies are difficult to tie nicely, especially when hackles suitable for the size of hook are used. This may account somewhat for the oversized hackles usually found on them. When you buy small flies, insist on the right-sized hackles. Also be willing to pay more for such flies than you do for the ordinary stock variety.

Not many patterns are needed in these midge flies, and I'm not sure that you need to be particular what they are. Remember that the smaller the fly, the harder it is to see on the water. In most cases a pattern easy to see may be best for you to buy. The most effective patterns as far as I am concerned are: Royal Coachman, Ginger Quill or Light Cahill, Adams, and any black pattern. The Blue Dun is excellent but very hard to see, and sometimes a Black Gnat will work wonders.

Speaking of black flies, there is need for them, and yet they are not in general use. I'll wager that if you took a census of the flies used on a dozen streams, you would be lucky if you found one angler using a black fly. I know thousands of anglers who never use one, and I know that I neglect them time after time even though I know from experience that they often produce much better than some other patterns to which we have become attached.

When you study and compare these two lists with the next list, now published for the first time in this 1952 revision of *Trout*, I hope that you will note that I always have aimed for the same objective; that is to present a workable selection of flies that will prove effective under all dry-fly conditions from coast to coast, without being so unwieldy that it confuses rather than helps.

This edition of *Trout* also includes a new color plate of dry flies (No. 16) which will be discussed following the latest list. This plate shows some local patterns that are excellent, besides some others that should prove to be generally useful. Added to the many other patterns shown in this book, most of them designed to meet a local condition, these should be helpful to any fly tier in creating something to please his own fancy or need, or perhaps in providing him with helpful information when asked to tie some particular pattern for a friend or customer.

Here is the new 1951 list—those marked † are shown on Plate 16.

Fly	Size of Hooks
Adams	10–12–14–16–18–20
Brown Bivisible	10–12–14
Black Angel or other black pattern	12–14–16–18–20
Blue Dun or Blue Quill	12–14
Badger Bivisible	10–12–14
Cahill Light	10–12–14–16
† Firehole	10–12–14–16–18
Gray Hackle Yellow Body	10–12–14
Ginger Quill	10–12–14–16
† Gyro-Pattern (in any of your favorite patterns)	8–10–12
Gray Wulff	8–10
Honey Dun or † Honey Quill	10–12–14
Irresistible	8–10–12
Quill Gordon	10–12–14
Royal Coachman Fan Wing	8–10–12
Royal Coachman Regular Wing	10–12–14–16
SPIDER TYPES	
Andalusian or Bronze-blue	14–16
Furnace or Brown	14–16
Badger or Grizzly if Badger not available	14–16

Fly	Size of Hooks
VARIANT TYPES	
Hopkins	12–14–16
Iron Blue	12–14–16
Lavender	12–14–16
Multi-color	10–12–14–16
White Wulff	8–10–12

Occasionally one will find need for extra-large flies and May flies. For this purpose the Bivisibles, Wulffs, Irresistible, Green May, and Royal Coachman patterns are good. Size 6 will usually take care of this need: and I also like some bushy short-shank hook Spiders for such conditions. The rough-water series as described, and shown on Plate 16, are also excellent.

Notes about the Dry Flies shown on Plate 16

BUZZ FLY. Sizes 10, 12, 14.

This interesting pattern was sent me about 1942 by Mr. L. B. Young, of San Francisco. It is a worth-while addition to anyone's fly kit and has produced for me on many occasions, both in the West and in the East.

BLACK WULFF. Sizes 8, 10.

Dan Bailey, of Livingston, Montana, is the originator of the variation of Lee Wulff's original patterns, the white and the gray. About it Dan writes: "This looks like nothing under the sun to me but the trout love it. It is used more on the lower Yellowstone and Boulder than any other dry-fly pattern."

Quite without any connection the writer had previously made up a Black Wulff that was so successful on occasion that I illustrated it in another work. This is differentiated from the Bailey pattern by the initials R.B. Here is the description: wings and tail, any suitable black hair; body, creamy-color wool, as on high-grade polishing glove or shoe brush; hackle, black.

BLUE WINGED SULPHUR DUN. Sizes 14, 16, 18—2X long.

Originated by Vincent C. Marinaro and tied by Bill Bennett, both of Harrisburg, Pa. It is one of the pale yellow varieties of flies encountered in some waters.

This fly may look unbalanced due to the position of the hackle and the body construction, but it isn't. Quoting from Mr. Marinaro's letter: "The wings are cut and shaped from the webby part of a broad neck hackle, taken as close to the tip of the hackle as possible to insure flexibility. Anchor them in the center of the hook, if anything closer to the bend than to the eye. Tie in the tail, not more than four fibres, and cock them very high, then split them by making a figure eight with the thread. Attach body material and turn on as far as the wings. Attach two very short fibred hackles and turn them separately at a low angle in opposite directions in the manner of an X. In this fashion the hackles are splayed very wide, thus giving maximum support and stability. Tie off in front of the wings and wind in front of the tie with the body material to form the thorax."

This is a fussy little job to tie as described, but some of my fly-tying readers will not have too much difficulty, I am sure, with the painting on the color plate to follow as well as this description. I think it to be an outstanding development in fly construction. But keep in mind that it is to simulate only certain flies and not all types. For instance, spinners and spent flies lie flat and so should be tied spent fashion. Mr. Marinaro tells me he is working on a book concerning this and other flies. It should prove very interesting.

CARROT. Sizes 10, 12, 14.

This was sent me by Mr. E. Hille, of Williamsport, Pa., whose name is well known to fly tiers. I asked him to send something new and yet good and which had a chance of living. His remarks are so interesting and logical that I'm passing them along to the readers of *Trout*.

As to new flies, they come and go; few stay with us for any appreciable length of time. My experiences in fishing are strictly limited to Central Pennsylvania, because I much prefer the local trout problems rather than find much easier or worse fishing elsewhere. The more I fish, the more I come to the realization that I know nothing at all about trout.

However the Carrot fly I've sent has produced results outstanding enough to make me hesitate being without one at any time. Of course it has been tested out only here in Pennsylvania. Early in 1942 Albert Eschenbach, then a beginner in fly-tying, gave me a new fly. As is so often the case with beginners, their early creations tend to be most colorful, and so was this fly. As originally tied it had a natural kapok body and one each orange and green hackle mixed—no wing. On my suggestion a hackle-tip tail and a light cream dubbing body were substituted and the fly was christened the Carrot. One cannot offend the creator by throwing such an atrocity away, and so it found a place in my "desperation" box.

Perhaps the 1942 trout season was productive, in any case not once did I have to fall back on the flies in the "desperation" box. But the last day of the season was different; very hot with the water warm and very low. Not a trout was even faintly interested in the parade of dries, wets, nymphs and even streamers that I staged. The trout in the last pool, a small one about ten by twenty feet, were just as contrary as the rest. I presented them with nearly all the different flies I had in the most approved manner but never got a sign of interest.

It all suggested the "desperation" box and somehow the first fly to pop out was the Carrot. I tied it to the leader and the first three casts produced three strikes and these fish ran ten, thirteen, and fifteen inches. The last fish slightly straightened the extra-fine wire hook on the fly and in trying to bend it back it broke. Mind you, this was the only Carrot I had.

Naturally, I didn't give immediate credit to the fly, assuming that the fish had simply started feeding. So I tried the old and proven patterns again, but in two more hours of fishing the best of water didn't get even one rise.

Experiences since then seem to indicate that this fly is peculiar in being mostly productive on sunny days. It never proves much good on cloudy days and the warmer the water the better the trout seemed to like it.

But it still lies in the "desperation" box. Somehow, as good as it is when needed, I cannot get accustomed to its looks.

BI-FLY YELLOW. Sizes 6, 8, 10.

An original by Dan Bailey of Livingston, Montana. Quoting Dan:

The name refers to its use either as a dry suggesting a large stonefly or a hopper, or wet like a streamer. It is now used wet more than dry and the shape of the hair gives it a breathing action when being retrieved. When used dry it floats very well. This fly accounts for many big fish, perhaps more than any other pattern we have.

BROWN QUILL SPINNER. Sizes 10, 12, 14.

Charles Wetzel, whose *Practical Fly Fishing* deals with Eastern American entomology and flies made in imitation of these naturals, is responsible for this pattern. In writing about it "Skipper" Wetzel comments:

> This fly is best known by the green ball of eggs attached to the tip of the abdomen. It appears over the water around the end of May and at dusk may be noticed flying back and forth over the riffles. The imitation is heartily recommended when this fly is on the water as it is one of the best of quill flies.

CALLENDER QUILL. Sizes 10, 12, 14.

This pattern, named after G. S. Callender, of Dalton, Pa., was originated by Charles Costa, of Scranton. It is recommended as a good early dry fly, particularly for brook trout. It is also fairly effective for later fishing for browns. It is a northeastern Pennsylvania pattern and the originality is not completely guaranteed.

CLYDE. Sizes 10, 12, 14.

This is another pattern sent me from California by L. B. Young, of San Francisco. It is, of course, a variation of the Royal Coachman and is very effective indeed, almost anywhere you may try it. Mr. Young advises that he did not originate the fly but has forgotten just who did. I know you will like it if you give it a try.

COOPER'S HOPPER. Sizes 8, 10, 12–2X long.

Ken Cooper, Michigan fly tier of note, sent me this one just before he left for the Happy Hunting Grounds. In his letter about it he remarks:

> If you cannot use it in the new color plates my heart will not be busted. It is the best I can do.

> One summer I spent four months camping on the banks of the Au-Sable, Michigan, and built a tar-paper shack for my fly factory. This was one of those summers when hoppers were everywhere, even getting in the soup if you didn't watch out. In a glass jar, with netting over the top, I most always had a couple of hoppers. I put a few stalks of hay in the jar so they'd have something to climb on and so had an opportunity to look at them from various angles. The hopper sent you was the one job that evolved from the observations.

As this hopper has proved to be a really successful pattern I felt that it was worth showing.

DEREN'S FOX. Sizes 10, 12, 14.

Jimmie Deren, well-known proprietor of the interesting Angler's Roost in New York City, is responsible for this one. But he gave us no remarks to quote.

EMERGENT DRY NYMPH (BROWN). Sizes 10, 12, 14.

This fly, another from Ernest Hille, is an interesting item. Let me quote from his letter about it:

In this part of Pennsylvania we have in June a hatch of the sub-imago of the coffin fly which we call the gray drake. I understand this is not the correct name for this fly but who cares? The flies do not hatch in large numbers for a short period of time, but instead they come off the riffles one or two at a time for a period of a few weeks. The trout take the emerging fly readily but are very selective to imitations. We have tried nymphs, dry flies and wet flies without results. Since even the large browns are on the feed when this fly hatches, a good imitation was most desirable.

The clue came when I tried a Gold Ribbed Hare's Ear and caught a very few fish. After much experimentation a variation of the Hare's Ear finally came into existence. This fly has a very rough and heavy body of the reddish brown fur from behind a rabbit's ear and upright slate mallard wings, no hackle and no tail. While it is similar to the Hare's Ear, experiments have conclusively shown that it is much more effective. Dry-fly dope is applied to it and it is fished dry. Evidently the trout take it to be the nymph case, as represented by the rough body, with the emerging fly on it as represented by the wings. In any case, results have been most gratifying; not only will every feeding trout take it on the first float, but many trout have taken it that were not actively feeding before. Even highly educated large trout will take it to some extent and I've busted up more often than I like to recall. Jack Knight, my steady fishing companion, has found this fly as effective as I have and I am looking forward to making further experiments with other subdued colors and in a variety of sizes. I think I shall call this the Brown Dry Nymph.

NOTE: I wrote Mr. Hille about this name and have changed it to the Emergent Dry Nymph (Brown). Thus one can keep the same name for any other pattern evolving from this, adding only the color.

Before passing along to the next fly pattern I wish to quote further from Mr. Hille's letter. He is an old-timer, knows well his local
waters, and his remarks make sense.

As to any other new flies, I don't know of any worth mentioning.
The standard patterns do well enough for me. The Hendrickson and
Gordon Quill when tied with a special hackle will induce many more
fish to take than will the ordinary blue dun hackle. [This hackle is a
very dark, smoky blue and bronzy color, almost black. It is the color
this writer has always liked and which reminds me always of a heavy
snow-cloud just before precipitation begins.]
The Light Cahill I can just as well do without. To me it is hardly
worth carrying. Trout will jump over it, slap at it with their tails,
swirl at it, but rarely will they take it. A local variation of it, with
yellow floss body and straw or honey dun hackle is better but still is
not right.

NOTE: Well, inasmuch as in some Eastern waters I have had exceedingly good results with a Light Cahill for many years, you can
see how locality effects the choice of fly patterns. For instance, on
some streams and at some times I've found a very light straw colored Cahill with pure white body the best. At other times and
places a bright ginger hackle has been best. Also we find a need for
a pink-body Light Cahill. Mostly it is locality and also the season.
But the old patterns are pretty good medicine.

FIFTY DEGREES. Sizes 10, 12, 14.
Designed by Jimmie Deren to fill an in-between need in the blue-
gray pattern series.

FIREHOLE. Sizes 10, 12, 14, 16, 18, 20.
This is one of my own and was so named because I had to invent
a special pattern one year in order to take trout in the Firehole
River. It was effective there mostly in the smaller sizes. However its
mixture of black, grizzly, and cream makes it a generally useful fly
anywhere, and in all the sizes ordinarily used for trout.

GOLDEN QUAIL. Sizes 12, 14.
Don Martinez, of Los Angeles, California is an old-timer even as
I, and his imagination and knowledge of insect life and trout pro-
duce some outstanding patterns. He says of this one: "It has noth-

ing special to recommend it but good looks, but that goes for quite a few things, and people in this world are becoming more philosophical. It is usually made in 12 and 14 because the wings are not available in sizes larger than 12 and still look right."

GREIG QUILL. Sizes 10, 12, 14.
By Elizabeth Greig, who learned her trade in Scotland at the age of seven. A variation of the divided Mandarin-winged flies, nearly all of which are good fish takers.

GRIZZLY WULFF
By Dan Bailey. He wrote:

Besides the Black Wulff, the Grizzly has definitely proven itself to be most effective throughout the Rockies, as well as other places. As you know, these are tied primarily for easy floating in fast water and for durability. They are used extensively in our big rivers such as the Yellowstone, Madison, Snake, and Flathead. They were developed by trial and error rather than by attempting to copy specific insects. I developed this pattern along with the Black Wulff while camped on the Madison at Hutchins Bridge in 1936, of course based on the original Wulff patterns. The wings and tail are of bucktail from the base of the tail, or from certain parts of the body of the whitetail. The darker, straight hair, rather coarse and pulpy, but not as pulpy as most body hair, is best.

GINGER QUILL. Sizes 8, 10, 12. Gyro-pattern. (Also called PARACHUTE, UMBRELLA, RIDE-RITE and perhaps others.)

GYROFLY. Of course every trout fly fisherman must know the Ginger Quill. It is shown here simply to let you see the way a Gyrofly is tied. The hackle is wound either on a hook made expressly for the purpose, or by tying the feather around its own stem. This places the hackle directly opposite to the regulation type, that is, horizontally along the shank instead of vertically.

Years ago, while I worked as a salesman for William Mills and Son of New York City, this type of fly was first introduced to the fly fishermen of America. Because it was a patented job I've never mentioned it in any of my writings until now, but as it has recently been turning up all over the pike and it has a place in fly literature,

I wrote to Arthur Mills, Jr., of William Mills and Son, for the facts of the case. He answered as follows:

Regarding the GYROFLY matter. First I will tell you that the name (GYROFLY) was original with Dad (A. C. Mills, Sr.) and used exclusively by us.

Originally, when these flies came out, we were the sole licensees by the patentee (a man by the name of Brush who has now been dead for some time). Later on Mr. Brush licensed several other fly makers to make his patented flies (which he called Parachute—which name was used by other licensees). I understand that after Mr. Brush died his Executors wanted to sell the patent, but they wanted such a big price that neither we nor any one else could see anything in it, as the sale of the flies was never too big, anyhow.

The style is particularly useful for fast waters, and if you use the stems of two hackles and then wind the hackles around their own stems it works out perfectly. You may also use wings on them. I would suggest the ginger color, some good rusty blue, a brown, and a grizzly or badger.

H. L. HOWARD. Sizes 10, 12, 14.

Designed by Herb Howard, of New Rochelle, N. Y. It wasn't made for any particular reason but on being tried it proved to be a most effective pattern, some Michigan folks using it extensively. I named the fly a long time ago. It really should have been called Badger Sedge because that would have been descriptive and a fellow could remember it easier.

HONEY QUILL. Sizes 10, 12, 14, 16.

I don't know who really originated this but Walter Argabrite, of Ventura, California, provided the reason for showing it. He uses it very extensively in size 14 and catches many large trout with it too. I like it in all sizes. It is really an offspring of the Paulinskill (*Just Fishing* list, 1932)—later the Honey Dun (*Trout* list, 1938). Walter had used these but found that on the waters he fished the quill body worked best. Also he decided the wing was useless, and likes it best tied on a heavy-wire hook with plenty of stiff hackle.

HOPKINS VARIANT. Sizes 10, 12, 14.

This is original with me but the idea is merely a combination of the Don Martinez Dunham and the ideas of Don Hopkins in connection with that pattern. The Dunham is illustrated in another book of mine. However I prefer this new variation with its wings.

IRON BLUE VARIANT. Sizes 10, 12, 14, 16.

This is another brainchild of mine. It serves me very well on many occasions when a very dark metallic blue is needed to get results. I have used it now for many years and I'm sure that it will work for others. I usually make it with a dull red raffia body but have found that a peacock quill body with a florescent red egg sack is sometimes better.

IRRESISTIBLE. Sizes 8, 10, 12–2X long is good.

As far as I know, Joe Messinger, of Morgantown, West Virginia, was the originator of this particular combination of clipped deer hair body and deer hair wings. But I have also been told that the first trout fly patterns made with this type of body were made by Harry Darbee, of Livingston Mannor, N. Y. I'm writing this as a reporter and nothing else.

JUNGLE VARIANT. Sizes 10, 12.

Another creation of the prolific Don Martinez. He also is frank about how it happened to come into being, and believe me many other patterns just happened in the same manner. He writes:

This was first dreamed up by me to use up otherwise wasted small jungle cock feathers. It caught on and now has a fairly good following. Used mostly in the Merced and other streams in Yosemite National Park. Makes a nice fly for precision dry-fly work; casting to feeding fish in thin water. It comes down lightly and has merit.

KILLER DILLER (GRAY). Sizes 8, 10, 12.
Remarks by Don Martinez:

I'm trying to rename this "Snake River Caddis" because it is very popular in the north fork of the Snake River. It is derived from the old Trude dry flies as made by Benj. Winchell of Chicago about 1915. It is not original with me. It is great for fishing deep, rough water, being an exceedingly good floater and durable.

MEAT BALL. Sizes 10, 12, 14, 16.
Designed by Herb Howard. This might be called a Dark Coty with a meaty-looking body, except for the speckled wing. Just a

remark to show how flies evolve. Anyway it is a good pattern and sometimes does an angler a good turn if he gives it a chance. The florescent materials of the woolly type will work well with this fly. The original is made with ordinary wool.

MORRIS QUILL. Sizes 10, 12, 14.

This was new at the time the first edition of *Trout* was written. It has proved to be a splendid pattern. The idea was given me by Bob Morris, of Morrisville, Pennsylvania.

PALE EVENING DUN—FOX.

This pattern, as far as I know, sort of grew out of correspondence between Charlie Fox, of Harrisburg and New Cumberland, Pa., and the writer, over a number of years. Its usefulness is in no way confined to the Pennsylvania streams. No matter where you are, if sulphury flies hatch, this one might turn the trick.

PALE EVENING SPINNER.

Here is another by Charles Wetzel. To quote from his book:

This fly carrying a mass of yellowish eggs at the tip of her abdomen may be noticed over the water, especially near sundown. I have opened trout whose stomachs were literally gorged with this insect. On some waters it is extremely abundant and appears in great numbers on dark and cloudy days.

PASTEL YELLOW SPIDER.

This was born from a material-shortage condition. I used up all my ginger furnace saddle hackles and couldn't get any, but had some white badgers. These were dyed ginger and thus the pastel shade. Queer thing though, it works sometimes when the regular doesn't—but mostly, I believe, because it is easier to see if your eyes aren't too good. So I thought I'd include it for that reason alone.

RED QUILL.

Here is one by Art Flick, who spent three years observing Catskill Mountain May fly hatches and then wrote a book about them, *Streamside Guide to Naturals and Their Imitations.*

He writes: "This Red Quill is supposed to represent the male of the Hendrickson. It is original with me."

TROUT

Of course there are a number of different Red Quills. This particular pattern is unique, however, and is particularly adapted to the Schoharie River watershed in the Catskills.

ROUGH WATER SERIES—in blue, yellow, white, or others if you wish.

By Don Martinez. Writes Don:

These are a composite of a number of similar flies, i.e., Cligan Bass Bugs, Emidas, Irresistibles, not to mention many others. They differ from those I know in being carried to rather extreme lengths in body bulk, this to achieve more buoyancy. They are almost unsinkable when dressed and will float quite well without any dressing. They are easily seen, almost until full darkness, and help to make it possible to fish extremely rough water as in the lower Madison in Montana, Snake in Idaho and Wyoming and so forth. They do not represent anything particularly, being merely a lure, but the fish seem unaware of this lack of similarity to actual insect life. They are effective and a downright pleasure to use even under most adverse circumstances, including swift rapids and poor light. Of course they are intended only for heavy fishing where big fish may be expected. They are heavy-duty flies, should be tied on heavy hooks, and are somewhat limited in use but mighty nice to have when needed.

SMOKY MOUNTAIN FORKED TAIL.

A fly for the Great Smokies sent me by the Reverend Edwin F. Dalstrom, formerly of Knoxville, Tenn. He doesn't say that the pattern is original with him but I am assuming that it is. While made for the Smoky Mountain country it also works well elsewhere. Other good flies for that country—at least in 1948—are given in the following excerpt from his letter:

The best flies this season have been Light Ginger Bivisible, a fly I tie called a Brindle (mixed grizzly and dark brown palmer—bivisible), Adams and another I call the Parson. This is a black quill with dyed black primary duck for wings and natural smoky black hackles and tail. The body is moose hair. Then there is the Blind Parson, like the above but with yellow wings. But the Forked Tail as an evening fly is irresistible.

NOTE: Well, I wrote the good Reverend that there is already a Parson—although a wet fly. See Plate 7 for picture and page 441 for description.

WAKE.

This is another of the writer's. It is a pale lavender job, and is sometimes quite successful when you see those pale gray-looking flies flying over the stream and dapping on the water, with trout frantically jumping all over the place after them. The name is but a vague remembrance. Somewhere and at some time in the past, some old fisherman called these flies Irish wakes as we watched trout jumping at them but not at our offerings. While the details of this incident have faded, the trout, the flies and the name have persisted.

Now to take up the second essential, that was sidetracked—the natural float of your fly. If you drop an artificial, which is not attached to anything, on the surface of the water, it will follow the current naturally, exactly like a real insect. But the instant you attach this fly to your leader, you create the problem that has caused anglers to grit their teeth and curse ever since dry-fly fishing first saw the light of day. You have assembled the causes of drag, that bugbear of the dry-fly fisherman.

It is easy sailing when the water currents between you and where you have cast your fly are of the same speed. In that case your fly, leader, and that part of the line on the water all travel along at the same speed and your fly will not drag, but the instant that any one of these three strikes currents of different speed than the rest, then drag set in unless it is offset by some previous counter tactics of the angler.

It would be impossible to segregate and explain the innumerable combinations of currents your cast will contact. Like human faces, it is hard to find exact duplications. Only experience and observation can possibly teach you how to cope with the majority of drag problems that present themselves, but the following remarks may help you get started and lift you over the first rough spots of your student days.

Before doing anything else, select your casting position so that you will be in the most advantageous position for floating your fly on the currents that are equal or almost equal in speed. By doing this you immediately reduce your drag hazard to the lowest possible degree besides adding something to your fund of stream lore.

Many apparently difficult drag problems may be solved by this simple, common-sense precaution, and once you see how well the system works, you will never start fishing any bit of water until you have looked it over carefully from every angle. It seems that every angler would do this instinctively, but because I've so often watched fishermen working a pool from the side that made the job difficult when the mere process of moving to a different position would have simplified matters, I thought it best to mention it here. Often important things are missed because they are so simple that one overlooks them.

It is my belief that a rigid adherence to this rule will put more fish in your creel than being able to cast excellent curves, loops, and whatnots.

But you will run into many conditions where it is impossible to find any position from which you can float your fly over a fish without drag when using a straight line. The first thing to learn in overcoming this is the slack-line cast. I wish I could so accurately describe this that you could immediately make the cast, but I've never read any description that you could visualize without practice and I cannot do any better. I accomplish this cast in two ways, sometimes using one and sometimes the other. One way is to check a normal forward cast just before it is completed, and then immediately follow through to a completion of the forward cast movement. The other way is to make a comparatively sloppy cast, that is, lazily and without the power usually used to make a perfectly straight cast. The best thing you can do is to get out your rod and try various timings in your cast until you make your line and leader lie on the water like a snake.

Making such a cast enables your fly to float naturally until the slack in the line straightens out. Frequently when fishing small pockets it is necessary to cast only a slight bit of slack in the leader, just enough to get the foot-or-two float needed to cover the pocket. After the fly gets out of the pocket it won't hurt your chances even if it does start to drag, but in this case it is best to let the fly float as it will until it finally comes taut below you, that is, if you are fishing across stream. If fishing upstream, keep retrieving line as far as the fly floats without pulling against it and make the pick-up when you can do it with a slight flip of the rod, or in other words a few feet in front of you. To lift a fly from the water prematurely, such as the moment it starts to drag or the very second it has passed the spot you think is "hot," will often put fish down quicker than anything else—not only those fish which might be in the particular pocket you are fishing, but those below, of which you may not even be conscious. Drag is not so likely to put fish down as the rip of the water caused by a premature lift when drag, sunken line, or perhaps too much line unite to cause an unnatural disturbance over a considerable area. Many times I have watched anglers put down rising fish and absolutely ruin a pool or glide because of needless haste in lifting the fly for the next cast. If they would only let the fly float, drag or no drag, or retrieve it very slowly once it had passed the objective, the fish would probably keep rising. Besides, often a fly being brought in by a slow retrieve will cause fish to follow and strike, while a fly drifting as it will with the currents and line pulling it in all sorts of crazy ways will sometimes take a fish. Perhaps there are instances when for a moment or two it passes in a natural manner over a trout. At any rate I know that I have taken many fish on my fly after it had floated perfectly over the rising fish and was dragging badly in water below.

Fish the cast out is advice that is sound and that will help to put fish in your creel. Many, many times trout will follow your fly for six or eight feet before taking. Just because the fly has floated over what you think is the lie of the fish without being taken does not mean that the trout has positively refused it. It may be a cagey old fellow. He may wish to investigate before he takes it. Because no artificial really imitates a natural, and the light may be such that he sees the fly clearly, he may be very suspicious and follow it instead of rising recklessly. If the fly starts dragging, or even gets sucked under from the pull of the line, he is not greatly concerned. He simply refuses to take it and goes back to his feeding spot. Sometimes, *if the fly is twitched ever so slightly at the moment it starts to drag, he might become momentarily incautious enough to take a chance at it.* But if the fly is lifted from the water so that it rips the surface ever so slightly, that fish not only refuses but actually gets frightened, and your chances of getting him or any others in the immediate vicinity are gone.

Even where no drag is apparent you must be extremely careful about making a premature lift. When fishing still waters you must use excessive caution in this respect. Suppose the trout are rising in the center of such a pool, say at a point where there is a slight current. Suppose your fly floats over the spot without any trout rising to it. Should you, the moment that fly passes over the hot spot, lift it and make a new cast so that it will immediately float over them again? Decidedly not. On the contrary you should let it ride as it will for several minutes or until the line sinks, if it does so before the several minutes have elapsed.

Then you should start retrieving, but *so slowly that the fly does not make a ripple you can see at the distance of a cast even if your eyes are extraordinarily sharp.* Often a trout will take the fly before it has been retrieved even a few inches; sometimes they won't take it until it has traveled several yards; and of course there are many times when they won't take it at all.

If no strike is forthcoming as you retrieve, simply continue the slow movement until you are able to take the fly from the water with a slight flip of the wrist. In this way you may keep fishing in such a place for an indefinite period without alarming the rising fish and so put them down.

As a momentary digression from fishing, let me call your attention to the fact that all wild life is extremely susceptible to sudden and quick movement. One may often get very close to wild animals if every movement is made slowly and evenly—practically imperceptibly. With a deer standing a few feet away I have raised my arm from its normal side position to the horizontal in front of me without disturbing the animal, but the movement was made so slowly that the animal was not conscious of it. That same deer bounded away when I quickly moved the fingers of that outstretched hand a bare inch.

In the same way fish are susceptible to movement, but here you have an added susceptibility to unaccustomed forms showing against light-colored backgrounds. Just as soon as your figure comes into relief in line with the trout's vision from beneath the water, you have spoiled your chances for the time being of fooling the trout in that area. It isn't likely they will even take a natural fly until they have recovered from the uneasiness caused by your appearance. With this in mind it must be remembered that even though your body may be out of this line of vision, your rod will be in it, and the movement of casting may apprise the fish of your presence. It is therefore well to limit your casts as much as possible to reduce this hazard to a minimum. Fishing out each cast to the last degree aids in this respect as well, and gives you a better chance to get a rise. By this time you must know that I believe in keeping the fly on the water rather than in the air, and I do hope that you will take this seriously. If you do, you will be more likely to say: "I've got a good one," than "Damn! I took that fly right out of his mouth. He rose just as I picked the fly from the water."

Often when fishing up and across stream, the slack line cast will not prove sufficient to stop drag long enough to be effective. In this case one must cast a loop. I have never had much difficulty throwing the right loop. I simply hold the rod off to the right, make the backcast as usual, but instead of straightening out the line on the forward cast, I leave it incompleted while it is still curved in the air. As a matter of fact the forward cast is made with a decidedly slow motion, adjusted according to the degree of loop desired. The left loop, however, has always been a bugbear. Sometimes I can make it, but more often I can't. However, I'll explain it the way it sometimes works with me. Aiming at a spot three feet or more above the fish, I direct the fly there. As the line is about to straighten out in front I pull back a trifle, just enough to stop the fly in its forward flight. When timed right, the fly falls downstream below the curve of the leader. I find that the best curves come when I hold the rod halfway or so to horizontal when making the cast.

However, loop or curve casts don't worry me much. In my opinion they're not so important as commonly supposed and as experts are inclined to make them sound. Unless you are really an expert caster, and there are very few that are, you are likely to put down more fish with your loop than you would if making a straight cast directly to the fish. Of course one real purpose of the loop is to float the fly over a fish in advance of the leader, the idea being that the fly coming into the line of sight first, the leader being behind, the fish sees only the fly and so takes it. (Fig. 1.) This is good logic and to be recommended if the angler has such control of his cast that he can make the loop without fuss and accurately—the same as the average good angler can make a straight cast. But in all sincerity I ask: "How many anglers do any of my readers know who are able to show you a consistently *perfect* and *delicately cast* loop in actual stream work?" Need I say more?

In other words the controlled loop cast is beyond the scope of

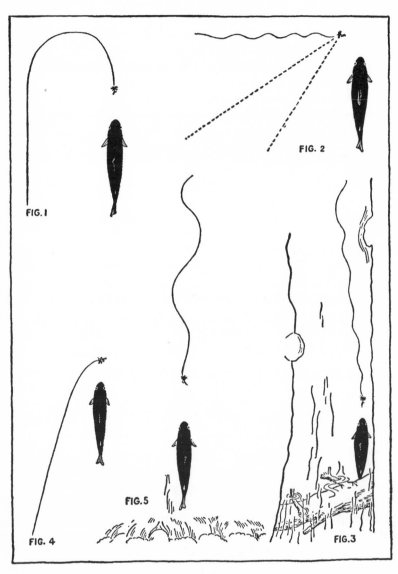

SHOWING VARIOUS CASTS

most of us. But I wouldn't feel badly about it. In most cases a cast across, or across and upstream at different angles, will do the same job as the loop, provided you cast a trifle short so that the fly alights close to but *on your side of the fish so that the leader does not go over him.* (Fig. 2.) Just as long as you can present the fly to the trout in this way without drag, it is really better than being able to cast a perfect loop because, having no slack to speak of, you are in better command of the situation when a fish does rise to your fly. Often when making a direct upstream cast it is best to cast behind a rising fish, that is, behind the disturbance you see in the water. Invariably I try this first over every rising fish I am directly below before trying other stunts to get him to rise my fly. Place the first cast so that the fly alights at least a foot behind the rise, then advance to within six inches of the rise. After that, advance no further with a straight upstream cast but follow the other methods of procedure as outlined.

It is also possible and sometimes very advantageous to fish a dry fly downstream. This calls for a slack-line cast since your fly must float, without being hindered by the leader or line, far enough to cover the section you wish to fish. (Fig. 3.) This method is particularly useful for casting to fish that are lying close to the upstream side of an obstruction. This might be a log, a mass of debris, a bank, a stand of weeds, or a rock. Many such places can't be fished satisfactorily either from the side or from below, but can be fished with slack-line cast from above. I also use the method frequently when fishing for trout rising at the very lip of the pool. (Fig. 5.) These are great places for good browns to frequent and are very difficult places to fish, but the downstream cast with a dry fly does the job better than almost any other known method. One doesn't hear so much about fishing downstream with a dry fly, but this doesn't alter the fact that the method is important.

As far as I can see, it is only on rare occasions that a real loop cast is necessary. At any rate most of us can make out very well without using it. At the same time a slight curve is often of decided advantage. (Fig. 4.) If you find yourself throwing a curve such as this, try to develop your skill. It is really good stuff and supplements admirably the cast that puts the fly on your side of the prospective quarry. However, don't worry about it if you can't make the curve consistently. If you do a good job of picking out the right place to cast from and put your fly in the best position for fooling the fish, you will have just as good a chance at a rising fish as the fellow who can throw corkscrews or write his name with the line.

So much for fundamentals. Let's go fishing and see what we can do on the stream under tough conditions without using any fancy methods—just using common sense. Here is an incident that happened in the Catskills. It was late in the season. The water was low and the fishing very poor—in fact no fish were being taken, even though rises to natural flies were in evidence every day. On our last afternoon a rise occurred on a long, rocky pool near camp. The deep water of this pool was at the far side of the stream, against a bank covered with heavy undergrowth. Our side sloped gently from shore to where the main current swept through. The background was open far enough to make any sort of a backcast possible, and altogether it was an ideal setup for the fellow who wants an easy piece of water to fish.

When we reached the place, I first took note of the position of the rises. Eighty per cent of them were on the opposite side of the current, close to the heavily wooded bank. When fishing for them from the shallow side, one had to throw across the current. Nevertheless, because it was traditionally the thing to do, four of us fished from that side. No matter what sort of loops or slack casts we threw, it netted us nothing. I saw some beautiful casts made—flies floated from two to three feet without apparent drag, right over rising fish, but they did not take them. Of course there might have been a drag that wasn't visible to our eyes—I can't be sure of that.

Anyway, at first we all thought that we didn't have the right fly, so we kept changing. I finally quit trying and started thinking instead. This is how my thoughts went: "Every single angler fishing this stretch always fishes it from the same side. Under normal conditions they take trout when casting from this side, which seems to prove that there's something wrong in low water when the fish hang so close to the bank on the other side of the current. Anyhow, trout are always more particular and fussy when the water is low. Perhaps if I fished from the other side—!"

So I waded across, directly to the overhanging bushy bank and started fishing the very water we had been vainly fishing from the opposite side. It was tough going. Here and there it was too deep for my waders and threatened to engulf me, while the branches of the trees were so low that the cast had to be made from the side and close to the water in order to avoid snagging.

With a cast barely longer than my rod I proceeded to catch trout, ten of them one after the other, and could no doubt have taken more if I had kept on fishing. However, this bit of success fired me with ambition to try places where the same conditions existed, just to see if this was simply a freak occurrence. Results seemed to prove that it was a good idea and worth adding to the book of experience. Out of five pools fished, four had traditional and easy sides to fish from. In each case it was necessary to throw either curves or slack-line casts to reach the rising fish behind the current tongue; otherwise the fly dragged so badly that no self-respecting trout would ever think of taking it. Although under normal conditions some trout usually rose on the regular casting side of this current, at this time there weren't any there. While we had made some beautiful casts across this current tongue, getting what appeared to be beautiful floats over rising fish, we hadn't caught any trout.

The opposite sides of these pools were heavily overgrown and the stream was treacherous wading, but you could make straight casts and have perfect floats of the fly. However, you had to cast so that you did not get snagged in the low-hanging branches. We didn't mind this difficulty because we caught fish readily when fishing from this position.

The one pool that was different couldn't be fished from the opposite side. Beyond the current tongue the water was too deep to wade and the bank too steep and heavily wooded to fish from. Although trout kept rising steadily under this far bank, all of our most perfect casts to them failed to bring results. In such a case a spinning outfit may solve the problem.

As far as our experiences in this particular experiment were concerned the loop and slack-line casts failed to produce, while fishing a straight, short line from a more advantageous position produced excellent results. Remember this when you come across conditions that call for fancy casting, and look for some way to fish the place with a short, straight cast. If you find it, I know you will be agreeably surprised with the results.

Much has been said about the way the line and leader should act on the water. Everyone seems to concede that the best combination is a leader that sinks and a line that floats. But it isn't always possible to make these things act as we want. Often the line sinks and the leader floats until the line carries it under, sometimes both sink at once, and at times both float.

It is true that in the sunlight a floating leader will cast a tremendous shadow. In the shade it doesn't matter whether it floats or sinks. When fishing in fast water it is often difficult to know whether the leader is floating or not, and I don't believe that it matters much but would concede that the advantage lies in having the leader float under such circumstances. Why? Because a sunken leader in fast water tends to drag the fly under the surface, and when floating, it does not cause any disturbance, owing to the many shadows thrown by the broken water itself, which effectually camouflage any disturbance your leader may make.

So let us see what happens on the stream. We come to still water. We want the leader to sink, so we rub it thoroughly with mud or some leader sink, and start fishing. Sometimes it sinks and sometimes it doesn't. Perhaps we get it sinking just right and at the same time get the line floating just right. Swell! It is ideal! Exactly what we wanted.

But the very next place we fish is quite different. The water is fast, the bottom covered with rocks that project upward close to the surface. The sinking leader pulls the fly under the surface, and we have a tough time making it float properly. We lessen the difficulty by putting on a heavy-hackled fly. This floats better, but the sinking leader catches on the tops of the rocks and pulls it under anyway. Sometimes it gets snagged between the cracks of the rocks and causes us considerable trouble.

After a time we get disgusted. We dry the leader, grease it, and start in again. Now it floats, and we have a few moments of pleasant fishing. After that we move on and perhaps come to another still water. We forget the leader is greased and have a terrible time. It doesn't sink. Then we remember that we have greased it, so now we rub it thoroughly with mud or sand to get rid of the grease so that it may sink again. We may even rub it with a wetting agent to help it sink. Some of the postwar items of this sort are excellent. However, one must keep in mind that to make the leader sink with either mud or a chemical product, it must be applied many times during a full day's fishing with a dry fly.

You have all experienced these difficulties. It is one thing to say that a leader should sink and another to qualify the statement as to what sort of water it should be sunk in or floated on. Besides, you should have the formulas for sinking or floating the leader at will. Otherwise you'll be right only when fishing the water you're fixed for. The solution? It's simple. Just fix your leader each time you change your position, or have two boxes of leaders—one fixed for floating and one for sinking—and change as needed. Is that what I do? I do not. I've been through it all, and now I do nothing but soak my leader so that it is pliable and usable. I've given up worrying whether it floats or sinks. Instead I spend the time figuring how to put the fly in any particular place to the best advantage. The leader and line may work just right. They both may act abominably. In the first case it gives me the advantage; in the second case my carefulness of approach and selection of delivery location offset the disadvantages of line and leader performance so that it isn't particularly important. Understand, I don't intend to belittle the advantage of having the line float and the leader sink. On the contrary, for certain waters the combination is ideal. But somehow I've never been able to control this sinking and floating proposition, so now I don't let it bother me too much. Instead I look for positions of vantage in relation to the location of the fish that may offset the need for such help.

However, I use both sinking and floating agents whenever conditions are such that their help makes my day more successful.

Making a line float satisfactorily is even more troublesome than making a leader sink. Most lines sink when you want them to float and perversely float when it is necessary for them to sink. (A sinking line is important only in some types of wet-fly fishing. As most anglers use the same line for both wet- and dry-fly fishing, they have plenty of trouble in this respect.)

But suppose you use one line only for dry-fly fishing. You start the day with a line that is well groomed for floating. After a few hours or less of steady fishing it begins to sink. This often happens just as the trout have started taking—after you have been getting nothing but undersized fish, or no fish at all, ever since starting. This definitely cramps your style, or to express it another way, prevents you from doing your best work and thus hurts your chances of getting fish.

Now if you stop fishing to dry and dress the line you will waste perhaps the most valuable time of the entire day, the very time when you would have your best chance to catch trout. Sometimes these opportune periods last several hours or even all day. At other times they are fleeting, lasting only a matter of minutes or at best an hour or so. And it takes anywhere from one to two hours to properly dry and dress a line after it has been sinking.

The answer is simple, though expensive as an initial outlay. It is to have duplicates of both line and reel. Carry the extra reel, with line thereon, in your pocket. Then when the line you are using becomes troublesome because of sinking, take it off and attach the alternate assembly that should be ready for use.

On the whole I prefer a nylon or hollow-silk fly line for dry-fly work. And here is a bit of sound advice. Do not use a dry-fly line for anything except dry-fly fishing. Many anglers use one fly line for all purposes, including dry-fly, wet-fly, spinner and even bait fishing, and then complain bitterly because it doesn't float when they expressly wish it to. Thus we have need for a third reel on which is a line that we use only for wet-fly, spinner and bait fishing, should we indulge in the last.

Here is what I would recommend for a well balanced set of lines:

Two double-tapers, for dry fly only—nylon.
One level or double-taper, for wet fly—silk.
One three-diameter, torpedo-head, or multiple-taper, for distance —either silk or nylon.

Remember that you can catch trout whether the line or leader sinks or floats. If you become too perturbed about the way these items of tackle "act up," you may easily let it become a big issue, and then you forget to see things that are really much more important. Years ago I worried a lot about such things. If the line and leader didn't work according to Hoyle, it spoiled my fishing. Today when something goes wrong and I begin to get a bit exasperated, I call a halt immediately. I quit fishing, compose myself somewhere overlooking good water, and observe. Usually doing this works out in the following manner. Some good fish are spotted rising in places that are hard to get at. I become so interested in the problem of reaching these fish that I forget about the jinx of sinking line and floating leader, or whatever happens to be the matter, and find myself figuring out a position from which I can make a short cast and a perfect float without alarming the rising trout. This serves to put me in a pleasantly relaxed state of mind which reacts favorably on my fishing. If I keep fretting through the entire day, I go home disgruntled and usually fishless, whereas taking time out for careful observation invariably produces some fish, if not a good catch.

So much for equipment. Perhaps a careful study of the chapter will give you some worth while ideas and help in the selection of various items.

CHAPTER VIII

Some Experiences with the Dry Fly

OFTEN Anglers ask: "What patterns and sizes of flies would you suggest for the blank country?"

One must be careful how this question is answered, even though he may know quite well a few streams in the territory concerned. So much depends on weather, time of year, fly hatches or lack of them, and also on the very streams themselves, because what may be an excellent fly on one river or brook may not be so good on another stream a few miles away. Besides, conditions change from time to time, and one can't possibly keep track of them all.

Of one thing I am positive: no one pattern or size can be used to the best advantage through the entire season at any one place. Neither does it follow that because one certain pattern and size was exceedingly successful one season, it will be as effective the following, although there are some flies that are consistently good on certain streams year after year. We can make general recommendations that serve very well, but unless you follow your own observations to the extent of using flies in conformation with your findings, it is quite likely that in many cases your success will be far from outstanding.

The real source of angling knowledge is experience. What happens to us on the stream builds up a fund of lore that is invaluable. Experiences are real. They actually happen. We live them—not only when they happen, but in memory. We apply and contrast one experience with another and so continue to grow.

So it is that interesting experiences find ready readers and by their movement teach more than plain statements of accumulated angling lore. To give you something to think about, I have in this chapter segregated a number of incidents from my experiences in which patterns and sizes had a definite bearing on the fishing. Being accurate accounts of what transpired they will be of real value. If they should help you solve some troublesome problem they will have served their purpose. After all, experiences take us away from dry technicalities, put action and romance in otherwise dull pages.

In northern New York, under the shadow of Whiteface Mountain, flows a river which has influenced the piscatorial thoughts of many Eastern anglers. Starting somewhere along the northern slope of MacIntyre, it gradually swells in volume as numerous tiny tributaries join it, and by the time it comes to an opening where the average fisherman sees it, the stream has become quite sizable. It pauses a while, after descending from the really high places, and meanders lazily through wilderness meadows, gouging out deep holes close to grassy banks where large trout like to lurk, and presents problems that tax the angler's utmost skill and ingenuity. Then it gathers together all its strength, and with a roar dashes and rages through the Wilmington Notch. It pauses momentarily here and there as obstructions or level spots slow its advance and provide ideal locations for fish, and then it tumbles wildly through the flume where once during my time a man lost his life while fishing. Finally it reaches the valley near Wilmington, where it becomes more dignified and provides some easier wading. After reaching the Wilmington bridge on the old road en route downriver, it changes into a stream of expansive riffles and large pools, with an odd stillwater pool here and there to add interest. At Hazleton it flows at excellent fishing speed, and spectacular are the rises I saw there. After a time it reaches the sand country—named, as far as I know, by Don Bell—where it again does some fancy stepping as it batters the tremendous rocks in its bed. Then comes Slant Rock Pool, where many things have happened of which some tall stories have been told.

What stream is this? You who have been these guessed it at the first. It is the west branch of the Ausable—a river rife with fishing legends, the home of numerous trout; a stream wildly fascinating, capable of giving you both a grand time and a miserable one; a stream possessing a Dr. Jekyll and Mr. Hyde temperament and a character strong enough to spread its fame from one corner of our country to the other. The Ausable commands your respect. It tests your skill and ingenuity. It is not a stream that will appeal to the timid, the weak, or the old. You like it best before you reach the age of forty. After that you wish you had youthful energy so that you could enjoy it as you did before the years of striving for existence had sapped your strength and made you a bit fearful of slippery rocks and powerful currents. But its fascination never dies—it lives forever in your consciousness. Perhaps the stories you tell of your youthful experiences there gain color and magnitude with the years. Perhaps you exaggerate when you relate some experiences of the earlier days. But this is just because you envy the youth that still can take it, and your exaggerations help you to keep a measure of self-esteem.

Fortunately, there is another branch of this splendid river—the east branch. This is of different type. It is more like the Catskill streams, being crystal clear and less tumultuous. In most sections it runs through fairly open country and is pleasant and friendly rather than compelling and somewhat terrifying. This branch suffered mightily from droughts some years back, and so did the lower part of the West River where truck-loads of dead fish were picked up. But both streams have, since then, recovered to a remarkable degree, thanks to intelligent stocking and reasonable weather conditions. Reports through 1948 from fly-fishermen indicated that the East River was producing almost as well as it did before the big drought, and that the West River had greatly improved. During 1949 some anglers had great catches in the West River, while in many instances anglers not too skillful had some periods of fair fishing. But only the dry-fly purists raved about the East River, and this was similar to the conditions of 1932–1933 when both rivers had started to show signs of deterioration. But through the intervening years the East River had gone through a very lean period, while before 1932 it had been a great producer to those who knew how to fish it. As I write this the 1950 season is in full swing. On the whole, reports from the Ausable show that the fishing is at least holding firm, if not improving. Keep in mind that weather conditions cause considerable variations in results.

Under the heavy pressure of present-day fishing, probably twenty times as great as in 1932, and I'm being conservative as of 1950, I think that the New York State conservation program has worked very well. Let me point out that back in 1932 we thought anglers were getting numerous, and yet we could fish almost anywhere on both rivers without encountering more than one or two fishermen a day. Usually we fished places where we never saw anyone except members of our own party. My estimate of the increase in anglers is based on the increase in the circulation of hunting and fishing magazines, and by this yardstick I am conservative because this circulation has grown more than twenty-five times over that of 1927.

The West River can take more punishment than the East River because it has a greater water supply. It never reaches the extremely low water-level of the other under natural conditions, and so, unless man cuts off some of the water supply as happened at Wilmington Dam during the former drought, I believe that between nature and intelligent stocking we can expect fair fishing there indefinitely. Beyond that ambiguous resumé I dare not predict. The fishing may get better, but it may also get worse. Who really knows? I know I don't, but I do know that so much water and food can supply just so many fish per average angler, and when there are too many anglers and not enough fish, then angling isn't much fun. However, when the fishing gets tough none but the true enthusiasts persist, and it is then that they may get the best fishing, provided they have the proper knowledge and skill. This doesn't necessarily mean that such anglers get limit catches, although they do more often than you might think. The thrill comes from outwitting an occasional good fish, or perhaps a few fair fish under adverse conditions. Rarely do such fishermen keep many fish even when they catch them. Their interest in the game is to get the fish to take their dry fly. Except for an occasional nice specimen so taken, they would rather return all the fish they land to the water. The sport of rising and hooking is the main objective.

When first I fished this country, both branches contained many large trout. Browns and rainbows were most common, but here and there one would find sections where brook trout were fairly plentiful although rather small compared to the other species. In these old days we had an unwritten law about the size we kept. Unless a brown weighed two pounds or more, it was returned to the water, and usually we never kept rainbows unless they weighed at least a pound and a half. With the brookies it was different. It all depended on whether we wished to eat them or not. If we did, then we'd keep a few eight- or nine-inchers, because to us they tasted better than the larger ones.

Trout of a pound or a bit more were then really quite common, and almost any sort of day produced enough fish to make a catch that under present-day standards would be raved about. It was a bad day indeed when at least two or three fish of two pounds or more did not come into camp and repose in cold grandeur in Byron Blanchard's icebox. And we all fished with dry flies too—exclusively! We disdained using such things as streamers, spinners, or bait. It wasn't necessary to do so.

As I delve into the recesses of my memory and read some of the many notes I made in those days, I find that the following flies were outstanding in performance: Brown Spider, Fan Wing Royal Coachman, Light Cahill, Whirling Dan, Badger Bivisible, Brown Bivisible, and Gray Bivisible.

Today these are still good flies for both Ausable branches, but the White Wulff, according to some anglers, seems to be giving them tough competition. I would also suggest some other good patterns which too are used by successful fishermen. Catskill is good. So is Wickham's Fancy, and if tied regular instead of palmer, as originally designed, it produces just as well—better in fact if the color of the body is the determining factor of success. The original Irresistible pattern and its offsprings are also favored. My present crush is on the variant forms in various colors and patterns, and one should not overlook the Gyro, Ride-Rite, and Parachute patterns, particularly for fast water.

I believe that I introduced the first Spiders to the Ausable, at least I have notes to the effect that I was badgered unmercifully by the fellows at By Blanchard's Adirondack Mountain House when I exhibited them and it was demonstrated that Ausable trout not only would take them, but that they also liked them better than many of the other patterns we had come to think perfect. After that it was common to hear the following conversation as a number of enthusiastic anglers looked over an especially good specimen of brown trout. "What a beauty! What did you get him on?" "Why, the Brown Spider, of course."

Let me now tell you of an August day to show an instance when both color and size were necessary to produce results. The weather was normal. The East River was low and clear, and I arose early to try my luck near camp. On the whole the fishing had been poor for some time because of an extended hot and dry period, and I had come to the decision that some before-breakfast fishing would produce results.

After due consideration I selected a stretch of water near Upper Jay—just about enough to fish carefully before breakfast. I started in below an island that divided the stream, and stood at the foot of the pool trying to decide which side to fish. One was fairly open and rocky, while the opposite side was overgrown and had a sandy bottom. Just as I had decided to fish the brushy side because I had figured it hadn't been bothered as much as the other, I spotted some fish upstream rising at the extreme left, where a smooth glide flowed glassily between large and showy rocks.

As our best flies up to this time had either been a Brown Spider or the Fan Wing Royal Coachman, with the honors going to the Spider, I started fishing with this fly.

For one hour I worked steadily over these fish. I didn't put them down, but neither did I rise one. Then I used common sense and tried something else, first a Fan Wing Royal and then, one after the other, ten patterns as far different from each other as my box could supply. Still no business. Then I happened to tie on a size 12 Badger Bivisible. Evidently it was more to the liking of the trout because it brought five rises from ten consecutive casts, but I failed to connect.

I felt I was on the right track but knew something was wrong. Perhaps the color was a bit off. Acting on this thought I changed to a Gray (Grizzly) Bivisible of the same size. This brought seven rises to ten casts, but still I hadn't felt a fish. Perhaps a change in size was needed. A size 14 Gray Bivisible was tied on the leader and this did a real good job, rising ten fish on ten consecutive casts and hooking five, an excellent percentage.

Of course I kept using this fly and by the time I had reached the upper end of the island I had hooked and released fifteen good trout and had kept two. I didn't want any more and it was time to go back, but because the entire stretch between the head of the island and the Upper Jay bridge was dotted with rising fish I kept at it. The fish still coming well, it occurred to me that it would be a good idea to try various flies to see whether the trout were now taking anything that came along or were still selective. The results proved selectivity. Nothing but Grizzly or Badger would work. A size 14 Badger Bivisible took fish just as readily as a size 14 Gray (Grizzly)

Hackle. It was a good example of selectivity, for while badger hackle differs considerably from grizzly (Plymouth Rock) some of it when wound on the hook has a definite gray cast and the Badgers I had were of this general coloration. Blue-gray, ginger, and others did not get any response. The selection of size was definite. When you got to the 14 you took trout consistently as long as the color was right. Brown, green, olive, gingers of several shades, blue-gray and the duns brought no response whatever, no matter what size was used. Unfortunately, I neglected to try flies in sizes smaller than 14's. It may be that they would have shown a better percentage of hooked fish than the 14's, especially if tied with hackles of grizzly (barred rock) or badger (silver-laced Wyandotte)—the two colors that produced in the 14's. Incidentally, I got back very late for breakfast and disrupted the planned schedules of some ten people because of that morning's fishing, but I have never regretted it, because if I had left the stream in time for breakfast, I would have missed the conclusive proof that the fish that morning wouldn't take any other flies except the two mentioned.

The success of this morning led me to try it again the next. Oddly enough, neither the Badger nor the Grizzly Bivisible worked. The only trout I took were four browns and two rainbows on a Brown Spider, and I didn't see a fish rise to a natural. Over each place where I knew trout lay I tried from six to ten patterns and sizes. I did get three rises to a Fan Wing Royal size 10, but missed them all. I'm inclined to believe that the general rise of the previous morning caused the selectivity. On this second morning there wasn't any rise at all, but individual fish here and there reacted favorably to flies that floated high on the water or were large enough to create interest.

The following season on this same stretch again I had several good days with both the grizzly and the badger flies, but ninety per cent of the catch were rainbows. This led me to think that a gray fly was best for rainbows. From the following experience it would seem that some gray in the fly is very acceptable to these fish, even though in this instance they would not take grizzly unless it was mixed with brown.

This next incident happened more than two thousand miles from the Ausable. The location was in the southeast corner of Wyoming, west of Snowy Range. We were camped on a creek named

Encampment, some miles downstream from a town of the same name. It was small water; companionable and cheery, easy wading, and plentifully populated with good-sized fish. Our host was an excellent fisherman from Colorado Springs, Glenn Jones. We had corresponded for a number of years previous to this time, about 1935, so when we decided to find out something about the Colorado country, we wrote to him for some suggestions. He responded by arranging the trip and personally conducting it. But we didn't start fishing in Colorado. He had previously been to Encampment and was so keen about it that he made it our first fishing stop, even though it was a long day's drive from the Springs.

Glenn knew this stretch of the creek very well. He had had exceptional luck in some of the pools, so naturally brought me to them first. There was one section to which he seemed very partial. It was down near an abandoned mica mine not far from a small canyon where, for some distance below, the stream was rough and turbulent.

To make this account more visual I am going to number the pools, starting with the one farthest upstream from the entrance to the canyon. We shall call this number one, and it was my favorite. It was large, with a perfect dry-fly run leading into it, and there one could always take a fish or two, no matter how unwilling the trout were in other sections of the creek. The next pool downstream, or number two, was small and situated in the center of a long and shallow flat. This pool was formed by some immense rocks that projected a number of feet above the surface of the water. It always harbored a few large trout that were hard to catch. There was deep water around the rock, but you had to wade a long way through shallows to reach it. Approach was the principal problem there, and if you took the time to wade into casting position a slow step at a time, and then waited a half hour or more before making the first cast, you usually took one fish. Pool number three was really the lower end of a shallow riffle where the formation of the bottom retarded the current and made a glide that spread out from bank to bank before concentrating into a solid volume of water that dashed down a short incline into the pool below. This pool wasn't much to brag about as far as looks go. The bottom was mostly sand, and the only cover was a few rocks at the point where the riffle above deepened and spread out into the basin.

Pool number three was Glenn's pet. He had made some really marvelous catches there. The first day we fished it he took one small rainbow. I caught nothing. The next day Glenn took two rainbows. I hooked and lost three. By this time we were both in a bad frame of mind. The trout kept rising steadily and in a business-like manner, but we couldn't seem to take them. The third day Glenn ignored the pool and went down into the canyon. Because the pool had aroused my curiosity I stopped at number three. As usual the trout were rising, but I couldn't take any. I tired of it after a while and went down to the fast water below. Here the water was too swift to see many rises, but occasionally I saw a dimple close to the opposite shore and knew that fish were working there. For an hour or more I concentrated on these fish, changing flies and sizes of flies until my patience was exhausted. Finally I tied on a size 14 Adams—why I hadn't used this fly before is inexplainable—and the first time this fly floated over one of the tiny eddies a fish was hooked.

I lost this fish. He was a good one and a hard fighter. He rushed downstream and wound the leader around a rock. He succeeded in snagging it so badly that it was a case of either wading in and taking a chance of spoiling the water for more fishing or losing most of it. I selected the latter alternative.

This incident upset me. In five minutes I hooked as many fish and lost every one of them because of faulty technique. Everything I did was wrong. I held the fish so hard that they tore out. I forgot I had a reel and played them with loose line held in the hand, which caused a break as soon as a fish made a long run, or I didn't hold them hard enough, and they wound the leader and line around the rocks. I did everything that one shouldn't do.

Fortunately the loss of the sixth fish brought me to my senses. I suddenly realized that I wasn't in any state of mind to land fish that fought like these did. So I quit and waded to shore, where I sat and considered the inconsistency of anglers in general and the dumbness of one in particular. I smoked two cigarettes until they burned my fingers, and finally I became tranquil.

This exercise of self-restraint did wonders. The first cast resulted in the landing of a seventeen-inch rainbow. The next fish was a combination of an aerial acrobat, speedboat, and submarine, but I landed him. This was because I was coldly calculating and could gauge how much strain the 3X leader would take without breaking, could calmly anticipate the moves of the fish and forestall them. After I'd taken a number of these scrappy trout the place suddenly went dead. Then I thought of number three pool, the one that had treated us so badly. Perhaps this Adams fly would also take them there.

So back I went upstream, and this time it was like taking candy from a baby. Every cast brought a rise, and at least fifty per cent of the rises meant a hooked fish, all rainbows ranging from ten inches to two and three-quarter pounds. "These grayish flies are the thing for rainbows, all right," I exulted.

Then Glenn came along. He also had a good catch, although he hadn't had nearly as many rises as I. "What did you get them on?" I asked, fully expecting him to name some gray fly. "The Royal Coachman," was the answer, and I was properly subdued. But evidently the trout in the canyon were interested in something different from these in number three. Glenn's Royal didn't produce any better than mine had when tying it earlier in the day, and he finally put on an Adams, which produced.

On a check-up after the excitement was over we figured that the Adams had taken about three times as many fish as the Royal Coachman. Whether it would have taken as many, if any, in the canyon we do not know as Glenn had not given it a trial there. He had started with a Royal, had taken his first fish on it, and had kept using it all through.

During the time that both Glenn and I were taking fish on nearly every cast, the "once in a couple of days or so" railroad train that chugged along the canyon walls came by, and the engineer, seeing us catching fish, stopped the train to let his passengers watch. We then started keeping instead of returning them to the water, and gave each passenger and employee a trout. We all got plenty of fun and satisfaction out of that particular incident.

On the whole the Adams proved most satisfactory on this Wyoming stream, appealing to the browns as well as the rainbows. Upstream from the ranch there were a couple of pools that contained mostly browns, and they were always rising any time between noon and sunset. Before using the Adams I didn't have any luck taking them, but with the Adams I always got a rise from any of the moving fish and they usually took it. As a rule a size 12 did the work, but occasionally a 14 or smaller was needed.

The following year very few rainbows were in the stream, although there seemed to be more browns than we had seen on our former visit. For the first four days we couldn't make connections with the trout on a dry fly, so we resorted to bucktails. Only one of our party stuck to the dry fly, and by so doing gave us the lead on what our trouble was. He kept changing flies, hoping to strike something that would work, and finally started taking a few fish on an Adams 14 that had been tied undersize. As I had been using a regular 14 between periods of bucktail fishing, and especially every time I came to a section where there were several trout rising, without having one response, I began to wonder if very small flies would work.

Acting on this thought I searched the duffel for a box of 18 and 20 flies I had put in for emergency but had forgotten. I found it, but it had no pattern that looked anything like an Adams. However, there were some Blue Quills, Flight's Fancys, Pale Evening Duns, and Royal Coachmans, and they were really small.

Because the Royal Coachman could be seen easiest, I tried it first, and it wasn't necessary to change. One could fish over any pool or riffle stretch with any other fly and not get an indication, then put on one of the 18 Royals and hook one fish after another. Whenever possible to see them on the water I tried the other three patterns of 18's, and they also took fish readily; but somehow I missed more rises to them than I did to the Royal.

The little fly was especially deadly when fished close to grassy banks whether you saw a trout rise there or not. It was rare sport to watch the little speck of white bounce along close to the grass and then see it suddenly disappear in a dimple so slight that you weren't even sure you saw it. A slight raise of the rod, and you were fast—usually to a good fish. This type of rise characterized all these rises to the 18 flies. To me it indicated that the trout took them surely, without suspicion, that they really imitated a natural so well that any feeding trout rose to them as long as the cast and the float were perfect. Of course 4X and 5X leaders were necessary, and this was a trial because the wind blew a veritable gale most of the time and downstream in most instances. There was only one bad feature to the use of the small hooks. The trout took the flies so deeply that it was impossible to get the hook out of most of them without injuring the gills. For this reason we didn't fish with them as much as we would have otherwise, spending the time instead trying for extra-large fish with a bucktail.

While flies as small as 18's are not needed as a general rule, conditions often make them a necessity. As a matter of fact this was the first time I had found a real need for them for at least five years.

Of course we had some troubles. When hooking large fish on very fine wire 18 and 20 hooks, we often lost them because the hook either bent out straight or broke. However, this happened only with fish of better than two pounds, or with slightly smaller fish when they got into fast, rocky stretches. On the whole we later found that regular fine wire, supported with a bit more hackle, was more satisfactory than 2X fine. This latter, however, was best for streams where the fish didn't run large or where they were partial to flies that were sparsely dressed, which demanded light wire hooks.

It so happened that after leaving the Encampment this year we had no more use for size 18 flies, but the memory of the need for them in this instance remained and I made it a point to stock up with a permanent assortment for emergency work. I have since had much reason to be thankful that I did.

For instance take an experience on the Firehole River of Yellowstone Park. We fished it first the latter part of September the following year and never saw more beautiful or accessible dry-fly water. The road paralleled it for miles. You could watch for rising fish as you drove along, and most of the current was just fast enough to provide a nice float.

It was filled with weeds dense enough to do credit to a warmwater lake. Wet-fly fishing was difficult and in many places impossible because the sunken fly was continually getting hung up. But most of the weeds were slightly under the surface, and between them ran many channels where the water flowed at medium speed and where the trout liked to lurk and feed. Also they seemed to be partial to small weed pockets in the centers of thick beds. As long as you kept your line floating or fished them with a short line, you could float your fly over the weeds without any trouble; but if you made too long a cast and the line sank the slightest, you got an infernal drag. This ruined the float of the fly, and besides some-times the line tangled up with the weeds. My first day on this stream was spent with Vint Johnson of West Yellowstone. Being comparatively new in this country at the time, Vint had been there only once, so knew very little about it. The only other information we had to go by was that gleaned from a short talk with Ranger Scotty Chapman, who knew the stream quite well. But this was sandwiched in during a party at Scotty's home, so it didn't register as well as it should have.

Vint and I didn't do very well. For at least three hours we fished with various flies in sizes 12 and 14, got perhaps a couple of dozen rises each, but never hooked a fish. Vint did prick several, but so far as I was concerned I never felt one of the rises I had.

Late that afternoon we were still struggling with the problem when some of Scotty's words of the night before penetrated the fog in my mind. "Use small flies," he had said. I started searching frantically for my emergency box of midges. It wasn't in my coat. I dashed up to the car, which was near by. It wasn't there. Nothing to do but search through the boxes I had on hand in hopes that a stray 16 or 18 could be located. I found one size 16 Adams.

As soon as I put this over the nearest rising fish I was fast—solidly. Also I took the next two fish I cast to, one of them a two-and-a-half pounder. The next fish looked considerably larger, and I struck too hard for the 4X gut and lost the fly. By this time it was four-thirty in the afternoon, and, as if arranged by schedule, the trout stopped rising; so we went back to camp.

That night we told Scotty of our experiences. He smiled as he said: "You sometimes need very small flies on the Firehole, as small as 16's and 18's would probably be better."

Fortunately I found my box of midges. They were in a duffel bag at camp.

It was two days before I again saw the Firehole. It wasn't my fault. If I'd had my way, the following morning would have found me there long before the fish even thought of rising. Vint Johnson was responsible. Disregarding my feelings, he approached my wife and sold her the idea that we should never think of leaving the Yellowstone without having seen Old Faithful, Fishing Bridge, Yel-lowstone Lake, the Canyon, and several other nationally known wonders—or whatever you call them. Just as if we couldn't come back another time to see these things, which would always be there. When trout are rising, fish for them; these are my sentiments. Old Faithful puts on a display every hour or thereabouts and never fails, but you can never tell about fish.

My wife fell for Johnson's sales talk. Even Ranger Scotty Chapman sided in with them—so what chance did I have? On the second day of this sight-seeing tour we were on our way to see Old Faithful. On the way we skirted the Firehole River. Vint was driving. This had been arranged beforehand. Both Grace and Vint mistrusted that if I did the driving we'd probably stop as soon as I saw a rising fish from the corner of my eye. This left me free to look about to my heart's content, but it didn't do me any good. Several times I nearly jumped from the car, but my hard-hearted companions wouldn't stop long enough to give me even an "eyeful."

To make matters worse Old Faithful had spouted some five minutes earlier, so we were told when we reached there. This meant a wait of some forty-five minutes before the next show. The time was posted but I've forgotten just what it was. I thought it would be a good idea to get in some fishing while waiting, but Vint said we should see other things instead. So again I was dragged hither and yon while we looked at boiling springs of various shapes, sizes, and colors and queer formations here and there.

Once in a while I got a glimpse of an enticing stream and expressed a wish to stop but it didn't do any good. It wasn't my day— it belonged to Vint and my wife. Finally we came to the Morning Glory Hole—one of Johnson's favorites. This meant that we stopped to look it over. Now I didn't mind. We had been following the course of the Firehole on the way there, and I had noted that it wasn't very far away when we stopped.

Pretending that I was enjoying the whole thing immensely, I looked into the Morning Glory Hole with the others, made a very few complimentary remarks, and while they were mentally losing themselves in the blue depths of the hole, sneaked away to take a look at the Firehole.

What I saw made my temperature rise several degrees. Grace and Vint might have been in raptures over the Morning Glory, but I was having an angler's dream of heaven. The scene had everything: reasonably shallow water, ideal flow of current, rising trout, and beautiful surroundings. A few casts distant upstream a boiling spring diffused its steam in picturesque white billows against a romantic background. As I looked a sudden snow flurry scattered a cluster of large flakes over the landscape. They sparkled gaily in the rays of a brilliant sun that momentarily peeked through the clouds. It was spectacular and thrilling but what thrilled me most was dimples in the water. No matter where I looked there were feeding trout! And me without a rod in my hand!

To go back to see Old Faithful was almost too much. I kicked over the traces and told them to go by themselves. But again they won and I meekly got in the car without having cast a single fly. "You'd never forgive yourself," said Vint dramatically, "if you left here without seeing Old Faithful." As if I couldn't see it the next time I went to Yellowstone—which I did many times.

We got back to the world's wonder about five minutes ahead of time. I figured this time should not be wasted so set up my rod. Before I got through I had the satisfaction of watching Vint doing the same. He wasn't as blasé about the fishing as he made out to be. Maybe he had planned this whole thing just to devil me.

Then Old Faithful performed, and I was glad, momentarily, that Grace and Vint had been so high-handed in their curtailment of my fishing. But even so, I was raring to leave the moment the force of the eruption had subsided—and Vint didn't do anything to hinder me this time. I suppose he felt that he had fulfilled his duty in bolstering my geographical knowledge first hand, and now figured I could play.

The trout were still rising when we got back to the Morning Glory Hole of the Firehole. This is my own name for this bit of water and is not official. Vint wanted me to have the pool to myself, so he went downstream to look things over while I stayed to see what could be done. I went down to the tail. Just as I got there the skies darkened abruptly and a thick wet snow pulled upstream on the wings of a gale. In the thick of it I saw trout rising a few feet above the lip of the tail.[1] It was an ideal setup for approach. The tail of the pool was a smooth glide that ended in a jagged natural dam about three feet high. With the gale lashing the smooth water, and my position being so much lower, I advanced within several feet of the little falls without disturbing the fish. Then I

---

[1] "Lip of the tail" means the short stretch where the water starts dropping, and it is usually smooth-topped.

knelt in the wash of the falls and could easily see the water above without being seen.

Despite Scotty's admonition about small flies and our experience of two days previous, I started fishing with a 12. I really thought the first experience had been a freak and that it was unnecessary to keep on using the midges. Some three dozen casts later I changed my mind. Although the trout kept rising to naturals, they would have nothing of my size 12 Adams, which was about the color of the naturals. The stream was covered thickly with these grayish flies, but they were so tiny that I could hardly see them.

I had tied a couple of size 16 Adams the night before, so put one on. This brought some three or four half-hearted rises but no hooked fish. So once again I brought out the box of "unseeables" that I hadn't used for more than a year. Having no Adams in this size, I tied on a Blue Dun. I couldn't see this on the water, but I think I got several rises to it because I felt one when I struck by guess. I could see the Black Gnat quite well, but nothing took it. I didn't bother trying any more of these dull patterns. I tied on the Royal Coachman, and on the very first cast I took a good trout.

Once again this old-time pattern proved its worth. I could see it better than the others, and despite the fact that the naturals on the water were gray, they took it better than those artificials which seemed to match the naturals from my point of view. It is quite likely that in this case, owing to certain light conditions, the Royal looked more natural than the others, but of course this is something I can only guess at. The fact is, I know that every rising fish I saw in the tail end of the pool took the Royal Coachman size 18, and that is conclusive proof it was O.K. for the time and the conditions no matter what the reason was.

In advancing above the tail I scared a lot of trout from the shallow water to my left, looking upstream. Immediately most of the trout for thirty feet above stopped rising; only those over at the extreme right and under the bank where the water looked extra deep kept dimpling away. Just about this time the heavy snow squalls that had been pestering us all day suddenly ceased and the sun changed drab colors into golden, pulsating life. The right bank proved very friendly. Practically every cast brought a rise, and about every third rise I hooked a good trout.

Then I came to the log jam, and above it I could see a rise that just spelled "size." It was a difficult place to fish from below, and I didn't want to get too far above for a down- or across-stream cast because other good fish were rising there. First I tried some loop casts. They seemed to fall well, but finally I got caught in the log; so I quit that. Figuring the fish was worth trying for, I cautiously worked upstream until opposite his lie, waited until he rose again, and then cast so that the fly dropped on the water about a foot above the log. It was perfect. I expected to see the trout rise and take my fly. I expected to see the fly disappear in the little hump this fish made. It disappeared all right—but under the log instead of a hump—and the trout never rose again, at least not while I was fishing this stretch of water. Fortunately my movements had not disturbed the fish in the water above, and here I was successful again. Then came an experience that was new to me. By this time I had reached within casting distance of a sizable boiling spring and could see its waters mingling with those of the stream. Close to the wrinkle caused by the meeting of the hot spring and the cold water I saw a trout rise. It was only a dimple, but from the suction I thought it a good fish. Conditions couldn't have been better for a good float of the fly. When the little Royal dropped to the water it drifted along in a lifelike manner until it reached the place where I had seen the dimple, and then it disappeared. I raised the rod and was fast to what felt like the best fish of the day. Vint came along just as the hook went home, and some minutes later I had the satisfaction of having him take my picture as I held up the seventeen-incher with white steam of the boiling spring for a background. It wasn't the best fish of the day, but it was the first time I had ever taken a trout where I could have boiled it within a few feet.

The catching of this fish seemed to be the signal for the rise to stop. Although both Vint and I fished hard for another half hour, we didn't rise another fish, nor did we see one rise. But after all it was time for this to happen, being about four-thirty on a cold afternoon.

And now I'm going to tell you why I feel that Old Faithful robbed me of some good fishing. I went back to this pool twice that season and never saw another trout. If we hadn't gone to see the geyser, I might have had a lot more to say about the Morning Glory Hole of the Firehole.

Incidentally, all through this stay in the Yellowstone the best fishing seemed to be between ten in the morning and four-thirty in the afternoon, with the last hour slower than the rest of the time. This was no doubt because of the coldness of the weather. It froze nearly every night, and as soon as the sun left the water, the air had the feel of a December day in southern New York. For me it was ideal. I've become old enough to appreciate the comforts of a warm camp early in the morning and a good dinner at a reasonable hour in the evening. But I forgive my wife and Vint. They were thinking only of me, and I must admit that I would have been embarrassed many times after getting back if I hadn't seen the things they insisted I should see. Just imagine having someone say: "So you've just come back from the Yellowstone. Wasn't Old Faithful simply gorgeous? What did you think of the Canyon compared to the Grand Canyon of the Colorado?"—and so on. Those who ask these things are never true fishermen, and they would have been horrified if I had had to say I hadn't seen them.

Since this first visit to the Yellowstone I've fished the Firehole many times. On some trips we've stayed in the vicinity for more than three weeks at a stretch and often stopped at the Glory Hole for a look. But I've never chanced to reach there when there were large trout moving and rising, although they were taking well in other parts of the river.

This same thing has happened to me in many other streams throughout the United States, and I am sure my readers will agree that, when a fishing opportunity comes up and the trout are taking freely, then one should take advantage of it and not spend time looking at scenic wonders that remain the same at all times. Even most geysers erupt at regular intervals, but the rise of good-sized trout is most uncertain. It can never be predicted accurately. Oh, you may arrive at a splendid formula and for considerable time have it live up to your expectations, but just about the time you get cocky about it you are heading straight to a fall.

All in all, during the season of the year I usually fished the Firehole, I found that small dry flies, say those running from 14 through 18 or even 20, were a necessity on many occasions. Usually the somber patterns were best.

It wasn't until my second season on the river that I found how to get the greatest sport from fishing it. You see it contains many rather flat and slow-moving stretches. Out in the current, often between heavy weed beds, trout were invariably rising, but most of them were small, ranging from keepers to fourteen inches, although at times the big fellows also rose in such places.

The first year I always noted that each time I waited along the banks of such stretches, or got into the stream in order to reach the feeding current tongue on the other side of the weeds, I invariably frightened sizable fish from the shallow water close to the bank.

One stretch in particular intrigued me, although I made out very poorly there. That first year I fished it perhaps a dozen different times and never succeeded in taking a trout better than a pound.

Let me describe this piece of water so that you will better understand the fishing that I experienced later on. Looking upstream, a slow-moving and shallow current hugged the left bank, which was mostly grassy and for the greater part treeless. Weed growth started about fifteen or twenty feet out and spread over to the edge of the main current almost in midstream. This formation held fairly constant for several hundred yards, so that there was plenty of fishing territory to play with.

Somehow my thoughts centered on that particular water all during the following winter. I couldn't think of trout without seeing the fish rising there, or the big ones wallowing out from the bank. So it was the first place I headed for when we reached Yellowstone Park the following year. Trout were rising in it, exactly as they had been on the last day I'd unsuccessfully fished it.

Starting below the good water I carefully waded up along the left-hand side of the weed bed, stopping when I got within reasonable casting distance of the lowest rising fish at the left-hand bank. Conditions seemed just right. The light was ideal, and a quartering wind came downstream at just the right angle and with just the right force to make a perfect loop without effort. Besides, the wind was strong enough to make a slight ripple on the water at the bank.

But something was wrong. Trout kept rising, but always just out of reach of the greatest distance I could cast and yet make the fly drop with perfect form. If I moved forward the few feet necessary to reach a fish it either stopped rising, or moved further up and began rising there. If I made a longer cast to reach the fish it was much worse. The trout not only stopped rising but usually got out of there in a hurry, making an exciting wake as they departed.

This finally resulted in my putting down every fish that had been rising along the bank to my left. By this time I had reached the upper limits of the feeding range along the bank, but there was still good feeding territory at my right. It extended at least another hundred feet upstream. A dozen of the actively feeding fish were within easy casting distance and were in the open water about six inches from the edge of the weeds, so I began fishing for them.

But I was disgruntled over my dismal failure and so made a poor first cast and promptly put down the half dozen fish that were working close by. This put me in an even worse state of mind, and just as surely as if I'd thrown stones at these fish they quit rising. With ire increasing every second I made a few more devastating casts, with the result that all fish within two hundred feet on all sides of me stopped feeding and the surface of the water became lifeless, without evidence of feeding fish.

I waited for a half hour and decided that I'd made a complete failure of my attempts at catching any fish that morning. It took about ten minutes to work out of the stream and walk to the car. When I got there I turned to look back. Then my eyes opened wide. Now that I had got out of the water, it looked as if every fish in it had started rising again; impudently, it seemed to me.

The ride to camp served to quiet my nerves. Before I had driven half of the twenty miles back to the village of West Yellowstone I was determined on returning to Weedy Flat, a name I'd given the place, that very afternoon. A new idea on how to outwit these fish had come to mind.

How different the reality! It was an afternoon I have always remembered, not from the success I achieved, but from the utter blankness as far as fishing was concerned. When I got back not a fish was rising. I spent several hours diligently casting over waters that I felt sure contained many sizable fish, and took exactly three trout that would at best have made only good bait.

It was two days before I got another chance to fish this water. I reached there about ten o'clock in the morning, which is about the time these trout started working. As I was setting up the rod the rise started, and by the time I got ready it was at its best.

Having what I thought was a fine idea, I selected a position near several good pockets among the weeds and also within casting distance of a choice bit of the left bank. Keep it in mind that "left" and "right" in this description are based on looking and fishing upstream, not on the correct "left" and "right" of a stream that are based on the flow of the current or directly opposite.[2]

Then I waded into the thickest of the weeds, where my legs would be hidden, and patiently waited. Of course all the fish for yards around quit rising when I did this, but after about fifteen minutes they started again. Things were working according to my calculations. The first fish to rise within range was one working in a weed pocket. He took my fly on the first chuck but the resulting fight, for it was a large fish, put all the other fish down. This necessitated another wait for action to begin again, a period of perhaps a half hour. When the next rise started the fish came up at the far side of the weeds, so I had to cast across the weed bed and drop the fly directly at the opposite edge.

The first cast was directed to the fish farthest downstream, or nearest to me. He took it and was landed. This time luck seemed to favor me. One after another I took four more, the last one weighing over three pounds. Fortunately, because these fish all fought on the right side of the weeds until tired out and then were slid over the weed tops to be released, the rest of the trout on the other side of the stream did not stop rising.

After the excitement attending the large fish had subsided I glanced to the left bank and saw several good fish dimpling there. I put the fly over the nearest one. It was, in my estimation, a perfect cast followed by a perfect float. But before the fly actually touched the water, the fish had fled for cover. I tried for the fish some four feet above this one. The same thing happened, except that this time I saw the wakes of three fish leaving the place. There were still a few more rises within casting reach above this. After I had made this third cast there were no more fish rising along the left bank. It was exasperating and challenging.

We went upstream a few miles and tried a nice stretch of fast water. I took several twelve- to fourteen-inch rainbows and one fifteen-inch brown, but all the time I kept thinking of that grass-covered bank which harbored a lot of good fish I had been unable to catch.

The fish in the fast water quit taking so we drove back to Weedy

[2] The reason I have stressed this point is that otherwise some readers would be confused. Some will be anyway, but if so it will be from reading without thought.

Flat. Trout were rising there, I believe all the fish located in the area. But now I used common sense, something I should have done at first. Instead of wading out into the stream and repeating the mistakes that had proved ruinous, I approached the bank with great caution, crawling on my hands and knees for the last twenty feet. Then on reaching the water I cautiously peeked upstream. About twenty feet above, a nice fish was rising. It was an accomplished trout. It never broke the water when taking a fly. A suction-hole appeared on the surface, making a dimple and a tiny ring, and that was all.

This trout was close to the bank and I knew that if in casting I waved the rod over the water it would immediately ruin my chances. So I moved back a foot or two and, guessing at the place where I'd seen the fish rise, made the cast over the grass. Only the end of the leader and the fly went to the water, and it had hardly got there when I saw the leader on the grass twitch. I struck, and was fast to plenty of fun in the way of a two-and-a-quarter-pound brown. I played this fish out without getting off my knees and took utmost care in landing and releasing it, not showing my person enough to be seen over the tall grass. This paid dividends, because the trout that had been rising just above this one was still on the job when I got ready to fish again.

I took three more good-sized browns before making an error and putting the rest down. But I was satisfied. I knew that from this time on I could take trout from under or close to the bank by fishing from the very bank under which they fed.

The method of fishing this bank proved most successful in many other stretches. Time after time I took splendid specimens from locations that were usually ignored, and from which most of the good fish were scattered by anglers who, having eyes only for the principal current of the water, never considered the possibilities offered near the banks.

Of course there were other problems because not all banks were similar. Often the fish located at the left bank of the stream (the bank to your right when looking upstream) which is troublesome for a right-handed fly fisherman.

Let me draw from some other experiences. Sometimes, to reach good locations, exhaustive and most painstaking stalking was required. For instance, there was a swampy left-hand bank (looking downstream) that harbored a dozen or more trout, all of them on the large side, that is from two pounds up. I never made out too well there, partly because it was the wrong side of the stream for a right-handed caster and partly because the bank was extremely wabbly and rough; deep and mucky holes were scattered all along the stretch, and many indentations where the fish fed were hidden

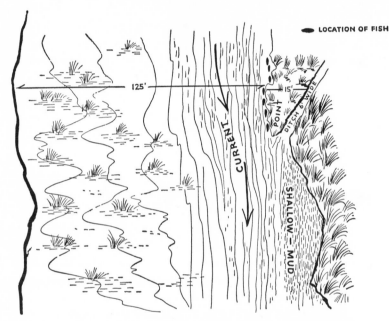

IT TOOK STALKING TO TAKE TROUT HERE. WEEDS SHOWN
TO LEFT ARE UNDER WATER.

by rank grass and other weeds. Thus, while you could see the outside of the rise ring when a fish took the natural, you could not actually present your fly at the most advantageous spot. However, I did manage to take a few bouncers, and lost perhaps the largest trout I ever hooked on a dry fly.

But let me elaborate. The bank could be reached only by wallowing through a natural ditch, full of muck, mud, and water up to my waist. Once on the other side you had to keep low down and crawl into position where it was possible to see the feeding fish. If you stood up or made excessive vibrations when crawling it frightened the fish, and once this happened they quit the place for considerable time, often not rising again for several hours.

The first time I saw this water I had worked up to the head of a favorite midstream pool and was gazing upstream, looking intently for signs of feeding fish.

The light was just right for this purpose, and for a quarter of a mile or more upstream the water was quite smooth-topped, although moving along at a rather smart rate. A number of splashes could be seen all through the stretch, but I figured them as small fish. But over to the right, along the bank I have described, I could see some rings that denoted sizable fish. This was at least three hundred feet distant, but in order to get to it I had to go back downstream some two hundred feet and then cross the river to get to the bank side. From there to the point where the lowest rises had been seen was another trudge of about six hundred feet because of the bay formed by the mouth of the natural ditch at this particular spot.

Before wading into the ditch, which looked like tough going, I decided to try a cast or two directed to the water just where it met the main stream. At the very edge of the point of land there was a trout dimpling steadily. He took the fly at the first float and dashed downstream directly to a batch of weeds. Just as he reached them he jumped and was gone. He looked to be about a two-pounder.

As no more fish were rising within sight and I now knew that I had been right in my conjecture about the fish rising here being large ones, I got into the mucky ditch; it smelled obnoxiously when my feet, tearing up the bottom, released the locked-in gases and brought them bubbling to the surface.

After considerable physical effort, I finally made the trip through the natural trench and across the extremely rough bogs to a spot where I could see the water fairly close to the edge of the bank. A little more than a rod's length below me I could see the outside of a rise ring. From its appearance I knew the fish was so located that it would be necessary to draw it out a foot or so by the proper presentation of the fly. The bank evidently had a considerable overhang and the trout was feeding underneath it. To attempt getting into a position from which I could cast under the bank was out of the question. Even if the feat could be accomplished, it would scare the fish. By this time I well knew from experience that even the tip of a rod projecting out over the bank would often drive these fish to cover in the weeds or some other place of security.

So after calculating the chances in relation to the exact distance, and allowing enough extra line to make a slack cast, I dropped the fly over the edge. It seemed to curve over the bank all right but nothing happened.

At the time I was using a size 14 Adams, and as it had hooked the fish rising at the point I thought it was just the ticket. Figuring that I hadn't allowed enough line to let the fly reach the water, I pulled off a few more feet. After this cast it seemed to me that the fly was touching the water all right so I kept on trying. I made perhaps five or six more casts with this fly. This took considerable time because in getting the fly back from the water I didn't dare pick it up as one would when fishing a more open location. If I had, the fly would have caught on the grass or perhaps the edge of the bank, in which case getting loose might have caused trouble in one way or another. So after each cast I carefully retrieved the line. Let me elaborate on this because it is very important. After I thought that the fly had been shown long enough I gently and slowly pulled it back to me. If you exercise enough restraint when doing this you will rarely get snagged, and it helps you greatly when fishing any water where you are likely to get hung up on logs, weeds, trees, grass, or whatnot. And it worked out right this time. I never did get snagged. However, neither did the trout respond to the size 14 Adams. I changed to a size 18, and a few seconds after the fly dropped over the edge I saw the outside ring of a rise. So I raised the rod, just in case. I came solid against a heavy fish.

For some reason this trout immediately started for the other side of the stream, nor could I turn him by using all the pressure I dared with a size 18, 2X fine hook and a 4X .006 leader. My rod, a seven-and-a-half-foot, three-and-three-quarter-ounce bamboo, was bent over excitingly and taking plenty as well. About eighty feet out the fish hung up in a mass of weeds and the line went slack. It was all over. The leader didn't break but the strain had proved too great for the extra-fine wire of the hook. (Let me repeat here that any wire size designation becomes of smaller calibration as the size of the hook gets smaller. In other words a size 18 2X fine hook is made of far lighter wire than a size 16 2X fine, and as the size of the hook gets larger so does the 2X fine wire get heavier. This is true of all basic make-ups, and it is based on a sensible formula.)

I didn't have any Adams patterns on stronger hooks, but I did have some Firehole patterns tied on size 18 regular fine wire hooks; about .001 heavier wire. By the time I'd found these flies I'd calmed down after the excitement of losing the big fellow; and seeing a suspicious-looking ring some twenty feet upstream I settled down to make a study of the situation.

As far as I could ascertain this fish was rising just above a rather high tussock that formed an indentation in the bank. There was only one way to fish for it, and that was to cast over the bog and trust that I'd guess right and strike at the right time, if it took. I made the try and connected. This time the trout did not get away. It weighed two and three-quarters pounds. It was a brown, as are most of the fish above the gorge, although many could be called Loch Levens if one got really technical.

Other wrinkles in the water were emanating from under the bank further upstream, but just then a strong wind started and it was too much for me. While I might have done some passable work on a different bank, or from a different angle, all I did here was to quickly put all of the rising fish down, either by slapping the stream with the leader or by getting so entangled in the grass and bogs that I had to move around a lot in getting free—which scared the fish even more than a bad cast.

Because of the rough and shaky earth, and because I am right-handed, I've never taken more than one fish at a time at this place. The closest I ever came to beating this was the first time, which I have just described. With the exception of one fish taken on a size 14 hook, all the rest were hooked and landed on sizes 16, 18, and 20.

Besides the fact that these bank-feeding fish often seem to prefer flies from size 14 to as small as they come, these small flies handle much better than large ones in the strong winds that so frequently lash this country. The reaches of the Firehole above the gorge, the water of which I write, are extremely vulnerable to these exasperating winds because of the river's meadow character. Flies of larger sizes, including the spider, variant, and fan-wing types, will also take fish there. They are particularly good in the open stretches and in water with a broken surface, but when the wind starts you will have the devil's own time in making a good cast with them because their construction and size lay them open to the full force of the wind. However, on occasion, I've found them most useful, when tied full hackled and with heavy, stiff tails, for fishing among log jams or in heavy weed and grass growths. By handling such flies gently you may easily fish waters you might otherwise find impossible because of continually snagging. Of course careless handling will get you into trouble regardless of what you use. Simply take it easy. If the wind carries the fly over a log or tough grass, draw it free with a slow and deliberate motion. Never pull it fast or jerkily, and above all, keep calm.

But it certainly seems as if the midge flies are entitled to plenty of praise. This is further borne out by some experiences in the High Sierras of California, although here the small flies suffered a setback when the Spiders showed that they too could give a good account of themselves.

We were at Arcularius Ranch on the upper reaches of the Owens River. Our cabin was in a swell spot. From the bedroom window I could see a sparkling riffle that ran directly toward the house. It was so close that its musical murmur lulled us to sleep at night. From the front of the house you could see the stream again after it curved gracefully around the two bends and then flowed away from you. In the background were some of the high peaks of the Sierras, jagged, spectacular, impressive, and inspiring except when the mists dropped low and gave one the sense of being isolated in the clouds.

At this point the stream was small but very fascinating. It was mostly narrow and bordered by grassy banks that had been undermined by the current. This made ideal resting places for good trout, and they were there if you were good enough to catch them. This condition had been the reason for a special method of fishing locally called "floating the bank." Frank Arcularius, brother of the ranch-owner, was a master at this type of fishing. It was really a form of dapping, except that the fly used was a wet one and was allowed to drift with the current as it would instead of being allowed to merely touch the surface at quick intervals as in true dapping.

I was much interested in the way Frank fished. He preferred a size 6 wet Coachman with the regular white wings clipped to short stubs. He also used a heavy leader, one capable of lifting a two-pounder from the water. When in action he stayed as far back from the bank as his rod allowed, and dangled the fly over the edge, letting the current carry it along as he followed it. It was fast fishing. One had to see that the fly was not dragged by restraint from the rod. He worked along with the current, always letting the fly seek the hidden cover under the grassy banks. To show how fast the method is, while I fished a hundred yards of stream in the regular dry-fly style, he covered a good half mile, perhaps more.

Of course this style isn't infallible, any more than others, nor is it applicable to every stream. Frank claims that even in the headwaters of the Owens if they don't strike right away, you might as well quit—or try something else. As a general rule, when they don't fall for Frank they don't for anything else, although there are exceptions as in everything else.

Watching Frank brought back memories of old days when I used to crawl up to a hole and dap a worm over the edge of the bank. The method was deadly, and I often mystified my friends because I sometimes took trout when they failed. There wasn't anything mysterious or skillful about it. The only secret lay in keeping out of sight and dropping a bait or fly as if it had fallen from the bank. It was really fundamental practice, and that is what all successful fishing is based on. We might create fancy names for different methods. We might invent fancy casts to overcome some problems, we might even make it appear that we have discovered a way to catch fish that transcends anything yet thought of; but when you really analyze all these things, you find that all they do is to arrive at fundamentals from different angles, that is getting a fly or bait to the fish so that they accept it.

The established methods of fishing on the Owens didn't completely coincide with the habits of the trout. There were glaring discrepancies between statements made and the things that actually happened. But let me tell you about it so that you may formulate your own opinion.

Everyone at the ranch when we were there, both visitors and residents, said that you had to get your fish before three in the afternoon or not at all. This didn't seem to check with the feeding habits of the trout. Every day we were there, between sunset and dark there was an excellent rise to naturals. On inquiring about this

I found it was a fairly regular occurrence but that the fish wouldn't take artificials at those hours. This suggested that we didn't fish as we should at this time of the day. Surely feeding trout can be taken if you fish for them in the right way; if you have what they want and present it as they want it.

It was also said that any dry fly larger than 16 would not produce and that flies smaller than 16 were the best. As Frank Arcularius made wonderful catches on his size 6 wet Coachman, I couldn't accept this as gospel. It didn't make sense to my way of thinking. Why should trout go wild about a really large wet fly and yet insist on the tiniest of dry flies? It wasn't logical. But let me tell you how things worked out.

As usual when visiting any new location I first spent some time watching someone do some fishing who knew the strem. In this case it was Bill Michael, of the California Institute of Technology. I find this system is a decided short cut to knowledge. It gives you a grand opportunity to line up the situation from the right perspective and also to get acquainted with any peculiarities of the stream.

Bill knew how to handle his dry flies and did a good job. Although fishing was exceedingly poor he managed to make a fair showing. There wasn't any doubt that the small dry flies were most productive. Occasionally I'd try a large fly over some particularly good-looking spot without getting any response, while Bill would at least get a rise in the same location and sometimes take a fish.

The fishing was poor. I saw at least a hundred trout rise but I took only two, and these I caught on a bucktail, size 8 long shank. Finally I had become discouraged over the indifference of the fish to my size 16 and 18 dry flies and had resorted to bucktails at the last moment. When I got these two fish I was sorry I hadn't tried them before. The entire day had been poor. Even Frank Arcularius reported the fish inactive, and the net catch of all concerned wasn't anything to brag about.

A short distance above our cabin the stream was dammed. Above the dam was a fairly large still water, with current so slow that you'd think it wasn't moving except for the drifting bubbles and the slight disturbance caused by the current when contacting banks and other projecting objects.

The following evening Bill decided to stay with me to try out this stretch. At least two hundred trout were rising within sight of us as we started out. I selected the lower pool, and Bill took the upper. While I fished, Lafe Brown, of Santa Paula, and Frank Arcularius stood by watching me. A few hours previously Lafe had experienced some really good luck there. I worked the stretch for all I was worth, and Bill Michael did the same on the stretch above, but we never got a fish worth keeping. I did get a few splashes that looked like good fish, but I have since wondered if they weren't really caused by trout that happened to rise to a natural floating close to my artificial. At least I must confess that I never felt a tug on any of these occasions, although I tried to set the hook.

The watchers didn't seem the least bit surprised over my poor luck, nor did they disparage my fishing technique. I became discouraged after a time and turned around to see Lafe Brown and Frank both smiling at me. "It's always that way here with the evening fishing," said Lafe soothingly. "If you can fish your fly so that it appears to flutter on the water, then you have a chance. Otherwise you can't do anything."

His remark gave me an idea. True to the traditions of the country, I had been using very small flies. Perhaps experts can flutter an 18 fly over the surface of the water, but I can't. But I can sometimes flutter a Spider or a well-tied Variant, and besides, the very construction of a Spider makes it look as though it were fluttering when being carried along by the current.

When Lafe saw me putting on a fly with a hackle spread of more than an inch, he looked at me dubiously. But his expression changed when I got four solid strikes in rapid succession. These strikes I missed, because by this time I was a bit upset and excited. I felt each one of these fish, but struck them all too fast and took the fly away from them. But I didn't mind much. Lafe Brown's remark—"I think you've got something there. Gad, but I think you're even a worse nut than I am"—more than compensated me for my failure.

The next evening I tried again, starting with the Ginger Furnace Spider I had been using the previous day. I took several trout with it, but had so many refusals that I knew it wasn't right. Then I tried some other patterns—Blue Gray, Grizzly, Honey, and Dark Brown. These were even worse than the Ginger Furnace. I didn't have much hope left when I put the last untried pattern on my leader. It was a Badger Variant, with peacock body. But the first cast changed all that. A trout took it on the first try. It seemed to be the complete answer for the time. Subsequent experiences also proved the fly excellent for evening fishing. The credit belongs to Lafe Brown. His remark about the fluttering fly had been the tip-off. Past experiences of my own with a spider fly had supplied the necessary connecting link that brought success.

Later experiments proved that a light honey or cream-colored Badger was better than the white. Incidentally this cream color, between ginger and white, became a killing pattern in a size 14, 16, and 12 (in order named) further down the river. Walter Argabrite, of California, considers size 14, with no wings and with a quill body, a top-notch taker of large trout. Because of the heavy fish hooked he always prefers these on rather stout hooks, and tied bushy so that they will float despite the heavy hook. This color in small flies is also very effective in central Pennsylvania waters. Sometimes it is used with a pale-green body, sometimes with a paper-match-stick yellow body.

These spider-type flies are simple but remarkable creations. Fluffy and ethereal, they fairly dance over the surface of the water. Time after time they have brought me success, when nothing else would. Consider the following experience, which took place on the North Branch of the Callicoon Creek in New York. It was during that period when I first became acquainted with the effectiveness of the Spiders, as far as I know at the very time when they first made their appearance as dry flies.

These early experiences on the North Branch were really wonderful. You could look into any hole, when the light was right, and see large numbers of trout. By actual count, one long and shallow pool near where we camped contained fifty, mostly rainbows, ranging in size from eight to twenty-two inches. I'm sure about the largest because I caught it. But they may have run larger.

The first day I fished the stream was unforgettable. At first sight I was unfavorably impressed. It was small and in some places unattractive. I had been told that the best fishing was right in the village of North Branch, so I went to that section.

The first thing I saw was a drowned White Leghorn chicken lying in a shallow riffle. It made me squirm a bit, but it was nothing to what I saw when I looked upstream. I saw three more White Leghorns above and two below. Because the first chicken lay near a good-looking pocket, I cast the fly there. No one was ever more surprised when the fly suddenly disappeared and I felt the tug of a really good fish, which presently made a spectacular jump and showed himself to be a rainbow of generous proportions. This fish balanced the scales at two and a quarter pounds. The resulting day's fishing was something to give any angler dreams for years to come. I can still see the flash of the rainbows as they rose quickly and dashed wildly away with the fly. I still thrill to the shadowy rise of the golden-colored brown trout as with self-satisfied assurance they sucked in the lure.

For three years the fishing on the North Branch was like that. Everyone you saw had a creelful, and although I never actually saw it myself, it was common gossip that many fellows took two or more limits a day. It could have been accomplished easily enough. The trout were there, they could be caught, and I never saw a game warden at the times I fished it. I do know that the toll was greater than the stream could stand. Gradually the fishing became poorer, and even now it seems as though the fishing had never recovered. Why? I'm not sure. Some say it doesn't get stocked enough; others say the fish are taken out as fast as they're put in. Personally I believe the trouble is more basic—a matter perhaps of less food supply owing to heavy spring freshets and the extremely low waters of late summer, plus overfishing.

It was about this time that I became really interested in the Brown Spider as a fly for interesting wary and much-fished-over fish. The North Branch had been very discouraging the last two times I had been there, and I thought it might be a good idea to try this high-floating Spider even though other patterns had formerly been so good on the stream.

However, I fished a half day before trying the Spider. Somehow I couldn't bring myself to forsake the flies I had used with such success previously. But a half day of inaction except for casting is enough to make you do anything. At the time I had reached the narrow stretch between the village and the next bridge crossing the main stream. I was just about to call it quits and go elsewhere when I thought of the Brown Spiders I had brought along to try but had neglected.

At this point the stream is brushy as well as narrow, but there are a few mighty swell holes that had always produced some good fish. Because the fishing was so low I skipped the lower end of the stretch and went directly to the first big hole, which was formed by shale rock. The last two times I had fished it I hadn't got a rise, but I felt sure there were still some fish left.

So the size 16 Brown Spider was cast tentatively on the lower end of the pool, where the water ran smooth-topped but quite swiftly. It hadn't floated two feet when a trout took it, rising leisurely and yet quickly and hooking himself against the rod as he went back to bottom with what he thought was a luscious bit of food.

The tough fishing suddenly became incredibly easy. Every trout in every pocket hole, pool, and riffle seemed to be waiting for the few wisps of brown hackle tied on a small hook. Action continued until dark.

But as I used this Spider on subsequent fishing trips I found out things about it that weren't so complimentary as this first account. Not always did the trout take it with such avidity. Often they jumped over it, splashed it, looked it over, and refused it— did everything but actually take it—until one became so exasperated that it would have been a relief to throw one's entire outfit at them.

For some time I wavered between discarding the fly and using it, but after stifling impulses and letting calm unprejudiced judgment settle the question, I decided that the good features of the fly far outweighed the bad. I found that even the exasperating features had meritorious effects. As an illustration consider the following experience.

The location? A stream in eastern Pennsylvania. The water was low and clear, with very few natural flies in evidence. For five hours the trout teased me almost beyond endurance. The only fly that could bring them to the surface was the Spider, but they wouldn't take it—they simply splashed at it, jumped over it, or bulged to it. Not once did they take it. A sudden notion supplied the key to success. It came after fifteen rises to the Spider in one pool had resulted in a positive rout. "Perhaps some juicy-looking fly would work right now," I thought. "Believe I'll try one of those large Bridgeville Olives."

No idea ever produced more immediate concrete results. The next fifteen casts brought six trout to net—trout anyone would have been proud to catch. Was the Bridgeville Olive entitled to all the credit? Or did the Spider deserve some recognition? In the light of subsequent experiments I am inclined to give the greatest credit to the Spider because it was the medium that aroused the trout from their lethargy. Exhaustive experiments under such conditions seemed to show that the fish first needed something to get them interested and then something that appealed to their appetite. The Spider seemed to have the power to arouse interest. After that, one could never tell what pattern would turn the trick. It might be the Spider itself, and often it was, but in such cases the completed cycle was of short duration. Usually a large and spectacular fly was needed. Any of the fan-wings were good, with the Royal Coachman and the Light Cahill usually taking the honors. Spiders and Variants of different coloration than the one used to create interest also served well as a follow-up fly. For instance, on many occasions I succeeded in getting the trout to start moving with the Brown Spider and then took them with the Badger Spider. There is no absolute rule covering this, nor was there a really logical reason for it, as would be the case if it always happened under identical conditions. But the big thing is that it worked whether it was sensible or not, and ever since I have found that it is a good method to try when the fish are not rising to any particular hatch. Putting your faith in a Spider when in doubt is good advice.

Here is definite proof that color and size have a bearing on success. The location was a northern New York stream. Brown, badger, and other colors brought no response, but light ginger was always productive—although it must be admitted that this was so only during the middle of the day. After exhaustive tests we also found that size 12 was most consistently successful. Between the period of the day when the sun first made its presence felt by the human body, and the first long shadows of afternoon started to appear, a light Cahill size 12 was by far the best bet; but before the sun touched the water in the morning and after it had left it at night a Fan Wing Royal Coachman or Dark Cahill size 10 produced most consistent results.

Why this was so is a mystery to me. The fly hatches during the period of this test were of blue-gray cast, relieved by an occasional hatch of straw-colored gingers. Of course it may be that the trout were partial to the light-ginger naturals and would take them at any time in preference to the blue-gray, but what about the evening fishing, when they preferred brown—and why should they take the Fan Wing Royal Coachman and the Dark Cahill with equal avidity? It is such things that put your brain in a turmoil of conflicting ideas. No matter what you figure is the right answer, it doesn't take much thought to pull it to pieces and prove that your carefully prepared thesis is as full of holes as a piece of chicken wire. Only the fundamentals stand the acid test.

Here is another instance where color certainly had plenty to do with getting the fish. I can't vouch for the size being a contributing factor, because we had only the one size in the fly that produced results.

This experience took place on the Neversink River at Oakland, New York. When we got there a green May fly hatch was in progress, and although we tried all sorts of patterns, including all the colors of natural fowl and some dyed, we couldn't take a trout until we put on a fly made with mottled, light-green wings, light blue-gray hackles, and a succulent-looking whitish-colored body.

On the same stretch seven days later we had a similar experience with a hatch of bluish-gray flies. In this instance two flies produced, and they were quite different in appearance from our standpoint—the Badger Bivisible and the Light Hendrickson. However, the Light Hendrickson proved most consistent, taking three fish to every one taken by the Badger. This was logical and consistent, as the fly on the water resembled the Hendrickson and not the Bivisible. Therefore it should have been better.

As I look over my notes I find many instances of this sort, but usually this selectiveness has occurred under specific conditions—such as during a large hatch of flies at any time of, or on any sort of, day, at any time the skies were clouded, or in the early morning and evening whether the natural fly hatch was large or not. Under other conditions it didn't seem to matter much what color or size of fly you used as long as it was presented properly.

However, on massing together a lot of similar experiences and comparing the flies used it seems to show that generally a brown fly of some sort is best on a bright, sunny day, and a blue-gray or gray fly is best on a dark day.

It was while I was considering these things that John Hillhouse and I had much correspondence about sunlight and its effect on the trout. John was one of the best fishermen I've ever known. The sum total of our findings in this respect is herewith given.

A rule of physics determines that when white, gray, or black is shown against a colored background, it appears to have a color complementary to the color of the ground it is shown against. On actual tests it was shown that brown was less changed than gray against a blue sky and therefore could be seen more plainly and as the color it really was. Gray was quite likely to lose its identity when shown against a bright, clear sky, and thus it may be that it wasn't so easily seen by the trout under these conditions.

On the other hand a gray fly is not complementary to gray sky at all. Therefore a gray fly does not change color in use, and so it can be readily seen on a gray day. This makes it a good fly for dark days or in the morning or evening if the trout will take gray and are not partial to some special hatch of another color.

Of course we might contend that natural flies are subject to the same changes because of color contrasts, but if you will consider the thing carefully you will readily see that they are not so much so if under certain conditions they are subject to the law at all.

The reason? Well, first of all natural flies vary from almost transparent to semi-opaque. When a body held between the eye and the sun transmits light without change, it is transparent—it is colorless. If the body is only translucent, it appears as white; or if it is of the right consistency, it will show tints of yellow, red, or whatever pigment is intermingled with the body substance. Unless it is transparent or translucent, a body is opaque—light does not show through it—and between a fish and the sun it will appear as purple or black. The artificial fly is practically opaque. Therefore when seen against the light it is nothing but a shadow. For this reason it is a question whether an artificial fly and a natural fly, lying side by side in your hand and appearing duplicates to you, are anything like duplicates to the trout. The fish sees the flies against the light; you see them against a non-luminous background. For this reason alone the matching of your flies means far less than your eyes tell you.

But there is another reason. Most natural flies have what may be called a glazed surface. This acts as a reflector. Your artificial fly does not have this surface and so is not a reflector. Of course we gain a fair effect by using glossy, stiff hackles and gold or silver bodies, but these materials do not have the life present in the make-up of the natural. I do believe that fur gives off a certain luminosity when seen against the light, and because of this I use it in my own flies considerably; but aside from the fact that they take fish like any other artificial, I have no proof that fur is better than wool or any other substances of which fly bodies are made.

In this connection the fluorescent fly-tying materials are of interest, but they are new, so that my experience with them is limited. However, under some conditions, where the colors available were suitable, I have had some luck with them when other materials didn't do so well. I have found flies made with them most useful for dark days, and before sunrise and after sunset.

It is said that some aquatic insects reflect ultraviolet light. Inasmuch as this fluorescent fibre absorbs the non-visible ultraviolet rays and sends out longer rays that are definitely visible to the human eye, it may be that it more nearly simulates some insect bodies, as well as making such flies more visible to the fisherman.

Of one thing I am positive. No artificial really ever looked like a natural to any human when compared side by side. Even though we could float our product with six points of hackle to simulate the six legs of a natural, these points would not be placed like the legs of a natural, they certainly wouldn't hold a hook above water—and who ever saw a natural possessing a body that looked like a hook?

No—our artificials do not do a good job of imitation. Even when tied with extended bodies they fail miserably, in fact I think more so than the regular dry flies that most of us use. They are clumsy, opaque—nothing like a real insect except to the human imagination. Personally I'll take my chances normally on high-floating flies—flies with small hooks and plenty of hackle to keep the hook above water. It seems to me that the more you hide the hook the better chance you have of fooling the fish.

Certainly if we give the trout the credit of being able to distinguish the difference between the slightest shades of color (and what dry-fly fisherman doesn't have this belief?), we should give them the credit of being able to see the hook and distinguish any artificial from a natural. Figuring along these lines, the Spider and

Variant flies score as being nearest to perfection. When tied on small hooks and with stiff, rather bushy hackle and tail, the hook will be held high enough so that it does not break through the surface film of the water, and besides, the hackle points distort the vision of the prospective quarry to the extent that it doesn't see anything above the water. This is logical reasoning, and yet it doesn't always work out as we think it should.

For instance, often we find that a fly floating low in the water is more effective than one floating high. Despite the fact that the hook of a low-floating fly must be plainly seen by the trout, they take it as willingly as they do a natural—as if it were a regular thing to see flies with hooks for bodies. Again, there are times when Spiders tied on short-shanked hooks without a tail will work better than those with tails, and yet the very construction of a fly without a tail makes it ride on the water with the hook plainly showing beneath. Then take the parachute or Gyro type of fly (see plate 16) which has the hook lying flat on the water with the barb of the hook underneath. This is a most effective construction. It may be, in this case, that the manner in which the hackle spreads tends to make the hook less noticeable. Incidentally I find that a fluorescent body is extremely effective on such a fly. It is, of course, more plainly seen by the fish than is the body of a conventional tie with hackle and tail, because it is underneath the hackle and so rests directly on the water.

The answer to it all? You have me there. Perhaps no one knows, not even the trout. Perhaps they take our artificials because they look good to them, because they look like food of some kind—in fact they must do that, otherwise they wouldn't take them at all. But do they take them because they look like a natural? I doubt it —in fact I can't believe it—and at the same time I believe that they can recognize slight variations in color or size. To my way of figuring we've got to accept one of two theories. Either the trout do not see as well as we think they do, in which case they mistake our artificial, hook and all, for a natural, or else they can see exceedingly well, know at once that our artificial is not an imitation of any real natural, but, not being capable of thinking, take it for a different sort of natural, and so rise when the color appeals and the fly is presented well enough to simulate the action of a real insect when it alights on the water. Now this theory appeals to me and answers for everything. It explains selectiveness to color and size, and yet doesn't outrage the senses by making one believe that our artificial looks like a natural. It gives us the freedom to believe that trout can recognize every little detail in a fly, even to one different degree in color or size, without making apologies for the presence of the hook.

I am fully convinced that trout have good eyesight for close work. From observation and study I would say that trout have a perfection of vision that far exceeds that of man and is probably more acute than that of birds when applied to objects close by. I do not believe that trout have very clear vision for objects more than a few feet away, but for microscopic close-up work no doubt they have at least as sharp vision as any fauna in North America. Certainly this belief is logical, considering the dense medium of water and the necessity for nearsightedness and the lack of need for farsightedness for the creatures that live in it.

This is the main reason why I can't accept our artificial flies as exact duplicates of naturals. At the same time I thoroughly recognize the selectiveness of trout to our artificials, which plainly shows that they have preferences for one thing or the other under certain conditions. Most of us will agree that trout are selective to our flies. Most of us will insist that they can readily tell the difference between light and dark shades of the same color. Then how in heaven's name can we account for their indifference to the hook in our artificial unless it is by saying they take it for some sort of a fly different from what we know the natural to be? Certainly eyes that see such small details as we insist they do and which almost every angler has, to his own satisfaction, proved they do, would see that one outstanding thing which sets our artificial apart from anything that nature directly created.

Have you ever put a natural fly and an artificial counterpart on the water and then looked at them from beneath?

If you should drop a natural fly and an artificial imitation at the same time into the water of a transparent bowl and then look at them from below, you would never credit trout with good eyesight and selective powers if you insisted that they couldn't tell the difference between the two flies. The difference is so obvious that unless we consider our artificials as flies that do not imitate nature, we must belittle the trout's vision and sagacity—something that would never do. This does not mean that the fish refuse to accept our artificials as something alive and therefore something to be eaten. It merely means that we have created something they like because it excites their appetite, even though it doesn't exactly simulate nature. I may be all wrong on this theory—I am not insisting that it really means anything. But I do claim it is much more logical and understandable than the theory that insists that our artificials take trout because they actually imitate naturals. They imitate flies to the extent that they are similar to them in *some ways*. That is true—otherwise the fish wouldn't have anything to do with them. But I can't believe that they take our artificial Blue Dun for a *natural* blue dun—unless they are so dumb that it doesn't matter much what we use, in which case all this talk is just so much babble. As far as I am concerned I feel that if a trout can't tell the difference between a natural and an artificial, then it can't possibly tell the difference between light and dark gray or any other closely matched colors—in which case all this fuss about patterns means nothing concrete. But the influence of light rays may affect the sight of fish to such an extent that they can't tell the difference between the two—and this gives us another angle on the question. This I shall go into later.

But here is another way to look at it, a way that uses the imagination instead of cold observation. Perhaps it is only occasionally that trout are particular and exceedingly careful. Perhaps when we take them easily with our flies, they are careless and reckless. Perhaps when they won't take our flies, they are in a careful mood. Even humans have these different moods, and some are more susceptible to reckless moods than others. Again, perhaps it is only the moron trout we catch with our artificials, or it may be that the ones we do take are caught off guard. I'm not trying to establish anything here. I'm just giving you some possibilities that might not have occurred to you.

There is another angle we must consider. As pointed out, our artificials, being of different consistency than naturals, may appear different to the trout, if identical to our eyes, and identical to the trout if different to our eyes. The light shining through a live organism of a certain color may easily create a different effect than when shining through an object of the same color that is not alive. Again, a combination of colors in a lifeless object that does not, to our eyes, even slightly resemble a natural we are trying to imitate may yet look more real to the trout when seen against the light. Therefore, even when leaving the hook out of our calculations, we can't be sure that our carefully tied artificial will, as far as the trout are concerned, look anything like the natural we are trying to imitate. It is this fact which may in some measure account for the successful careers of some fancy flies that do not imitate anything in nature as far as we can see.

The late Phil Gootenburg advanced an interesting and quite logical thought in this respect—that contrasts in colors and broken body lines create life in a fly through the application of light rays. Marvin Hedge and he made a step forward in the creation of a fly that eliminated the hook fault. This is the Visa-Phledge fly, named jointly from Phil and Hedge and the "visa" donated by me, so Gootenburg claimed. He said I named it when we floated it on the basin in our bathroom the night he first tied the fly at my bench so that I could see it. I don't remember the naming but I do remember the floating, and if Phil said so, I must have done it.

This fly construction never took hold in a big way, but personally I have found it to have some merit. I have taken quite a number of fish with such flies during low and clear water conditions when a large fly was needed to interest them. I believe that their effectiveness at such times was mostly because the hook, being inverted, could not be seen by the fish. However, I also noted that with the barb and point of the hook skyward instead of down in the water I missed a greater percentage of rises. This is something to consider.

The whole thing is a jumble of conflicting ideas. When you really start thinking about it, you are left dazed and confused and your pet theories suffer some knockout blows. Perhaps some day we shall know all the answers, but I hope we never do. If ever we eliminate theory, conjecture, and imagination from fishing and make it an exact science, we will rob it of the charm that has made it the refuge of minds seeking relief from life's burdens.

Fancy being able to fish by formula as you might mix a drink. Suppose you could pick up a book and find just what was needed, written something like this: "For condition B, use formula 1XYT," or something similar. It would be tragic if fishing could be put on such an exact basis. As it is, we never know when we're guessing right, and what seems absolutely right today may be all wrong tomorrow. Just when we feel we have everything figured out to our satisfaction, something comes along to upset all our calculations and makes us believe we don't know a thing about fishing. When you find someone who answers all the questions, you can be sure that he doesn't fish enough to know what it's all about, or else—well, just or else.

One of the best ponds for fly fishing that I've ever fished is Trapper's Lake, Colorado. This wasn't because the trout ran large but because they rose to flies so well.

It is a beautiful spot, some nine thousand feet above sea level and surrounded by picturesque mountains. No camping is allowed on the lake, although you may camp some distance below, so that the shore line is as nature made it except for a small area on one side where the State has a building and a boat livery. I'm a bit vague about this because we used a boat only once, and Glenn Jones got it for us that day.

The afternoon my wife and I first saw the pond was one of those gorgeous mountain days that no pen can describe, but that affect both our physical and mental being like a strong stimulant. Glenn knew the lake well. "The best way to fish it," said he, "is from the shore. Let's stop here a while and I'll show you why."

We were at the edge of the lake on a quiet weedy bay. "There," said Glenn. "Did you see that dimple? I think a fish is working toward us."

I saw the riffle and watched the clear water carefully. Glenn's eyes, being more tuned to the situation than mine, saw the fish before mine did. "There are several of them," he exulted. "Cast your fly in front of them." I saw them and made the cast so the fly alighted right in the range of their course. As soon as the fly touched the water one of the trout started for it, and a few moments later I landed my first cutthroat.

We took several trout that night although it wasn't particularly fast going—due to being a bit late, as we found later on. Because I had taken the first fish on a bucktail I stuck to it, but Glenn changed to a dry fly and took three times as many fish as I.

It didn't take me long the following day to find out what it was all about. You didn't fish promiscuously. You did more observing than you did casting, but when you did cast, it was to a rising fish. Walking along slowly or standing in one location by which you knew trout traveled, you watched for rises or for the fish themselves. If you saw a rise you waited until you ascertained the direction the fish was moving and then cast your fly some distance ahead, provided you could do so without putting the leader over the trout. Putting the fly directly over the trout rarely brought a response, in fact it sometimes made the trout move away from you and in some instances put him down. In the case of a fish swimming along but not rising, the same procedure was followed.

As a rule it didn't matter what fly was used, but occasionally you would discover a fish that was cagey and had to be coaxed. One good specimen fooled around my location for an hour before I got him. He would look over each one of my offerings, coming right up to each one as if he had decided to take it and then go back to his swimming level with an impudent flip of his tail. One of the most effective flies for me had been a Royal Coachman. The one I had been using was badly chewed up, and this fish had refused it. I had tried nearly everything by this time, so I decided to give him up. I went back to the Royal, but selected a new fly instead of the bedraggled specimen. After tying it on I couldn't resist taking one more try at the big fellow, especially as at this time he was lazily swimming by me. I dropped the fly about two feet in front of his line of progress. To my surprise he rose and took it deeply as if it was just what he wanted. Was the new Royal the reason for his change of mind? I don't know, and your guess is as good as mine.

Of course I wanted to try the boat fishing, so we spent a half day at it. The dry fly did not work well here because of the movement of the boat, which prevented one from handling it correctly. Just when you had made a cast in front of a fish the boat swung or moved and spoiled the entire effect. However, wet-fly fishing was better from the boat, although the fish did not average as large as those caught from shore on a dry fly.

This September fishing at Trapper's Lake was best between ten in the morning and five in the afternoon, with a clear sky. The last day there a storm was brewing. Until the sun was swallowed by the clouds there was a goodly number of cruising fish along the shore, and fishing was good. After that they seemed to retire to deeper water, the rises stopped, and we couldn't do a thing. Whether this means anything I do not know, because we left the following morning to escape bad weather. It was lucky we did. Before we got back to Colorado Springs we had a tough ride through a blinding snowstorm, one bad enough to get pictured in a newsreel. Some day we're going back. No one could ever fish this lake without longing to return, not because of the size of the fish—the average was really quite small—but because of the intensely interesting shore fishing and the delightful atmosphere of the surroundings. The visit there remains one of our cherished memories. And the fish are gorgeous in appearance and fine eating.

Typical of midsummer pond trout fishing in the East is our experience in a little pond in Vermont. At this time I was fishing with George Donovan, of East Charleston, Vermont, who has a camp on Echo Lake. Neither George nor I had ever fished the pond, so we didn't know where to look for the trout; but George had obtained some information, and that together with our instincts in the matter took us right to a spot where there were plenty of trout.

We saw rises, had a lot of strikes, but caught only one small trout, the honor of which goes to George. Two anglers never worked harder than we did. We changed flies, methods, and position until we had used up every bit of pond-fishing lore we had ever accumulated. Something was wrong. Either we didn't strike the right fly or else we failed to use the right method. But then this is a common experience among anglers. We all have times when we can't catch them, and no one knows all the answers. But from later experiences I feel sure that we would have taken fish that day if we had only used dry flies. As is often the case when fishing for brook trout in Northern waters, we had figured that they would take wet flies without question, and we had failed to take dry flies with us.

That the dry fly is decidedly a good bet in some lakes is further illustrated by the following notes about Maine fishing during the fall of 1948 and 1949.

The place was Little Kennebago. The water was low, the weather showery. There are only limited hot fishing areas there in the fall and although we reached the place at nine in the morning, after a long trip from the head of Kennebago Lake, another canoe was already located on the current hot spot.

They were catching trout one after the other, but none better than a pound. Where we fished, several very large fish rolled about, but we couldn't get them to take our flies. Apparently there were no small ones concentrated there. Finally Ken Crocker, our guide, struck up a conversation with the other fellows. They had also tried for these large fish, but because they couldn't do anything with them, they had changed their position and had started catching the smaller fish, mostly on the dry fly. One of the two was using a large streamer and doing very poorly.

Things remained static for about an hour, and then the smaller fish quit striking. Just about that time another canoe, with two occupants, came and anchored directly below us. Some ten minutes later the streamer-caster in the upper boat took a good fish. Then, with the exception of a large fish wallowing about now and then and giving all observers palpitation of the heart, things went dead. Another boat arrived. They anchored opposite us, near enough so that our lines could snag if we both reached the same spot at the same time. Inasmuch as the canoe below us could also reach into our water, I refrained from casting as much or as far as I could have, because I didn't want to hook the other fellow's line.

Considerable time passed. We had a borrowed boat which we had promised to bring back to the owners about three that afternoon. The weather became very threatening, and off to the southwest we could see rain shrouding a few of the hills. The fellows upstream had taken time off to eat lunch; one of the fellows below was working hard and the other was eating. My wife and I kept steadily plugging away, hoping for a rise before our time was up, and wishing it would happen soon so that we could put our teeth into the inch-thick steaks Ken was going to broil for lunch. Besides, we did want to catch one good trout before the canoe had to be delivered to the owners. Allowing for the cooking and eating of lunch, we had decided on two as the zero hour.

Just when all parties concerned had about lost their enthusiasm because of the inactivity of the fish, one of the men below us took a good trout. Not three casts later he took another, and then after five minutes another. By this time the rest of us were all pepped up again, but it didn't do us any good. We didn't catch

The Fly Plates

There is a wealth of design in the color plates of this book. It is perhaps the greatest collection of flies ever gathered together and reproduced in color, so that one may easily copy them. Among the many hundreds of patterns shown, any fly-tier may find inspiration. It should be pointed out that many of the wet patterns lend themselves to dry fly construction. Keep that in mind and do not think of them as only wet flies.

To keep up with the flood of new patterns, new at least in name, is definitely impossible in these days of widespread amateur and professional fly-tying. But here is a suggestion that would simplify things if it were followed. There are a great many well-known patterns such as Cahill, Royal Coachman, Professor, Adams, and Blue Quill, to mention a few. If, when any new pattern starts from a basic design, it were given that name plus some descriptive name showing the change, it might help a lot. For instance, suppose someone put a Red Quill body on an otherwise basic Blue Quill, and called it Blue Quill—Red Quill Body. The addition of the words Red Quill Body would tell the person reading or hearing about it exactly what it was. Or take the Gold Body Cahill. This could have been named Sammy or something else equally undescriptive. Instead I called it just what it really is, and thus anyone can easily visualize it. If you carry this idea along, you can see that it would be very helpful. Of course naming fly patterns that way would be impractical in many instances; but such flies could be called by the basic pattern name plus the name of the stream or territory for which they were specially made, or plus the name or initials of the designer—for example, AuSable Cahill or Hank's Cahill. While names like these would not be descriptive, they would indicate a variation on a basic pattern; and those bearing the name of a stream or locality would clearly be specially designed for that territory. Of course I know many, if not all, of the objections and the weaknesses of this idea; but at least it is a step toward simplification of fly names that is sorely needed, not only by harassed fly-tiers, but by beginners at fly fishing and others as well.

The strange thing about this pattern business is that the average good fisherman rarely uses many flies, but he is very particular about the ones he does use. And from year to year his pet pattern for a particular season may change. It is quite possible that, if we confined ourselves to an assortment of twelve to eighteen sensibly selected colors, styles, and shapes, in sizes from 6 or even 4 down to 18 or smaller if possible, we'd catch just as many fish as we would with a hundred or more. In fact I believe we'd do better with only a few, because then we'd concentrate on using skill and knowledge to catch fish, instead of wasting valuable time searching through a confusingly large number of flies for the one pattern that the fish couldn't refuse. Often a rise is limited to a very short period. Much of it can be lost if you spend too long a time changing patterns. This does not mean that you should not try to match the hatch. It simply means that there are definite limits as to what can be accomplished in this respect.

You must have faith in any fly to be really successful with it. The Royal Coachman is about the most popular fly used, and yet there are a good number of anglers who have never had any real luck with it; they definitely think it is a very poor pattern, simply because they do not have any faith in it, regardless of how many fish it catches for the other fellow. Hence the need of many patterns. Just refrain from carrying so many that you can't locate the one fly you want.

A NOTE ABOUT

The Spinning Lure Plates

In a game as young as spinning, at least in the United States, new lures spring up like oats on fertile soil. When these plates were painted every effort was made to get representative lures from all the makers that we knew and we got them, but now there are many others, some very good indeed.

Any of the lures shown in the plates, or reasonable facsimiles of them, should be obtainable in any well equipped sporting goods store. I am also listing the names of some recent additions to the trout spinning lure family, all of which have served me well and that should also be easily obtainable from dealers.

LIST OF SOME NEW LURES

C. P. Swing Spoon	Phoebe	Spinnaire
Flirt	Plucky	Tail-lite (Dize)
Fuzzie-Wuzzie	Rublex-Devon	Wobl-L-Rite
Gold-Fish (Stuart)	Side-Winder	Actual Lure

There are also many others, not generally distributed, that are very good. The main requisite of a good spinning lure is that it is heavy enough to cast with the outfit and that it handles satisfactorily when being retrieved.

PLATE NO. 1

WET FLIES

Abbey	Academy	Adder	Adirondack	Admiral	Alder
Alexandra	Allerton	Apple Green	Arthur Hoyt	Artful Dodger	Babcock
Barrington	Baldwin	Beauty	Beamer	Bee	Beamis Stream
Beatrice	Beeman	Belgrade	Big Meadow	Bishop	Bisset
Black Dose	Black Gnat	Black Gnat Silver	Black Palmer Red Tag	Black June	Black Moose
Black Prince	Black Quill	Block House	Blue Blow	Blue Bottle	Blue Dun
Blue Jay	Blue Professor	Blue Quill	Bob Lawrence	Bog Pond	Bostwick

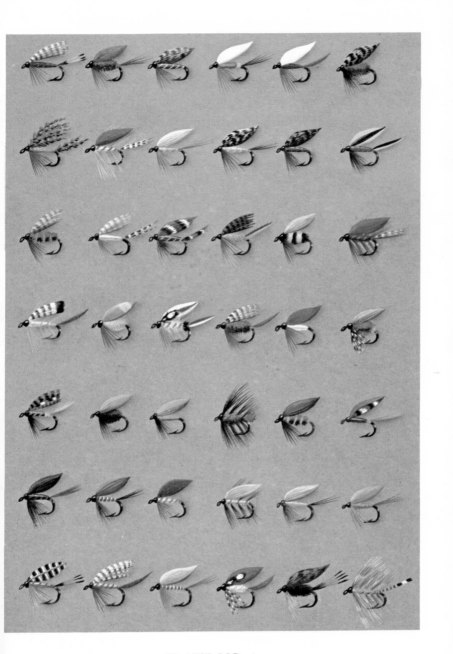

PLATE NO. 1

WET FLIES

PLATE NO. 2

WET FLIES

Bouncer	Bonnie View	Bootes Black	Bottle Imp	Brandreth	Bright Fox
Brown Hen	Brown Mallard	Brown Sedge	Brown Turkey	Brunton's Fancy	Bunting
Butcher	Cahill	Calder	Caldwell	Canada	Captain
Caperer	Cardinal	Carter Harrison	Cassard	Cassin	Catskill
Caughlan	Chamberlain	Chantry	Chateaugay	Cheney	Cinnamo
Claret Gnat	Coachman	Coachman Leadwing	Cobler	Colonel Fuller	Concher
Cooper	Cornell	Cowdung	Critchley Fancy	Critchley Hackle	Cupsupti
Dark Spinner	Down Looker	Deacon	Deer Fly	Denison	Dolly Varde

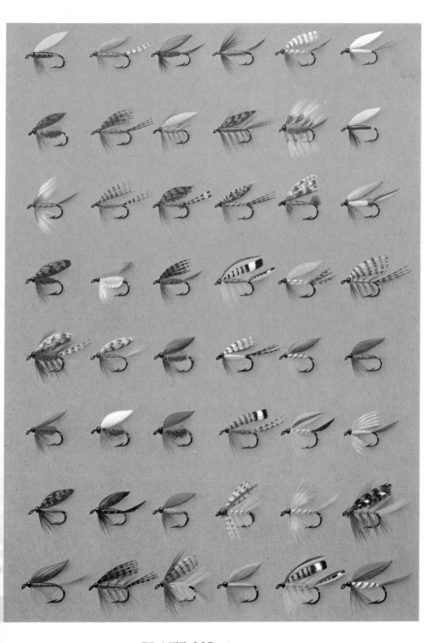

PLATE NO. 2

WET FLIES

WET FLIES

Darling	Dorset	Dr. Breck	Dr. Burke	Dugmore Fancy	Dusty Miller
Durham Ranger	Edrington	Elliot	Emerald	Emma	Epting
Esmeralda	Ferguson	Fern	Fiery Brown	Feted Green	Fisher
Fish Hawk	Fitzmaurice	Flagger	Flamer	Fletcher	Flight's Fancy
Florence	Forsyth	Fosnot	Francis Fly	General Hooker	Getland
Ginger Palmer	Gold Ribbed Hare's Ear	Good Evening	Gold Monkey	Gold Stork	Gordon
Golden Doctor	Golden Duke	Golden Dun	Golden Ibis	Golden Dun Midge	Golden Pheasa
Golden Rod	Golden Spinner	Gosling	Grannom	Gray Marlow	Grouse Spider

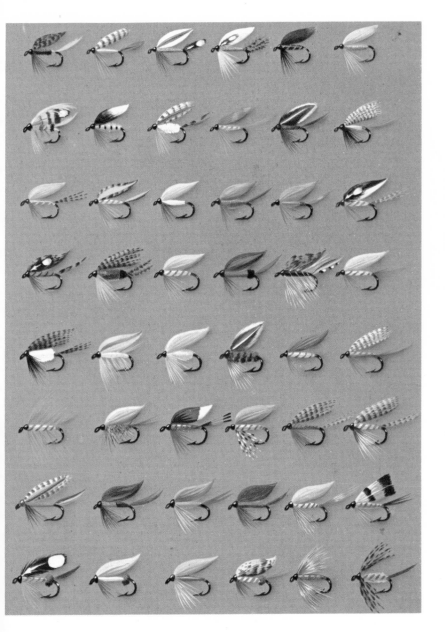

PLATE NO. 3
WET FLIES

PLATE NO. 4

WET FLIES

Guinea Hen	Governor	Gov. Alvord	Grackle	Gravel Bed	Green Midge
Gray Drake	Gray Midge	Gray Miller	Great Dun	Green Coachman	Green Drake
Green Mantle	Greenwell's Glory	Grizzly King	Gunnison	Harlequin	Hawthorn
Heckham Green	Heckham Red	Hemlock	Henshall	Herman Fly	Hofland's Fancy
Hoskins	Howell	Holberton	Hopatcong	Hudson	Hunt Fly
Ibis and White	Imbrie	Indian Rock	Indian Yellow	Ingersol	Irish Grouse
Irish Turkey	Iron Blue Quill	James	Jay Blue	Jay Yellow	Jay Silver
Jennie Lind	Jock Scott	John Mann	June	June Spinner	Kamaloff

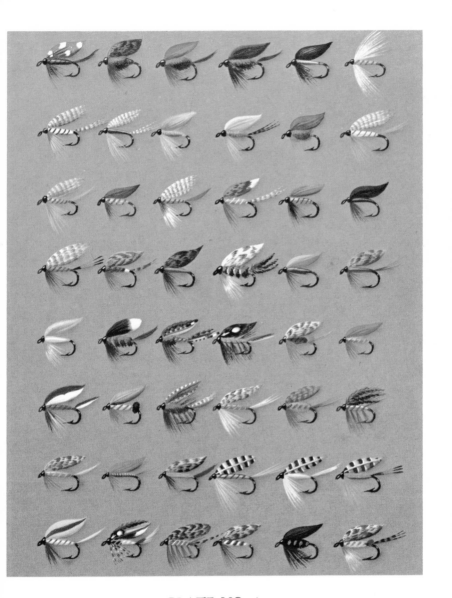

PLATE NO. 4

WET FLIES

WET FLIES

Kate	Katydid	Kendal	Kiffe	Kineo	King of the Waters
Kingdom	Kingfisher	Kinross	Kitson	Knowles' Fancy	La Belle
Lackey's Grant Lake	Lachene	Lady Gray	Lady Merton	Lady Mills	Lake Edward
Lake George	Lake Green	Langiwin	Laramie	Lanigan	Last Chance
Liberty	Light Blow	Light Fox	Light Polka	Lister's Gold	Lord Baltimore
Logan	Lowery	Loyal Sock	Luzerne	Magalloway	Magpie
Major	Mallard	Mark Lain	Marston's Fancy	March Brown American	March Brown English, Female
March Brown English, Male	March Dun	Marlow Buzz	Mascot	Marsters	Martin

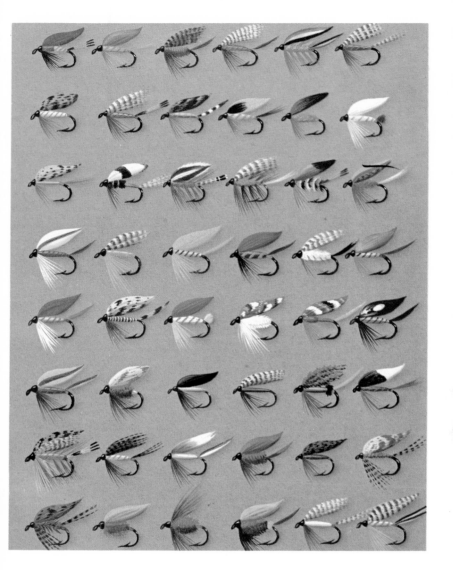

PLATE NO. 5

WET FLIES

WET FLIES

Maurice	Maxwell	Maxwell Blue	McAlpin	McGinty	McKenzie
Mealy Moth	Mershon	Mershon White	Midge Black	White Miller	Mills No. 1
Mohawk	Moisic	Mole	Montreal	Montreal Silver	Montreal Yellow
Moose	Morrison	Moth White	Moth Brown	Munro	Murray
Nameless	Neversink	Neverwas	Nicholson	Nickerson	Nonpareil
Oak	Olive Dun	Olive Quill	Olive Wren	Onondaga	Oquassac
Orange Black	Orange Blue	Orangto	Orange Miller	Orange Sedge	Orvis Gray
Page	Pale Evening Dun	Pale Sulphur	Pale Watery Quill	Park Fly	Parmachene Beau

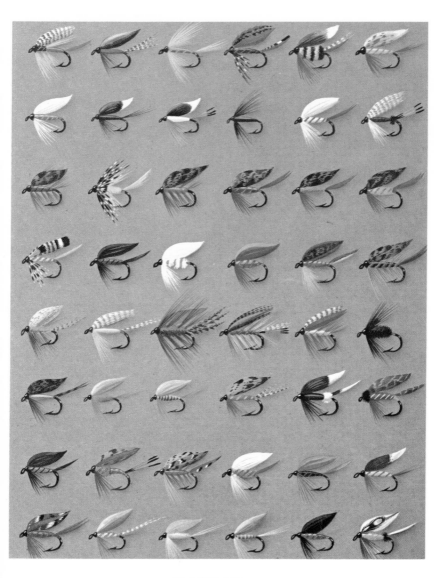

PLATE NO. 6

WET FLIES

PLATE NO. 7

WET FLIES

Parmachene Belle	Parson	Pathfinder	Partridge	Passadunk	Peacock
Pea Jay	Pebble Beach	Pellee Island	Perkin's Ideal	Perkin's Pet	Perry
Peter Ross	Piker	Pink Wickham's Fancy	Plath	Plummer	Polka
Poorman	Pope	Post	Portland	Potomac	Potter
Premier	Preston's Fancy	Priest	Prime Gnat	Professor	Prouty
Quack Doctor	Quaker	Queen of the Waters	Rainbow	Ray Bergman	Rangeley
Red Ash	Red Fox	Red Quill	Red Spinner	Red Tag	Richardson
Rich Widow	Riley	Rio Grande King	Romaine	Romeyn	Roosevelt

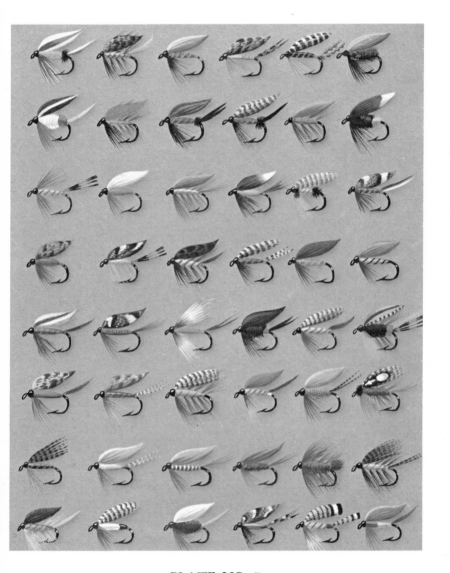

PLATE NO. 7

WET FLIES

PLATE NO. 8

WET FLIES

Ross	Round Lake	Royal Coach-man	Rube Wood	Sabbatus	Sage	Sallie Scott
Saltoun	Sanctu-ary	Sand Fly	Saranac	Sassy Cat	Scarlet Gnat	Scarlet Ibis
Schaefer	Sheenan	Seth Green	Shad Fly	Shoe-maker	Skookum	Silver Black
Silver Doctor	Silver Fairy	Silver Ghost	Silver-Gold	Silver Jungle Cock	Silver Stork	Silver Sedge
Sir Sam Darling	Soldier Palmer	Some-thing	Soo Nipi	Spencer	Split Ibis	Stebbins
St. Law-rence	St. Pat-rick	St. Regis	Stone	Secret Pool No. 1 Dr. Burke Pattern	Strachan	Stranger
Sturte-vant	Sunset	Swift-water	Teal	Teton	Thistle	Thunder
Tomah Joe	Toodle Bug	Tele-phone Box Dr. Burke Pattern	Turkey	Turkey Brown	Turkey Silver	Tuthill
Tycoon						

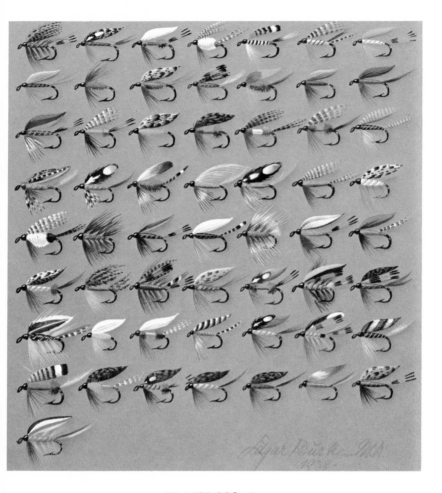

PLATE NO. 8

WET FLIES

PLATE NO. 9

WET FLIES

Undertaker	Union	Utah	Vance	Vanity	Victoria Green
Volunteer	Von Patten	Walker	Walker-Hays	Walla-Walla	Wanderer
Warden	Warwick	Wasp	Waters	Watson's Fancy	Webbs
Whirling Blue Dun	Whirling Dun	White Hackle	White Jungle Cock	White King	White Miller
Montreal White Tip	White Water	Whitney	Wickham's Fancy	Widow	Wilderness
Willow	Wilson	Wilson Ant	Winters	Witch Gold	Witch Silver
Witcher	Wood Duck	Wood Ibis	Woppinger	Wren	Yankee
Yellow Coachman	Yellow Drake	Yellow Dun	Yellow Sally	Yellow Spinner	**Zulu**

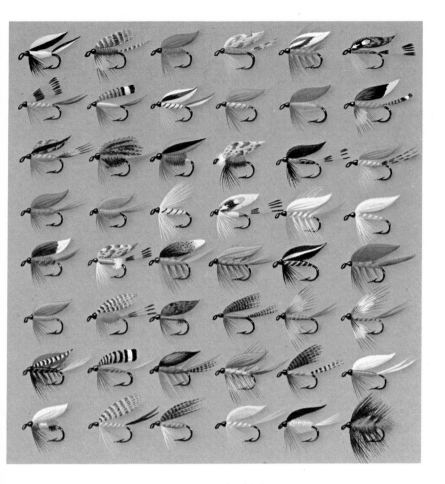

PLATE NO. 9
WET FLIES

WET FLIES—STREAMERS AND NYMPHS

Fontinalis Fin	Bergman Fontinalis	Grasshopper	Bob Wilson
Griffen	Gray Squirrel Silver	Red Squirrel Gold	Bell Special

Jess Wood

R. B. Nymph No. 1	R. B. Nymph No. 2	R. B. Nymph No. 5	R. B. Nymph No. 6
R. B. Caddis	Leaf Roller Worm	Hewitt Nymph No. 1	Hewitt Nymph No. 2
Hewitt Nymph No. 3	Water Cricket	Ackle Shrimp	Ed Burke Nymph

R. B. Trans-lucent Amber Nymph	R. B. Trans-lucent Red Nymph	R. B. Trans-lucent Green Nymph	R. B. Trans-lucent Brown Olive	Kol-Ray Caddis	Strawman Nymph

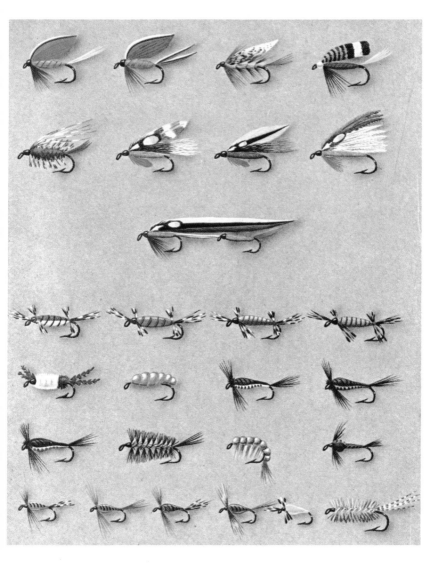

PLATE NO. 10

WET FLIES—STREAMERS AND NYMPHS

PLATE NO. 11

SPINNING LURES

Weighted Bucktail
  copper wound body

Weighted Spin-Fly
  minnow
  Gray

Ross McKinney
  weighted streamer

Weighted Bucktail
  copper wound body

Quilby Minnow
  series 50

Kopermino
  green

Gray Ghost
  weighted streamer
  smooth silver body

Butterfly Spinner
  orange

Chief Needabeh
  weighted streamer

Silver Tiger
  weighted streamer
  embossed silver body

Spin-Devil

Red Fin Spinner Fly

PLATE NO. 11

SPINNING LURES

ADDITIONAL STREAMERS AND BUCKTAILS

Scott Special	Summer's Gold	Wesley Special
Gootenburg's Jersey Minnow	Dr. Burke	Black-White Optic Bucktail
Blue Devil	Capra Streamer	Chief Needabeh
Estelle (Gootenburg)	Fraser	Black Ghost
Gray Ghost	Lady Ghost	Nancy
Spencer Bay	Three Rivers	York's Kennebago

Marabou (White)   Marabou (Yellow)

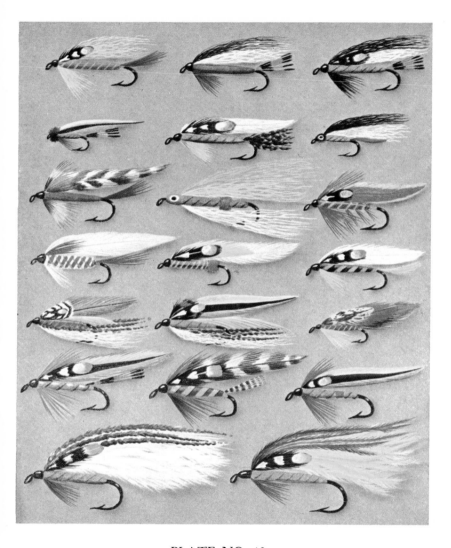

PLATE NO. 12

ADDITIONAL STREAMERS AND BUCKTAILS

SOME SPECIAL DRY FLIES

Ausable	Black Angel	Brown Olive	Gray Translucent	Grizzly Tango
Honey Dun	Light Cahill Translucent	March Brown American	Pink Lady Translucent	Tango Triumphant
Woodruff	Multi-Color Variant	Light Multi-Color Variant	Multi-Color Variant No. 2	Badger Variant
Brown Variant	Furnace Variant	Ginger Variant	Grizzly Variant	Blue Variant
Adams	Coffin	Spent Blue	Spent Olive	Spent Yellow
Gray Wulff	Royal Wulff	White Wulff	Green May	Yellow May
Fan Wing Royal Coachman	Fan Wing Silver Coachman	Green Fan Wing Coachman	Ginger or Petrie's Royal Coachman	McSneek

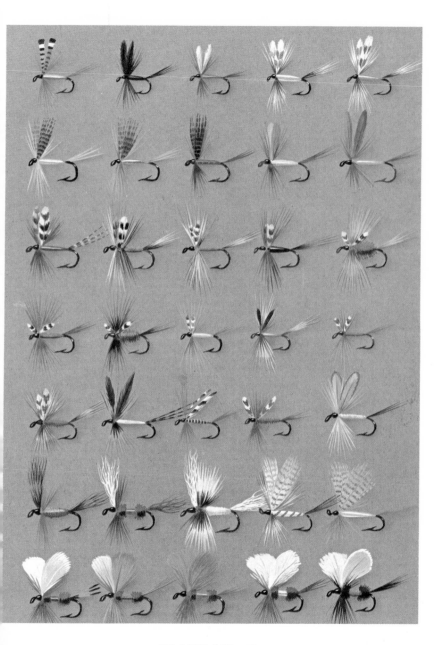

PLATE NO. 13

SOME SPECIAL DRY FLIES

PLATE NO. 14

DRY FLIES

Badger Bivisible	Black Bivisible	Brown Bivisible	Brown and Gray Bivisible	Blue Bivisible
Gray Bivisible	Pink Lady Bivisible	Black Spider	Blue Spider	Brown Spider
Ginger Furnace Spider	Orange Fish Hawk	August Dun	Black Gnat	Blue Quill
B. V. Booth	Blue Dun	Bradley	Bronze Quill	Caddis Light
Campbell's Fancy	Cahill	Cahill Gold Body	Cahill Light	Cahill Quill
Light Cahill Quill	Coty Dark	Coty Light	Coachman	Dark Coachman Lead Wing
Cochy Quill	Ginger Quill	Gordon	Quill Gordon	Gray Drake

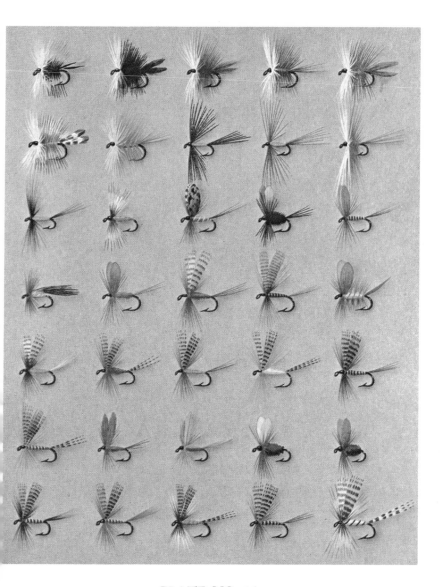

PLATE NO. 14

DRY FLIES

DRY FLIES

Gray Quill	Gold Ribbed Hare's Ear	Dark Hendrickson	Light Hendrickson	Housatoni Quill
Iron Blue Dun	Lady or Female Beaverkill	Mallard Quill	Mosquito	McGinty
Olive Dun	Olive Quill	Pale Evening Dun	Parson's Dun	Petrie's Eg Sack
Ramapo Special "Gooten-burg"	Royal Coachman	R. B. Fox	R. B. Blue Fox	Red Fox Beaverki
Red Fox Stoddard	Squirrel Tail	Tup's In-dispensable	Turner's Green	Westbrool
Whirling Blue Dun	Will's Spinner	Wortendyke	Yellow Creek	Yellow Mallard
Yellow Spinner	Stillwater No. 1	Stillwater No. 2	Stillwater No. 3	Cooper-B

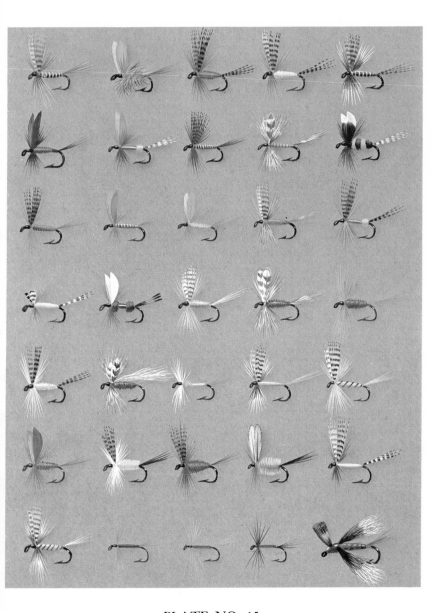

PLATE NO. 15

DRY FLIES

NEW DRY FLIES

Buzz Fly	Black Wulff (Bailey)	Blue Winged Sulphur Dun	Carrot	Bi-Fly Yellow
Brown Quill Spinner	Callender Quill	Clyde	Coopers' Hopper	Deren's Fox
Emergent Dry Nymph	Fifty Degrees	Firehole	Golden Quail	Greig Quill
Grizzly Wulff Bailey	Ginger Quill Gyro	H. L. Howard	Honey Quill	Hopkins Variant
Iron Blue Variant	Irresistible	Jungle Cock Variant	Killer Diller	Meat Ball
Morris Quill	Pale Evening Dun (Fox)	Pale Evening Spinner	Pastel Yellow Spider	Red Quill (Flick)
Rough Water (Blue)	Rough Water (Yellow)	Rough Water (White)	Slate Drake Dun	Smoky Mountain Forked Tail
	Sterry Special		Wake	

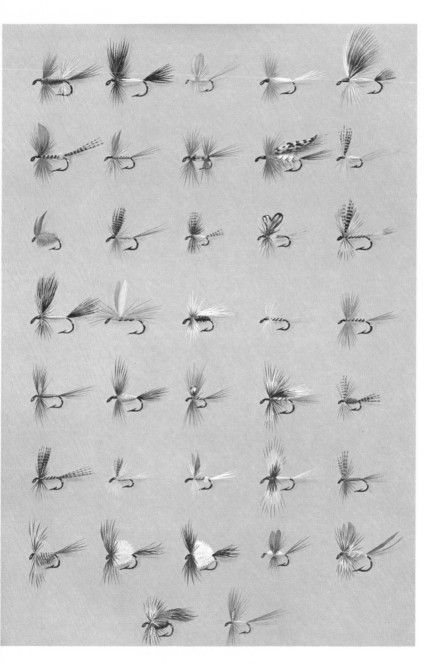

PLATE NO. 16

NEW DRY FLIES

anything, but the one fellow fishing below took another fish. By this time he was satisfied, so he quit fishing to have his lunch. His partner had been leisurely eating during this time, but never got excited enough to do any fishing.

Everything had been quiet for some time when a fish jumped close to their boat. The indolent fellow, who hadn't as yet caught a fish, and who also hadn't fished very much, suddenly came to life. He made a few casts and was soon fast to the best fish caught that day. After this display of action and skill he quickly reverted to his sluggish character and settled down to enjoy more food, making my mouth water, both for the fish and for the food.

During all this time the party opposite us had been working like mad, with streamers and wets, but didn't get a strike. They decided, finally, that they'd had enough and quit. A few large fish still wallowed in the water near us, so we kept trying.

The fellow below, who had taken four fish, called out to us: "Have you tried a small, dark dry fly; a black gnat? That is what I took most of mine on."

"No," I called back, "but I shall."

Well, I didn't have a dry black gnat, but I did have some size 14 Dark Cahills. I tied one on. "It's ten minutes to two," announced Ken Crocker. Just then a good trout rose in front of us. A second later the little Cahill dropped over the rise ring. Then came a wrinkle on the water, my wrist twitched automatically, and the day was saved. I had taken a good fish.

Incidentally, we had our steaks and mashed potatoes as well as hot biscuits and other things, but how Ken Crocker did such a splendid job of it in the rather heavy rain that came down during this time was surprising—an outstanding example of outdoor cookery. I recommend him highly as a wonderful guide for middle-aged or old folks who enjoy good food along with some fishing. Somehow the food tasted even better because of the pure and sweet rain water that mingled with each mouthful. As a youth and a young man I had gloried in doing this sort of thing myself. But to a man in the last decade of his three score and ten, or popularly allocated span of life, it helps to have a professional comrade for all the necessary odd jobs; said helper also being well experienced in the territory being fished. This one was only a few years younger than I. He was a good guide in every sense of the word.

TROUT

This day we spent at Little Kennebago was the next to the last one we would be there. The previous days had been spent fishing with wet flies and bucktails. The last day dawned with a threatening look. It was cold and windy, and the water looked most uninviting. It was black, with whitecaps. Grace, my wife, stayed in to get our duffle ready for departure the following day and I was glad, because she doesn't like rough water. But Ken Crocker got me up extra early. The reason was that he wanted to take me to Blanchard's Cove. This was a very popular fishing spot, so popular in fact that we had fished it only twice during the time we'd been at Kennebago. It was always crowded before we started out, except for this one time.

The bad weather helped us. When we got there the place was ours; not another person was in sight, nor did anyone appear by water, although one party did come by land and caught a few eight- or nine-inchers from shore after the big stuff had quit taking.

The wind had increased in velocity by the time we reached the cove and the waves were high but unbroken. Now it seems that common sense would indicate the use of a wet fly or streamer on such a day. But remembrance of that one good fish taken on the dry fly at Little Kennebago the day before still colored my desires. Being dry-fly-minded anyway, that is the way I decided to fish.

Because the water was so rough, I selected a fly for easy floating and visibility. It was a light-ginger, multicolor Variant size 12. I glanced at Ken as I did this, rather expecting disapproval. On the contrary, he beamed approval.

A good cast's distance toward shore we both saw the flash of a trout. The fly dropped near the spot, and a second later he was on—a nice two-pound male. It was the start of a glorious session. The fish didn't take every cast, but they came so frequently that I never found myself wishing one would hit. For about an hour and a half I cleanly hooked every fish that rose, and they were all of a nice size, although none were goliaths. Then I started missing now and then, and they started to run smaller, until suddenly it was all over. Only then did I notice that the wind had become twice as strong as when we had started, and that it had also grown much colder. But it was a grand climax to my fishing at Lake Kennebago.

The following fall we were at Penobscot Lake, in the Moosehead country. While on the whole I took most of my fish there on a wet fly or a spinning lure, there were a couple of days when we would have been fishless except for the dry fly. The first time was the day we started fishing. It happened in a bay fed by a small creek. A number of fish were rising but they wouldn't have anything to do with wet flies, so I changed to dry. The first one tried brought several investigating swirls but no actual takes, so I switched patterns. After a number of changes that brought further rises but no hooked fish, I finally picked an acceptable fly. It was a Ginger Variant, made with wings cut from the brown mottled feathers of an English pheasant. But after taking four trout we never saw another rise, nor could we get any more response to our artificials, either dry, wet, or streamer.

This happened one other morning in another bay, and on each day Mrs. Woodward, owner of the camp, reported experiences of a similar nature. She said that she'd been plagued with rises that were missed. She was blaming her technique, but as she is an accomplished angler I felt that the misses were not her fault, that the trouble lay in the fact that she hadn't used a suitable fly. I offer as a logical reason for my belief the fact that I'd also missed every fish that rose to every fly I had used except the Ginger Variant. When I used this fly I hooked every fish that rose to it.

There are many small ponds that provide excellent dry-fly fishing if you fish them at the right time. The trout must be feeding in comparatively shallow water, and must be interested in taking flies from the surface. On the whole I like best to fish close to weed beds, stumps, or other types of cover, and prefer not to try at all with a dry fly if there are not any fish rising or jumping. When they are active on the surface and keep moving about in a limited area that you can easily reach, then I find that making a cast, letting the fly lie quietly for a time, and then twitching it a bit before lifting is about as good a method as any.

In all good fishing the main requisite is to first locate the fish. If they are cruisers, sometimes the dry fly will work very well, and of course so will the wet fly. Fish the flies so that they are presented ahead of the course of the fish. If the fish are concentrated in a few spots, one must work these places carefully and thoroughly. If they are in deep water, either a deeply sunken fly, spinner, or natural bait must be used. If they are in shallow water, they may respond equally well to either a wet fly or a dry fly, provided you do not frighten them in the fishing. But learn your pond well, or have someone take you who knows the pond well. This is the best advice I can give for this sort of fishing.

◄§ CHAPTER IX ֍►

Spinning Tackle for Trout

B ACHE BROWN and A. R. Beverley-Giddings introduced me
to spinning. One snowy and frigid December day they brought
me a complete outfit and insisted that I try it out on the snow
that was a foot or more deep in my yard. At that time spinning was
practically unknown in the United States and Canada. Of course
my first casts were abominable, but I could readily see the advantages of the fixed-spool reel and was instantly sold on its possibilities.

But I didn't get to use this outfit seriously the next year. Both
fly and plug fishing were so good that I used it very little—only
when conditions were so bad that you couldn't catch fish with
anything except dynamite. Of course it didn't produce, but I did
learn how to use it.

The next year was different. Wherever my wife and I fished it
seemed that conditions were bad, and the spinning outfit saved the
day in many instances. Thus I became really interested in the use
of the spinning reel, particularly the open-spool type in which the
axis of the reel is parallel to the rod.

At first the lines caused much trouble. They are now greatly
improved, so much so that it has become pleasurable to fish with
them. Even so, as of 1951 there is still need for further improvement.

One of my original lines was made of "Jap" gut, a leader-like
material that persons young at fishing have perhaps never seen or
used. Unless it was thoroughly soaked you couldn't fish with it,
and unless you wound a piece of wet rag around the spool to keep
the line wet you couldn't even start fishing. The line would jump
off the spool like a spring, and then you spent valuable fishing time
trying to get it pliable enough to use. Most of the time I com-
promised by cutting off the more objectionable twists. Even then

I got into trouble. As every angler knows, it becomes necessary to spend time walking from one fishing spot to another. I'd forget to put on the wet rag, and the line would dry out between the reel and the lure, so that when I got to the next fishing hole and impulsively made the first cast, I got all messed up. About the only way I could keep the line usable was by soaking the reel in the water every once in a while, while steadily fishing, and taking time out to thoroughly wet both the reel and the line between reel and lure when moving from one place to another. This prevented it from getting too dry between pools, so that I could start fishing almost at once when I reached the new location.

My other early line was made of untreated, braided silk, of five-pound test. (Remember that this was before the introduction of nylon.) The part that was in the water most of the time when casting lost its strength in a few hours. I would always forget to test it in time, and just when it got too weak to take much strain, invariably I'd get a strike from a large fish, and the line would break somewhere between the rod tip and the lure. It was abominable when the wind blew hard; it acted like a cobweb, so that you hardly knew where you were casting. It also picked up water like a sponge, so that after a dozen casts or so you got sprayed in the face, something that was most exasperating. All in all, it was so bad that I finally quit it completely and reverted to Jap gut. As long as I dipped this in water often enough to keep it well soaked and pliable, I made out reasonably well.

The fixed-spool method of spinning is the missing link between bait-casting and fly-casting. With this tackle you can fish satisfactorily with lures too light in weight for the one and too heavy for the other. It is the reel that makes this possible. As it has a fixed spool, that is, one that does not revolve, the line flows off freely; there isn't anything to hold it back except the slight friction on the guides between the reel and the tip-top. Thus you can cast lures as light as one-eighth of an ounce without much effort, and if the bait is sufficiently compact you can do quite well if it weighs only one-sixteenth of an ounce.

The progress of the lure is stopped, when using a reel of manual pick-up type, by the forefinger; or by a quick forward turn of the handle when using one with a mechanical pick-up device. You can use the forefinger for the pick-up on *some* mechanical types, so I would suggest that you check this if you think your own finger is better than a mechanical one. In either case you must turn the reel-handle forward to get the line on the spool once more.

Personally, I prefer the mechanical device. For one thing it prevents your getting into the troubles attending the use of the manual, such as missing the line with your finger, when you can get "balled up" quite badly—a troublesome thing for persons with short fingers and small hands, like me. There is another reason too. When walking or wading from one fishing hole to another the mechanical finger keeps the line in place better than the small device used on the manual pick-up. Thus you are not so likely to have trouble with the line getting loose, out of bounds, and in a tangle.

The most up-to-date reels are equipped with a device that enables you to lock the handle so that it doesn't turn backward, and I recommend that anyone buying a spinning reel make sure that it is so equipped. This device makes easy the landing of a fish, the laying down or carrying of the set-up rod, and trolling. Because you cannot thumb a spinning reel as you can a bait-casting reel, this is a most constructive improvement. When I first used them none were made that way.

Fixed-spool reels require lines of small calibration to give satisfactory results to the user. Such lines naturally have a lower breaking strength than lines with a large calibration, but because spinning reels are made with drags that allow the line to slip when you reel in or hold the reel handle tight, it is possible to use these low-test lines with reasonable impunity.

The secret lies in setting the brake, or drag, of the reel. It should be adjusted to give just before the pressure becomes more than the line can take. When you have it set just right, you can either keep reeling in or hold the handle steady against even a large fish. When he pulls hard, the line slips out against the drag; and the instant he relaxes and you start reeling as fast as is necessary, in he comes.

But remember that any line gets progressively weaker with use, particularly that part near the lure. Test this part frequently, and if it shows signs of losing strength, then break it off in small pieces until you get above the weak section. Ordinarily this testing isn't necessary more than three times in eight hours unless you are using extra-heavy lures, or catching extra-heavy fish. Always after you have had a long and hard fight with a fish, you should test the line and look at the hooks on the lure. When they show that the fight has impaired their strength or hooking ability, do something about it. When fishing over jagged rock you may also get into trouble. Under such conditions take time out frequently to test the line, and look over the lure for dull or broken hooks. When testing the line be careful not to jerk or snap it. Simply pull steadily and reasonably, according to the pound test of the line you happen to be using. Jerking may break the line, and will always weaken it.

I would suggest that you first experiment at home, if possible, to get accustomed to the feel of your tackle. You might do this in your yard, in a field, or even in a city park. Have someone play being the fish, so that you get to know how much strain the rod and line can take without breaking. If you are too gentle in playing a fish it may get into a tangle of roots, the branches of a fallen tree, or a mass of weeds or debris. If you know just how much resistance to apply without breaking the line it will aid greatly in keeping fish from such hazardous locations.

Keep the rod pointed upward when testing a line or playing a fish. If you point the tip of the rod at the fish or the water, naturally the entire strain will be on the line. This may be O.K. if the line is of heavy weight, but spinning lines are of small calibration and limited strength. The rod should always act as a foil when playing a fish. That is part of its function. It will serve this purpose only when you hold it so that it bends when a fish is fighting.

Of course the brake should be set so that it aids you in getting the best results. It should give just under the test of the line, I'd say at least a pound under, to take care of possible deterioration between testings. When you strike conditions in which a brake set to the full breaking strength of the strongest usable spinning line fails to hold the fish, then spinning tackle is definitely not suitable for that fishing. I have run into such situations a number of times, when bait-casting or fly-fishing did a better job.

It is impossible to get a backlash with a fixed-spool spinning reel. However, you can get into other difficulties. One is to have a bunch of line come off the spool all at once, in a mass of coils. Of course it makes a tangle, and a bad one. This, in my experience, is generally caused by one of two specific factors. For one, the line is too stiff, too heavy, or both. For the other, when fishing a lure by the jerk-and-reel method (something often necessary to get best results) the line spools loosely instead of tightly, as it should. In this last case you may do fine for many casts; and then suddenly one cast makes such a mess of the line that the easiest way out is to cut off the tangle and start over again. Of course the softer and finer the line the better off you are, and with extreme care in handling the slack when jerking you may be able to get by for a long time without getting into difficulties. Perhaps there are experts who can handle the jerk method without getting into trouble, but I'm certainly not one of them. I get too interested in the fishing to be careful. But at that, I do not have the trouble I had when I started spinning, so perhaps one of these days I shall be able to fish one entire day without having any difficulties whatsoever. But I doubt it. I imagine that a very calm and non-excitable person would make out best in this respect. But if I couldn't get excited over fishing I'm sure that, for me, it would lose its greatest charm.

There is another trouble experienced with some open-spool spinning reels. If you make the slightest error in handling them YOU MAY SUDDENLY FIND THAT THE LINE HAS SLIPPED BEHIND THE SPOOL AND BECOME WOUND AROUND THE MECHANISM. If you catch this quickly you can usually remedy the trouble in a short time, but often the line jams into the parts in such confusion that the only way you can extricate it is by cutting it loose. Unfortunately this happens most often when the fishing is good, and you are in a hurry to unhook a fish so that you can start casting for the next one. Mostly it occurs when you lay down the rod to unhook a fish, and then make the next cast without first checking to see that everything is in working order. Some reels are made with replaceable chenille guard that prevents the line from getting behind the spool. All spinning reels should be made in such a way that the line cannot get so entangled. Otherwise they do not perform to the best advantage. It is quite likely that in time all manufacturers will have overcome this fault. I hope so, because it is a most exasperating one.

A heartfelt objection, raised by many prospective buyers of a spinning outfit, is that it is a left-handed affair. This perhaps is the most persistent objection of all. But it is unreasonable, and the anglers who really should complain are the left-handed casters. They have only a few reels to choose from, and must always pay extra for those that are available.

I am right-handed, but I have never found left-hand reeling awkward. In fact, it is the most logical procedure. As early as 1917 I questioned the sense of both casting and retrieving with the same hand. Later I switched to reeling the fly reel left-handed. I'm sorry now that I didn't do the same with the bait-casting reel—that is, purchasing a left-handed model, casting with it right-handed, but reeling in with my left hand. Anyway using the fly reel left-handed so many years made the use of the open-spool spinning reel relatively easy for me to master. It is simple to use the hand opposite the casting one for the reeling-in operation. True, it may seem awkward and unnatural at first, but just a little serious practice makes it comparatively easy, and if you persist you will soon do it automatically. But I would suggest that you change the spooling of the line on your fly reels accordingly; otherwise you will get mixed up when shifting from fly rod to spinning rod.

Of course I now have a gripe against fly reels. Most of them are made for right-handed reeling, and the heavy click or extra resistance works only when the line is spooled for this. I use such reels reversed, and of course they do not give me the aid of mechanical pressure against a fish just when it is needed most. I must do my reeling in against the click, and that makes it a bit more tiring. However, I do have a fly reel that can be set for either right- or left-hand use. Believe me, I use this reel in preference to any other when fishing waters where you may hook large fish.

But if you insist on casting and retrieving with the same hand there are spinning reels to accommodate you. One is an open-spool reel that sets on top of the reel-seat instead of underneath. It is the bait-casting spinning reel. The other is a reel that sets below the reel-seat like an orthodox spinning reel, but that is otherwise different. In shape it is much like a fly reel, and the line comes out from a hole in the side of the casing. In using it, you both cast and retrieve with your right hand. If you prefer to spin with your fly rod, then this last is the best possible, as it fits on the fly rod reel-seat. All in all I prefer the regulation, open-spool, under-the-reel-seat spinning reel, but these other innovations may be just what you want. That is up to you.

I have already mentioned that spinning lines are much better than when I first started using them, but can be still further improved. The greatest trouble lies in being able to get lines that are strong enough, in a calibration that will perform properly when being cast. To date (early 1951) the strongest lines I've ever been able to use satisfactorily with open-spool fresh-water spinning reels are eight-pound test in the braided nylon yarn, and five-pound test in the monofilament nylon. These strengths are rarely needed, except for heavy trout fishing. Incidentally, some five-pound mono-filament lines calibrate as small as .0086. When casting with quarter-ounce lures you can use monofilament as heavy as .011 or .012, but this definitely tends to be troublesome.

For the average trout stream a three-pound test monofilament is ample, even if the fish average quite large. This means a line with a calibration of approximately .008. The last line I used calibrated .0079 and tested three and a half pounds. Another one, used just previous, calibrated .008 and tested only three pounds. As both lines were equally pliant I naturally favor the one that showed the greater test. But I also use lines much lower in test and calibration when fishing clear water for wary trout. For instance I have found two-and-a-half- and one-and-a-half-pound tests, .0071 and .0047 respectively, necessary at times. You may take large trout with these very light lines providing that conditions allow it and you properly handle both line and fish. But do not expect too much from material as light as .0047. It will not take much punishment, and weakens rapidly in use.

During the past season (1951) I have found the following lines very satisfactory. They really fill the entire need of the trout fisher-man.

Material	Test	Calibration	Remarks
Monofilament	2½ to 4 lbs.	.0071	For wary trout and very light lures
Monofilament	3½ lbs.	.0079	For all-around fishing
Monofilament	4 lbs. to 5 lbs.	.0086	For use when trout run large and hazards are present
Braided nylon	4 lbs.	.009	To replace four-pound monofila-ment if desired
Braided nylon	6 lbs.	.011	For tough conditions where a strong line is needed
Braided nylon	8 lbs.	.012	For really heavy work

NOTE—*The variations in pound test for calibration were the differences as marked by the manufacturers on the lines. But I have found that the 2½ pound test on some makes was as strong as the 4 pound on others. The same applies to the 4 and 5 pound test.*

The six-pound test braided is a line that I tried first in 1950, and it is excellent. The slight difference in calibration makes it better for casting lures lighter than one-quarter ounce than the eight-pound, and yet it gives you much greater security than the four-pound. However the four-pound, being two one-thousandths of an inch (.002) smaller, is sure to be more effective than the heavier line when fishing low and clear water.

One of the outstanding qualities of an open-spool reel is the easy interchange of spools. For instance, if you wish you may have a separate spool for each of the aforementioned lines. You may change from one to another in a matter of minutes. However, for the average fisherman I would suggest only three lines, wound on spools and ready for use.

SPOOL 1—To be used for low and clear water and for very wary fish.
           Monofilament—Two-and-a-half to four-pound test. .0071

SPOOL 2—For average all-around trout fishing
           Monofilament—Three-and-a-half to five-pound test. .0086

SPOOL 3—For heavy fishing
           Braided—Six to eight-pound test.

In the softer monofilaments you may use as heavy as .010 but it will not cast as easily nor as smoothly as the smaller sizes recommended.

You might include a ten-pound braided—something to take care of situations where eight-pound test is insufficient. You may not care for the way a line of this weight handles on a fixed-spool reel; but it won't be too bad if you use lures a bit heavier than usual or weight lighter lures sufficiently, and practice a bit so that you get the feel of it. However I recommend this weight of line with some reservations. As far as I'm concerned, I'll use heavy fly-rod tackle if anything greater than eight-pound test is needed to land a trout. Note I do not say *play* a trout. The need for greater strength in a line comes after a fish is played out and for any possible reason must be dragged upstream to the angler against surging waters. In such cases I've seen even twelve-pound and heavier lines and leaders break under the strain. However, remember that this condition is an isolated one, occurring only in such places as certain sections of the Sault Sainte Marie rapids of Michigan and other large, roaring, and potentially dangerous rapids. In such waters one may possibly hook a fish of four to seven pounds or larger and not be able to follow it to a point where it can be landed without interference from the current.

The spinning rod has an in-between action. That is, it is neither a fly rod nor a bait-casting rod—quite the proper position for a casting instrument made expressly to fill the needs of an intermediate method. The action has been usually referred to as parabolic, which means that the butt runs limber and the tip runs stout, so that the bend of the rod under strain is quite even from grasp to tip. The rod is made with a slow taper instead of a fast one, and that is about as simply as I can describe "parabolic."

In a light spinning rod you will find a reasonable similarity to a heavy fly rod of the same length. For instance, if you could add an ounce of bamboo, evenly distributed from butt to tip, to a three-and-a-half-ounce limber-butt fly rod, plus a long spinning grasp without a conventional fly-rod reel-seat, you would have a pretty good spinning rod. But it would make a very stiff fly rod, one rather unpleasant to use. Personally I've never handled any spinning rod that pleased me when used for fly fishing. It can be made to work, with the proper line, but it fails to perform the way you need it to. In other words it is just a makeshift when it comes to fly-fishing.

The same thing applies to the adapter handles that convert joints of both fly and bait-casting rods into spinning jobs. They work, and you can catch fish using them. I know because I've tried all these things. But keep in mind that spinning is a separate method of angling, just as necessary and as sporting as the other two major methods, fly casting and bait casting. It also needs specific and tailor-made tackle in order to provide top performance and pleasure in the using. Under some conditions you could do wonders with a cane pole. But you would be limited to the potentialities of such a crude tool. You can use an old-style telescopic rod for bait fishing, fly fishing, and spinning, but it has its limits in providing you with good performance. It has its purpose but that is not to act as a fly rod or a spinning rod. So I could not conscientiously recommend a spinning rod for fly fishing, or a fly rod or a bait-casting rod for spinning, even though all are interchangeable to a limited degree.

But if you do not wish to buy a rod specifically for spinning until you are sure that you will like the method, then the purchase of an adapter handle for use on some rod you already own is a good idea. This cost is small and they do work, provided you own rod joints that fit and have reasonably good action. I have fished a lot with these makeshift jobs, and have caught lots of fish with them. Two in particular pleased me most. One was an old bamboo bait-caster a few inches longer than six feet when set up with its original independent handle. It weighed four and three-quarters ounces. When set up with the adapter handle it was six inches longer and weighed about a half ounce less. Another was made from the two upper joints of a three-piece, nine-foot bamboo fly rod. It was slightly longer than the other and weighed a full ounce less. The bait-caster proved too stiff for lures less than one-quarter ounce, and the fly rod was too limber to long take the strain of spinning lures. Nevertheless they both worked well enough for me to catch my share of fish. But I must admit that while using them I kept wishing I was using one of my rods especially built for spinning instead.

If you do decide first to try an adapter handle instead of buying a spinning rod, I would suggest that you do not use a good fly rod for the purpose. If you have only fly rods that you like, then I would recommend that you spend a few dollars more and get one of the many low-priced spinning rods now being manufactured. One thing I can promise. If you are an enthusiastic fisherman without prejudice as to methods of fishing and keep at spinning long enough to understand it, eventually you will buy a good spinning rod, as well as the best of other spinning tackle. Otherwise, like many others, you will cast it aside, or sell what you have to someone else.

I now have nine spinning rods and a number of reels. The rods range from six to eight feet in length, and from three and a half ounces to five and a half ounces in weight. I'm still a bit undecided as to which rod I like best for all-around fishing. From the most recent experiences I favor an experimental rod of bamboo, weighing four ounces. It is six feet ten inches long, and constructed like a bait-casting rod, that is with a short butt and a long tip. With it I am able to cast lures from a quarter ounce to an eighth of an ounce in weight with equal ease, provided the right line is used with each and the lures themselves are not too air-resistant. This rod would be better if it did not have a fancy-shaped handle that prevents setting the reel nearer the butt end when using light-weight lures. A built-in spinning-rod handle should be so constructed that you may attach the reel high or low, according to the weight of the lure; that is, high for the heavier baits, low for the lighter ones. This change in position definitely changes the action of some rods. When the reel is set low the rod is appreciably more limber, hence better able to cast the lighter lures.

For accuracy I seem to do best with a rod less than seven feet long. I believe this is mainly because my eyes pick up the progress of the lure better with a short spinning rod than they do with a long one. It may be the same with others.

Some of the lowest-priced rods are made of metal. I've used both six- and six-and-a-half-footers of this type and made out right well with them, except that with lures of less than one-eighth of an ounce it is difficult to get reasonable distance. For an all-around trout rod I will stand by my first suggestion, a rod slightly under seven feet and weighing not over four ounces—this to be used for nothing but spinning and made with a proper handle. If you wish to use a spinning rod as an emergency fly rod as well, then I would suggest more length and less weight per foot, in order to get the limberness necessary to properly handle a fly. You might have a combination made up, say a seven-and-a-half-footer with two tips, one tip made for spinning and the other for fly fishing. Such rods aren't too bad, but in my opinion you haven't got the right action in either tip. One tip makes a mediocre spinning rod, the other a most ordinary fly rod. Always remember that when you get one rod to do two entirely different things, you can't expect it to be just what you want for either.

The last addition to my stock of spinning rods is a tubular glass job. It is six and a half feet long and weighs three and five-eighths ounces mounted. I've now used it enough to say that it compares favorably with my pet action split bamboo and of course has the advantage of being lower in cost and capable of taking more abuse.

Lures should be selected with the different types and conditions of water in mind. However, if you do not wish to get too involved here to start, it is possible to make out very well indeed with a shrewd selection of spoons. One should be of the spinning type, that is with its blade revolving on a shaft. There are a number of excellent designs on the market. One with a willow-leaf-shaped blade is very popular in some waters, while a broader and more rounded blade is extensively used in other places. These spoons should have sufficient weight to cast easily. Most of them are best cast on the lightest weight monofilament line.

Next you need what I consider a very important lure. It was one of the very first to show up in America, and came from France. It is a spinner with a different shape than any other I've ever seen, and the metal is on the heavy side and not very large. The body is constructed of rubber or rubber substitute in various colors. This lure has outstanding qualities. First it casts easily; second it spins readily so that it can be reeled in very slowly; third you can fish it in shallow places without continually getting hung up. It comes in two styles, both similar except that one has a wool tag. It comes with single, double, or treble hooks. I much prefer the single-hook models, and usually cut off whatever extra points there may be. The single hook normally rides upright, and the best of this arrangement is that you can drag the bottom or even fish the edge of grass and weeds without readily snagging. Thus you can often take fish with it where other lures can't be used. It is a must for fishing in very shallow water.

Next, a deep-running spoon with a revolving blade is a good thing to have. It should work readily at low speed, and be heavy enough to get really deep. Of course you can use any one of the other spoons for this, and get the depth by attaching a sinker a slight distance above it. But if you can get one that does the job without a sinker it is somewhat better, simply because it can be more easily fished. But unless a deep-running lure has good action, then it is better to use a shallow-running lure that performs well, and get depth by the aid of a sinker. When doing this allow at least six inches between sinker and lure, so that the action is not impaired.

The wabblers and the darting-type spoons are always in order.

There are times, conditions, and places where these are better than revolving spoons. In the last two years some splendid lures of this sort have come on the market. Before then it was very difficult to obtain them.

All of these spoon types should be purchased in at least two colors. I prefer nickel or silver, and brass or gold. Some also like copper, and if you can get pearl then I would recommend it. I used one in 1950 while fishing in the Ozarks, but have been unable to find out where to get any more up to this writing.

An assortment of lures with different bodies is also recommended. You may have some with white beads, red beads, or orange beads,

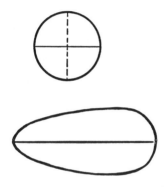

SPINNING SINKER AND KEEL

or with different-colored rubber bodies. Once I dyed a white rubber a deep green, and it took fish when red and yellow failed. At times a lure with a rubber hula dress at the end is more effective than the conventional types, while feathers, animal-hair, and scarlet wool tied to the end of any lure may be most attractive on occasion. You can always make up a good spinning lure if you have sinkers, spinners, and flies on ringed hooks. The only trouble with most spinning blades is that they will twist a line unless measures are taken to prevent it. A keel of some sort is necessary. If the spinner is heavy enough for easy casting, then a plastic keel will do the job. There is at least one company that makes these. If the spinner is too light for good casting, cut a piece of sheet lead into a circle having a diameter of about three-quarters of an inch. Cut this in half. Then make a groove from the middle of the straight edge to the middle of the curve on the other side—this so that bending the material will be easy and accurate. You attach the keel by simply bending the groove over the line and pressing the edges together. An oval-shaped piece of lead simply scored lengthwise in the middle will form a keel of additional weight. The whole idea is to make a streamlined article that slides easily through the water straight ahead but resists the side-pressures that tend to turn it over. Of course if the spinner overcomes the resistance of the keel, so that it also spins, you will soon have a badly twisted line. I've often seen lines so twisted that getting them straightened out was a hopeless task. This will not happen if the keel has enough flat surface to overcome the power of the turning spoon. Freely running swivels will aid the keel in keeping the line from twisting, so make sure that you have good ones.

In choosing lure colors you may use your imagination. What may be good for one day, one stream, or even one individual fish, may not be good for another. On the whole, reds, yellows, and white are all good in addition to nickel, brass, and copper. Occasionally green and blue will do better than others.

Do not overlook Devon-type lures. These are fast spinners, and very effective if you like them. Anglers have used them for ages, but most of them are devilish line twisters. If you buy them in rights and lefts and switch from one to the other frequently, you can keep out of trouble. There is also a special Devon made that is equipped with a non-twisting device. It works, too, but it does not take the place of some of the other Devons, perhaps because of its action, perhaps because of the colors. But neither do the other Devons take the place of these. So to be fully equipped you really need both. Years ago I used Devons that had reversible fins. You could make them spin either right or left at will. I haven't seen these in recent years, and it is too bad because they were very good.

Small plugs are often excellent. This is particularly true of plugs that have a good action when reeled at low speed, and that can be kept working steadily in one spot where the current pull has sufficient power and is flowing in the right direction in relation to your position to let it operate as it should. This sounds rather involved, and it is. You see, you must co-operate with even the most perfectly designed lure, and you cannot expect it to do the job if you fail to fish it properly. This means placing it in the right place from the right position. Only then will it give top performance.

On the whole I prefer using lure of this type with a sinker attached from ten to eighteen inches above it. However, if the plug has sufficient weight to be cast the required distance, then sometimes not using a sinker brings better results.

I would suggest the following colors for these very good lures:

Orange (or *yellow*, or *both*): A generally effective coloration.
Silver: Particularly effective for some conditions, as when fish are feeding on minnows.
White and Red combination: Not necessary but a good fish-getter. If you are a devotee of this mixture, be sure to include it.
Rainbow: This should be a mixture of primary colors, and the more the variations in the different colors the better. How best to have them arranged on the lure depends on the light. So get some that are dark on bottom and light on top, and vice versa. As long as I can remember, this mixture of all the primary colors has at times been the open sesame to very good luck.

Weighted flies are sometimes good, but for my part, unless it is a case of deep trolling, I prefer fishing a fly with a fly rod. Any fly weighted enough to cast with a spinning rod is a lifeless sort of thing, and hard to fish with. An unweighted fly of identical pattern, used on a fly rod, has definite life and buoyancy. But the addition of a dressed trailer-hook fly will make the weighted fly better. You can also improve it by attaching a spinner at the front end. Some flies are made with a built-in spinner, but the ones I have used are a trifle light for average fishing conditions where a spinning outfit is necessary. They could easily be made better.

There are some spinning lures made with bodies that resemble quills. These are excellent, and certainly resemble minnows more than many other baits. I believe these should be added to your assortment.

To make the spinning-lure assortment complete you should have something in the way of bugs that may be fished on the surface. Unfortunately such lures, when of a weight suitable to be cast with spinning tackle, are mostly too large to be very satisfactory for trout fishing. But you should have a few anyway because you may wish to fish for bass. Besides, these surface bugs can be used in a unique and often effective manner. To the hook, tie a leader from twenty to thirty inches long. To the end of the leader, tie either a wet fly, a dry fly, or a streamer. Fish the dry fly without motion, or at most just twitch the bug slightly now and then. But fish the other two flies by making the surface bug cause considerable disturbance on the surface of the water. It is surprising how effective this method can be. Sometimes you can even get doubles, one on the bug and another on the trailing fly. On the whole, however, I have taken more trout on the trailer than on the bug.

Also, in this connection, you may purchase plastic globes (balls) that can be filled with water to give the necessary casting weight. To these you may attach a leader and fly, as described for the bug. If you choose, you can also attach a hook to the globe. As these globes cast more easily than surface bugs, you may like them better.

You may desire to fish with natural bait. For spinning there are special gangs made for use with minnows. Often this natural-minnow bait will take trout when everything else fails. But it also demands the chore of either buying or gathering minnows, and then keeping them fresh after you get them. Of course you may use preserved minnows, but fresh ones are far more effective, even if they are dead. Of course they should not be spoiled, unless you wish to use them for catfish bait.

If you want to fish with worms or natural bait other than minnows, you can use the spinning outfit with success. But for such work I prefer a fly rod unless I need to fish very deep, in which case I believe I'd favor an old-time bait or a bait-casting rod with suitable accessories. As a matter of fact I believe a fly rod is best for fishing with a minnow, when the fish is on a single hook and not pierced with a gang.

Since the advent of spinning in the United States, many boxes have been designed to carry the lures, though when the method was introduced we used whatever boxes we had on hand. When purchasing boxes for this purpose, simply consider how you wish to use them. If you want a box for carrying lures on the stream, you should select one that will fit nicely in the pocket of your fishing coat, or whatever garment you use when fishing. For stock, or for boat fishing, select the box that will segregate as many different lures as possible, simply because it will then be possible for you to find just what you want in less time.

An assortment of small swivels both snap and plain, wire split rings, beads, spoon blades, and sinkers are all part of a balanced spinning kit. With them you can repair or perhaps improve the lures you have. I wish some firm would make up a kit of various lure parts from which a person could assemble a lure as needed. I'm sure that it would be enthusiastically received by anglers who like this method of fishing.

CHAPTER X

Spinning Methods and Experiences

THE methods used in spinning embrace both plug- and fly-fishing techniques. The differences, actually, lie only in the type of reel, used in conjunction with a rod that has action suitable for casting lightweight lures. To describe each method of fishing spinning lures in detail would be merely to repeat many of the methods of wet-fly fishing already described in these pages. Suffice to point out that you should handle a spinner or a plug in all the different ways you can use with a fly, plus whatever extra methods may be especially suited for use with a reel that can retrieve very fast.

For this reason I shall confine this chapter mostly to actual fishing experiences wherein certain lures or methods produced, while others failed or didn't do too well. I believe this will give you a more digestible, enjoyable, and thus more interesting chapter than it would otherwise be.

It seems right that I should start with my first outstanding experience with spinning tackle, rather than mediocre previous trips. This took place on the Rising River in California. My wife and I were fishing out of Burney, which is not far from Mount Lassen— a most interesting and picturesque country, well worth visiting. For companions we had Mr. and Mrs. Harold Tarter, natives of California.

Fishing had been extremely poor, so on the last day of our stay I wasn't a bit annoyed when a huge batch of correspondence caught up with me, and I found it necessary to reduce the pile before starting on our next jaunt down to Bishop, not far from the Yosemite country.

Harold and our wives went off to Rising River early in the morning, with the understanding that I would join them in the afternoon. I spent more time at the work than I'd originally intended. Even though I rushed when I realized it was late, I reached the stream only a scant hour and a half before dark.

Tarter reported trout rising off and on all day, but no luck in catching them. Let me mention here that he is an excellent fisherman, and when he hadn't been able to take any fish with a fly, I knew that I wouldn't have taken any either except by some lucky chance.

If Harold had told of taking trout with his flies, then this particular incident would not have occurred, because I also would have fished with a fly. Even as it was, I had to fight my desire to rig up the fly rod. But common sense finally prevailed, and the spinning outfit was soon in action.

I went to the upper end of the stretch in order to fish down, and Harold went to the lower end so that he could fish up. I decided on a systematic covering of the water, fishing across and downstream. I could easily cast to the opposite shore, which I did, dropping the lure as close to the bank as I could at a quartering downstream angle. Sometimes I let the lure sink a bit before retrieving, sometimes I did not. As the stream at this point was unreadable from the surface, being somewhat canal-like in appearance, I simply moved a couple of feet after each cast and so covered the entire water thoroughly.

There was sufficient current to make possible the rather slow reeling of the rubber Devon minnow I chose to use. After it got under the surface, the Devon would make a graceful sweep across stream while being retrieved. Not knowing which method might be best, I alternated between steady and jerk retrieves.

The first sign of action came on the ninth or tenth retrieve—one of the steady ones. I saw a large shape appear under the lure just as I lifted it from the water. Of course I spent the next two dozen or more casts over the same place, trying the lure deep and high—jerking it, reeling it fast, and what not. But he wouldn't come back, so after much valuable daylight had been wasted in this vain attempt, I resumed the methodical covering of the water. Perhaps thirty feet further down I got a decidedly hard snub but failed to connect. After that came a dead period, and I reached a point where to get further downstream would have meant walking a considerable distance around a dense piece of brush. I decided to retrace my steps the hundred yards or so back to where I'd seen that big fish come up under my Devon. I felt that it was as good a place as any to spend the little bit of daylight left.

By this time it was quite dusky, and the water looked black and mysterious. I was ready to quit, but decided to make one last cast. It was time for the jerk retrieve, but I was a bit discouraged and used the easiest way—the steady retrieve. Then came the strike, a heavy and exciting one. The bank was high and undermined, I had no net, and darkness was descending with incredible speed.

The fight was about over, and I was trying to figure out a way to get hold of the fish with my hands when I was relieved to find Harold, with his net, at my side. The line broke as the big fish, approximately a four-pounder, flopped in the net, and the loose end became hopelessly jammed in the mechanism of the reel. Later we tested the line and found that it couldn't take more than a pound pull. And it had tested five pounds when I started fishing that afternoon!

Although I have written up this experience before in *Outdoor Life*, though never in detail as I have here, I felt that it was necessary to do so because it marked the turning point in my attitude toward spinning. This is something that must be experienced by all fly-fishing enthusiasts before they really accept the method. It gave me the jolt I needed to make me realize that here was a way of fishing deserving of every angler's consideration. Surely, I reasoned, if it could turn a bit of success like this once, then it could do it again. From then on I began using this spinning outfit more frequently, sometimes even choosing it in preference to the fly rod.

I find that in fast water the natural-drift method as used in wet-fly fishing will produce far better than any other except in isolated cases. It isn't hard to do this providing you have the right lure to conform with the speed and depth of the water. Only you can decide this by experimentation on the spot. But here is what should happen in order to do it right. When the lure hits the water it should be carried along and prevented from sinking rapidly by the force of the current. *If it is too heavy for the water it will not carry properly.* As it is being thus swept along you should be able to release line just fast enough to let the drift proceed naturally; yet you should also keep just a slight bit of pressure, enough to be in control of the strike if a fish hits. The lure should be performing as this is going on, that is a spinner should be spinning and a wab-

bler should be wabbling and so forth, each according to its character. Sometimes the current is so strong that the lure comes to the
top at the slightest pressure of the line. In such cases you may try
feeding out line very fast, and you may let the lure drift for a considerable distance. Of course this procedure means having short
periods of slack line during the drift, and so you may miss a strike.
After you have let out all the line you wish to or can, then retrieve.
If the lure comes to the top, try giving it jerks, hard enough to
splash. This sometimes gets results. Or try a heavier lure that will
go down despite the water's power. It all depends on how the fish
are acting. If they are taking at or near the surface, fish a lure that
rides there, or vice versa.

Often it is best to get the natural drift by casting upstream instead of across and down. But sometimes it takes exceptional skill,
not to mention physical endurance, to fish a lure that way. This is
true when the water is so fast and heavy that you must reel like
mad to keep up with the drift of the bait. In such cases it may be
best to use extra-heavy sinkers and fish downstream, something
that would be better to do with a bait-casting ensemble than a
spinning one. But to show how well this upstream natural drift
works, when applied right and in water where it is possible without
extreme effort, let me tell you of a most exciting incident that took
place in the Laurentides Park, Quebec.

The exact location was Bergman's Pool on the Trompeuse-
Ecorces River. This feeds into a beautiful body of water called Lac
aux Ecorces, on which the main camp for the territory is located.
It was our last day at the park, and next to the last day of the trout
fishing season, September 29. As we had portaged out from Big
Lake Metascouac that day and had had numerous unpacking
chores to complete, it was late afternoon before we got started for
the pool. By the time we reached it, only about an hour and a half
of fishing time remained.

My comrade was Laurent Talbot, well known by many guests
of the park, and well liked for his helpfulness to them in arranging
their vacation time. My guide was Roger Durocher, and Laurent's
was Rock, a young Indian with a fine personality who showed
promise of becoming topnotcher in the guiding profession.

Of course we started off hopefully fishing with flies. In the first
half hour I got only one touch, which I missed, and Laurent had

had a big fellow make one pass at his flies although it did not take. Neither of these fish would make a second crack. It was especially exasperating because every once in a while a large trout would come to the surface and make a terrific commotion—often not more than a dozen feet from us, sometimes much less.

Reluctantly I set up the spinning outfit, attaching a favorite fly-rod plug and rigging it for deep water and easy casting by attaching an eighth-ounce sinker about twelve inches above it. Then I made a cast almost directly upstream. The water surface was smooth-topped but speedier than I realized, so I had to reel quite fast in order to make the plug wabble instead of merely snagging on bottom. It was almost under the boat and really deep when I felt a very hard pull and was fast to a nice fish. As this trout was brought fighting to the surface, several others could be seen flashing about it.

The first fish landed, I quickly made another short cast directly out from the boat. As I reeled the lure in and it came to the surface, a large male came up with a great splash. I was startled, and took the lure away from the fish, but dropped it quickly back into the water. Instantly the water boiled and the trout came into the air so that everyone saw him. But I did something wrong and never felt him strike. Guess I took the plug off the water too quickly. I imagine this trout would have taken it on the way down. But, recovering my poise, I made another short cast, and a few seconds later I was fast to a very nice male, whether the same one that had jumped near the boat I do not know.

One might suppose, from the way that one fish struck on the surface and the boiling of the others on the top, that a surface lure or fly would have been the best, but it wasn't. We got the same idea and tried a number of surface creations, but nothing happened. So I quickly changed back to the original set-up, and on repeating an upstream cast and retrieve had the gratification of again feeling the pull of a heavy fish just when the plug had drifted, with my slight help, back to the boat. When the trout took, the plug was very deep and almost under the boat.

Laurent, not having a spinning outfit, tried a plug of the same design and size as mine on his fly rod. He got one good rise to it, but the hooks failed to go home, something quite understandable when you consider that he was using a very light rod, one not intended for use with plugs. It didn't have the *power* to set the hooks. Also, without a sinker this particular lure did not go deep enough to be perfectly satisfactory in meeting the mood of these fish. A silver or aluminum finish seemed to be the best for the time and place. I've found this finish excellent in many waters from coast to coast.

When it was time for us to leave Bergman's Pool I had caught seven beautiful trout, none under two and a half pounds or over two and seven-eighths pounds. We kept two of these fish for food. The others were released uninjured, in hopes that they would eventually give some other angler a thrill.

This is only one of the many experiences I've had that illustrate the effectiveness of this method. I had several during 1950, one so outstanding that I believe it to be worth telling. It took place on the Snake River in Wyoming, within sight of the rugged Teton range. Three of us had fly-fished the fast-water stretch of a long and deep hole. We each took a few trout, and then couldn't get another touch.

The others moved downstream to fish the more quiet water where some fish had been seen rising, but I thought I'd put aside the fly rod for awhile and fish over the fast water again with the spinning outfit. Starting at the head or upper end, I worked downstream three times, changing lures each time. On the third trip down, using a quarter-ounce wabbling spoon, gold in color, I took a two-pounder. This was the only strike received fishing the regular across-and-downstream way.

Then I faced about and fished upstream. The lure was easy to cast and I could reach one hundred feet without any difficulty. This allowed me to cover the entire stretch from the head of the rapids to where I stood where I had landed the fish on the way down. It required fast retrieving to keep up with the water's speed, both to give the lure action and to keep it from snagging. When the lure had been brought in to a point not more than fifteen feet above me I felt a heavy weight, and was fast to a two-pounder. On the next cast I hooked a larger fish, just a few seconds after I started to retrieve. Then, in three successive retrieves, I hooked three more good fish, none under two pounds, and all within fifteen feet of where I stood, in water that I had covered a short time before fishing downstream from above with the same lure. I believe that it was the depth of the lure, achieved by fishing it upstream, that turned the trick.

I have had many interesting spinning experiences among these great mountains of the West. I remember vividly one large hole, also on the Snake, but on the Idaho fork not far from Big Springs. I'd fished it half a dozen times without getting anything bigger than a one-pounder on a fly rod, but did some real execution there when I worked it over with a spinning ensemble.

It is a mixed-up piece of water. The main current rushes straight toward a forested bank, but before it actually assaults the land, it meets another rather strong minor current at right angles. Of course the water makes a considerable mix-up at that point.

These conflicting currents at the upper part of the pool make the proper handling of flies there very difficult, in fact just about impossible, from the only side that can be reached by land. And each time we fished the river from a canoe, we drifted over the hole so fast that we never did get time to fish it correctly.

As mentioned, I had fished this hole half a dozen times without taking a decent fish. Twice this was done from a canoe, three times from the heavily forested side that could be reached by land. Finally I took one good fish. This was after Scotty Chapman, Don Bell, and I decided it might be a good idea to park at the head of this pool awhile and to use three methods fishing it, just to see what would happen.

We embarked in the canoe at the railroad trestle below Big Springs, Idaho. The hole in question is the first one of any size that is reached after you leave the railroad. We approached it on the main current stem which, contrary to the regular flowage of the stream there, makes a sharp left-hand turn, with the fast water starting immediately after the turn. We landed on the right-hand side not very far from the head of the fast water. The shore is sandy and reasonably flat for nearly the entire length of the run, or to the point where this fast water meets the other current that follows the general stream direction, and then, mingling with it, turns almost at right angles. Below this the big pool gradually became similar to any other normal hole.

It was nice fly fishing the main current stem from shore. Don went below and fished up with a dry fly, while Scotty started in from above and fished down with a wet fly. They fished carefully and well and both are intelligent, skillful fishermen. Scotty took one small fish, Don failed to get a rise.

After they had given up I went to work with the spinning outfit, using a small fly-rod plug, in fact the same one I have mentioned using in the Laurentides, although this incident happened many years previously. Because of the heavy water I used a quarter-ounce sinker ahead of the lure. The run was quite narrow, and when I fished the lure from shore it would not hold in the current but insisted on pulling around and in to shore again. I worked around for awhile and finally found a place where I could wade out into the water for a number of feet. Then I made a cast of some sixty-five feet across and downstream, and let the current pull the lure along, giving just enough line so that it kept going deeper. I must have fed out at least forty more feet of line when I got a hard snub, and a second or two later a boil appeared in the mixed-up water where the two currents met. Some time later I beached a cutthroat of about three pounds. Later I got another strike at the same place, but missed the fish. There seemed to be a small eddy in that particular spot, because when the line was held steady at that point the lure would keep working around and around without taking out any more line.

In the deeper and more quiet part of the hole around the bend, Scotty pricked three fish with a streamer fly and I pricked one on the plug. Spinning lures were scarce at that time, so I didn't have many different kinds to play with. Those I did try failed to get any response. The dry flies failed entirely. Not one fish even rose to investigate them.

Incidentally I believe that fish missed on the strike are inclined to disturb the fishing in a pool more than does the actual hooking and playing of one. A pricked trout gets thoroughly frightened and dashes for cover, thus scaring the rest of them. But while the hooked fish temporarily startles the others, they soon get over it and become interested in trying to get the thing the hooked fish seems to be fighting, or perhaps chasing. Often they follow a hooked member of the pool, and if you have a cast of two lures or flies you will sometimes get a double. Of course this doesn't always hold true, but if you have fished long enough you will have witnessed other fish following and darting around the trout you are playing. They will follow in that way directly to a boat, or to a bank if conditions are suitable.

A number of years later, fishing this same pool, I not only landed many good fish from it, but had some doubles as well. World War Two had intervened in the interim. But as soon as the war had ended and it was possible to make long trips, I got back to this country again. By that time I had become much enthused over spinning, so at the first opportunity went to this pool on the Snake, this time without a canoe. As mentioned, the left bank can be reached on foot and it is heavily forested. It is thick and tangled enough to make fly-fishing very limited, in fact there are only a couple of small areas where you can get into the water far enough to make any cast at all. Here is where spinning tackle comes into its own, and using it in this hole had been in my mind all through the war.

At first I fished the head, just where the main and secondary currents met; the very spot from which I'd taken the three-pounder when fishing from the other side several years before. From this side it meant casting up into one current and across another. Using the same sinker-and-plug combination as before, I made a cast that placed the lure about four feet beyond the spot and into the swift main current leading to it. By the time I got control and felt the lure for a second I was fast to a fish. I took two more with the identical tactics and lure, then couldn't get another hit although I tried other locations and lures. Of course I believe that the way the lure sank and acted from this particular casting position and over this particular spot accounted for the three fish, all cutthroats, each one better than a pound and a half in weight. From the same casting location, I fished across and downstream as far as I could manage to get fair action out of the lures I used. This netted two rainbows of approximately one and a quarter pounds each. They took the little plug in preference to other lures I tried.

Then fish started rising in the more shallow and rather fast water at the foot of the hole. It took considerable time and maneuvering to get into casting position for them, but they were still hot at it when I got situated. I did wish that I had my fly rod instead of the spinning outfit. The trout were taking flies from the surface, and my position was such that I had to fish upstream.

These trout would not look at the plug or any of the spoons in my kit. Fortunately I happened to have one floating bass bug in the tackle box, and also some streamer flies. I snapped the bug on the line swivel, tied a two-foot leader to its hook, and then selected the most meaty-looking fly I had to tie onto that. It was a rather large fly and nameless. Someone had given it to me. The body was bloody red, the wings and hackle very soft dark furnace. It looked like a cross between a streamer and a nymph. On the third or fourth drift of this combination, fishing it quartering up and across and giving it a slight twitch now and then, a large rainbow took the bug. I set the hook, and he jumped, throwing the lure some six feet through the air in less time than it takes to write the words. I didn't have time to recover from this shock, because as the thrown bug dropped back to the water another fish grabbed it and was hooked. Hardly had he settled down to fighting than another fish jumped close to him, and in its mouth was the trailer fly. Both were landed.

For the next half hour I was fast to one fish after another, some-times two at the same time, and there were many instances where two fish struck but only one was hooked. Then suddenly the fish-ing went dead, not only there but everywhere else along the stream that I could reach from shore or by wading. This experience would have been perfect except for one thing. While the fish hooked and landed ranged from one to three pounds each, not one of them came anywhere near the size of the one that had thrown the bug. As is usually the case, I would have settled for that one fish alone. Much better that than all the others.

Lest you think that here is the answer to an angler's prayer, let me mention that although I have fished this water four times since, I never took more than two fish on any occasion—and those were one-pounders or less.

At another time three of us were drifting downstream in a canoe. One of my companions was fishing wet, one dry, and I was using the plug-and-sinker combination. Nothing of particular in-terest happened until we reached a long, medium-fast run that bordered a meadow. All over this stretch, from some fifteen feet out to the edge of the bank, fish were rising and dimpling nicely, a definite challenge to any dry-fly man.

Before the other fellows had time to think of going to the bank so that they could fish the water thoroughly, I had sent the plug over one of the dimples. Instantly I was fast to a good-sized and stout brownie. We drifted quite a bit while fighting this fish, in fact beyond the hot section. Due to the natural formation of the bank, it seemed best to retrace our course to a point above the active feeding area in order to get to shore without alarming the rising fish.

On the way back Don intended to fish with a dry fly, while I kept fishing with the spinning outfit. Scotty was paddling the canoe. The fly never had a chance. On the first cast, over the first rise we saw, I hooked a good fish. This happened before the rise could be reached with a fly-rod cast. We kept moving upstream while I played this fish to a finish, but even so I had time to take one more good trout and lose two others because I deliberately played them too hard, before we could safely shoot to shore without scaring the feeding fish.

On shore I retired to let my friends get in their innings. They got into casting position without putting down a single rising fish, and started to work. Both were skilled and experienced fly fishermen. I know that I couldn't have done any better job than they, nor perhaps nearly as good. And what happened? Not a single trout was taken. They ignored everything that was offered. Not only that, but after the flies had been cast to a fish a few dozen times or so it would stop rising completely.

My friends finally quit and asked me to try the plug. There were still three dimpling fish for me to cast to. In great confidence I dropped the little plug just right to the nearest fish. It seemed an absolutely perfect delivery, but the trout didn't take. I tried again. The cast wasn't quite as perfect but was very good. This made the trout stop rising. Almost the same thing happened with the other two, except that they didn't stop rising until the fourth cast for one and the eighth cast for the other.

What was the trouble? I do not know positively, although I could present a few logical theories. Perhaps some of my readers will get interested enough in this incident to think it out and arrive at their own conclusions. I've given you the facts of the case. Perhaps you have had similar experiences; I know that I have; although none so definite as this incident where a dry fly and a spinning lure were compared when used for fish feeding on flies. Keep in mind that these surface feeders took the plug when it was cast to them from the canoe, but refused it when it was offered to them from the shore. Also that in similar conditions I've experienced the opposite reaction.

Sometimes it is quite amazing how some spinning lures will take trout that are rising to natural flies floating on the surface of the water. In my experience good spinning lures for this purpose should have the following characteristics. They should cast easily. They should act or perform properly when reeled at low speed. They should not sink when in motion, nor come to the top. They should ride in such a way that the hooks do not catch bottom continually. (This is almost impossible with either spoons or spinners equipped with treble hook. But certain plugs so equipped will miss some hazards due to the nose of the lure digging sharply down into the water on the retrieve.)

Please do not ask me to recommend any specific lure in this respect. I do have a few favorites, and have cut off the extra points of others to make them better for such work. Unfortunately when a treble hook is cut it changes the weight and balance so that the lure doesn't perform as well as it should. However a double hook, set so that the points are directed upward, is very good for many lures.

Manufacturers tell me that they have great sales resistance to lures that are not equipped with treble hooks. I realize that this is true, but it isn't right. If all manufacturers would get together and use nothing but single hooks, then the resistance would be broken. Personally I wish all lures were made with single hooks, or at least with one, two, or three single hooks instead of one, two, or three trebles. I return nearly every fish I catch to the water. Once in a while I keep a couple of pounds to eat. When a fish is caught with a treble it is very difficult to unhook it without injury, no matter how careful I am in doing it. Moreover the time element enters the picture, and three barbs take longer to release than one. If the lure has two treble hooks it makes matters that much worse. This is bad enough when the fish are big enough to keep. It is deplorable when the fish are small. And don't overlook the fact that many undersized fish are caught, far more than the number of good fish, perhaps even of legal fish. A single hook will hold a fish just as well as a treble, perhaps better; and a lure constructed to operate best with a single hook instead of a treble would serve both those who wish to keep their limits and those who fish for the fun of it. Besides, it would save many small fish that would otherwise be too badly injured to survive.

To illustrate how a spinning lure will take rising fish in shallow water, let me tell you of an experience that took place on a stream that should have been restricted to fly fishing some time ago and has since been so restricted. I had located six sizable trout that fed daily at the edge of a weed-patch, in water that barely covered their dorsal fins. The bank on their side was low and covered with short grass, so that no matter how good a stalking job I did, I always scared them away before getting into fly-fishing position. From the other side of the stream I could get no nearer than seventy feet without scaring them. Now that distance is too great for me to cast a fly and consistently have it alight softly, especially a dry fly. I tried it, and also tried a wet, but each time I succeeded only in chasing the fish away.

Consequently I finally decided to try the spinning outfit. Using a spinner of the type last described, that is one that handles nicely in shallow water, I dropped it close to, but not over, the nearest rising trout. It alighted without any discernible splash. As the water was shallow and there were many weeds, I started the retrieve the instant it landed. Immediately the water bulged near the lure, changed into a turbulent V, and then I felt the strike. It was a fish that weighed two and three-quarters pounds. Far up on a bank some distance away, my wife Grace cheered. At least she told me she did after I got back to the car. I was too far away to hear her.

Three others were hooked at this time. All ran above two pounds, but I weighed only the single fish I killed so do not know if they weighed more than the one I kept. The other two fish that I knew were there did not take. I took the trouble to cross the stream and investigate but could see no sign of them.

Three days later I fished this place again, using the same spinner. Three good fish were hooked, landed, and released. One was certainly a fish that I'd caught the first time. He'd been marked by the lure when I took it from his mouth. Again I investigated the spot from the other side. Again I saw no trout, nor any sign of one leaving the place at my approach. Whether new fish had come in, or whether I had hooked the same fish twice, is not determinable, except for the one that had been accidentally marked. I haven't fished this particular place since, so must end my case history here. But I couldn't help feeling that this spinning method could definitely hurt the fishing in some streams.

But let me clarify this. In my personal experience with spinning I have found that certain streams that had in the past afforded at best very spotty fly fishing, reacted remarkably well to spinning technique and lures. This holds true in both the East and the West. Also, occasionally in excellent fly streams there are pools or deep holes where fly fishing isn't too productive. Now here is where I believe that spinning is to be highly recommended. It fills a long-felt need. But I also find that streams which afford consistently good fly fishing throughout the season, provided one has reasonable skill and knowledge, yield readily to the offerings of the spinning angler too. Thus, far more fish are taken from such streams than would be the case if fished only by fly fishermen. In other words, many anglers who are not able to take trout on a fly make out quite well with the spinner, thus adding to the fishing pressure that in recent years has become very great. Now while I like to see everyone catch his share of fish, it is obvious that in some cases spinning can materially lower the quality of an originally good fly stream.

Some states recognize the need of restricting some of their waters to fly fishing—Maine and Connecticut to mention two. Yellowstone Park now has a new rule restricting two of its most popular waters to flies. While it is rather difficult to enforce such specific laws, the very fact that they exist acts as a sufficient check to most anglers, particularly if they are shown that such regulations are designed to help their fishing and not to discriminate against them.

I like spinning very much indeed, both for its sportiness and for the large fish it so often attracts. And I also believe that, regardless of how good it is, it will not deplete our waters any more than any other method in the hands of a meat-getter. But it does seem tough for a good fly stream to be subjected to additional pressure by the spinning enthusiasts, when there is so much water that is poor fly fishing and yet excellent for spinning.

This is merely a thought. I have no special stake in fly fishing, or bone to pick with spinning. All I wish is that folks would use the latter with discretion, that they would spare those waters well known for providing good fly fishing. Certainly the fly fisherman is entitled to some consideration.

In any stream fishing, knowing the lures you have is a necessity for really successful spinning. Only by completely understanding each one can you possibly derive the greatest returns from their use.

To illustrate the need for such knowledge, let me tell you of some experiences on the Yellowstone River, somewhere below the Grand Canyon of the Yellowstone. Much of the water where this experience occurred was rather fast. There were places where the rapids ran straight and true. Here I used a deep-running, quarter-ounce lure that was about right for them. It could be fished for a bit with a natural drift as already described, and afterward could be reeled in slowly. Both the natural drifts and the retrieves brought their quota of strikes and worked out very satisfactorily, although the whitefish were a bit of a nuisance.

But occasionally I would come to runs where this lure hung up; and then had to be fished with a lighter lure, sometimes even with a different type of spinner. One thing was usually needed to get results. The lure had to make a natural drift of at least thirty feet—more was usually better—or else you didn't catch any fish. I must confess that I lost a lot of time trying lures to get the right one for each different condition, something that would have been avoided had I known all of my lures intimately.

Occasionally we came to an eddy where lures that had proved good in the rapids, glides, and ripples failed to work. Here a fly-rod plug, with an action that fought the water hard so that you could always feel the throbbing, worked best. It took different weight sinkers to get the best results in different holes, simply because each eddy or pool was unlike any other. When the right combination of lure and sinker was achieved, one could, with sympathetic reaction to the current pull, search out all parts of the hole. That is what is needed to consistently get strikes in such places. Sometimes you must release line fast, sometimes slowly; often it is best to hold the line taut. What to do is all telegraphed up your rod. Keep the lure working at an in-between speed, neither too fast nor too slow. You can, by testing, soon get to know by the throbbing when a lure is working most effectively. Remember, if possible, just how the throbs felt when you got a strike. Learning to recognize these things when they happen is an important must in successful fishing.

Feeding trout, in holes and eddies where there is a decided whirlpool action, tend to lie near the edge of the currents where they can pick up the food that is gradually being drawn toward the comparatively static center. The better your lure works around near the edge of this static spot, the better your chance of taking fish. Clever worm and minnow fishermen know this fact well. For instance, take Allie Murray of Vermont. All through the season, come high water or low, Allie can get results on the local streams he knows so well. When he fishes a worm he weights it just right for a particular hole. If it doesn't work right at the start he keeps changing weights and sometimes hooks as well, until the bait can be manipulated all over the bottom of the hole. Of course a spinning outfit can be used for bait as well as for lures. The idea is to have either artificial lures or bait work around the hole close to the bottom.

But to get back to the Yellowstone River. Well, whenever my combination of plug and sinker fitted the waters of any whirling pool, then I got a fish or two; but when it didn't, when the lure failed to properly search the edge of the current close to bottom, then it was rare that any strike was received.

The sinker-and-plug combination worked well in a very wide, lakelike part of the river. Where we could reach it with our casts from shore there wasn't any whirling eddy, but there was a slow downstream movement. I first tried the lures that had done well in the fast-water stretches. As these did not produce, I eventually used the combination, a one-sixteenth ounce plug with a one-eighth ounce sinker.

I made the first cast slightly upstream, and as far as I could throw. Pausing a moment before starting the retrieve, I reeled in just enough to keep from getting hung up. Every once in a while I let the sinker touch bottom, just to make sure that I was fishing deep.

On the third retrieve I got a hard hit but failed to connect. On the sixth retrieve I missed another, but this was followed a few seconds later by the exciting pull of a heavy-feeling fish. For a few moments the line sang and hissed as it cut through the water. Perhaps five or more minutes later I had the pleasure of steering a three- and three-quarter-pound cutthroat into a tiny harbor between two large rocks jutting out from shore.

During 1950 and 1951 I spent several days on the Yellowstone, below the park. Here the wabbling and darting spoons seemed to work best, taking a good number of fish, including browns, rainbows and cutthroats.

When it comes to pond and lake fishing, the spinning outfit is excellent. Often, except at certain periods of the year, such waters provide little or no fly fishing, but fishing with spinning lures can produce amazing results. Don't overlook trolling in this connection. I know the method isn't very exciting by most angling standards, but many times it is a necessary method if you would like to catch any fish.

On the whole it is wise to troll quite slowly—just fast enough to bring out the action of the lure being used. Also, before trying any other depth, fish as close to the bottom as you can. This means you must touch bottom quite a bit and so may get hung up now and then. This trouble must be taken in stride, because if you don't get near bottom you may not get a strike. There are some types of sinker that do not catch as easily as others. Also some lures hook up worse than others. If you have too much trouble getting snagged, it may be for this reason. Then try some other styles.

Once you get to know any water well, you can troll close to bottom very neatly, seldom getting snagged. But this smoothness of operation comes only from experience, not only with the specific waters, but also with various lures and sinkers. And a very sensible method, if perhaps not esthetic in the eyes of some, is a slow troll with worms or minnows or some other natural bait. I mean really slow—barely moving in fact—and if you do it without the aid of a sinker, all the better.

Of course there are times and places when the trout lie neither on bottom nor on top, but instead stay in between the two. It is said that one can find out where the different fish are by taking the temperature of the water at different depths. It is claimed that each variety will seek the degree they like best. Now generally speaking this is true, and I imagine that some ponds and lakes could be charted along these lines. But for general practical use the idea leaves one floundering. There are so many variations, so many factors bearing on each individual piece of water, that applying the idea becomes very complicated. Even if a fellow knows enough about it all to correctly test and diagnose a case it take a lot of time, something most anglers have the least of. But by intelligently trolling you can definitely find out at what depth and what location the fish are feeding, and at the same time be fishing.

The spinning outfit is excellent for trolling, provided your reel can be locked so that it won't turn backward. (See Chapter IX.) When you locate some fish by trolling you may stop and cast over the place, if you so choose. You may ask: "Why not cast all the time? Wouldn't you locate fish just the same, or better?" The answer is no, and the reason is that casting fails to give adequate depth coverage. You see, just as soon as you start retrieving, the lure starts to work toward the surface, thus traveling away from the fish feeding in deep water. When trolling you can keep a lure working at any definite depth you choose, depending on the length of line let out, the weight of the lure, and the speed of the boat. You can consistently fish the bottom for long distances, or any level between bottom and the surface.

When it comes to fishing the surface of shallow water then casting definitely does the best job, but when it comes to fishing deep then trolling gives the best coverage. In very deep water casting is almost a total loss, although fish can be caught that way. In my experience I find that when fish are feeding deeper than twenty feet, I usually do better if I stop casting and troll instead. At the same time I must admit that by letting a lure sink to bottom and then retrieving with alternate spurts and pauses, I have made some excellent catches in water as deep as thirty feet.

Regarding the idea of testing water temperature in reference to locating fish, let me point out that there isn't anything new about it. As long as I can remember, anglers knew that when summer warmed the waters you had to find spring-holes or cold locations in a lake or stream if you hoped to catch a fish. I wrote about this in the 1920's. But while a certain temperature seemed best for one piece of water, another did just as well somewhere else. There isn't any doubt that trout will leave water that becomes excessively warm; they will stay in warmer water that is highly oxygenized, but not in water of the same temperature where the oxygen content is low. I've had excellent trout fishing on the surface with water temperatures ranging all the way from 50° to 70°. But I've also had some very poor fishing with the same temperatures, particularly at both the top and bottom extremes. On the whole I believe I prefer a temperature ranging from 57° through 65° for all-around shallow-water and surface fishing, of course excepting special cases. For instance, where streams are fed by hot springs the trout seem to do well at temperatures several degrees higher than in other streams.

Deep lakes have a fairly definite pattern. For awhile, say for two or three weeks after the break-up of the ice, the waters of such lakes are sufficiently mixed to be compared with a well-mixed drink, that is, all the component parts are thoroughly intermingled. This period may be longer than the time mentioned, depending on the weather. A very warm, sunny, and windless period in early spring might easily reduce the time, while cloudy skies, strong cold winds, snow, and cold rain might hold the condition static for longer than three weeks.

It is while the water is so completely mixed that trout take best and are also comparatively near or right close to the surface. But as the surface water becomes higher in temperature, it also becomes lighter in weight, thus preventing a complete circulation in lakes of thirty feet or more in depth. It is then that the water in such bodies becomes gradually stratified into three layers. The upper, or epilimnion, ranges in depth from about fifteen to thirty feet, according to the openness of the country and the amount of strong wind, sunshine, and other factors. Naturally the more open and windy the country, the more circulation occurs, and the more likelihood of the surface waters remaining cool and filled with oxygen. This upper layer, whatever its depth, is quite uniform in temperature throughout its entire area. Then comes the middle layer, or thermocline. This is a section of rapidly changing temperature, dropping, according to some records, as much as 1.8° Fahrenheit per 3.28 feet in depth. (See Bulletin 63, State of Connecticut, Public Document #47.) This layer may vary in depth approximately as much as does the upper layer. All water deeper than this layer, which will probably bring you down below sixty feet, is called the hypolimnion. This remains shut off from circulation, and so keeps cold during that period of the year when hot weather makes the surface water unfit for some species of fish. Of course this condition remains more or less static until sufficient cold air and wind conspire to completely mix the waters again.

On the whole, during the period when the three layers are in evidence, or perhaps I should say in operation, bass and similar fishes inhabit the top layer, rainbow and brown trout might likely be found in the middle area, while lake trout and whitefish will be at some good feeding location in the lower layer. Where will the brook trout be? Well, perhaps in the lower section of the middle area, but more likely in some spring-hole in the upper area. Trolling is best when they are in the lower or middle section, usually out in the deeper parts of the lake; casting, when they are in comparatively shallow-water spring-holes.

A spinning outfit is about the best job of all for fishing most lakes and ponds from shore. It doesn't always take the place of a fly rod, but in most lakes it is usually more effective. Not only can you reach out farther, but you can also cast easily from wooded shores where it would be very difficult, if not impossible, to cast properly with a fly rod.

The need for different types of lures is just as great in this fishing as it is in any other. You should have lures that work well at very low speed, and stay well down when being retrieved. You should have others that tend to stay up when being reeled slowly. Some you should be able to reel at high speed and yet have them perform properly, that is, not slide through the water with mediocre action, or spin around when they are supposed to wabble or dart. Manufacturers should concentrate on making these different actions as well as on trying to outdo each other in colors and finishes, and in advertising.

Sometimes trout will take a lure traveling at high speed but will refuse the same lure when it is going slowly. This may be due to several causes; the mood of the fish, the degree of light and the direction from whence it comes in relation to the angler's casting position, and the clarity of the water. The more colored or muddy the water, the less accurate the vision of the fish.

Even hungry trout may be suspicious on occasion, and if they have time to look a lure over enough, they may refuse to take it. I can't believe that any trout, except the immature or foolish, ever mistake a spoon or plug for a minnow IF THEY TAKE TIME TO IN-SPECT IT. But any animal may be easily fooled by something that is moving too fast to be clearly seen, or that is obscured by the rays of the sun or by discolored water. Of course I do believe that all game fish will many times deliberately go out of their way to strike strange things, sometimes taking them rather than the things they know well and live on. Trout get angry as well as bass. This is particularly true of brook trout, as I have often observed when spending many hours watching instead of fishing for them. And we all know that something about the flash of a spinner, and the wriggle or wobble of a plug, excites the interest of game fish. Even when you can't get them to take such artificials they will often follow them, dart at them, and otherwise tease the the angler.

Sometimes flies will fool the trout in ponds more than spinners and plugs. Therefore, if it is necessary to use a spinning outfit when fishing such waters, you should be equipped with the plastic globes so that you can throw flies that simulate insects and minnows. You may even attach a two-fly cast to the globe and simulate the action of the hand twist retrieve fairly well by proper manipulation of the reel handle.

There is a definite need for the spinning outfit. With it you can use some lures and reach some places better than is possible with other tackle. I believe that every angler should own, and be able to use with reasonable skill, all three major ensembles—that is, outfits for fly fishing, spinning, and bait-casting. Incidentally I'm listing the three in the order of my preference.

CHAPTER XI

Sunshine and Shadow

Under certain conditions trout do not see clearly. What the conditions are we shall now investigate. Bear in mind that this is theory although it has been applied to actual fishing, and as far as the writer is concerned it aids considerably in bringing success. But let us start at the beginning.

"Trout are selective to color and shape in inverse ratio to the intensity of light." In other words trout are more selective in the early morning and in the evening and on dark days than they are when the sun is shining brightly on the water. For this reason, if the trout will feed at all during the middle of the day, then a bright day will be the best sort of a day on which to fool them.

Before you rise up in arms over this paragraph I ask you to go back over your fishing experiences and see if you haven't had the following typical experience with flies many times. The early-morning fishing proves disappointing, and until the sun hits the water here and there, you don't do much better. But the moment the high and low lights made by reflections from the sun, or the sun itself, cast bold rays on the water, you begin to rise trout. While you don't take fish fast or see any spectacular rises, somehow you keep getting a fish here and there and have a really fine day. And then in the evening, after the sun has set and you expect fishing to be at its best, you suddenly find that you have a tough time fooling even a couple of ordinary specimens, if any at all. You change patterns time after time and cast, cast, and cast, but only occasionally do you strike the right fly and make a really good catch—that is, good compared to the number of fish breaking the water.

To explain how this might happen, let us start at the beginning. Under certain circumstances and on clear days trout cannot evaluate either the size, color, or shape of objects on the surface of the water. These certain circumstances are caused by bright light. Let me show you what I mean by making a simple experiment. Let us hold a fly directly between the sun and our eye. What happens? Color vanishes, shape is obscured, size becomes an uncertain quantity. About all we are conscious of is a black or purple indefinite shape and an uncontrollable eyestrain. But as we move the fly from the direct line between our eye and the sun, we see color and shape become more distinct and eyestrain become less. Further movement of the fly brings it to a position where the fly can be seen fairly well and eyestrain vanishes. In this position we cannot elaborate the little details of our artificial, but we get a good general effect. The vision is not so clear that we can tell exactly what the fly is, but it is clear enough so that we could make a good guess. Now if we stand with our back between the sun and the fly, we will note that we can see it very plainly indeed. We can see each hackle point, the hook, and the barb. We can also distinguish the pattern without effort.

In making stream experiments along these lines we find that when the fly is directly between the eye of the trout and the sun we get very few rises but that it makes no difference what fly is used. The fish, if they rise at all, will take a Scarlet Ibis as well as anything else, even though the natural on the stream may be gray, black, brown, or any other color.

In the area where the fly is somewhat indistinct and yet where the light isn't strong enough to cause bad eyestrain (the second position), we find the trout rise readily and are not particularly selective. This is because in this position they see quite well, but not so well that they can distinguish the little departures from the naturals.

In the third position, where the trout looks at the fly away from the sun, we find that we need to exercise excessive caution and use the right fly in order to get results. The fly and the cast must be about perfect. This is in direct contrast with the first position, where one doesn't need to worry either about the cast or the fly, or the second position, where any reasonable care is exercised.

In my opinion we have here the reasons why so often we have good catches during the sunny hours of a bright day, even when there isn't a general rise to naturals, and why so often when the tremendous evening rises occur we have such a difficult time to take fish. It is the rises occurring when the light is dull that cause most of our troubles and that make so many fly patterns necessary.

In my estimation, fishing on sunny days, when the fish in a stream will rise at all during this time of the day, requires less effort and fewer patterns of flies than fishing on dull days and only in the morning and evening. It is not necessary to fish in direct sunlight to get results. Reflections may easily form that distraction which prevents the trout from seeing too plainly what you are offering them. Understand, I'm not insisting that this theory is unassailable. I know that it is and could tear it apart without too much effort myself. But I do know that experience has consistently upheld my views in this respect, so that I consider them worth while passing along to you, to make use of or ridicule as you like.

Remember that on gray days there is no area where the fly is indistinct, and that this applies to any day when the sun does not cast a clearly defined shadow. On bright days, even under the shadow of the trees, the water may catch the reflection from a rock or cliff or the leaves of trees on which the sun is shining brightly, and so obscure the vision of the fish when a fly floats by in that area affected by the reflection.

All these things must be taken into consideration when choosing the most advantageous position to fish from, and the combinations you run into are many and complicated. In fact the subject is so big that it would take a lifetime of experimentation on this idea alone to definitely arrive at some perfect conclusions. I will say this, if you can ascertain the exact location of a large trout, the depth of water he lies in, and then figure out the angles of sunlight so that you can place your fly in that area of sufficient but some- what indistinct vision, you stand a good chance of taking him, perhaps not the first time you try, but eventually, if you keep at it and make sure you have the thing figured out correctly. At any rate I have given you the thought. Some of you may go further with it; most of you will simply read it and then forget it; the rest of you will no doubt consider it mere twaddle. All I can say is that the original idea came from the mind of one whom I considered one of the best anglers of my time.

Just what constitutes a good fishing day? Ask a dozen anglers, and you're likely to get a dozen different answers. Of course each one will insist that his choice is the best. It is, because at these times he has had his best fishing. I have my own choice—right or wrong. It is a bright sunny day with a snappy, cool air, and a northwest wind. This has been my favorite ever since I've started fishing, and I've never had any occasion to change my mind. I don't care if it blows a gale as long as the skies are blue and the air invigorating. This sort of weather makes my blood move faster. I feel vigorous, optimistic, capable of moving mountains. But when I put the cold light of registered facts on experiences, I find that I've had poor fishing on such days as well as excellent fishing. As a matter of fact no matter what type of day I pick out I find that both good and poor fishing have been experienced on them. Nevertheless I still prefer the snappy day, probably because I feel so good on such days, and besides they really do show a positive record of providing more good fishing than poor. But enough of this. Let me tell you of some experiences along these lines.

First, the Neversink at Oakland, New York. The time, May 30th. Weather, cold and squally, sometimes blowing so hard that it was impossible to cast except during a lull. We had been fishing on the Mongaup but hadn't done a thing, so on the way home thought we'd go Oakland way and take a look from the bridge. By the time we reached the bridge the day had grown worse. It was much colder, and the periods between terrific gusts were shorter. We had no hope of seeing any action, but because we had plenty of time we parked by the bridge and leaned over the railing to look at the Ledge Pool, which could plainly be seen from this point. A white slash in the center of the hole caught my eye. It was a considerable distance away, so that really I couldn't tell what it was, but some inner sense told me it was a rise. I didn't say anything to the others at the moment—just kept my eyes glued to the tail of that pool where I had seen that peculiar streak of white. Then I saw another, and immediately after that two more. It was enough for me. Without wasting any more time I made a bee line for the car to get my rod. As I went I shouted to the others: "There's something doing down there." They looked at me as if I'd gone crazy. I didn't blame them. Instinct rather than sight had told me that those white streaks were caused by trout.

So we went down to the pool and assembled our rods. While doing so we saw a half dozen of the slashes; and now, being so close to the pool, I could see that there wasn't any mistake about their being the rises of fish. Then I saw the reason for them. There was a large hatch of green May flies in evidence. The wind was blowing so hard that it made many of them skate over the surface of the pool, and the trout rising to take them sometimes had to chase them across the surface when the squalls struck. In doing this they make a slash of white spray, which the wind caught and accentuated.

The only fly in my box that in any way imitated this May fly was the Bridgeville Olive, a nondescript fly of the fan-wing type I had adopted and named because it had brought me success on the Neversink on the stretch just below Bridgeville. It really should have been called the Green May because it imitated this fly very well indeed. My first cast with it was a failure. A strong gust of wind struck the ledge on the opposite side and backed across the stream with a vengeance, fairly throwing the fly back in my face. This made me cautious, so I waited until a momentary lull occurred before making the next cast. The fly alighted perfectly, but I had misjudged the currents and got an immediate and bad drag. I tried several more times from the same position but could not get a float that did any business—I presume because of the drag. The fish were feeding in midstream, and to get the fly to them required a cast that put the line on three currents of different speeds.

There was only one thing to do. Out in the center of the stream was a flat rock that divided the main current of the deep hole. It was a mean place to get at, but I felt sure one could get a perfect float from that position, and determined to make a try for it. I made it and found that from this location I could not only put the fly over the rising fish, but could also fish the extreme right-hand side, which had been absolutely unreachable from the first position.

Then, after taking all this time and going to all the trouble, I make a fiasco of a splendid opportunity. Although in six casts I rose six good fish, I never had a chance to feel them. In each case I struck too hard and too fast, missing four completely and leaving a fly in the mouth of each of the other two. This seemed to end any further chances. Either there were only six trout feeding in the pool, or else I had put the rest down. At any rate, even though the natural May flies kept floating down with ever-increasing numbers, they did so without any molestation.

It took fifteen minutes to reach the next place where I could do any fishing. I saw a few rises here and there, but the water was very high and I could not wade out far enough to reach them. Coming to a hole where I knew a large fish lived, having had previous experiences with him, I was just about to try for him even though he wasn't rising when from the corner of my eye I saw one of the slash rises some distance out in the swirling current. It could be reached by a long cast from where I stood, but feeling sure that it was impossible to make a satisfactory float, I decided to make an attempt to get into better position. This took another ten minutes, but it was worth it. There was a shallow spot of small area some twenty feet below and to the left of the rock near which the trout was rising. From this place one had all the control of the short cast, something of distinct advantage any time and of particular advantage on this day with the wind so troublesome and the water currents so contrary.

All during this time the wind buffeted and howled, and the trout kept rising. He hit so viciously that several times the wind took the spray from his rise and sent it flying several feet in the air. Watching my chances with the wind, I sent the fly out on its mission, confidently expecting to take the fish on the first cast. But I found that a normal cast in line with the side of the rock and slightly above did not float the fly close to the rock where the fish seemed to be rising. While trying to figure out how to make the right float, I saw that the trout was not lying at the side of the rock but in front of it and that the occasional slashes were caused when a fly got by him and he rushed after it.

As I made the cast to this point the wind took the fly, deposited it just above the rock, then skated it alongside. I saw the trout come for it, and as the slash was completed I felt the pleasant sensation of a heavy fish fighting.

This entire afternoon was a succession of incidents similar to this. The greatest difficulty was getting in a location where you could reach the rising fish and then waiting your chance to cast it between squalls. The fly hatch was continuous until sunset, when they disappeared and the trout stopped moving. I kept three fish that weighed a total of ten and a quarter pounds, and this at a distance of about seventy-five miles from New York City.

According to common belief this shouldn't have been a good fishing day. It was positively wintry. The next week I went back again, and it was just the sort of a day the average person would call perfect. It was warm, partly cloudy, and there was a light breeze. And yet there wasn't a fly hatch to speak of and we didn't see a trout rise, either to a natural or to our own flies.

Only twice in the years since have I found this water just right for dry-fly fishing. On each occasion it was very windy and cold and May flies were hatching. On one of these occasions I left my fly in the mouth of a brown trout that jumped clear of the water after feeling the sting of the strike. I'm positive it weighed six pounds or better. I'd be willing to wager that right now, if you got to this stretch of river at just the right time, you'd have some rare sport. This sort of thing happens all the time. It is where luck plays such a part in the game. A fish or a number of fish suddenly decide to feed, and as suddenly decide to quit. If you are there at the right time you make a good catch or at least have the opportunity to do so. But get there before or after and you might swear there isn't a fish in the place. This is more likely to happen on the large streams. The small, intimate brooks are usually not so temperamental.

But you can't lay down any positive rules about the weather and fishing. When you get dogmatic about it, nature often slaps you down. However, I must say that a day when the humidity is low has usually been best for me when fishing with a dry fly. Of course this is weather when the skies are blue, when you feel like doing things, when you do not easily perspire and feel uncomfortable. Mostly this sort of day comes with a rising or steady barometer, but I have also experienced them, with good fishing, on a falling barometer.

In many cases a strong wind with cool air and a rising barometer has made excellent dry-fly fishing. Often it knocks many flies from the bushes and trees and this makes the trout surface-minded, at least in places where bushes or meadow grasses overhang the water.

This overall condition is not confined to any one locality or section of the country. Almost always I have found the sort of day you wax enthusiastic about a good day for fishing with dry flies. When the day is muggy and dark I have found other fishing methods more productive, for instance wet flies, streamers, spinners, or bait. Of course this hasn't always held true, but it has worked that way with me the great majority of times.

Water temperature has a lot to do with the way trout rise, but to arrange their reactions to the different temperature degrees into a consistent table is well nigh impossible. I would say that on the whole 70° Fahrenheit marks the top. Sometimes you can get good fishing at this level or even up to 72°, but it depends on the character and setup of the stream and the type of trout. When it goes higher it is usually very poor indeed. About your only chance then is to find where springs cool certain areas or where cold-water streams enter the lake, river, or creek.

To illustrate this, let us go to the lower Neversink again, in the middle of summer after a long, hot, and dry spell. The water was so warm that you could bathe in it without gasping at the first plunge. We knew that we couldn't possibly catch any fish in the usual haunts, so we headed for a small, cold brook where I had had some rare sport with brook trout at another time under similar conditions.

This brook entered at the shallow part of a very deep and large pool. One never knew if the fish would be there, as they didn't use the place regularly—only on certain occasions. To get at them without scaring them, you had to wade out and around and approach from the pool side.

On this day I was lucky. There were about thirty fish in the hole, about twenty-five brookies and five browns. You could see them facing the cold water of the little stream. I managed to take five before they took fright and disappeared. I waited three hours in the hope that they would return, but my wait was in vain. Where they went is a mystery, but I imagine that somewhere near by there must have been a deep spring-hole in the main river. Certainly they couldn't stay long in the main currents with the water temperature what it was. Incidentally, this same day I saw some fish breaking out in the big pool and finally succeeded in getting them on a salmon dry fly, of which I usually carry two or three for night trout fishing. They were small mouth bass. I caught eight. Two of them were somewhat better than legal size—the others ranged between eight and nine inches.

The Eastern streams are yearly subjected to these intense heat spells. The miles of open, rocky streams absorb the devitalizing heat of long days, and the nights are not cold enough to balance the condition. Low water does not make fishing bad in itself. Trout will rise just the same when the water is excessively low as they will when it is normal if the water temperature doesn't get too high and you use the extra caution and skill needed for fishing under such conditions. If you don't believe this, take a thermometer with you and notice the difference in activity between the streams where the water averages 65° or below and those where it ranges 68° or above. And, let me tell you, it is always possible to catch trout in the upper reaches of the streams where the cold springs and dense shade offset the extreme heat of the sun on long summer days.

It is the effect of this extreme heat that so often, if not always, causes Eastern fishing to taper off at the end of June, and why, when the nights of late August become longer, with an occasional cool one, that the fishing sometimes picks up. Of course there is no set rule about it. It all depends on seasonal conditions.

In the trout country from the continental divide westward, the streams are not subjected to these high temperature conditions. In much of this section the summers are too short to cause trouble, or else the entire season is moderate enough to equalize things. In all the Rocky Mountain country I've ever fished, you rarely get any good dry-fly fishing before July. Before then the streams are flooded and filled with snow water. Then, after the fishing does start, the nights stay cool if not positively cold, and by the latter part of September, you are almost sure to have snow again, and at certain altitudes you will have freezing weather at night. In other words, streams in the mountain country (continental divide westward) stay cold in every instance, as far as my personal experience goes, so that your problems are those of finding the right method and lure for successful fishing—solvable problems if we can find the solution, and not unsolvable ones as is the case when confronted with excessively high water temperatures.

The only exception to this in my experience is the Firehole River in Yellowstone Park. Here the trout rise well with water temperatures of 74° or higher. There may be other streams like this. As Ranger Scotty Chapman says: "Those Firehole trout have become accustomed to warm water and thrive in it. The temperature remains fairly constant, and the fish rise quite consistently at all times." He is absolutely right. I have fished this stream at every opportunity ever since my very first visit, and find no change in this respect, although the flies the trout prefer change from time to time. The last time they refused the tiny midges they had so often insisted on, and took rather bushy Variants in the bluish shades.

In the season of 1935 we took a trip from Colorado Springs to the southeastern part of Wyoming and back via Trapper's Lake and Independence Pass. It was between September 15 and 27. During this period we had frost or ice every night except two, and ran into a real snowstorm at the pass, which made us trek for home. There was a good twelve or fifteen inches on the ground when we reached Colorado Springs, and many of the trees of the city were losing limbs and splitting in half from the terrific weight of the wet snow that clung to everything it touched.

The following year we stayed in the southeastern corner of Wyoming ten days during the latter part of September. Each morning we saw the thermometer hovering between 20° and 25° above zero, and then after the sun came out strong, a rise to 50° or 60° made you shed everything but the necessities. We never had much luck fishing the few times we tried it early. Usually the trout did not start feeding until the sun had warmed things up a trifle. If we did get out early we had to use a fresh pair of wading-sox and -shoes unless we brought the wet ones indoors the night before. Otherwise they were frozen as hard as bricks and took considerable time to thaw out.

On this occasion we left just in time. We were working west to Oregon by way of Ogden, Utah, which we reached the first night. Although the snow blanketed the mountaintops the following morning, it did not descend to the valley we drove through. The wind on this trip was terrific. All across Wyoming we saw countless miniature tornadoes—or "twisters," as they call them there. They ranged from a few feet to fifty yards in width at the base (these are guesses), and when we rode through one of them, it was all I could do to hold the wheel straight. The ride through the valley west from Ogden was real fun. The mountains were blanketed in a snowstorm but we rode mostly through sunshine. Occasionally the wind would blow some of the storm across our path, but it was merely like a squall and soon passed. But one can readily understand why the water in the streams in this country stays cold. The mountain peaks where they originate don't have many weeks without snow. I have noted that the trout in this country will rise to the dry fly when the water is at much lower temperature than in the Eastern streams—that is, striking an average based on the tabulations of actual experience. Of course this is logical and understandable. Any living thing becomes acclimated to certain average conditions. These trout of the high-altitude streams become accustomed to colder water than do the trout of the Eastern streams. It is quite likely that they would also quit rising at a lower water temperature than do the Eastern trout, which are subject to excessively high water temperatures. All in all, the Eastern trout have the toughest time of it. The water they live in touches extremes each year. The trout of the high altitudes suffer some differences in water temperature, but it is much more equable than that experienced by the trout in the East.

Incidentally, a friend who was fishing with us in Wyoming stayed over after we left. He was to stay two days longer, but when he got up the next morning a regular blizzard was raging and he decided to leave before he got stuck. He wrote us that he had a tough trip getting out and had to go around the long way instead of over the Snowy Range to Laramie.

In the Yellowstone we usually have snow in September. On two occasions we struck storms of such intensity and length that anyone in the East would have called them small blizzards.

Since these first trips to the mountain country I've learned to expect almost anything in the way of weather. It is in fact one of the fascinating charms of the high altitudes. You might start out on a gorgeous sunny summer morning and by noon or before be tramping or riding through a snowstorm. It is fascinating, exciting, and sometimes a bit terrifying because you're not sure what is going to happen. I love it and thrive on it and so must everyone else who loves nature as she is—not only when she is smiling. When someone tells me of climate where the sun always shines, where the temperature doesn't have much variation, where the wind never reaches high velocity, I can't get particularly enthused, even though it does seem to be what the majority wants.

It's nice to stay in such places, but too much sameness would bore me if I had it too long. I'd rather be chased to cover by a sudden shower, see huge black clouds streaked with awesome lightning, witness a blizzard attack with irresistible fury, have a fog isolate me from my surroundings, see the sea rage along a barren stretch of coast, swelter in heat one day and shiver the next—anything where contrasts give one an extra appreciation for what follows. It is inclement weather that makes you more thoroughly enjoy a perfect day when it comes. It takes hot, dry weather and parched soil to make you really appreciate the rain.

Yes, I can live a lifetime in several hours of raging storm. Have you ever walked in the dense forest when the snow shrouded everything except those objects in your immediate vicinity, when there was no trail to follow, when you knew that only by your woodsmanship and compass you could ever expect to reach camp? If you haven't, you have missed one of the greatest thrills that life has to offer to a lover of the outdoors. It is a dangerous thrill unless you know what you're doing or have someone with you who knows. I imagine everyone who has ever traveled the wilderness gets lost temporarily now and then. It is knowing what to do and how to get out of it at such times which is the test of woodsmanship.

But aside from the thrill of this uncertainty, heavy snowstorms bring another which you feel no matter where you are. It muffles all sound, brings the sky to earth, and you walk in a world from which all strife seems to have fled. Even cities seem less harsh and forbidding at such times. The swirling clouds of snow envelop the buildings, making them look like mountains and the deserted streets resemble the floors of canyons. I must admit I like them best when nature is buffeting them—those times when everyone is avoiding the streets and going on them only for necessity.

Truly, no one can say that he likes camping until he has been through a siege of really inclement weather and is still eager to go again in spite of it. As a matter of fact it is the things we consider bad that give us the most pleasurable memories. Do we ever keep talking about the trips on which no hardship occurs, when nothing goes wrong? It seems to me that we quickly forget such trips. But how we do gloat over an adventure of some kind—a terrific storm that washed out the roads, getting lost in a big swamp at night, making a dangerous mountain ride through snow or fog, having a blowout and escaping with minor injuries or none at all. It doesn't need to be much, but it can be big. Even running short of food on a wilderness canoe trip can provide the chief topic of an entertaining evening. One thing leads to another and the party is a huge success.

If anything in nature affects the feeding habits of fish besides food, temperatures, and water conditions, it is probably the barometric pressure. It probably affects us too, as we'd find out if we checked it up carefully. Of course I'm not sure that air pressure has an effect under the surface of the water, although I've read somewhere that it has. One can't always be checking on the barometer when fishing, so that often our theories are guesses. But I can and will relate some experiences dealing with storms and their effect on trout fishing. These are not guesses, but actual happenings.

First, let us go back to 1914. I was somewhat afraid of eletrical storms at that time, and, besides, believed absolutely that they ruined the fishing before and throughout the storm and sometimes for the balance of the day. I really thought that trout were frightened by the thunder and lightning the same as I.

But one day I happened to be fishing with a fellow who didn't believe these things and who had no fear of thunderstorms, or anything else for that matter. I heard the first rumble of the shower and wanted to back-track because we were a long distance from shelter, but my friend wouldn't stop fishing.

"They're not rising now," I pointed out, "and they surely won't rise with this storm coming. There's no use in getting soaked for nothing."

"Perhaps the storm might wake them up," was the only satisfaction I got.

Came the dead calm that so often precedes a violent summer storm. The black clouds were towering over our heads, and it was getting quite dark. With the crash of a bolt that landed in some near-by timber the storm suddenly broke, and at the very moment it started, my friend hooked the first trout of the day. Not only that but he kept getting them one after another during the storm and after it had passed. I couldn't do anything while the storm was at its height, but after it had dwindled to a light patter I too started to catch trout.

The storm circled and came back, joining another coming from the northwest. This time there was a deluge. The trout suddenly stopped rising and the stream started to discolor. We dug out some worms from the banks and took several more fish, and then even worms wouldn't work. We worked hard until evening, when it cleared; but we didn't catch another trout, no doubt because of the flooded conditions. Drenched and bedraggled, we plodded through the wet brush to our bicycles and then pedaled eleven sodden, weary miles home. We worked for our fishing in those days.

A similar experience took place on the north branch of the Callicoon Creek many years later. It was an extremely hot and sultry morning, the sort that only the Eastern seaboard states know how to deliver. We left Nyack early and arrived at the stream just as dawn was breaking. The air was so oppressive that I felt quite indifferent about fishing. The water looked lifeless, and conditions did not seem right.

My friend, not being so susceptible to climatic conditions as I, came down with his rod all set for action. "Boy, it's hot!" he snorted, "but that's just the time you get some good dry-fly fishing." With that he cast his Brown Spider over the most productive spot in the pool we were standing by.

But nothing happened. He fished the pool until daylight fully arrived, and then moved upstream to the next bit of good water. We went along slowly. My friend fished energetically and perspired freely while I moped along behind, bathing my face and hands frequently but not even bothering to put my rod together, although I did carry it along.

Two hours passed—three, four. We stopped in a shady spot to have a bite to eat. "It's queer," said my friend. "I'd say this was a perfect day for dry-fly fishing. There are plenty of flies on the water, the stream is in perfect condition, and yet I haven't taken a fish nor seen one rise."

"You've got me," I replied, "unless it is that the trout feel this weather as we do and are depressed and indifferent. For a long time I also thought that hot, muggy weather was good fly-fishing weather, but I've had poor fishing so often under these conditions that I'm beginning to have my doubts. Sometimes I blame the poor fishing on my own indolence, but this time we've got real proof because you fished hard and well."

My friend laughed. "You have some queer ideas at times. As if atmospheric conditions that depress you could have any effect on the fish! It's just a case of coincidence—you just happened on the stream under such conditions when the trout were off feed."

"That may be the reason," I admitted dismally, "but anyway I still know that we won't get any trout today—unless the weather changes."

Until two-thirty that afternoon conditions remained the same. We both fished steadily after lunch, but all we saw were a few hungry infants. I was about ready to quit when I sensed a change in the air. A slight gust of wind had drawn through the valley, and it smelled of rain—of sodden fields and steaming roads cooling under a deluge.

Instantly my indifference vanished and I began to fish hard. At the moment my friend happened to be resting. He noticed my change in attitude and gave vent to his feelings in the matter.

"What has come over you?" he asked. "One moment you are moping along like a sick cat, and the next you act as full of ambition as a robin gathering worms after a rain."

"It's the wind—the wind!" I exclaimed impatiently.

"The wind what!" snorted he in disgust. "Have you gone crazy?"

"Don't be so stupid." I retorted. "Conditions are changing. There has been a rain! The humidity is disappearing if not gone. *We're going to have some fishing.*"

He shook his head in despair as he looked at the still, blue heavens.

"The boy's gone mad," he said in mock sadness. "It has rained! The trout are going to rise! Can you imagine that? With the sun getting hotter by the minute?"

But I ignored his ravings. I felt sure that something was going to happen. I could smell it.

Then off in the distance we heard the rumble of thunder, and with it another gust of moisture-laden air swept down the brook.

"Did you say it was going to rain," asked my friend, "or that it had rained?"

I turned to answer him but never did. I heard a splash and missed a good fish.

That started the fun. We took trout after trout during that period when the storm was working toward us. A yellowish darkness settled down on the valley and it became deathly still. Then came a subdued moaning from the distance that quickly gained in volume. After that came a roar which had an ominous sound. Intermittently the thunder grumbled and growled. I heard all this as I rose trout and played them.

With a suddenness that was appalling the storm descended upon us. The wind blew a veritable hurricane, the rain came down in torrents and then changed to hail, which pelted us unmercifully. Until the hail came, the trout kept rising, even to our sodden flies.

The deluge lasted twenty minutes or thereabouts. Then it stopped as abruptly as it had come. But the trout had stopped too. We couldn't get another rise. The water began to color and soon became the shade of cream-filled coffee. It was the end as far as we were concerned. A quiet rain then started in, and we saw the worm fishers appear as if by magic. This would give them their innings, which come seldom enough in the average summer.

Another incident, somewhat similar, took place on Forbidden Brook, so called because four fellows who fished together did not wish to advertise it. It was in the latter part of July, and between claps of thunder and pelting hailstones as big as marbles we filled our creels until the stream became discolored and they stopped taking our flies.

These are just a few of the experiences I have had that seem to prove thunder showers do not spoil the fishing, but on the contrary may even improve it.

On the other hand there have been many other instances where the direct opposite was the case—where the fishing was excellent until the storm broke, after which the trout went down and wouldn't start rising again, or when the approach of a storm seemed to stop the rise long before it arrived. I remember one incident in particular. It was a threatening day, and when we got to the stream it seemed as if every trout in it was willing to take our fly. We were exultant—it was to be one of those banner days we are always looking for, but which come so seldom. I had just landed my third trout, a plump fourteen-incher, when a black cloud poked its head over the edge of a near-by mountain. Three minutes later a squall carrying a mixture of rain and hail assailed us. Immediately the trout stopped rising, and although the shower did not make any difference in the water of the stream, they did not rise again that day.

My notes show many such instances, which of course vary, but which are similar enough to make one feel that the fish should react in a similar manner—but they don't. Many times before a big storm, not a shower, we have experienced very poor fishing when conditions seemed perfect, even with a rising barometer. At other times we've had wonderful fishing under the same setup. Now there may be some underlying forces that cause these differences. But they are so inconsistent that I've never been able to work out any definite rules concerning them.

And do not overlook the danger of fishing in a thunder storm. Do not stay out on the open lake; do not seek shelter under a solitary tree. If you are in an open meadow, you are safest if you lie down. Lightning seems to seek out isolated high points. If you keep this in mind it will reduce your chances of being struck.

I've had both good and bad fishing in all sorts of weather—cloudy days, muggy days, rainy days, and clear days—but when I sum it all up, I find that I can still give the most credit to clear, snappy days when it feels good to be alive. There I rest my case. What do you think?

There is one water condition I have found almost infallible for good dry-fly fishing. It is just as the stream clears after a storm that has raised and muddied it. Let us examine an actual experience on the Ausable in New York State.

To begin with, the water was low and the fishing poor. The storm started with intermittent showers, and during this period the trout started rising a bit. Just when we thought we were going to have some good sport, a deluge came and we quit because there wasn't any fun fishing in it. It lasted the rest of the day, and the next morning the stream had risen several feet and was the color of chocolate malted milk. Rain was still coming down.

For three days we killed time by playing cards, looking at the stream every little while to see the progress of the freshet, and doing plenty of cussing about the tough break we were having. We got tired of this and began to get quite impatient. Then Don Bell suggested that we give the girls a picnic and at the same time do a little fishing. He suggested Stiles Brook. "The fish don't amount to much," he said, "but there's a good place to eat and the falls are quite pretty."

This brook runs into the East River. It was clear and attractive-looking. Before lunch I fished up from the river to the camp site and took a half dozen nine- to ten-inch rainbows. While lunch was being prepared Don showed me the best spot on the brook—the deep hole under the falls.

The first cast to the foot of the falls produced the rise of a twelve-incher, and for the next twenty minutes we had quite some sport with fish ranging from eight inches to eleven inches. Then came the call for lunch.

I could see Don getting restless. He finished eating first and said he was going down to look at the river—to see if conditions had changed. I knew this small-stream fishing was getting his nerves. He was always looking for big fish, and there wasn't much chance of taking them in Stiles Brook. But I was a bit intrigued by the falls pool and went back there. Three times I rose what looked like a pound-and-a-half brown but did not connect. That ended it. Not another fish would rise.

There didn't seem to be much use of wearing out the casting arm, so I went back to chat with the picnic party. I don't know how long we whiled away the time, but it was well along in the afternoon when above the chatter and the murmur of the brook I faintly heard a shout. It sounded like Don's booming voice, so I left the camp site and started down the road. On the way I heard the call again and knew it was Don.

When I got down to the river I saw him standing at the edge of a good-looking pocket stretch. I thought the water looked a bit lighter in color. Don's eyes were riveted on the river. He heard me but didn't turn to look at me. "They've started rising," he said. "Look there!" and he pointed to a rise near a rock in midstream.

It was the truth. The waters of the river had cleared a trifle. While they were still quite murky, you could now see undersurface rocks that before had been completely invisible. And I had left my rod back at the camp site! You may be sure that I didn't bother to talk about it with Don. I went back to get both Don's rod and my own. Don showed his vast experience by the way he took all this. I was so excited that I puffed and trembled, but he took it so calmly that he never changed the speed of the puffs of his pipe.

By the time I got back and we set up the rods, the stream had become almost entirely clear; and when I reached a location where I could cast to the nearest rising fish, I could see my feet when wading in two feet of water. The rest of that afternoon has always remained with me as a most delightful memory. Rainbows, browns, and natives (brook trout) all seemed in wonderful humor and took our flies with reckless abandon. As I remember it, we each kept four fish, and they filled our creels. We kept only the best specimens.

Another incident of this sort occurred on the Beaverkill at Lew Beach, New York. There had been a cloudburst in the early morning while we were on the way, and when we reached the stream it was over the banks, raging and sullen. To pass the time we fished with wet flies and streamers, sinking them by casting upstream and then letting them float with the current on a slack line. We took several trout this way, but it was hard and slow work. So we finally quit and passed the time doing other things until the water had a chance to clear.

At six in the afternoon it was still dirty and high. We started to eat our dinner leisurely, but something happened to make us finish in a hurry. I sat facing a window that provided a view of the stream, and I was watching as I ate. It seemed to me that the water changed color as I looked. I called Bill's attention to it.

"I believe you're right," he agreed. "Let's get through and see."

It was true. The water had dropped several inches according to our improvised gauge, and it was clearing—there wasn't any mistake about that.

Our very first casts brought results. As our flies floated on the still-milky water, dark shapes came up from the bottom and took them. The trout were definitely on the feed. As we fished, the water cleared rapidly, and as it cleared, the trout took more readily. By dusk it was so clear that in eighteen inches of water the reflected light from the western sky plainly disclosed the bottom to our view. Before sunset the trout took any fly we cast over them. After sunset they became more and more choosy, until at the last we couldn't do a thing with them—even though it seemed as if every fish in the stream was out to gorge on the large hatch of naturals.

These two experiences have been duplicated in various degrees many times. On the average I find that it is a pretty safe bet to consider such circumstances well worth taking advantage of.

The condition of the water is quite pertinent to the sort of fishing we may expect. In neither of these incidents is there mention of the fishing in the other stages, aside from the little wet-fly fishing on the Beaverkill. However, as a general rule it works out this way. At the very start of the rise we may have a short period of fly fishing. This is very uncertain. In the intermediate stage between the start of discoloration and extreme muddiness we may do good work with streamers, bucktails, large wet flies, worms, and minnows. During the height of the rise we are likely to find our best fishing by putting on a sinker and some bait. The thing to do then is to get to bottom, preferably the bottom of deep holes. However, there is another alternative, one that has often produced for me. It is to fish the shallow back eddies that are formed by the high water. At times I have even taken trout by fishing a fly well up in the grass that has become flooded. During midsummer rises of water, I have found that there always seem to be some venturesome—or foolish—trout who follow the rise wherever it goes. By doing so they find some extra tidbits that evidently tickle their palates. It is a dangerous pastime for them, because they sometimes get caught when the waters recede. Sometimes I have found them landlocked in puddles because they delayed departure too long. Most of the fish caught this way speedily become the victims of vermin, which is perhaps a good thing, because otherwise they would die a more lingering death. However, if the muddy water continues for a considerable time, it is quite likely that all sporting methods of angling will fail. Under such circumstances I would rather wait for the freshet to subside.

This angling game is so involved that it is almost impossible to segregate any number of incidents dealing with one particular problem without overlapping on some other. Here I have been talking about the weather and suddenly find myself involved in a discussion of water conditions that are a direct result of weather. Having started, we might as well delve deeper into the subject and see where it leads. After all, that is the charm of fishing and of fishing literature, and at this moment I have no more idea where it will take us than you have. What we are doing is making random casts and hoping that they bring a worth-while rise.

Now let us see where we left off—the effects of a summer rise in water. What about the effects of high water in spring? Does it affect the fishing in the same way? Here we have a question requiring some real thought and a journey into memory for experiences that might help us to make a decision. What do I find? First, that high water in spring is a normal condition, while in midsummer it is abnormal. Therefore the effect can't be the same. Besides, the water is cold and the fish sluggish. Excessive rain in spring will retard the fly fishing, because the trout will go to favored deep holes, where it requires less effort to fight the current. A worm at this time, sunk so that it drifts in front of them, will usually bring a response. As the waters recede they become a bit more active and take flies, but they are not particularly interested in surface food, being more susceptible to minnows or something that imitates them. They will also be interested in worms and grubs. Perhaps the reason for this is that they need bulk in food after the long winter. It is only rarely that I have had any dry-fly fishing of any account in the Eastern streams before May 15, no matter what the condition of the water.

This leads to another question. If a person likes fly fishing, what is the best time to go? Another brain teaser, because so much depends on the weather and the location. However, I've started this, so will lead with my chin, basing my recommendations on the personal experiences I've had.

There are many things to consider. Latitude, longitude, and altitude all have their effect, not to mention the sort of season we're having—wet or dry, hot or cold. However, there are a few generalities that are fairly uniform and will aid us in striking a good average.

For instance, streams located in the southern range of trout will become warmer earlier than those in the northern range. So too will the streams in the low altitudes become warmer more quickly than those in the high altitudes. You can see how complicated it's getting. Fortunately, the really high altitudes are confined to the West, which simplifies it to some extent. Even so we have some altitude differences in the East that make considerable difference in fishing.

About the only way to make sense is to localize. First let us take a heavily wooded stream in the Catskills, of New York. In such a stream we are likely to find poor fly fishing during April and May due to the usual *unusual* belated spring rains and cold, frosty nights that frequently run through to the first of June. If you do get a break in weather, the best fly fishing during this early period will probably come during the warm part of the day, when the sun has a chance to get in its work. June is quite likely to be the best month in this territory. However, if the stream is fairly open and on the east side of the range, you may get some fair fly fishing during May, although this is absolutely dependent on the weather. Even during June, the best month, you will run into extremes of good and bad fishing according to the influence of the weather and the fly hatches. However, for any of the Catskill territory I would say that the safest time to go would be between May 25 and July 5. Ordinarily the slope to the Delaware is a trifle later than the slope to the Hudson or the Mohawk, with the exception perhaps of the upper reaches of the Rondout and Neversink, the waters of which are exceedingly cold even in August.

During July and the greatest part of August the fishing in this entire section is likely to be poor, except for spurts during or after summer rains, as pointed out earlier in this chapter. If the streams do not have any rise in water and the weather is hot, then the best chance of getting fish is to confine your operations to the early morning after the night has lowered the temperature of the water, or at night after the sun has been set long enough so that the cooling rocks and soil exert their influence on the water temperature. Also remember that night allows the cooling waters of springs to work their way downstream without being heated by the sun-blasted rocks, as is sure to happen in the day. All these things have an effect on the activity of the trout. During the latter part of August, conditions may easily change again. The water is likely to remain low and clear; but with increasingly shorter and cooler nights the water temperature lowers, and thus the daytime fishing is quite likely to improve.

Even as I write, numerous exceptions, both in streams and seasons, continually arise in my mind. As far as a general statement of the conditions in the Catskill country is concerned, I think you have as accurate a description of the seasons as can be given.

As one moves southward, the setup varies a trifle, on the average about two weeks earlier at the opening. Jersey has had a September open season for years. With reasonable precipitation and weather not too hot, the Jersey fishing will remain good throughout June; but it doesn't take much hot weather to ruin it. My notes show excellent dry-fly fishing throughout May on Flat Brook, with the early June fishing even better but tapering off quickly with the arrival of hot days. During July at Flatbrookville I've registered water temperature at 88°. I have no record of any higher than that, nor have I any complete data covering it. I just mention the fact to show what may be expected of Jersey trout fishing after June 15. Of course showers will sometimes pep up the streams for a short time, but when they get too warm it takes more than one summer shower to bring them back. The wonder to me is that so many fish survive the hot months. No doubt the survivors from the fishermen find many cold spots under banks and debris jams, as well as spring holes here and there. On the whole the September fishing doesn't average as active as the early season, although some dry-fly fishermen like it better and get excellent fishing now and then. The reactions of the trout and the average water conditions are similar to the Adirondack-Ausable River country some two weeks earlier, or between the middle of August and Labor Day.

Pennsylvania is similar to New Jersey except that in the northeast the streams will coincide with the western slope of the Catskills. Northern Michigan seems to run about the same as the Adirondacks, but on the whole I believe that the water stays colder there than it does in northern New York. In the trout lake sections of Maine, the Adirondacks, and the province of Quebec, as well as trout lakes elsewhere in similar conditions, the season opens when the ice goes out, and it is usually good then for about a month although this period may be shortened by adverse weather conditions. Then it tapers off gradually until summer, when it really gets tough except for spring-hole locations where the fishing is often extremely good. Then, as fall advances and the waters cool, one may often get good fishing again, sometimes excellent, according to the weather.

As a rule the season on the Ausable and streams of similar type in the Adirondacks will run from one to two weeks later than the Catskills, with the chance that the fishing will stay more uniform through the season. Right here, to show how difficult it is to give worth-while general information in this respect, I wish to call your attention to the fact that I know some streams in this section where the conditions are different—where the best fishing is between the time the ice goes out and the heat of summer begins—where the July and August fishing is distinctly a matter of spring-hole fishing. You will always find varying conditions. In some ponds and streams where the water remains cool, fishing is likely to be consistently good throughout the season, but streams that are subject to the direct rays of the summer sun and that do not have enough cold-water springs to offset this heat will be devoid of trout except where such springs keep the water suitable for their existence.

In the southern end of the original range of trout, that is, Virginia, the Smoky Mountain region, and so forth, you will likely find the best fishing in May. From the data I've gathered concerning these waters I would place the fishing conditions about two weeks ahead of New Jersey and Pennsylvania. This means, of course, that it also ends earlier because of temperature conditions. Naturally altitude makes a great difference, but in the Southern uplands the higher altitudes usually mean smaller waters and the trout do not get large.

There is a new angle to this Southern trout fishing. During 1950 I spent one day on the Norfork River, a short stretch of stream below Norfork Dam, Arkansas. The fishing there was made possible by the damming of the river, which formed a lake of considerable depth. Because of this depth, the water feeding into the river below the dam from the bottom of the lake was cold enough for trout.

Wisely, this water was stocked with trout, and in a remarkably short time rainbows up to four and six pounds were being regularly taken, with some larger ones coming along now and then. The browns also seem to be doing well. I saw one of fifteen inches, weighing a good pound and a half, that was the prettiest as well as the best-conditioned brown trout I've ever looked at. The rainbows are mostly broad, fat, and good fighters.

As the water supply of this stream comes from the bottom of the deep lake, the temperature remains fairly constant, a condition that makes it particularly suitable for the well-being of trout. There is still a question as to whether the fish spawn in this short stretch of trout water. Jack Bonner, of Norfork, who knows the river better than anyone else, claims they do. All I know is that the day I fished it I caught five small trout, from eight to nine inches long, that seemed more like hatchery products than native-born fish. I also hooked one large fish that I lost and caught several six- to seven-inch fish that might have been spawned there.

Except when the water is low, usually only on Sunday, there is very little good water that can be reached except by floating through. Even at low water the boat is the only practical method, unless you can take lots of punishment in the way of tough shore walking and wading. The boat makes it easy, but you must either get out to do your fishing, or else have a guide retard the drift of the boat enough to let you fish the good spots. Incidentally, before the dam was built this river was a great black-bass stream.

During 1951 I spent two more days on the river. I did a little better, taking a couple of fourteen-inch rainbows while my guide took a four pounder. Mr. and Mrs. Gene Benson of Oklahoma fish this stream a lot and have the deserved reputation of taking trout from it more consistently than anyone else. From what they said, and from what I observed while watching them fish, part of their success was due to the fact that they had their guide hold the boat consistently all along the way and at the proper spots for fishing. It is hard to get most Ozark guides to do this because they want to fish all the time.

Wabbling and darting spoons and plugs with excellent action at low speed seemed to be the best lures at this time.

There is a possibility (claimed by some to be a certainty) that the Bull Shoals Dam, which has been constructed across the White River, an excellent bass stream, a number of miles above Cotter, will make the same perfect set-up for trout. This would provide considerable trout water in this part of Arkansas. If the White River section grows trout comparable to the Norfork, then they will be well worth while fishing for. (Incidentally the Norfork runs into the White River some distance below Cotter, Arkansas.) Here is hoping that the predictions regarding the White River come true. It will compensate somewhat for the disappearance of many miles of stream that will always be remembered in legend and story as some of the most fascinating bass water in America. (See *Fresh-Water Bass* for the writer's experiences on this river and on the Buffalo.)

As far as I can tell from experience, from discussions, and from correspondence with other anglers, I would say that the Western trout country, at least in Colorado, Wyoming, Montana, and Idaho, does not offer fly fishing until July, or at best late June. Unless you get hampered by an early September snow, you may expect fairly good fly-fishing conditions until around October 1st. The September snow is likely to be troublesome only as long as the storm lasts, but the next storm is quite likely to cause considerable trouble. During the 1950 season in the Yellowstone area we got there just after the early September snow had melted enough to be off all the roads. For some ten days we had the most glorious weather. Then another snow started and it kept on day after day, not continuously, but never clearing up for more than a few hours.

However, in both Montana and Wyoming the trout waters descend low enough to provide fishing well into October, depending of course on the season. As you know, weather has a way of upsetting calculations and one can only generalize about conditions, no matter where.

One thing is sure. In the high-altitude country, where the mountain peaks are rarely completely barren of snow, one does not need to worry about streams that get excessively warm. Altitude as well as longitude makes a difference. Most of Colorado's streams are so high that perhaps July and August will prove the top months. On the other hand Wyoming and Montana may be snowed under while the High Sierras in California may be simply snappy and invigorating. For instance we have fished the Yellowstone the first week of October, tramping along the streams in from six to eight inches of snow. Some ten days or more later we have fished the Owens River on the east slope of the High Sierras, at an altitude approximately the same, under the most pleasant conditions. Of course the nights were extremely frosty and chill, but we had no snow and at mid-day the sun became so warm that one had to shed clothes. Sometimes the conditions were like late summer in the Adirondacks of New York State. Of course, we have seen the conditions reversed.

No one can ever be one hundred per cent accurate regarding weather and fishing conditions. However, generally one will find the foregoing general resumé reasonably correct, allowing for differences in seasons, altitudes, and latitudes.

✎§ CHAPTER XII §✎

Water Types and How to Fish Them

PROBABLY every angler has his pet type of water. It is all right to have this preference; but it leads to neglect of other types, and that is sure to reduce your chances of success. In the old days this didn't matter much. When you went fishing you usually had the stream to yourself—or nearly so—and you could skip from one place to another with the surety that all your favorite locations would produce.

Conditions of recent years have changed this. Now the streams are so crowded that you must make the most of whatever bit of water you find unoccupied. Therefore, even though it has always been important that the angler knows how to fish intelligently all types of water, now it becomes vastly more important if we hope to make our angling days something more than periods of walking and casting.

The most obvious places to fish are the good-looking pools. Being so evident, they are fished by every passer-by. Thus they are less likely to produce under tough conditions than locations that are overlooked by the majority. But even though these attractive-looking pools are fished extensively, most anglers do not fish them thoroughly. In many cases they fish only the obvious and easy parts and let the rest alone.

One day I stopped fishing with the intention of resting a bit and watching a pool until some good fish started rising. I became so intrigued over the action passing before my eyes that I spent a half day watching instead of fishing. I selected a cool, comfortable spot on the brushy side of the stream from which one could not fish, but where I was in a position to see everything that happened without being seen except by the most keen and educated eyes.

To help you follow the action I show a sketch of the pool, marked with letters for guidance. It was somewhat complicated, but it will be worth your while to study it. Generally speaking this advice is offered only to the inexperienced, but the experienced who are open minded may be interested if only because they know the difficulties that attend the writing of this type of fishing knowledge.

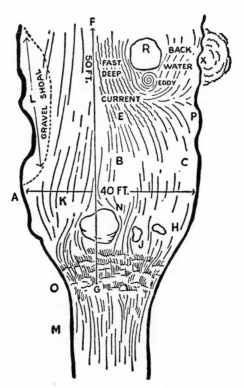

SHOWING HOW SOME ANGLERS FISH

I sat comfortably at X. The entire shore on this side was densely covered with growth, and the water was deep down to the point where it began to pick up speed above the tail of the pool, just slightly upstream from H. It was impossible to fish from this side.

During the time I watched ten anglers came through, yet all except one followed the same general procedure. After fishing the water below the little falls they went directly up to A, and from there fished the water bounded by B, C, P, and E. Invariably they first cast to the far side, to C and P, and afterward fished the water closer by—a method that is wrong, as it is always best to fish the near-by water first and then reach out for distance. The reason for this, of course, is that in making long casts first you will probably disturb the fish lying between you and the farthest point. After that they waded up the gravel shoal and fished the fast current between F and E. From this position they could not properly fish the backwater behind rock R.

But let me describe the actual fishing of some of the anglers I watched. The first two came through within twenty-five minutes of the time I had relaxed on the bank under the heavy foliage. After that at least two hours elapsed without anyone's disturbing the water. During that period several things occurred that excited my interest and almost served to end the observation. The first was a jump of a good fish in the eddy behind rock R. This fish did not rise again so I curbed my desire to cast over it. Experience had taught me the futility of trying for fish acting in this manner, especially with a dry fly.

About an hour later something else occurred to whet my appetite for fishing. One after another, eight good-sized fish slowly but surely made their way over to the gravel shoal L and started feeding on nymphs and small minnows. At the same time two really large fish entered the backwater directly under my observation post.

I had stood the strain just about as long as I could, and was about ready to get into action when angler number three came along. He paid no attention to anything until he reached position K, where he stopped and made ready to cast. Of course all the trout feeding in the gravel shoal L scattered as soon as he arrived there, in fact they had become frightened by the time he reached position O. This fellow cast beautifully, had good control over drag, and creditably fished the main current F to E, the shore between C and P, and the eddy behind rock R. He took one fair fish at the left behind rock R, and had two rises in the main current between E and F. After this he went on. He had not tried to fish the backwater where I sat, and had missed a good bet by neglecting the gravel shoal.

The pool was kept busy for the next two hours. Five anglers fished it in that time—every one of them covering only the main current between E and F. Not one rose a fish. The two large fish in the backwater stayed put and did not seem to be feeding. The passing of the anglers had not bothered them, because all had stayed on the opposite side of the stream and not one had sent an inquisitive cast to the eddy.

About a half hour after they had passed by, I saw another fellow approaching. Every one of the others had plunked along to position A before starting to fish, thus spoiling all the lower water and the gravel shoal L; but this angler first stopped at M to look things over. Between M and O he worked small pockets below the falls, taking one fair fish from this water.

Then instead of advancing further upstream he waded carefully to position G, crouching low and finally getting on his knees. The water then came dangerously near his wader tops, but he kept well down; hence there was less chance of the fish in the glide water above seeing him. From this position he made a short cast to the smooth glide at N just a few inches above where the water tumbled down at the side of the rock. A fish was waiting there. It rose but missed. I almost shouted with admiration. Here was a real angler and no mistake. When the fish rose and missed his fly he didn't react with a fruitless and damaging strike. Instead he let the fly go over the falls and did not attempt lifting it until he could do so with a slight flick of the wrist.

He then deliberately dried out the fly, taking plenty of time in the process, and then made another cast to the identical spot where he made the first cast. This time the trout seemed to take it before it had touched the water. As soon as it felt the hook it made a dive over the falls and a few moments later was neatly beached. I was a considerable distance away, but from the way it looked, the fish was a good one.

After creeling the fish on shore he returned to position G, from which he carefully fished the rest of the water between J and H. At J he hooked a fish that jumped and tore loose, and at H he rose another one, and this time I believe he took the fly away from it. At least he attempted to set the hook because the fly went sailing through the air back to him. Then he did a wise thing. Instead of casting the same fly right back, he changed it—I suppose to another pattern. I couldn't see plainly enough to be sure of this, but I know I couldn't see the second fly on the water, and the first had been plainly visible. But I saw the splash when the fish rose and saw his rod bend in a perfect arc as the fight began. This fish fought in the glide above the falls between N and H, but after a time the angler got it over the rapids and then proceeded to lead it to shore where it was beached.

The angler then advanced slowly on his knees until he reached a point about halfway to A. From here he worked the left side of the tail glide and covered the gravel shoal L. Of course he didn't do anything because the fish had been scared out, but had he happened along before the other men had spoiled the water I feel sure he would have taken one or more of the trout that had been feeding in the shallows.

After exhausting the possibilities of the gravel shoal he moved carefully and slowly to K. From there he worked the pool systematically, starting with short casts and gradually lengthening them until he had fished the entire stretch from B to E and from C to P. He did not get a rise in this section.

After that he fished the current from E to F. This also failed to produce. I was getting anxious now. I wondered if he'd fish for the trout I could see in the backwater below me. He looked the situation over carefully and started to cross at K, but stopped when the water got to the top of his waders and he saw he couldn't make it. I breathed a sigh of relief because I wanted to try for those big fellows myself.

But he had seen the backwater and the eddy behind the rock R. Instead of going on upstream, he stopped at the head of the pool and started wading across in the shallow rapids above. He finally reached the rock R and found a standing-place on the upstream side. From here he fished over the backwater. His fly alighted on the water below me. There wasn't any current to speak of, so it simply floated there motionless. I saw one of the big fish start for it, and here the angler made his mistake—although he didn't know it. Before the fish fairly started he lifted the fly, and the disturbance made the trout scurry for cover. The other trout also took fright and disappeared. Of course the angler knew nothing of this—he was fishing the location because he knew that sometimes that type of water produced good fish. He covered it thoroughly, but since no fish were left in it he failed to get any response. The incident made me realize the harmful effects of too quick a lift from the water. If this angler had let his fly rest on the surface for another thirty seconds, he would have had a rise even if he didn't hook the fish—and the chances are that he would have hooked it.

Now for the first time the angler considered the eddy behind the rock R. Using the rock as a shield, he fished it from that position. Not having any crosscurrents to bother him, he got a perfect float, and I wasn't a bit surprised when he hooked a really good fish. Having accomplished this, he seemed satisfied and departed. That coup of the little eddy intrigued me. When fishing the same water from the gravel-shoal side, one could get at best only a few inches float without drag. If you got a rise during the time the fly was floating these few inches, all well and good; but if you didn't your chance was gone, and frequently the dragging fly put all the fish in the eddy down. When fishing the eddy from above, you could cover the entire spot with a twenty-foot cast and get a perfect round-the-circle float. If there were any interested fish there at all, the ruse was certain to bring results.

It was getting late, and I figured that if I wanted a trout to bring home I'd better get busy. I was getting ready to leave when another angler appeared. I waited to watch. But my movements preparatory to leaving my hiding place had caught his eye. Evidently my presence bothered him, because he whipped his fly carelessly and hurriedly over the water a few times and then went on upstream without having got a rise. But from my subsequent experience I feel that he might have failed to get any results even if he had fished it carefully and thoroughly.

When he left I went downstream a few hundred yards and started working back over some water that I knew was exceptionally good. Whether the amount of fishing had made the trout quit striking, or whether I did a poor job, I can't say. At any rate, no rise materialized; and while I considered the time well spent, it did not put any trout in my creel.

Here are some of the important things to be learned from this afternoon of observation—methods of procedure that mean so much but that are ignored by so many.

Brown trout do go into shallow water to feed, and unless the angler is mighty careful about the approach, he will frighten them from such locations long before he comes within casting distance. I have always found such places highly productive and well worth taking time and thought to consider, for fish on the feed in thin water are always ready to take a properly presented dry fly. Even if you are not sure that the fish are feeding in these shallows along shore, it usually pays better to give them a try than simply to race from one deep pool to another and fish only the main part of each hole.

True, it is a game requiring the utmost patience, not to mention hard work and effort. It is possible to spend a half hour making a distance of fifty to sixty feet on your knees and then spoil your chances by one poor or wrongly directed cast. Or you may hook a good fish on the first cast and have it make so much disturbance in the fight, or when you are landing it, that all other feeding trout in the section are put to rout.

The great increase in the number of fishermen has aggravated this condition. Often you do not have a pool to yourself long enough to figure out how to fish it properly. Besides, trout that would normally feed in the shallows are often kept from doing so by the continual procession of anglers barging along just where they would like to feed. Often, too, just when you have spent a half hour or so getting into a position where you can effectively cast over feeding fish in such areas, someone comes along and walks boldly along the shore, showing himself to the trout you have been stalking; and of course away they go to deep water. So your time is wasted and you feel disgusted.

But ignoring these modern deterrents let me describe a few methods of successfully fishing gravel shoals as shown in the diagram.

Of course it all depends on the particular situation. In the one described it was possible to get within working distance of the fish from below, as long as the angler kept low, either by crouching or by advancing on the knees. True, you may be disappointed when you do this, as was the angler who correctly fished it after others before him had scared the fish out. But perhaps you actually see signs of fish feeding in such shallows, as I did again the next time I fished the water. By sneaking up to a point about halfway between O and A, I caught two of them before the rest became frightened. And it always pays to go along slowly, using your eyes intelligently and taking advantage of every possible lurking place for one or more trout. Often they are seen in the most unlikely places.

Another way to fish the shallow gravel bars is to deliberately wade in the main current, if it isn't too deep or heavy, and fish the shore waters from this position. If the trout are feeding in the shallow water you will not scare them by wading in the deep waters. As a matter of fact the fish feeding on or under the surface in the deep waters do not scare for long. This you may easily prove. How many times have you had fish start rising behind you after you had fished the water and waded on upstream? Often, I'll warrant. On the other hand the trout in the shallows scare easily and remain frightened, or at least most suspicious, for a long time. Another thing; when you hook a fish in the shallow water from a deep-water position it will immediately dash for the deep water; thus it doesn't make a fuss on the surface to make the rest of the fish there suspicious. But if you connect with fish from the shore side they are inclined to make plenty of disturbance at the start of the fight, and this frequently sends the rest of them back to deep water, where they often (but not always) remain for the balance of the day.

Still it is sometimes necessary to fish these gravel shoals from the shore side. For one reason or another it may be impossible to wade the deep water, or you may not be able to wade it at a proper distance from the trout; that is, you may be so close as to scare them, or else so distant that current movements spoil the floats of your fly. Also, conditions may be such that you can't approach either from down- or upstream, even if you get down on your knees, without having the trout become aware of your coming— which will, of course, send them back into deep water.

In a case of this sort you must stay far enough back from the water's edge to keep the trout from seeing you. The distance will vary with the background and the slope. Generally speaking you can get closer with a high and dark background than you can with a low and light one. The reason? It is simple enough. A dark and high background will obscure your figure, a low and light background will accentuate it. Just think of this in terms of silhouettes and it will help you to understand, if you question this advice. You must grasp the principle and figure it out from there, because each location is at least just a little bit different from any other. When the differences are obvious I'm sure that even the tyro will readily recognize them. When you figure them out correctly it will help you to get close to feeding fish without scaring them.

Once you have the distance between your casting position and the feeding trout computed reasonably correctly, then you may start fishing. It will pay off best if you drop only leader and fly on the water; and often, if the feeding fish are close to shore, the less leader showing the better. This usually means that both line and leader are subject to excessive punishment because they contact the ground. When they are scraped over gravel, sand, or anything else abrasive or dirty, it may cause considerable damage. So after fishing one or two of these gravel shoals from the shoreside it will pay you to dry, to clean, and if after that you have the patience, to dress the line. Also examine the leader carefully. If it shows scores, or looks a bit marred, it will be best to either repair it by replacing the injured strands or substitute a new leader. Unless you are skilled in repairing I would suggest the substitution. It takes less time, and you can always do the repair job when you are relaxing at home. But be sure that you carry extra leaders along so that you won't be stymied. You must also be sure to have all the strands with you that are necessary for repairs, in case you prefer doing this on the stream. But I would advise carrying extra leaders. It is much easier, doesn't cost any more money, and definitely saves time, the most valuable thing in fishing.

Here is another important thing to learn when fishing any shallow water. Often the trout will travel some distance in order to take the fly.[1] When they do, you can see the wake they make as they come after the fly. This is exciting, so that your reactions may cause you to strike too quickly and hard. Whereupon you either take the fly away from the fish; or break the leader, leaving the fly in its mouth. Until you can control this violent reaction you will never become consistently successful at fishing for large trout in shallow water. From my experience I find that it usually pays to wait until a fly disappears from the surface before you strike; or more efficiently, just manage to bring the line taut, something that hooks the fish but doesn't break the leader. I'm not claiming I can

---

[1] From my personal experience I can say that trout will often travel as much as six feet for a fly that they see floating on the surface in clear, shallow water. But just as often the distance traveled is only a few inches, and they may even take the fly the moment it touches the water. All these things must be synchronized if you would be successful. Of course only persons with super-intelligence and quick reflexes can hope to score anything approaching one hundred per cent perfect, and most of us, including the writer, do not come under that classification. But I do insist that the more you know about these things the more successful you will be, if not in actually catching fish, at least in knowing why you weren't able to catch them. And if you know why you don't score, it will definitely help you in future attempts.

always control my own reactions. As a matter of fact I can't. But when I do I hook the fish, and when I don't I invariably lose out.

Usually pulling a fly or lure from a fish when you strike will frighten the rest of the feeding trout in the section more than breaking a leader in its mouth. This because the missed strike causes considerable fuss on the water surface, while leaving a fly in the mouth of the trout doesn't make any disturbance whatever. In most cases of this kind the angler can hardly realize what has happened until he discovers that the fly is gone. The trout that took the fly may be momentarily nonplussed, but the rest of them are rarely disturbed and keep on feeding as though nothing had happened. Sometimes, indeed, the fish taking the fly has been caught not long after, the proof being the lost fly in its mouth. However, incidents of this sort are not common. They happen only once in a while.

When fishing the tails of pools that are shallow and the water clear, it is sometimes difficult to approach near enough for a cast without scaring the fish, even if you go to the effort of advancing into position on your knees. Not so many years ago I chanced on the Beaverkill when conditions were abominable. Not a fish had been taken for two weeks, and everyone was in the doldrums. Obviously it was a waste of time to fish in the ordinary manner. Better men than I were doing it without getting anywhere, so I started wandering along the stream looking for something that might give me an inspiration.

I noticed that at the tail of every pool at least two or more trout were rising, but I also noted that you couldn't get at them without putting them down long before you could make a cast. Once down they didn't start rising again for some time. But here and there was a pool that was grass-bordered at the tail. When I came to the first one the experiences of old days came in good stead. I remembered sneaking through the long grass on the banks of a meadow stream and dapping a worm over the edge to a hole where I knew the trout lay. The method was infallible, no matter how low the water or what time of the year it was done. Here was a setup where the same thing could be done with flies.

I had been using a fourteen-foot 4X leader, thinking that it would help in taking these trout under the low-water conditions. Of course I couldn't handle such a leader when making short casts, or in trying to spot a fly on the water over the top of the grass, so I changed to a seven-and-a-half-footer tapering to 2X (.008). I wanted a leader strong enough to immediately hoist a small fish out of the water, so that landing it would not disturb larger fish that might be interested but not so anxious to take. At kneeling position the grass was about six inches higher than my head. I couldn't see the rising trout, and I was effectually hidden from them.

Figuring the approximate length of line needed, I made a tentative cast and hoped I'd figured it right, for even though it was nearly a case of dapping, it was necessary to make a flip of the rod and send out enough line to clear the grass and have the fly alight on the water without any more leader than I could help. A few seconds passed. Then I felt a tug and was fast to a fish, and had him out so quickly that I surprised myself. It was a ten-incher. The next fish resisted more, and I had to wait until he got a bit tired before landing him via the air route. This one was eleven and a half inches. Two more fish came from this pool before I hooked into one that wouldn't lift, and when I tried it he tore loose. That was the end as far as this pool was concerned. By looking for such places the rest of the day I managed to have a mighty exciting time of it at a period when fishing was admittedly at a standstill. It was a simple stunt, as old as fishing itself, and yet I see thousands of anglers fishing all the time who never use the idea.

Sometimes the bushes and grasses are too high to fish so simply. In this case you can sometimes stand behind them and cast over the tops with excellent results. In making a cast from such a position it is necessary to use considerably more line than would be used for an unimpeded cast of the same distance. (See diagram.) Saying X is the place where the fly should land, you can readily see why an overcast is necessary.

There was a section of the Encampment Creek in Wyoming that was perfectly adapted to this sort of fishing. The bushes were high, the water clear and shallow. You couldn't get in the stream to wade without scaring trout as far as you could see. Of course in this case the hooking of one fish usually finished the section, because it took clever maneuvering first to keep the line from snagging in the bush, and then you had to get through it to land your trout. However, this method produced some of the best fish caught by dry fly on the stream, so I considered it worth while.

It is the same old story. When streams are fished hard and conditions are tough, you might better spend an entire day overcoming the obstacles in the way of one "hard-to-get-at" spot than to fish a couple of miles of open water. No matter how poor the fishing may be in the open, you may always be sure of taking trout in the secluded places provided you give the time and study necessary to fish them. Don't marvel at the angler who always

CASTING OVER BUSHES

seems to have some measure of success no matter how bad fishing is. Instead, cultivate the habit of working the tough places that the average person passes by. Sometimes an entire day's search reveals only two or three such places, but if these three places yield one trout each, the day will be a success; whereas a day of hard, persistent work over the other waters may result in no fish at all. On more than one occasion this plan has given me a happy day when otherwise it might have been a discouraging one. It wasn't because of any skill on my part. It was because I spent the time looking for apparently unfishable water and then working out a method of fishing it. Just to show you how it works out, let me tell you of an experience.

The spot was a deep pocket thoroughly surrounded and almost covered with alders. It took me slightly more than an hour to work my way into the brush until it was possible for me to get my fly on the water. Then it took me another half hour to get the rod in position so that I could both drop the fly properly and handle the fish if one was hooked. In doing this I lost parts of two leaders and several flies. But the instant the fly touched the water an eighteen-inch brown took that fly so deep that the only way I could have lost him would have been by breaking the leader. Of course the landing of this fish caused so much commotion that there wasn't a chance to take another there. In the bargain I got pretty well soaked because I had to get into the hole to land the fish, and the water went over the top of my waist waders; but even so, don't you think it was worth it? I did that night, when the net results of the day were compared.

One word of advice about such fishing. You need a heavy leader and short one. It need never be longer than seven and a half feet, and shorter is better. 1X is a good size. As a rule a large fly—size 10—will do the trick, and in the majority of cases no leader will touch the water anyway. Trout in such locations are not so angler-wise as the ones in open water. They are rarely molested and feel secure because of their almost impregnable position. They will take more chances than those fish in open water, where everything from fishermen to hawks continually strive to end their existence. Of course 3X and 4X gut may be used if you insist on it, but it is almost a sure bet that with gut as fine as this you will lose any fish of decent size. The place for this fine gut is on open water when it is low and clear. It is needed then because the gut is on the water, and the finer and longer it is, the less noticeable.

The backwaters of any pool, or in fact any large pocket, may easily give you a chance at a good fish, provided that you fish it properly. Never cast a fly into such a location without first considering it from every angle. A little thought often prevents you from doing the wrong thing. It takes a long time to learn the lie of the fish in these backwaters, and while experience aids you in fishing them, nothing succeeds like knowing the location from personal observation. If you don't get any indication the first time you fish a backwater, try it from a different angle the next time. If you know there are large fish in a stream, go a bit further and spend some time investigating and observing such locations. I remember fishing one backwater fifteen times without getting a single hit simply because I always fished it from the wrong angle. One day I fished it from the right position and took one of the finest browns I've ever caught. It has since yielded me several that anyone would be proud to catch.

I cannot stress too emphatically the importance of this "correct-position" detail. Each bit of water in a stream should be fished from the position that will give your fly the most natural float, regardless

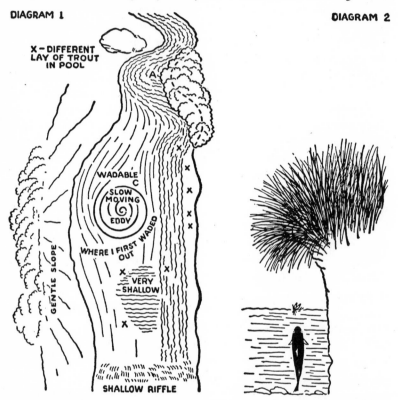

of how well you may be able to cast. It takes plenty of observation plus experimentation to get to know some types of water. For instance, on the Encampment Creek there was a pool of which I never got the full benefit until I learned exactly how to fish it. Looking upstream the left bank was a shallow slope with a background of bushes. All this side of the pool was comparatively quiet water. The neck of the pool was narrow and fast. This current at the upper end first shot over to the right bank which was canopied with heavy foliage, and then gradually left the bank and ran straight away to the tail of the pool. (See Diagram 1.) This left a rather slow-moving stretch between the current and the right bank, which was decidedly grassy and overhanging. (See Diagram 2.) While a few fish lay in the main current the best ones, and most of them, lay in the quieter water close to the bank.

I had no difficulty taking fish rising in the current, but I couldn't seem to do anything with those rising against the bank. I did fairly well by fishing from the very shallow water near the tail, but could fish only a part of the water from this section because of an abominable downstream drag that came with a long line. The solution was rather simple once I found it. There were two narrow but wadable spots both above and below the deep, slow eddy. From the lower one, where I first waded out, all but the upper stretch could be fished nicely with a short line and a long rod, which enabled you to cast over the current and yet hold the line away from the current. From the upper position C you could fish that part close to the overhanging trees in the same way. Of course I always fished the tail and current first before wading in.

This sort of condition is typical of many streams, and you should be able to recognize the general characteristics of them from the diagram. Of course the specific details will vary, but the problem as a whole remains the same.

Even in open water there are excellent fishing places that are missed by many anglers. Along the banks many pockets are formed, pockets just large enough to make a suitable resting- and feeding-place for a single trout. If you proceed carefully and fish every inch of a bank as well as the obvious places, you will see or rise many more fish than if you only fish the obvious places. I have taken many a good trout from pockets that could not be recognized as such until experience had brought the locations to my attention.

Then there are the shallow riffles. I wager that nine-tenths of the anglers skip them, considering them unworthy of notice. Some of them are—no doubt about it. But others have from one to ten pocket holes that contain fish. Are you sure that the riffles you skip do not have such pockets that might produce trout for you? Here again is water that is not molested. It will pay you to investigate their possibilities. Even if you find only one productive spot in a half dozen you try, that place may some day prove valuable to you; and the chances are that after a time you will catalogue in your mind a number of such locations on every stream you fish, and so have an advantage over the other fellow when conditions are bad.

And don't forget that brown trout in a feeding mood will go searching for food all over the place. They will run boldly into very shallow water, particularly to the edges of sand and gravel bars. They will seek the edges of grassy meadows, often in water that won't even cover their dorsal fins. But watch out for them in such places. They tend to be extremely wary, so that the slightest error on your part will send them scurrying for cover. Also, you may possibly misinterpret the surface movements. They may look like rises, but instead be caused by the dorsal or caudal fins as the fish take nymphs beneath the surface. Sometimes they stand on their heads when doing this, and you may make many casts with dry flies without getting any response, while a deftly drifted nymph will bring a strike. And I feel sure that usually you need not worry about having a certain pattern for the work. The principal thing is to place it just right, so that it sinks and drifts at the right level for the trout to take.

In a previous chapter I wrote of an experience on the Firehole River in Yellowstone Park and mentioned the weeds. These deserve more attention. As a general rule the strips of weeds ran lengthwise with the stream current, with open channels in between and small pockets that seemed like eddies in the midst of the beds. The entire stretch was fishing water, that is, there were no barren places here and there where you might sneak up on the next location where the trout lay. Because of this it was very easy to put fish down by alarming others you were bound to disturb as you made your way to some objective.

The secret lay in first getting into the most strategic position possible, and then waiting there quietly for twenty minutes or more without casting a fly or otherwise causing any disturbance. Usually, by that time, the trout you had put down by getting into position would have started rising again, often within easy casting range.

From then on, by being careful in moving and waiting patiently before fishing after each change in position, it was possible to go from one side of the stream to the other and upstream as long as the rise was on, and to catch fish. Of course in many cases the weeds served as ideal blinds, and one of the most deadly methods was to stalk some rising fish on the opposite side of a particularly heavy weed-bed and then dap the fly along the edge of the bed. The trout also used the weeds for hiding places when alarmed.

On one occasion I rose eighteen good fish in about thirty minutes by following these tactics. By good I mean fish weighing a pound and a half and up. However, I was off the beam on striking that day. I hooked the first ten very lightly—just held them for a moment or two and then they were gone. Then I missed the next five completely—definitely struck before they even got the fly in the mouth. However, I didn't go down in utter and dismal defeat. The last three fish to rise I hooked solidly and in good form, the best of them weighing better than three pounds.

Incidentally, if you fished this stretch of water in any other manner than over the tops of the weeds, you invariably made out quite poorly, in fact rarely did you hook into a fish better than twelve inches, even though the trout were generally in a very taking mood. It was clearly a matter of concealment by the weeds, which made it possible to catch the larger fish with apparent ease —provided, of course, you hooked them securely when they rose.

I hope you will understand my reason for devoting so much space to this angle of trout fishing. The reason is that I know it is very important if you wish to make the most of your fishing time in these days of crowded fishing waters. Most of us have so little time to spend at the sport that it defeats our purpose. Having so little time, we think we must fish the best-looking spots where everyone else fishes because they must be good or no one else would fish them. This is false reasoning, because we are relying on precedents established by easy fishing and in most cases by anglers who have followed the established rules rather than the dictates of their own minds. It would pay larger dividends if we spent more time at thinking and observing than at fishing. Remember that locating fish is more than half the battle. When you know exactly where they are, then you can intelligently fish for them. Otherwise you are simply trusting to luck. I have often observed anglers wading through a shallow stretch, chasing trout out all around them, heard them talk about all the fish they saw, and then seen them neglect such a place and fish a deep hole near by. The chances are that all the fish in this deep hole were out feeding in the shallows. When scared by the angler they rushed back to deep water or hid under rocks and of course wouldn't feed for some time. The thing to do is to stop short when you start scaring trout in the shallows. Look the situation over, take a half hour or more to do it, and then fish the shallows with all the skill and care you can muster.

As an instance of this, let me again give an illustration by relating an actual experience. The location was a rocky riffle below a beautiful pool, one that was impossible to pass without fishing. To reach the pool it was necessary to wade to one side of this riffle, and frequently one would see good trout dart away from the very shore in water not over four inches deep. And yet only one out of every thirty anglers fishing this stream ever fished the riffle. They were too anxious to get the pool that looked so enticing. However, the riffle produced three fish to every one caught in the pool, regardless of the difference in the number of anglers fishing each place. Obviously the anglers fishing the riffle had an advantage over those fishing the pool. The fish in the fast-water pockets had not been bothered very much, and so were less angler-wise. Of course if the riffle had been fished as hard as the pool, it would no doubt be much poorer fishing than the pool because it would not have the capacity of supporting as many fish.

Whenever you find a small stream entering a larger one, it will pay to investigate the locality. Sometimes there isn't any hole at the point where it enters, but there may be one or more in the immediate vicinity. Usually the best water will be below such streams rather than above.

There are always a certain number of good trout that will run up into these little streams at certain times of the year, as a general rule in the spring when the freshets are on, and in the late summer when the waters of the larger streams become cold. Often, at either of these periods, you may profitably fish these small spring brooks. I like best to fish them in the late summer. At this time they are down as low as they ever go. All the water in them comes direct from the springs, which keeps them cool. It requires the utmost caution, careful and skillful casting, and plenty of thinking to get results in these brooks at this time, but if you do it properly you will be surprised at the results.

Speaking of this brings back memory of one spring brook that I love. Although one could jump across it in most places, it always contained a reasonable number of trout larger than ten inches and quite a few running up to eighteen. The amazing thing about this brook was the productiveness of the shallow riffles. If they were more than three inches deep on the average, it was a common thing to take twelve-inch, or better, fish from them. It had one large hole that would have done credit to a big stream. It was more than eight feet deep on one side, was thoroughly covered with thick brush, and even on the other side the water was a foot deep at the edge of the bank. At the tail the depth held until the last few feet, and at the head, after sliding through what looked like an old sluiceway for running logs, which was covered by a farm bridge, it deepened quickly to six or seven feet.

The best fish were taken when a fly was cast directly to the edge of the sluiceway or at the very edge of the heavy brush that was on the deep side, the right when you looked upstream. The biggest fish I ever caught there was a two-pounder, but I would have been happy had I been offered the chance that came to my Dad. He is basically a bait fisherman and was brought up on bass, Northern pike, and pan-fish in the waters of Lake Ontario, near which he was born. Business brought him to Nyack where he met my mother, and they brought me into the world in 1891. Three near-by lakes and the Hudson River kept him occupied with fish other than trout, and it wasn't until I had become a regular writer about angling subjects in the 1920's that he ever gave trout or artificial-lure fishing a thought.

Well, it happened that Dad went with me on a camping trip to the stream mentioned. The water was low and clear, and while I made out splendidly with dry flies, he didn't do very well with worms.

At the time we were near this hole and I got a bright idea. It was to drop a grasshopper into the water from the bridge, from a height of some sixteen or more feet. So I rustled up a hopper and baited Dad's hook with it. Then I told him to get cautiously to the center of the bridge and drop the hopper over. He crept to the center and lowered the hopper to the water. Just as it touched, a brown trout of easily eight pounds in weight came for it. Dad reacted too fast. The big trout got the grasshopper but not the hook because of the quick and hard jerk given to the line. It was enough to make the fish come clear of the water so that we both saw him plainly, but all Dad had was an empty hook sailing through the air from the pressure of the strike.

Dad actually turned a bit pale, and he wouldn't leave the place for an hour or two after. But after drowning a couple more hoppers without getting any response, he finally gave up. I tried for that fish several times afterward, but never again saw any sign of it. Perhaps it moved out, perhaps someone else caught it. I don't know. But I do wish that I could have caught it on a fly.

Incidentally we never caught any good fish from the tail of this pool. And pertinent to the subject of pool fishing, this one never produced as well as many other sections that didn't look nearly as fishy. For instance, a short distance below it there was a shallow sandy riffle. If I hadn't seen a trout rise there the first time I fished the brook, I'd probably never have tried it. But once I did, I never passed it up; and it never failed to produce, although the big pool did.

By far the most intriguing stretches of the brook were the upper reaches, which ran through a large cow pasture. The water was slow-moving and on the whole very shallow, but the banks were considerably undermined, giving plenty of cover. Besides, in many places the bottom was covered with moss and silt in which the trout hid when frightened.

The best way to fish this stretch was to crawl along the bank and cast carefully some distance upstream and to the other side. If you fished standing up, you not only did not rise a fish, but neither did you see any. The moment a fish saw you it ruined all the water between you and the next upstream curve. This fishing from the bank from a hidden position was a necessity on the still waters or slow-moving stretches, but it wasn't so good on the riffles. When fishing them one had to sacrifice the upper stretches and had to do it without sending the frightened fish up through the riffle. In order to accomplish this I would get as near the foot of the riffle as possible, hoping that most of the fish in the pool were behind me. Then I would fish that part of the pool with sloppy casts before getting in the water. Usually this resulted in the fish there going downstream, although it wasn't a sure bet by any means. After that I would ease down to the water, all previous movements, of course, having been made on the knees or lower, and, after getting in the stream, would wade on my knees until in position to fish the riffle.

It was a lot of effort and perhaps for nothing, but at least fifty per cent of the riffles produced, sometimes only one trout but frequently two or three. Often narrow, insignificant-looking riffles would net fourteen- and fifteen-inch fish. To show what unusual places will produce, I must tell you of an experience.

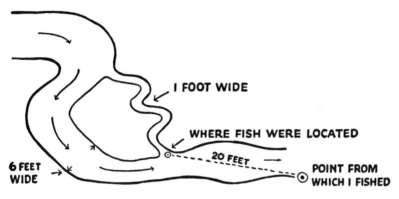

AT ONE POINT A NARROW CHANNEL CONNECTED TWO BENDS

At one point a narrow channel connected two bends. It was barely twelve inches wide and looked like nothing more than a surface drain. But as I fished the water into which this led, I saw what looked like the wrinkle caused by a fish. So I tentatively cast my fly to the place. It no sooner hit the water than a wake appeared, and the next instant I was fast to a trout that gave me a grand tussle. It was sixteen inches long. I never expected to get another rise in this place, but one usually casts a fly back to a spot that has produced; and I did it this time. Again the wake appeared, and again I was hooked to a grand fish. This one went sixteen and a half inches. But the climax came when I made still another cast, this time sending the fly as far as I could up the narrow channel. It caught on a blade of over-hanging grass, wobbled there a moment, and then dropped when I twitched the rod slightly. I didn't see it hit the water, but I did see a splash as a fish struck. In less than ten seconds he had me tangled up in the grass and the bank. I saw him once as he raised himself from the water with a violent shake of his body, and then it was over. He had broken the leader.

After that I went over to look at the place. It was just about deep enough to float the fish that had been in it. I imagine they had gone in there to take grasshoppers and bugs that fell or jumped into the water from the overhanging grass. Several times, in later years, I found fish there and managed to hook and land some nice ones, simply because of the original experience from which I learned plenty.

This stream is in New York State and it is small. But out West I've encountered conditions that were closely similar to this spring brook. The Firehole River is a lot like it, although some ten times larger. It also contains many more fish, with the average running heavier and longer. Some of these Western streams are most exciting, and sometimes you run into very interesting experiences while fishing them.

One day Don Bell, of Hillsdale, New York, and I stopped to look at a stretch of the Grayling, a rather small stream that runs into an arm of Hebgen Lake, Montana. There in a pool, within sight of the car window, we saw a large trout. It was large enough to look quite silly in the small pool which wasn't more than two feet deep in the center, nor more than fifteen feet wide.

Don got his rod together, went below the pool, and started fishing for it with a dry fly. From his casting position he couldn't see the fish, but from my position in the car I could, so I directed his casts with words. Well, he finally got the fly over the fish just right. The trout came for it lazily and the water formed into a little vortex under it from the sucking action of the take.

I had advised Don what was happening and when the fly disappeared from sight I called out "Strike!" Don, an old-time dry-fly man more than twenty years older than I, set the hook like the maestro he is and then the fight was on. That fish surely made a fuss in the small and shallow pool, but because both ends of it were only a few inches deep he didn't leave it, and in time was subdued. I forget the exact weight of this trout, a cutthroat, but I remember that it was better than four pounds. We discovered later that there had been a half dozen or more of these big fish in the stream, that this was the smallest taken. However, the others had been caught with natural bait.

One of the most difficult spots to fish with a dry fly—but the easiest for a good bait fisherman to fish—is a deep hole at a time when the trout are not rising. Now there are times when persistently making cast after cast over such water will bring results. But this doesn't happen frequently—at least to the extent of making a good catch. On the other hand the bait man, provided he is clever, usually can and often does take some good fish here. To watch a good man at this game is quite fascinating. He is just as fussy about what he uses as the fly fisherman. He must find the right combination of weight and bait to properly work the deeper currents. Once he does this, he can keep his bait swirling about in the pool for a considerable time, and if patient enough he will eventually get a hit. You can fish a weighted fly in this same way. I've done it many times and occasionally have taken fish by the method. But an artificial fly has no taste or meaty odor, and there are many times when trout are quite plebeian in this respect, preferring real meat to feathers.

Fly fishing big streams, if the water is fast, turbulent, and unwadable except near shore on one side or the other, requires special attention. On the whole in such waters streamer, bucktail, and wet flies produce better than dry flys, but one should not overlook the possibilities of the latter.

No matter how deep and swift the stream there are always quiet stretches and small eddies here and there near shore, and if you watch them carefully you will often see trout rising. Many of these surface-feeding fish will be small, but among them there are usually a fair percentage of large ones. Sometimes a cast over a small dimple will take an undersize trout, sometimes a ten- or twelve-incher; and I've also seen it produce fish of two to four pounds.

And do not overlook the fast, deep water itself, even if white-topped, providing you can reach it and satisfactorily fish it. Sometimes this is impossible unless you are in a boat or canoe that is properly controlled as you drift. When the boat drifts too fast you hardly get a chance to fish a fly correctly, therefore it should be stopped completely or else slowed down so that you can. Of course haphazard casts as you drift quickly by will take a fish now and then, but slowing up or stopping the drift at strategic places will help the angler to rise and hook many more fish.

Look for small dark spots in any stretch of tumbling water. If you can float a dry fly over them you may be surprised at the results, especially if there are large rainbows in the river. If you fish such water with dry flies it will pay you to have them tied heavily hackled and on heavy dry-fly hooks, say regular or fine wire, or even stout wire if the conditions will allow it.

It all goes to show that you can't overlook any possibility when fishing. With all one's experience, there is always something else to learn. If you fish intelligently, inquiringly, thoroughly, and carefully, you'll always get plenty of surprises to pay for what you put into the effort. The person who fishes with his head, regardless of whether he is an accomplished caster or not, will get some real joy from the game, and it won't all come from catching fish. Most of it will come from ideas and memories that can't be erased.

◦§ CHAPTER XIII §◦

Vision–Striking–Rise Types–
Stream Rules

Vision

Trout can see farther under water, if it is clear, than they can see above it. When the angle of sight is obtuse enough the surface of the water acts like a mirror and turns the line of sight back into the water again. The deeper the fish lies in the water the larger his window of sight on the surface.

For this reason when you are wading at any considerable distance from a fish you may forget all of you that is above the water but must watch out for your legs which are under the water. Of course in riffles and broken bottoms this is not so important. Fish cannot see far under such conditions any more than we can through heavy mist.

In still waters, that part of you which is in the water may be more disturbing to the fish than the rest of you. For this reason it is best to fish from the shore wherever possible provided your figure is not so high that it is silhouetted against the background, in which case the trout see it and become alarmed. Keeping back, keeping low, and selecting backgrounds that absorb your figure are all necessary if you would successfully fish clear, still waters.

Trout see objects more clearly under the water than they do those upon its surface or above it. This is easily proved. The surface of the water is never perfectly flat, and when it is not flat it acts as a poorly-shaped lens and distorts anything above it. Besides, objects on the surface create surface distortions themselves and so provide their own concealment. A fly, for instance, creates depressions where its feet rest on the water, and is looked at by the fish through a system of concave lenses. This principle may be applied to glass. Plate glass is perfectly flat—therefore it is perfectly clear. Old-fashioned window glass is not perfectly flat and therefore causes distorted vision.

From this we may reason that trout cannot distinguish the color, shape, and size of flies floating on the surface as they can those beneath the surface. If we use the ideas set forth in the chapter dealing with dry-fly construction and have some of our dry flies made so they float high, it is less necessary to consider color than it is when using low-floating flies in which the body is submerged. In other words, when a low-floating fly is necessary, then it is quite likely that the fish will be more selective to color, size, and shape than when a high-floating fly can be used. So too we feel that flies fished under the surface, being more visible to the fish, may need to have more color to meet some special need than any fly floating on the surface.

Size is the most important consideration in a dry fly. Even though trout may not be able to distinguish the colors of a fly that is distorting the vision by its hackles resting on the surface, they can tell something of its size by the shadow caused by its density. This varies according to the degree of light. As a rule, when fish are rising steadily to a large hatch of flies of the same size, if you imitate the size in any neutral shade, it is quite likely to produce. So too when you can't seem to imitate the hatch so that the trout will take your artificial, an extra large fly of almost any sensible combination will sometimes turn the trick. In this latter case it is probably a matter of attracting attention by means of a large mouthful of food.

But on working toward direct imitations of the natural we are often more prone to match color than size. I've often witnessed anglers fishing with size 12 when they should have been using 18, and 14 when they should have been using 10. Rather than carry a large assortment of patterns, a small number, in all sizes from 18 to 6 especially suitable to the waters you fish, is much more sensible. Keep in mind that hook size alone does not make a small fly. To be really small the hackles, wings, and so on should also conform with the hook size. Of course sometimes you want a large fly on a small hook. That is the principle of the Spiders and the Variants. It is my opinion that you would benefit by an assortment of this kind, and you will have plenty of flies in your box if you carry six assorted patterns. Choose them wisely and with an eye to real variety. For instance, don't buy both Whirling Dun and Dark Cahill. If the trout will take one of these patterns, they will rise to the other. The fly plates in this book will aid you to make your choice in this respect, as you will be able to select a diversified assortment by comparing the colors and selecting only one each of any definite color. The descriptions will give considerable aid in making your choice.

Striking

As far as I can ascertain, the reasons for missing a rising fish come from faulty reactions. When we miss a fish we are either too fast or too slow. I'm inclined to react too fast and a bit too hard, and this is a common fault that causes a lot of trouble for trout fishermen in general, especially if they react quickly to emergencies. In all my experience I have fished with only three anglers whose reactions were too slow and who missed rises because of it.

Usually one's reactions are based on the fishing of the day. If trout rise surely and deliberately, as well as frequently, we have little trouble in hooking them, no matter whether our reactions are fast or slow. If we make a few false moves at the beginning we soon overcome them, and once this is done we wonder how it is that we so often miss rises and frequently leave our fly in the mouth of a fish because we strike too hard.

But when we meet with an off day, it is different. On such days we get many strikes from small fish. No matter how much we are determined to strike deliberately and without force, a continuation of these rises from small fish gets us into a state of nervousness that causes us to strike with a quickness and verve that are disastrous when a good fish rises. We either take the fly away from him or else leave it in his mouth.

In all my experience and years of observation I've never yet found a good sizable fish that wasn't hooked if the strike was deliberate, but I've seen countless others lost because of a fast and forceful strike. By a deliberate strike I mean the simple raising of the wrist or forearm to bring the power of the rod taut against the pull of the fish. Naturally the more slack line on the water, the greater distance the wrist or arm must move to accomplish this. For this reason it is good practice to have full control of your slack —to fish with as small an amount of slack line as you possibly can. If you do this, you do not need to worry about striking. When a good trout takes a fly he immediately starts to bottom with it, and the speed of this movement is considerable, so fast in fact that a taut line against a reasonably stiff rod will force the barb of the hook through the flesh of the mouth. From the observations of many experiments I have learned that as long as no pull is exerted against an artificial fly a trout has taken, he will continue to carry the fly until he has reached his normal and accustomed feeding position. At that time he will eject an artificial unless the line becomes positively taut and is held that way while he is on the way down, in which case the pressure exerted sets the hook. If the angler augments this pressure by a strike that is the least bit excessive he will readily break gut calibrating smaller than .009 (1X) and so lose both fish and fly. In making a decision on which method you wish to select, consider what you would rather have—a large mess of small trout or from one to a few large trout. In view of the fact that almost everyone who fishes is always looking for that big one, I fail to see why anglers don't continually concentrate on control of the strike rather than on anything else.

Keep this fact in mind and try to control your reactions accordingly. Remember that when a good fish takes the fly, all you need for a perfect strike is a line handled so well that the downward movement of the taking fish sets the hook. A good fish is a wise one who has survived the onslaughts of anglers, and he always takes surely and deeply or not at all; so you always have plenty of time to take in slack and exert the slight pressure necessary to set the hook—if this exertion is necessary, which I doubt unless the rod is a very limber one. This holds true with all large fish, either trout or salmon, and the larger the fish the more careful you must be about striking.

Rise Types

There are a number of rises we see that can be identified if we observe closely enough. In this brief discussion of the subject I hope to get others thinking about the possibility of being fully conversant with the most common rise types and so be in a position to take advantage of the conditions they suggest.

DIMPLE, also SUCK and SIP RISE: Indicative of large fish but looks somewhat like the rise of a minnow. However, if you observe closely you will note a movement to the water that distinguishes it from the rise of a very small fish. These rises often leave a bubble or two, and if close enough you can see a slight depression in the center of the ring caused by the process of the fish sucking the fly under the surface without breaking the water. This is a rise to be careful of and to refrain from striking at too hard. It usually means something worth while if you handle the situation properly. It has the appearance of a small pebble dropping in the water.

SLASH: Usually occurs during the hatch of large flies, especially the May flies, also happens to flies that run across the surface, of which there are a few. It is caused when the trout goes for the fly as it leaves the water, especially when the wind affects the movement of these flies. It has the appearance of a stick being slashed through the water.

BULGE: The resulting disturbance caused by a quick turn of the trout after it has made a dash for a nymph or some other underwater prey that happens to be quite close to but not on the surface. There are some who distinguish this from a mount or hump, but it is practically the same thing and for our purpose may be considered as such. There are different degrees of this rise, depending on the way the trout has taken the nymph or other food. At times larvæ may be floating along just under the surface, and a trout may be feeding steadily on them but without fuss. In this case the bulge or hump would be barely noticeable. A rise similar to this is caused by a fish taking a minnow, but in this case you are quite likely to witness a wake besides the bulge and you surely will if the fish persists in his feeding. It looks like a mound of gelatin, of course with animation.

TAILING: Every angler of any experience is acquainted with and knows this one. Of course it isn't a rise at all but is the tail of a trout disturbing the surface as it feeds on the bottom, dislodging and eating nymphs and small crustaceans from the rocks or weeds. When the water is shallow the tail itself may show a trifle now and then. When the water is slightly deeper the tailing may look like a mixture of a ripple and suction. This is usually easily identified by the wavering ripple, but when the tail is touching the surface only occasionally and slightly, it is often mistaken for a genuine dimple rise.

SATISFACTION RISE: Similar to tailing except that it isn't continuous. Caused by a little wiggle of the tail as the fish drops beneath the surface after the rise, it is a genuine surface rise and is really preceded by an elongated dimple. Often the large selective rises in the Wyoming country are of this type and perhaps express entire satisfaction with the fly being taken.

SPLASH: Caused by two entirely opposite reactions—overeagerness to get the fly or sudden refusal after having decided to take it. In the natural fly it is almost always overeagerness; in the artificial it is more likely to be for the other reason. The name is descriptive.

INVESTIGATING REFUSAL: Purely my own term for the rise of a fish that comes directly to the fly, makes a dimple or swirl, but does not take it. It happens mostly to artificials, but I have seen it with naturals.

DOUBLE-ENDER: In appearance similar to the satisfaction but has no tail wiggle. Sometimes it is combined with the satisfaction. Likely to show a very slight wake followed by the tail disturbance, it is caused by a trout rising from a position very near the surface instead of perpendicularly from considerable depth.

ROLL: I'm not sure just what causes this. As a matter of fact I've never been able to take many fish when such a rise was in progress. Sometimes I almost believe that they are playing rather than feeding, but this is purely guesswork. On more than one occasion I have fished over fifty trout doing this roll without getting one of them. It looks like a porpoise rolling in the ocean. Of course the back is often plainly visible.

Coming back to the investigating refusal, this is sometimes caused by the effect of sunlight on the vision of the fish. When a trout starts rising to an artificial it may be partially obscured by the rays of the sun; but by the time the fish reaches the fly it may be in the range of total visibility, and so he recognizes it for the fraud it is. A change in your position when casting to this fish may result in getting him. Consider the diagrams to get the drift of my thought. The center black spot is the location of total invisibility or at best very poor visibility, as shown in a previous chapter. The circle of lighter color around this black center is the section of sufficient visibility where the trout can see fairly well but not too well to recognize discrepancies in our artificial. On the opposite side of the fish he has positively clear sight to the limit of his range of vision. If the sun is directly overhead, as in the circular diagram, then the point of invisibility would be directly above and both sides would have areas of partial and total visibility. If you give this a little thought in connection with the other remarks on the subject in Chapter Eleven, I am sure you will see the advantage of trying to figure out the position of the trout and the sun and if possible cast your fly so that it will float in the range of sufficient visibility without first being in the range of total visibility.

SUNLIGHT AND ITS DIRECT EFFECT ON THE VISION OF A FISH. THE DARKER SHADING IS THE AREA OF LEAST VISIBILITY, HENCE A TROUT MAY BE EASIER FOOLED BY AN ARTIFICIAL LURE FLOATING IN THIS AREA.

Stream Rules

Let us sum up some of the important rules of stream trout fishing—those principles which are so vital to success:

1. Make all approaches to the stream with care and caution. Remember that once you are seen you are at a great disadvantage if not completely defeated.

2. Be prepared with any size fly needed. The box should contain every size between 6 and 18, including Spiders and Variants.

3. Develop a gentle delicate cast so that your fly alights softly. This calls for skill as well as suitable tackle to bring about such results.

4. Study the water before fishing it. Select the most advantageous spot to fish from. Remember that the obvious places in the hard-fished streams are less likely to produce than the tough spots that no one fishes.

5. If you fish a place you do not know and fail to take a fish, don't leave it until you examine it carefully. It is possible that you didn't fish the right spot or from the right position. A careful investigation is quite likely to reveal the reason you failed.

6. Use the longest leader you can handle. Usually you can handle one much longer than you imagine. Remember that the purpose of the leader is to conceal artificiality. If you believe a leader is at all necessary, then you must admit that the longer the leader the better chances you have for success.

7. Flies, lines, and other equipment of the right sort are not absolutely necessary in the rising of fish, but they are very important in that they make it easier to do the things that bring success and in some cases are essential to success. Once a person fishes with the best, he will never again be satisfied with inferior tackle. If you can't afford the best, get the best you can and be critical when you buy it. Be sure the leaders taper as they should, that your line is the right size for your rod, that your dry flies will float. These are all aids to good fishing, and everyone who loves the game wants tackle that performs smoothly and efficiently.

8. Fish slowly and thoroughly. Haste never paid dividends. Don't worry about the fellow ahead of you. If you start racing to get ahead of him he'll probably try to beat you, and from then on it will be nothing but a foot-race instead of a contemplative and inspiring recreation. If you like a certain section it may pay you to wait if someone else is fishing it. Wait until he goes, and then wait some more and do some observing. When you see fish commence to move, then start fishing. Don't whip the stream to a froth. Make fewer casts, make them to places that count, and fish each cast out instead of lifting it prematurely.

9. Be courteous even if the other fellow isn't. To lose your own temper and become discourteous because the other fellow started it doesn't help matters. Instead it will lessen your normal angling ability. A calm, peaceful mind and the knowledge that you have been a gentleman will do much to make your fishing successful.

Perhaps some of my viewpoints will be considered radical to those who consider technical skill above anything else. I bow to their skill, admire it, wish I were in the same class with them. But underneath I am still the instinctive, natural fisherman of my boyhood, and from this angle the nine rules mentioned seem most important. It seems to me that the fundamentals are the necessities, and the other things are accessories that aid in bolstering the fundamentals. Once the fundamentals become instinctive you do the necessary things without thought. Then you can elaborate to good advantage. But to start out with highly technical ideas without the groundwork of lowly experience is to start wrong. It is putting the cart before the horse.

❧ CHAPTER XIV ❧

Steelhead of the Umpqua

HAVING been born and raised on the East Coast and not being wealthy, it took me a great many years to satisfy my desire to fish in waters west of the Mississippi. The first trip, with a five-year-old Model A Ford, took us to that river, from Canada to New Orleans, and out into the Atlantic as well: that is, to the island of Ocracoke, North Carolina. The next year, with a new car, we made a trip that brought us plenty of fishing in Michigan, Colorado, Wyoming, Missouri, Arkansas, and Mississippi.

During these years Clarence Gordon, of Oregon, had been corresponding with me. His letters about the steelhead fishing on the North Umpqua, in the vicinity of Steamboat where he had a delightful camp, painted such fascinating pictures that my wife and I couldn't resist them. We put aside other projects we had considered and surrendered to the lure of Oregon, California, and West Texas for that year. We have always been glad that we did. We feel that we owe Clarence a debt of gratitude for having hastened our first trip to the Pacific Coast.

A friend, Fred Gerken, of Tombstone, Arizona, also had a great desire to fish for steelhead, so the result was a meeting at the Wilcox Ranch on Encampment Creek, Wyoming. I'd become attached to this stream from a previous trip, and after ten days of splendid fishing there, we started for Oregon.

We went by way of the Columbia River Highway. My first glimpse of Mount Hood was enthralling. It fulfilled all my dreams of what a high mountain should look like. There were many forest fires raging at the time, and by some freak of the air-currents the smoke obscured the lower part of the mountain, but not the valley, leaving the peak suspended in mid-air—pointed, majestic, and fascinating. We'd seen higher mountains before but none more spectacular, for Hood rises from comparatively low country while the others rise from very high altitudes to begin with, thus losing much impressiveness. Next to Mount Hood, the Tetons hold my memory most. They are so rugged and jagged, and rise so high above the surrounding country, that they get your nervous system responding with inward heart quivers.

We had another thrill when we left Roseburg for the trip up the North Umpqua to Steamboat. The first few miles were not so much, but once above Glide it was as picturesque and tortuous a route as one could imagine. You felt sure you were going places, and you really were.

The river is wild and beautiful, and at first sight a bit terrifying. You wonder how you are going to be able to wade it without getting into difficulties. Despite this it isn't so bad once you learn to read the bottom. On the bottom are narrow strips of gravel that wander here and there and crisscross like old-time city streets. By walking in these and stepping only on reasonably flat, clean rocks or on other rocks where you can see the mark of previous footsteps, you wade with fair comfort and safety. The rocks of the routes between most of the good pools are plainly marked by the tread of many feet, and as long as you know what to look for you have no trouble. But do not hurry—watch each step closely unless you have the activity and sure-footedness of a mountain goat or a Clarence Gordon. When he gets to a hard spot he makes a hop, skip, and jump and lands just where he wants, while you gingerly and sometimes painfully make your way after him, arriving a few minutes later. He waits apparently patiently, but probably in his heart wishing you would move quicker. He finds it so easy it must seem ridiculous to him for anyone to be so slow and faltering. I once thought I was agile (I was, from what others tell me), but Clarence—well, just ask those who have fished with him.

Never having fished for steelhead, I decided to watch Gordon a while before trying my luck. From experience I know that you can learn plenty by watching someone who knows the water from concentrated fishing. The time of the year may make a difference in the places where the best fishing is found. At the season we have fished the North Umpqua, steelhead were found only in certain sections of the main channel. In addition, not all waters containing large steelhead were suitable for fly fishing. If of greater depth than six to eight feet, the trout were not much interested in a fly, although now and then one would take.

I fished first at the Fighting Hole, so named because it was all fast water and short, with white and fast water below, so that there was always a good chance of the fish getting out of the hole and into the rapids and thus taking you for a ride that often led to disaster in some degree. Usually this meant only the loss of the fish, but sometimes it meant the loss of a bit of tackle as well.

The first thing I noted was the way Clarence handled the fly. He cast quartering across and slightly downstream. When the fly touched water his rod tip began to dip and rise rhythmically about every three seconds. At the same time he retrieved a little line with his other hand—about a foot or two all told during the entire drift of the fly. On the first cast the fly did not submerge. Before making the next cast he soaked it thoroughly, and from then on it sank readily. He explained that in low, clear water a fly dragging over the surface was likely to spoil your chances. This was good trout-fishing lore. Many times I have soaked flies in mud to make them sink quickly for the same reasons when fishing for wary browns.

The Fighting Hole did not produce, so we moved down to the Mott Pool. This was a long fast run that terminated in a fairly wide basin. Almost at once Clarence hooked a fish. As it struck he let go the slack line he had been holding. The reel screeched as the fish dashed downstream. He broke water some hundred and fifty feet below and then started a dogged resistance. At this time Clarence gave me a little more information: "Most trout fishermen after steelhead for the first time make the mistake of stripping line when playing them. They do it with other fish and think they can do it with these, but you have got to play them on the reel: otherwise there is sure to be trouble." As I watched I knew this was true. As with Atlantic salmon, it would be certain suicide to your chances to attempt to play them by stripping. Those strong rushes—some as long as a hundred and fifty feet—those vicious tugs when like a bulldog they figuratively shook their heads savagely, would make it well-nigh impossible to handle them in any other way except on the reel. The slightest kink, the slightest undue pressure, and something would break.

Watching Clarence fight this fish was too much for my resolve not to fish until I learned something about the game. Besides, I had learned how to manipulate the fly; the rest would be the same as grilse or landlocked salmon—or at least so I thought.

The lower end of the Mott failed me. Clarence said it was probably because his fish had run into it several times and so disturbed the rest located there. I hooked a steelhead in the next hole—I think it is called the "Bologna" for the reason that when a fish goes over there it is gone; and as they usually do go over, it is just bologna to fish the hole; but I did not know it at this time. There was an irresistible vibrant pull at the strike, the reel screeched a few seconds, and then the line was slack. I had lost my first fish.

"You'd have lost the fish when he went over anyway," soothed Clarence. "It is usually over quickly in this hole," and then he told me why. "Going over" on the Umpqua means that a fish leaves the pool it has been hooked in and runs into the white water below. If this stretch of bad water is of any great length, a fish that "goes over" is usually lost. When it gets away the fish is said to have "cleaned" the angler.

It seemed as if the Umpqua steelhead had it in for me—at least I made a poor showing the first three days. I hooked five fish and lost them all. Three pulled out after a short fight, and two cleaned me out good and proper. I was in the doldrums. The only thing that cheered me at all was the fact that Clarence Gordon insisted my hard luck was due to bad breaks and not to poor fishing. "Besides," he said, "I have really been giving you the works—bringing you to places that always mean trouble when you hook a fish. Take that hole right here—I've never landed a fish here yet, and I have hooked plenty."

On the other hand Fred Gerken seemed to take the game with the greatest nonchalance and was making a record for himself. On the first day he used his four-and-a-half-ounce trout rod, thirty yards of line, and a 3X leader, went out on the Kitchen Pool, and took a five-pounder as if he were catching a one-pound rainbow. But he did not tempt fate by continuing the use of the trout outfit. The next day he assembled his nine-and-a-half-footer and really went after business. Well did he uphold his grand start—a fish the second day, and no others were brought into camp. He did the same thing the third day, although he wasn't the only one. Phil Edson, of Pasadena, brought one in about four pounds bigger than

Fred's. But still I had nothing to show. It was always excuses—this happened, that happened—well, you know how it is. To make it look worse my wife took a five-and-a-quarter-pounder at noon on the fourth day, and while she is a good bait-caster she had never done a lot of trout fishing. We started her out with the bait-casting rod, and she did not like it a bit. But to be a good sport she kept using it for three days. Then she rebelled—she wanted to fish with a fly like the rest of us. So I took her out on the Kitchen Pool to give her a little coaching. About a half hour of this and she decided she could go it alone. I had seen a steelhead jump at the lower part of the pool, so was only too glad to rush ashore for my rod. I had just reached the tackle tent when I heard my wife give a call. I rushed back and found her fast to a fish—I believe the very one I went in to get my rod for. As I say, she had not had much experience fly fishing, but she had turned the trick and handled the hooked fish like a veteran. She was proud of her five-and-a-quarter-pounder, but not as happy about it as I thought she had a right to be. I soon learned why. She said: "It was all luck. The cast that took him was the worst I made." I knew exactly how she felt. Dr. Phil Edson, a guest at the camp who had been an observer of the operations, remarked; "A sloppy cast—in the Kitchen Pool and at mid-day in a bright sun. That's something to make us think. Morning and evening, say the experts, and be sure to drop your fly lightly. I wonder what they will say about this?" (To my knowledge no one ever questioned this. They couldn't, as a matter of fact, because it actually happened.)

To make Phil's remarks even more pointed, immediately after lunch I slipped down to the Mott Pool and about halfway through hooked a fish. The singing of the reel was music to my ears. Nothing went wrong this time, and I had the satisfaction of looking toward the end of the fight to see Fred, Grace, and Phil watching me. Phil was so anxious that I save the fish that he took off his shoes and stockings and with bare feet waded that treacherous water between us, just so that he could be on hand to help me land it in a most difficult spot. That is sportsmanship to commend. I shall never forget this spontaneous act of his as long as I live. It showed the real soul of the man, his unselfish desire to see that I got my fish. It was all very satisfying.

Now Clarence showed his angling acumen. For several days he

had been planning his next move so that it would be most advantageous to me. He explained it, now that it was time to carry it through. It seems that when steelhead are not moving much, they become indifferent to flies fished repeatedly from one side of a pool. Mott Pool had been fished hard from the camp side for some time and was going a bit sour. But it hadn't been fished from the opposite side for at least a week—first because not many would tackle it from that side alone, because of the difficulty of wading, and second because Clarence always made an excuse when anyone mentioned going there. He wanted it to get *hot* before taking me there. Even after being taken to the other side by canoe there was plenty of rough wading before reaching the place from which you started fishing. If it hadn't been for Clarence showing me the bad spots and how to avoid them, I'd probably have floundered many times. As it was I never lost my footing.

When we reached the upper end of the hole that I was to fish, Clarence gave me some sage advice. "There are big fish here," he warned. "When one strikes, just keep a taut line and let him go. Don't strike back." Nothing happened until my fly drifted and cut across the tail of the pool. Here I felt a tug but did not connect. But on the next cast I hooked a heavy fish. For the moment he simply held steady, then moved to the center of the pool. Once there he sulked for five minutes or more, and I could not move him. Suddenly he started doing things, and I have but a vague idea of what happened. The reel screeched, its handle knocked my knuckles, my fingers burned as the line sped beneath them as I was reeling in frantically to get the best of a forward run. At the end of this exhibition, in which were included several jumps, he started a steady and rather slow but irresistible run that made the backing on my reel melt away. Clarence was by my side looking at my reel drum. "He's gone over," he said. My heart sank. Then for some unaccountable reason, perhaps an unknown ledge below, he stopped running. I started to pump him—work him—and he came right along. I reeled as fast as I could, and still he kept coming. My spirits revived with this chance of success. By this time he was only thirty feet away. But the fish suddenly decided he had come far enough and started edging off sideways. I could not stop him. He made a short fast run into shallow water at the right, and then all I felt was a vibrant weight. "I'm hung up," I groaned. I walked from one side of the ledge to the other, I knocked the rod, gave slack line, did everything I possibly could, but he did not come loose. I could feel the fish, so I knew we were still connected.

It was partly dark by this time, and the water between me and the fish was treacherous. I had never waded it in daylight and could not attempt it in the dark. But Gordon took the chance even though he had never waded the place before. "The leader is caught on a board," he called. "There—he is all yours." I felt a tug, saw and heard a splash, and the fish was gone. "About a twelve-pounder," said Gordon. "It's a wonder the leader didn't break the instant you snagged." For this is what happened: the leader had finally frayed on the board and broken. The board had floated down from some bridge-construction work upstream.

And that night Fred brought in another fish. But fortune treated me better from then on. The very next evening I brought in two fish, one weighing seven and a half pounds and the other ten and three-quarters. The latter was the largest fish of the season, although a week after we left, Phil Edson took one of ten and a half pounds. From then on my luck ran better than average, but Fred's held true to form to the last day. At that time his score was seven hooked and seven landed—some record when fifty per cent is an excellent score. Clarence and the rest of us decided something must be done about it. The result of this conference was a trip down to the opposite side of Mott Pool. That night Fred hooked one he couldn't do much with, but even so he might have upheld the honor of his standing except for an unlucky break. The fish had been hooked lightly and pulled out. Anyway, he came in without his fish—the only day out of eight that this happened.

It is strange the way things sometimes happen. Dr. Dewey, of Pasadena, arrived at camp a few days before we did, took his limit of three fish two days in succession, and never lost one. But after that it was different. He hooked a number of fish, but something always went wrong. Some "pulled out," and one "went over." He tried to follow the latter, stumbled, and fell in. He came in wet, bedraggled, and muddy. He hooked a number of other fish on flies from which the points of the hooks had been broken on rocks, and of course he held these only a second or two. Twice his leader frayed on sharp rocks and broke at a critical moment. But this was good medicine. It taught him that it pays to inspect tackle frequently to avoid such needless losses. The complaints, "If I had only changed my leader," or "If I had only looked at my fly to see if the hook was all right," should never have to be made.

I experimented considerably with flies. I tried streamers, standard salmon patterns, and all sorts of flies that had brought me success in various sections of North America, but none of them produced. The best fly of all was the Umpqua. It had been designed especially for this stream. The Cummings was a close rival and often effective when the Umpqua would not produce.

From my own experience and from many talks with the fellows who fish the North Umpqua every season I gathered that only two sizes were needed—numbers 4 and 6. I used 4's most, but when a fish was missed I would change to a 6. Sometimes the smaller fly worked.

The day before we left Steamboat I concentrated on two pools, the Sawtooth and the Surveyor's. The Sawtooth got its name from the sharp-topped rocks that divide it. If a fish ever ran your leader over the center or sawtooth rock, it was good-by to fish and whatever part of your terminal tackle below where it was cut by the rock.

The first time I had fished this pool both Clarence and Phil Edson were watching me. There was a suspicious smirk on their faces, but at the moment I didn't tumble to the reason. When I hooked a fish I could fairly feel their expectant joy in my downfall. I almost played directly into their hands too. I led the fish upstream, and only their uncontrolled chuckles put me wise that this might spell disaster because of the sharp rocks. In time I changed my tactics and landed the fish, and so spoiled their chance for a horse-laugh on me.

But on this last day I took my first trout from this hole with incredible ease. It was a fair fish, a bit over six pounds, and took the fly on my side of the sharp rock. By giving it the butt of the rod and showing no quarter I kept it from crossing the dangerous spot, and for some reason it gave up not long after. But the next fish gave me a taste of what a Sawtooth trout could really do. This one took in the center of the hole, on the other side of the sharp-edged rock. When he struck the shock was so great that it almost took the rod from my hands, and after getting hooked he quickly wrapped the leader around the rock and it cut through as if it had been a piece of cheese. It happened so fast that it temporarily dazed me. That was all the action I got from the Sawtooth that day.

At the Surveyor's Pool it was not necessary to make a long cast. The first one I made wasn't more than twenty feet, and a six-pounder took it at the very moment it touched the water. Landing this fish made me feel quite satisfied with myself. Two six-pounders in an hour was mighty good fishing no matter how you looked at it.

I rested the pool a half hour and then tried again. This time I had four rises that I missed, and then I connected with a fish that took slowly but surely. He was the heaviest one I had yet come in contact with. For twenty minutes I just held on. The fish didn't either run or tug; he simply bored to bottom and stayed there. Nothing I could do would budge him, even the taking of the line in my hand and pulling with that. But finally he must have become tired of the continual strain, because he suddenly started to kick up a general rumpus. First, he came direct from the bottom with express-train speed and continued into the air until the force of his rush had been expended. When he hit the water he did so broadside, making a splash that might have been heard a quarter of a mile. He then lashed the pool to a froth, made a few more less spectacular jumps, and finally came to rest out in midstream and near the surface.

It looked to me as if he had used up his energy, so I put on all the pressure the rod would bear, thinking he'd come in docilely. Vain hope. I couldn't move him any more than I could when he had been hugging the bottom. He just lay there with a wicked look in his eye and sapped the strength from my arm. Finally I had to release the pressure a bit. I couldn't take it. As I did this he started fanning his tail and his fins. I knew something was going to happen, but I didn't know what. I soon found out. Turning quickly he started downstream, and this time I could tell he was going places. There was no stopping him. I braked as much as I dared, burned my fingers as well as knocked my knuckles, but the line melted away. When I looked at my reel the end was near. He was in the fast water below the pool and gaining speed each instant, so I pointed the rod tip at him and prayed that only the leader would break. Then something snapped, and the strain was gone. The leader had broken at the fly, and the fish had "cleaned" me.

The landing of the ten-and-three-quarter-pounder in the Mott Pool had been thrilling, but it did not affect me like this complete rout. Now that time has lent perspective to the experience, I know that this particular incident was my most memorable angling adventure. And it is that way all along the line. In every species of fish I've angled for, it is the ones that have got away that thrill me most, the ones that keep fresh in my memory. So I say it is good to lose fish. If we didn't, much of the thrill of angling would be gone.

The following year after this exciting incident found me on the way to the North Umpqua again. This time we went through Yellowstone Park and then took the northern route through Montana, Idaho, and Washington. It was remarkably clear the day we drove down the Columbia River valley. Mount Hood stood out so plainly that we decided it was the time to drive around her base. The sight of this mountain did things to me again—put a lump in my throat, a tremble in my nerves. Anyone who is fascinated by towering peaks should never miss the Mount Hood ride. As much as I love fishing I'd give up a day or two any time just to gaze at this pile.

But Mount Hood is capricious. After smiling at us for a couple of hours she suddenly veiled her face with a reddish smoky cloud, and with the coming of this cloud our spirits changed from gaiety and cheer to gloom and depression. On the west side of the mountain it was dismal and oppressive, but as we neared Oregon City the sun broke through the clouds and it was cheery again.

The fishing conditions on the North Umpqua weren't very good. The water was so low that the fish could not get over the racks of the commercial fishermen at the mouth of the river. As a consequence there were comparatively few steelhead in the water, and the ones that were there had been fished over so much that they had become decidedly wary and particular. It was tough fishing, and no one could deny it.

On this occasion I had the good fortune to become acquainted with Jay Garfield, of Tucson, Arizona. He and his wife had the cabin room next to ours at Gordon's Camp. He had been fishing the river for about five weeks straight and had been consistently successful, with a top fish of some eleven and a half pounds. Of course this might have been luck, but his success seemed too

consistent to be the result of luck. As usual when contacting anything of this sort I proceeded to discover just what there was to
Jay's fishing that might account for his good luck.

In this particular case the job was both easy and enjoyable. Jay
is the sort of fellow you warm up to as soon as you meet him, and
he was not only willing but eager to show me everything he knew
about steelhead fishing. So that I might get this idea about it at first
hand, he asked me to fish with him.

The first place we tried was the Plank Pool. I had always fished
it from the opposite side of the river, but Jay went to it from the
camp side. "I like it best from this side," he said. "I think you have
a better chance to fish it right. Besides, I have a special method
which works best from this side."

So we waded across the bend just below the junction of the
North Umpqua and Steamboat Creek. The spot was both fascinating and fishable, especially where the currents of the two
streams united to form the Plank Pool.

Jay did not wade directly to the edge of the hole. He stayed
back some distance from the edge so that he wouldn't alarm any
fish that might be near his side and perhaps high enough in the
water to see him. Then he made a cast up and across stream, dropping the fly so that it floated close to the ledge that skirted our side
of the pool. As the fly drifted with the current he followed its
progress with the tip of his rod, keeping the line on the verge of
being taut and yet not pulling against it or giving the fly any action.

It was the old natural-drift method that I had used for brown
trout for many years. Of course this lent added interest as far as
I was concerned, because I hadn't expected anything of the sort.
He got a follow on the first drift. I saw the flash of the fish, but
Jay said it did not touch his fly. After that came at least a dozen
drifts in the same current, but they were ignored. But he didn't
seem to mind. He just kept working the edge of the ledge on our
side of the current.

As usual, when the strike came it was unexpected. I was standing about fifteen feet below Jay and could see the lower part of
the drift perfectly. One moment I saw the fly; the next moment it
had disappeared and I saw a flash of color. At the same instant
came the screech of the reel. Jay had hooked the fish and

had proved that his method of fishing the Plank had real merit.

As I watched Jay fish other steelhead locations around camp I realized why he was a successful angler. He was painstaking, methodical, experimental, and extremely patient. He fished every inch of a pool, and if one style of fishing failed to work he changed methods. He never hurried a cast or a drift, never lifted the fly prematurely. Above all he never seemed to get discouraged, even when all his efforts drew blanks. He would not quit. He used Eastern brown trout methods on Western steelhead, and they worked. At the same time he did not neglect the regulation steelhead methods. So of course he caught fish.

As I watched him that old saying kept running through my mind: "The Colonel's lady and Judy O'Grady are sisters under their skins." It struck me that it was much the same with trout. Fundamentals of fishing for them remain the same regardless of the specific details necessary for individual species. And Jay was fundamental and instinctive in his fishing rather than spectacularly skillful; hence he was a successful fisherman.

Because the Sawtooth Pool had fascinated me from the beginning, it was the first place I fished after watching Jay Garfield do his stuff. At first I fished it from the camp side of the stream. The regular method failing, I then tried the natural drift. A good fish rose when the fly skirted the tall of the left-hand glide, but I failed to connect. No other fishes resulting from my further efforts there, I decided to go to the opposite side, a good quarter-mile walk around. Here again I first tried regulation steelhead tactics. Because this didn't bring any results I changed to the natural-drift method.

Because the day was bright and the water clear and smooth-topped where I wished to fish, I knew I was up against a difficult proposition. I had to get closer in order to reach under the ledge with a sunken and naturally drifting fly. So I approached cautiously and crouched low and when in position to do the job stayed down on my knees, knowing that one little glimpse of me by the fish would ruin all chances for success.

The fly drifted along and sank out of sight as the undercurrent pulled it into the hole. I felt a peculiar slow tug and thought the fly had snagged. Instead it was a steelhead, and when I exerted pressure he came out of the water with snap and action. While he was in the air the line went slack and I thought I saw my fly sticking from the side of his mouth. I had seen correctly. My fly was gone. And all because of a faulty knot. I had carelessly tied it to the leader with a simple jam instead of a turle. Because of such things we anglers so often fail.

I was angry and disgusted with my carelessness and stupidity. I sat down, smoked a cigarette, tied on an Umpqua size 4, and made up my mind to try another natural drift even though I thought my chances were nil.

I misjudged the second cast and dropped the fly a few inches away from where the first started. This changed the drift. Instead of following the current, the fly started dragging across current almost at once and headed straight for the fissure in the rocks. I saw the danger of snagging and made an attempt to prevent it, but I was too late. I succeeded in jamming it well in the rocks.

It took a half dozen switch casts to release the fly, but this was finally accomplished. Then, instead of lifting it from the water to make another cast, I let it settle down in the pocket. What happened immediately is a question. My thoughts about it are confused and uncertain. All I can really remember is burned finger tips and the sound of a screaming reel. When full realization really returned, I was holding the rod tight and the line stretched out in the distance. Some hundred and twenty-five feet below me the fish had gone under a rock and snagged there.

I thought the fish was gone. Nevertheless I decided to handle the situation as if he were still there. So I reeled in, kept the line taut, and walked toward the place as I reeled. On getting there, I tried releasing the line by exerting pressure from all angles. I failed. The feeling of being inextricably snagged remained. I saw Clarence Gordon downstream. He was working toward me. I knew he would be with me shortly to aid me with his valuable counsel. But I became impatient. If the fish was gone, I might as well break the line or leader, whichever was caught; and if he was still on, I certainly couldn't get any place simply by applying pressure with the rod.

So I laid the rod on the ledge, where I stood and took hold of the line itself. At the greater pressure something gave away. I felt a pulsating throbbing and pulled some more. The fish was on, and these direct pulls on the line had dragged him from his stronghold.

As he came free I dropped the line and grabbed the rod, and fortunately made a smooth connection. The fight was still on when
Clarence arrived. Some minutes later I had the satisfaction of admiring the fish as he lay in shining splendor on the rock ledge.

Following this practice of careful approach and natural drifts
netted me two more fish when I fished Fred Gerken's Pool, so
named because the year previous it had been the one place that
made it possible for him to make his record perfect for seven consecutive days. It was the next good hole below the Ledge Pool.
The usual way of fishing this pool was to make a long cast from
above and across to the Key Rock, and then to follow through
with the regular dip-and-lift method of fly manipulation. I had
fished it several times in this manner, but it hadn't produced for me
even though it had for Fred; so after the Sawtooth experience I
thought I'd try something different.

Instead of starting in from above I went directly opposite the
rock, crawled on my knees to a fair-sized rock on shore, and from
its shelter cast toward the Key Rock, letting the fly drift downstream, or rather across and toward me. Of course I took in the
slack as it did this. About halfway across a fish took, hooked himself solidly, and made a rush back into midstream. He didn't fight
hard enough to make me get off my knees, so I simply held on
until he tired and then led him to a little landing harbor near the
rock that was shielding me. Although I didn't have any real hope
of rising another fish in this water after the disturbance of the
fight, I thought I'd make a few more casts to make certain about
this. In almost the identical spot I hooked a second fish, and this
time not only did I have to get on my feet, but also I had to follow
the fish downstream for considerable distance.

There were other incidents that proved the value of the natural
drift in steelhead fishing, but this does not mean that it was better
or even as good as the regular method. It simply gave me an extra
chance at any piece of water and was better for certain locations
and certain fish. On various occasions other anglers on the stream
took fish with the regulation method after I had failed with the
drift method. For instance, consider the following. Late one afternoon both Jay and I fished the Kitchen Pool with the natural-drift
method. We did not get a rise even though we did see one fish
jumping. After we left the pool we met Ed Dewey and told him

about the fish we had seen but didn't get. He went back there and took it—or at least he took a fish, and we like to think it was the one we saw.

My own fishing for the entire stay on the river was about evenly divided, and I believe that adhering exclusively to either method would have reduced my final score. On the whole I think that many steelhead anglers get so accustomed to fishing far off that they often neglect the "hot spots" near by. The peculiar thing about this obsession is that whichever side the angler fishes from, the opposite side is the one he feels he must reach to get his fish. This is a natural reaction, but it isn't logical or sensible. Although the other side of the stream may look better, it doesn't necessarily mean that it is. The side you are on may be where your luck lies. So approach any bit of water with the utmost caution, and keep out of sight until you have exhausted the possibilities under your feet. Not that long casts aren't necessary for a complete coverage of the average pool. They are. But don't neglect the side you are fishing from.

And here is something else to think about. When fishing is good it doesn't matter if you fish far off and neglect the places near by. You'll get all you want no matter where you fish. But when fishing is bad—when you are fortunate to get even one strike in a hard day's fishing—then the man who covers both sides of the pool and fishes them with varied methods is the angler who is most likely to answer: "Good," when someone asks him: "What Luck?"

Recommended Tackle for Steelhead

ROD. Nine to nine and a half feet, weighing from six to seven ounces on the average. Or you might try lighter-weight glass rods of less length. Some fishermen think they are tops. Recently I've been using some five-strip bamboo rods. I would think that an eight-and-a-half-footer of four and three-quarters ounces of this construction would be suitable for steelhead, salmon, and bass-bug fishing. It has the needed power without the extra weight.

REEL. This should be large enough to hold thirty or forty yards of fly line and three hundred feet of backing, in my estimation of about ten- or twelve-pound test, but not less than eight. The average steelhead rod will take a GBF torpedo-head or an HCH double-taper, of nylon. You might go one size smaller in double-taper when using a silk line. The eight-and-a-half-foot five-strip rod will handle the GBF nylon, but if silk is used, then HCF will be best.

LEADERS. Nine feet, tapered according to personal needs, desires, and the size of the fish one might hook, from .019 or heavier to .015, .014, .013, or .012. Often size .015 may be best, when the water is swift and the fish large. Sometimes .012 is best, when the fish are wary and the water low. The other sizes can be useful also, for in-between conditions. It is quite impossible for anyone to make an exact table concerning these things. There are too many variations involved, and to tabulate all the numerous complications would require the services of an experienced and understanding statistician.

CHAPTER XV

Lake Trout [1]

Surface Fishing

SURFACE fishing for lake trout is exciting sport. To cast with a light rod to a rock shoal or to a picturesque shore line and catch fish ranging anywhere from two to twenty pounds is an experience well worth seeking, and returning for, once you've had a taste of it.

The outfit need not be elaborate. It is quite likely you have everything you need in your bass, trout, and spinning outfits. A five- to six-foot bait-casting rod, preferably of medium weight, a regulation bait-casting reel, and fifty yards of eighteen-pound bait-casting line cover the casting tackle. In lures, almost any sort of a spoon will do, although I would suggest a wabbling or darting type of spoon about four inches long. Or you may just as well use the equivalent spinning tackle, and lures to match it. (See Chapter XI).

While shallow-water lake-trout fishing does not require any particular skill or finesse in casting and anyone who can cast a plug at all will get his share of fish, still there are certain methods of procedure that will tend to increase your catches, especially at times when conditions may be a bit difficult.

Probably the most important thing of all, unless you are depending on a guide who knows his business, is to be able to select good fishing grounds. Usually you will be told of, or will know from observation, some particularly popular location, but while the fish are found in such places there are others not so well known, and consequently less fished, that are quite likely to provide better fishing if you have an idea of what you are looking for. There is also a decided thrill in exploring waters and finding fish in unexpected places, and it is quite easy once you become accustomed to reading a lake.

[1] Some of the incidents in this chapter were used as a basis for articles that appeared in *Outdoor Life* and *Field & Stream*.

First of all, remember that lake trout are primarily deep-water fish and that no matter how suitable a reef or shore may be, it will not yield any fishing unless it is in direct contact with the section of the lake where the trout live during their sojourn in deep water. They usually come into shoal water only in the colder months of the year—for a short time after ice-out in spring, and again in the autumn. For this reason it is best to confine your operations to localities that either border or are directly in the deep sections of the lake.

In searching for possible fishing grounds, in other words reefs or shoals, look for light spots in the water. The lighter they are, the more shallow they will be; and the larger in extent they are, the more fish they will harbor.

The laker seems to prefer boulders to anything else, but will be found wherever the rocks form gullies or holes. Flat rock shoals or shore lines where the rocks drop sheer to the deep water are never productive for surface fishing. Islands with boulder-strewn shores are ideal, but even around such islands you will find one place the trout prefer most. It will usually be where a boulder shoal reaches out into the lake.

As a rule the larger trout will stay on the outside of a shoal while the smaller ones will be scattered all over it. As an illustration of this consider an island shoal on Crow Lake, Ontario. It literally swarmed with small to medium-size trout. They were so eager to take a spoon that there wasn't any fun catching them. This was when fishing from the outside toward shore. When we reversed the procedure I took two really large ones in a half hour of fishing. On the other hand, when fishing another shoal close by, the outside failed to produce and a deep pocket near shore gave me a really large fish.

A reef surrounded by deep water is something to get enthusiastic about. The outer edges of such a place should be trolled for large trout, and the visible portions, that is the shallow parts, should be covered by casting. Look for deep pockets in the shallows. You can easily recognize them because the water will look darker than the surrounding, more shallow parts. These holes are good bets, usually yielding fish even though the rest of the shoal may prove a disappointment. These outside reefs are quite likely to give you the first surface fishing of the fall. They are sometimes productive two or three days before the mainland shoals. Once I took a twenty-pounder in such water on a bait-casting outfit.

Lakes where the shore lines are not rocky present a real problem. Such a lake is Dog Paw, at least the end we fished. Not one of our party had ever been there before, so Harry Nordine, our guide, throttled the motor low and we stood up looking for possible fishing locations. We both spied one at the same instant. It lay some three hundred yards out from an island, and to all appearances the water was deep on all sides.

This reef was about one hundred and fifty feet long by eighty feet wide. The shallowest part was about two feet deep, and the outer edges about eight feet deep. Then it dropped abruptly to considerable depth. We took two fish from the center and three from the outside, two of these by trolling. They all ran to good size—about sixteen pounds. My wife lost one, just when it was tuckered out, that looked to be about twenty-five pounds.

In my experience it has never paid me to waste any time fishing over shallows having smooth bottoms. The more rough and uneven they have been, the better they have produced.

As a rule, lakes having few visible rock shoals are not very adaptable for casting. They are better for trolling, and of course during the times of the year when lakers are in the shallows trolling may be done with light tackle. However, it is difficult to find the shoals in such cases, and to have any success it takes plenty of observation, sounding, and experiment before you discover where the fish are.

No matter how long it takes, be sure you are in good water before you waste time fishing it thoroughly. A dozen well-placed casts in the most likely spots will tell the story. If the fish are there, you will get a strike, or at least a follow, quickly, and if you get one, there are sure to be more.

There are two ways to fish either a reef or an island shore. One is from the outside in to the center of the reef or to the shore, and the other is from the center or the shore to the outside. For best results both methods should be used on each reef. The reason I shall explain, and have illustrated by diagrams.

Lake trout usually, if not always, hang close to the bottom. If you cast from the outside, as in Fig. 1, your lure is seen only by those fish in the shallow part to which you cast. Your lure travels away from the fish in the deeper sections. No matter what type of reef you fish, it is best to cover it in this way first.

After the possibilities of the shallowest parts have been exhausted, then move your boat into the place you had been fishing and work the outside from this position (Fig. 2). In this latter you let the lure sink to bottom before starting the retrieve. Then when you start, your lure will naturally follow the contour of the slope of the shoal and thus reach the fish that are on the outside edges. Of course this method scares the fish in the shallows, and that is the reason why you should fish it from the outside in.

If the entire reef is shallow and does not have much slope, then it is best fished from the outside entirely, with the first round of casting taking place with the boat held a good casting distance from the outer edge. After you have been around the outside a couple of times, then move in and circle again. Do this as many times as is necessary to cover the entire water. At the end work out slowly and around, and when you get to the outer edge try the deep water beyond. More than once such practice will result in a good trout or two, besides occasionally a musky, as both are sometimes found in the same waters.

Always fish as deep as you can without getting snagged. But if you don't get snagged occasionally, you're not fishing deep enough. Lake trout are not surface feeders, and even when in the shallow water they do not tend to come to the surface for food.

From my experience I would advocate a fast retrieve, provided the spoon travels at proper depth. Some spoons when retrieved fast will rise to the surface and are not too good. They should stay under to bring best results. A slow-moving lure tends to bring many follows and hits but not so many hooked fish. This may be due to the fact that they have too much opportunity to examine a slow-moving lure and so recognize it for the fraud it is. On the other hand, a trout following a fast-moving lure may be induced to strike by suddenly stopping the retrieve for an instant and then immediately resuming the speed.

During my experience I have many times proved that fast reeling will often produce when slow reeling fails. Here is one graphic instance.

We had gone to shore to warm up and get a bite to eat prepara-

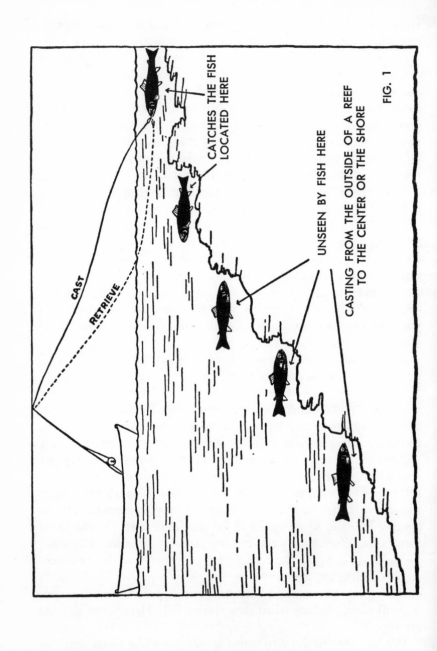

CAST

RETRIEVE

CATCHES THE FISH
LOCATED HERE

UNSEEN BY FISH HERE

CASTING FROM THE OUTSIDE OF A REEF
TO THE CENTER OR THE SHORE

FIG. 1

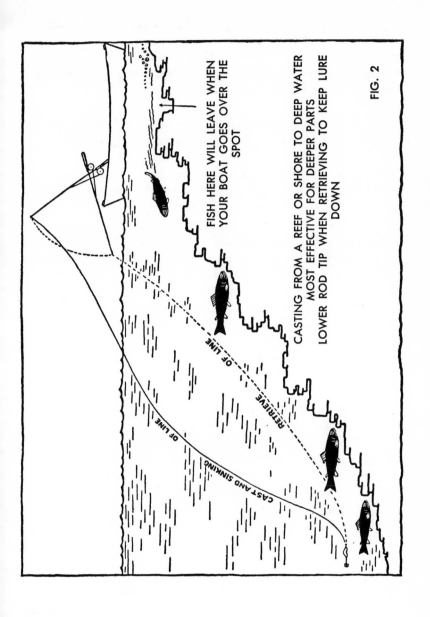

FISH HERE WILL LEAVE WHEN YOUR BOAT GOES OVER THE SPOT

CASTING FROM A REEF OR SHORE TO DEEP WATER MOST EFFECTIVE FOR DEEPER PARTS LOWER ROD TIP WHEN RETRIEVING TO KEEP LURE DOWN

RETRIEVE OF LINE

CAST AND SINKING OF LINE

FIG. 2

tory to fishing a reef close by. While we sat there toasting our frozen hands and feet, two other boats fished the reef, one about twenty minutes after the first. They worked it thoroughly, cast excellently, but did not take a fish. Our guide was downcast. "Not much use fishing there," he said. "And I thought it would be a good bet."

But I had noticed something. Every one of the fellows who had fished the reef had reeled in their lures slowly. "Let's try it anyway," I suggested. "You can never tell what will happen."

It was only a good cast away from where we sat so we were soon fishing. Both my wife and I reeled with great speed. On my very first retrieve I hooked a fish, and Mrs. Bergman wasn't far behind. Within a half hour we had our limit and, because we were half frozen, went in. Incidentally, it looked as if the other parties were using the same lure as we, a Wisconsin-made spoon. The only difference in their fishing and ours was in the speed of the retrieve.

At times a quick darting movement of the lure, followed by a pause and then a repetition of the darting, is a very effective method. When in a boat it is accomplished by a quick sideward movement of the rod. At the completion of the movement the slack line must be reeled in very fast at the same time that the rod is being brought forward for the next side movement. Follow the action throughout the retrieve. When fishing from the shore make the movement downward instead of sideways. That is, from an approximate forty-five-degree angle upward bring it straight down to your feet with a forceful stroke. When bringing the rod back for the next downward stroke you must reel exceedingly fast to take up the slack. It is the same type of lure movement used when fishing for spotted weakfish along the Gulf of Mexico coast. Incidentally, whenever fishing for lakers from the shore while standing up, always reel in with the rod pointing down to keep the lure as deep in the water as possible. Of course straight reeling-in sometimes produces.

Lake trout are frequently called dirty-weather trout, and the title is pertinent. The worse the weather, the better they seem to strike—if you can stand the weather long enough to do any fishing. I believe the reason is that bad weather obscures their vision rather than that they feed better because of the inclement weather. Because they can't see the disturbing things above the surface they become a bit reckless and unsuspicious. I am inclined to this belief because experiment has proven that even in the calmest water on a shallow reef you can get good fishing until the disturbance caused by your hooked fish has alarmed the rest of the fish on the shoal. When it is rough the catching of fish does not disturb the rest, nor does your boat drifting over them seem to cause much alarm. As when fishing a quiet pool in a trout stream, you must use extreme care when surface-fishing for lakers on a calm, clear day. Naturally, the more shallow the water, the more difficult it is to fish without alarming the game under these conditions.

I've fished all day for lakers in a blinding snow and had them strike so readily that the first cast over any reef brought immediate response, and so did the second cast; but it was always almost impossible to reel in the second fish because the hands became too numb. I can usually make a cast no matter how numb my fingers get, but when it comes to hooking or playing the fish it is a different proposition. On one occasion, with the temperature at 20° above zero, I hooked five good trout one after the other and did not have enough power in my fingers to handle them. In each case they took the reel handle out of my fingers on the strike and got away. I then figured it was time to get my fingers thawed out.

Fishing in this type of weather makes you think of ways and means to combat it. After a day or two of misery we went to shore every hour or so and heated some rocks. One would be put under our feet and the other would be handled after each fish was caught. One rock would usually do for two fish—sometimes three, according to how fast they came along. We once spent ten days fishing in snow and with temperatures ranging between 18° and 28°. There were no modern hand warmers then. Believe me, these gadgets help when fishing under frigid conditions.

Either in the spring or the fall you will need warm clothing when fishing for lake trout. Anything that will add to your physical comfort will aid you in the catching of fish. No one yet ever made a good job of fishing when he felt miserable.

Once we got to the Lake of the Woods country too early in the autumn. The trout were still in deep water. Our guide, Bill Burke, suggested Height of Land Lake, otherwise Kisskuteena. This meant canoes and an extra guide, so we got Oliver Gaudry. Our headquarters were at Ernie Calvert's Cedar Island Camp. The reason for

Height of Land was the fact that the trout there were supposed to come up earlier than those in Whitefish Bay. "Of course," said Bill, "they don't run so large there, but we've got a better chance than we have here. I know they are still in deep water at Whitefish and certainly won't be up for a week or ten days, if not more."

We got to Height of Land Camp in time to get in an hour's fishing while Oliver and Grace fixed up camp. But it didn't look very good here either. We fished a lot of water without getting an indication, and then Bill suggested trying for a musky. We picked up one small one and then came to a weedy bay in which was one large rock and a cluster of small ones. On the first cast to the big rock I hooked a fish. "Small musky," said Bill. Then: "No, that don't act like a musky." Meanwhile I was having a grand time. When it tired we saw we had a lake trout. It weighed twelve pounds. "I never saw a trout come from that place before," said Bill. And we didn't catch another from it either, or anywhere else in the lake. According to Burke we were still too early. On the way back to camp we saw a bunch of fish breaking on a reef, and he drew in close to shore to look at them. "Now I know what's the matter," he declared. "The trout have just moved into their spawning beds and won't strike for a few days yet."

I wanted this explained and he obliged me. I take no responsibility for the following quotation. All I can say is that it sounds reasonable, is interesting, and may be the truth. At least I've never found out anything to refute it—or prove it either for that matter. Anyway, this is what Bill told me. I questioned him about it again at camp that night and wrote it in my notebook almost word for word. "The trout usually come up in the shallows about October 1. The male comes first and cleans off the beds, and the female arrives shortly after. During the time when the nests are being prepared they won't strike. I believe it's because they're too busy to bother about eating. Of course one is picked up now and then, but mostly they won't strike at all. Sometimes they start taking the second day after they get through the job, but the fishing don't start much until the fourth or fifth day. Once they start taking, they hit fast until spawning really begins. Then they slack off."

As stated, I'm not able to vouch for the authenticity of this statement, but Bill was observing, and several others I talked to agreed with him regarding it. And if fishing is any proof, then we proved it. We were there six days and the last day had six strikes from lakers. Two were nearly landed but got off when they wound themselves up the leader, as they so often do. The reef on which we got these strikes was one we had tried religiously every day because it was one of the best in the lake.

Another guide said the lakers wouldn't take until the leaves were off the birches. Bill's theory had more sense. The most canny guide we ever had in the matter of understanding lakers was Eric Lungrin—I believe that was his last name, anyway it sounded like that. I know after he had told us he grinned and added: "Ay Swedish."

The strange thing about it was that Eric never fished himself. But as he explained: "Ay luk for fish. Ay see wut they do."

There wasn't anything doing the first day, but we saw some fish breaking on the outer edge of one shoal. "Bin doin' that four day," said Eric. "Ay tank maybe tomorrow." It made me think of Bill Burke's theory.

The following day we went directly to this reef. We circled it and worked it carefully. The wind was blowing hard and it was tough fishing. All the trout seemed to be congregated in a deep hole of small area. In order to get a strike it was necessary to cast to the shallow water beyond the hole and then reel the lure through it at high speed. By doing this we took four fish and missed five.

The next reef we tried was between two islands and in the wash of the surf. For this reason Eric worked like a Trojan to keep the boat directly in the surf. I figured he knew what he was doing, so I got in all the casts I could. Then it happened. As I was just about to pick the lure from the water for another cast, a huge shape swallowed it. It was a long, dogged fight, and we drifted a half mile or more before the fish was landed. It was the first and the largest trout of the season that came into this camp, twenty pounds or a bit better. Eric was justly proud, and the rest of the guides properly envious, especially as some of them had been poking fun at Eric as a guide.

Flies may also be used for this surface lake-trout fishing. In my experience the best patterns have been streamers and bucktails, the same used for landlocked salmon fishing in the east. (See colored fly plates.) I've had some very good fishing with Marabous and intend experimenting with different color combinations of these flies the next time I go for lakers when they are on the surface. A size

4 long-shank hook is about the right size for the flies. For a leader you need something stout, either a regular bass-bug leader or something similar. Personally I prefer the steelhead leader, a nine-footer tapering from .019 to .014 or .015. Either the fast-jerk method or the hand-twist retrieve is a quite satisfactory way of fishing the flies. You may also use fly-weight spinners and lures if you choose, but for me give me a spinning rod or a bait-casting rod for a lure of this type. When I use a fly rod I prefer to use a fly with it.

As I mentioned at the start of the chapter, I prefer wabbling lures for lakers, those which will not come too much toward the surface when reeled fast. There are a number of such spoons on the market, and the same lures may be used for either surface fishing or trolling.

Deep Trolling

I am going to ignore the trolling done with a line controlled by a winch attached to the stern of a boat. Even though it is necessary —perhaps—in exceedingly deep lakes, I could never work up any enthusiasm over the practice and so really know nothing about it. If the water is too deep for me to reach with my light outfit, then I willingly give up the fishing.

A regular six-and-a-half- to seven-foot trolling or heavy bait rod is excellent for this work, and so are light salt-water rods. I prefer an ordinary bait-casting rod, mostly because when we go fishing we go for months at a time, and by using my bass and musky rods I can save that much space. However, I would not advise the light or medium-weight bass rods for this purpose unless they are made of steel or glass. Dragging from seventy-five to a hundred yards or more of wire line, or fabric line to which is attached a heavy sinker, is a tough strain on any material, and while I like bamboo best for fly and light-lure fishing, I would definitely recommend steel or glass for trolling or for casting heavy lures.

For deep-trolling lines I would suggest wire. My favorite is solid Monel metal. It is very small in diameter for its strength and sinks very fast, so that you can get deeper with less length. I find the fifteen-pound test, calibration .016, quite satisfactory for most lake-trout fishing. Size .018 or twenty-pound test will be better for conditions where great depth is essential, say where more than a hundred and fifty yards of fifteen-pound test is needed.

There is a twisted line that is more flexible than the solid wire. Some anglers may like it better. I use it to some extent and prefer the lightest I've been able to get, twenty-seven-pound test. But you need a larger reel for this. The calibration is greater, and you need more length to get the depth reached with the same length of solid wire. Twisted and braided lines capture air and this, added to the fact that the stuff is lighter per foot and diameter than solid wire, means it doesn't sink as fast; therefore you need heavier wire and more of it to get down to the required depth. This calls for heavier tackle all around, in order to have balanced equipment.

In experimenting with wire, linen, and silk lines during the past twenty-five or more years, I have found that solid-wire line takes some fifty per cent more fish than the others when tested in the same water and with the lure at the same depth. Consider this experiment made in 1936, one of many that were similar. The time spent was eighteen hours, scattered over a period of six days. Silk, solid-wire, twisted-wire, and braided-wire lines were used equally and were fished at the same depth, this being accomplished by sounding the same lure continuously over the same bottom with the different lines. The fine solid-wire line accounted for ten fish, the twisted for six, the braided wire and silk for four each.

Noting these differences in results I wondered about the cause. If all lines were bringing the lures down to the same depth and location, then why did we catch more on one line than on the others?

This led to more experiments; and these revealed that a wire line, particularly if solid and rather fine, gave us a better hooking percentage because we could feel the slightest take of a fish, and as there was a minimum of slack to take up and our reactions were naturally quicker, we rarely missed connections. On the other hand we found that while we got as many strikes with silk lines we missed at least half of the fish that took; that with the braided wire we got fewer strikes than with silk and solid wire; and that with twisted lines we got less strikes than with silk but hooked more fish with more regularity, almost as well as when using the fine solid wire.

My deductions were as follows. The fine solid-wire line, with little water displacement, taut, unhindered by any foreign weight, enabled us to sense the very first touch of a striking fish. The silk line, not having any weight, and being sunk with the aid of a sinker, had a decided belly which delayed the feel of the strike and also delayed our response when we attempted to set the hook. When the fish took hard, it was all right; but when the strike was easy or perhaps to the very end of the lure, then this belly caused missed strikes. Another thing that was very noticeable was the better fight of the fish on a wire line after it had been brought up to the surface. After all, as the wire line was reeled in, the weight became much less, and so the fish had a better chance to fight. With the silk line, even when it was reeled in close to the boat, the fish always had the drag of the heavy sinker. The twisted line did not get to the depth needed until excessive length had been released, which also meant considerable belly. Thus, when striking, one missed fish because the strike didn't carry through fast enough to offset this curvature of line. However, this trouble was later overcome by using heavier and stiffer rods than those needed with the fine solid-wire line. As I personally prefer to use the lightest tackle possible, this was the thing that sold me on Monel metal for a deep-trolling line.

It is a good idea to use a piece of braided nylon line or solid nylon leader material between the wire line and the lure. For one thing, it allows more freedom of action for the lure; and it tends also to save your wire line if you get hooked on bottom, that is if the leader has a lesser breaking strength than the wire line. For instance, suppose your lure is tied directly to the wire, and you get hung up. Wire won't cut on a rock, but fabric or leader material will. So if you can't get loose without breakage you may easily lose part of your line, as it will be likely to part where a bad kink has occurred. And kinks do get into wire lines. It is true that sometimes the break may occur directly at the lure, so that no loss of line is involved, but it can happen the other way. On the other hand, when using from two to three feet of braided line or leader material that has a lower test than the wire, then usually you lose only the lure and a part of this leader.

But even more important is the fact that soft material between wire line and lure allows the lure to have greater freedom of action, and thus appear more lifelike. It is a good idea to tie a short and flexible wire trace with a snap swivel to the end of the leader.

This allows you to make quick changes of lures and also prevents the leader from becoming frayed by the teeth of a fish that has taken it deep.

Remember that if you want to catch lake trout in summer, you must sink the lure down to them. Once you get where the fish are, there is always a good chance to lose terminal tackle. It catches on sharp rocks, and these cut the best of lines or leader materials except those made of wire. To illustrate, let me tell of an experience in Quetico Park, Ontario, Canada.

When fishing over the most productive spot there we invariably either caught a good fish or lost a lure. Of course we couldn't get down to the bottom and actually see what was causing the trouble, so I can't insist that what I figured out is correct. But here it is, the only logical reason I could think of. The fish evidently lay near a rock having a very sharp edge. When they took the lure it steered the leader away from the sharp rock and so we didn't get into trouble. When no strike occurred at this particular spot, the lure struck the rock and there caught fast. This brought the leader taut against the knifelike edge and quickly cut it. We tried trolling from the opposite direction. Then we never lost a lure, but neither did we get any fish, although we bumped something there each time we crossed. Evidently it was caused by the rock formation on this particular bottom. At least, that is the only explanation I can give.

But you must take these lure-losing chances if you hope to be successful. Many, many times I have caught fish simply because of taking a chance on losing tackle. And many other times I've lost tackle that way too. In many cases it has been impossible to get a strike when fishing a ledge unless the spoon bumped bottom occasionally, and on one occasion we couldn't get a fish in one particular spot unless the lure snagged and we had to back up to release it. The strike was made always as the bait came free. Of course we lose lures doing these things, but it is better to do that than to fish in a way that doesn't give you a chance to get anything.

I remember one trying day when I lost every favorite lake-trout spoon I had. In addition we were some four days' travel away from the nearest possible chance of picking up a lure of any kind. It was a situation to call forth every bit of inventive genius in our party of three. It was then that we found various other lures and combinations of lures effective. The large musky plugs were surprisingly good, especially the "float when not in action" type. Because of their buoyancy, even a wire line needed a small sinker to keep them down. We tied this sinker on a piece of old silk line, and it was good we did. The lure didn't snag because of its buoyancy, but the sinker did; and if it had been attached with a line stronger than the copper, each time it happened we would have lost more than the sinker.

On this occasion I assembled also a combination lure, using an old copper wabbler, a nickle wabbler, and on the very end a quarter-ounce red-and-white wabbler. This turned out to be a honey and took fish readily. As a matter of fact any string of lures is likely to be attractive to lakers. They are inclined to be voracious feeders, and nothing seems to be too large for them to tackle—in fact sometimes it seems that the larger the lure, the better it works. If you ever get in the lake-trout country without the necessary lures, remember this—and while you are about it, why not put a reel and wire line in your kit? After all, July and August are frequently poor fishing months for other trout and for bass; and if it's too bad, a few hours a day trolling does take the curse off, especially if you happen to land a husky laker.

There was another day, again while far from any source of supply, when we lost both of the two lures that were catching fish. My wife lost hers first, when a large musky cut the line. I lost mine a few minutes later by stupidly dropping it overboard while changing a swiveled trace. This time nothing else would work, and we tried everything in the tackle box.

There are times when live bait works better than anything else. I have used both worms and minnows with good results. Fishing from a ledge in Partridge Lake, Algonquin Park, I picked up a nice one simply by sinking a worm to bottom. In this instance I didn't even use a sinker. We were killing time preparatory to making a canoe trip, and I just tried the worm for the fun of it. As I was using my trout fly rod I had a bit of fun. Phantom minnows, either of the porpoise hide or the celluloid type, are also good if the fish are not in water too excessively deep. I've also had fair success with a bass spinner-and-fly combination.

Lake-trout locations are usually small in area and somewhat scattered, at least this applies to places where the angler catches fish. If you are not acquainted with the water and have no one to tell you the approximate locations of the hot spots, you will have a tough time finding them. You can do it if you go at it systematically, but it takes a lot of time; and if you have only a week or two for vacation, this is a serious item.

Once you locate a hole, line it up with objects on shore. (See sketch.) If your memory for such things is excellent, you will be able to remember these locations; but if it is only ordinary and you

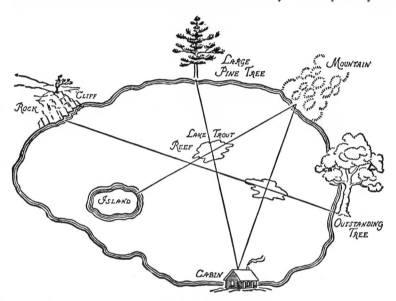

fish a number of different places, it is a good idea to make a record of each good hole so that you may readily go there the next time you fish the lake. Put this record in a notebook and put the notebook in your tackle box—then you'll have it when you need it. This is a good idea to follow in all lake fishing, and it makes an interesting log as well as a source of information.

Speaking of this prompts another word of advice. Always keep extras of all necessities in your tackle box. By necessities I mean: knife, file, pliers, line, reel, waterproof match box with matches, fly dope, and a repair kit. Having these in duplicates will often save you from irritation and loss of temper.

Lake trout are sometimes baited—that is, the fishermen put out buoys and then bait the water near them. I don't subscribe to the practice, but I will say that you can often get excellent fishing in these baited spots. Only once have I fished near one of these buoys. I had been fishing for walleyes with a nine-foot four-and-a-quarter-ounce fly rod and a minnow. Coming to the buoy, I let the minnow go to bottom. I'm not sure that it reached there, for after a short time I felt a tug, set the hook, and had a real battle on my hands. The fish went around twenty pounds, and the fight became rather tedious and tiring before it ended.

It is rare indeed to find lake trout in discolored water. I don't mean dirty water either, but simply dark-colored. As a matter of fact, in every lake I've ever found them, the water has been very clear. Of course you will never find them in lakes that are shallow. They need clear water with depth enough to give them coolness in the heat of summer. I know of several lakes having holes not greater than forty feet that have been stocked with lakers, and in every case nothing has ever resulted from the stocking. One example is Cranberry Lake in the Adirondacks, a natural brook-trout lake, although enlarged by a dam. This lake was stocked with lakers many years ago, but from what I can find out only two were ever taken—and these were caught in the river below the dam. Evidently the fish that survived the stocking went downstream, probably headed for Lake Ontario. At any rate I've fished this lake at all seasons for brookies and often have taken time out to try for the lakers; but I never caught one, although I have taken some mighty good *fontinalis* while fussing. I am sure that if there were any survivors of this original stocking, one would be caught now and then, especially in the spring when the entire lake shore is fished with spoons, flies, and bait.

You who know lake trout well consider them worth fishing for. They are good to look at and in my opinion very good indeed to eat. At any rate I consider them swell fish to have on tap when those more widely sought species are off their feed or out of season.

↜ CHAPTER XVI ↝

Grayling

As far back as I can remember, grayling have fascinated me and I always looked forward to that day when I might be fortunate enough to fish for them.

There came a time, in 1933, when it looked as though this ambition was to be realized. We were going to Colorado and had been told we could get some grayling in Elk River.

When we got to Colorado Springs, our meeting place with Glenn Jones, with whom we were to fish, we immediately inquired about the grayling. "Of course," said Glenn. "The boys were up there a few days ago and took a swell catch on bait. We'll go there in a few days."

So we went to Elk River and caught some of these Colorado graylings; at least Glenn did. I started out with good intentions of trying, but spotted some rainbow trout and promptly forgot all about the fish we had come there for. But Glenn didn't. When it comes to persistency in fishing he has plenty, and having made up his mind to catch Colorado grayling, he proceeded to do so. While I fished a mile of stream and had some grand sport with trout, he stayed in one spot and solved his problem.

He proudly displayed his catch when I returned. I looked at the fish and experienced a feeling of keen disappointment. These fish did not have large and colorful dorsal fins as I had expected, and besides they had awkward suckerlike shapes and mouths.

"Had to use size 18 flies," said Glenn, "and they take so lightly that you hardly know when you get a rise. Lost quite a few. Come on, try it."

I did, but made out poorly. For one thing I wasn't particularly interested any more. I should have been warned by this feeling that something was wrong with the picture. My book knowledge had led me to expect a different fish than what we had caught here. But after all, I had never seen either a live grayling or a mounted one, so wasn't in a very good position to doubt the statements of fellows who were supposed to know. So I accepted them with reservations and promptly crossed them off my list of preferred game fish. Later on I wrote an article for a sportsmen's magazine and mentioned this experience on the Elk. I didn't say very much, but what I did say was far from complimentary.

The few sentences were enough to start something, and I'm glad they did, as it led to my final acquaintance with a grand fish. Shortly after the article appeared I received some letters from men who really knew what grayling were, as well as the fish we had taken in the Elk. The first letter came as a reproof because I had compared grayling with suckers. It was deserved. It also stated that the fish we had caught were Rocky Mountain whitefish. In the letter were drawings that compared the two fish. I knew then why the fish Glenn caught had struck a responsive chord in my memory. Years ago I had fished for Adirondack Mountain white-fish, and they had been very similar to these Rocky Mountain whitefish, although the latter seemed trimmer built. A little investigation proved conclusively that we had caught whitefish and not grayling. Of course I wrote him at once with apologies. Let me quote from his second letter.

I was pleased to get yours in answer to my recent outburst concerning grayling. The confusion in the fish seems to be widespread. Last Sunday we had guests who formerly lived in Wyoming. The man is an ardent fisherman and better informed than most. Naturally the conversation turned to fishing so I mentioned our correspondence. I asked him if he had ever caught grayling. He said that he had, but when I asked him for a description he described the Rocky Mountain whitefish. I mentioned the difference in the two fishes and asked him if he didn't think that the fish he had caught were whitefish. He replied, "Well, they are the same thing, aren't they?" This was a new one on me as I had not realized that some considered them the same fish. When I declared they were not the same he did not argue but I think the reason was from politeness and not from any conviction. The next day I received a letter from him which showed he had doubted me. He said he had looked up the fish on getting home and had found illustrations which proved I was correct. The fish he had caught were whitefish.

Another letter stated that almost everyone in the state of Colorado called the Rocky Mountain whitefish a grayling and that there were no grayling in the United States except in Montana and Yellowstone Park.

All this made me more determined than ever to catch some grayling. About this time I received a letter from Vint Johnson, of West Yellowstone. He spoke of grayling and said we should come there for them, so we speedily made arrangements to do so.

It was September 19 when we arrived at West Yellowstone, and by this time some of the grayling waters were closed. I had thought we'd find some in the Madison, but was told this was exceedingly uncertain. But Scotty Chapman, park ranger, came to the rescue. He had a pet pond where he said we'd be sure to catch all we wanted. This was Grebe Lake, deep in the forest. After a two-mile drive on a lumber road, you still had a long two miles and a bit more to walk to get to the fishing.

All that Scotty said about the pond was true. The location was beautiful and wild, and there were plenty of grayling in it. When I saw the first one I wondered how I had ever confused them with whitefish. They were graceful, racy, and colorful. When you looked at them in the water preparatory to landing them, they looked like fish-shaped, animated purple flowers.

Fishing for them was similar to spring-hole fishing for brookies in the Adirondacks. It was necessary to let the fly sink until it almost touched the tops of the weeds. Then you used the hand-twist retrieve as described on page 22. In using the method for these fish, seventeen thumb movements to the minute seemed most effective, although variations were advisable from time to time.

Most of the strikes were touches so light that you were barely conscious of them, and if you didn't respond immediately you missed the fish. When missing a hit it was advisable to immediately give a bit of slack and let the fly settle back in the water before continuing the retrieve. If you hadn't used too much force in the strike so that the fly moved too far away from the fish, doing this invariably brought another hit. Often a fish would follow and keep nudging all the way in, until the fly was about ready to be lifted from the water.

Besides doing these things correctly it was also necessary to watch your line closely as the fly sank to bottom preparatory to the retrieve. Often a fish would take a fly as it sank, in which case you did not feel the hit but could see the part of your line that was on the surface make a slight twitch. When this happened you had to act quickly and a bit violently in order to take up slack and set the hook. However, the retrieve was the most important thing. If you got that deliberate and slow jerk timed right, you got plenty of touches even if you didn't connect with half of them. A line that sank readily was absolutely necessary. When I tried a dressed line that would not sink I could not take a fish with it, but on going back to the water-logged one, I began to take fish immediately.

One might suppose that a split shot would serve the purpose in the case of the dressed line, but while it did produce, it didn't work nearly so well as a water-soaked one without the shot. The slow descent of an unweighted fly or line seemed to have an appeal the weighted fly or line lacked.

Certain limited areas were "hot spots" from time to time. Then they would suddenly become dead, and another place ten to fifteen feet away would give you action. This appeared to prove that the grayling were moving about in schools.

The best fishing seemed to be in water ranging from six to eight feet in depth, and in every case, as far as my experience goes, over a mossy, weedy bottom—much the same sort of bottom found in Eastern brook-trout ponds. These weeds were literally swarming with small insect larvæ and fresh-water shrimp. There is a grayling hatchery on the lake, and the eggs for propagating are taken from the lake, many from where we made our best catches.

Fishing from a boat did not produce nearly so well as fishing from shore. Probably this was due to the fact that you could not manipulate the fly properly when in the boat. It was forever moving one way or the other and spoiling the effect of your retrieve. At any rate, experimenting with both mediums seemed to prove this. One evening, with the lake dimpled with rising fish, Scotty and I fished from the boat while Vint fished from shore. Vint took fish readily. The only change he made in daytime methods was that he did not let the flies sink as deeply before starting the retrieve. We got one strike, and this came when I had my only opportunity to make a cast and start the retrieve without the boat sheering off in the wrong direction.

In my opinion, grayling are not particularly selective to fly patterns, but I must admit that some flies produced better than others. The one that took the most and the largest fish for us this first time was a Royal Coachman streamer. Despite the fact that grayling have small mouths and strike so lightly, a size 4 medium-long-shanked hook fly seemed to give perfect satisfaction. Blue Dun, Blue Quill, Olive Dun, and Cowdung were all very effective in sizes 10, 12, and 14, and I have no doubt that many other trout patterns would be excellent if tried. It is interesting to note that our most effective patterns here are universally used and are old-timers that have stood the test of time and keen competition. The boys who started these patterns knew something, and there's no mistake about it.

Sometimes these fish rise best just as the fly touches the water. Often when they do this it is extremely hard to hook them. On one trip, for instance, I counted seventy rises of this type, out of which I caught only ten grayling. But this isn't always true. Since those days I have fished Grebe Lake many times, and on some occasions have struck it when both rainbow trout and grayling would hit hard and sure almost the very instant the flies touched the surface. One day, for instance, with the wind blowing against the casts so badly that one had to make them between gusts, I hooked thirty assorted rainbows and grayling out of thirty-five rises, with the majority of hits coming just as the flies touched the water on a seventy-five-foot cast.

I do not know of any pond that is more consistent in providing good fishing as long as you follow the methods of wet-fly fishing described in this book, and fish in spots where the grayling feed. In the few cases when I observed anglers fishing there with little or no success and catching mostly small fish, I noted that they either didn't cast far out enough, didn't handle the retrieve properly, failed to sink the flies when the fish were working deep, or wasted time casting over places where the chances of taking any fish were poor or nil.

At these same times, those who fished with the necessary knowledge and skill took limit catches of the largest grayling found in the lake. The catching of rainbow trout was always incidental as far as I was concerned; that is, I always hooked or raised them between grayling. They always gave me a shock because they strike so much more viciously and fight much harder, inch for inch.

The only times we've ever had poor fishing at Grebe have been days when the snow lay deep and the wind blew so cold that the guides froze up and one's fingers became numb. I imagine that the reason fishing is then poor is not that the fish are unwilling, but that the human body fails to react properly under the conditions. At least this is true as far as I am concerned. When it is freezingly cold I simply cannot fish right. My fingers won't work properly, and I get impatient and miserable. This is quite likely to make your fishing efforts unsuccessful. A fire on shore, if allowed and if you can find the wood without breaking a conservation law, helps in such instances. So does the modern hand-warmer. But as for me, when I can't fish more than ten or fifteen minutes without spending a comparable time in warming up, then I prefer not to fish. This is no doubt a matter of age. Fifteen or twenty years ago the cold didn't bother me.

Besides the flies I originally found good for grayling, which I have already mentioned, the following patterns have proved excellent, sometimes better than the original list: Grizzly King, March Brown—including American and both male and female English, brownish nymphs, Light and Dark Cahill, Alder, Mallard Quill, and once in a while some fancy pattern, such as Logan, Wilson, and Warwick, (all shown in the plates of *Trout*). Many of these odd patterns are great trout and grayling takers. If you are a fly tier, try some of them. The results may surprise you.

For eating I like the grayling as much as any fresh water fish, and better than many others. The flesh is firm and not too sweet, and it has a distinctive flavor. Of course this is only the way I feel about it. Folks vary a lot in their likes and dislikes of fish for food, and I'm not too enthusiastic about fish to begin with. I also like the Rocky Mountain whitefish, not quite as much as grayling but almost. I think my favorite of all fish is an Eastern brook trout, native born, not smaller than eight inches or larger than twelve. Of course if hatchery fish stay in the stream long enough they too become suitable eating, as far as I am concerned. But I do not enjoy the flesh of recently stocked fish.

If you ever have a chance to fish for grayling I think it is worth your while to do so. But if you catch a fish that has a mouth like a sucker, then you may be sure that you haven't caught a grayling. It is probably a Rocky Mountain whitefish, or maybe even a variety of sucker.

⤐ CHAPTER XVII ⤏

On Tying Flies

I LEARNED how to tie flies by experience, my sole start being an hour's observation of another fly-tier at work. After that I procured an outfit and got to work and since that time have tied approximately two hundred thousand flies. It is with the thought that perhaps what I have learned will aid someone else in fly-tying that this chapter is being written. It's not going to be elaborate or exhaustive, but I hope to drive home to the person wishing to take up fly-tying some essentials which go into the making of a well-tied fly.

One thing I do know. If you want to make good flies, you must have both good tools and good material to work with. If you try to save money by buying cheap merchandise, it is an easy matter, but the flies you make will reflect just what you have put into them. Once you see and know what goes into the making of a well-tied fly, you will readily understand why you pay five dollars a dozen or more for the best grade you can buy.

The tools actually needed are so few that there isn't any reason why one cannot afford the best. The first item is the vise. Of course anything of this nature will answer the purpose after a fashion, but the best products are made with the special needs of the fly-tier in mind and will give you far more satisfaction as well as aid in turning out a workmanlike product in the shortest length of time. Nothing gives you more enjoyment or more assistance in the development of any hobby than good tools to work with and fine material to create with. To see the ideas of your brain materialize in the vise is the prime reward of fly-tying. After you have once created, it may become drudgery to keep reproducing that creation. You will find it much more satisfactory to have someone else do this work for you. But the creation is the thing that gets you. It stimulates your imagination and ingenuity, and incidentally makes you appreciate the work of a professional who knows his business and who puts workmanship and quality above production. Once having done the job yourself, you consider the price he charges very reasonable indeed, because you know just what it means in effort and material to produce a fly that is well built in every detail.

NAACC [1] OFFICIAL STANDARD TABLE OF
REGULAR FLY HOOK MEASUREMENTS
WITH SIZE DESIGNATIONS, DEVIATIONS AND
PERMISSIBLE TOLERANCES

SIZE Number	LENGTH In Inches	WIRE DIAMETER In 1000ths Inches
2/0	1⅝	.045
1/0	1½	.043
1½	1⅜	.041
1	1¼	.039
2	1⅛	.037
4	15/16	.033
6	13/16	.030
8	11/16	.027
10	9/16	.024
12	7/16	.021
14	11/32	.018
16	9/32	.016
18	7/32	.014
20	5/32	.012

NOTE

1. The length is the over-all measurement of the shank, excluding eye. (See Diagram)

2. Sizes No. 22 to 13 increase in size by 1/32 inch for each number. Sizes No. 12 to 3 increase in size by 1/16 inch for each number. Size No. 2 to 5/0 increase in size by 1/8 inch for each number.

The maximum permissible tolerances, plus or minus, shall be one-half of the difference between sizes.

3. Odd number sizes, in all respects, measure midway between the even number sizes.

4. Deviations from regular sizes are indicated by X's, either long, short, stout or fine. Each X denotes a single number size either above or below the standard. Size 12-2X fine is size number 12 on a number 14 wire. Size 10-4X long is size number 10 with a length of size number 6.

A good vise should facilitate quick changing from one fly to the next and it should also be adjustable to any hook, from a large, stout, streamer size to the smallest made. You may start out trying

[1] NAACC means National Association Angling and Casting Clubs.

only 10's and 12's, but sooner or later you'll be jumping on both sides. Of course, if one is not particular about speed, a thumb-screw or knob-operated vise will do good work and cost less than the lever-operated type. Material dealers have a number of different types and qualities to choose from. Take your time in choosing, and make the decision with your own particular needs and desires in mind.

Hackle pliers must be good, or else they are most exasperating. The jaws should be narrow and yet have enough surface to hold, and the grip should be tight without being sharp. In other words they should hold tight without cutting. This calls for a high-quality, finely adjusted tool. Unfortunately a good pair is not easy to find. Once I bought eight before I got one that worked properly. If you want to tie flies in sizes 18 or smaller, it will help if you can get a pair of good small hackle plyers.

The scissors should be small and sharp, especially at the points. Unless they cut at the points they are an abomination for this work. Either curved or straight blades are all right. I like them both. The more narrow the points the better they are for close work. Scissors get out of adjustment with heavy use, and also dull quickly if employed for cutting tinsel and other hard material. I find it both economical and efficient to have two pairs on hand at all times— one for the fine work of cutting off hackle ends and so on, and another, a bit larger, for cutting off the coarse materials that raise such havoc with a delicately adjusted pair of scissors. If you do a lot of tying, it will also pay to have a second pair of good fine ones in reserve.

A stiletto or bodkin may be easily made by inserting a needle in a cork or a piece of wood. It is a simple tool and exceedingly useful. With it you may pull out any hackles you have inadvertently tied under, finish off the whip knot neatly at the eye, perk up the hackles after they are all wound in, varnish the head, and clean out the eye if it gets clogged with varnish. It is also useful for picking out fur, wool, or other material used in dubbing bodies, so that it may be spun on the thread. If magnetized, it is also great for picking up hooks, either from the box or the table.

A thread-holder, either attached to your vise, to a board on which your vise is fastened, or to your workbench in the position you find most convenient, is exceedingly helpful when tying bodies on long-shanked hooks, for instance on streamer and bucktail patterns. (See illustration of setup on my tying table, showing vise, thread-holder, and reel full of waxed thread.)

As far as fly-tying silk is concerned, I prefer the finest I can obtain. It makes a much more delicate-looking fly, enables you to tie off after each operation without adding noticeable bulk, and is less inclined to unwind, thus making a more substantial fly. In my opinion this fine silk should be waxed in bulk before it is needed, using hot melted wax to do the job. If you cut off each piece you wish to use and wax it individually with cold wax, you will find that you break many pieces and also weaken those pieces you don't

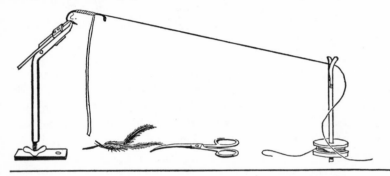

break. In the sketch I show you the simple little gadget I use for waxing my thread. All you need is an ordinary tin can fitted as shown, a clip clothespin, and a cheap reel to hold the waxed thread. With this outfit you can wax approximately five hundred yards of thread in thirty minutes. The flame for melting the wax should not be too hot. Personally I find that ordinary refined beeswax is very good. Many, however, prefer shoemakers' wax or something similar. This contains resin, beeswax, and refined tallow. Once the wax is melted, turn the flame down just high enough to keep the wax from congealing.

Most tiers use heavier thread for streamers and bucktails than they do for dry flies and small wet flies. I prefer 6/0 (000000) for all dry and wet flies up to and including size 8; 5/0 (00000) for larger dry flies, say sizes 4 and 2; 4/0 for large wet flies and small streamers and for making any of the smaller clipped-hair bodies, such as the Irresistible pattern. Considerable pressure is needed against the deer or similar body hair to make it flare out from the shank of the hook, hence extra strength is needed in the thread. For streamers and bucktails in the larger sizes, where considerable material must be used to make a good-looking fly, I would suggest thread size A.

There are other tools used by many tiers but the writer doesn't find any need for them. If a thread is waxed to sufficient stickiness you do not need to hold it firm by the aid of extra hackle plyers or some other tool when adding material. If you do not like to use

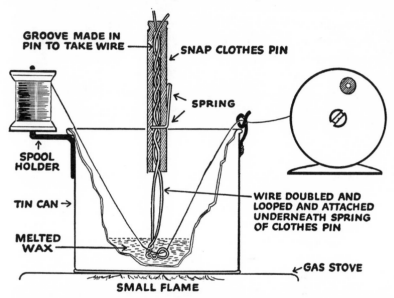

GROOVE MADE IN PIN TO TAKE WIRE → SNAP CLOTHES PIN

SPRING

SPOOL HOLDER

TIN CAN →

WIRE DOUBLED AND LOOPED AND ATTACHED UNDERNEATH SPRING OF CLOTHES PIN

MELTED WAX

GAS STOVE

SMALL FLAME

sticky wax and wish to make a more substantial fly, a simple half-hitch at the end of each specific operation will hold everything tight. When tying flies with 6/0 thread the half-hitches are not noticeable even on small flies, and 5/0 does all right on slightly larger sizes. In the same manner each set of larger sizes can stand a little heavier weight of thread.

Don Martinez advocates and is the designer of a hand vise. Tiers who use this vise need no other tool than a pair of scissors, and they produce flies faster than tiers using any other method. This way of tying is excellent for wet flies, streamers, and hackle dry flies. Not only that, but you can sit relaxed and comfortable in an arm chair while tying, thus avoiding the fatigue attending tying flies at a vise where you must sit at a desk, table, or bench.

But let me describe how I tie a dry fly. The photographs (following page 416) are arranged in the order that I follow when tying. The whip knot, used only when finishing off at the head, is shown on an unfinished fly so that it can be seen better.

Tying a Light Cahill—Dry

Of course the first operation in tying any fly is attaching the thread to the hook. Use either a half-hitch or whip knot (Fig. 1).

Second—Tie on the tail. See Figs. 2, 3, 4, 5, 6—which also show the jam knot or half-hitch.

Third—Tie on wings—Figs. 7, 8, 9.

Fourth—Tie in hackles—Fig. 10.

Fifth—Tie in body material—Figs. 11, 12, 13.

Sixth—Wind on body material—Fig. 14.

Seventh—Wind in hackle—Fig. 15.

Eighth—Finish off with whip knot—Figs. 16, 17, 18, 19.

Now let's go back and take up each operation separately. We will assume that the thread has been attached to the hook, and the tail wound on (Fig. 1). We secure it with a jam knot, or half-hitch, first at the tail. (Note: The different operations in the jam knot show different positions on the hook. This was due to the difficulty of holding the positions for a photograph. So several were taken of each position at different times, and we picked the best in each instance. As a matter of fact, position so that the camera could get what we wanted was considered rather than keeping each step in the same relative position. Forget the location of the thread and remember only that the operations in each step are what we are trying to make plain to you. In tying a single jam, naturally the thread would at all times be located at the same spot on the hook.) Now let us tie the jam knot.

First, take thread in the right hand, pulling it straight toward you. Then put the left forefinger on top of the thread with pressure slightly downward, and with the right thumb and forefinger bend the thread upward and back to the hook. Continue this around the hook and bring thread back toward yourself, keeping it taut at all times (Fig. 2). This makes a loop held by your left forefinger with the end of the thread held by the right hand. Now with the

first or second or both fingers of the left hand exert pressure downward on the left thread of the loop (Fig. 3), and with the left
forefinger pull the thread held by the right hand to the left and
toward you, at the same time holding the end taut with the right
hand. By this simple operation the thread becomes crossed and
makes the start of the jam. Now, keeping the place where the
thread crosses taut, pull with the left-hand finger and release, but
keep taut with the right-hand finger until the crossed threads jam
against the shank of the hook. Fig. 5 shows thread at start of way
down. Fig. 6 shows jam completed, with the left hand pulling the
end of the thread through to finish the knot.

We now wind the thread quickly up the shank of the hook into
position to tie on the wings. Tie off here with the jam knot. Now
take about half of a speckled Mandarin feather from the flank of
the bird and lay it in the hook (Fig. 7). Tie it fast with the jam.
Then wind close against the base of the feather *in front* enough
times to make the feather stand up nearly perpendicular, and cut off
the butt end (Fig. 8).

In the next operation we divide this feather exactly in half with
our thread, and by a few crisscross windings between the divisions,
and a knot to hold, we get the wings set permanently (Fig. 9).
Note: many tiers cut each side of the wings separately from the
Mandarin feathers. In my opinion this makes extra work and does
not make any better job than the method described here.

We now have the tail and wings tied on and completed. The
next step is to tie in the hackle. Picking out one or two, according
to what you wish, the fibres are spread (Fig. A—showing hackle
as taken from neck, and then stripped of its down and spread) and
tied on hook close to back of wing as shown (Fig. 10). Two hackles are better than one because you can face each one differently
when tying on, making a better-balanced, better-looking, and
better-floating fly. If you desire a sparsely hackled fly, make only
two winds of each hackle instead of four winds of one hackle. This
may run more or less according to how much hackle you wish to
have on the fly. This is more expensive than making sparse flies
with single hackles, but the results attained in the finished product
are far better as far as floating quality is concerned.

After the hackles are tied in (not wound on) the next step is to put on the body. If the material is wool, silk, tinsel, or some other material that may be handled as it is, then it is tied directly to the hook. However, in this particular fly we are now tying I am using fur, and this must be spun on a thread. The fur used is taken from the soft part between the outside hairs and the skin. To aid you in plucking it from the hide, you may clip the long hairs. However, I take the fur off without doing this and pull out any of the long coarse fibres if they come with the downy under-fur.

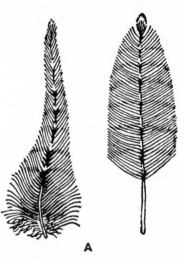

A

This plucked fur may be tied on in two ways. The illustration shows the knee method. This is done as follows. Lay a pinch of fur on your knee. Cut off a piece of waxed thread about six or seven inches long and hold as shown. Then roll the thread over the fur in about the same way you would work a rolling-pin over dough. (Perhaps you should ask a woman about this.) About half as much fur as shown in the photograph, but spread out in the same manner, is sufficient for a fly of the size shown in Fig. 10. (More fur than necessary was used in this case simply for picture-taking.) After the fur is spun on the piece of thread, tie this to the hook, wind on, and tie off, as in Fig. 14.

The other way to do this trick is to simply loosen up a bit of fur about as shown on the knee in the picture, and rub this directly on the tying thread when you come to that stage of tying a fly. You do this with the fingers, rolling the dubbing on the thread with thumb and forefinger while holding the thread taut with the other hand. When you get proficient at this it is very helpful in making for speed, as it eliminates one entire step. Instead of tying on the fur-wound piece of thread, you simply wind on the main thread which has had the dubbing added, and proceed from there as if you had been simply winding on the thread. Your first attempts will probably be clumsy, and the bodies distressingly bulky,

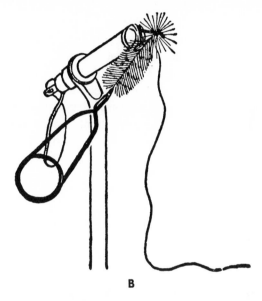

B

but with practice you can soon learn to make both a neat and substantial job.

The thread must be a bit on the sticky side for the plucked fur to adhere to it. To make the most neat and tapered body, use the dubbing material most sparingly. When dubbing a fly as small as size 16, the fur should increase the diameter of the thread by only a trifle. Of course, if you want a rough and heavy-looking body, then use more fur and spread it out loosely.

It is now time to make the final operation. Grab the tip of the hackle with the pliers and wind around the hook close to the wing, being careful to keep the hackle fibres standing out verticle to the shank of the hook. (See Fig. B.) If two hackles are being used, take the one tied in nearest the tail and wind that in first, tying off, of course. Then do the same with the forward hackle. Manipulate

[409]

the fibres as you do this so that they do not press over each other, and make the last wind or two in front of the wings to tie in there. To make sure everything is set tight against the body after finishing this, take your thumb and forefinger and, with your fingernails tight against the shank of the hook near the eye, push back toward the tail against the wings. This not only sets everything up tight, but helps in spreading the hackles a trifle fanwise so that they rest on the water better.

You may find that it is difficult to get the results you wish by following the instructions. Materials make a difference. One hackle will wind on without trouble, another will refuse to wind on properly. When you get one of the latter you may be sure that most of the feathers on that particular hackle neck will do the same. Hackles or any material used for the tails of dry flies should be glossy, stiff, and if desired long, the stiffness should extend well down into the stem of the hackle. Some furs adhere to the thread easily and smoothly but others do not. With some, in fact, it helps to use rather sticky thread, or use two threads. To do this last first lay a piece of waxed thread on your knee. Then fluff out the fur to be used and lay it on top of this thread. Take another piece of thread and lay on top of the fur, and twist the two together. This is a good stunt for making fluffy and bulky fur bodies, but it can also be used for making sleek, tapered ones also. To my knowledge this is simply one of my own little ideas, which I stumbled on when trying to make the Gold Ribbed Hare's Ear pattern.

As aforementioned, the photograph of the finish-off knot shows a hook without body, hackle, and wings. To start this knot, first hold the thread in left thumb and forefinger taut against the hook, of course pulling the thread toward you. Then place the right forefinger against the bottom of the thread, again toward you; and at the same time bend the thread in the left hand under your right finger, away from you, and over the top of the hook shank (Fig. 16).

Go around the hook shank and directly back toward you, and at the same time take the thread strand that was just bent over the hook in your left thumb and forefinger along with the thread you are bringing back toward you, and hold the two strands firm. This will leave a loose loop on the right (Fig. 17). With the right hand, wind the loose loop forward around the hook and over the thread several times. Then take all three strands in the thumb and fore-finger of the left hand, leaving the loop as shown (Fig. 18).

You are now ready to finish the knot. This can be done by placing the finger on the thread at the head as in illustration, or by placing the shaft of a bodkin needle in the loop that shows in Figs. 18 and 19, and putting pressure on it toward you while you pull the end thread to close up the loop against the hook. When the needle contacts the hook shank, pull it out. The tension on the thread pulls the knot tight. It takes from four to six seconds to tie this knot, including picking up the bodkin, and it is as secure as any other whip finish. If you wish to make doubly sure of a lasting finish, make a second knot over the first. This will take less time,

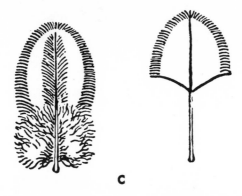

C

at least one second less than the first one, simply because rhythm was established in making the first.

There are tools available for making a whip-finish knot. They are inexpensive. Thus you need not learn how to tie this knot without one. But the knot I use is excellent and easy to make, although most difficult to describe in words.

Figures 20 and 21 show a method of putting on fan wings. First select two feathers from the breast of a Mandarin or domestic duck, taking care that they have identical shapes and sizes. Strip off the soft, fluffy feathers at the base. Fig. C shows both the feathers as pulled from the skin, and as they look after being stripped. Now turn these back to back, match evenly together (Fig. D), and then place as shown in Fig. 20. With the tying thread, bind the two ends of the feathers together *on the hook*. Then bend them back toward the vise and tie (Fig. 21). If you have done this correctly, the wings will set as shown in photograph. If they do not set just as you want, further manipulation of the thread will make them either spread further apart or fit closer together, according to the way you make them go with the thread. It is impossible to explain this point—you must learn it from experience. If the wings are not straight when you put them on, nothing you do will straighten them. Either you didn't set them straight to begin with, or else the quills of the feathers are flat on the wrong side and so

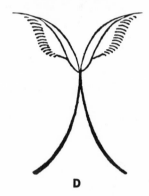

D

won't set straight, in which case you might better get another set of wings and start over again.

To me the worst task in putting on fan wings is the selection of the feathers for uniformity in shape and equal size in a pair. As a rule it is best to take two feathers that are together on the bird. Even then you will sometimes get two that do not match; and unless they do, the fly will not look right or cast well. A drop of varnish on the hook between the wings will make them more rigid and durable. However, I do not like wings fortified in this way because it makes them too stiff, too rigid for casting. If you do a really good tying job with perfectly selected feathers, they will be durable enough to catch several fish before going to pieces, look better, and cast far easier. Of course the ends of the wings are clipped off after being tied in, and a few figure eights between and to both sides of the wings will help to make them rigid and hold their position. I have found that if the wings go on smoothly and straight in the beginning, they stay that way, very seldom getting out of place in use. On the other hand, if they are a bit contrary and I must fuss with them to make them set straight, I rarely find that they stay straight in use. For this reason I discard any feathers that do not have stems that tie on straight. If I can get forty-eight pairs of perfectly matched wings from one duck for flies ranging from 10 to 14, I feel that I've done very well. While being so particular is costly, at least one has the satisfaction of having a nicely balanced fly when in use. Sometimes a duck is very poor, yielding few if any feathers that will make a really nice fly.

When putting on quill or tinsel, the shank of the hook must first be made tapered with the winding silk—otherwise the body will be unsightly. You cannot build up with these materials and make them look like anything, so it is necessary to have a base of perfect proportions to wind on. Besides, in the case of tinsels, to build up with them, even the finest, will add extra weight that will make it difficult to float the fly, no matter how stiff the hackles are.

Peacock quills are used for bodies more than any other kind. The best quills come from the eye of the tail feather. They vary in color and density of edging line, so that it is possible to get almost any shade of quill you want between light gray and very dark gray. In addition they may be dyed olive, green, red, or any other color you desire. Many other birds including hackle feathers of chickens have usable quills—the condor being one of the best. In this respect, do a bit of experimenting with whatever feathers you can secure. It is all fascinating research when you have time and look on fly-tying as a hobby. Of course the quills when taken from the feather are covered with feathery barbules. These must be scraped off, either with the fingernails or with a dull razor-blade. When using a steel edge to do the job, lay the quill on a telephone book, celluloid, or anything that will give slightly as you scrape. If you try it on a hard surface that does not give, you are sure to have considerable trouble with breakage and cutting. My wife uses the thumb and second finger of her hand to do the work and can do it in re-markably quick time. Condor quills cannot be stripped in this way. A commercial product named Clorox will eat off the fuzz, but you must watch the job closely so that you don't over-do it. When through, wash the quills thoroughly and then repeat.

Raffia grass makes a succulent-looking body that trout like, but it is a poor floater because it absorbs moisture. If you wish to take the time, lightly coating the body with a good line-floating preparation will aid in this respect. Of course for wet flies the material is ideal. To use the stuff, first wet it, and then split it into narrow strips so that it may be evenly and smoothly wound on the hook shank. The natural color makes an excellent May fly or Light Cahill body, and of course you may dye the material to suit your needs.

Of all the materials used for bodies of dry flies, I think silk is about the poorest. The only time I use it is when absolutely necessary, as when making some special pattern that can't be duplicated with anything else. Most silk changes color when it gets wet, becoming much darker. Some grades are better than others. Silk imitations enter into this category. The material is good for wet flies.

There are new fluorescent body materials that shine when exposed to ultraviolet light and which are most lustrous and bright during all daylight hours, being particularly brighter than other material about a half hour before sunrise, and a half hour after sunset. (This according to the sunrise and sunset hours as officially given each day for your particular locality. Of course the material may be brighter for a longer time at any day's end if conditions are just right. The time given is the minimum.) You get them in the form of threads. Unfortunately the colors available in these materials are very limited, but they are tough and hold their color. They are definitely a good material for some patterns.

Fur is one of my favorite body materials. Scraps can be picked up in the oddest places, and all come in handy at some time or another. Bluish grays in various shades are usually obtainable. I like the under-fur of muskrat and blue fox for some patterns, for instance Dark Cahill and Adams. The fur of a red fox has three distinct shades, all making excellent bodies that trout like; one for instance being ideal for the Light Cahill in the lightest creamy shade. I could go on and on about various furs (don't overlook rabbit) but this is not a complete treatise on fly-tying, so I think you can easily pick up from here and go deeper into the subject. Incidentally white or any light-colored fur may be dyed another color. This will aid you in getting many colors not found in the natural.

Body materials may be picked up almost anywhere—a piece of yarn from a carpet or a coat; some fur from cats or hair from dogs; threads from shirts and underclothes. In fact anything that you can wind on, either directly or as dubbing, can be used, and may possibly be just the body you need for some particularly tough condition. The charm of fly tying comes in the creation of something that pleases you. Anything you produce that takes fish becomes a super-production in your eyes. But fly tying becomes work, as does everything else, when it is used as a way to earn dollars.

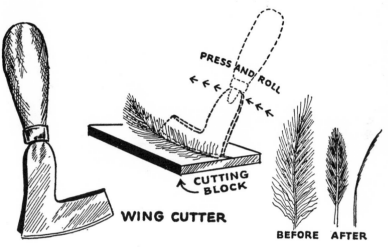

DRY FLY WING CUTTER

Two recent tools, made in the U.S.A., have helped in the making of wings for both dry and wet flies. One cuts perfect wings, with stem in center, from the breast and other small feathers of any bird, and also from the soft and fuzzy centers of large hackles. For instance, from the breast feathers of pheasants you can cut the most beautiful wings for the English March Brown pattern. From other birds you can cut wings equally good for other patterns. The best thing about these wings is that you can match them perfectly and they are extremely durable, far more so than any other wing, except the hackle point type. From discarded and otherwise unusable white fan wings from the breast and side feathers of any duck you can cut perfect wings. You can get white for perfect Royal Coachman patterns, blue-gray for Blue Quill and similar flies, slate for patterns that call for that shade, speckled and mottled wings from all kinds of game birds including the grouse, pheasant, and woodcock. In fact, with this tool, none of the soft feathers plucked from a bird need be wasted, and from them you can fashion patterns that otherwise would be almost impossible to make. You can also cut wings from the surplus feathers on hackle necks, after you have used up all that are suitable as hackles. It is the most useful tool that has been made for the fly tier since the invention of the hackle plyers, whenever that was. The wings cut with this tool are

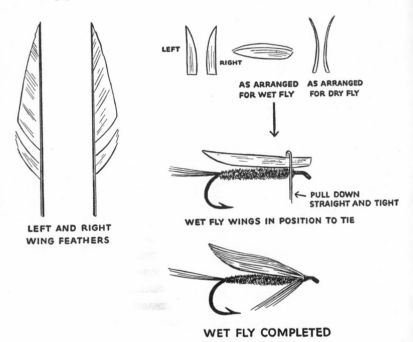

LEFT

RIGHT

AS ARRANGED
FOR WET FLY

AS ARRANGED
FOR DRY FLY

PULL DOWN
STRAIGHT AND TIGHT

LEFT AND RIGHT
WING FEATHERS

WET FLY WINGS IN POSITION TO TIE

WET FLY COMPLETED

tied in, in the manner shown by the illustrations of tying a fan wing.

The other tool is made to cut wings from the sides of flight quills. Instead of doing them one at a time, as with scissors, this tool cuts out a large number at once, all of them the same shape. For most wet-fly patterns wings are indispensable. To make wings otherwise than by cutting with this tool, let me describe the process. First you need a pair of well-matched flight feathers, one from the right wing, the other from the left wing. From each feather, cut out a section about one-quarter inch wide. For wet flies, place the two even and concave edges together, with the tips pointing inward and touching each other. Incidentally, wetting them in the

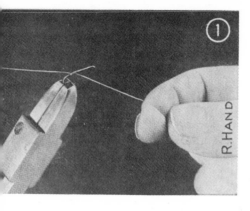

First step in tying a fly

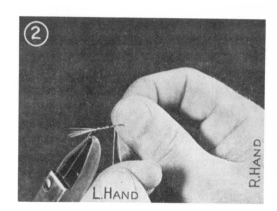

rst step in making a jam knot

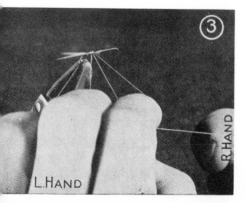

Second step in making a jam knot

Center thread being pulled taut against right-hand thread with left index finger

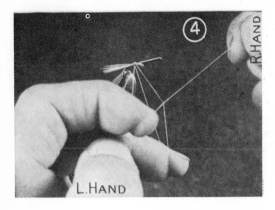

Third step in making a jam knot

Pull is exerted with the left hand. Restraint given by right finger keeps everything taut

Fourth step in making a jam knot

Really a continuation of third step, showing tautness kept until reaching the hook, where it jams the thread against the hook

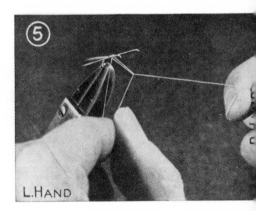

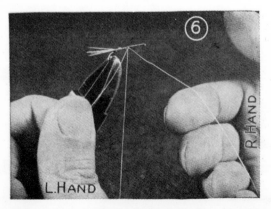

Fifth step in making a jam knot

Knot completed and thread being pulled through with left hand

First step of tying on wings of mandarin, mallard, teal, etc.

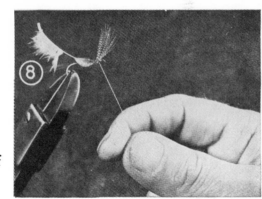

Second step of tying on wings of mandarin, etc.

Third step of tying on wings of mandarin, etc.

Tails and wings tied on hackl[e]

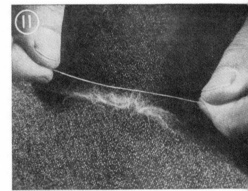

First operation of spinning fur for bodies

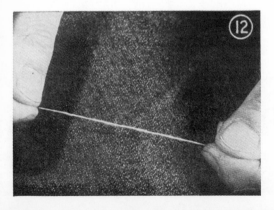

Second operation of spinnin[g] fur for bodies

See instructions for another metho[d] of using dubbing

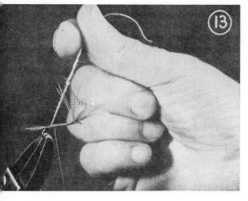

After hackle is tied in, the tier returns to the tail and ties in the body, which is wound on at the time

Body wound on—
The next step is to wind in the hackle

Hackle all wound on and ready to tie off

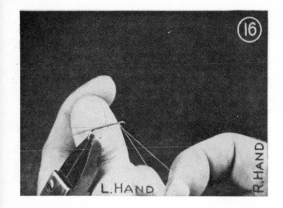

First step of whip knot

Second step of whip knot

Winding thread. Wind thread in right fingers

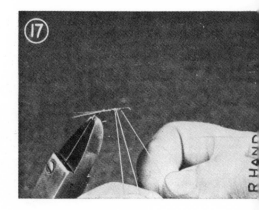

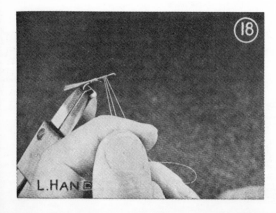

Third step of whip knot

All threads taken in fingers

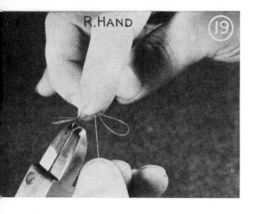

Fourth step of whip knot

Pulling key thread and keeping taut with finger of right hand

Tying on a pair of fan wings

Fan wings tied on—ready to cut off stems

mouth after getting them set together will aid you in getting them tied on the hook properly. To tie in the wings, grip the matched pair tightly in thumb and forefinger of the left hand and place horizontally on top of the hook, with the tips reaching just about to the bend. In making the tie the thread must pull all the fibres down, one on top of the other, or else they will split or be otherwise unsatisfactory. Once you pull down on the wings and make a couple of extra turns your future procedure is destined. If the wings hold their shape and lie nicely horizontally along the hook shank, then make one or two more turns around the hook and tie off. Otherwise take them off and try a new pair.

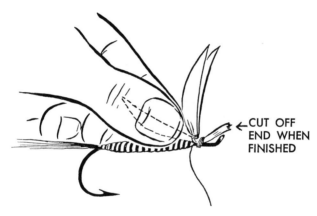

←CUT OFF END WHEN FINISHED

In tying a dry fly with wings cut from flight feathers, have the wing-tips pointing outward. To tie in the dry-fly wings use the same starting procedure as when tying a wet. Make the first turn over the feathers to bind them to the hook, make another turn or two before releasing your grip on the wings, and then let them go. If they look even and flare out on each side nicely, then bring them to a vertical position and make two or three turns around the base of the wings close against the hook and then one or two turns, or as many as needed, around the shank of the hook in back of the wings. This is to make them stand erect. At first you may have lots of trouble, but if you persist you will get there.

Speckled feathers, such as those found on mandarin, mallard, teal, and other ducks make beautiful wings. The Cahill, Quill Gordon, and others are made with such wings. These can all be tied as shown in Figs. 7, 8, and 9. Such wings are very effective and durable. And to come back again to the center-stem-wing cutter, this will cut a pair of wings from two of the left-over feathers after you have used the fibres as shown in the photographs.

I also like wings made of hair (squirrel, deer, caribou, woodchuck, and so on). Wings made from such material are exceedingly durable and, while a trifle rough-looking, make exceedingly effective flies. The Wulff patterns are of this construction, and several years ago I made one I called the Squirrel Tail that proved effective even in very low and clear water conditions. The wings were gray squirrel, the hackle grizzly (Plymouth or Barred Rock), the body blue fox, the tail grizzly.

The ends of hackle feathers also make good wings. I much prefer them to quill wings. Of course in spent flies these hackle wings are used more than any other. Spent wings, you should know, are tied with wings spreading out flat, crosswise on the hook shank, instead of upright.

Soft hackles are best for wet flies, stiff hackles best for dry flies. It is the stiff hackles that are difficult to obtain. The old birds yield better feathers than young birds, and all roosters produce their best feathers after the advent of cold weather. The pick of the crop is when the new feathers have just reached their prime. Later than that the quills become heavier and stiffer and make the using of them difficult. The sweetest hackle to use is one with a slender quill and yet with short stiff fibres that hold fairly uniform throughout the length of the feather. There should also be a minimum of denseness in the center (see Fig. E). However, some hackles with apparently dense and fibrous centers are very stiff and usable. Naturally, feathers with dark centers are of this type. When you open them up for use (see Fig. E) you can readily tell whether the quality is good. If the hackles keep snapping forward regardless of your stroking them the other way, they are pretty good stuff, even though they may not look it. If they are wishy-washy when stroked, they are useless for dry flies. Good dry-fly hackles should be glossy, but glossiness does not necessarily mean that they are stiff. They may have soft and fuzzy centers and so be unsuitable for dry-fly work, although excellent for wet flies. The ability to select good necks comes only from much experience. These hints will help, but won't make you an expert without experience teaching you the hard way. And even the most canny expert cannot tell whether a hackle will wind evenly on the hook until he tries it. Some of the stiffest hackles I ever had were useless for tying flies because they twisted sideways when being wound on, and there wasn't anything you could do about it. You don't hear much about these things, of the high-priced neck you buy that may turn out to be useless because of this trouble. All these things add to the cost of tying a top-grade fly and help to explain why you can buy some flies for three dollars a dozen and pay from four to five

E

and a half dollars or more for others. Aside from the care used in tying, which takes time, first grade dry flies are made only with the most select materials, chosen from the best obtainable.

In making streamers, bucktails, and wet flies the steps of construction are changed a little. Personally I prefer to start with the tail, if any, then the body. Hackle can be next tied on if desired, or you may put this on last. Use glossy side toward eye. After the hackle has been wound in, pull all the fibres downward with moistened fingers. Wind the thread over the top of the hackle, forcing in back toward the hook, and the job is done, except for placing the wing as already described. You may tie on the wings first, if you choose, either on wet flies or streamers and bucktails, then tie in the hackle as described. Or if you do not want to wind the hackle on, you may pull out a cluster of it and tie it as a bunch directly under the head of the fly. I call this "bearded." You can use tips of feathers for this purpose as well as bunches of hackles. Chenille makes a good body for streamers and bucktails, so does any other bulky material; and of course tinsel bodies are very good because these flies are supposed to more or less simulate minnows,

WET FLY HACKLE
WOUND ON HOOK

WET FLY HACKLE TIED
BACK AND READY FOR WING

PLAIN BEARDED HACKLE -
HACKLE NOT WOUND ON

COMPLETED STREAMER AND BUCKTAIL
ONLY DIFFERENCE IN CONSTRUCTION FROM WET FLY ARE IN THE WINGS

and tinsel gives a glitter that is like the flash of a minnow's scales. In putting on tinsel bodies, care must be taken to build up the shank of the hook smoothly. Then start winding the tinsel on near the eye of the hook, leaving enough space between for tying in the hackle and the wings. Now wind the tinsel back to the bend of the hook and then back to where you started and tie off. This will make a smooth, good-looking, and durable body. Winding first with flat tinsel and then winding over that with oval tinsel makes an effective body for some conditions, but on the whole I do not consider it necessary. However, the more tinsel that catches the light rays, the more the body will sparkle and look alive, thus using the oval or embossed tinsel has its points, because it has a broken surface.

Hooks should be purchased according to the need. Dry-fly hooks should be light in weight and delicate. Wet-fly hooks should be heavy so the fly sinks readily. Streamer hooks should have longer shanks according to the length of the fly desired. Some anglers prefer the bend of the hook to be near the end of a streamer fly. I prefer it a bit behind the center. Many fish hit from the side rather than from behind, and a hook with too long a shank misses such fish. If you have it about two-thirds from the eye of the hook in relation to the fly, you stand a good chance of getting the fish whether they are striking from the side or from behind. Of course when fish strike from the front, you are out of luck except when using a short-shanked hook. Spider flies without tails should be tied on short-shanked hooks.

Dyes are obtainable for fly tying in any color desired, even to the duns and other delicate shades. This is a great help. When I first started fly tying I had to mix up the primary colors to get the effect desired.

Moths are the bane of the fly-tier's existence, but they can be controlled if you use sufficient care. If you keep every container well protected with moth flakes, inspecting for evaporation frequently, you will find that you can escape the ravages of this pest. However, if you miss one box or container, you may be sure the moths will find you out. One year I missed one box that contained three finished flies. When I next went over the boxes I found that in this one only the hooks of the flies were left. When you get new materials, look them over carefully. If you are doubtful about them, wash in a mixture of carbolic soap and lysol. Then rinse in pure water and dry.

If you get bucktails direct from the source and uncured, be mighty careful about them. Moths simply go crazy about such a feast. First, you should cure them and set the hair. This is done by several washes with the following solution: 2 ounces alum, 1 pint water, ½ pint salt. Boil, let cool, and then apply. You may put the tails directly in this solution for a period of five to fifteen minutes, but this leaves a deposit on the hair that must be worked off with the fingers. I prefer to rub it on the hide with a rag, giving it from one to four dressings as desired. The final result is a clean whitish-looking hide. If you do this after the hair has started to slip from the hide, it will not stop it from coming out; but if you do it before it starts to slip, it will hold tight indefinitely. Once cured and dried out thoroughly, place in a box with a tight cover and sprinkle heavily with moth flakes, and you won't have any trouble keeping them.

When dyeing necks on the skin, the hide gets hard and brittle and difficult to handle. A mixture of half alcohol and half glycerine rubbed into the hide softens it and makes it much easier to handle.

Fine and compact hair is best for making hair-winged flies. Before World War II small deer tails of excellent quality and texture were obtainable. Impali tails are the next best, but I have been unable to get these in brown, so have been dying them that color.

This chapter covers only the most essential details of fly-tying. There are other books that go into detail on the subject. But this can serve to get you started. If you like the hobby, you will soon be buying everything in sight that is related to it.

APPENDIX
by
EDWARD C. JANES

Basic Tackle

Rods

During most of the time that Ray Bergman fished—from early in this century until the mid-1960's—and wrote, bamboo was the universally favored material for the manufacture of fishing rods. It had superseded the former rods made of lancewood, greenheart, and bethabara, just as they in turn had superseded the fir rods popular in Izaak Walton's day.

The first bamboo rods were made of Calcutta cane, which originated in various parts of the East but was shipped from Calcutta. Bamboo—actually a variety of grass—when split into strips and glued provided rods greatly superior to those made of lengths of tapering wood. However, Calcutta cane is pliant to the point of limpness, as anyone who has flexed a rod made of this material can attest. It is also vulnerable to attack by worms.

The next forward step in the manufacture of rods came around the turn of the present century with the change from Calcutta to Tonkin cane, superior in every way to its predecessor. Tonkin cane (*Arunden aria* Amabilis) does not grow wild but is cultivated in a small section of Kwangsi Province in China, near North Vietnam. It is not only straight and durable, but its elastic ligneous fibers are much more tightly compacted than those of other canes. So far, attempts to grow Tonkin cane in other areas, such as Puerto Rico or the Deep South, have met with failure.

The use of Tonkin cane in rod-making was pioneered in the United States by Gene Bartlett at his factory in Montague, Massachusetts. So popular did his rods become that the entire industry soon converted to the newer material and today practically all bamboo rods are made of it.

With the advent of this tougher, stiffer material, manufacturers began experimenting with rods made of three to six strips. Among the three-stripped was Abbey & Imbrie's so-called steel vine rod made up of three rounded sections. This proved less efficient, however, than the six-sided rod which has become almost universally adopted today.

Tonkin cane also allowed more latitude in rod-making, and manufacturers began experimenting with different types of actions. These experiments brought forth the steep taper rod in which most of the action is located in the tip section and the parabolic action rod with most of the action in the butt. Today, however, most rod-makers and the majority of anglers prefer a universal taper that provides a smooth flowing action throughout the entire rod from tip to butt.

Many of the early rods, turned out by such craftsmen as Hiram Leonard, Edward F. Payne, Frank E. Thomas, and William Devine, were beautiful examples of the rod-maker's art, but by today's standards they were too willowy and soft in action and too prone to coming apart at the ferrules. They also took a "set" easily.

In Ray Bergman's early fishing days a wide variety of bamboo rods could be purchased in an equally wide price range. This situation continued until China became a Communist nation and the flow of Tonkin cane to America abruptly ended. As stockpiles dwindled, a number of rod-makers were no longer able to supply inexpensive or medium-priced bamboo rods, although a few continued to be produced here and some were imported from Japan.

Today limited supplies of Tonkin cane are again finding their way into the country but its high price, combined with rising labor costs, have practically done away with low-priced bamboo rods. Therefore, the only custom-made bamboo rods on the market now are expensive ones. Among the best are the resin-impregnated rods such as those developed by the Orvis Company of Manchester, Vermont.

It takes the better part of two months of crafting to fashion one of these fine bamboo rods. First, the individual canes must be carefully sorted for straightness and also for the density of their fibers. Canes whose fibers do not extend nearly to the center of the stalk are rejected, and those which meet the specifications are then divided into groups representing various types of actions.

In the next step the selected sticks are tempered over an open flame to seal in their native strength and elasticity and also to give them a rich brown luster. The tempered cane is then split into segments which are rough sawn to shape preparatory to milling. Six cane segments are required for each rod section.

Two milling operations follow—the first a rough milling to remove excess stock and to form the general taper of the segment, and the second a fine milling to a tolerance of a quarter of a thousandth of an inch. A second inspection of the milled sticks for straightness and strength rejects any flawed segment.

Next comes the important step of "mismatching" so that the natural nodes are correctly placed to assure a perfect flex in the finished rod. The mismatched segments are then collected into bundles of six.

Now the six segments are ready to be dipped in a special glue and wrapped together both clockwise and counterclockwise to insure uniform pressure throughout their length. When the sticks are dry, the wrappings are removed and the glued sections are ready for immersion in a week-long bath of specially formulated Bakelite resin which renders them impervious to moisture and heat. The sections are then buffed to a high polish which can be maintained indefinitely by occasional rubbing with a soft cloth.

Matched ferrules are then mounted on the impregnated sections in a manner that assures a perfect fit. Next, cork grips are mounted, shaped on a lathe, and sanded to satin smoothness, and then the reel seats are added.

Guides are wrapped by hand and the wrappings given four coats of varnish. Now the finished rod is ready for final inspection and testing for proper action. Small wonder that the price tag on such rods is high.

This is the high point of development which bamboo rods have reached today, and they are a far cry from the rods turned out by the pioneer manufacturers or the mass-production rods of pre-World War II days. Custom-finished, these rods represent the highest standards and traditions of the rod-maker's craft. One hopes they will be around for a long time to come.

In his writings Ray Bergman makes frequent mention of steel rods, and here again the picture has changed considerably. The first steel rods appeared around the turn of the century and enjoyed a wide vogue during the next four decades. Their chief virtue lay in their comparatively low cost and the fact that they required less care and were somewhat more durable than contemporary bamboo rods. However, they left much to be desired in their balance and action. Some were solid, others tubular in construction, and at least one manufacturer produced a tapered steel rod.

A popular favorite, especially among young anglers of a generation or so ago, was a telescoping steel rod. The tip and midsection could be extended to any desired length, making this a sort of all-round tool, suitable for fishing small, brushy brooks as well as large streams and lakes.

The manufacture of steel rods was interrupted for several years by World War II, and by the time the industry returned to peacetime production fiberglass had appeared on the scene. The advent of fiberglass rods—poor though they were by present-day standards—marked the beginning of the end for steel rods. They have now practically disappeared.

The Shakespeare Company of Kalamazoo, Michigan, introduced the first fiberglass rods in 1947. These consisted of solid blanks of glass fiber bonded with plastic. They were not entirely satisfactory in taper and action, yet these early progenitors exhibited the traits which were universally hailed in their successors. They did not rust, they did not take a set, they required almost no care, and they could take punishment that no bamboo or steel rod could endure.

Soon after the appearance of solid glass rods, the Conolan Corporation of Costa Mesa, California, introduced a line of hollow glass rods. These proved to be far superior in every way to the solid type, and the tubular construction design was quickly adopted by other manufacturers. Some rods were made by wrapping woven glass cloth around a tapered core, others by shaping glass fibers in a mold.

Today the better glass rods are made of closely woven fiberglass cloth tightly bound on steel mandrels under tremendous pressure. Walls have become lighter and more uniform, but laminations are tighter with more fibers for added strength.

The quartz-cured rod blanks are then heat treated from the inside which results in a uniform action with no soft spots to give way or break when casting or playing a fish. Finally, a hard epoxy finish is applied to the blanks and windings to make the rod impervious to heat and moisture. The best rods provide carbide guides and at least one manufacturer supplies fiberglass ferrules, proof against corrosion and breakage.

Thus we have the characteristics of glass rods: they are rugged, impervious to moisture, heat, and hard fishing—and they are relatively inexpensive. Moreover, unlike bamboo rods, the less expensive glass rods are almost as good as the most costly ones, since all glass rods are mass produced from blanks. The higher price of the so-called custom glass rods results from the grade and type of grip, reel seat, ferrules, guides, and other fittings used in finishing them. Basically, the rods are, or ought to be, of uniform quality.

Today glass rods outsell bamboo rods at a ratio of at least twenty to one. Balance and action continue to improve and it seems entirely possible that in time glass may entirely replace bamboo, just as bamboo replaced the earlier rods made of various woods.

But nothing is certain, for, meanwhile, another material is being used today in rod manufacture: graphite filament. It may well turn out to be as revolutionary in its day as fiberglass was when introduced three decades ago. Graphite, also known as black lead or plumbago, is a soft, lustrous form of carbon long used in the manufacture of lead pencils and more recently in lubricants and electrodes. Rods made from graphite filaments appear to have several advantages over fiberglass and bamboo. Perhaps the greatest of these is the graphite rod's strength of backbone in proportion to its weight. One of the new graphite fly rods, for example, comes in an eight-foot length and weighs only one-and-three-quarter ounces. It takes a number-6 line (for an explanation of line numbers, see page 438) and packs a surprising recovery speed into its stiff action.

This high recovery speed makes for high line velocity which in turn makes possible longer controlled casts. In tests this rod proved capable of shooting line as far as fiberglass sticks of considerably heavier weight. This, of course, means more effortless and hence less tiring casting over a long day of fishing. The same action and power have been built into graphite spinning and bait-casting rods as well.

Graphite rods, incidentally, appear to be frail, owing to the small diameter of their butts. But manufacturers declare that graphite blanks are even more durable than fiberglass and will stand up better to hard usage.

A second advantage lies in the delicate response of the light, stiff tip to a strike. Even the hardly noticeable touch of a trout taking a deeply sunken wet fly or sucking a dry from the surface is instantly telegraphed to the angler.

Several manufacturers today are making graphite rods, and new methods along with computer-programmed designing have resulted in a large number of varying actions to meet all angling requirements. And, as in the case of fiberglass rods earlier, the makers of graphite rods are taking different approaches to design. Some are using tubular construction, others solid blanks, and at least one is combining graphite with older materials.

A disadvantage is price. Graphite rods at present compare in cost with top-quality bamboo rods. As more manufacturers go into the production of these rods, however, prices may well come down.

Whatever material they are made of, modern rods are called upon to perform feats never demanded of the rods of an earlier time. For this reason, certain features should be looked for in buying a rod today. Two of these features are power and action. This might be a good place to clear up the existing confusion between these words.

The two terms are often used interchangeably, frequently by the manufacturers themselves, as though power and action were synonymous. Actually, they are not. *Power* is the amount of flexing strain a rod can sustain before losing its efficiency—or breaking. Instead of speaking of trout-action, bass-action, and muskie-action rods, the makers might better substitute the word *power*. *Action*, on the other hand, is the curve a rod takes on when casting a lure or playing a fish. Action is the built-in flexibility which helps to propel the line and lure through the air and to play a fish without breaking terminal tackle.

Where the curve of a flexed rod begins is important. As mentioned earlier, a rod can have a so-called steep action (with most of the action in the tip), a parabolic action (with the action in the butt), or a universal action (which flows evenly through the entire stick, with the curve itself beginning just short of midrod).

The steep-action rod, sometimes known as the Hewitt tip action after the well-known angler and writer who developed it, was popular some years ago when most fly fishing was done with wet flies. It is inefficient for today's more sophisticated fishing with flies and fly-rod and spinning lures.

The parabolic action caused a furor when it was first developed a few decades ago, and it too is generally unsuitable nowadays because when used with modern lures and methods, it makes for awkward casts and is likely to break all but heavy-test monofilament leaders and lines. Also, the lifespan of parabolic-action rods is shorter, because of their tendency to weaken and ultimately break at butt or ferrule when playing a fish.

The ideal action for today's rods—fly, bait-casting, or spinning —is the universal taper, which flows in an even arc from midrod to tip during the casting of lures and the playing of fish. This type of rod will cast farther and more accurately than rods with other actions. There is, perhaps, one exception. Some expert dry-fly men prefer an action that begins nearer the tip. This, they claim, enables them to cast a more versatile line. However, it is a difficult action to handle and for most anglers the universal action is the proper one, whether in ultra-light, medium, or heavy-power rods.

Actual casting, of course, is the best way to check the *action* of a rod. It is possible, however, to gain an idea of its curvature and flexibility by stringing it up and tying the end of the line to some fixed object. Then, moving back twenty feet or so, pull gently on the rod until a curve results. If the curve begins at midrod and arcs evenly to the tip, the rod has a universal action.

It is difficult to determine the *power* of a rod without actually using it. Rod-makers give some indication of a rod's power by designating it as ultra-light, light, medium, or heavy "action" (confusingly—what they actually mean is *power*).

An ultra-light rod is so constructed that the lightest fly line or spinning lure, as the case may be, is sufficient to bring out its action during the cast. Light rods are somewhat less delicate but are still designed for light lures and, except in the hands of expert anglers, small fish. Medium-powered rods will handle medium-sized lures and will subdue most freshwater fish that one is apt to encounter.

Another clue to a fly rod's power lies in the maker's recommendation about the weight of line to use with it or, in the case of a spinning rod, the specified weight range of the lures for which it was designed. Too light a line or lure will underpower a rod; too heavy a line or lure will overpower it. In either case it will be an inefficient tool.

This is why rod balance is so important today in fishing with all the new types of flies, fly-rod lures, and spinning lures. And there is more to this business than having a fly line that will bring out the action of your fly rod or lures of a weight suited to your spinning rod, important as these factors are.

The rod must be balanced to the reel, the reel to the line, and the line to the lures as well as to the rod. The result is an outfit that enables the angler to drop a fly delicately upon the water or to cast a lure farther and more accurately with spinning tackle.

We'll have more to say about this subject after we look into some of the new developments that have come about in reels and lines during recent years. Before leaving the subject of rods, though, we should explore a bit more fully the subject of rod lengths and weights for various types of modern trout fishing. No hard rules can be set forth since several X factors, including the angler's age, build, sex, and skill, enter into the problem. The perfect rod for one person might prove to be a disaster for another. Top-flight anglers can handle six-pound trout on six-foot, one-and-a-quarter-ounce rods while less accomplished anglers have difficulty in landing a one-pound bass on an eight-and-a-half-foot, five-ounce rod. A six-foot man weighing 190 pounds could cast for hours with a nine-foot six-and-a-half-ounce rod which would tire a slightly built man or a woman angler in a very short time.

It is possible, however, to make one or two general rules. A seven- to eight-foot fly rod of three to four ounces makes an excellent tool for small trout brooks. For larger lakes and streams with (presumably) bigger fish, an eight-and-a-half- to nine-foot rod weighing four-and-a-half to six ounces would be preferable. Steelhead waters, where it is necessary to cast larger lures considerable distances, often against the wind, require a nine- to nine-and-a-half-foot rod of five-and-three-quarters to six-and-a-half ounces.

What has been said of fly rods holds equally true in the case of spinning rods. The six-footers are light-power rods designed to cast the smallest lures while the eight-foot sticks are built to handle larger lures and larger fish.

A good spinning rod should have a cork grip at least sixteen inches long so the reel can be moved back and forth by means of rings to achieve proper balance when casting lures of various weights. Guides should be offset, that is, raised above the rod's surface instead of being wound directly to it as is the case with fly rods. Manufacturers of better type spinning rods today are using polished aluminum-oxide guides, a distinct forward step.

Reels

Reels, too, have changed with the changing times. These ingenious devices, known to the ancient Egyptians, had become common in Izaak Walton's day. The "winch" that he used was a single-action affair not too different from the fly reels of today. Its primary purpose was to store excess line, a function shared by contemporary reels, but modern reels also act to tire fighting game fish and prevent the line from snarling.

Through the years, most fly reels have been single-action, that is, the spool revolves once with each complete turn of the handle. Most fly reels are equipped with a click device which keeps an even tension on the line, and the best clicks are made of metal rather than plastic. The pawl, too, preferably of a triangular shape so that it may be rotated as its corners become worn, is best if made of metal. To some fly reels a light drag in the form of a knurled screw is added.

Fly-reel spools are narrow to keep line from snarling or building up at one spot while a fish is being played. Spindles average seven-eighths of an inch in width. The reel's diameter should be wide enough to accommodate sufficient line for the kind of fishing being done. A reel two-and-three-quarter inches in diameter carrying ninety feet of fly line is sufficient for fishing small trout waters, but on steelhead rivers a reel with a three-and-a-half-inch diameter capable of spooling ninety feet of fly line plus at least one hundred fifty yards of backing is required.

Actually, fly reels have not changed in their essentials since Ray Bergman's day; only a few refinements have been added. One of these is the substitution of magnesium—an especially light but also strong and rigid metal—for steel in the manufacture of modern fly reels. Another is the change, in some models, from single-action to a geared 2-to-1 retrieve so that the spool revolves twice to one turn of the reel handle. This increases line control in playing a fish and requires only half the reeling necessary with the older-type fly reels.

As an added aid to line control and also fish control, improved braking or drag devices have been added to the former click. Orvis's Madison fly reels, for example, offer an adjustable drag consisting of eight lever settings plus a pressure adjustment screw on the rim cage to increase or decrease the eight settings for the exact degree of tension desired. Also, some reels are made with a one-sided frame for easier removal of the spool.

As might be expected, it is in the field of spinning reels that recent changes have been more pronounced. Fixed-spool spinning reels go back to 1905 when A. F. Illingworth patented the first one in England. The new-type reel, in which the spool remains stationary while the line spirals from a fixed spindle, gained immediate popularity in Europe. It was not until the end of World War II, however, that spin fishing began to gain favor in this country. Since then a number of innovations have been added to spinning reels, both those of European manufacture and also to the fine reels manufactured in the United States.

Basically, spinning reels consist of a spool which is fastened by a brake screw into a revolving cup. A bail (a loop-like structure attached to opposing sides of the cup) or finger extends from the cup and is folded over the spool when in the closed position. A housing behind the cup holds a set of gears and a crank mechanism with an antireverse lock, which prevents the handle from revolving when a fish takes line. (In higher-priced reels, gears are machined from high-grade metals unlike the poorly fitting gears made of cheaper materials in inexpensive models. It is false economy to choose from among the latter.)

When casting, the folding bail or finger is opened outward to allow free passage of the line. At the end of the cast when the lure drops to the water, a turn of the crank closes the bail, engaging the line in a roller situated at one end of the bail. When line is retrieved it passes over this roller and onto the spool. As the crank is turned, the cup revolves and an eccentric gear causes the spool to move in and out for even winding of the line. The brake consists of a wing nut which fastens the spool to the spindle and which can be turned to exert the desired amount of pressure in playing a fish.

The first open-face spinning reels had a so-called finger bail which merely thrust out over the spool in closed position. Besides lifting it to cast, the angler also had to close it manually before reeling, and, all too often, finger bails failed to pick up the line, resulting in snarls and imprecations.

Today most all spinning reels have full bails—that is, a semihoop instead of a finger folds over the spool in closed position. This type of bail, with crank activated closing, is practically foolproof and has gone far to increase the popularity of spin fishing.

A newer modification of the original spin-casting reel is the closed-face reel in which the line feeds through a hole in the middle of the reel face. These reels provide an oscillating spool and a trigger device which frees the line for casting and locks it at the end of the cast. Closed-face spin-casting reels are somewhat easier to operate than open-face spinning reels, and they can be used with conventional rods with small guides since the line does not spiral widely as it comes from the spool but, instead, flows out straight.

Closed-face reels with their quick release feature are especially useful in bait fishing. The reel is in gear when the fish takes the bait and by just pushing the release button the angler can throw it into free spool. This allows the fish to hold the bait and begin to swallow it or to run with no suspicious tightening of the line. As soon as the reel handle is turned, the gears again mesh and put pressure on the fish. The push-button release is handy, too, in fishing deep pools or deep-water ponds. It is possible to cast a light lure and let it sink to any desired depth, or to drop it over the side of a boat and let it go right to the bottom in free spool.

In streams one can cast into the bankside shallows where trout so often lie, and by holding the rod high on the retrieve, it is easy to fish in two- or three-foot depths. When the lure comes to deep water, you can push the release button and let the lure sink before continuing the retrieve.

Most spin-casting rods, as well as bait-casting rods, are made with recessed reel seats, and this type reel seat is especially advantageous for the closed-face reels because it places the release button right under one's thumb where it is easy to reach. Spin-casting rods come in various lengths, and for casting lures the longer rods give more delicacy and accuracy—and more action to the lure on the retrieve.

A new refinement recently added to spinning reels of the open-face design is a trigger-like release that automatically opens the bail and picks up line for the cast, something one formerly had to do with one's forefinger. A variation of this is a new model which is operated by pressing the index finger against the bail to release line. Still another feature found on the newest open-face spinning reels are skirted spools designed to keep dirt and debris out of spool housings.

Those who prefer spin-casting with closed-face reels also have some new refinements to choose from. One is a device that permits the user to release exactly the same amount of line at each cast, an excellent feature when one has found the range of a hard-to-get-at pocket and wants to place a lure in exactly that same spot again— or when one wants to fish at a predetermined depth.

Another new model spin-casting reel provides two drags. One is preset to the pound test of the line being used. Then, if one tightens down too much on the second drag, it is automatically overridden as the strain nears the line's breaking point.

In spin-casting, lines of four- to six-pound test are probably best for trout fishing since these lines will cast light lures efficiently but are still strong enough to land sizable fish. Heavy lines cut down on casting distance, and it's better to get your lure to a fish and take a chance of losing it on a light line than not to be able to reach it at all.

Lines

There have been several new developments in the lines used for trout fishing in recent years.

The earliest fishing lines were made of vines, woven grasses and sinews, followed by the horsehair lines in vogue in Izaak Walton's day. Then came silk, of which—up until World War II—almost all modern fly lines were made. Also, until a few years prior to World War I, most of these were level lines, at least in this country, for tapered lines weren't made here and few fishermen had heard of them. It wasn't until the mid-1920's that American manufacturers began turning out single-taper, then double-taper, and finally, torpedo or quick-taper fly lines. Level lines are still in use for bait fishing or for trolling, but fly-casting calls for tapered lines for best results because it is the weight of the line that gives distance and accuracy to the cast.

Single-taper lines, which taper from a heavy butt section to a fine tip, are not generally available in the United States today, but it is possible to make one by cutting a double-taper line in the middle and splicing it to a number of yards of backing to fill the reel.

In general, today's tapered lines fall into two categories: straight-taper lines, or those which taper evenly from mid-section to end; and quick-taper (also called forward-taper) lines, or those which taper only close to the end and which carry a heavier weight forward. Most quick-taper lines are level for the first five or six feet from the end, increasing to their greatest diameter over the next fifty or sixty feet and then gradually tapering to level at the other end. Straight-taper lines can drop small flies to the water's surface more delicately than quick-taper lines, but the latter are better for casting large flies or streamers, especially on windy days.

Two recent variations of the quick-taper line are the wet-tip and wet-head lines. In the wet-tip, the first ten feet sinks while the rest floats. This makes a good line for fishing shallow streams when trout are lying near the bottom. In the wet-head line, the first thirty feet sinks while the rest floats. This is for use in deeper waters when you want to fish near the bottom. Another variation, especially popular in the West, is the shooting-head line. This line consists of a single taper of about thirty feet made up of number 11 (or 340 grain weight) (for an explanation of line numbers and weights, see page 438) followed by one hundred fifty feet of level line. With this type line and a suitable rod, casts of a hundred feet or more can easily be made.

Here is a short table of suggested rod lengths and new-type wet-tip and wet-head lines:

Rod Length	Line
8 ft.	No. 6
8½ ft.	No. 7
9 ft.	No. 8 or 9

Early braided fly lines were "enameled" to give them a smooth finish for frictionless passage through the guides. However, these finishes tended to chip and peel and today they have been replaced by an impregnation and heat process which lasts indefinitely.

There are a few silk lines still to be found, but by far the majority of fly lines today are made of nylon or the newer dacron. The specific gravity of silk lines caused them to sink and it was necessary to keep them well greased to make them float when dry-fly fishing. Nylon lines, however, tend to float, which makes them ideal for dry-fly fishing.

Dacron lines, on the other hand, sink readily and hence are ideally suited to wet-fly fishing or trolling. Also, both nylon and dacron lines are more resistant to rotting and wear and tear so that their normal lifespan is considerably greater than that of the former silk lines.

As Ray Bergman pointed out in 1952, processes came along to improve the quality as well as the durability of nylon from when it was first made, and the same is true of dacron fly lines. Further improvements continue to be introduced. Among the more recent is a change in the consistency and weight of the finish through the adoption of vinyl finishes. Originally, the fly lines themselves were tapered; today the lines are level and the finish is tapered instead. In manufacturing lines, dies open and close to form the taper. Today, too, most fly lines are hollow. The newer vinyl-plasticized finishes have also taken some of the former stretch out of nylon and dacron lines.

A few years back, when all fly lines were made of silk, they were classified by diameter and identified with letters indicating their size. A, for example, represented a diameter of .060 of an inch and the size decreased in alphabetical progression to the smallest size, I, which was .022 of an inch. Under this system tapered lines were marked HCH, HDH, HCF, and so on, depending upon whether they were double-tapered or forward-tapered. (See page 157.)

This system of calibration was carried over at first to nylon lines, but today the American Fishing Tackle Manufacturers Association has come up with a new code for nylon and dacron lines based on the weight in grains (there are 437.5 grains in one ounce) of the first thirty feet of tapered line. This system is used because dacron weighs more than silk while nylon weighs less than silk and because floating finishes tend to decrease the weight of nylon lines and sinking finishes tend to increase the weight of dacron lines.

Today, however, probably 95 percent of all fly lines are made of nylon. Dacron is more often used in the manufacture of saltwater big-game fishing lines.

Under the new code, lines are given a number from 1 through 12, showing the weight of the first thirty feet of line and also indicating the taper—L for level, DT for double-taper, and WF for weight-forward (or quick-taper). After the weight number there is another letter denoting whether the line floats (F) or sinks (S) or is intermediate (I), which means it can be made either to sink or float by dressing it for the intended use. Thus, for example, WF6F signifies a weight-forward line whose first thirty feet is 6 weight and which floats.

Here is a table showing weights, in grains, of floating lines:

AFTMA Number	Level	Double Taper	Weight Fd.
1	60		
2	80		
3	100		
4	120	120	
5	140	140	140
6	165	165	165
7	190	190	190
8	215	215	215
9	240	240	240
10	290	290	290
11	340	340	340
12		380	

Some line manufacturers add to these numbers the older designation of silk-line diameters (for example, HDH).

Line fit is extremely important for any fly fishing, but especially for dry-fly fishing. Here are recommended matchings of rods and lines under the new code.

Rod Length	Line
6–7	DT4F or WF4F
7½	DT4F or WF4F
8	DT5F or WF5F
8½	DT7F or WF7F
9	DT8F or WF9F
9½	DT9F or WF10F

Early spin fishermen in America experimented with various types of braided lines as well as monofilament, but within a short time the latter definitely proved its superiority for this kind of fishing for trout, at least. Among its advantages are the fact that it creates less friction than braided line, both in leaving the spool and in traversing the rod guides, thus adding 20 to 30 percent more distance to the cast.

Another advantage lies in the virtual invisibility of monofilament line to the fish, making the entire line one long leader. The bait or lure seems to be swimming freely of its own volition. Also, monofilament lines are longer lasting than braided lines since they absorb less water and are less vulnerable to abrasion. And, finally, they have a tendency to spring from the reel spool during a cast rather than being pulled from it as is the case with braided lines.

As the name implies, monofilament is a single strand of nylon (or dacron) extruded to make a complete line. It can be manufactured in any diameter from .006 to .045 inches with a test strength of from one-and-a-quarter to sixty pounds. Nylon fibers vary in structure: some are stiff, others limp, some are thin in relation to strength, some thick; some are round, some are oval in shape or flattened. These various types all have their special functions, but for trout fishing the average spin fisherman should select a round monofilament of a strength sufficient to fit his lures and the size fish he expects to catch, and of a sufficient limpness to cast efficiently and drop a lure delicately, but not so limp as to stretch unduly or cling to the spool instead of springing from it.

Leaders

No fly-rod outfit is complete until a leader is attached to the line. Formerly, Spanish silkworm gut was the material universally used for leaders. With the Spanish Civil War, the supply of silkworm gut practically dried up but, fortunately, nylon came along just in time to replace it, and in a number of ways the new material has proven to be greatly superior to silkworm gut.

Since gut is brittle when dry, it cannot be tied until it has been thoroughly soaked. Furthermore, in order to insure that strands of leader were of uniform diameter the gut had to be drawn through diamond dies, a process which frequently weakened the leader by peeling its surface. Tapering leaders of gut had to be made in short lengths tied together by knots, causing weak spots. Nylon leaders, on the other hand, can be extruded to any length, can be tied dry, are much more resistant to wear and tear, and are slower to deteriorate.

Ten-yard coils of nylon leader can be bought in all practical pound test sizes and in lighter weights is ideal for bait fishing and fly-rod trolling. Three or four feet is ample for a bait-fishing leader in spring, but as waters drop and turn clearer, leaders should be lengthened to eight or nine feet and in midsummer to at least twelve feet. A ten- to thirty-foot leader is adequate for trolling, depending on the turbulence, depth and clarity of the water, and the time of year.

A tapered leader is a definite asset in fly fishing. Tapered nylon leaders are sometimes knotted, but it is also possible to obtain them in knotless single strands up to twelve feet and tapering to 5X.

For early-season wet-fly fishing a nine-foot leader tapering to 3X is adequate, while late-season fishing requires a twelve-foot 4X leader. A nine-foot 3X leader is also adequate for spring dry-fly fishing, but in summer a twelve- to fifteen-foot 5X or 6X leader is often a necessity. It is customary to tie a short length of nylon, called a tippet, to the leader's end to obtain a finer point, if desired, and also to avoid having the leader become shorter each time a fly is replaced.

This might be a good place to include a table of nylon tippet sizes and their pound test breaking points:

Tippet Size	Pound Test
7X	1.2
6X	2.1
5X	3.3
4X	4.3
3X	5.2
2X	6.3
1X	7.2
0X	9.0

In order to achieve the best balance in a fly-fishing outfit the leader should be tapered so that it becomes an extension of the line.

The butt section should be of only slightly less diameter than the end of the fly line and the rest of the leader should taper gradually to the tip. It is the heavy butt that turns over the lighter strands behind it.

It is possible to cast a well-tapered leader of twelve to twenty feet without difficulty. A well-tapered leader of this type consists of a thirty-pound test butt section tapering through twenty-five and twenty to fifteen, then eight and then the X calibrations. Nylon leader material can be obtained in both stiff and limp forms. In making up long leaders many anglers like to use both types—stiff for the butt half and limp for the terminal half.

Nylon leader material brought with it a need for somewhat different knots from those formerly used with silkworm gut—at least modifications of the earlier knots—for monofilament is cranky. It is by nature wiry and slippery, even in its limp form, and to some extent elastic. Limp nylon is especially so. Also, the tight pull of one strand of nylon against another in certain knots can cause one or the other strand to be cut through or at least weakened. Finally, nylon is harder to hang on to when making loops or twists. However, it can be subdued and formed into tight, well-holding knots when properly handled.

There are three basic knots which the trout fisherman should master. These are: the blood knot, used for tying two strands of monofilament together; the improved clinch knot to tie line or leader to the eye of a hook or lure or to the ring of a swivel; and the monofilament end loop which is useful in making leaders. These are all knots known to earlier generations of anglers who worked with silkworm gut. However, they are now tied with extra turns that enable them to hold when tied with monofilament. Otherwise they will slip or break.

In tying the blood knot, it is necessary to make five or six turns of each end before pulling the ends through the loop. Draw the twists slowly until they come together. Be sure that one end protrudes upward and the other end downward. If both ends face in the same direction the knot will slip. Clip the ends to within one-sixteenth of an inch from the knot.

The clinch knot also requires five or six turns of the end around the line and then the end must be thrust through *two* loops in order to make it hold securely.

The end loop is made by placing the end alongside the main strand to form a four-inch loop. Make five twists of the doubled strands and then insert the single loop through the double loop and pull it tight. This makes a small, neat loop that will slip easily through the guides. A smooth, slow pull is the secret in tying all knots in nylon monofilament.

Balanced Fly-Fishing Outfits

And now, after discussing modern developments in rods, reels, and lines, it might be well to return for a moment to the matter of balanced outfits mentioned earlier.

The first step in matching a fly-fishing outfit is that of obtaining a reel of a weight to balance one's rod. This is especially important in the case of a fly-rod outfit, for here the reel is mounted at the very end of the butt behind the caster's hand. One way to get a good idea of a fly rod and reel's balance is to string up the rod and then balance it across the index finger. The point of balance should be about eight inches from the reel. If the reel is too heavy, balance can sometimes be achieved by removing some of the fly line and replacing it with light backing. If the reel is too light the problem can often be remedied by adding a suitable amount of lead core line to the backing.

This type of balance is not so important in the case of spinning outfits since here the reel is suspended below the rod with the casting hand grasping the reel foot. Also, the reel can be moved forward or backward as required on the long cork grip. The important thing here is to use a small light-weight reel for an ultra-light rod, a medium-weight reel for a medium rod, and so on. Spin-casting reels mounted on top of the rod on a fixed reel seat only require that the angler choose as light a reel as possible to do the job the outfit is designed to do.

Line balance is another important factor to consider. In a fly-fishing outfit it means line weight, for it is the line rather than the lure that is cast. Too light a line will fail to bring out the rod's power and the result will be that the line will billow in waves rather than straightening out on the backcast and forming a tight S on the forward cast.

A too heavy fly line that overpowers the rod can be felt as a weight rather than a pull at the end of the backcast, a weight that threatens to break the tip—and sometimes does. The resulting forward cast is low and sluggish. The only way to choose the correct line is to cast with it, bearing in mind that in most cases accuracy is more important than distance and that casting should be an effortless, rhythmic motion.

Line weight is also important, though in another way, to the spin fisherman. Too heavy a line on a spinning reel is apt to cause trouble during the cast because the overly stiff line tends to spring too rapidly from the spool under the slightest slack. Too fine a line on a larger reel is all too apt to slip under the spool flange, and also a fine line requires a light drag seldom found on any but the smallest reels.

More important in the case of spinning outfits is their balance to the weight of the lures they will cast. Each spinning rod has its range of lure weights, usually designated by the manufacturers. Ultra-light rods, for example, are designed for lures from one-sixteenth to one-quarter of an ounce, medium rods for one-eighth- to one-half-ounce lures, and heavy-duty rods for lures weighing from one-half to three-quarters of an ounce. Lures in these ranges will bring out the action of the rods with which they are recommended to be used. However, since each individual casts differently, only he can determine the weight lure in these ranges which will give him the most distance and accuracy.

Fly Floatants

While not really basic tackle, fly floatants are of importance to dry-fly fishermen and this seems to be a good place to mention them.

The silicone preparations Ray refers to are still in wide use and have been improved; their costs have come down. The invention of aerosol spray cans has added the convenience of a new precision to the application of dry-fly floatants. Flies can now be sprayed without matting the most delicate hackles. There are preparations on the market today which not only cause flies to float but also clean them of slime, dehydrate them, and cause them to float perfectly, trout after trout. These preparations come in liquid, paste, and powder forms in aerosol cans, plastic squeeze bottles, and jars.

Waders

Mention should be made of the present-day plastic waders, which are relatively inexpensive, and the nylon waders, which aren't. Both are lightweight, waterproof, and can be obtained in both boot and stocking-foot styles.

Flies and Lures

Dry flies and nymphs have become so popular in America today that anglers have tended to overlook the wet fly, their respected progenitor. Its long and illustrious history goes back into ancient times, and up until fairly recently when anglers spoke of fly fishing, at least in this country, they meant wet-fly fishing. They did their fishing with a cast of three snelled flies tied to a looped leader, just as their forebears had fished for two centuries and more.

When *Trout* was published in 1938, snelled flies were still popular with some fly fishermen, especially those of middle age or older. Today, however, they have been almost completely superseded by eyed flies without snells, and it would be extremely difficult, if not impossible, to find snelled flies in this country.

The reasons for this are several. For one thing, as Ray Bergman notes, you can carry more eyed flies than snelled flies. For another thing, the silkworm gut used in the snelled flies of the time tended to become brittle with age and was prone to break. Even when new it had to be soaked for an hour or more before use. And, finally, gut snells were subject to the same weak spots as gut leaders as a result of being drawn through diamond dies. Some of the problems of silkworm gut could have been overcome by the use of nylon snells, but by the time it replaced gut, snelled flies had been pretty much discarded by the fishing fraternity. And with the passing of snelled flies, looped leaders also virtually disappeared from the American angling scene.

Wet flies, of course, are fished beneath the surface and are tied today either with wings and hackle or with hackle alone. In either case they are designed to imitate drowned insects. As far back as 1420 Dame Juliana Berners listed twelve wet flies which have their close counterparts in patterns still in use. In former times feathers were the principal material used in the tying of flies, but in recent years wool and fur have become increasingly popular. Hair flies are especially favored in Northwestern trout waters.

To aid a wet fly to sink readily and to give it additional action, modern fly-tiers slant the wings back and slightly upward along the shank. The use of soft hackles and heavy wire hooks also help wet flies to sink.

Wet flies can be divided into two general categories: those which imitate a natural insect, and those which attract by their flashiness or color. Trout strike the former, obviously, because they look like food. Trout probably strike the latter out of annoyance or curiosity, although even these flies have enough of the contour, size, and color of natural insects to make them appear edible. There are also some anglers who believe that these wet flies may imitate tiny darting minnows.

Closely akin to wet flies are nymphs, which someone has described as ultra-wet flies. These wingless and wispy hackled flies are tied to imitate the pupa stage of aquatic insects, one staple of the trout diet. During every month of the year some form of nymphal life is hatching, and, as these small organisms rise to the surface to burst their nymphal cases and complete their life cycle as mature insects, the trout feed greedily upon them. Like wet flies, nymphs are fished beneath the surface and therefore are tied on heavy wire hooks to make them sink readily.

Nymph fishing had its genesis in England. The father of the sport in America was Edward Ringwood Hewitt who brought the British patterns to this country and used them on his native Catskill streams. He learned, however, that patterns successful on English chalk streams were less effective on our larger, faster waters, and, as a result, he began collecting native specimens and experimenting with them. He found that most nymphs common to our waters are brown on top and gray, green, or yellow on the underside. These colors in various combinations and shades have been basic ever since. Adding to the nymphs Ray Bergman discusses and the ones illustrated in Plate 10, in recent years new types, as well as new patterns, of nymphs have been created.

From the angler's point of view, nymphs can be divided roughly into three groups: the May flies, stone flies, and caddis flies.

May flies (Ephemerida) are found in practically all trout streams, not only early in the season but throughout most warm months, despite their name. The artificials include the March Brown, Hare's Ear, Beaver, Coachman, Cahill, and Pale Evening Dun.

Stone flies (Plecoptera) are usually found in fast-flowing streams. Growing to large size, they are apt to attract large trout. Eggs, laid individually, sink to the bottom, and, after hatching, the nymph remains on the bottom for a year, growing legs and wings. When they are ready to emerge, they make their way onto the shore where the adult insect breaks out of the nymphal case and crawls under a rock or log. Its wings dry in a couple of hours and at this time the male finds a female, the two mate, and the female flies away to lay her eggs, thus renewing the cycle. Stone fly nymphs are in the water throughout the season. Productive artificials include Early Black, Early Brown, Little Yellow, Peria, Giant Black, Giant Golden, Damsel, and Dragon.

Caddis flies (Trichoptera) lay their eggs by touching the surface of the water or by crawling down a reed or stick and fastening the eggs to its base. The larva builds a case of sand, pebbles, or twig fibers around its body and creeps about in this protective covering, enlarging the case as it grows. After a year it builds a cocoon wherein it grows legs and wings. Upon emerging, it bites the end from the cocoon and rises to the surface as an imago, or adult insect. At once it flies away to mate. In this fly we have both the larval and pupa forms for trout food. They have been imitated by the Small Dark Pupa, Small Green Pupa, Little Sand Sedge, Speckled Sedge, Dark Gray Larva, White Larva, Yellow Larva, Pale Olive Larva, Olive Sedge, Grannon Pupa, and Giant Brown Sedge.

Considerable expertise has gone into the tying of these and other nymphs since G. E. M. Skues, the English barrister, pioneered this type of lure around the turn of the century. New materials, new studies of living nymphs, and new tying techniques have resulted in making a wide variety of nymphs available to today's anglers.

Still other types of wet flies are the streamers and bucktails that have gained great popularity in recent years. For the benefit of beginning anglers, perhaps it should be explained that streamers are flies tied with feather wings and tails while bucktails are fashioned from bucktail or other hair, such as bear, fox, squirrel, etc. Some flies, like the muddler, combine both feathers and hair. Both streamers and bucktails are tied on long-shanked hooks.

Most streamers today are tied with the wings high on the hook shank, pointing outward so that when the fly is drawn through the water, the wings tend to draw close to the shank. When forward motion is stopped, the wings move outward again. Thus a start and stop retrieve causes the fly to "breathe," giving it a most attractive action. Marabou feathers are especially conducive to this breathing action. Bucktails can also be tied so that they breathe—by placing the wings on top of the shank, causing them to move up and down when the fly is retrieved.

Ray speaks of bucktails with glass or plastic eyes; these seem to have lost favor in recent years, the former perhaps because of their weight and tendency to break and the latter (as Ray points out) because of their lack of transparency.

While on the subject of streamers and wet flies in general, mention should be made of the Shimmer Fly developed by Joe Kvitsky of Westfield, Massachusetts. While not a new creation, it is one that too few anglers use and one that can often put trout in the creel when other flies fail. It is a built-in fly-and-spinner lure; that is, tied in all conventional patterns, the Shimmer Fly has a tiny propeller fastened to the hook shank just behind the eye. Ray does not mention this lure in *Trout* but he knew about it, and this is what he said about it in *Outdoor Life* magazine:

"The Shimmer Fly is a fly-and-spinner lure. In small sizes it casts as easily as a fly with an appreciable degree of air resistance. Large sizes handle as well as bass bugs and are equally effective. I find this type very useful when used as a dropper on a two-fly cast. The spinner-headed fly touches the surface, goes under a trifle, and then flies or jumps into the air. Air as well as water will spin the light propeller which makes a purring sound.

"Thus the two flies together simulate buzzing insects hovering over and dropping into the water. Try it for rainbows in white water and for browns in fast glides. You may get an unexpected thrill. For trout, use sizes 4 through 8. You may not find these lures in all stores, although they should be there for they are among the top performers in the spinner class."

The most popular fly-fishing method today is dry fly, and there have been a number of changes and developments in dry flies in recent years. Among them is the hackleless dry fly pioneered by Doug Swisher and Dr. Carl Richards of Rockford, Michigan. It was their theory, backed up by considerable research, that especially in smaller fly sizes the hackles tend to hide the outline of the body and wings so that the fly loses its natural look. Therefore they began tying flies without hackles, using dubbed bodies to make them float. Dubbing consists of twisting and rolling small scraps of waxed fur and then winding them around the tying thread which attaches them to the hook shank. When light wire hooks are used, dubbed flies are practically unsinkable, requiring no hackle to keep them afloat.

However, these flies will not float upright unless a tuft of fur is tied on top of the hook near the bend and tail fibers are split around the fur tuft, one on each side, to act as stabilizers. For wings on small-sized flies (18 to 28) they used a clump of hackle fibers, but for larger sizes they found paired duck shoulder feathers to be better. Today their efforts have been expanded and commercially tied hackleless flies are available from many tiers. Some of the most popular are Dun-Brown Spinner, Dun-Crea, Dun-Yellow Spinner, Slate-Tan Parachute, Slate-Olive Parachute, Slate-Tan Hackleless, Gray-Olive Hackleless, Dun-Olive Hackleless.

Another new variation of the traditional dry fly is the modern thorax-type fly. Bodies of these flies are dubbed like hackleless flies. They are hackled in conventional fashion except that the hackle is spread wider and then clipped from the underside. This results in a broad base and good flotation yet, as in the hackleless flies, the body remains clearly visible to the fish. Perhaps these flies should be called demihackle, but, in fact, they take their name from the fact that the wings are attached at what would be the thorax location on the natural insects. Forked tails are added to make them float high and to stabilize them and keep them upright, the same as the split fibers on the hackleless flies. They come in common May fly patterns, such as Quill Gordon, Iron Blue, Hendrickson, Green Drake, Cahill, Red Quill, March Brown, etc.

A sort of outgrowth of the Visa Phledge Fly mentioned by Ray

Bergman is the new Keel fly created by Bing McClellan of the Keel Fly Company in Traverse, Michigan. The Keel fly floats with the hook point facing upward and the shank acting as a keel. This certainly does away with Ray's complaints about the unnatural-looking hook being visible to the trout. It also enables these flies to slip through weeds without snagging, an excellent feature in certain types of trout water.

Midge flies in sizes smaller than Ray recommends have come into great popularity in recent years. These flies will take trout in the shrunken, gin-clear streams of midsummer when nothing else will. They can be divided into two groups—the true midge flies, and the even smaller minutiae flies. The former are tied on number 20 or 22 hooks in conventional patterns such as Olive Dun, Blue Dun, Adams, Variant, etc. and are useful when trout are feeding on hatches of tiny flies. The minutiae, usually tied on number 22 to 24 hooks, are for use when trout selectively feed on the minuscule insects which these flies imitate. Actually, they ride *in* the surface film rather than floating above it. Twelve-foot leaders tapering to 6X or 7X are necessary to fish these flies and delicacy is the watchword in striking a trout. They are the best and often the only answer to fishing quiet, late-season waters for wary, educated trout.

Mention should also be made of another variety of flies which have lately come into vogue—the terrestrials. These, as the name implies, imitate land insects—ants, crickets, wood beetles, leafhoppers, grasshoppers, jassids, spiders, beetles, and so on. In the trout diet these insects fill in gaps between hatches and are especially effective in the summer months when they are most abundant and when the earlier May fly and other hatches have slowed. Thousands of these insects are blown or fall into the water and are eagerly taken by feeding trout.

It was Vince Marinaro of Mechanicsburg, Pennsylvania, who first brought the attention of anglers to the possibilities of artificial flies tied to imitate these land-based insects, even though the naturals had been used by fishermen for many years. Vince tied his first fly, the jassid, without body and with a flattened junglecock wing. This resulted in a silhouette-type fly with opaque wings that represented the appearance of many different variations of the Jassidae family. The fly proved immediately successful and has since been copied and altered by other tiers into a variety of forms

imitating a number of terrestrial insects. Among them are the Black
Beetle, Crow Beetle, Letort Cricket, Letort Hopper, Wood Beetle,
Green Leaf Hopper, and Inch Worm. A selection of these terres-
trials belongs in every serious angler's fly box.

One last development that should be mentioned in regard to dry
flies is for making fly bodies. It consists of a sheet of thin, flexible
polypropolene fiber which is excellent for dubbing. It is easy to use,
easy to store, and does not deteriorate. It comes in twelve colors
which can be blended into a limitless variety of shades and can be
mixed with natural fur.

Lures

The sports of spinning and spin-casting have brought in their train
dozens of new light lures and their number continues to grow. In
fact, as in the case of flies, there are so many lures available today
that one would need a trunk to carry them all. Fortunately, for all
practical purposes, a basic supply of various types of lures will
suffice.

The main thing to make sure of is that the weight of the lures
selected fit the rod and line with which they will be used. Too
heavy a line for the weight of the lure will shorten the cast considerably; too light a line for the lure's weight will noticeably affect one's accuracy and may result in a snapped line. So far as the
rod is concerned, as mentioned earlier certain rods are designed
for certain weight lures and it is best to stay within the weight
range specified by the manufacturer.

Spinning lures may be divided into several classifications: spinners, wobblers, plugs, and flies. Each type has its place in the
angler's box.

Spinners, which require only a slow, steady retrieve, are effective
in both streams and ponds. So are wobbling spoons, which can be
fished deep or near the surface, depending on how far they are
allowed to sink. Sometimes a slow, steady retrieve works well; at
other times a fast retrieve or an erratic one will prove more productive. There are myriads of plugs—floaters, sinkers, poppers, and
divers. As for flies, the angler has a choice between weighted ones
—whose built-in weight seems to detract somewhat from their ac-

tion—and regular flies fished with a plastic bubble or buckshot added to give them weight. The latter, to my mind, work better.

Among popular effective spinners are the C. P. Swing, St. Clair Tail-Lite, Mepps, and Birdwing. Some of the newer ones include E. P. Spinn, Special Spin, and Flat Spinner. There are also several wobblers which continue to produce well. Among them are the Goldfish, Wob-L-Rite, Dardevle, Trix-Oreno, and Johnson Silver Spoon (a weedless lure). To these in recent years have been added the Panther, Martin, Wiggle Jig, Little Tiger, Normal Spoon, and Muddler Jig. Plugs that produce well include Tulsa Bee, Tiny Runt, Tiny Torpedo, Midg-Oreno, Flatfish, Eelet, Moosehead Minny, and Quilby Minnow. Also now on the market are Number 9, Floating Flo, Gizmo, and Diver Dart.

Methods

Ray Bergman was a master of all the trout-fishing techniques known during his long and distinguished career and he describes them thoroughly in this book. However, certain innovations in angling practices have been brought about by changed conditions and new developments in tackle. It is these innovations that will be discussed in this section.

Wet-Fly Fishing

Wet-fly fishing was the original type of fly fishing practiced in America, and it was conducted under prescribed traditions inherited from the Old World where its beginnings trace back to antiquity. Among them was the tenet that one fished wet flies downstream. But today's anglers have found that at times it is advantageous to fish them upstream; for instance, when one is fishing fast-flowing riffles. Standing downstream, the angler can pick out likely looking lies and cast to them for a quick drift with better success than would be possible trying to cover these spots with a downstream drift. It is also easier to approach wary trout this way, from their rear.

It is really no more difficult than fishing a dry fly upstream. It requires, however, a short line and a fast retrieve. The idea is to drop the fly on target and then strip line fast enough to match the speed of the current. Otherwise the line will belly toward the angler and sweep the fly downstream before a feeding trout can catch a glimpse of it. The short line is also necessary so that if a trout rises to the fly, the angler's strike will be instantly relayed to the hook. If it isn't, the fish will eject the fly before the slack line is taken in sufficiently to implant the barb.

This is also a good way to fish big pools where the current runs along the opposite bank. In upstream wet-fly fishing, however, there is little chance to see the rise as in dry-fly fishing, and little chance to feel a solid tug as in downstream wet-fly fishing. Therefore, it is imperative to stay alert and to strike instantly at any pause or sudden forward motion of the line.

The "line retrieve" that Ray describes in detail in his wet-fly chapter is today called the "strip retrieve" and has been slightly altered. The line is held between the right thumb and forefinger at the reel while the left hand pulls line between the thumb and forefinger. At each pull, the right thumb and forefinger hold the line tight while the left hand reaches up for the next pull. This can be used for slow as well as fast retrieves since it gives continuous control of the line.

The wet fly, it has been learned, can be fished in such a manner as to imitate not only a drowned insect, but also as a nymph and, in some cases, a tiny shiner. The methods of fishing it depend on what one is attempting to simulate.

The traditional "natural" downstream drift imitating a drowned insect is still the basic method of fishing wet flies, especially on small streams. A new technique is to let the fly drift with the current for a few feet and then give it a couple of hard jerks to make it bounce back upstream before allowing it to drift freely again. This motion is repeated to the end of the drift when the fly is again caused to dart upstream in a series of twitches before being lifted for another cast. Sometimes these emphatic jerks catch the eye of a trout and goad it into taking the fly.

Another productive method is to impart as much varied action as possible to the fly during its drift and subsequent retrieve. Short jerks, followed by pauses, long jerks and a series of twitches all help to call attention to the sunken fly and add to its attraction at times when the trout seem not to be interested in drifting drowned insects.

Certain wet flies, when retrieved in short jerks, probably give the appearance of bite-size shiners darting in the current. Others, when activated, look like spiders or other insects that have fallen into the water and are struggling to escape. Sometimes if the fly is raised to the surface and held there to flutter in the current for a time, a trout will surge up to smash it.

Still other flies, especially wingless ones, may very well appear to the trout to be nymphs. Such flies can be very productive when trout are bulging or tailing. Actually, at such times a nymph is the proper answer, but in the midst of a frenzied hatch when there is no time to change flies, a wet fly of this type fished with a leader greased to within two or three inches of the fly makes a good substitute.

Often large trout, especially rainbows, live in pocket water in a stretch of foaming rapids. These places have to be fished more or less by feel rather than by sight except where boulders break the surface to reveal likely trout-holding water. For the rest of these stretches you have to hope your fly will find the trouty hotspots. One good way to accomplish this is to cast wet flies directly across the current and then to raise your rod as soon as the fly or flies have touched the water. Hold the rod tip high while you bring the fly skittering across the surface as fast as you can retrieve. When trout hit under these conditions, they do so with a jolt, and in this kind of white water fishing, a leader of at least six-pound test is a necessity.

The wet fly is a very versatile lure and present-day anglers are learning to exploit its potentials to the fullest. Formerly, a cast of three flies was commonly employed in wet-fly fishing, but today many anglers use only one or at most two. They prefer the accuracy and delicacy of casting a single fly and the challenge of making that fly the right one. When two flies are used today, it is customary to have the dropper fly a size or two larger than the tail fly, partly for better visibility of the dropper and partly to give the trout a choice of two sizes of morsels. Seven and a half to nine feet is the usual leader length, with tail fly and dropper separated by a distance of about two feet to avoid tangling. The dropper strand should be about ten inches in length. It is fastened to the leader by a barrel knot.

Nymphs

Nymph fishing, a newer form of wet-fly fishing in this country, has undergone as one might expect some new developments in recent years. Not only are there a number of new patterns and types of nymphs, but also there are new or altered ways of fishing them.

It is more difficult to fish a nymph correctly than it is to fish either a conventional wet or a dry fly, but often this is the only lure selectively feeding trout will take. The ideal time to fish nymphs, of course, is when trout are either bulging (i.e., taking nymphs just below the surface) or tailing for somewhat deeper nymphs that are rising to the surface. When they are feeding thus on nymphs, trout will often completely ignore the hatching adult flies leaving the water.

When trout are bulging it is best to fish a nymph as one would a dry fly, that is, upstream on a floating line. The leader should be greased to within a couple of inches of the nymph so that while the line and most of the leader float, the nymph itself will swim just below the surface, the point at which the bulging trout are feeding. Sometimes you will see a bulge near your leader's end as the trout takes your nymph. More often you will see the line pause or shoot forward. In either case you must strike instantly. This, incidentally, is a modern refinement of Ray Bergman's "upstream drift."

When trout are taking nymphs somewhat deeper, often their tails will break the surface. And sometimes, especially in slow-moving shallow water, you can see their sides flash as they nose down and turn to grab a nymph near the bottom. At such times you will have to go deeper. You can still use a floating line, but with an un-greased leader. You will need plenty of slack to get the nymph down to the proper depth, so an upstream cast is advisable.

At still other times, the trout feed on nymphs in deep water and to reach them then you must turn to a sinking line or one of the newer wet-tip or wet-head lines. This fishing calls for a shorter leader—about six or seven-and-a-half feet instead of the nine- to twelve-foot leaders used for fishing with a floating line. If a long leader is used in deep nymph fishing, the current is all too apt to lift it above the trout's feeding level. Ray Bergman mentions adding a shot or two to the leader to sink the nymph. Today most anglers prefer to use nymphs with weighted bodies, thus doing away with the frustration of casting a fly and sinker combination.

In any event, the nymph should be fished on a slack line so that it bumps along the bottom. This is the most difficult of all nymph fishing since it is impossible either to see or feel the strike. Again, the only indication of a taking fish is the action of the line either stopping or shooting forward. In either case, you must strike instantly and firmly enough to take up the slack bellying down the current.

In the still waters of deep pools it is best to give the nymph action by jerking it a foot or two with pauses in between. Often this will attract the attention of a trout that otherwise might not have seen the lure lying on the bottom.

Another method, somewhat similar, is to let the nymph sink to the bottom and as it nears the end of its drift, instead of jerking it, retrieve it by slowly drawing it a foot or two toward you and then letting it sink again. This undulating motion which resembles a nymph rising to the surface and sinking back to creep along the bottom often proves irresistible to the trout.

Streamers and Bucktails

The conventional method of fishing streamers and bucktails is to cast them diagonally upstream and let them sink as they drift down with the current. The strike may come at any time during the downstream drift, but perhaps most frequently as the fly sweeps in an arc across the current at the end of the drift. If no strike is forthcoming, the fly is left to flutter in the current for a moment and is then retrieved in short jerks with pauses in between.

A refinement of this natural drift method described by Ray Bergman is the broadside presentation of the fly invented by A. H. E. Wood to use in fishing his native British salmon rivers. In this technique the line is greased and the cast made across and only slightly upstream. As the fly drifts down the current the rod tip is pointed slightly ahead of it. If a belly appears in the line it is mended upstream by a sort of half-roll cast. By this means, instead of being dragged down-current by the bellying line, the fly drifts naturally and broadside to the current. This is the way trout prefer to take a shiner.

Anglers experimenting with new tackle have come up with other productive ways to fish these versatile flies which imitate all sorts of trouty foods from minnows to crawfish to grasshoppers. Incidentally, the natural drift has been found to work better with bucktails than with streamers. This is because bucktails, by their nature, resemble grasshoppers, crawfish, or large nymphs such as the stone fly nymph, and hence look natural as they drift along the current.

Streamers, on the other hand, more resemble minnows and when they drift motionless look less like natural minnows because their feathers tend to droop in a sort of matted mass. To look natural they must be made to "breathe" by imparting jerky action which will cause the feathers to open and close against the hook shank.

However they are fished, it is important in using streamers and bucktails to cover all the water thoroughly. Too many anglers content themselves with drifting their flies through the middle of pools, completely ignoring the bankside runs and pockets which are equally as productive and often more so. This is especially true in evening fishing since trout tend to move into the shallows toward dusk.

The first cast should be a short one of fifteen to twenty feet diagonally upstream, and it should be fished until the fly has drifted to a point directly downstream from the angler. And, as mentioned earlier, fishermen today have found that their success is often improved by giving twitches to a streamer as it drifts downstream. It should be retrieved in short jerks until it is within ten feet before lifting it for another cast. Line should be lengthened about a foot on each subsequent cast until a range of fifty or sixty feet is attained. Then move downstream fifteen feet or so and begin again. As a general rule of thumb, the faster the current the less need to twitch the streamer on the drift, for the action of the water causes the fly to flutter and dart like a minnow. However, even under these conditions a quick jerk now and then will cause the fly to look like an injured minnow and, hence, a likely meal.

While bucktails and streamers are usually fished at least a few inches under water, there are times when certain types will produce when used as surface lures. This, in effect, is what Ray Bergman did when he "slapped the fly over them, bringing it back so fast that it skipped over the water." Sometimes a good trick when trout are surface feeding but won't take your dry flies is to grease the underside of a muddler minnow or similar bushy bucktail and retrieve it in fast jerks that cause it to dart across the surface.

The size of a streamer or bucktail can be very important. In general, the larger the water and the trout that dwell therein, the larger the fly should be. This is only common sense, since large trout, especially browns and rainbows, prefer their food in sizable chunks. It is on the converse side that many anglers make the mistake of using too large a fly on small streams inhabited by small trout. A large streamer drifting through a run holding small trout is more apt to frighten them than to attract them. A trout that can see a number 22 midge in fast water will have no trouble spotting a number 10 streamer.

Small streamers and bucktails demand light tippets. Not only can trout see heavy tippets, but, also, the stiffer nylon in such tippets detracts from the natural drift and action of the fly. For small trout in small streams 4X or 5X tippets are ideal.

Large streamers and bucktails, however, call for 3X or 2X tippets to prevent them from snapping off on the cast and also to prevent breakage of the tippet when playing a heavy fish. Even a 1X tippet may be required on waters that hold king-size trout.

One important point to keep in mind when fishing streamers and bucktails is to hold your rod at a 45-degree angle when retrieving the fly. If you do so, the rod tip will do its job of absorbing the shock of the strike and will help to plant the barb solidly in the trout's jaw. If the rod tip is held low and pointing at the fish, the combined jolt of the strike plus the pressure of setting the hook will pop all but the strongest tippets.

Dry Flies

Changes in dry-fly construction as well as changes in trout waters and today's hard-pressured trout have brought new refinements to the craft of fishing with a dry fly, even though the basic methods still remain. For one thing, just as anglers today have learned that there are times to fish wet flies upstream, so they have found there are occasions when it is advantageous to fish dry flies downstream. One of these times, for example, is when you have fished a pool and have moved on upstream. Suddenly, behind you you hear the slurp of a feeding fish and, turning, you see the spreading rings of its rise beside the bank. In order to fish for that trout in the conventional upstream manner you would have to wade ashore very cautiously so as not to disturb the fish, take a long detour well back from the bank and then enter the stream and maneuver yourself into position. This would take time and energy and might well result in putting the fish down despite your precautions.

There is, however, a technique with which you can reach the trout from your present position. A downstream cast with an S curve which drops the fly about three feet upstream of the rising fish should float the fly over it without drag. If the fish takes on a downstream float you should hesitate a couple of seconds before striking rather than setting the hook instantly as on an upstream cast. This is because the trout is coming toward you with its mouth open to grab the fly. If you strike at the rise you will pull the fly out of its mouth. If you hesitate before setting the hook, the trout will turn downward, holding the fly in its jaws, at which time a strike will set the hook.

It is also well to remember that when a trout sees a fly floating toward it, it leaves its lie to inspect the fly, sometimes drifting several feet downstream before taking it. Also, the ring of its rise is drifting down the current. Therefore, the fly should light several feet above the rise. Otherwise, it may drop below the fish or on top of it.

Still another situation in which fishing a dry fly downstream is more productive than upstream fishing is in skating spiders, a new refinement of an older form of fishing originally conceived by Edward Hewitt in the mid-1930's. He used number 10 spiders and cast them upstream but anglers today tend toward smaller number 12 and 14 flies. Skating spiders consists of casting these long-hackled, bodyless, tailless flies and then retrieving them in a series of skips and jerks across the surface over a trout's lie. The modern way to fish them is to cast straight across stream and skate them through likely water. Start at the head of a pool and work downstream into the tail which is the most likely hotspot. Both line and leader should be greased for this kind of fishing.

In his chapter Dry-Fly Fundamentals and Tackle, Ray describes the conventional method of making an S or serpentine cast by checking the normal forward cast just before its completion and then immediately following through again. Another method is to make the usual forward cast and then as the fly nears its target spot to impart a side-to-side motion to the rod, putting a series of curves in the line as it drops to the water. Care must be taken to keep the curves reasonably small, for otherwise it is hard to control the line and also the curves themselves add to the dangers of drag. All you need is a two- or three-foot float over a feeding trout. This slack line cast is probably the most important one, aside from the basic forward cast, for the aspiring dry-fly angler to master.

Under most circumstances an S cast will take care of your downstream dry-fly fishing. There are times, however, when a fish is rising close to the bank across and somewhat below you. At such times you can achieve a dragless downstream float by casting a right or left loop. The right loop is made by stopping the forward cast just before the tip imparts its final thrust. The result is a rather sloppy cast in which the line goes out without speed in a lazy curve to the right. This drops the fly ahead of the tippet and lets it float over the fish on a slack line. Modern dry-fly rods enable the angler to accomplish a left loop cast without too much trouble by using a simple technique. The rod is held to the side at a 45-degree angle, pointed to the right of the proposed target. The cast is snapped forward with more power than would normally be used for a similar distance and then at the end of the cast the fly is stopped abruptly by a quick backward movement of the rod. This causes the leader to curl around to the left with sufficient slack to permit a float of several feet.

There are situations where the only way you can put a dry fly over a trout is by fishing downstream. This happens frequently on fast broken water where drag would set in on an upstream cast before the fly had hardly touched the water. A dry-fly cast downstream with an S or a loop cast will often give you the necessary slack to float it across a pocket before the current whisks it away. A slightly heavier tippet is advisable and, in fact, almost mandatory in this kind of fast-water fishing. Fortunately, trout don't see the leader as well under these circumstances and also must make up their minds quickly if they are to grab the fly before it disappears from their vision.

Ray makes a point of the invisibility of tiny flies in swifter waters and if he were fishing under the same conditions today he would in all probability be using even tinier flies—the true midges and minutiae tied on number 20 to 24 hooks. Few anglers have keen enough eyesight to follow a number 24 Black Ant as it floats down the current. Most of us must depend on seeing the rise and hoping to set the hook without breaking the 5X or 6X tippet. This is why, when possible, it's best to use a fly with a touch of white (like the Coachman), red, yellow, or some other vivid color that can better be seen during the float. Unfortunately, the trout do not always show a like taste for colored flies.

In this type of fishing it helps to watch your floating line and to project your gaze to a point some twelve to twenty feet beyond its end—depending on the length of your leader. This will give you some idea where your fly is and enable you to strike quickly at the least glimpse of a commotion in that area. Also, in retrieving the fly, never pull it from the water at a distance, for the line and leader may be over the trout's lie. Instead, bring the fly in slowly and quietly until it is within ten or twelve feet before lifting it for another cast.

Even in Ray Bergman's day, taking sizable brown trout out of hard-fished waters on dry flies had become a formidable task. It is even more difficult today. For one thing, there aren't as many trophy brown trout in our streams as there were two or three decades ago. For that matter, there aren't as many top brown trout streams as there were then, either. For another thing, there are at least ten times as many anglers competing for these fish as there used to be. Despite these changed conditions, there are present-day anglers who consistently take big brown trout, a number of them on dry flies.

It is true that much of the diet of old cannibal brownies consists of other fish and small creatures unfortunate enough to fall into the water near their lies. But it is also true that at times even these wary old lunkers appear to relish a diet of insects. At such times, knowledgeable dry-fly fishermen can take them.

The first prerequisite for success is the use of extreme caution in approaching the fishing spots. Trout don't grow to king-size proportions without becoming very wary of any sight or sound that could spell danger. In getting into casting position it is imperative to step carefully, to keep low and, when possible, to keep the sun at one's back. Smaller trout, fleeing at the angler's approach, can effectively spook large fish and send them into hiding. Therefore, it is best to cast from the bank whenever this is feasible. When it is not, great care should be taken to wade as quietly as possible and then it is wise to stand motionless for five or ten minutes before making a cast.

Large trout seldom rise to small flies. This is, of course, only a generality, for occasionally in clear, low waters sizable fish will take midge flies. But for all practical purposes, the angler fishing for trophy browns should use flies in number 8 to 10 sizes—the Wulff flies, large millers, golden spinners, golden variants, and white caddis flies. Dusk is the most favorable time to fish, for browns are nocturnal feeders and on fair days only leave their resting places with the setting sun. Sometimes on dark or rainy days they will feed on and off during the daylight hours.

Ray Bergman discusses at some length the importance of caution in approaching and fishing pools and runs where trout may be expected to lie. Such caution is even more essential in angling for today's educated trout and especially when using dry flies. This is so because of the very nature of dry-fly fishing with its specialized techniques. Many anglers blame their lack of success on "fished out" streams when actually the fault lies with themselves. A clumsy approach and slipshod casting is guaranteed to put down the most eagerly rising trout.

The necessity of quiet, deliberate wading has already been mentioned and also the advantages of casting from the bank when possible, and keeping the sun at one's back. But this is only an initial step toward success. Before making the first cast, it is important to look over the water to be fished, to decide where you want to place your fly and how best to accomplish this design. Standing or kneeling motionless while you mull these matters over in your mind is itself helpful in quieting the uneasiness of any trout that may have been alerted to danger by your approach.

Having made up your mind what you want to do and how you want to do it, it is important to make your first cast good, especially when the cast is made to a rising trout. A poor first cast may even put the trout down, but, if not, it will certainly cause it to become suspicious and less inclined to take the fly. In fact, each time you make a sloppy cast and have to retrieve it, your chances of success decrease. But no matter how poor the cast, the fly should be allowed to float several feet beyond the target area before it is lifted. Otherwise the trout will see and hear the line, leader, and fly being ripped from the water and the chances of its rising again will be slim. It is best under these circumstances, after the fly has floated beyond the target spot, to strip in line until the fly is within twelve feet and then it can be lifted without disturbing your fish.

Every dry-fly angler recalls those occasional enchanting evenings when the rings of several rising trout spread across a favorite pool. At such times the temptation is great to cast blindly into the pool and let chance decide which trout will take the fly. But just as shooting blindly into a covey of quail seldom grasses a bird, so in this kind of casting chance usually decrees that no trout will take the fly.

Instead, it is essential to pick an individual trout and cast to it as though this were the only trout in the pool. The one to choose is the nearest one, even though a larger fish is rising just upstream. The larger trout will wait but if you cast to it first, the nearer fish will be put down. When the nearest trout is hooked, you should try to keep it from running upstream if possible. Often if you can get its head out of water you can skid a trout close enough to net or beach it. If not, keep the rod tip high and pull slowly, exerting as much pressure as you can to turn the fish downstream. And if the first fish does put the others down, all is not lost, for usually if the pool is rested for a while they will start rising again.

When a hatch is taking place trout seem to display a definite rhythm in their feeding instead of rising at random. This is doubtless because of the way they customarily take a fly. Underwater photography, which has been perfected to a high degree in recent years, has made it possible to observe trout feeding activities and has shed new light on their behavior. As a fly floats into view in a trout's conical window (the wedge-shaped field of vision from eye to surface), the fish rises slowly under it and drifts backward downstream with the current, almost touching the fly with its nose. Having determined that it is edible, the fish sucks in the fly —causing the dimpling rise—and swims back to his former position.

This all takes time and sets up a sort of rhythm which can be pretty well measured by the angler. Therefore, if you see a trout rise two or three times, you can tell with considerable accuracy when he will be ready to rise again. A fly cast too soon will drift over the fish before it is prepared to take and may even put it down. This is why, too, as mentioned earlier, the cast should be made a few feet upstream of the spot where the rise took place.

Spinning

During the later years of Ray Bergman's career, spinning had become an accepted and popular angling method. Ray was quick to appreciate the potential of this new craft and to take advantage of its possibilities. In the revised second edition of *Trout* published in 1952 he added two chapters on the subject. However, in the years since his death, spinning, more than any other form of angling, has seen numerous changes brought about by new tackle and new techniques. Ray would undoubtedly have helped in the development of this new tackle and would have mastered and, indeed, pioneered in these new techniques. Since this was not to be, let us here suggest some of the new ideas in tackle and methods that the past decade has brought.

First, though, let us look at some of the basic fundamentals of spinning upon which these recent developments have been built. The fact that in spinning the line is released from a fixed rather than a revolving spool at once changes the concept of modern angling. It gives the angler a versatile new tool, easy to use and offering several advantages over older methods, among them the virtual elimination of backlashes and the problem of backcasts. It makes possible, too, the accurate casting of lures too heavy for fly rods and too light for bait-casting rods, lures which often appeal to trout when nothing else does. Finally, it makes it possible for fishermen to place these lures accurately at greater distances and into spots that they could not reach by any other means. Small wonder that this new angling method was greeted with enthusiasm by American anglers.

In another section we have discussed the subject of spinning tackle. Now let's see how this tackle is put to use on today's trout waters.

The first thing to learn about its use, obviously, is how to cast properly. One of the chief advantages of spinning is that it is a skill rather easily mastered. It takes considerable practice and experience to become an accomplished fly caster, but a few hours with a spinning outfit is sufficient to enable the novice to become at least proficient enough to catch fish consistently. Of great importance in spin fishing is the use of the forefinger in casting. Whether one is using a manual pick-up or full bail, one should learn to run the line over one's forefinger slightly crooked to hold the line in place. Then at the completion of the cast, extending the forefinger allows the line to slip off freely as the lure flies toward its target.

As in the case of fly-casting, there are several different deliveries available to the spin fisherman. Unlike fly-casting, however, one permissible cast in spin fishing is the side cast and, indeed, sometimes it is the best possible cast. This type of throw permits long casts when needed with the lure traveling in a comparatively low trajectory, thus preventing excess bellying of the line. To execute it, the lure should be reeled to within six inches of the rod tip. The cast is made almost entirely with the wrist, aided somewhat by the forearm with the upper arm remaining close to the body and motionless. Facing the target, point the rod toward and slightly above it. With the bail open and the forefinger holding the line, snap the rod downward to the right, causing it to flex. When it is fully flexed, snap it forward and upward, releasing the line at the precise instant that the rod is pointing at the target. Too early a release will cause the lure to fly to the right, too late a release will send it to the left. In most fishing situations accuracy is more important than distance.

The overhead cast is also a useful one, especially where obstructions prevent the use of a side cast. Its chief disadvantage lies in the fact that it results in a high trajectory with consequent slack through bellying of the line. This can be frustrating on windy days. To make this cast the rod is lifted sharply to the twelve o'clock position, powering the rod by flexing it, and then, while it is still flexed, the rod is snapped forward and the lure released when the rod tip is pointing toward and slightly above the target. With heavier rods, some forearm action should go into the overhead cast; light rods require only a snap of the wrist.

The backhand cast, made across the body from the left instead of the right as in the side cast, is often useful, too. Hold the rod pointing downward to the left and then with the wrist flip it back and then quickly forward and upward in the direction of the target.

For short, accurate drops into pocket water or between obstructions the flip cast is invaluable. In this cast, about a foot of line should be left between the rod tip and the lure which acts as a sort of pendulum. Point the rod toward and below the target. Flip it slightly upward and then immediately down again to flex it. While it is thus bent, bring it quickly up again and release the line toward and above the target.

With these casts mastered, the angler is prepared to meet any situation likely to arise in his fishing.

The original method of fishing spinning lures was to cast them across and slightly upstream, allowing them to drift through a pool or run and then to retrieve them by reeling them in against the current. This is still a very effective method, but experimentation soon proved the efficacy of upstream fishing with spinning lures, a practice adopted by many spin fishermen today. Upstream fishing, especially in fast water, enables one to sink the lure deep where larger fish often lie. The best lures for this kind of fishing are light ones which require no extra weight above them—lures such as wobbling spoons.

The trick is to cast directly upstream and then, by reeling, to keep the lure moving at a speed slightly faster than the current. This causes the lure to swim just off the bottom without snagging. If the lure is fished properly, it can be felt bumping bottom now and again. Of course, snagging can't always be prevented but lures are expendable when good-sized trout are the reward for deep fishing.

Somewhat akin to this type of fishing is the method known as "scooting" which spin fishermen have developed in recent years. This has proven to be a very effective trout-fishing method both in streams and ponds. The lure used in scooting is a small lead jig, either bullet-shaped, round, or oval, sparsely trimmed with bucktail. It is fished by bouncing it along the bottom of pools or rocky shoals. It can be retrieved in various ways to simulate a variety of trouty foods. A brown jig, for example, can be handled to imitate a nymph moving jerkily across the bottom, a silvery jig can be maneuvered to look like an injured minnow, and a black jig can be fished in such a way as to resemble a crawfish or a mollusk seeking escape. In general, the way to fish jigs is to cast them straight upstream and let them sink to the bottom. Then retrieve them in short hops of an inch or so with pauses in between. However, there are other refinements that can be added to this basic method to meet various circumstances.

Any fisherman is sure to lose a number of these lures to snags but they are inexpensive and many anglers make their own. All that is required is a set of jig molds, hooks, silk thread, bucktail, lead, and a small pot and burner. Hooks should be fastened so that they ride with the point up to help avoid snagging.

When spinning first became popular it was customarily carried on in larger streams and rivers where it enabled spin fishermen to reach spots inaccessible to fly-rod anglers. But today more and more fishermen are finding spinning tackle highly effective for fishing small brooks which, incidentally, are gaining new popularity as the last strongholds of wild native trout, some of surprisingly large size. This sort of fishing requires some of the new light or ultra-light tackle for best results, such as a five- or six-foot rod weighing from two-and-a-quarter to three-and-a-quarter ounces and using two- to three-pound test monofilament. Lures run from one-sixteenth to one-quarter of an ounce in the form of tiny spinners or wobblers. These small lures will drift in shallow currents and can be guided beneath undercut banks and through debris-covered eddies with ease.

Ray Bergman mentions but does not discuss the possibilities of fishing wet flies, nymphs, and dry flies with spinning tackle by means of a bubble float. This has become an increasingly popular facet of spin fishing in recent years. The bubble is a plastic ball much like the float or bobber familiar to everyone. The spinning bubble, however, has a cap which can be removed to pour water into the bubble in order to sink it to any desired depth.

In wet-fly fishing, for example, the bubble can be partially or completely filled with water to make it drift as deep as conditions warrant. It is rigged by fastening it to the end of a four-foot leader and then tying a one-foot dropper to the leader about six inches above it. Or you can add two droppers, if you like, about two feet apart. The bubble will drift down the current, taking the flies with it in a very natural manner. Even when completely filled, the bubble will not snag bottom but will continue to float just above it.

For nymph fishing the bubble can be rigged to drift near the surface with the nymph an inch or two below, or it can be partially filled with water for deep nymph fishing.

In dry-fly fishing a short dropper is fastened to the leader three or four feet behind the empty bubble. The bubble is cast across stream and allowed to float with the current. The rod should be held high to keep the fly at the surface and line can be paid out by leaving the reel bail or pick-up finger open and regulating the flow of line by pressure of the forefinger against the spool. The same problems of drag apply to dry-fly fishing with a bubble as they do to conventional dry-fly fishing, but the bubble often helps to prevent drag by its buoyancy and natural drift along the current.

For really deep fishing the versatile bubble can be rigged through one eye only, instead of the usual two. Then when the lure is cast, the bubble will be close to the hook but when it lights on the water the lure will sink while the bubble slides up the leader until stopped by a swivel tied between leader and line.

FULL DESCRIPTIONS OF

FLIES SHOWN IN COLOR PLATES

PLATE 1
WET FLIES

Fly	Body	Ribbing	Tip	Tail	Hackle	Wing
ABBEY	Dark Red Floss	Gold Tinsel	Gold Tinsel	Golden Pheasant Tippet	Red (Light Brown)	Gray Mallard
ACADEMY	Peacock Herl		Red Floss	Crimson	Brown	Claret
ADDER	Brown Floss	Orange Floss	Orange Floss		Brown	Brown Turkey
ADIRONDACK	Gray Fur		Yellow Floss	Black Hackle Tips	Orange	White
ADMIRAL	Dark Red Floss	Gold Tinsel	Gold Tinsel	Scarlet	Scarlet	White
ALDER	Peacock Herl				Black or Brown	Brown Turkey
ALEXANDRA	Silver Tinsel Flat	Round Silver Tinsel Optional	Dark Red Floss Optional	Peacock Sword and/or Scarlet	Deep Wine, Dark Claret or Black	Peacock Sword May have dash of scarlet on ea. side.
ALLERTON	Yellow Floss	Gold Tinsel	Gold Tinsel	Teal or Barred Wood Duck	Dark Blue Tied Palmer	Scarlet
APPLE GREEN	Highlander Green Floss	Yellow Silk		Brown	Brown	Slate
ARTHUR HOYT	Bright Green Floss	Yellow Silk	Yellow Silk	Dark Brown	Dark Brown	Brown Turkey
ARTFUL DODGER	Dark Claret Floss	Gold Tinsel	Gold Tinsel		Light Claret	Pheasant
BABCOCK	Crimson Floss	Gold Tinsel	Gold Tinsel	Black and Yellow	Black	Black Stripe over Yellow
BARRINGTON	Peacock Herl	Gold Tinsel	Gold Tinsel		Brown	Gray Mallard
BALDWIN	White Floss			Teal	Claret	Teal or Mallard
BEAUTY	Dark Gray Floss	Silver Tinsel	Silver Tinsel	Guinea Fowl	Black	Guinea Fowl
BEAMER	Dark Blue Dubbing	Silver Tinsel	Silver Tinsel	Crimson and Dark Blue	Mixed Crimson and Dark Blue	Brown Mallard
BEE	Alternate Yellow & Black Chenille				Dark Brown	Dark Slate
BEAMIS STREAM	Dark Claret Dubbing	Gold Tinsel	Gold Tinsel	Mixed Gray Mallard & Brown	Brown Tied Palmer	Brown
BEATRICE	Yellow Floss		Green Floss	Scarlet	Yel'w and Crimson Mixed-Tied Palmer	Barred Mandarin
BEEMAN	Light Green Chenille				Brown	Gray Turkey

PLATE 1 (Continued)

Fly	Body	Ribbing	Tip	Tail	Hackle	Wing
BELGRADE	Yellow Wool or Dubbing	Gold Tinsel	Black Chenille	Crimson and White	Claret Tied Palmer	White Red Stripe Jungle Eye
BIG MEADOW	Peacock Herl		Gold Tinsel	Crimson	Brown	Gray Mallard
BISHOP	White Floss				Brown	Dark Red or Claret
BISSET	Peacock Herl		Yellow Silk		Guinea Fowl	Dark Slate
BLACK DOSE	Black Silk Floss	Silver Tinsel	Yellow Floss and Silver Tinsel	Golden Pheasant Crest	Black	Brown Turkey Brown Mallard Guinea Stripe
BLACK GNAT	Black Chenille				Black	Dark Slate
BLACK GNAT SILVER	Silver Tinsel				Black	Dark Slate
BLACK PALMER RED TAG	Peacock Herl		Scarlet Tag— Wool		Black Tied Palmer	
BLACK JUNE	Peacock Herl	Silver Tinsel	Silver Tinsel		Black	Black
BLACK MOOSE	Black Silk Floss		Silver Tinsel	Green		Guinea & Purple
BLACK PRINCE	Black Silk Floss	Gold Tinsel	Gold Tinsel	Crimson	Black	Black
BLACK QUILL	Black or Dark Gray Quill			Black Hackle Fibres	Black	Very Dark Slate
BLOCK HOUSE	Yellow Silk Floss	Gold Tinsel	Gold Tinsel		Scarlet	Scarlet
BLUE BLOW	Blue Silk Floss		Gold Tinsel		Black Tied Palmer	Slate
BLUE BOTTLE	Blue Silk Floss	Silver Tinsel Optional		Black Hackle Fibres	Black	Slate
BLUE DUN	Blue-Gray Fur Dubbing			Blue Gray Hackle Fibres	Blue Gray	Blue Gray
BLUE JAY	Orange Floss Silk	Gold Tinsel	Gold Tinsel	Gldn Ph. Tippet	Orange	Blue Jay
BLUE PROFESSOR	Blue Silk Floss	Gold Tinsel		Crimson	Brown	Gray Mallard
BLUE QUILL	Blue Gray Quill			Blue Gray	Blue Gray	Light Slate
BOB LAWRENCE	Cinnamon Dubbing	Silver Tinsel	Silver Tinsel	Scarlet	Guinea Fowl	Scarlet Jungle Cock Eye
BOG POND	Black Chenille			Golden Pheasant Tippet	Grizzly	Brown Pheasant
BOSTWICK	Silver Tinsel			Barred Mandarin	Mixed Brown & Griz. Tied Palmer	

PLATE 2
WET FLIES

Fly	Body	Ribbing	Tip	Tail	Hackle	Wing
BOUNCER	Black Floss	Gold Tinsel	Orange Tag		Orange	Yellow
BONNIE VIEW	Brown Wool	Gold Tinsel	Gold Tinsel		Brown	Gray
BOOTS BLACK	Maroon Wool or Fur	Gold Tinsel	Gold Tinsel	Gray Mallard	Black	Very Dark Slate
BOTTLE IMP	Blue Gray Wool or Fur			Black	Black	
BRANDRETH	Yellow Wool	Gold Tinsel	Gold Tinsel	Scarlet	Scarlet and Yellow	Gray Mallard
BRIGHT FOX	Yellow Floss			Brown Hackle	Brown	White
BROWN HEN	Peacock Herl		Gold Tinsel		Brown	Brown Turkey
BROWN MALLARD	Brown Wool	Gold Tinsel	Gold Tinsel	Brown Mallard	Brown	Brown Mallard
BROWN SEDGE	Dun Fur				Brown Tied Palmer	Light Slate
BROWN TURKEY	Brown Floss			Brown Hackle	Brown Tied Palmer	Brown Turkey
BRUNTON'S FANCY	Peacock Herl			Scarlet	Badger Tied Palmer	
BUNTING	Black Floss		Silver Tinsel		Black	White
BUTCHER	Scarlet Floss	Yellow Silk		Scarlet	Badger	
CAHILL	Blue Gray Fur Dubbing		Gold Tinsel if desired	Mandarin or Dyed Mallard on low price flies.	Brown	Mandarin or Dyed Mallard on low price flies.
CALDER	Orange Floss	Gold Tinsel	Peacock Herl Tag	Barred Mandarin	Brown	Peacock Sword over Light Brown Turkey
CALDWELL	Brown Floss	Yellow Silk		Brown Mallard	Brown	Light Brown Turkey
CANADA	Red Floss	Gold Tinsel	Scarlet Tag		Red	Gray Turkey or any mottled Black & White
CAPTAIN	White Floss		Peacock Tag	Scarlet and Yellow	Brown	Slate

[472]

PLATE 2 (Continued)

Fly	Body	Ribbing	Tip	Tail	Hackle	Wing
CAPERER	Red Brown Wool				Scarlet	Copper Pheasant
CARDINAL	White Chenille				White	Cardinal
CARTER HARRISON	Black Seal Fur	Gold Tinsel	Gold Tinsel	Scarlet	Brown	Brown Mallard
CASSARD	Scarlet Floss	Gold Tinsel	Gold Tinsel	Scarlet Yellow Insect Green Barred Mandarin	Yellow Tied Palmer	In order Scarlet Yellow Insect Green Barred Mandarin
CASSIN	Yellow Floss	Gold Tinsel	Gold Tinsel	Peacock Sword and Scarlet	Brown	Yellow
CATSKILL	Orange Floss			Mandarin or Dyed Mallard	Brown Palmer	Dyed Mallard or Mandarin
CAUGHLAN	Dark Claret Chenille or Wool			Gray Turkey	Dark Claret Palmer Tied	Gray Turkey
CHAMBERLAIN	Orange Wool	Gold Tinsel	Gold Tinsel	Golden Pheasant Crest	Brown	Gray Turkey
CHANTRY	Peacock Herl		Gold Tinsel		Black	Dark Slate
CHATEAUGAY	Pale Yellow Floss			Brown Mallard	Brown	Gray Mallard
CHENEY	Yellow Floss	Scarlet or Red Silk			Yellow	Slate
CINNAMON	Dark Brown Floss	Gold Tinsel	Gold Tinsel		Brown	Cinnamon
CLARET GNAT	Dark Claret Wool or Chenille				Dark Claret	Slate
COACHMAN	Peacock Herl Green		Gold Tinsel if desired		Dark Red or Brown	White
COACHMAN LEADWING	Peacock Herl Green		Gold Tinsel if desired		Dark Red or Brown	Dark Slate
COBLER	Brown Wool	Gold Tinsel	Gold Tinsel	Mandarin	Brown	Barred Mandarin
COLONEL FULLER	Yellow Floss	Gold Tinsel	Gold Tinsel	Black	Yellow	Yellow with Scarlet Stripe
CONCHER	Insect Green Floss			Scarlet	Insect Green Floss	Insect Green Floss
COOPER	Orange Floss				Black	Brown Turkey

PLATE 2 (Continued)

Fly	Body	Ribbing	Tip	Tail	Hackle	Wing
CORNELL	Black Floss	Gold Tinsel		Black	Black	Black
COWDUNG	Olive Green Wool				Brown	Cinnamon (Orpington Cock)
CRITCHLEY FANCY Peacock Herl Head	Yellow Floss or Wool	Gold Tinsel			Yellow Tied Palmer and faced with Gray Mallard	Narrow Strip of Scarlet over Gray Mallard
CRITCHLEY HACKLE	Yellow	Gold Tinsel	Gold Tinsel	Yellow	Pale Yellow mixed with Grizzly	
CUPSUPTIC	Silver Tinsel			Yellow Hackle	Crimson Tied Palmer	Narrow Guinea over Brown Turkey
DARK SPINNER	Dark Claret Floss	Purple Silk		Purple Hackle	Purple	Dark Slate
DOWN LOOKER	Brown Floss		Orange Floss	Brown Mallard	Brown Tied Palmer	Brown Mallard
DEACON	Yellow				Scarlet at Shoulder and Yellow Tied Palmer	Gray Mallard
DEER FLY	Blue Gray Floss				Blue Gray	Blue Gray
DENISON	Orange Floss		Green Floss Tag and Gold Tinsel Tip	Barred Mandarin on Crimson, Yellow and Green	Yellow Tied Palmer	Crimson, Yellow & Green Topping Barred Mandarin
DOLLY VARDEN	White Floss	Gold Tinsel	Gold Tinsel	Cinnamon	Brown	Cinnamon (Orpington Cock)

NOTE—Many of these patterns shown in the wet plates make excellent dry flies. Because any pattern shown in color is designated as **wet** or **dry** does not mean that they may not be tied in either manner.

[474]

PLATE 3
WET FLIES

Fly	Body	Ribbing	Tip	Tail	Hackle	Wing
DARLING	Black Dubbing		Orange Floss	Golden Pheasant Crest	Furnace Brown	Brown Turkey
DORSET	Green Floss			Furnace Hackle	Light Brown Furnace	Teal
DR. BRECK	Silver Tinsel			Jungle Cock Eye	Crimson	White with Crimson Stripe
DR. BURKE	Flat Silver Tinsel	Silver Tinsel		Peacock Sword	Yellow	White—also Jungle Cock Eye
DUGMORE FANCY	Black Floss	Silver Tinsel			Black	Bronze Black
DUSTY MILLER TROUT	Gray Wool				Blue Gray	Blue Gray
DURHAM RANGER	Crimson and Orange Floss	Silver Tinsel	Black Chenille Tag—Yellow Silk and Silver Tinsel Tip	Golden Pheasant Crest	Dark Blue Face Deep Wine Tied Palmer	Jungle Eye G.P. Crest-Top-G.P. Tippet Blue Shoulder
EDRINGTON	Orange Chenille	Black Floss			Brown	Black with White Tip Turkey
ELLIOT	White Chenille			Pheasant and Scarlet	Green	Gray Mallard Scarlet Stripes
EMERALD	Light Green	Gold Tinsel		Light Brown	Light Brown	Pale Brown Mottled
EMMA	Dark Red Floss	Gold Tinsel	Gold Tinsel	Light Claret	Light Claret	Jungle Body Feather
EPTING	Yellow Floss		Red Floss	Orange	Black	Gray Mallard
ESMERALDA	Light Green Floss	Yellow Silk Rib		Brown Mallard	Brown	Light Slate
FERGUSON	Yellow Floss	Gold Tinsel	Gold Tinsel	Yellow and Crimson	Green Hackle	Brown Turkey Yellow Stripe
FERN—As Shown	Pale Pink Floss—Gold Tip—		Gold Tinsel		Brown	Light Slate
FERN—As Also Tied—(Marbury)	White Floss	Silver Tinsel	Silver Tinsel		Gray	Slate

PLATE 3 (Continued)

Fly	Body	Ribbing	Tip	Tail	Hackle	Wing
FIERY BROWN	Fiery Brown Wool		Gold Tinsel	Crimson Tail	Brown Hackle	Brown
FETED GREEN	Medium Dark Green Floss		Crimson Floss	Green same color as wing	Green same as wing	Medium Dark Green
FISHER	Yellow Wool	Gold Tinsel		Wood Duck or Mandarin	Claret	½ Black, ½ White Married Jungle Eye
FISH HAWK	Gold Tinsel	Brown Silk		Brown Turkey	Brown	Brown Turkey and Jungle Eye
FITZMAURICE	Crimson Chenille		Black Chenille	Peacock Sword	Yellow Hackle	Brown Mallard
FLAGGER	Pale Yellow Floss	Gold Tinsel	Gold Tinsel		Blue Gray	Slate
FLAMER	Gold Tinsel		Black Chenille	Crimson	Brown	Crimson
FLETCHER	Black Floss		Silver Tinsel	Scarlet Yellow Guinea	Gray Tied Palmer	Light Brown Turkey
FLIGHT'S FANCY	Pale Yellow Floss	Gold Tinsel	Gold Tinsel	Brown Tail	Brown	Light Slate
FLORENCE	Pink Chenille		Silver Tinsel	Brown Mallard	Black	Brown Mallard
FORSYTH	Yellow Wool		Light Blue Floss		Yellow Tied Palmer	Yellow with Brown Stripe
FOSNOT	Yellow Wool or Chenille				Light Blue	Light Slate
FRANCIS FLY	Peacock Herl	Dark Red Floss			Gray (Dark Grizzly)	Jungle Body Feather
GENERAL HOOKER	Yellow Floss	Green Silk			Brown	Dark Slate
GETLAND	Green Floss	Gold Tinsel	Gold Tinsel	Brown	Brown	Gray Mallard
GINGER PALMER	Pale Yellow Floss	Gold Tinsel	Gold Tinsel		Ginger Tied Palmer	
GOLD RIBBED HARE'S EAR	Rabbit Fur— Not Plucked	Gold Tinsel		Brown	Formed by the long fibres of unplucked Rabbit Fur as it is wound on.	Slate

PLATE 3 (Continued)

Fly	Body	Ribbing	Tip	Tail	Hackle	Wing
GOOD EVENING	Scarlet Floss or Wool	Gold Tinsel		Golden Pheasant Tippet	Brown	Dark Blue—White Tip
GOLD MONKEY	Pale Yellow	Gold Tinsel	Gold Tinsel		Guinea (Black and White)	Slate (Gray)
GOLD STORK	Gold Tinsel			Gray Mallard	Brown	Brown Mallard
GORDON	Yellow Floss	Gold Tinsel	Gold Tinsel	Brown Mallard or Mandarin	Badger	Brown Mallard or Mandarin
GOLDEN DOCTOR	Gold Tinsel			Scarlet Yellow Green	Claret	Gray Mallard Blue, Red
GOLDEN DUKE	(Front)—Gold Tinsel—2/3rds (Back)—Black Floss—1/3rd			Crimson	Black	Crimson
GOLDEN DUN	Orange Floss or Wool			Gray	Gray	Gray (Slate)
GOLDEN IBIS	Gold Tinsel			Scarlet	Scarlet	Scarlet
GOLDEN DUN MIDGE	Pale Green Floss	Gold Tinsel		Gray	Gray	Light Slate
GOLDEN PHEASANT	Orange Floss	Gold Tinsel	Gold Tinsel	Black	Orange	Golden Pheasant Tippet
GOLDEN ROD	Orange Floss	Gold Tinsel	Peacock Tag	Crimson	Orange	Jungle Eye
GOLDEN SPINNER	Pale Yellow Floss		Peacock Tag		Brown	Light Slate
GOSLING	Green Floss			Gray	Gray	Slate
GRANNOM	Pale Yellow Wool	Gold Tinsel	Peacock Tag		Brown	Light Brown Turkey
GRAY MARLOW	Red Floss or Wool	Gold Tinsel	Gold Tinsel		Grizzly Barred Rock	
GROUSE SPIDER	Orange Floss or Chenille	Gold Tinsel	Gold Tinsel	Scarlet	Grouse	

PLATE 4
WET FLIES

Fly	Body	Ribbing	Tip	Tail	Hackle	Wing
GUINEA HEN	Crimson Fur or Wool	Gold Tinsel	Gold Tinsel	Crimson	Claret Light	Guinea
GOVERNOR	Peacock Herl		Scarlet Floss		Brown	Brown Turkey
GOV. ALVORD	Peacock Herl			Dark Scarlet	Brown	Slate Married to Cinnamon
GRACKLE	Peacock Herl			Dark Scarlet	Black	Dark Scarlet
GRAVEL BED	Dark Slate Floss		Gold Tinsel		Black	Black
GREEN MIDGE	Green Floss	Gold Tinsel	Gold Tinsel		Light Blue Dun	
GRAY DRAKE	White Floss	Black Floss		Gray Mallard	Gray	Gray Mallard
GRAY MIDGE	Crimson Floss			Gray Mallard	Light Gray	Gray Mallard
GRAY MILLER	Blue Gray Wool or Fur		Silver		Light Gray	Slate
GREAT DUN	Brown Cast Fur or Wool			Brown Mallard	Blue Gray	Slate
GREEN COACHMAN	Peacock Herl		Gold Tinsel		Green	Slate
GREEN DRAKE	Pale Yellow Floss	Brown Silk		Green	Green	Gray Mallard Dyed Yellow Green
GREEN MANTLE	Green Wool	Gold Tinsel	Gold Tinsel	Green	Green	Gray Mallard
GREENWELL'S GLORY	Olive Floss	Gold Tinsel	Gold Tinsel		Dark Brown Furnace	Very Dark Slate
GRIZZLY KING	Green Floss	Gold Tinsel		Scarlet	Badger Gray	Gray Mallard
GUNNISON	Green Floss	White Floss		Gray Mallard	Brown	White Tipped Turkey
HARLEQUIN	½ Blue Floss ½ Orange Floss	Black Silk			Black	Dark Slate
HAWTHORNE	Black Floss				Black Mixed with Light Claret	Black
HECKHAM GREEN	Green Floss	Gold Tinsel	Gold Tinsel	Golden Pheasant Tippet	Brown	Teal

PLATE 4 (Continued)

Fly	Body	Ribbing	Tip	Tail	Hackle	Wing
HECKHAM RED	Scarlet Floss	Gold Tinsel	White Floss	Turkey Brown	Light Red	Bittern or Light Turkey Brown Mottled
HEMLOCK	Dark Gray Floss				Brown	Dark Brown Turkey
HENSHALL	Peacock Herl	White Floss	Gold Tinsel	Peacock Sword	Grizzly " Barred Rock "	Light Gray Turkey
HERMAN FLY	Crimson Floss		Gold Tinsel		Brown	Slate
HOFLAND'S FANCY	Dark Claret Floss			Brown	Brown	Bittern Light or Light Turkey
HOSKINS	Yellow Floss				Gray	Light Slate
HOWELL	Peacock Herl	Gold Tinsel	Gold Tinsel	Light Claret	Deep Wine	White Tipped Turkey
HOLBERTON	½ Peacock Herl ½ Orange Floss	Gold Tinsel	Gold Tinsel	Barred Mandarin, Crimson, Yellow, Peacock Sword	Crimson	Peacock Sword, Crimson, Yellow—Barred Mandarin
HOPATCONG	Silver Tinsel			Scarlet and Yellow	Black Tied Palmer	Brown Turkey Jungle Over
HUDSON	Dark Brown—Almost Black Wool	Gold Tinsel	Orange Floss Tag	Green	Orange	Light Brown Turkey
HUNT FLY	Green Floss	Yellow Silk			Brown Hackle	Cinnamon Orpington Cock
IBIS & WHITE	Crimson Floss	Gold Tinsel	Gold Tinsel	Red and White	Red and White Mixed	Red and White
IMBRIE	Yellow Floss	Gold Tinsel	Black Chenille Tag		Brown	Slate
INDIAN ROCK	Peacock Herl			Crimson over Gray Mallard	Crimson Palmer	Gray Mallard and Crimson
INDIAN YELLOW	Very Light Brown Floss	Pale Yellow Silk		Very Pale Ginger or Dark Honey	Very Pale Ginger or Dark Honey	Grouse

PLATE 4 (Continued)

Fly	Body	Ribbing	Tip	Tail	Hackle	Wing
INGERSOL	Orange Chenille	Gold Tinsel		Pheasant	Brown	Turkey
IRISH GROUSE	Orange Floss	Gold Tinsel			Furnace Tied Palmer	Peacock Herl
IRISH TURKEY	Green Floss	Yellow Silk		Yellow	Brown	Light Brown Turkey or Bittern
IRON BLUE QUILL	Dark Blue Quill			Dark Iron Blue	Dark Iron Blue	Dark Slate
JAMES	Silver Tinsel			Scarlet	Light Claret	Brown Turkey or Bittern
JAY BLUE	Light Blue Floss	Gold Tinsel		Light Blue	Light Blue	Blue Jay
JAY YELLOW	Yellow Floss			Yellow	Yellow	Blue Jay
JAY SILVER	Silver Tinsel	Oval Silver Tinsel if desired		Golden Pheasant Tippet	Ginger	Blue Jay
JENNIE LIND	Yellow Floss	Gold Tinsel		Light Purple	Scarlet	Light Purple, Scarlet Stripe
JOCK SCOTT	Black Floss at head Yellow Floss at tail	Silver Tinsel		Golden Pheasant Crest and Scarlet Tuff	Guinea Fowl— Black and White	Peacock Sword ; Blue, Yellow, Scarlet, White-Tipped Turkey— Married ; Jungle Cock Eye
JOHN MANN	Yellow Floss	Gold Tinsel	Scarlet Tag	Brown Turkey	Brown Tied Palmer	Dark Brown Turkey or Bittern
JUNE	Alternate Scarlet and White Floss				Black	Light Brown Turkey
JUNE SPINNER	Black Chenille	Broad Silver Tinsel			Black	Black
KAMALOFF	Yellow Wool	Gold Tinsel	Red Floss Tag	Brown Mallard	Grizzly "Barred Rock"	Light Brown Turkey or Bittern

PLATE 5
WET FLIES

Fly	Body	Ribbing	Tip	Tail	Hackle	Wing
KATE	Scarlet and Yellow Floss	Gold Tinsel		Golden Pheasant Tippet	Black	Cinnamon "Orpington"
KATYDID	Green Floss "Highlander"	Gold Tinsel		Green	Green	Bright Green
KENDAL	Deep Wine Chenille				Scarlet	Brown Mallard
KIFFE	Dark Green Floss Silk	Gold Tinsel		Scarlet	Scarlet	Gray Mallard Dyed Yellow
KINEO	Scarlet Wool	Silver Tinsel		Black, White Scarlet—Married	Scarlet Tied Palmer	Scarlet, White, Black—Married
KING OF WATERS	Crimson Floss	Gold Tinsel		Gray Mallard	Brown	Gray Mallard
KINGDOM	White Floss	Bluish Green Floss	Gold Tinsel		Brown—sometimes Scarlet	Brown Turkey or Gray
KINGFISHER	Crimson Floss	Gold Tinsel	Gold Tinsel	Golden Pheasant Tippet	Brown	Gray Mallard
KINROSS	Olive Green Floss	Silver Tinsel		Barred Wood Duck or Mandarin	Olive Green	Dark Brown Turkey Wing
KITSON	Yellow Floss or Wool	Gold Tinsel	Gold Tinsel	Black	Light Claret	Yellow-Black Cheeks
KNOWLES' FANCY	Light Brown Wool	Silver Tinsel			Brown	From Black Cock's Tail Feather
LA BELLE	Light Blue Floss	Silver Tinsel		Scarlet Wool Tag	Light Blue	White
LACKEY'S GRANT LAKE	Olive Green Floss		Gold Tinsel	Light Brown	Light Brown	Light Brown Turkey
LACHENE	Shoulder—Black Chenille—Tail End Embossed Silver Tinsel	Silver Tinsel		Gray Mallard Dyed Pale Yellow	Dark Claret	Amherst Pheasant
LADY GRAY	Blue-Gray Rabbit Fur	Silver Tinsel		Barred Mandarin	Scarlet Tied Palmer	Jungle Body Feather

[481]

PLATE 5 (Continued)

Fly	Body	Ribbing	Tip	Tail	Hackle	Wing
LADY MERTON	Blue-Gray Rabbit Fur	Silver Tinsel		Golden Pheasant Crest	Black Tied Palmer Scarlet Shoulder	Gray Mallard
LADY MILLS	White Ostrich	Silver Tinsel & Black Ostrich		Golden Pheasant Tippet	Blue Gray	Cinnamon with Black Tip
LAKE EDWARD	Light Brown Wool or Fur	Gold Tinsel	Gold Tinsel	Yellow	Scarlet	Yellow, Dark-Blue, Brown Turkey
LAKE GEORGE	Scarlet Floss	Gold Tinsel	Gold Tinsel	Scarlet	White	White with Scarlet Stripe
LAKE GREEN	Yellow	Insect Green Silk			Light Ginger	Teal
LANGIWIN	Yellow Floss	Black Silk		Bright Yellow	Bright Yellow	Bright Yellow
LARAMIE	Deep Wine Wool	Silver Tinsel	Silver Tinsel	Deep Wine	Black	Dark Gray or Speckled Dark Gray
LANIGAN	White Chenille			Black	Light Claret Tied Palmer	Gray Mallard
LAST CHANCE	Yellow Floss	Black Silk	Gold Tinsel	Crimson	Light Brown	Light Slate
LIBERTY	Pale Blue Floss	Gold Tinsel		Dark Blue	White	Scarlet
LIGHT BLOW	Quill—Pronounced Stripe			Light Brown Turkey	Crimson	Light Brown Turkey
LIGHT FOX	White Wool	Gold Tinsel	Gold Tinsel	Yellow Wool Tag	Yellow	Slate
LIGHT POLKA	White Chenille				White	Guinea
LISTER'S GOLD	Dark Claret Wool at Shoulder—Gold Tinsel Rear	Gold Tinsel		Yellow	Orange	Guinea
LORD BALTIMORE	Orange Floss	Black Silk		Black	Black	Black—Jungle Eye
LOGAN	Brown Floss	Gold Tinsel	Gold Tinsel	Crimson, Orange Married	Dark Brown	Orange, Crimson Stripe
LOWERY	Peacock Herl		Yellow Floss		Brown	Mixed Gray or Cinnamon

PLATE 5 (Continued)

Fly	Body	Ribbing	Tip	Tail	Hackle	Wing
LOYAL SOCK	Pale Yellow Floss				Black	Black
LUZERNE	Dark Claret Floss				Black	Gray Mallard
MAGALLOWAY	Light Brown Wool		Black Chenille Tag—Gold Tinsel Tip	Yellow	Brown Furnace	Peacock Sword
MAGPIE	Brown Floss	Gold Tinsel		Brown	Brown	Magpie or Black Turkey, White Tip
MAJOR	Purple Wool	Gold Tinsel	Blue Floss Tag—Also Gold Tinsel Tip	Golden Pheasant Tippet	Scarlet Tied Palmer, Blue at Shoulder	Brown Turkey Gray Mallard
MALLARD	Yellow Wool	Gold Tinsel		Brown Mallard	Brown	Brown Mallard
MARK LAIN	Yellow Floss or Wool		Gold Tip	Scarlet and White	Scarlet	Cinnamon— White Tip
MARSTON'S FANCY	Peacock Herl					
MARCH BROWN American	Brown	Gold Tinsel	Gold Tinsel	Dark Gray	Brown	Dark Gray
					Brown	Brown Turkey
MARCH BROWN English, Female	Gray-Brown	Gold Tinsel		Partridge	Partridge	Pheasant (Light)
MARCH BROWN English, Male	Gray-Brown	Gold Tinsel	Gold Tinsel	Partridge Dark	Partridge Dark	Pheasant (Dark)
MARCH DUN	Medium Green Wool		Gold Tinsel			Light Slate
MARLOW BUZZ	Peacock Herl		Gold Tinsel		Brown Furnace	
MASCOT	Peacock Herl		Yellow Floss Tag	Scarlet	Black	Slate
MARSTERS	White Floss or Wool		Gold Tinsel	Gray Mallard	Scarlet	Widgeon or Gray Mallard
MARTIN	Yellow Floss	Gold Tinsel		Yellow and Black Alternate	Deep Yellow	Widgeon or Gray Mallard

PLATE 6
WET FLIES

Fly	Body	Ribbing	Tip	Tail	Hackle	Wing
MAURICE	1/3 Black Floss 2/3 Scarlet Floss			Scarlet	Yellow Tied Palmer over Black Floss	Teal
MAXWELL	Copper Tinsel			Teal	Brown	Iridescent Green Wood Duck
MAXWELL BLUE	Medium Dark Blue-Gray Floss	Silver Tinsel	Silver	Light Blue	Light Blue	
McALPIN	Claret Wool	Gold Tinsel	Gold Tinsel	Wood-Duck (Barred) Topping Scarlet	Guinea	Peacock Herl Topping Scarlet
McGINTY	Alternate Black & Yellow Chenille			Gray Mallard Topping Scarlet	Brown	Black Turkey— White Tip
McKENZIE	Light Olive-Green Wool	Gold Tinsel	Gold Tinsel	Brown	Brown	Mottled Slate and Brown
MEALY MOTH	Lightest Gray Wool	Silver Tinsel			White	White
MERSHON	Black Silk Floss			Black	Black	Dark Blue, White Tip
MERSHON WHITE	White Silk			Golden Pheasant Tippet	Light Brown	Dark Blue, White Tip
MIDGE BLACK	Black Floss				Black	
WHITE MILLER	White Silk Floss	Gold Tinsel	Gold Tinsel	Scarlet	White	White
MILLS NO. 1	Crimson Floss	Gold Tinsel	Black Tag, Gold Tinsel Tip	Golden Pheasant Tippet	White	Mallard Dyed Yellow
MOHAWK	Light Claret Floss			Brown	Brown Tied Palmer	Brown Turkey
MOISIC	Black Wool Shoulder, Yellow Wool End		Gold Tinsel	Golden Pheasant Crest	Guinea Face, Yellow in Back	
MOLE	Gray Wool				Brown Tied Palmer	Brown Turkey

[484]

PLATE 6 (Continued)

Fly	Body	Ribbing	Tip	Tail	Hackle	Wing
MONTREAL	Claret Floss Silk	Gold Tinsel	Gold Tinsel	Scarlet	Claret	Brown Turkey
MONTREAL SILVER	Silver Tinsel (Flat)			Scarlet	Claret	Brown Turkey
MONTREAL YELLOW	Yellow Wool	Gold Tinsel	Gold Tinsel	Scarlet	Claret	Brown Turkey
MOOSE	Yellow Floss Silk	Gold Tinsel	Gold Tinsel	Yellow	Guinea and Yellow Intermingled	Barred Wood-Duck—Golden Pheasant Tippet Eye
MORRISON	Claret Wool	Black Silk		Black	Black	Black
MOTH-WHITE	White Chenille	Silver Tinsel	Silver Tinsel		White	White
MOTH-BROWN	Cinnamon Wool	Gold Tinsel	Gold Tinsel		Brown	Cinnamon Dark Orpington Cock
MUNRO	Green Floss	Gold Tinsel	Gold Tinsel	Scarlet and Yellow	Yellow	Scarlet with Brown Turkey Stripe
MURRAY	Black Floss	Silver Tinsel		Scarlet	Orange Tied Palmer	Brown Turkey or Pheasant
NAMELESS	Embossed Silver Tinsel			Mallard Dyed Yellow	Scarlet Tied Palmer Half Way	Light Pheasant Light Brown Mottled
NEVERSINK	Pale Yellow Floss			Gray Mallard	Yellow	Gray Mallard
NEVERWAS	Peacock Herl			Peacock Sword	Dark Green Tied Palmer	Orange
NICHOLSON	Claret Wool	Gold Tinsel		Gray Mallard Golden Pheasant Tippet	Light Blue and Claret Mixed Tied Palmer	Brown Mallard Blue Stripe
NICKERSON	Yellow Wool				Brown Tied Palmer	Gray Mallard or Teal—Scarlet and Brown
NONPAREIL	Black Chenille		Gold Tinsel		Black	
OAK	Orange Floss			Brown Turkey	Brown	Brown Turkey
OLIVE DUN	Olive Wool			Olive	Olive	Slate
OLIVE QUILL	Quill Dyed Olive			Olive	Olive	Slate

PLATE 6 (Continued)

Fly	Body	Ribbing	Tip	Tail	Hackle	Wing
OLIVE WREN	Olive Brown Wool	Silver Tinsel	Silver Tinsel	Gray Mallard	Brown Furnace Preferred	Light Brown Turkey or Pheasant
ONONDAGA	Black Silk Floss		White Chenille	Black and White Turkey Tip	Black	Black and White Turkey Tip
OQUASSAC	Claret Wool	Pink Silk	Yellow Silk Floss	Pheasant Tail	Claret—Black Chenille Collar	Pheasant Tail
ORANGE BLACK	Orange Floss	Black Silk		Black	Black	Black
ORANGE BLUE	Orange Chenille and Blue Floss	Gold Tinsel	Gold Tinsel	Golden Pheasant Tippet	Claret	Light Brown. Turkey or Pheasant—Orange Stripe
ORANGTO	Gray Wool		Gold Tinsel	Scarlet and Guinea	Yellow Face and Brown Tied Palmer	Pheasant—Guinea Stripe
ORANGE MILLER	Orange Wool or Chenille	Gold Tinsel	Gold Tinsel	Scarlet	White	White
ORANGE SEDGE	Black or Dark Gray Wool	Gold Tinsel	Gold Tinsel	Orange		Orange
ORVIS-GRAY	Olive Yellow Wool	Gold Tinsel	Gold Tinsel	Blue-Gray	Blue-Gray	Black Turkey with White Tip
PAGE	Crimson or Scarlet Floss	Gold Tinsel	Gold Tinsel	Scarlet	Scarlet	Guinea with Scarlet Stripes
PALE EVENING DUN	Pale Yellow	Gold Tinsel	Gold Tinsel	Gray Mallard	Blue-Gray	Light Slate
PALE SULPHUR	Pale Yellow Wool			Pale Yellow	Pale Yellow	Yellow or Pale Yellow
PALE WATERY QUILL	Peacock Quill			Greenish Yellow (Pale)	Greenish Yellow (Pale)	Light Slate
PARK FLY	Crimson Floss	Gold Tinsel	Gold Tinsel		Black	Black
PARMACHENE BEAU	Pale Yellow Floss	Silver Tinsel	Black Ostrich Herl	White and Scarlet	Mixed Scarlet and White	White with Scarlet Stripe Jungle Eye

PLATE 7
WET FLIES

Fly	Body	Ribbing	Tip	Tail	Hackle	Wing
PARMACHENE BELLE	Yellow Wool	Silver Tinsel	Black Ostrich or Chenille	White and Scarlet	White and Scarlet	White with Scarlet Stripe
PARSON	Gray Wool	Silver Tinsel	Orange Floss	Golden Pheasant Crest	Black Tied Palmer	Light Brown Turkey
PATHFINDER	Scarlet Wool	Gold Tinsel	Gold Tinsel		Brown Furnace	Light Slate
PARTRIDGE	½ Pale Yellow Floss ½ Silver Tinsel			Gray Partridge	Honey	Partridge Tail (Gray)
PASSADUNK	Black Floss	Green Silk Floss	Green Silk Floss	Peacock Sword	Olive Yellow Hackle	Teal
PEACOCK	Peacock Herl				Black	Slate
PEA JAY	White Chenille		Red Chenille Tag	Yellow	Orange	Scarlet with White Stripe
PEBBLE BEACH	Dark Claret Floss or Wool	Silver Tinsel	Silver Tinsel		Black Shoulder, Brown Tied Palmer	Orange
PELLEE ISLAND	Scarlet Floss	Gold Tinsel	Black Chenille Tag	Black	Black	Scarlet
PERKIN'S IDEAL	Scarlet Floss	Gold Tinsel	Black Ostrich Herl	Black	Black	Gray Mallard
PERKIN'S PET	Silver Tinsel				Brown Tied Palmer	Slate
PERRY	Black Chenille		Pink Chenille		Black	Black Turkey with White Tip
PETER ROSS	Yellow Floss	Gold Tinsel	Gold Tinsel	Golden Pheasant Tippet	Light Ginger	
PIKER	Orange Wool		Gold Tinsel		Brown	White
PINK WICKHAM'S FANCY	Pink Floss		Gold Tinsel	Light Brown	Light Brown Tied Palmer	Dark Slate
PLATH	Bright Green Wool		Gold Tinsel	Crimson	Crimson	Gray Turkey— White Tip

PLATE 7 (Continued)

Fly	Body	Ribbing	Tip	Tail	Hackle	Wing
PLUMMER	Black Ostrich Herl—Butt Yellow Floss	Gold Tinsel	Black Ostrich Herl		Yellow	Teal
POLKA	Scarlet Floss	Gold Tinsel	Gold Tinsel	Brown and White	Scarlet	Guinea
POORMAN	Brown Olive Wool		Gold Tinsel		Brown	Tan Mottled Turkey
POPE	Yellow Floss (Pale) Silk		Gold Tinsel	Golden Pheasant Tippet	Green Shoulder and Yellow Tied Palmer	Guinea
POST	Pink Floss	Gold Tinsel	Gold Tinsel	Crimson	Black Tied Palmer	Dark Brown Turkey
PORTLAND	Scarlet Floss	Gold Tinsel	Gold Tinsel	Teal	Crimson	Teal
POTOMAC	Bright Green Floss	Yellow Silk Floss			Brown	Cinnamon
POTTER	Blue Green Floss	Black Silk	Black Silk		Dark Brown	Slate
PREMIER	Scarlet Floss	Gold Tinsel	Gold Tip	Scarlet	Scarlet	White with Scarlet Stripe
PRESTON'S FANCY	Gold Tinsel			Brown	Brown	Guinea Fowl
PRIEST	Silver Tinsel			Scarlet	Gray Badger	
PRIME GNAT	Black Ostrich Herl		Orange Floss or Wool	Black	Black	Black
PROFESSOR	Yellow Floss	Gold Tinsel	Gold Tinsel	Scarlet	Brown	Gray Mallard or Teal
PROUTY	Black Chenille		Orange Chenille	Blue and Golden Pheasant Tippet	Yellow Shoulder and Brown Tied Palmer	Married Slate, Scarlet and Yellow and Gray Mallard
QUACK DOCTOR	Flat Silver Tinsel			Scarlet	Scarlet	Light Brown Turkey
QUAKER	Gray Silk Floss	Gold Tinsel	Gold Tinsel	Gray Mallard	Grizzly	Gray Turkey
QUEEN OF WATERS	Orange Silk Floss				Brown Tied Palmer	Teal or Gray Mallard

[488]

PLATE 7 (Continued)

Fly	Body	Ribbing	Tip	Tail	Hackle	Wing
RAINBOW	Light Blue Silk Floss	Gold Tinsel	White Floss	Scarlet	Grizzly	Cinnamon
RAY BERGMAN	Rusty Orange Wool			Brown Mallard	Brown	Slate
RANGELEY	Light Claret Dubbing	Gold Tinsel	Gold Tinsel	Orange	Orange Shoulder Light Claret Tied Palmer	Gray Mallard Jungle Eye
RED ASH	Red Floss	Gold Tinsel	Gold Tinsel		Blue Dun	Brown Mallard
RED FOX	Light Red Fox Under Fur		Gold	Gray Mallard	Brown	Slate
RED QUILL	Tawny Quill sometimes Red			Brown	Brown	Slate
RED SPINNER	Dark Claret Wool	Gold Tinsel	Gold Tinsel	Brown	Brown	Dark Gray
RED TAG	Peacock Herl			Scarlet Tag (Wool)	Brown Tied Palmer	
RICHARDSON	Light Blue Floss		Gold Tinsel	Brown Mallard	Black Tied Palmer	Brown Mallard
RICH WIDOW	Light Blue Floss	Gold Tinsel	Gold Tinsel	Yellow	Yellow Tied Palmer	Black
RILEY	White Wool		Black Floss Silk and Gold Tag		Brown	Teal or Gray Mallard
RIO GRANDE KING	Black Chenille		Gold Tinsel	Yellow	Brown	White
ROMAINE	Green Wool		Gold Tinsel	Guinea	Black	Guinea
ROMEYN	Green Floss Silk	Gold Tinsel	Scarlet Silk Floss Tag—Gold Tinsel Tip	Barred Wood- Duck or Mandarin	Grizzly	Barred Wood- Duck or Mandarin
ROOSEVELT	½ Claret Wool ½ Yellow Wool			Brown	Orange (Dark)	Slate

[489]

PLATE 8
WET FLIES

Fly	Body	Ribbing	Tip	Tail	Hackle	Wing
ROSS	Brown Silk Floss	Gold Tinsel	Gold	Green, Golden Pheasant Tippet	Brown Furnace Tied Palmer	Peacock Herl over Brown Mallard
ROUND LAKE	Claret Wool	Gold Tinsel	Orange Chenille or Wool Tag	Blue	Orange	Brown Turkey Jungle Eye
ROYAL COACHMAN	Peacock Herl with Scarlet Floss Center		Gold if desired	Golden Pheasant Tippet	Brown	White
RUBE WOOD	White Chenille		Scarlet Floss	Teal	Brown	Gray Mallard
SABBATUS	Alternate Black and White Floss Ribbing		Scarlet Silk Floss	White and Black	Yellow	Barred Wood-Duck, Kingfisher Cheeks
SAGE	Yellow Wool	Black Silk Thread	Silver Tinsel	Scarlet, Insect Green, Gray Mallard	Orange	Dark Gray Mallard
SALLIE SCOTT	Palest Yellow Floss	Orange Floss		Pheasant Tippet	Pale Yellow	Light Blue Parrot
SALTOUN	Black Floss	Gold Tinsel	Gold Tinsel	Ginger Hackle	Ginger	Slate
SANCTUARY	Dark Hares' Ear Fur	Gold Tinsel	Gold Tinsel		Brown	
SAND FLY	Gray Fur			Blue-Gray	Brown	Lt. Brown Turkey
SARANAC	Claret Floss	Gold Tinsel	Gold Tinsel	Golden Pheasant Crest	Claret	Golden Pheasant Tippet
SASSY CAT	Peacock Herl			Scarlet	Yellow	Yellow with Scarlet Cheek
SCARLET GNAT	Scarlet Wool		Gold Tinsel		Scarlet	Slate
SCARLET IBIS	Scarlet Floss	Gold Tinsel	Gold Tinsel	Scarlet	Scarlet	Scarlet
SCHAEFER	Reddish Brown Wool	Gold Tinsel	Gold Tinsel	Golden Pheasant Tippet	Grizzly	Scarlet, Dk. Blue, Bright Green
SHEENAN	Yellow Silk Floss		Pink Chenille Tag	Golden Pheasant Tippet	Black	Gray Mallard
SETH GREEN	Green Silk Floss	Yellow Silk Floss			Brown	Lt. Brown Turkey

PLATE 8 (Continued)

Fly	Body	Ribbing	Tip	Tail	Hackle	Wing
SHAD FLY	Peacock Herl—Gold Tinsel Center				Brown	Brown Turkey
SHOEMAKER	Gray Ostrich—White Silk Floss Center			Brown Mandarin Speckled	Brown	Brown Mandarin Speckled
SKOOKUM	Scarlet Chenille—Silver or Gold Center			Scarlet	Mixed Bright Green and Scarlet or Claret	Teal
SILVER BLACK	Black Floss	Silver Tinsel	Silver Tinsel	Gray Mallard	Grizzly	Light Widgeon
SILVER DOCTOR	Flat Silver Tinsel	Oval Silver Tinsel	Scarlet Floss and Gold Tinsel	Golden Pheasant Crest—Dash of Blue	Blue and Guinea	Brown Turkey, Teal, Blue, Yellow
SILVER FAIRY	Silver Tinsel			Scarlet	Guinea	Jungle Cock Eye
SILVER GHOST	Peacock Herl	Silver Tinsel if desired		Barred Mandarin	Grizzly	Silver Condor, Black Tip
SILVER-GOLD	Silver Tinsel			Golden Pheasant Crest	Badger	Golden Pheasant Crest
SILVER JUNGLE COCK	Orange Silk Floss Shoulder—Silver Tinsel Back			Golden Pheasant Crest	Grizzly Tied Palmer over Orange Section	Jungle Cock Eye
SILVER STORK	Silver Tinsel			Gray Mallard	Brown	Gray Mallard
SILVER SEDGE	White Wool	Silver Tinsel	Silver Tinsel		Light Ginger Tied Palmer	Light Brown Turkey
SIR SAM DARLING	White Chenille		Black Chenille	Brown Mallard	Brown	Gray Mallard
SOLDIER PALMER	Scarlet Wool	Gold Tinsel	Gold Tinsel		Brown Tied Palmer	
SOMETHING	Black Silk Floss	Gold Tinsel	Gold Tinsel	Golden Pheasant Tippet	Black	Green, Scarlet, Purple, Yellow Married
SOO NIPI	Black Silk Floss	Gold Tinsel	Gold Tinsel	Barred Mandarin	Light Blue	White
SPENCER	Gray Fur	Gold Tinsel	Gold Tinsel, Yellow Wool Tag		Gray Badger Tied Palmer	

PLATE 8 (Continued)

Fly	Body	Ribbing	Tip	Tail	Hackle	Wing
SPLIT IBIS	Silver Tinsel			Golden Pheasant Tippet	Brown	White Scarlet, White Scarlet Married
STEBBINS	Green Wool		Gold Tinsel	Widgeon	Brown Furnace	Dk. Gray
ST. LAWRENCE	Yellow Floss	Gold Tinsel	Scarlet Tag Chenille	Scarlet	Scarlet	Light Gray Turkey—Topping Brown Turkey
ST. PATRICK	Silver Tinsel			Peacock Herl	Light Blue-Gray Dun	Peacock Herl
ST. REGIS	Very Dark Gray Fur			Guinea and Golden Pheasant Tippet	Brown Tied Palmer	Brown Mallard Golden Pheasant Tippet over
STONE	Blue-Gray Fur	Yellow Silk		Blue-Gray	Blue-Gray	Very Light Gray Turkey
SECRET-POOL NO. 1 (Dr. Burke Pattern)	Peacock Herl—Gold Tinsel Center			Golden Pheasant Tippet	Claret	Slate, Jungle Eye
STRACHAN	Cinnamon Fur	Gold Tinsel	Yellow Wool Gold Tinsel	Golden Pheasant Tippet	Light Blue at Shoulder—Black Tied Palmer	Yellow, Dk. Blue Golden Pheasant Tippet
STRANGER	Dark Brown Wool	Gold Tinsel	Gold Tinsel	Brown	Brown	Brown Turkey Golden Pheasant Tippet
STURTEVANT	Black Wool	Gold or Silver Tinsel	Gold or Silver Tinsel	Scarlet, Gray, Mallard	Blue-Green Tied Palmer	Jungle Body Feathers
SUNSET	Yellow Wool				Yellow	White
SWIFTWATER	Peacock Herl Orange Center			Gray Mallard	Brown	White
TEAL	White Floss Silk	Black Silk		Teal	Grizzly	Teal
TETON	Yellow Silk Floss	Gold Tinsel	Gold Tinsel	Brown	Brown	Slate, Jungle Eye

PLATE 8 (Continued)

Fly	Body	Ribbing	Tip	Tail	Hackle	Wing
THISTLE	Green Silk Floss	Gold Tinsel	Gold Tinsel	Golden Pheasant Crest, Scarlet—Golden Pheasant Tippet	Mixed Yellow and Scarlet Tied Palmer	Jungle Eye Golden Pheasant Tippet
THUNDER	Black Silk Floss	Orange Silk		Golden Pheasant Crest	Yellow	Guinea
TOMAH JOE	Gold Tinsel or Silver Tinsel		Peacock	Yellow	Mixed Scarlet and Yellow	Barred Wood-Duck or Mandarin
TOODLE BUG	½ Yellow Wool ½ Blue Silk Floss		Gold Tinsel	Gray Mallard	Brown	Brown Turkey
TELEPHONE BOX (Dr. Burke Pattern)	Orange Silk Floss or Wool	Black Silk	Peacock Herl Tag	Golden Pheasant Tippet	Brown	Brown Turkey Jungle Eye
TURKEY	Yellow Wool	Gold Tinsel	Gold Tinsel	Scarlet	Brown	Brown Turkey
TURKEY BROWN	Brown Floss	Scarlet Silk	Gold Tinsel	Scarlet	Brown	Brown Turkey
TURKEY SILVER	Scarlet Floss	Silver Tinsel	Silver Tinsel	Scarlet and Yellow	Green	Gray Turkey
TUTHILL	Purple Floss Silk	Orange Silk		Golden Pheasant Tippet	Brown	Light Brown Turkey
TYCOON	Orange Floss	Gold Tinsel	Scarlet Floss	Scarlet and Yellow	Claret Shoulder Yellow Tied Palmer	Black White, Scarlet White Married

PLATE 9
WET FLIES

Fly	Body	Ribbing	Tip	Tail	Hackle	Wing
UNDERTAKER	White Wool			Black and White	Black	White and Black
UNION	Unstripped Brown Condor	Gold Tinsel		Teal	Grizzly	Teal
UTAH	Cinnamon Wool				Ginger	Cinnamon
VANCE	Gold Tinsel			Light Mottled Turkey	Yellow	Light Mottled Turkey
VANITY	Orange Floss	Gold Tinsel			Brown Tied Palmer	White—Jungle Body Feather
VICTORIA GREEN	Green Floss	Gold or Silver Tinsel	Gold or Silver Tinsel	Golden Pheasant Tippet	Yellow	Brown Turkey Jungle Eye
VICTORIA REGULAR	Blue Floss	''	''	''	''	''
VOLUNTEER	Yellow Silk Floss	Gold Tinsel	Gold Tinsel	Scarlet	Green	Golden Pheasant Tippet
VON PATTEN	Yellow Floss			Scarlet	Brown	Barred Mandarin
WALKER	White Floss	Black Silk		Scarlet and White	Yellow	White with Gray Turkey Stripe
WALKER-HAYS	Yellow Floss Silk	Scarlet Silk Floss	Scarlet Silk Floss		Brown	Slate
WALLA-WALLA	Yellow Mohair or Wool		Gold Tinsel		Brown	Cinnamon
WANDERER	Amber Wool	Gold or Silver Tinsel	Gold or Silver Tinsel	Barred Mandarin	Badger Gray	Black or Brown Feather—Wh. Tip
WARDEN	Tan Wool	Silver or Gold Tinsel	Silver or Gold Tinsel	Guinea Dyed Yellow	Ginger	Light Brown Turkey—Black Stripe
WARWICK	Peacock Herl	Gold Tinsel		Orange	Orange	Black—Peacock Herl over
WASP	Alternate Black and Brown Ostrich Herl		Orange Floss		Brown	Tan—Black, Tan

[494]

PLATE 9 (Continued)

Fly	Body	Ribbing	Tip	Tail	Hackle	Wing
WATERS (White at Head)	Peacock Herl				Black	Light Gray Turkey
WATSON'S FANCY	½ Scarlet Silk Floss—½ Black Silk Floss	Gold Tinsel		Golden Pheasant Tippet	Black	Black
WEBBS	Very Pale Green Wool	Gold Tinsel	Gold Tinsel	Grouse	Pale Yellow	Green Parrot
WHIRLING BLUE DUN	Blue-Gray Fur	Gold Tinsel	Gold Tinsel	Blue-Gray	Blue-Gray	Dark Slate
WHIRLING DUN	Blue-Gray Fur			Brown	Brown	Slate
WHITE HACKLE	White Floss Silk	Black Silk or Silver Tinsel Optional			White	
WHITE JUNGLE COCK	White Wool		Scarlet Tip	Pheasant Tippet	White	Jungle Cock Eye
WHITE KING	White Silk Floss	Gold Tinsel	Gold Tinsel	Orange	Orange Shoulder White Tied Palmer	White
WHITE MILLER	White Silk Floss	Silver Tinsel	Silver Tinsel		White	White
MONTREAL WHITE TIP	Claret Wool	Gold Tinsel	Gold Tinsel	Scarlet	Claret	Black Turkey White Tip
WHITE WATER	White Ostrich Herl—Green Silk Center			Pheasant Tippet	Light Blue Gray	Grouse
WHITNEY	Tan Fur	Gold Tinsel	Gold Tinsel	Yellow	Orange at Shoulder—Brown Tied Palmer	Turkey—White Tip
WICKHAM'S FANCY	Gold Tinsel			Brown Hackle Tips	Brown Tied Palmer	Slate
WIDOW	Black Silk Floss	White Silk			Black	Black with White Stripe
WILDERNESS	Green Wool	Gold Tinsel	Silver or Gold Tinsel		Brown Tied Palmer	Dark Red over Brown
WILLOW	Olive-Gray Silk Floss		Gold Tinsel		Brown	Dark Slate

[495]

PLATE 9 (Continued)

Fly	Body	Ribbing	Tip	Tail	Hackle	Wing
WILSON	Orange Wool		Gold Tinsel	Golden Pheasant Tippet	Orange	Gray Mallard
WILSON ANT	Medium Brown Floss		Peacock Herl Tag		Brown	Pheasant Wing
WINTERS	Claret Floss Silk			Brown Mallard or Light Gray Mallard	Brown Furnace or Dun	Brown Mallard
WITCH GOLD	Light Gray Silk Floss	Gold Tinsel or Yellow Floss Silk	Gold Tinsel	Scarlet	Honey Badger	
WITCH SILVER	Gray Silk Floss	Silver Tinsel	Silver Tinsel	Scarlet	Gray Badger	
WITCHER	Black Wool	Gold or Silver Tinsel	Yellow Tag or Gold Tinsel	Golden Pheasant Crest	Black Tied Palmer	Gray Mallard Stripe over Slate
WOOD DUCK	Bright Green Wool	Gold Tinsel	Gold Tinsel	Yellow	Bright Green	Barred Wood-Duck
WOOD IBIS	Dark Claret Wool			Orange-Brown Mallard	Orange Tied Palmer	Iridescent Black
WOPPINGER	Gray Silk Floss			Blue-Gray	Dark Grizzly Tied Palmer	Slate
WREN	Light Gray Floss	Yellow Silk	Yellow Silk	Gray Mallard	Brown	Brown Mallard
YANKEE	Light Blue Floss Silk	Gold or Silver Tinsel	Gold or Silver Tinsel	White	Scarlet	White
YELLOW COACHMAN	Peacock Herl Yellow Center		Gold Tinsel		Brown	White
YELLOW DRAKE	Yellow Floss Silk	Gold Tinsel	Gold Tinsel	Black	Yellow	Gray Mallard Dyed Yellow
YELLOW DUN	Gray Fur	Yellow Silk			Yellow	Brown Mallard
YELLOW SALLY	Yellow Floss Silk	Gold Tinsel	Gold Tinsel	Yellow	Yellow	Yellow
YELLOW SPINNER	Yellow Chenille		Gold Tinsel	Yellow	Scarlet	Black
ZULU	Peacock Herl		Scarlet Wool Tag		Black Tied Palmer	

PLATE 10
WET FLIES—STREAMERS AND NYMPHS

Fly	Body	Ribbing	Tip	Tail	Hackle	Wing
FONTINALIS FIN "Phil Armstrong"	Orange Wool	Gold Tinsel		White Hackle Wisps	Furnace	White and Gray Stripe Married to and Topping Orange
BERGMAN FONTINALIS "Phil Armstrong"	Alternate Ribs of Gray and Orange Wool			White, Gray and Orange Married 2 Sections	Dark Blue-Gray	White and Gray Stripe Married to and Topping Orange
GRASSHOPPER	Yellow Wool Tied to Overhang Hook			Scarlet Hackle Wisps	Brown Sparse Palmer	Light Brown Turkey
BOB WILSON (Yellow Head)	Copper Tinsel			Golden Pheasant Crest	Black	Barred Mandarin
GRIFFEN	Peacock Herl			Scarlet Hackle Wisps	Clipped Grizzly Tied Palmer and Clipped	A Few Long Wisps of Grizzly Hackle
GRAY SQUIRREL SILVER R.B.	Silver Tinsel	Silver Tinsel if desired			Scarlet Tied in Whole—Not Wound Around Hook	Gray Squirrel Hair—Grizzly Hackle—Jungle Cock Eye
RED SQUIRREL GOLD R.B.	Gold Tinsel	Gold Tinsel if desired			Scarlet Tied in Whole—Not Wound Around Hook	Fox Squirrel Hair Honey Badger Hackle—Jungle Cock Eye
BELL SPECIAL	Silver Tinsel				Scarlet Tied in Whole—Not Wound Around Hook	Brown Ostrich White Ostrich Jungle Eye
JESS WOOD May be tied on single hook	Silver Tinsel			Scarlet	Furnace	Yanosh Tied Streamer Jungle Eye
R.B. NYMPH No. 1	Buff Wool, Brown Enamel on Back	Black Linen Ribbing		Guinea Fowl Also Feelers from Body Feathers	Guinea Fowl Legs from Wing Feather	

PLATE 10 (Continued)

Fly	Body	Ribbing	Tip	Tail	Hackle	Wing
R.B. NYMPH No. 2	Rust Wool	Gold Tinsel		Guinea Fowl Also Feelers from Body Feathers	Guinea Fowl Legs from Wing Feather	
R.B. NYMPH No. 5	Gray Wool	Gold Tinsel		Guinea Fowl Also Feelers from Body Feathers	Guinea Fowl Legs from Wing Feather	
R.B. NYMPH No. 6	Dark Olive Wool	Gold Tinsel		Guinea Fowl Dyed Olive from Body Feathers	Guinea Fowl Legs from Wing Feather	
R.B. CADDIS	White or Light Gray Chenille		Black Chenille or Ostrich Tag	Peacock Herl Also Peacock Herl Feelers		
LEAF ROLLER WORM	Cork Painted Insect Green					
HEWITT NYMPH No. 1	White, Brown Back	Black		Black	Black	
HEWITT NYMPH No. 2	Deep Yellow Brown Back	Black		Black	Black	
HEWITT NYMPH No. 3	Gray, Brown Back	Black		Black	Black	
WATER CRICKET	Pink Silk Floss			Black Hackle Wisps	Black Tied Palmer and Clipped	
ACKLE SHRIMP	Tan Colored Rubber	Segmented by Bucktail		Bucktail		
ED BURKE NYMPH	Black Wool Heavy at Head	Gold Tinsel Back End of Body	Gold Tinsel	Black Hackle Wisps	Black	
R.B. TRANSLUCENT AMBER NYMPH	Amber Composition Flattened	Black Silk		Guinea Fowl Body Feather Wisps	Badger	
R.B. TRANSLUCENT RED NYMPH	Tango Composition Flattened, Amber Under	Black Silk		Brown Hackle Wisps	Brown	

PLATE 10 (Continued)

Fly	Body	Ribbing	Tip	Tail	Hackle	Wing
R.B. TRANSLUCENT GREEN NYMPH	Dark Green Composition, Amber Under	Black Silk		Olive Dyed Guinea Body Wisps	Brown Olive	
R.B. TRANSLUCENT BROWN OLIVE	Brown Olive Composition, Amber Under	Black Silk		Unstripped Brown Quills from Mandarin Duck	Grizzly	
KOL-RAY CADDIS	Very Pale Yellow Cellophane or Composition Tapered				Guinea Body Feather Wisps	
STRAWMAN NYMPH	Deer Body, hair tied to stick out from book and clipped	Yellow Floss Silk		Gray Mallard		

PLATE 12
ADDITIONAL STREAMERS AND BUCKTAILS

Fly	Body	Ribbing	Wing	Tip	Hackle	Tail
SCOTT SPECIAL	Light Brown Wool	Silver Tinsel	Yellow Bucktail Jungle Eye	Silver Tinsel	Yellow	Scarlet
SUMMER'S GOLD	Gold Tinsel		Brown Bucktail Topping White Bucktail		Scarlet	Golden Pheasant Tippet
WESLEY SPECIAL	Silver Tinsel	Round Silver Tinsel	Slate Bucktail Topping White Bucktail Jungle Eye		Black	Golden Pheasant Tippet
GOOTENBURG'S JERSEY MINNOW (Peacock Herl Head)	Gold Tinsel		Dark Honey Badger Hackle Feather		Ginger or Brown Mixed with Pink	Golden Pheasant Tippet
DR. BURKE	Silver Tinsel	Round Silver Tinsel	White Hackle Feather Jungle Eye	Gold Tinsel	Yellow	Peacock Sword
OPTIC BUCKTAIL (Painted Eye Head)	Silver Tinsel (Flat)	Round Silver Tinsel	Brown or Black Bucktail over White Bucktail Jungle Eye			Scarlet
BLUE DEVIL	Gold Tinsel		Grizzly Hackle Feather with Blue Peacock & Kingfisher Cheek		Grizzly, Golden Pheasant Crest Added Underneath	Golden Pheasant Breast or Crimson
CAPRA STREAMER	Silver Tinsel Scarlet Sac About 2/3 from Front	Round Silver Ribbing	Light Slate Capra Topping Yellow Capra Jungle Eye		White Capra Tied Same Length as Wing	
CHIEF NEEDABEH	Scarlet Floss	Silver Tinsel	Orange over Yellow, Hackles Tied Streamer Jungle Eye	Silver Tinsel	Yellow and Scarlet Mixed	
ESTELLE (Gootenburg)	Alternate Scarlet and White Chenille	Gold Tinsel Wound Opposite to Chenille Stripes	White Hackle Tied Streamer Scarlet Cheek	Gold Tinsel	White	Scarlet

[500]

PLATE 12 (Continued)

Fly	Body	Ribbing	Wing	Tip	Hackle	Tail
FRASER	Green Wool	Silver Tinsel	White Hackle Streamer with Short Yellow over Jungle Eye	Orange Chenille Tag		
BLACK GHOST	Black Wool or Floss	Silver Tinsel	White Hackle Tied Streamer Jungle Eye		Golden Pheasant Crest	Golden Pheasant Crest
GRAY GHOST	Orange Floss	Silver Tinsel	Blue-Gray Hackles Tied Streamer Silver Pheasant Cheek, Long Golden Pheasant Crest, Jungle Eye		Peacock Herl White Bucktail Tied Streamer	
LADY GHOST	Silver Tinsel		Honey Badger Hackle Tied Streamer, Brown Pheasant Cheek Golden Pheasant Tied Streamer and Low Jungle Eye		Peacock Herl and White Bucktail Tied Streamer	
NANCY	Copper Tinsel	Silver Tinsel	Green Hackle Long, Orange Short, Both Streamers Light Brown, Mottled Cheek	Silver Tinsel	Yellow Tied Under Only	
SPENCER BAY	Silver Tinsel	Silver Tinsel (Round)	Honey Badger Streamer, Brown Pheasant Cheek, Jungle Eye		Mixed Light Blue and Yellow	Golden Pheasant Tippet
THREE RIVERS	Claret Wool Body	Wide Silver Tinsel	Grizzly Streamer Jungle Eye	Wide Silver Tinsel	Scarlet	Teal
YORK'S KENNEBAGO	Silver Tinsel	Round Silver Tinsel	Honey Badger Jungle Eye	Scarlet Floss Tag 2/3 from Eye	Scarlet	

[501]

PLATE 12 (Continued)

Fly	Body	Ribbing	Wing	Tip	Hackle	Tail
MARABOU (White)	Silver Tinsel	Silver Tinsel (Round)	White Marabou Peacock Herl on Top (5 Strands) Jungle Eye		Scarlet Under Only	
MARABOU (Yellow)	Silver Tinsel	Silver Tinsel (Round)	Yellow Marabou Brown Ostrich Herl on Top Jungle Eye		Scarlet	

PLATE 13
SOME SPECIAL DRY FLIES

Fly	Body	Ribbing	Tip	Tail	Hackle	Wing
AUSABLE	Blue-Gray Hard Body			Light Blue-Gray	Light Blue-Gray	Barred Mandarin or White Tipped Starling
BLACK ANGEL	Black Hard Body			Black Hackle Wisps	Black	Black Hackle Tips
BROWN OLIVE	Brown Olive Hard Body			Brown Olive Dyed	Brown Olive Dyed	Brown Olive Hackle Tips
GRAY TRANSLUCENT	Yellow Cellophane or Composition			Grizzly (Barred Rock)	Grizzly	Grizzly Hackle Tips
GRIZZLY TANGO	Tango Cellophane or Composition			Grizzly Hackle Wisps	Grizzly	Grizzly Hackle Tips
HONEY DUN	Cream Cellophane, Composition, Wool or Fur			Honey Hackle Wisps	Honey	Mandarin Speckled
LIGHT CAHILL TRANSLUCENT	Deep Yellow Body, Cellophane or Composition			Ginger	Ginger	Mandarin Speckled
MARCH BROWN AMERICAN	Brown Cellophane or Composition	Gold Tinsel		Brown Hackle Wisps	Brown	Brown Mallard
PINK LADY TRANSLUCENT	Pink Translucent Composition			Brown Hackle Wisps	Brown	Dark Slate Hackle Tips
TANGO TRIUMPHANT	Tango Cellophane or Composition Body			Brown	Brown	Ginger
WOODRUFF (Usually Tied Spent)	Green Cellophane or Wool			Gray Mallard	Brown	Grizzly Hackle Tips
MULTI-COLOR VARIANT R.B.	Gold Tinsel			Dark Badger or Black, Ginger & White Mixed	White at Eye Dk. Ginger Center, Black Rear	Grizzly Hackle Tips

PLATE 13 (Continued)

Fly	Body	Ribbing	Tip	Tail	Hackle	Wing
LIGHT MULTI-COLOR VARIANT	Silver Tinsel			Red Mixed Grizzly Natural	Red Mixed Grizzly Natural	Grizzly Hackle Tips
MULTI-COLOR VARIANT—No. 2	Black Silk			Blue-Gray, Red & Black Inter-mingled	Blue-Gray, Red and Black Inter-mingled	Grizzly Hackle Tips
BADGER VARIANT	Peacock Herl			Badger	Badger	Grizzly Hackle Tips
BROWN VARIANT	Gold Tinsel			Brown Hackle Wisps	Brown	Grizzly Hackle Tips
FURNACE VARIANT	Blue-Gray Ostrich Herl			Furnace Brown Hackle Wisps	Furnace	Grizzly Hackle Tips
GINGER VARIANT	Cream Silk Floss, Wool or Cello-phane			Ginger Hackle Wisps	Ginger	Grizzly Hackle Tips
GRIZZLY VARIANT	Tango Cellophane or Light Claret Silk Floss			Grizzly Hackle Wisps	Grizzly	Brown Hackle Tips
BLUE VARIANT	Gold Tinsel			Grizzly Hackle Wisps Dyed Blue-Gray	Grizzly Hackle Wisps Dyed Blue-Gray	Grizzly Hackle Tips
ADAMS	Blue-Gray Fur			Grizzly	Mixed Grizzly and Rhode Island Red	Grizzly Tied Either Spent or Upright
COFFIN	White Silk Floss			Pheasant or Black	Badger—Very dark & speckly if possible	Black Hackle Tips
SPENT BLUE	Quill Body			Blue-Gray Hackle Wisps	Blue-Gray	Grizzly Hackle Tips Spent
SPENT OLIVE	Unstripped Condor Dyed Olive			Olive Hackle Wisps	Olive	Grizzly Dyed Blue-Gray Tied Spent
SPENT YELLOW	Pale Yellow Wool Body			Black Hackle Wisps	Pale Yellow	Badger Hackle Tips, Dyed Yellow Tied Spent

PLATE 13 (Continued)

Fly	Body	Ribbing	Tip	Tail	Hackle	Wing
GRAY WULFF	Blue-Gray Fur			Brown Bucktail	Blue-Gray	Brown Bucktail
ROYAL WULFF	Peacock Herl Scarlet Silk Floss Center			Brown Bucktail	Brown	White Bucktail
WHITE WULFF	Cream Color Fur, Wool or Something of that Nature			White Bucktail	Light Badger	White Bucktail
GREEN MAY	Cream Body of Cellophane, Composition or Silk Floss	Gold Tinsel	Gold Tinsel	Dark Blue-Gray	Grizzly Dyed Light Blue-Gray	Gray Mallard Dyed Pale Green
YELLOW MAY	Cream Cast Cellophane or Composition or Cream Floss Silk			Ginger Hackle Wisps	Mixed Ginger and Grizzly	Gray Mallard Dyed Yellow
FAN WING ROYAL COACHMAN	Peacock Herl Scarlet Silk Floss Center			Golden Pheasant Tippet	Brown	White Mandarin or Domestic Duck
FAN WING SILVER COACHMAN	Peacock Herl, Silver Tinsel Center			Blue-Gray Hackle Wisps	Blue-Gray	Light Blue-Gray Dyed Mandarin Fan Wings
GREEN FAN WING COACHMAN	Peacock Herl Green Silk Floss Center			Green Hackle Wisps	Green	Dyed Green Mandarin Fan Wings
GINGER or PETRIE'S ROYAL COACHMAN	Peacock Herl Pale Yellow Silk Floss Center			Ginger Hackle Wisps	Ginger	White Mandarin or Domestic Duck
McSNEEK	Black Dyed Peacock Herl, Silver Tinsel Center			Black Hackle Wisps	Black	White Fan Wings

PLATE 14
DRY FLIES

Fly	Body	Ribbing	Tip	Tail	Hackle	Wing
BADGER BIVISIBLE				Badger Hackle Tips	Badger Tied Palmer, White Hackle at Eye	
BLACK BIVISIBLE				Black Hackle Tips	Black Tied Palmer White Hackle at Eye	
BROWN BIVISIBLE				Brown Hackle Tips	Brown Hackle Tied Palmer, White Hackle at Eye	
BROWN AND GRAY BIVISIBLE				Mixed Brown and Blue-Gray Hackle Wisps	Mixed Brown and Blue-Gray Tied Palmer, White at Eye	
BLUE BIVISIBLE				Blue-Gray Hackle Tips	Blue-Gray Hackle Tied Palmer White at Eye	
GRAY BIVISIBLE				Grizzly Hackle Tips	Grizzly Hackle Tied Palmer White at Eye	
PINK LADY BIVISIBLE	Gold Tinsel			Ginger Hackle Wisps	Ginger Hackle Tied Palmer Pale Yellow or Pale Green Hackle at Eye	
BLACK SPIDER	Gold Tinsel			Black Hackle Wisps	Black	
BLUE SPIDER	Gold Tinsel			Blue-Gray Hackle Wisps	Blue-Gray	
BROWN SPIDER				Brown Hackle Wisps	Brown Tied Palmer, White at Eye	
GINGER FURNACE SPIDER	Gold Tinsel			Ginger Furnace Hackle Wisps	Ginger Furnace	

PLATE 14 (Continued)

Fly	Body	Ribbing	Tip	Tail	Hackle	Wing
ORANGE FISH HAWK	Orange Floss	Gold Tinsel	Gold Tinsel		Badger Light	
AUGUST DUN	Light Brown Floss	Yellow Silk	Yellow Silk	Dark Brown	Dark Brown	Pheasant or Light Brown Turkey
BLACK GNAT	Black Chenille			Black Hackle Wisps—Some Prefer Without Tail	Black	Slate
BLUE QUILL	Gray Peacock Quill			Blue-Gray Hackle Wisps	Blue-Gray	Slate or Blue-Gray
B.V. BOOTH	Olive Wool	Gold Tinsel			Brown	Dark Woodchuck Tied Flat Along Hook
BLUE DUN	Blue-Gray Fur			Blue-Gray Hackle Wisps	Blue-Gray	Blue-Gray or Slate
BRADLEY	Blue-Gray Fur			Brown Hackle Wisps	Brown	Gray Mallard
BRONZE QUILL	Dark Quill			Dark Flame Hackle Wisps	Dark Flame (Bronze)	Gray Speckled
CADDIS, LIGHT	Olive-Yellow Wool or Mohair			Brown	Brown Tied Palmer	Slate or Blue-Gray
CAMPBELL'S FANCY	Gold Tinsel			Golden Pheasant Crest	Furnace	Gray Mallard
CAHILL	Blue-Gray Fur		Gold Tinsel if desired	Mandarin Speckled	Brown	Mandarin (Speckled)
CAHILL, GOLD BODY	Gold Tinsel			Brown Hackle Wisps	Brown	Mandarin Speckled
CAHILL, LIGHT	Creamy White Fur			Mandarin Speckled Light Shade if possible	Ginger	Mandarin Speckled Light Shade If Possible—Not Important
CAHILL QUILL	Peacock Quill			Brown	Brown	Mandarin Speckled
LIGHT CAHILL QUILL	Light Colored Imported Condor Quills or Peacock if desired			Mandarin Speckled	Ginger	Mandarin Speckled

PLATE 14 (Continued)

Fly	Body	Ribbing	Tip	Tail	Hackle	Wing
COTY DARK	Blue-Gray Fur Mixed with a Mite of Scarlet Wool			Dark Blue-Gray Hackle Wisps	Dark Blue-Gray	Dark Blue-Gray Hackle Tips
COTY LIGHT	Blue-Gray Fur Mixed with a Mite of Scarlet Wool			Light Blue-Gray Hackle Wisps	Light Blue-Gray	Light Blue-Gray Hackle Tips
COACHMAN	Peacock Herl			Brown Hackle Wisps if desired	Brown	White
DARK COACHMAN LEAD WING	Peacock Herl			Brown Hackle Wisps if desired	Brown	Dark Slate
CCCHY QUILL	Peacock or Condor Quill			Cochy-Bondhu	Cochy-Bondhu	Mandarin Speckled
EINGER QUILL	Light Colored Imported Condor Quill			Ginger	Ginger	Mandarin Speckled or Blue-Gray Last my choice
GORDON	Golden Floss Silk	Gold Tinsel		Mandarin Speckled	Badger	Mandarin Speckled
QUILL GORDON	Peacock Quill			Bronze Blue-Gray	Bronze Blue-Gray	Mandarin Speckled
GRAY DRAKE	White Silk Floss	Black Silk		Teal	Light Grizzly	Teal

PLATE 15
DRY FLIES

Fly	Body	Ribbing	Tip	Tail	Hackle	Wing
GRAY QUILL	Peacock Quill			Dark Grizzly Hackle Wisps	Dark Grizzly or Blue-Gray	Gray Mallard or Teal
GOLD RIBBED HARE'S EAR	Fur from Hare's Ear	Gold Tinsel	Gold Tinsel	Brown Hackle Wisps		Slate
DARK HENDRICKSON	Dark Blue-Gray Fur			Speckled Mandarin	Dark Blue-Gray	Speckled Mandarin
LIGHT HENDRICKSON	Cream Colored Fur			Speckled Mandarin	Light Gray	Speckled Mandarin
HOUSATONIC QUILL	Quill			Speckled Mandarin	Gray Badger	Speckled Mandarin
IRON BLUE DUN	Blue-Gray Fur		Scarlet Floss Silk	Furnace Hackle Wisps	Furnace	Dark Blue Slate
LADY or FEMALE BEAVERKILL	Gray Silk Floss		Yellow Chenille Tag or Egg Sack	Gray Mallard	Brown	Slate
MALLARD QUILL	Peacock Quill			Dark Brown Hackle Wisps	Dark Brown	Brown Mallard
MOSQUITO	Dark Peacock Quill			Dark Grizzly	Dark Grizzly	Dark Grizzly Hackle Tips
McGINTY	Alternate Stripes Yellow & Black Chenille			Gray Mallard or Teal	Brown	Black Turkey with White Tip
OLIVE DUN	Fur or Unstripped Condor Quill Dyed Dark Olive			Olive Hackle Wisps	Olive	Speckled Mandarin or Slate
OLIVE QUILL	Peacock Quill			Olive Hackle Wisps	Olive	Slate
PALE EVENING DUN	Greenish Yellow Wool			Pale Blue-Gray	Pale Blue-Gray	Slate or Blue-Gray
PARSON'S DUN	Brown Olive Wool Body			Honey Grizzly Tail	Honey Grizzly	Gray Mallard
PETRIE'S EGG SACK	Gray Wool or Fur Body		Pale Green Chenille Egg Sack	Speckled Mandarin	Medium Blue-Gray	Speckled Mandarin

PLATE 15 (Continued)

Fly	Body	Ribbing	Tip	Tail	Hackle	Wing
RAMAPO SPECIAL "Gootenburg"	Red Fox Fur Cream			Gray Mallard	Mixed Ginger and Blue-Gray	Gray Mallard Clipped Short
ROYAL COACHMAN	Green Peacock Herl, Scarlet Floss Center		Gold Tinsel if desired		Brown	White
R.B. FOX	Gray Fox Fur			Honey Hackle Wisps	Mixed Honey and Ginger	Gray Mallard
R.B. BLUE FOX	Blue-Gray Fur			Grizzly Hackle Wisps	Mixed Grizzly and Blue-Gray	Grizzly Hackle Tips
RED FOX BEAVER-KILL	Blue-Gray Fur from Red Fox	Gold Tinsel	Gold Tinsel	Ginger	Ginger Faced with Pale Blue-Gray	
RED FOX STODDARD	Cream Fur from Red Fox			Speckled Mandarin	Honey	Speckled Mandarin
SQUIRREL TAIL	Blue-Gray Fur	Gold Tinsel	Gold Tinsel		Grizzly	Squirrel Tail Tied Flat Along Hook
TUP'S INDISPENSABLE	Yellow Floss Silk with Pink Wool Tuft at Shoulder			Ginger	Ginger Faced with White	
TURNER'S GREEN	Pale Green Wool			Dark Honey	Grizzly Dyed Blue Dun or Badger	Gray Mallard Dyed Light Green
WESTBROOK	Pink Wool	Black Silk		Dark Honey	Dark Honey	Gray Mallard
WHIRLING BLUE DUN	Blue-Gray Fur or Wool			Brown Hackle Wisps	Brown	Dark Slate
WILL'S SPINNER	Unstripped Condor Dyed Yellow			Black Hackle Wisps	Cream White	Gray Mallard or Speckled Wood Duck
WORTENDYKE	Smoky Gray-Brown Fur			Black Hackle Wisps	Black	Gray Mallard or Speckled Mandarin
YELLOW CREEK	Light Gray Ostrich Herl			Black Hackle Wisps	Light Blue-Gray	Badger Hackle Tips
YELLOW MALLARD	Yellow Wool or Fur			Gray Mallard	Ginger	Gray Mallard

PLATE 15 (Continued)

Fly	Body	Ribbing	Tip	Tail	Hackle	Wing
YELLOW SPINNER	Yellow Floss	Black Silk		Yellow	Honey Badger	Gray Mallard Dyed Yellow
STILLWATER—No. 1	Copper or Silver			Sparse Blue-Gray	Sparse Blue-Gray	
STILLWATER—No. 2	Copper			Sparse Light Ginger	Sparse Light Ginger	
STILLWATER—No. 3	Copper or Gold			Sparse Furnace or Black	Sparse Furnace or Black	
COOPER-BUG	Green Wool or Floss Silk	Gold Tinsel	Gold Tinsel	Scarlet Hackle Wisps	Gray Squirrel Tuft at Head	Gray Squirrel Tied Spent

PLATE 16
NEW DRY FLIES

Fly	Body	Ribbing	Tip or Tag	Tail	Hackle	Wing
BUZZ FLY	Peacock Herl		Optional—Silver or Gold Tinsel or None	Bright Red or Crimson	Rear, Grizzly or Barred Rock. Front, Brown. Wind over Top of Peacock	
BLACK WULFF Bailey	Pale Pink Floss—Lacquered for Durability			Moose Hair	Furnace	Moose Hair
BLUE WINGED SULPHUR DUN Best Size 16, about 1X Long	Sulphur Yellow Spun Fur			Pale Blue Dun	Dark Cream	Pale Slate—Dyed Blue—from Webby Part of Neck Hackle
CARROT	Light Cream Fur Dubbing			White Hackle Wisps	Orange and Green Mixed	
BI-FLY YELLOW	Bright Yellow Rubber			Deer Hair, Same Color as Wings	Grizzly—Plymouth or Barred Rock	Deer Hair, Flared
BROWN QUILL SPINNER 12 Good Size	Peacock Quill		Green Chenille Egg Sac	Mandarin Speckled	Red Brown	Light Mallard Slate
CALLENDER QUILL	Quill Tinted a Bit Yellow or Cream			Grizzly or Barred Rock Hackle Wisps	Grizzly—Barred or Plymouth Rock	Red Brown Hackle Wisps, Upright
CLYDE	Peacock Herl Fore and Aft. Royal Coachman Red Floss Silk in Center		Optional—Either Gold Tinsel or None	Red-Brown Hackle Wisps	Red-Brown as in Royal Coachman, Wound Fore and Aft Over the Peacock Herl	

PLATE 16 (continued)

Fly	Body	Ribbing	Tip or Tag	Tail	Hackle	Wing
COOPERS' HOPPER	Light Tan Chenille, Palmered with Green Hackle			Red, (Dark Claret, as in Montreal)	Red-Brown	Mottled Turkey with Pinch of Red Squirrel Between the Wings
DEREN'S FOX	Light Cahill Cream from Red Fox. Scored Crosswise on Top with Brown Lacquer. This Does not Show on Plate			Light Multi-color Hackle Wisps	One Cream and One Light Multi-color Mingled Together	Pale Yellow Mallard Plate Shows Mandarin
EMERGENT DRY NYMPH	Rough and Fat Dubbing Made from Fur of Rabbit's Ear					Slate, from Mallard Duck Flight Feathers, Tied Upright
FIFTY DEGREES	Muskrat Mingled with Some Brown Beaver Fur		Blue Dun	Blue Dun		Fine Speckled, from Teal Pin Feather
FIREHOLE	Cream Fur from Fox or Other Animal			Speckled Black and White Teal or Mallard or Wood Duck, as Shown in Painting	Mixed Grizzly (Barred Rock etc.) and Black	Speckled Mallard, Teal or Wood Duck as Desired. Fly Is O.K. with Any of Them

PLATE 16 (continued)

GOLDEN QUAIL	Rear Half Flat Gold Tinsel. Front Half Light Orange Chenille	Golden Pheasant Crest	Plymouth or Barred Rock (Grizzly)	Fan Wings from Necks of Cock California Valley Quail
GREIG QUILL	Quill Peacock or Similar	Badger Hackle Wisps	Badger Honey List	Speckled Wood Duck
GRIZZLY WULFF Bailey	Pale Yellow Floss, Lacquered to Make More Durable	Same as Wings. Select the Darker Straighter Hair Which May Be Less Pulpy than Regular Body Hair	Mixed Brown and Grizzly	Deer Hair from Near the Base of the Tail or from Certain Parts of the Body of a Whitetail
GINGER QUILL GYRO Mills—See Text	Any Regular Quill Material, to Make the Effect Desired	Optional—Brown or Gray Speckled Mallard or Mandarin if Desired	Ginger	Spent Whitish or Pale Blue-Gray Hackle Tips. Can Also Be Made Upright as Painting
H. L. HOWARD	Black Wool or Fur		Badger, Whitish if Possible, Otherwise Cream	White Bucktail or Impali Calf Tail
HONEY QUILL	Stripped Condor Quill	Same as Hackle, Using Wisps	Very Light Ginger or Honey or Cream	Optional—If Used, Blue-Gray Hackle Point Is About the Best

[514]

PLATE 16 (continued)

Fly	Body	Ribbing	Tip or Tag	Tail	Hackle	Wing
HOPKINS VARIANT	Light Condor Quill, Stripped of Most of the Fuzz			Red-Brown Hackle Wisps	Front—a Silver Doctor Blue Sometimes Called Teal Blue. Rear—Red-Brown. Painting too Purple for the Blue That Is Right	Slate or Starling, or Blue Dyed Fish Skin Cut to Wing Shape. Make Stubby
IRON BLUE VARIANT	Raffia Grass, Dyed a Dull, Deep Red			Same as Hackle	Very Dark Blue-Gray, Almost Black	Blue Dyed Fish Skin Cut to Wing Shape. Make Stubby
IRRESISTIBLE	Deer Body Hair, Light Gray in Tone			Deer Body Hair, Same as Wings	Blue-Gray as in Quill Gordon	Deer Body Hair, Dark Brown in Tone
JUNGLE COCK VARIANT	Yellow and Blue Macaw Quill			Brown Hackle Wisps, Rather Long and Heavy	Only One Rather Long Furnace, Tied Sparse	Small Jungle Cock. Neck Feathers Tied Back to Back
KILLER DILLER	Light Yellow Silk or Rayon Palmered with Small Plymouth Rock (Barred Rock or Grizzly)			Brown Hackle Fibers	Plymouth or Barred Rock (Grizzly)	Eastern Gray Squirrel Tied Horizontal to Shank
MEAT BALL	Deep Meaty Pink or Dark Rose Wool			Speckled Mallard or Mandarin, Brownish	Blue-Gray but Bronzy	Teal, Speckled Mallard, or Mandarin— Wood Duck if You Choose

PLATE 16 (continued)

Fly	Body	Ribbing	Tip or Tag	Tail	Hackle	Wing
MORRIS QUILL	Peacock Quill			Mixed Mandarin and Ginger Hackle Wisps	Mixed Ginger and Badger	Speckled Mandarin or Wood Duck—Same as the Cahills and Gordons
PALE EVENING DUN—FOX	Very Pale Green Fur Dubbing or Wool			Same as Hackle	Light Cream or Honey Mixed with Pale Blue-Gray	Teal or Gray Mallard, Well Speckled
PALE EVENING SPINNER	Pale Yellow Floss Silk	Gold Wire	Yellow Chenille	White Hackle Wisps	Pale Yellow	Starling
PASTEL YELLOW SPIDER	Gold Tinsel			Same as Hackle, or Variation if Desired	Light Badger Dyed Very Pale Ginger	
RED QUILL Flick	Stripped Quill of Large Rhode Island Red Hackle Feather. Must Be Well Soaked to Tie			Dun Spade Hackle Wisps	Natural Blue Dun	Flank Feather of Mandarin or Wood Duck Drake
ROUGH WATER Blue	Caribou Body Hair Dyed Blue; Clipped to Size as Shown Original Blue of Fly not as Purple as the Artist's Version			Brown or Dun Hackle Wisps	Light Grizzly, Barred or Plymouth Rock	

[516]

PLATE 16 (continued)

Fly	Body	Ribbing	Tip or Tag	Tail	Hackle	Wing
ROUGH WATER Yellow	Caribou Body Hair Dyed Yellow, Clipped to Size as Shown			Black or Grizzly	Light Grizzly or Brown	
ROUGH WATER White	White Caribou Body Hair, Clipped to Size as Shown			Black	Black	
SLATE DRAKE DUN	Reddish Tan Spun Fur, Tied to Make Thorax as Shown Artist Made Color a Bit too Yellow			Same as Hackle	Bronze-Blue or Dark Blue Dun	Darkest Slate from Webby Part of Neck Hackle (Cock Dyed)
SMOKY MOUN-TAIN FORKED TAIL	Lynx Fur Dubbing	Yellow Tying Silk		Two Fibers of Mallard Primary, Tied Forked	Grizzly or Barred Rock	Mallard Drake Primary Flight Feather
STERRY SPECIAL	Peacock Herl Tied *Fat*		Flat Gold Tinsel— Optional		Plymouth Rock	Haido Squirrel Tail
WAKE	Pale Lavender Silk Floss Painting too Pink			Pale Lavender Artist's Color of This Fly too Brown	Pale Lavender	Blue Dyed Fish Skin Cut to Shape, or Slate. Painting too green

Index

1· TACKLE AND EQUIPMENT

INDEX

INDEX

I · TACKLE AND EQUIPMENT [cont'd]

INDEX

INDEX

II · METHODS AND TACTICS [*cont'd*]

lake trout, fishing waters adjacent to reefs and islands, 380, 381; diagram, 382, 383

lake-trout locations, taking notes of, 393

lake trout, surface or shallow-water fishing, 378–388

lake trout, types of water to fish, 379, 380

large flies, advantage of, in wet-fly fishing in fast water, 19, 20

large flies, useful to start trout moving, 249

leader material, between wire line and lure, in lake-trout fishing, 390

leaders, frequent examination of, 165–167

leaders, heavy vs. light, in bucktail fishing, 121, 122, 125, 129

leaders, importance of sinking, in clear water, 73

leader, sinking or floating of, in dry-fly fishing, 211–215

leaders, long and light, best for casting downwind, 158

leaders, longest that can be handled, advised for most waters, 360

leaders, long vs. short, in bucktail fishing, 114–117

leaders, short and heavy preferred, for brush-grown streams, 341

left-handed reeling, advantages of, 270

lifting cast from water too soon, 333

line, floating of, in dry-fly fishing, 212–215

"line retrieve," 23

lining up lake-trout holes with objects on shore, diagram, 393

live bait, for lake-trout fishing, 392

locating fishing grounds, important in lake-trout fishing, 378, 380

long rod best for bucktail fishing, 141

loop casts, in dry-fly fishing, 207–209

"mending," in the wet-fly cast, 16

midge wet flies, often esential, 104

minute details, importance of observing, 109

muddying water, to start trout feeding, 97

narrow channels, productive of large trout, 349, 350; diagram, 349

"natural drift," in spinning, 284, 285, 296

"natural drift," in steelhead fishing, 373–375

"natural drift," in wet-fly fishing, 14, 98, 125, 140

nymph a likely lure, after missing trout on dry fly, 101

nymph drift, timing speed of, with dry fly, 55, 100, 101

nymph fishing in still waters, 56, 57

nymph-fishing methods, as differing from wet-fly, 51

nymphing by trout in shallows, mistaken for fly rises, 344

nymphs, small sizes often essential, 103, 104

observation of stream, value of, 6, 12, 13, 63, 214, 215, 335, 341, 342, 345, 360

pick-up of dry-fly cast, 204–206

pockets in stream, wet-fly methods of fishing, 17–20

pool-fishing techniques, 329, 331–334

pool, typical, diagram showing how fished by most anglers, 330

position of angler, as related to water, 341–343, 358, 359; diagram, 342

quiet eddies in turbulent streams, good feeding spots, 351

reel, carrying extra with rigged line, in dry-fly fishing, 214

releasing snagged fly with switch cast, often productive of strike, 138

retrieve, preferred methods, in casting for lake trout, 381, 384

retrieve, with reel, 21

rocks, sunken and surface, casting to, 19

rules of stream fishing, summarized. 359–361

self-discipline, in fishing tactics, 113

sinking wet flies by soaking in mud, 364

size of natural fly, more important to imitate than color, 354

slack-line cast, to avoid drag, 204, 207, 209

slack line, control of, 356

small-brook fishing, 347–350

spinning line, importance of frequent testing, 267, 268

INDEX

III · FLY-TYING TOOLS, MATERIALS, AND METHODS

IV · PERSONS, PLACES, AND LITERATURE

INDEX

INDEX

INDEX

v · MISCELLANEOUS

This book was set on the Linotype in Janson, a recutting made direct from the type cast from matrices made by Anton Janson some time between 1660 and 1687. Janson's original matrices were, at last report, in the possession of the Stempel foundry, Frankfurt am Main.

Of Janson's origin nothing is known. He may have been a relative of Justus Janson, a printer of Danish birth who practiced in Leipzig from 1614 to 1635. Some time between 1657 and 1668 Anton Janson, a punch-cutter and type-founder, bought from the Leipzig printer Johann' Erich Hahn the type-foundry that had formerly been a part of the printing house of M. Friedrich Lankisch. Janson's types were first shown in a specimen sheet issued at Leipzig about 1675. Janson's successor, and perhaps his son-in-law, Johann Karl Edling, issued a specimen sheet of Janson types in 1689. His heirs sold the Janson matrices in Holland to Wolffgang Dietrich Erhardt, of Leipzig.